FEATURE	MENU SELECTIONS	KEYSTROKES	PAGE
Equation (Create)	Graphics ➤ Equation ➤ Create	Alt-F9 E C	680
Equation (Edit)	Graphics ➤ Equation ➤ Edit	Alt-F9 E E	690
Exit WordPerfect	File ➤ Exit	F7	18
Export to Text File	File ➤ Text Out ➤ DOS Text	Ctrl-F5 T S	779
Flush Right	Layout ➤ Align ➤ Flush Right	Alt-F6	98
Font (Appearance)	Font ➤ Appearance	Ctrl-F8 A	136
Font (Size)	Font ➤ choose size	Ctrl-F8 S	133
Footers	Layout ➤ Page F	Shift-F8 P F	232
Footnote	Layout ➤ Footnote	Ctrl-F7 F	725
Force Odd/Even Page	Layout ➤ Page O	Shift-F8 P O	236
Fully Justify Text	Layout ➤ Justify ➤ Full	Shift-F8 L J F	96
Generate	Mark ➤ Generate	Alt-F5 G	752
Go to Character/Page	Search ➤ Goto	Ctrl-Home	31
Graphics Print Quality	File ➤ Print G	Shift-F7 G	281
Hard Page Break	Layout ➤ Align ➤ Hard Page	Ctrl-↵	221
Headers	Layout ➤ Page H	Shift-F8 P H	229
Help	Help	F3	71
Hyphenation On/Off	Layout ➤ Line Y	Shift-F8 L Y	357
Import Text File	File ➤ Text In	Ctrl-F5 T	780
→Indent	Layout ➤ Align ➤ Indent ->	F4	99
→Indent←	Layout ➤ Align ➤ Indent -><-	Shift-F4	99
Index (Define)	Mark ➤ Define ➤ Index	Alt-F5 D I	741
Index (Mark Block For)	Mark ➤ Index	Alt-F5 I	739
Keyboard Layout	File ➤ Setup ➤ Keyboard Layout	Shift-F1 K	811
Left-Justify Text	Layout ➤ Justify ➤ Left	Shift-F8 L J L	95
Line Draw	Tools ➤ Line Draw	Ctrl-F3 L	154
Line (Graphic)	Graphics ➤ Line	Alt-F9 L	155
Line Height	Layout ➤ Line H	Shift-F8 L H	663
Line Spacing	Layout ➤ Line S	Shift-F8 L S	89
List (Define)	Mark ➤ Define ➤ List	Alt-F5 D L	743

Computer users are not all alike.
Neither are SYBEX books.

We know our customers have a variety of needs. They've told us so. And because we've listened, we've developed several distinct types of books to meet the needs of each of our customers. What are you looking for in computer help?

If you're looking for the basics, try the **ABC's** series. You'll find short, unintimidating tutorials and helpful illustrations. For a more visual approach, select **Teach Yourself,** featuring screen-by-screen illustrations of how to use your latest software purchase.

Mastering and **Understanding** titles offer you a step-by-step introduction, plus an in-depth examination of intermediate-level features, to use as you progress.

Our **Up & Running** series is designed for computer-literate consumers who want a no-nonsense overview of new programs. Just 20 basic lessons, and you're on your way.

We also publish two types of reference books. Our **Instant References** provide quick access to each of a program's commands and functions. SYBEX **Encyclopedias** and **Desktop References** provide a *comprehensive reference* and explanation of all of the commands, features, and functions of the subject software.

Sometimes a subject requires a special treatment that our standard series don't provide. So you'll find we have titles like **Advanced Techniques, Handbooks, Tips & Tricks,** and others that are specifically tailored to satisfy a unique need.

We carefully select our authors for their in-depth understanding of the software they're writing about, as well as their ability to write clearly and communicate effectively. Each manuscript is thoroughly reviewed by our technical staff to ensure its complete accuracy. Our production department makes sure it's easy to use. All of this adds up to the highest quality books available, consistently appearing on best-seller charts worldwide.

You'll find SYBEX publishes a variety of books on every popular software package. Looking for computer help? Help Yourself to SYBEX.

For a complete catalog of our publications:

SYBEX, Inc.
2021 Challenger Drive, Alameda, CA 94501
Tel: (510) 523-8233/(800) 227-2346 Telex: 336311
Fax: (510) 523-2373

▼ ▼ ▼ ▼ ▼ ▼ ▼ ▼ ▼ ▼ ▼

MASTERING WORDPERFECT 5.1

For DOS

. . . .

MASTERING
WORDPERFECT® 5.1
For DOS®

Alan Simpson

SYBEX®

San Francisco ■ *Paris* ■ *Düsseldorf* ■ *Soest*

ACQUISITIONS EDITOR: *Dianne King*
DEVELOPMENTAL EDITOR: *Christian T. S. Crumlish*
EDITOR: *Richard Mills*
TECHNICAL EDITOR: *Maryann Brown*
WORD PROCESSORS: *Ann Dunn and Susan Trybull*
BOOK DESIGNER: *Amparo del Rio*
PRODUCTION ARTIST: *Helen Bruno*
TECHNICAL ART: *Delia Brown*
SCREEN GRAPHICS: *Cuong Le*
POSTSCRIPT ICON TYPEFACE *created with CorelDRAW by Len Gilbert*
DESKTOP PUBLISHING SPECIALISTS: *Len Gilbert, M. D. Barrera, and Deborah Maizels*
PROOFREADERS: *Patsy Owens, Lisa Haden, and Catherine Mahoney*
INDEXER: *Nancy Anderman Guenther*
COVER DESIGNER: *Thomas Ingalls + Associates*
COVER PHOTOGRAPHER: *Michael Lamotte*

SYBEX is a registered trademark of SYBEX Inc.

TRADEMARKS: SYBEX has attempted throughout this book to distinguish proprietary trademarks from descriptive terms by following the capitalization style used by the manufacturer.

SYBEX is not affiliated with any manufacturer.

Every effort has been made to supply complete and accurate information. However, SYBEX assumes no responsibility for its use, nor for any infringement of the intellectual property rights of third parties which would result from such use.

An earlier version of this book was published under the title *Mastering WordPerfect® 5.1* copyright ©1991 SYBEX Inc.

Library of Congress Card Number: 89-51776
ISBN: 0-89588-670-7

Manufactured in the United States of America
20

To Richard G. and Rosemary Sickles

Every book is a team effort, but this one was especially so. Words alone cannot express my appreciation for this opportunity, or my indebtedness to the many people whose skills, talents, and hard work brought this book from the idea stage into your hands. But at least words can give credit where credit is due.

Christian Crumlish served as developmental editor, mentor, friend, advisor, and sounding board throughout the long and demanding project.

Richard Mills, editor, maintained editorial quality and kept things moving.

Maryann Brown, technical editor, checked each keystroke to make sure everything I said was correct and precise.

Among the other professionals who demonstrated great talent and devotion in this project are Amparo del Rio, book designer; Helen Bruno, production artist; Len Gilbert, M. D. Barrera, and Deborah Maizels, desktop publishing specialists; Patsy Owens, Lisa Haden, and Catherine Mahoney, proofreaders; Susan Trybull and Ann Dunn, word processors; Delia Brown, technical artist; Cuong Le, screen-graphics technician; and Nancy Guenther, indexer.

Gladys Varon deserves special thanks for being a true (and timely) friend in an hour of need.

Rodnay Zaks, Rudolph Langer, and Alan Oakes made the whole thing possible.

Talented writers Elizabeth Olson, Martha Mellor, Eric Stone, Dan Gookin, Mary Taylor, and Neil Salkind contributed much of the material of the original manuscript.

Bill Gladstone handled business matters (as he does for all my books).

Susan and Ashley provided love, support, sustenance, comfort, and lots of patience.

CONTENTS AT A GLANCE

TABLE OF CONTENTS

Chapter 3

PART TWO

Formatting Your Documents

Chapter 4

SPACING, ALIGNING, AND INDENTING TEXT **89**

Chapter 5

FONTS, LINES, AND SPECIAL CHARACTERS

Chapter 6

PART THREE

Tools To Simplify Your Work

Chapter 9

Chapter 10
CHECKING YOUR SPELLING AND FINDING THE RIGHT WORD . . . 333

Chapter 11
HYPHENATING TEXT 357

Chapter 12
MANAGING YOUR FILES 373

Chapter 13
CUSTOMIZING WORDPERFECT 401

PART FOUR

Automating Your Work

Chapter 14

USING STYLES TO SIMPLIFY YOUR WORK 435

Chapter 15

PART FIVE

Office Tools

Chapter 16

FORM LETTERS, MAILING LABELS, AND OTHER MERGES **501**

PART SIX

Desktop Publishing

Chapter 19

USING GRAPHICS IN YOUR DOCUMENTS 595

Chapter 20
WORKING WITH COLUMNS AND CREATING LAYOUTS 645

Chapter 21
ADDING EQUATIONS TO YOUR DOCUMENTS 679

PART SEVEN
Managing The Big Jobs

Chapter 24
USING MASTER DOCUMENT TO WORK WITH LARGE FILES 755

PART EIGHT
Techniques For Power Users

Chapter 25
INTERFACING WITH OTHER PROGRAMS 767

Chapter 26
ADVANCED MACRO AND MERGE COMMANDS . . . .

Chapter 27
CUSTOMIZING THE KEYBOARD LAYOUT . . . .

PART NINE

Hands-On Lessons

Lesson 1

Lesson 2

Lesson 3

Lesson 10

CREATING A POWER MACRO

APPENDICES

Appendix A

Appendix B

ordPerfect Corporation never ceases to amaze the computer industry with products that combine incredible power with a remarkable ease of use. WordPerfect 5.1 is no exception. Not only is it bigger and better than its predecessors, it's even easier to get along with, for beginners and old hands alike.

This is a book about using WordPerfect. The purpose of the book is twofold. On the one hand, the book is designed to teach you how to use WordPerfect productively and efficiently, even if you've never touched a computer in your life. On the other hand, the book serves as a reference to all the big features and little details when you just need a quick reminder.

WHOM THIS BOOK IS FOR

As a super-successful software product, WordPerfect has two kinds of users: throngs of newcomers who are finding out just what this terrific program has to offer and experienced users (several million of them!) requiring in-depth information on new and improved features. This book is designed to help both kinds of users.

ARE YOU NEW TO COMPUTERS OR WORDPERFECT?

One of the toughest parts of learning to use a program is just getting the basic "feel" of the thing. For this reason, I've included ten hands-on lessons near the back of the book, designed to help newcomers get up and running fast. I've also avoided the buzzwords and technobabble that often make the manuals that accompany software so incomprehensible. Even in the general chapters outside the hands-on lessons, I offer clear step-by-step instructions for using all of WordPerfect 5.1's many useful features.

ARE YOU AN EXPERIENCED WORDPERFECT USER?

If you are an experienced WordPerfect user but are new to version 5.1, you'll appreciate the in-depth descriptions of important new features in WordPerfect 5.1, like tables, pull-down menus, the Equation Editor, and other changes and refinements that will make your job easier.

The section titled "Tips for Experienced Users" near the end of this Introduction summarizes the new features and points you toward specific chapters that you'll want to focus on if you're upgrading to version 5.1.

FEATURES OF THE BOOK

This book is designed both as a tutorial and as a quick reference to the many features of WordPerfect 5.1. Special features of the book, designed to simplify and speed your mastery of WordPerfect, and to provide easy access to information when needed, include the following:

Endpapers Inside the front and back covers you'll find a quick reference to the techniques for performing common tasks.

Pullout Template You'll find a handy template near the back of the book, which you can remove and attach to your keyboard to use as a quick reference to WordPerfect commands.

Margin Notes Margin notes provide cross-references to where related features are covered in the book, "hot tips" for added insight on creative ways to use features, and cautions about problems that can occur when using a feature.

Fast Tracks The Fast Tracks at the beginning of selected sections provide a quick summary of techniques for using a specific feature, when you need just a quick reminder rather than a lengthy explanation.

Pull-Down Menu Steps WordPerfect offers two methods of accessing its features: You can use the function keys (found in earlier versions), or you can use the new pull-down menus. This book covers both methods, and you can use whichever you feel most comfortable with.

Hands-On Lessons Everyone knows that the best way to learn something is by doing it. If you want to get the feel of creating a document, or creating and using tables, styles, macros, or form letters, try the accompanying hands-on lessons near the back of the book (Part 9). The lessons also refer you to specific sections and chapters where you can get additional information.

Optional Companion Disk You can purchase a copy of the various sample documents, styles, and macros presented in this book in ready-to-use form on a disk. The disk is not required to use this book, but it may come in handy if you want to use some of the examples as a starting point for your own work without keying everything in from scratch. See the coupon in the back of the book if you're interested.

STRUCTURE OF THE BOOK

This book is designed to supplement the densely packed and somewhat technical manual that came with your WordPerfect package. The purpose of the WordPerfect manual is to document every available feature in great detail. The purpose of this book is to show you how to use WordPerfect and put it to work for your own purposes, whatever they may be.

To make things easier for you and to help you focus on information that's relevant to your own use of WordPerfect, I've divided the book into nine parts:

Part 1: Getting Started The first part covers all the basics of typing, editing, saving, and printing documents with WordPerfect. If you are a beginner, you'll find that this part will help you ease into WordPerfect and become comfortable with the differences between using WordPerfect and using a typewriter.

Part 2: Formatting Your Documents This part takes you beyond basic typing, editing, and printing skills, and teaches you how to start controlling the exact appearance of your documents.

Part 3: Tools to Simplify Your Work This part covers tools and techniques to make your work easier, such as search and replace, automatic spell-checking, automatic hyphenation, managing your documents, and customizing WordPerfect for your own needs.

Part 4: Automating Your Work This part covers two of WordPerfect's more convenient features, designed to simplify your work and increase your productivity: styles and macros.

Part 5: Office Tools This part covers those features of WordPerfect that are particularly useful in business settings, including merges, which are useful for mass mailings and fill-in forms, and the handy Math feature, which is useful for invoices, financial statements, and other documents that require some calculations.

Part 6: Desktop Publishing Desktop publishing is the wave of the '90s, and this part covers all you need to know about using lines, graphics, and columns to produce documents that are visually exciting and interesting.

Part 7: Managing the Big Jobs This part covers tools that help you to create and manage bigger projects that require multiple chapters or sections, cross-referencing, footnotes, outlines, and other advanced features.

Part 8: Techniques for Power Users This part covers advanced topics for power users, including interfacing with other programs, using advanced macro and merge commands, and customizing the keyboard layout.

Part 9: Hands-On Lessons When you need a little extra help in getting started with a particular feature, refer to this part for the appropriate hands-on lesson, which will take you step by step through a practical application of the feature. This helps give you an edge in learning new skills.

ADDITIONAL SUPPORT

Much of the success that WordPerfect Corporation enjoys is based on its dedication to customer support. Phone numbers for answers to specific questions are listed below:

Installation	(800) 533-9605
Features	(800) 541-5096
Graphics	(800) 321-3383
Networks	(800) 321-3389
Printers	(800) 541-5097

You should be at your computer when you place the call and should have your WordPerfect license number (included with your WordPerfect package) handy. You should also know the make and model of your printer.

In addition to *Mastering WordPerfect 5.1* and WordPerfect Corporation's support lines, you have another resource for getting help with WordPerfect: the WordPerfect Support Group. This is a national user group that publishes *The WordPerfectionist,* a monthly newsletter that provides useful tips and keeps you posted on new developments at WordPerfect Corporation. The group also provides product discounts, disk subscription services, and a user's forum on CompuServe. For information about the group and subscription rates, contact

WordPerfect Support Group

Lake Technology Park

P.O. Box 130

McHenry, MD 21541

Phone: (800) USA-GROUP

INTERIM RELEASES

From time to time, WordPerfect Corporation provides interim releases of WordPerfect 5.1 to members of their Software Subscription Service (the phone number is (800) 321-4566). These releases include minor fixes and enhancements to previous releases.

In some cases, WordPerfect Corporation may change the information presented on your screen, add a feature, or change a feature slightly. Though every attempt has been made to keep this book up to date, there may be slight variations between this book and the interim release you are using.

The interim release date of your copy of Word- Perfect appears in the upper-right corner of the Help screen when you press Help (F3).

If you find a discrepancy between a figure in this book and what you see on your screen, chances are it's because of a change made in an interim release. If an option that appears on your screen is not mentioned in this book, your best bet for getting information on that new feature is simply to press the Help key (F3).

TIPS FOR EXPERIENCED USERS

If you've worked with WordPerfect 5.0 and are upgrading to 5.1, you should have no trouble using your old files in the new version of WordPerfect. The following sections explain what special steps you'll need to take, if any.

COMPATIBILITY WITH OTHER VERSIONS

Word-Perfect 5.1 documents can also be edited, without conversion, in WordPerfect for Windows.

If several people in the same office use different versions of WordPerfect, they can still share documents. To edit a document in 5.1 format that was created in an earlier version, simply retrieve the document as you normally would. When you save that document, it will be stored in 5.1 format.

To save the WordPerfect 5.1 document that's currently on the screen in 5.0 or 4.2 format, press Text In/Out (Ctrl-F5), select Save As, then select either WordPerfect 5.0 or WordPerfect 4.2. Hidden codes that are incompatible with earlier versions will be stripped, replaced with [Unknown], or converted to older codes that handle a similar feature.

UPDATING MERGE DOCUMENTS FOR 5.1

Primary and secondary merge files from WordPerfect 5.0 are fully functional in 5.1, just like other documents. However, the merge codes in 5.1 are different, so you may want to convert them from 5.0 format. This is especially desirable if you'll be adding new codes while working with the merge document in 5.1. That way, you won't have two different types of merge codes in the same document.

To convert 5.0 merge codes to 5.1, retrieve the 5.0 merge file to the Edit screen, press Merge/Sort (Ctrl-F9), and select Convert Old Merge Codes. The conversion takes place immediately. Remember to save the document after the conversion so that the changes are made permanent.

USING 5.0 MACROS AND KEYBOARD LAYOUTS IN 5.1

To specify a directory for storing 5.1 macros and keyboard layouts, press Setup (Shift-F1) and choose Location of Files.

There's no special conversion needed to use your WordPerfect 5.0 macros and keyboard layouts in 5.1. But because some keystroke sequences have changed in 5.1, you may need to make changes to a macro to get it to work properly. Also, to make a macro or keyboard layout more accessible in WordPerfect 5.1, you should move or copy it to the keyboard/macros directory for 5.1. You can use the List Files feature (F5) to do so.

USING 5.0 GRAPHICS IN 5.1

WordPerfect has provided an entirely new set of sample graphics (.WPG files) in 5.1, but your 5.0 graphics are still fully functional. To put a .WPG graphic from 5.0 in a 5.1 graphic box, simply select Filename from the Definition menu for the box, and type the complete file name of the 5.0 graphic, including any necessary directory information.

You can make things a little simpler by copying the 5.0 .WPG files into whatever directory your 5.1 graphics are stored in. Use the List Files feature (F5). (To specify a directory for storing 5.1 graphic files, press Setup (Shift-F1) and select Location of Files.)

CONVERTING FONTS FOR USE IN 5.1

WordPerfect has changed the way in which leading (the space between lines of text) is managed in version 5.1: All proportional fonts now receive 2 points of leading, and monospaced fonts receive no additional leading.

Your best bet for updating third-party fonts (such as Bitstream's) to 5.1 is to contact the font manufacturer for an update of their fonts. Optionally, you can use the PTR program to update existing fonts to 5.1 format. See Chapter 8 for more information.

SUMMARY OF NEW AND IMPROVED FEATURES

WordPerfect has a number of new and improved features. Some of the features not found in earlier versions of the program are

FEATURE	DESCRIPTION	CHAPTER
Dormant Hard Return	Prevents an extra blank line at the top of the page	7
Equation Editor	Allows you to create and edit equations	21
Mouse Support	Mouse control of menus, the cursor, and blocking	2, 3
Pull-Down Menus	Menu alternatives to the function keys	3
Spreadsheet Linking and Importing	Links spreadsheets to documents dynamically	25
Tables	Simplifies typing columns, printing lines, and doing math	6

There are also a number of improved features:

FEATURE	IMPROVEMENT	CHAPTER
Help	Context-sensitive	3
Hyphenation	Can be based on the Speller dictionary	10, 11
Installation	Fully customizable	Appendix A
Justification	New Center, Left, Full, and Right options	5
Keyboard Layout	Sample keyboards and macros provided; Map feature	27
Labels	LABELS macro and simplified label formatting	7
Location of Files	Locations of document, graphic, and other files can be specified	13
Long Document Names	More descriptive document names allowed (up to 68 characters)	12
Macros	Numerous new commands	15, 26
Merges	Numerous new commands	16
Outlines	Outline styles can be defined	22
Page Numbering	New numbering styles available	7
Paper Size	Simplified; comes with predefined sizes	7
Printing	Selected pages, multiple copies, and back-to-back pages can be printed	8
Reveal Codes	Screen size can be specified	3
Special Characters	Over 1500 characters can be printed	5
Speller	Finds suspect capitalization	10

FEATURE	IMPROVEMENT	CHAPTER
Tabs	Can be absolute or relative to margin	4
Units of Measure	Fractions converted to decimals	4

PART ONE

Getting Started

The first three chapters of this book are written specifically for beginners. You'll learn how to start WordPerfect on your computer, and how to create, edit, print, save, and retrieve WordPerfect documents. The skills you'll learn in this part are the most important and fundamental, because you'll use them in every document you create. They also will pave the way to learning WordPerfect's more advanced features.

CHAPTER 1

Creating and Printing Your First Document

ordPerfect is a word processing program that helps you to create and edit *documents*. A document is anything you might type with a typewriter: a memo, a letter, an envelope, or a mailing label (or several hundred of each!); a schedule, an itinerary, an invitation, or a legal brief; or a coupon, an advertisement, a magazine article, a newsletter, or an entire book. No matter what kind of writing or typing you do, WordPerfect is sure to make your work easier and more productive.

Perhaps the single most important feature that WordPerfect offers can be summarized as simply this: *You can change anything in your document without retyping.* For example, you can

◆ Insert, delete, move, and copy words, sentences, paragraphs, and entire pages without retyping

◆ Change the spacing, margins, and format of your document without retyping

◆ Automatically check and correct your spelling in an entire document in a matter of seconds

◆ Print dozens or even hundreds of personalized form letters, mailing labels, and envelopes

◆ Embellish your documents with typefaces, tables, graphics, and multicolumn layouts

But this is just the beginning. As you'll see, WordPerfect offers much more than can be summarized in a few sentences. And no matter what sizes, types, or formats of documents you create, WordPerfect is certain to make your work much easier.

In this chapter, you'll learn how to create and print a document, and how to save the document for future use. This will bring you "up to speed" in using WordPerfect, whether you're an absolute beginner or an experienced computer user.

INSTALLING WORDPERFECT

WordPerfect is a *computer program,* a set of instructions that tells your computer how to act. Like all programs, WordPerfect must be purchased separately and installed on your computer before you can use it. You need to install WordPerfect only once, not each time you want to use it.

If you don't know whether Word-Perfect has already been installed, follow the instructions in this section to try starting it. There's no harm in trying!

There are two ways to know whether WordPerfect is already installed on your computer. You do not need to install WordPerfect if

◆ You share a computer with other people, and someone else is already using WordPerfect on that computer.

◆ You have already installed WordPerfect on your computer, or your computer dealer has done this for you.

You can find complete installation instructions in Appendix A.

GETTING STARTED

YOU MAY BE ABLE TO START WORDPERFECT

simply by typing C:\WP51\WP and pressing ↵ at the DOS command prompt (depending on how your system is configured).

In this section, you'll get WordPerfect up and running on your computer. Typically, when you first start your computer, its *operating system* (usually DOS) is in control. You need to enter commands that tell the operating system to turn control over to WordPerfect.

The exact steps you'll follow to start WordPerfect depend on whether your computer has a hard disk or just two floppy disks. Follow only those instructions that are appropriate for your computer.

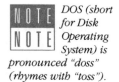 *DOS (short for Disk Operating System) is pronounced "doss" (rhymes with "toss").*

STARTING WORDPERFECT FROM A HARD DISK

If your computer has a hard disk, follow these steps to start WordPerfect:

1. Start your computer in the usual manner to get to the DOS command prompt (usually *C >*).

2. Type **C:** and press ↵.

3. Type **CD \WP51** and press ↵.

4. Type **WP** and press ↵.

 *Be sure to type **CD \WP51** (with a backslash, \), not **CD /WP51**, in step 3. CD is short for Change Directory.*

When you first start up WordPerfect, a copyright notice will appear briefly, and then the nearly blank WordPerfect Edit screen, with only the cursor, the status line, and perhaps the mouse pointer displayed.

STARTING WORDPERFECT FROM FLOPPY DISKS

 To prevent damage to your disks, always use felt-tip pens—never ballpoint pens or pencils—to write on disk labels after you have affixed them to disks.

If your computer does not have a hard disk, you will start WordPerfect from the disk labeled *WordPerfect 1*. You must already have installed WordPerfect before you can start it from floppy disks. You also must have two high-density disk drives, 720K or greater. (If you have a laptop computer, you may need to run WordPerfect from floppies.)

You'll also need a blank, formatted floppy disk for storing the documents that you create. If you're not sure how to format a floppy disk, see your DOS manual or *Mastering DOS 5,* by Judd Robbins, SYBEX, 1991. Typically, a box of blank disks comes with a set of blank labels. Write **WordPerfect Practice** on one of the labels and affix it to the blank, formatted disk.

When you're ready to start WordPerfect, follow these steps:

1. Start your computer in the usual manner to get to the DOS command prompt (usually *A>*).

2. Remove the disk currently in drive A of your computer.

3. Put your WordPerfect 1 disk in drive A.

4. Put your blank, formatted disk labeled *WordPerfect Practice* (as described above) in drive B.

5. Type **B:** and press ↵ to switch to drive B.

6. Type **A:WP** and press ↵.

You should see a copyright notice appear on the screen. You will then be prompted to

Insert diskette labeled "WordPerfect 2" and press any key

Remove the disk currently in drive A, and insert the WordPerfect 2 disk. Then press any key to continue (for example, press the spacebar).

You will see the WordPerfect Edit screen, with the cursor, the status line, and perhaps the mouse pointer displayed. Once you've started WordPerfect from floppy disks, leave the disks in drives A and B until WordPerfect instructs you to change them or until you've exited WordPerfect (as discussed later).

UNDERSTANDING THE EDIT SCREEN

When you first start WordPerfect, your screen will look something like Figure 1.1. The large blank area is where you will do your typing and editing (it's like a blank sheet of paper). The other parts of the screen pointed out are described below.

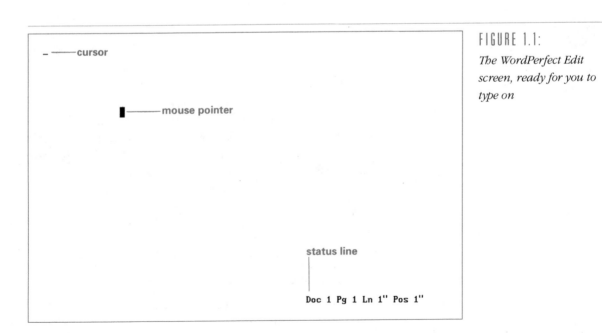

FIGURE 1.1:

The WordPerfect Edit screen, ready for you to type on

cursor

mouse pointer

status line

Doc 1 Pg 1 Ln 1" Pos 1"

THE CURSOR

The *cursor* is a small, blinking underline that appears near the upper-left corner of your screen. It shows where the next character that you type will appear on the screen. As you'll see later, you can also move the cursor through existing text without typing in order to position it under letters or words that you want to change, delete, or move.

THE MOUSE POINTER

If you have a mouse but don't see the mouse pointer, try moving the mouse. If this doesn't work, make sure the mouse driver has been loaded (see the manual that came with your mouse).

If your computer has a mouse attached, you'll also see a *mouse pointer*. Unlike the cursor, which is a small, blinking underline, the mouse pointer is a solid, unblinking square, which moves in whatever direction you move the mouse.

Using a mouse with WordPerfect is optional, but in case you have one and like it, I'll talk about ways you can use it, particularly in Chapter 3.

THE STATUS LINE

At the bottom of your screen is the *status line*, which provides information about the position of the cursor on the screen in relation to its position on a printed sheet of paper, as summarized below:

If you share a computer with others, someone may have changed the units of measurement from inches (") to centimeters (c) or some other scale. Don't worry about that.

Doc: shows which document you are currently typing or editing, Doc 1 or Doc 2. Chapter 3 explains how to work with two documents at a time.

Pg: shows which page you are currently typing or editing. In Figure 1.1, the Pg indicator shows *1,* because the cursor is at the top of the first (currently blank) page.

Ln: shows which line you are currently typing or editing, as measured in inches from the top of the printed page. In Figure 1.1, the Ln indicator shows *1",* because the cursor is automatically placed 1 inch below the top of the printed page. (Above the cursor, there is an invisible 1-inch margin, which appears only on the printed copy of the document.)

Pos: shows the cursor position, as measured in inches from the left side of the printed page. In Figure 1.1, the Pos indicator shows *1",* because the cursor is in the leftmost screen position. (To the left of the cursor, there is an invisible 1-inch margin, which appears only on the printed page.)

As you'll see in Chapter 4, you can easily change the standard 1-inch margins at any time. WordPerfect uses 1-inch margins as *defaults* (predefined settings) for your convenience, since these are standard settings for many types of documents, such as letters and memos.

The 1-inch margins will appear on the printed copy of the document, but don't appear on the screen.

THE PULL-DOWN MENUS

The Edit screen acts as a blank piece of paper for you to type on. Other tasks, such as printing your document, saving it for future use, and so forth, are available through *pull-down menus* (so named because you pull them down from the top of the screen).

To get to the pull-down menus, you must first display the menu bar, shown in Figure 1.2, using either of these techniques:

I'll discuss using the mouse and additional menu techniques in more detail in Chapter 3. For now, however, you just need to know the basics.

◆ Press **Alt-=** (hold down the **Alt** key, press **=**, then release both keys).

◆ Press and release the right button on your mouse.

To view a pull-down menu, you first need to make a selection from the menu bar. You can use any of three methods:

*You can use either uppercase or lowercase letters to choose options from the menu bar; for example, you can type either **F** or **f** to choose **F**ile.*

◆ Press the highlighted (or colored) letter of the appropriate option (e.g., press **F** to view the **F**ile pull-down menu).

◆ Use the ← and → keys to move the highlighted bar to the option you want, then press ↵ to select it.

◆ Move the mouse pointer to the option you want, and click the left mouse button.

Figure 1.3 shows the File pull-down menu.

Making a selection from a pull-down menu is exactly the same as making a selection from the menu bar. You can press the highlighted letter, move the highlight to an option and press ↵, or position the mouse pointer and click the left mouse button.

Removing the Menus

If you accidentally call up a menu that you do not understand or for any reason want to leave the menus without making a selection, you can do either of the following:

◆ Press **Alt-=**.

◆ Click the right mouse button.

The menus will disappear, and you'll be back at the normal Edit screen.

```
File Edit Search Layout Mark Tools Font Graphics Help        (Press F3 for Help)




                    menu bar






                                             Doc 1 Pg 1 Ln 1" Pos 1"
```

FIGURE 1.2:

The menu bar appears at the top of the Edit screen after you press Alt-= or click the right mouse button.

You'll make some useful menu selections a little later in this chapter. For now, you can use either method to remove the menus. As mentioned, you'll learn about the menus and the mouse in more detail in Chapter 3. For now, however, focus on building your typing and editing skills.

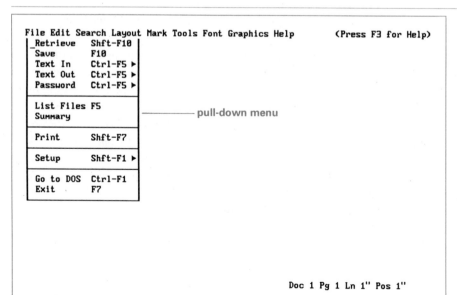

```
File Edit Search Layout Mark Tools Font Graphics Help        (Press F3 for Help)
 _Retrieve   Shft-F10
  Save       F10
  Text In    Ctrl-F5 ▶
  Text Out   Ctrl-F5 ▶
  Password   Ctrl-F5 ▶

  List Files F5
  Summary                ———————— pull-down menu

  Print      Shft-F7

  Setup      Shft-F1 ▶

  Go to DOS  Ctrl-F1
  Exit       F7



                                             Doc 1 Pg 1 Ln 1" Pos 1"
```

FIGURE 1.3:

When the menu bar is displayed, you can pull down the File menu by typing the letter F or by moving the mouse pointer to File and clicking the left mouse button.

USING YOUR KEYBOARD

If this is the first time you've used a computer, you'll undoubtedly notice that its keyboard is different from that of a standard typewriter. The computer keyboard is divided into four main areas:

◆ The function keys

◆ The typing keys

◆ The numeric keypad

◆ The cursor-movement keys

Figure 1.4 shows these areas on three popular computer keyboards.

The figure also points out the locations of the Tab, Backspace, Shift, and Enter (↵) keys. Before actually putting WordPerfect to work, let's take a look at a few special keys on your keyboard and how they work in WordPerfect. Be aware that different keyboards use different symbols for some keys. For example, the ↵ key is sometimes labeled *Enter* or *Return*. Refer to Figure 1.4 if you have trouble locating ↵, Tab, Shift, or Backspace.

THE NUM LOCK KEY

The arrows and other special keys don't do anything until you have typed some text on your screen, so don't worry too much about these keys right now.

Some keyboards also have separate keypads for cursor movement and other special keys.

The Num Lock key has no equivalent on a typewriter. It determines whether numbers or other special keys are used when you press keys on the numeric keypad. When Num Lock is on, the numbers work. When Num Lock is off, the arrow keys and other special keys work.

As you'll learn in Chapter 2, the arrows and other special keys are important because they allow you to edit existing text. The numbers on the numeric keypad are not so important, because you can use the numbers at the top of the typing area (as on a typewriter) to type numbers. I recommend that you leave Num Lock off when using WordPerfect and always type numbers by using the top row of keys on your keyboard.

When the Num Lock key is in the On position, the Pos indicator on the status line blinks and, on some keyboards, a light is also illuminated on the keyboard (near the Num Lock key). Although you won't have to be too concerned with the arrows and other special keys in this chapter, you should start making it a habit now to press the Num Lock key whenever you see the Pos indicator blinking on your screen. This will turn Num Lock off.

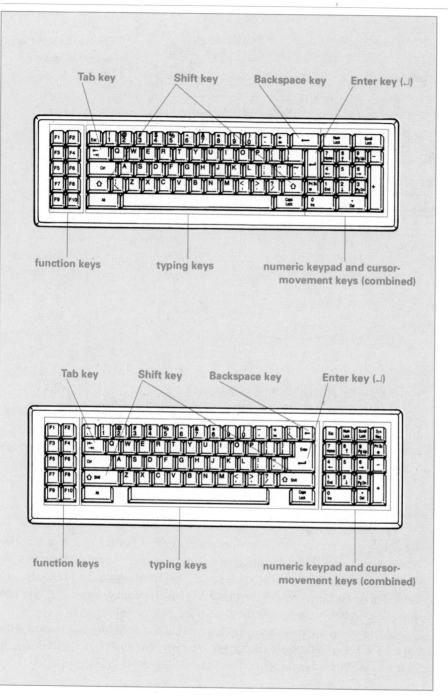

Popular computer keyboards

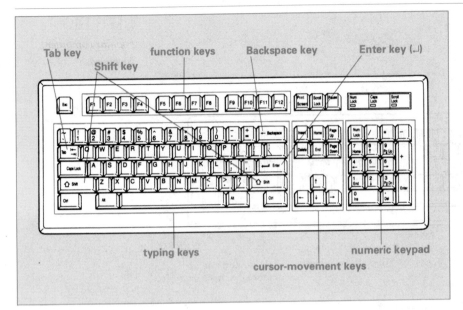

THE CAPS LOCK KEY

The Caps Lock key works much like it does on most typewriters. When Caps Lock is on, letters are typed in uppercase (the Pos indicator on the status line appears in uppercase letters). When Caps Lock is off, letters are typed in lowercase (Pos appears with an initial capital). The Caps Lock key has no effect on numbers or punctuation marks.

THE SHIFT KEY

The Shift key serves the same purpose in WordPerfect as on a standard typewriter. It's used to type uppercase letters or other special characters. For example, to type a single capital letter *A,* you hold down the Shift key, type the letter **A**, and then release the Shift key. To type an asterisk (*), you hold down the Shift key and press the * key (the number 8).

Unlike many typewriters, the function of the Shift key is reversed when Caps Lock is on: Letters are displayed in uppercase, but if you hold down the Shift key and then type a letter, the letter is displayed in lowercase.

THE TAB KEY

The Tab key works the same on the computer keyboard as it does on a typewriter: It indents to the next tab stop. Press Tab whenever you want to indent the first line of a new paragraph.

The Tab key is also very useful in controlling other types of indentations and alignments, as you'll learn in Chapter 4. You'll also learn to control how far the Tab key indents text, so you can gain more precise control over the appearance of your documents.

 On some keyboards the Tab key is marked with two opposing arrows; it is usually to the left of the letter Q.

THE BACKSPACE KEY

The Backspace key lets you back up and make corrections as you type, much like the Backspace key on a typewriter with a correctable ribbon.

Don't confuse the Backspace key, which is in the typing-key area, with the ← key, which is one of the cursor-movement keys. The Backspace key erases text as the cursor backs up. The ← key simply moves the cursor back through existing text without erasing anything.

 On many keyboards, the Backspace key is marked only with an elongated ←.

THE ENTER KEY

The Enter (↵) key is the computer's equivalent of the typewriter's carriage-return key. On some keyboards the key may be labeled as simply ↵ or Return. You press it when you've finished typing a line of text or to select a currently highlighted item, as you'll see throughout this book.

When typing a document in WordPerfect, you use the ↵ key to end short lines of text, to insert blank lines, and to end paragraphs. Unlike with a typewriter, however, you do not need to press ↵ to end each line of text within a paragraph. I'll discuss this in more detail in the section "Typing with WordPerfect."

THE CANCEL KEY

The Cancel key (F1) might just be the most important function key in WordPerfect. It's the universal "I want to get out" key, because it lets you cancel unfamiliar operations and return to more familiar territory. For example, if you inadvertently make a number of incorrect menu selections and end up at a screen that you don't understand, you can usually press the Cancel (F1) key (perhaps a few times) to work your way back to the more familiar Edit screen, without making any choices from the menus that appear. As you'll learn in the next chapter, the Cancel key also lets you restore accidentally deleted text in your document.

Function keys (labeled F1 through F12 on your keyboard) are also known as shortcut keys.

You can also escape from just about any situation by using your mouse. For example, to cancel a menu without making a selection, click the right mouse button.

COMBINATION KEYSTROKES

Combination keystrokes are often used as optional shortcuts for selecting pull-down menu options. Shortcuts are handy when you become proficient with your keyboard and want to activate frequently used commands by pressing a key or two, rather than by selecting options from menus.

 For best results, don't try to press the combination keys simultaneously. For example, to press Ctrl-F5, hold down the first key (Ctrl), then, while you're holding it down, press the second key (F5). Then release both keys.

On WordPerfect screens, a hyphen between two keys indicates a combination keystroke. For example, Ctrl-F5 means "hold down the Ctrl (Control) key, press the function key labeled F5, then release both keys." The combination Alt-F7 means "hold down the Alt (Alternate) key, press F7, then release both keys." Likewise, Shift-S means "hold down the Shift key, press the letter S, then release both keys."

If you experiment with these combination keystrokes, you may bring up menus you are not familiar with yet. If so, just press Cancel (F1) to cancel any selection.

TYPEMATIC KEYSTROKES

Unlike some typewriters, all the computer's typing keys are *typematic*. This means you can repeat a keystroke simply by holding down the key. You can see this for yourself by holding down any letter key on the keyboard for a few seconds. To erase the letters you typed, hold down the Backspace key.

TYPING WITH WORDPERFECT

TO TYPE A DOCUMENT WITH WORDPERFECT,

type as you normally would, except remember that when typing paragraphs, press ↵ only at the end of each paragraph, not at the end of each line.

Typing with WordPerfect is almost identical to typing with a regular typewriter, except for these three differences:

◆ Do not use the letter *l* in place of the number *1,* and do not use the letter *O* in place of the number *0;* they are not the same to a computer, and they do not look the same when printed by most printers.

LESSON 1

If you want some quick, hands-on experience in typing and printing a WordPerfect document, refer to Lesson 1 in Part 9, near the back of this book.

*If you want to add a blank line between paragraphs, press ↵ twice at the end of each paragraph. If you accidentally press the ↵ key and catch the error right away, just press the **Backspace** key, once for each ↵ you entered.*

◆ Because WordPerfect already assumes that 1-inch margins will be needed on the printed document, you need not do anything to add margins to your text.

◆ As you type past the right margin on your screen, WordPerfect automatically *word-wraps* text to the next line. You should only press ↵ to end a short line that does not reach the right margin, to end a paragraph, or to add a blank line.

This last difference between typewriters and WordPerfect is perhaps the hardest one for experienced typists to get used to. But it's important to let WordPerfect handle the right margin automatically, by not pressing ↵ until you've finished typing a paragraph. This gives you maximum flexibility to add, change, or delete words or sentences in the middle of the paragraph later.

To illustrate, Figure 1.5 shows a sample printed business letter typed with WordPerfect. Figure 1.6 shows the same letter, but with ↵ keystroke symbols that indicate where you would press ↵ while typing the document.

HOW LARGE CAN YOUR DOCUMENT BE?

Don't let the size of the WordPerfect Edit screen fool you into thinking that you can create only small documents—this entire book was created with WordPerfect! As you'll see when you do the hands-on lessons in Part 9, WordPerfect automatically *scrolls* text to give you more room when you need it.

You can easily review and change text that has scrolled out of view by using the mouse or the various scrolling keys, such as ↑, ↓, Page Up (PgUp), Page Down (PgDn), and others.

One word of advice, though: The larger a document is, the longer it takes to perform basic operations like printing, saving, checking spelling, and so forth. Therefore, if you plan to create a *really* large document, like a book, it's best to treat each chapter as a separate document.

PRINTING A DOCUMENT

LESSON 1

Lesson 1 in Part 9 takes you through all the steps of creating and printing a document.

TO PRINT YOUR WORDPERFECT DOCUMENT,

select Print from the File pull-down menu, then select Full Document (or press Shift-F7 F).

You can print the document that you are currently working on at any time, using the menus. To print a document that's currently on your screen, follow these steps:

1. Press **Alt-=** or click the right mouse button to display the menu bar.

2. Select **F**ile from the menu bar, either by pressing **F** or moving the mouse pointer to File and clicking the left mouse button.

3. Select **P**rint just as you chose File, either by pressing **P** or moving the mouse pointer to Print and clicking the left mouse button.

4. On the next screen, select **F**ull Document by pressing **F** or by moving the mouse pointer to Full Document and clicking the left mouse button.

As the Fast Track at the beginning of this section indicates, you can optionally use the shortcut of pressing **Shift-F7** and then **F** to print a document. Again,

August 7, 1991

Sidney R. Jackson, M.D.
Bayside Medical Group
5231 East Statton Drive, Suite 106
Los Angeles, CA 92312

Dear Dr. Jackson:

The update on your insurance policy is as follows. I am including a letter from the Regional Manager of Farmstead regarding the information specific to your occupational and medical concerns. Pending receipt of a referral letter from your previous doctor, this letter serves as an important part of your policy and should be safeguarded with your other documents.

I have turned over your policy to a full-time insurance agent, Bastien Cole. He will be able to serve you more adequately and provide the detailed information you may need for your specific problems. This will also allow me to relinquish my commissions in order to better serve you in a consultant capacity. In the meantime, however, you do have coverage in effect.

As indicated earlier by phone, I will be out of town for the next three weeks. Should you have any questions, please feel free to leave a message for me at my Florida office. I will be in contact with them daily for messages. Rest assured that I hope to continue to be of service to you.

Sincerely,

Edna R. Jones, M.D.

ERJ:ess

cc: Bastien Cole

deciding when to use a shortcut or when to use the menus is entirely up to you.

There may be a few seconds' delay while WordPerfect prepares the document for printing. But, assuming that your printer is properly connected, turned on, online, and ready to accept output from the computer, your document should start printing soon.

When the printing is finished, you'll be returned to the Edit screen. But don't turn off your computer! You'll probably want to save your document for future use, and you should always properly *exit* WordPerfect before turning off your computer, as discussed in a moment.

Incidentally, you'll notice that your printed document has 1-inch margins all the way around, which do not appear on the Edit screen. These are the *default* margins, which WordPerfect uses for every printed document. You can change these margins if you wish (you'll learn how in Chapter 4).

Your printed document will also have a smooth right margin, which can cause some extra space between words in each line. The smooth right margin

```
August 7, 1991⏎
⏎
Sidney R. Jackson, M.D.⏎
Bayside Medical Group⏎
5231 East Statton Drive, Suite 106⏎
Los Angeles, CA  92312⏎
⏎
Dear Dr. Jackson:⏎
⏎
The update on your insurance policy is as follows.  I am
including a letter from the Regional Manager of Farmstead
regarding the information specific to your occupational and
medical concerns.  Pending receipt of a referral letter from your
previous doctor, this letter serves as an important part of your
policy and should be safeguarded with your other documents.⏎
⏎
I have turned over your policy to a full-time insurance agent,
Bastien Cole.  He will be able to serve you more adequately and
provide the detailed information you may need for your specific
problems.  This will also allow me to relinquish my commissions
in order to better serve you in a consultant capacity.  In the
meantime, however, you do have coverage in effect.⏎
⏎
As indicated earlier by phone, I will be out of town for the next
three weeks.  Should you have any questions, please feel free to
leave a message for me at my Florida office.  I will be in
contact with them daily for messages.  Rest assured that I hope
to continue to be of service to you.⏎
⏎
Sincerely,⏎
⏎
⏎
Edna R. Jones, M.D.⏎
⏎
ERJ:ess⏎
⏎
cc:  Bastien Cole
```

FIGURE 1.6:

The ⏎ symbols show where you would press ⏎ while typing the letter: at the ends of short lines, at the ends of paragraphs, and wherever you want blank lines.

is another default setting (called *full justification*). You'll learn how to switch to a ragged right margin (left justification) in Chapter 4, which removes the extra space between words in each line.

PRINTER PROBLEMS

*If your printer refuses to print, you may be able to find out why simply by pressing **Shift-F7** and then **C** to get to the Printer Control screen (see Chapter 8).*

If WordPerfect cannot print your document or prints gobbledygook, it may be because the printer is not properly connected or installed. Refer to Chapter 8 for more information on printing if you have problems.

SAVING YOUR WORK

> **TO SAVE YOUR WORK AND EXIT WORDPERFECT,**
>
> select Exit from the File pull-down menu, or press Exit (F7). Then press Y when asked about saving, and enter a file name (or press ↵ to reuse the previous file name). Then select Yes twice when asked about replacing and exiting.

It's important to understand that the document shown on your WordPerfect Edit screen is stored in the computer's *memory* (also called *RAM* for random access memory). When you turn off your computer, everything in memory is immediately and permanently erased.

Chapter 12 discusses general file management techniques, including erasing files.

Therefore, it's important to *save* a copy of your document in a file on your disk, in case you want to make changes to it later. Information stored on-disk is permanent—it is *not* erased when you turn off your computer. In fact, it is erased only if you take specific actions to erase it.

Before saving a document, you must first think up a *file name* for the document, as discussed in the next section.

NAMING DOCUMENTS

Anything that you save on a hard or floppy disk, including a WordPerfect document, is considered to be a *file*. Individual files are often stored in groups, called *directories,* on the disk. Every file in a given directory on the disk must have a unique name. That is, no two files in the same directory can have the same name.

The name you assign to a file must conform to the following rules and conventions:

◆ The name can be up to eight characters long and can contain letters, numbers, or both.

◆ The name can be followed by a period and an *extension* up to three characters long. The period that separates the file name from the extension is the only period allowed.

◆ Neither the name nor the extension can contain blank spaces.

◆ The name can contain underscores (_) or hyphens (-), but none of the following characters: * ? + = [ ] : ; ^ " / \ ¦ > <.

◆ The name can be typed in upper- or lowercase. All file names are converted to uppercase; hence, the file names *SMITH.LET, Smith.Let, Smith.let,* and *smith.let* are all the same.

Examples of valid and invalid file names are shown in Table 1.1.

When deciding on a file name, try to use a descriptive name that will make it easy to find the file in the future. For example, the file name *XXX* tells you nothing about the contents of that file. But the file name *SMITH* (albeit brief) at least gives you a clue that the file contains something about somebody named Smith, perhaps a letter to that person.

Furthermore, although the extension to a file name is optional, it can be handy for remembering the type of information stored in the file. For example, you might want to use the file extension *.WP* when saving WordPerfect documents so that in the future you can tell which files on your disk are Word-Perfect documents simply by looking at the extensions.

Using consistent file-name extensions also makes it easier to select a group of files, based on their extensions, when you use the List Files feature (Chapter 12).

SAVING AND EXITING

Once you've decided on a file name for your document, here's how to save the document:

1. Press **Alt-=** to display the menu bar.

2. Press **F** or click on File to display the File pull-down menu.

3. Press **X** or click on Exit to select the option.

4. The screen displays the prompt "Save document? **Yes** (**No**)". Press **Y** (or just press ↵) to select Yes. The screen displays "Document to be saved:".

FILE NAME	VALID/INVALID
LETTER	Valid
LETTER.1	Valid
SMITH.LET	Valid
1991TAX.QT1	Valid
QTR_1.WP	Valid
QTR-1.WP	Valid
MyLetter.wp	Valid (but converted to MYLETTER.WP)
QTR 1.WP	Invalid (contains a blank space)
QTR1.W P	Invalid (extension contains a blank space)
12.1.91.WP	Invalid (too many periods)
MYFIRSTLETTER.TXT	Invalid (too long, but will be accepted and converted to MYFIRSTL.TXT)
WON'T.WP	Invalid (contains a punctuation mark)

TABLE 1.1:

Examples of Valid and Invalid File Names

If you've worked on the current document before, the existing file is probably just the previous draft of this document.

WP is an abbreviation for WordPerfect.

5. Type the file name you've decided on, and press ↵. If a file with the name you entered already exists on the current drive and directory, you'll see a prompt asking whether it's OK to replace the existing file with the one you are currently saving, followed by the options "**N**o (**Y**es)".

◆ If you want to replace the existing file with the document that's currently on your screen, answer Yes by pressing **Y**. You would want to do this only in a situation where you don't care to keep the "old" existing file, for example, when the document currently being saved is an improvement on the previous draft that already exists.

◆ If you don't want to replace the existing file with the one currently on your screen (or are not sure), select No by pressing **N**. You'll be prompted to enter a different file name for this document. Repeat step 4 above, but enter a different file name. This new version of the document will have the new name you provide; the original document (or previous draft) will keep its original name.

6. Next, you'll see the prompt "Exit WP? **N**o (**Y**es)".

◆ If you want to leave WordPerfect and turn off your computer or run a different program, press **Y** to answer Yes. You'll be returned to the DOS prompt.

◆ If you want to stay in WordPerfect and work on a different document, press **N** (or just press ↵) to select No. Your document will be saved on the disk, then cleared from the Edit screen. If you want to continue working on the document, press **F1.**

 *Failure to save and exit before turning off your computer almost always leads to lost work and wasted time.*

Again, let me stress that it's important to remember to save your work and exit WordPerfect before you turn off your computer.

TAKING THE ON-SCREEN TUTORIAL LESSONS

TO START THE WORDPERFECT TUTORIAL,

Return to the DOS prompt, then type C: and press ↵. Type CD \WP51\LEARN and press ↵. Then type TUTOR and press ↵.

As an adjunct to the hands-on exercises in Part 9 of this book, you might want to try using the WordPerfect Tutor program, which comes with your WordPerfect package. If you've installed the tutorial (as described in Appendix A), you can give it a try right now.

STARTING THE TUTOR FROM A HARD DISK

 *If you experience a problem that prevents the tutorial from running on your computer, it may not have been installed on your hard disk. However, you might want to try running it one more time, just in case you mistyped one of the commands.*

If your computer has a hard disk, be sure to exit WordPerfect. Make sure the DOS command prompt (usually *C >*) is displayed, and follow these steps to start the WordPerfect Tutor:

1. Type **C:** and press ↵.

2. Type **CD \WP51\LEARN** and press ↵.

3. Type **TUTOR** and press ↵.

4. When prompted to type your name, do so and press ↵. You can type up to nine letters, using your first or last name (or any name you wish, for that matter).

STARTING THE TUTOR FROM FLOPPY DISKS

If your computer does not have a hard disk, you can follow the steps below to take the tutorial. First, make sure that you've already exited WordPerfect and that the DOS command prompt (usually *A>* or *B>*) is displayed on your screen. Then follow these steps:

1. Insert the *WordPerfect 1* disk in drive A (if it is not already inserted).

2. Insert the WordPerfect *Learning-Images* disk in drive B.

3. Type **B:** and press ↵.

4. Type **PATH A:** and press ↵.

5. Type **TUTOR** and press ↵.

6. When asked for your name, type your name (up to nine letters).

7. Press ↵.

USING THE TUTOR PROGRAM

Figure 1.7 shows the tutorial screen as it first appears after you enter your name (though you may need to wait a few seconds before you see this screen). The

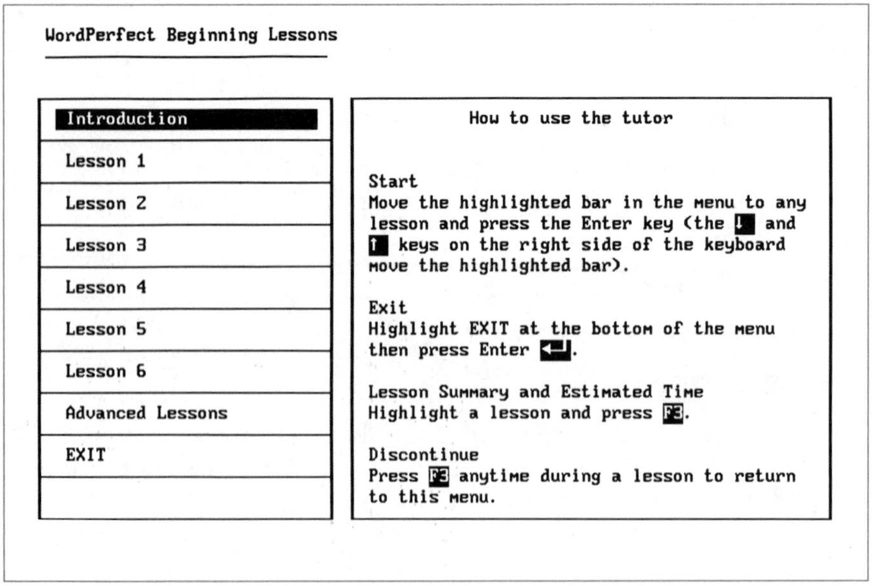

FIGURE 1.7:
The Tutor's first screen

program is quite self-explanatory, as everything you need to know is displayed right on the screen. Remember these points:

◆ On some machines the ↑, ↓, →, and ← keys on the numeric keypad work only when Num Lock is off. If you press one of these keys and nothing happens, press the Num Lock key, and then try pressing an arrow key again.

◆ When the Tutor tells you to "Press Any Key to Continue," press a regular typing key, like a letter, the spacebar, or ↵. Don't press Ctrl, Alt, or Shift, as these keys do nothing by themselves.

◆ When asked to type a number, use the numbers at the top of the typing keys, not the numbers on the numeric keypad.

To take a lesson from the Tutor program, use the ↑ or ↓ key to move the highlight to one of the lessons in the list. Then, press ↵ to take the currently highlighted lesson. It's probably best to start with the introductory lesson. Follow these steps:

1. If *Introduction* is not already highlighted, press ↑ until the highlighter is on the Introduction option.

2. Press ↵.

3. Follow the instructions that appear on the screen.

The tutorial will guide you through your first lesson. Follow the instructions presented on the screen as they appear, and try to look toward the top of the screen while pressing any keys that the Tutor instructs you to press. When you've completed the lesson, you'll see a review of the topics covered in the lesson; then you can press any key to return to the Lessons screen.

After you take a lesson and return to the Lessons screen, a check mark appears to the left of the completed lesson's name. Even though the lessons you've taken are marked with a check, you can still take any lesson again just by highlighting its name and pressing ↵.

When you've finished taking a lesson (or lessons), move the highlight to the EXIT option by using the ↓ key and then press ↵. You will be returned to the DOS command prompt. At that point, you can either turn off your computer or use WordPerfect again. (But don't forget to follow *all* the steps necessary to start the WordPerfect program, as described near the beginning of this chapter.)

In the next chapter, you'll learn how to retrieve a saved document and make changes to it. As you will see, the real beauty of word processing is that it allows you to change anything in your document, without ever retyping.

While taking a lesson, it's sometimes difficult to read the instructions on the screen, follow those instructions, and watch what's happening on the screen all at the same time. Therefore, you might want to repeat each lesson a few times.

CHAPTER 2

Editing Your Documents

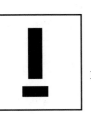

!n this chapter you'll learn how to edit a WordPerfect document by adding, changing, moving, and deleting text. As you'll see, you can make almost any change imaginable. And you can edit a document at any time: while you are creating it or long after you've printed and saved it.

HANDS-ON
....
LESSON 2

Lesson 2 in Part 9 provides hands-on examples of editing the document you created in Lesson 1.

If you have already saved your document and exited WordPerfect, you'll need to do two things to get started:

◆ Start WordPerfect and get to the Edit screen (described in Chapter 1).

◆ *Retrieve* the document you want to edit (described in the next section).

RETRIEVING A SAVED DOCUMENT

TO RETRIEVE A DOCUMENT,

select Retrieve from the File pull-down menu or press Retrieve (Shift-F10), then type the name of the file you want to retrieve and press ↵.

If you've already saved a document and no longer have it on your Edit screen, you'll need to retrieve that document to make changes to it. If you have a different document on your screen at the moment, you may want to save that document first and clear the screen. If the document that you want to edit is currently on the Edit screen, skip all steps below (you don't need to retrieve the document, since it's already on your screen).

If another document is on the Edit screen, you should save it (if you haven't done so already), then clear the screen as described in "Saving and Exiting" in Chapter 1. Briefly, the steps for saving a file and clearing the screen are as follows:

1. Select E**x**it from the **F**ile pull-down menu, or press Exit (**F7**).

2. When asked whether you want to save the document, press **Y** for Yes or **N** for No.

3. If you answered Yes to the previous prompt, type a file name and press ↵. If the file already exists, you'll be asked whether you want to replace it. Press **Y** if you want to replace it. If you don't want to replace it, press **N**, then type a new file name.

4. Finally, press **N** (for No) when asked whether you want to exit Word-Perfect. The screen will clear and you'll be ready to retrieve your document.

To retrieve your document, follow these steps:

1. Pull down the File menu as shown in Figure 2.1 (press **Alt-=** or click the right mouse button, then press **F** or move the mouse pointer to the File option on the menu bar and click the left mouse button).

2. Select **R**etrieve by pressing **R** or by moving the mouse pointer to Retrieve and clicking the left mouse button.

3. When you see the prompt "Document to be retrieved:", type the complete file name and press ↵.

The document appears on the Edit screen, ready for editing. If you can't find the file, or you see a message indicating that the requested file cannot be found, perhaps you misspelled the file name when typing it in. If you have problems retrieving files, refer to Chapter 12 for more information.

*Every document you save is stored as a **file** on the computer disk.*

As you'll see in the next chapter, Word-Perfect also lets you edit two documents at once.

*You can complete steps 1 and 2 with a single keystroke by pressing Retrieve (**Shift-F10**) instead of using the pull-down menu.*

POSITIONING THE CURSOR

TO MOVE THE CURSOR TO ANY CHARACTER IN THE DOCUMENT,

use the cursor-movement keys listed in Table 2.1, or move the mouse pointer to the character where you want the cursor to appear and click the left mouse button.

The arrows and other special keys on your keyboard let you move the cursor through a document *without changing any text*. Keep in mind the following points when moving the cursor:

◆ You can move the cursor through existing text only; that is, you cannot move down past the last line in a document (though you can press ↵ to *add* a line). Similarly, you cannot move past the end of a short line (though you can insert more spaces at the end of a line by pressing the spacebar).

◆ You can use the arrow keys to move and position the cursor, but the ones on the numeric keypad work only if the Num Lock key is off.

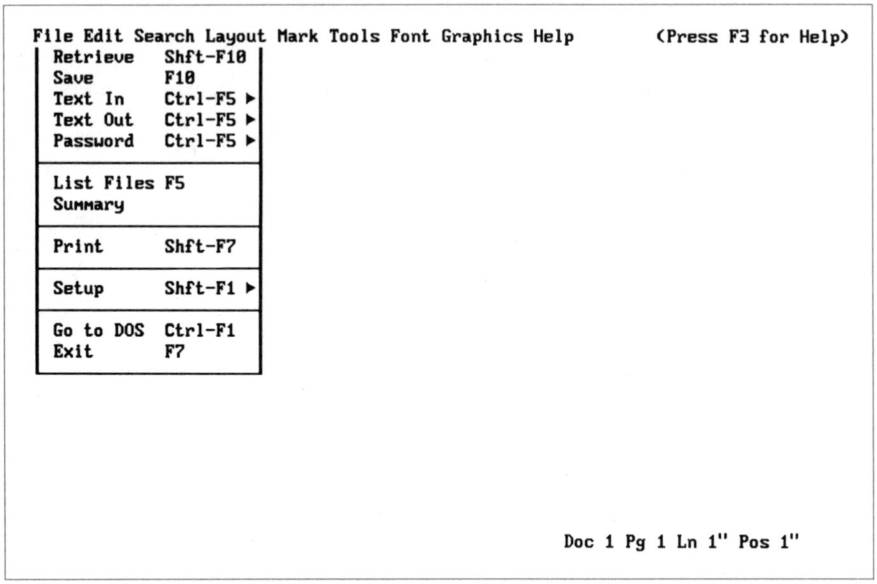

```
File Edit Search Layout Mark Tools Font Graphics Help        (Press F3 for Help)
  Retrieve    Shft-F10
  Save        F10
  Text In     Ctrl-F5 ▶
  Text Out    Ctrl-F5 ▶
  Password    Ctrl-F5 ▶

  List Files F5
  Summary

  Print       Shft-F7

  Setup       Shft-F1 ▶

  Go to DOS  Ctrl-F1
  Exit        F7




                                    Doc 1 Pg 1 Ln 1" Pos 1"
```

FIGURE 2.1:

The File pull-down menu lets you save and retrieve files.

◆ You can also quickly position the cursor under any character on the screen by moving the mouse pointer to that character and clicking the left mouse button.

◆ Remember that most of the keys on the keyboard, including the cursor-movement keys, are typematic and will repeat if you press and hold them (see Chapter 1). For example, if you press and hold the ↑, ↓, ←, or → keys, you can quickly move through your document.

◆ Remember, a hyphen indicates a combination keystroke. For example, Ctrl-→ means "hold down the Ctrl key and press →."

◆ A space between two keystrokes indicates separate keystrokes. For example, Home ← means "press and release the Home key, then press and release the ← key."

Figure 2.2 shows the basic cursor-movement keys on the numeric keypad. You can also use the arrow and other special keys next to the numeric keypad, if your keyboard has them. These keys move the cursor regardless of whether Num Lock is on or off.

Table 2.1 presents a more detailed description of the cursor-movement keys. You may notice that the Home key can be used to exaggerate the effect of the key you press next. For example, pressing → moves the cursor one

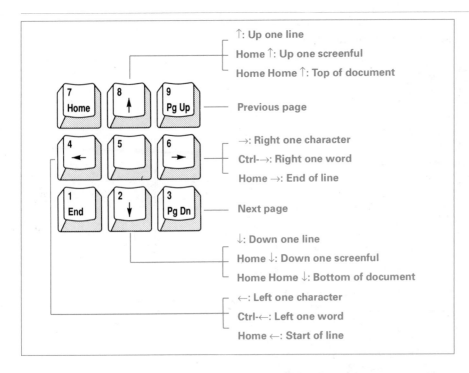

FIGURE 2.2:

Keys for cursor movement on the numeric keypad

↑: Up one line

Home ↑: Up one screenful

Home Home ↑: Top of document

Previous page

→: Right one character

Ctrl-→: Right one word

Home →: End of line

Next page

↓: Down one line

Home ↓: Down one screenful

Home Home ↓: Bottom of document

←: Left one character

Ctrl-←: Left one word

Home ←: Start of line

TO MOVE	PRESS
Left one character	←
Right one character	→
Left one word	Ctrl-←
Right one word	Ctrl-→
To left edge of screen	Home ←
To right edge of screen	Home →
To beginning of line	Home Home ←
To end of line	Home Home → (or End)
Up one line	↑
Down one line	↓
To top of screen	Home ↑ (or gray −)
To bottom of screen	Home ↓ (or gray +)
To previous page	Page Up
To next page	Page Down
Up one paragraph	Ctrl-↑ *
Down one paragraph	Ctrl-↓ *
To beginning of document (after codes)	Home Home ↑
To beginning of document (before codes)	Home Home Home ↑
To end of document	Home Home ↓

* Available on enhanced keyboards only

TABLE 2.1:

Cursor-Movement Keys

NOTE NOTE *If Num Lock is on, pressing an arrow or another special key on the numeric keypad types the number instead of moving the cursor.*

character to the right, but pressing Home and then → moves the cursor all the way to the end of the line.

If you press ← or → and the cursor does not move, or moves erratically, it's not a malfunction: WordPerfect is moving the cursor through "hidden codes" that you cannot see at the moment. I'll discuss these codes in the next chapter (which also clarifies the difference between Home Home ↑ and Home Home Home ↑). In the meantime, you can just press the arrow key until the cursor does move.

You can easily try most of the cursor-movement keys on your own, so long as there is a document on your Edit screen to move the cursor through. A couple of general techniques, however, are described in more detail below.

NOTE NOTE *If you don't have an enhanced keyboard, Ctrl-↑ and Ctrl-↓ do nothing. But you can "remap" the keyboard (see Chapter 27) to activate these keys.*

MOVING THROUGH PAGES

TO SCROLL THROUGH DOCUMENTS THAT ARE LARGER THAN THE SCREEN,

use the gray + and – keys or the Page Up and Page Down keys, or press the right mouse button and drag in the direction of the text you want to see.

As you gain experience with WordPerfect, you'll undoubtedly create documents that are several pages long. As you continue to type past the bottom edge of the screen, the existing text will scroll off the top edge of the screen to make room for the new text.

When you get to the end of a page, a long dashed line appears across your screen indicating the start of a new page, and the status line indicates which page the cursor is currently on. For example, in Figure 2.3, notice that the cursor is below the page-break line; the status line indicates that the cursor is on page 2 (*Pg 2*).

```
WINTER ACTIVITIES

The Moonlight Inn is just minutes away from some of Southern
California's best ski resorts. Whether you're a beginner, or a
black diamond bump basher, you'll find the slopes that are right
for you.


RESERVATIONS

Reservations should be made at least a month in advance -- two
months for peak ski weekends. Call 1-800-555-MOON. Please have
a credit card handy.

CANCELLATIONS

In the even of a cancellation, deposit is refundable 15 days
prior to your scheduled visits. Within 15 days of your scheduled
visit, deposit is not refundable, but may be applied toward a
---------------------------------------------------------------
-  ——— Cursor is on page 2                    |
                                       page break

D:\WPWIN\FIG2-3.WP                    Doc 1 Pg 2 Ln 1" Pos 1"
```

FIGURE 2.3:

The cursor is on the second page of the document.

When you have more than one page (or one "screenful") in a document, you can use the Page Up, Page Down, gray plus (**+**), and gray minus (**-**) keys on the numeric keypad to scroll up and down. Pressing **Home Home** ↑ moves you to the top of the first page. Pressing **Home Home** ↓ moves you to the bottom of the last page.

You can also use your mouse to scroll through text. Here's how:

1. To scroll to parts of the document that are not visible on the screen, press the right mouse button and drag in the direction of the text you want to see.

2. As soon as the document begins scrolling, you can simply hold down the right mouse button, without moving the mouse itself, to continue scrolling.

3. To stop scrolling, release the right mouse button.

MOVING TO A SPECIFIC CHARACTER OR PAGE

*If you want to move the cursor back to its previous position, press **Ctrl-Home Home** (that is, hold down the Ctrl key and press the Home key twice).*

You can use the Goto key (**Ctrl-Home**) to move the cursor to a specific character or page (or you can select **G**o To from the **S**earch pull-down menu). When you press Ctrl-Home, you'll see the prompt

Go to

near the bottom of the screen. Type the punctuation mark or letter that you want to move the cursor to. For example, if you want to move the cursor to the end of the current sentence, type a period. If you want to move the cursor to a specific page, type the page number and press ↵.

INSERTING AND REPLACING TEXT

TO SWITCH BETWEEN INSERT AND TYPEOVER MODES,

press the Insert (Ins) key.

When editing a document, you can choose between two basic modes of adding text: *Insert mode* and *Typeover mode.*

◆ In Insert mode, new text is inserted between existing text.

◆ In Typeover mode, new text replaces (overwrites) existing text.

In the example below, three uppercase X's were inserted in the word *Word-Perfect,* by placing the cursor on the letter *P* and typing *XXX* in Insert mode:

WordXXXPerfect

In the next example, three letters were replaced by placing the cursor on the letter *P,* switching to Typeover mode by pressing the Insert key, and then typing *XXX:*

WordXXXfect

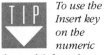

*To use the Insert key on the numeric keypad (often abbreviated as **Ins**), Num Lock must be off.*

Normally, WordPerfect is in Insert mode. To switch to Typeover mode, press the **Insert** (Ins) key once. You'll notice the message "Typeover" appear near the lower-left corner of the Edit screen. To switch back to Insert mode, press the Insert key again; the Typeover indicator disappears from the status line. The Insert key acts as a *toggle*—that is, it switches between Insert mode and Typeover mode each time you press it.

INSERTING TEXT, SPACES, AND LINES

To insert text (or spaces or lines) in a document, follow these basic steps:

1. Use your cursor-movement keys or mouse to move the cursor to where you want to insert text, spaces, or lines.

2. Make sure you're in Insert mode (if "Typeover" appears in the lower-left corner of the screen, press the **Insert** key).

3. Type the text to be inserted as you would normally type (all other text will move to the right and down to make room).

◆ To insert a blank space, press the spacebar.

◆ To insert text, just type your text.

◆ To insert a blank line or to break a line into two pieces, press ↵.

When you insert new text, be aware that some existing text may scroll off the right edge of the screen and seem to disappear. Don't worry about that. When you've finished typing your new text, just press ↓ or ↑, and WordPerfect will automatically readjust all the text to fit within the margins.

If you make mistakes while inserting new text, you can make corrections as usual with the Backspace and Delete keys (described in more detail in a moment).

CHANGING TEXT AND LINES

If you want to change or replace existing text, follow these steps:

1. Use the cursor-movement keys or mouse to move the cursor to where you want to replace existing text.

2. Make sure you're in Typeover mode (if "Typeover" does not appear in the lower-left corner of the screen, press the **Insert** key).

3. Type your new text—it will overwrite (replace) existing text.

In many cases, you'll probably want to replace some text and insert other text. No problem—just press Insert when you want to switch from Insert mode to Typeover mode, or vice versa.

HOW INSERT AND TYPEOVER AFFECT BACKSPACING

There's a slight difference in the way the Backspace key operates in Insert mode and Typeover mode. In Insert mode, pressing Backspace deletes the character to the left of the cursor and drags all characters to the right along with it (this fills in any "holes" that would otherwise be left by the deleted text). In Typeover mode, the Backspace key still deletes the character to the left, but does not drag the characters to the right with it. Instead, it leaves blank spaces in place of the characters it deleted.

BLOCKING TEXT

TO MARK A BLOCK OF TEXT,

move the cursor to the first character in the block, press Block (Alt-F4 or F12), and move the cursor to the last character in the block. Or, move the mouse pointer to the first character in the block, hold down the left mouse button, and drag the pointer to the last character in the block.

You can block (or "highlight," or "mark") any section of text to work with in a document. A block can be as small as a single character or as large as the entire document. Once you've marked a block of text, you can perform many operations on it, including deleting, moving, copying, printing, and so forth.

BLOCKING TEXT WITH THE KEYBOARD

If you prefer to use the keyboard rather than the mouse, here's how you can block any section of text:

1. Move the cursor to the first character of text that you want to block.

2. Activate the menu bar (**Alt-=**), pull down the **E**dit menu, and select **B**lock (or press **Alt-F4** or **F12**).

You can continue to extend your block by repeating this action as many times as necessary.

3. Use the cursor-movement keys to extend the highlight to the last character you want to select for the block, or type the last character. (For example, to extend the highlight to the end of the current sentence, type a period; to extend the highlight to the end of the paragraph, press ↵.)

BLOCKING TEXT WITH THE MOUSE

To mark a block of text using your mouse, follow these steps:

1. Move the mouse pointer to the first character of text that you want to mark as a block.

2. Hold down the left mouse button, and drag the pointer to the last character in the block you want to mark.

3. When the block you want to work with is highlighted, release the left mouse button.

Here are several tips to remember when highlighting large blocks of text:

◆ If the highlight gets to the edge of the screen, you can just continue dragging or moving the cursor with the cursor-movement keys. Text off the edge of the screen will scroll into view and will be included in the highlighted block.

◆ If you run out of desk space while rolling the mouse, keep the mouse button depressed, lift and reposition the mouse, then resume rolling the mouse.

◆ If you get tired of dragging the mouse around, you can always mix mouse techniques with keyboard cursor-movement techniques. For instance, you can start a block by dragging with the left mouse button, then use the cursor-movement keys to finish blocking the text.

Regardless of whether you use the mouse or the keyboard to highlight a block, the block you select is highlighted on the screen (as in Figure 2.4), and the message "Block on" blinks in the lower-left corner to remind you that you can perform a *block operation*.

SUMMARY OF BLOCK OPERATIONS

Once a block is highlighted and the Block On message is blinking, you can perform quite a few operations on the block. In this chapter I'll discuss moving, copying, deleting, and changing the case of blocked text.

Chapter 3 discusses abbreviated menu sequences, like Font ➤ Appearance, in more detail.

For future reference, Table 2.2 lists all the operations you can perform on a block and includes references to where these operations are covered in more detail. Note that the ➤ symbol shows a sequence of menu selections. For example, Font ➤ Appearance means "Pull down the Font menu and select Appearance, either using your mouse or by typing **Alt-=**, then **O**, then **A**.

CANCELING A BLOCK

If you highlight a block of text, then change your mind and want to unhighlight it, do one of the following:

◆ Press Block (**Alt-F4** or **F12**) again, or press Cancel (**F1**).

◆ If you have three mouse buttons, click the middle button. If you have two buttons, click the left button.

```
                    MEMORANDUM TO FILE


TO:      Raymond Peters's file

FROM:    Robert Dolan

SUBJECT: Meeting with John Brown

DATE:    July 21, 1990
                                           highlighted block of text

Met with John Brown at his office in Newport.  Discussed the
possibility of expanding his clothing business at the Brick
Shopping Mall downtown.  He is not in total agreement with the
proposed contract sent by Ray Peters, as there appear to be too
many loopholes.  It is still unclear who is going to take the lead
on this project, whether it be Brown's office or Peters's office.

It was suggested that he and I meet with Peters in the very near
future.  Brown was advised to make revisions to the above-mentioned
agreement and present it at that next meeting.

Peters should again be contacted as to the plan of action.  Set up
Block on                                 Doc 1 Pg 1 Ln 3.83" Pos 7.5"
```

FIGURE 2.4:

An example of a high-lighted block of text

ACTION	MENU CHOICES	SHORTCUT	CHAPTER
Append to file	Edit ➤ Append ➤ To File		3
Boldface	Font ➤ Appearance ➤ Bold	F6	5
Center	Layout ➤ Align ➤ Center	Shift-F6	4
Change appearance	Font ➤ Appearance	Ctrl-F8	5
Change case	Edit ➤ Convert Case	Shift-F3	2
Change size	Font ➤ *choose a size*	Ctrl-F8	5
Comment	Edit ➤ Comment ➤ Create	Ctrl-F5	3
Copy	Edit ➤ Copy	Ctrl-Ins *	2
Copy to Clipboard	Edit ➤ Append ➤ To Clipboard		12
Delete	Edit ➤ Delete	Delete or Backspace	2
Flush right	Layout ➤ Align ➤ Flush Right	Alt-F6	4
Mark for Reference	Mark ➤ *choose reference type*	Alt-F5	23
Move	Edit ➤ Move (Cut)	Ctrl-Del *	2
Print	File ➤ Print	Shift-F7	8
Protect	Edit ➤ Protect Block	Shift-F8	7
Save	File ➤ Save	F10	12
Search/Replace	Search ➤ *choose option*	F2 (or Alt-F2)	9
Sort	Tools ➤ Sort	Ctrl-F9	17
Spelling check	Tools ➤ Spell	Ctrl-F2	10
Style	Layout ➤ Styles	Alt-F8	14
Table	Layout ➤ Tables ➤ Create	Alt-F7	6
Underline	Font ➤ Appearance ➤ Underline	F8	5

* Available on enhanced keyboards only

TABLE 2.2:

Operations That You Can Perform on Blocked Text

REDEFINING THE SAME BLOCK

After you perform an operation on a block, the highlight disappears. If you want to highlight the same block again for another operation, follow these steps:

1. Select **E**dit ➤ **B**lock from the pull-down menus, or press Block (**Alt-F4** or **F12**).

2. Press **Ctrl-Home Home**.

MOVING AND COPYING TEXT

TO MOVE OR COPY A BLOCK OF TEXT,

1. **Block the text you want to move or copy.**

2. **Select Move (Cut) or Copy from the Edit menu, or press Ctrl-Del (to move) or Ctrl-Ins (to copy).**

3. **Position the cursor at the destination for the text, and press ⏎.**

One of the most common editing operations is moving text around to reorganize it. Copying is also fairly common. For example, when typing a list of names and addresses of people in the same neighborhood, you might want to copy just the street address, city, state, and zip code from one person to the next, without retyping. Or, you might need to copy certain passages, such as standardized paragraphs, from one document to another.

The basic steps for moving and copying are practically identical. The only difference, of course, is that moving text takes it from one place and puts it in another, as shown in figures 2.5 and 2.6.

Copying, on the other hand, leaves the text in its original position and places a copy of that text in a new location, as demonstrated in figures 2.7 and 2.8.

To move or copy a block of text, follow these steps:

1. Highlight the block of text you want to move or copy, as described under "Blocking Text."

2. Press **Alt-=** or click the right mouse button to activate the menu bar, and select **E**dit to pull down the Edit menu.

3. If you want to move the selected text, select **M**ove (Cut); the selected text disappears. If you want to copy the selected text, select **C**opy.

LESSON 2

Lesson 2 in Part 9 provides a hands-on example of moving text.

 *If you have an enhanced keyboard, you can perform steps 2 and 3 from the keyboard: Press **Ctrl-Del** to delete (cut) the block, or press **Ctrl-Ins** to copy the block.*

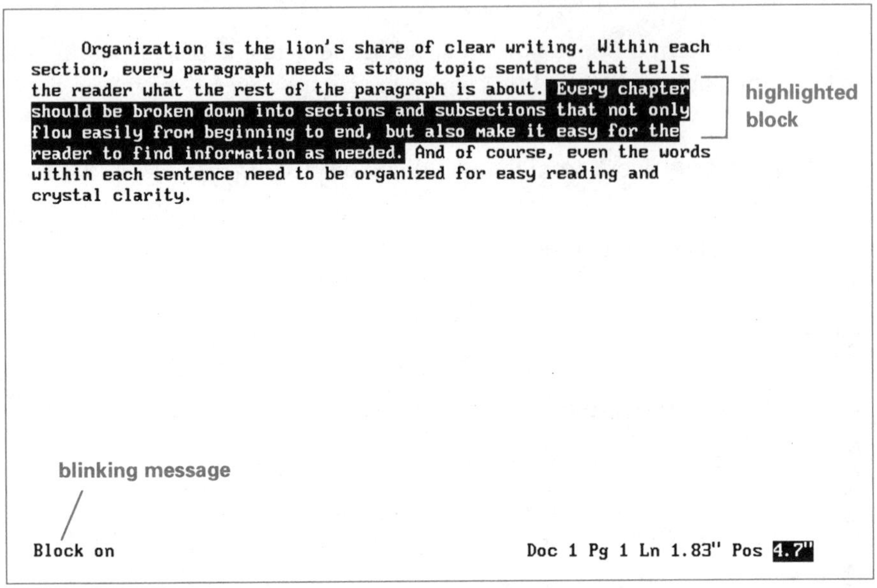

Organization is the lion's share of clear writing. Within each section, every paragraph needs a strong topic sentence that tells the reader what the rest of the paragraph is about. Every chapter should be broken down into sections and subsections that not only flow easily from beginning to end, but also make it easy for the reader to find information as needed. And of course, even the words within each sentence need to be organized for easy reading and crystal clarity.

highlighted block

blinking message

Block on   Doc 1 Pg 1 Ln 1.83" Pos 4.7"

FIGURE 2.5:
A highlighted block of text

Organization is the lion's share of clear writing. Every chapter should be broken down into sections and subsections that not only flow easily from beginning to end, but also make it easy for the reader to find information as needed. Within each section, every paragraph needs a strong topic sentence that tells the reader what the rest of the paragraph is about. And of course, even the words within each sentence need to be organized for easy reading and crystal clarity.

Highlighted block from Figure 2.5 moved here (at cursor position)

D:\WPWIN\FIG2-5A.WP   Doc 1 Pg 1 Ln 1" Pos 6.5"

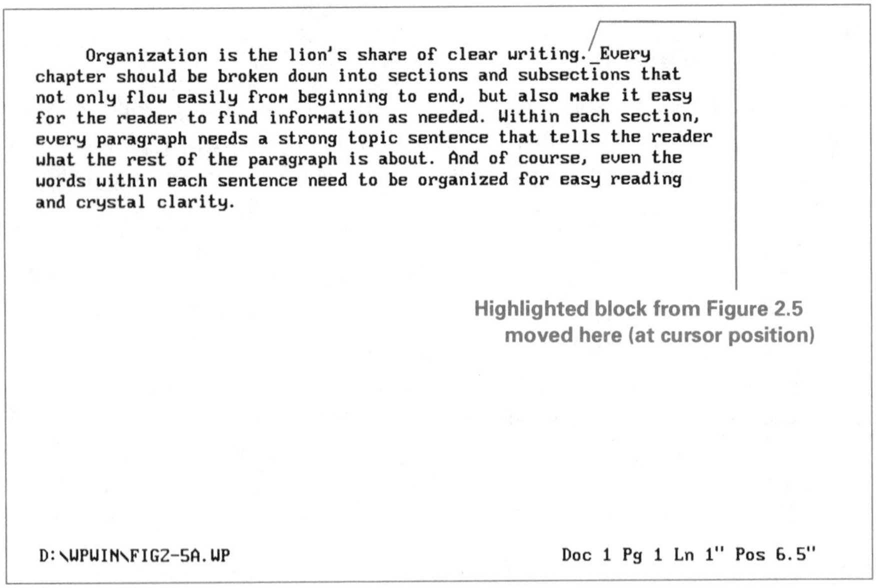

FIGURE 2.6:
The highlighted block of text in Figure 2.5 was moved up and is now the second sentence.

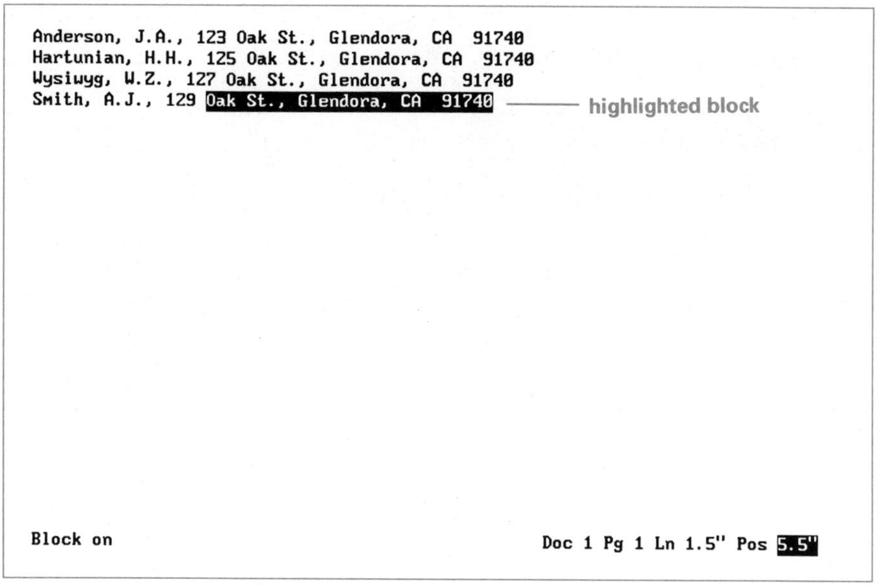

```
Anderson, J.A., 123 Oak St., Glendora, CA  91740
Hartunian, H.H., 125 Oak St., Glendora, CA  91740
Wysiwyg, W.Z., 127 Oak St., Glendora, CA  91740
Smith, A.J., 129 Oak St., Glendora, CA  91740    ——— highlighted block




Block on                              Doc 1 Pg 1 Ln 1.5" Pos 5.5"
```

A highlighted block of text

```
Anderson, J.A., 123 Oak St., Glendora, CA  91740
Hartunian, H.H., 125 Oak St., Glendora, CA  91740
Wysiwyg, W.Z., 127 Oak St., Glendora, CA  91740
Smith, A.J., 129 Oak St., Glendora, CA  91740
Oak St., Glendora, CA  91740 ———————— copied block of text




D:\WPWIN\FIG2-8.WP                     Doc 1 Pg 1 Ln 1.67" Pos 1"
```

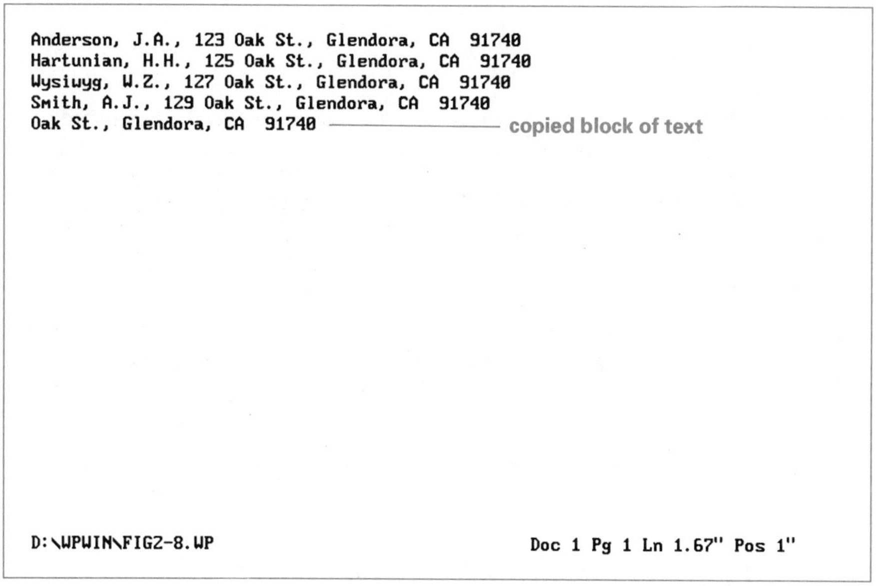

FIGURE 2.8:

The highlighted block of text in Figure 2.7 was copied to the next line.

4. Note the message in the lower-left corner of the screen:

Move cursor; press **Enter** to retrieve.

5. Move the cursor to where you want to move or copy the text to, and press ↵, or select **P**aste from the Edit pull-down menu.

If you are trying to move the text to the end of the document, but cannot move the cursor down to a new line, don't worry about it. Just move the cursor as far down and to the right as you can (either by pressing **Home Home** ↓ or scrolling with your mouse), and press ↵ to retrieve the blocked text. Then you can move the text down by pressing ↵.

Note that the general steps above are useful for moving and copying text in normal, paragraph format. If you need to move a rectangular block of text, such as a column in a table, refer to chapters 4 and 6.

SHORTCUTS FOR MOVING AND COPYING

If you want to move or copy a single sentence, paragraph, or page of text, it's not necessary to block it first. Instead, you can use a shortcut method:

1. Move the cursor to anywhere within the sentence, paragraph, or page you want to move or copy.

2. Pull down the **E**dit menu and choose the **S**elect option, or press Move (**Ctrl-F4**).

3. Select **S**entence, **P**aragraph, or P**a**ge, depending on which amount of text you want to move or copy.

4. Select **M**ove or **C**opy.

The Append option on the Copy/Move menu is covered in Chapter 3.

5. Move the cursor to the destination for the selected sentence, paragraph, or page, and press ↵ (or select **P**aste from the **E**dit menu).

Note that, in step 4, you can also choose to delete the selected sentence, paragraph, or page. The sections that follow describe still other options for deleting text.

MAKING ANOTHER COPY OF THE SAME BLOCK

If you just moved or copied a block of text and want to make another copy of that same block, you don't need to go back and highlight the same block again. Instead, just position the cursor where you want the next copy to appear, and select File ➤ Retrieve (**Shift-F10**). When WordPerfect asks for a file name, just press ↵ instead of entering a name. You can make as many copies of the same block as you wish in this manner.

DELETING TEXT

TO DELETE A CHARACTER,

move the cursor to that character and press the Delete (Del) key.

As you'll see, you can easily delete blank spaces and lines, as well as text.

WordPerfect offers a great deal of flexibility in deleting text from a document. Of course, when deleting text, there is always the chance that you will delete the wrong letter, word, or group of words. For that reason, WordPerfect also allows you to undelete the text you've just deleted. That way, you don't have to be nervous about deleting, because you can always bring back what you've deleted.

You've already seen how to use the Backspace key to delete text to the left of the cursor. This technique works pretty much the same way it does on typewriters that automatically white out text as you press Backspace. In this section, we'll look at other techniques for deleting text.

DELETING CHARACTERS

You can use the Delete key to delete an individual character or a group of characters. However, unlike the Backspace key, which deletes the character to the left of the cursor, the Delete key deletes the character above the cursor.

The Delete key is abbreviated *Del* on many keyboards. To use the Del key on the numeric keypad, the Num Lock key must be off (otherwise, pressing Del types a period). To delete text using the Delete key, follow these steps:

A blank space is simply a character in WordPerfect, so you can delete a space just like any other character.

1. Use the cursor-movement keys or mouse to position the cursor wherever you want to start deleting text.

2. Press the **Delete** key to delete the character above the cursor.

3. You can press Delete repeatedly (or hold it down) to delete as many characters as you wish.

DELETING A BLOCK

As an alternative to pressing Delete repeatedly, you can simply highlight any block of text, of any size, and then press Delete or the Backspace key once to delete that block.

1. Use the keyboard or mouse to block the text you want to delete (see "Blocking Text").

2. Press **Delete** or **Backspace**, or select **D**elete from the **E**dit pull-down menu.

3. You'll see the message

   Delete Block? **No (Yes)**

4. To delete the block, click on Yes (or press **Y**). Optionally, click on No (or press **N**), then press Cancel (**F1**) to retain the block.

The block is removed from the screen. Figure 2.9 shows an example of a block of text highlighted within a paragraph. Figure 2.10 shows the same document after deletion of the highlighted block.

Text surrounding the gap left by the deleted text is reformatted automatically to fill the gap. However, if the gap is not immediately filled to your liking, just press the ↑ key or ↓ key so that WordPerfect readjusts the format.

Also, you may need to insert or delete blank spaces after deleting text if there are too many, or too few, blank spaces at the beginning and end of your highlighted block. For example, if you delete a word from the middle of a sentence, but delete neither the blank space in front of nor behind that word, two extra blank spaces will remain. Delete one of the extra spaces by moving the cursor to it and pressing **Delete**.

```
                MINUTES OF SCHEDULED REGULAR MEETING

                        Conservation Commission
                        San Fernando, California

7:00 p.m.                                     Conference Room 5
Monday, February 25, 1991                     Community Building

CALL MEETING TO ORDER/ROLL CALL:  Meeting was called to order at 7:00
p.m. by President Jones.  Present:  Commissioners Abbott, Bates,
Carter, Smith.  Absent:  Dory, Edwards.  Excused:  Fox.

APPROVAL OF MINUTES:  It was MSP (Bates/Carter) to approve the
minutes of February 12, 1991.

A.   NEW BUSINESS:

     Guest speaker Dave Garcia, City of Los Angeles Park & Recreation
     Dept., updated the Commission on the proposed renovation of
     Swift Park.  Residents have complained about the poorly
     maintained sports fields, and parents of younger children are
     calling for a play area for toddlers.  The estimated cost for
     the first phase of the project is $2.9 million, to include
     enhancement of the existing parking lot.
Block on                            Doc 1 Pg 1 Ln 4.5" Pos 5.1"
```

FIGURE 2.9:

A highlighted block of text

DELETING A WORD

As a shortcut for pressing the Delete key repeatedly (or holding it down), you can delete an entire word and the blank space that follows it:

1. Move the cursor to any character in the word you want to delete.

2. Press **Ctrl-Backspace**.

*If you have an enhanced keyboard, you can also press **Ctrl-Del** to delete a word and the blank space that follows it.*

To delete several words, you can hold down the Ctrl key and press the Backspace key repeatedly.

DELETING A BLANK LINE

If you press ↵ to insert a blank line when typing your text, then decide to delete a blank line, follow these steps:

1. Move the cursor to the blank line that you want to delete.

2. Press the **Delete** key.

That's all there is to it. However, if the blank line contains spaces, tabs, or other "invisible" characters, you may need to press Delete more than once to delete these characters before the blank line disappears.

```
            MINUTES OF SCHEDULED REGULAR MEETING

                  Conservation Commission
                  San Fernando, California

7:00 p.m.                            Conference Room 5
Monday, February 25, 1991           Community Building
←——————————————————————————————————————————————————→
CALL MEETING TO ORDER/ROLL CALL:  Meeting was called to order at 7:00
p.m. by President Jones.  Present:  Commissioners Abbott, Bates,
Carter, Smith.  Absent:  Dory, Edwards.  Excused:  Fox.

APPROVAL OF MINUTES:  It was MSP (Bates/Carter) to approve the
minutes of February 12, 1991.

A.   NEW BUSINESS:

     Guest speaker Dave Garcia, City of Los Angeles Park & Recreation
     Dept., updated the Commission on the proposed renovation of
     Swift Park.  The estimated cost for the first phase of the
     project is $2.9 million, to include enhancement of the existing
     parking lot.


                      Doc 1 Pg 1 Ln 4.17" Pos 2.5"
```

FIGURE 2.10:

The document after deletion of the highlighted block shown in Figure 2.9

DELETING THE REST OF A LINE

Another shortcut for pressing the Delete key repeatedly to delete text is to delete the rest of a given line of text. Follow these steps:

1. Position the cursor wherever you want to delete the rest of a line (or at the first character of a line to delete the entire line).

2. Press **Ctrl-End**.

The Ctrl-End combination keystroke is often referred to as *Delete EOL,* which stands for *Delete to End Of Line.*

DELETING THE REST OF THE TEXT ON A PAGE

If you want to delete all the text from the current cursor position to the bottom of the page, follow these steps:

1. Move the cursor to where you want to start deleting text.

2. Press **Ctrl-Page Down**.

3. You'll see the message "Delete remainder of page? **N**o (**Y**es)".

4. Press **Y** if you're sure you want to delete the rest of the text on the page, or press **N** (or ↵) if you change your mind.

If you press Y to delete the remaining text on the page, any text on following pages will be "pulled up" onto the current page.

SHORTCUTS FOR DELETING

The shortcuts for moving and copying specific sentences, paragraphs, and pages also work with deleting. The steps are as follows:

1. Move the cursor to anywhere within the sentence, paragraph, or page you want to delete.

2. Pull down the **E**dit menu and choose the **S**elect option, or press Move (**Ctrl-F4**).

3. Select **S**entence, **P**aragraph, or P**a**ge, depending on which amount of text you want to delete.

4. Select **D**elete.

SUMMARY OF DELETION TECHNIQUES

Table 2.3 summarizes the techniques used to delete text. Keep in mind that, in addition to or as an alternative to these techniques, you can simply block *any* portion of your text, then press Delete to delete it.

UNDELETING TEXT

> **TO UNDELETE ACCIDENTALLY DELETED TEXT,**
>
> **press Cancel (F1) and select Restore.**

Now, let's suppose you delete some text (or spaces, or blank lines), then suddenly realize, "Whoops! I deleted the wrong text!" (or too much text, or whatever). No need to panic—WordPerfect is quite forgiving. You can undelete text just as easily as you deleted it, providing you do so soon after you realize your mistake. Here's how:

1. If you moved the cursor after realizing your mistake, put it back to wherever it was when you made the incorrect deletion.

2. Select **U**ndelete from the **E**dit pull-down menu, or press Cancel (**F1**).

3. The deleted text reappears on the screen, highlighted, with two options at the bottom of the screen:

   Undelete: **1** Restore; **2** Previous Deletion: **0**

4. If the highlighted text on your screen is indeed the text you want to restore, click on Restore or press **R** or **1** (you can skip the remaining steps).

5. If the highlighted text on your screen is *not* the text you want to restore, click on **P**revious Deletion (or press **P** or **2**) until the text you want to restore appears (though WordPerfect only "remembers" your last three deletions).

6. When the text you want to undelete appears highlighted on the screen, click on the Restore option (or press **R** or **1**). If it's too late and the text you want to undelete does not reappear, press ↵ to cancel the undelete operation. You'll then need to retype the text you accidentally deleted.

It's important to remember that WordPerfect only remembers your last three deletions and to realize that WordPerfect restores previously deleted text

TO DELETE	POSITION CURSOR AT	AND SELECT	OR PRESS
Character	Character	Edit ➤ Delete	Delete
Word	Word		Ctrl-Backspace or Ctrl-Del *
Blank line	Blank line	Edit ➤ Delete	Delete
Rest of Line	Start of deletion point		Ctrl-End
Sentence	Sentence	Edit ➤ Select ➤ Sentence ➤ Delete	Ctrl-F4
Paragraph	Paragraph	Edit ➤ Select ➤ Paragraph ➤ Delete	Ctrl-F4
Rest of page	Start of deletion point		Ctrl-Page Down
Entire page	Page	Edit ➤ Select ➤ Page ➤ Delete	Ctrl-F4

* Shortcut available on enhanced keyboards only

TABLE 2.3:

Summary of Text Deletion Techniques

*Word-Perfect "remembers" deleted text by storing it in an area of memory called a **buffer**.*

wherever the cursor happens to be at that moment. So to avoid becoming confused, your best bet is to review the remaining text on your screen immediately after making a deletion (before you move the cursor); if you change your mind, you can easily recover text simply by pressing Cancel (**F1**) and selecting Restore.

REPEATING A KEYSTROKE

As you know, you can repeat a keystroke simply by holding down the key. Another way is to press the Repeat key (**Esc**). When you do, the status line shows

Repeat Value = 8

The number *8* is a suggested value that WordPerfect displays automatically.

You can type in any number, then press the key you want repeated. For example, if you want to delete the next 100 characters of text, you can press Repeat (Esc), type *100,* then press Delete.

SPLITTING AND JOINING PARAGRAPHS

The discussion of hidden codes in the next chapter sheds more light on these techniques and will help you solve other kinds of formatting problems.

The general techniques described so far make it easy to split a lengthy block of text into two paragraphs or to combine two short paragraphs into one. As anyone who works with written words knows, these are pretty common tasks when editing the first draft of a document.

SPLITTING ONE PARAGRAPH INTO TWO

If you decide that a single paragraph in your document should be split into two paragraphs, you can easily make that change:

1. Move the cursor to the beginning of the sentence that you want to split off as the start of a new paragraph.

2. Press ↵.

3. If you want to insert a blank line above this new paragraph, press ↵ again. If you want to indent this new paragraph, press **Tab**.

This technique also works for rejoining a line that was accidentally split in two by pressing ↵, as demonstrated in Figure 2.11, after the word *also.*

JOINING TWO PARAGRAPHS

If you break text into two paragraphs, then change your mind and decide to incorporate the two paragraphs in one, just delete the blank lines or spaces that separate the paragraphs.

1. Move the cursor to the uppermost paragraph of the two you want to join.

2. Press the **End** key to move the cursor to the end of that paragraph.

3. Press the **Delete** key until the lower paragraph reaches the cursor.

4. If necessary, insert blank spaces by pressing the spacebar while in Insert mode to separate the sentences.

Figure 2.11 summarizes the basic techniques for joining and splitting text. In Chapter 3, you'll learn about the Reveal Codes screen, which gives you a behind-the-scenes understanding of why these techniques work and provides more flexibility in controlling the appearance of your text.

CHANGING UPPER- AND LOWERCASE

It's not uncommon to inadvertently type a long passage of text without realizing that Caps Lock is on, or to type something in lowercase and decide later to change it to uppercase. For this reason, WordPerfect offers a simple means of changing text from lowercase to uppercase, and vice versa:

1. Block the text that you want to change to upper- or lowercase.

2. Select Con**v**ert Case from the **E**dit pull-down menu, or press Switch (**Shift-F3**).

3. If you want to convert to uppercase, choose To **U**pper (or **U**ppercase). To convert to lowercase, select To **L**ower (or **L**owercase).

The term ***globally*** *means "throughout the entire document."*

This technique is fine for changing a single block of text. But if you want to *globally* change case—for example, change "Arco corporation" to "ARCO Corporation" everywhere in a document—use the Search and Replace feature, described in Chapter 9.

```
July 28, 1991

Mrs. Adrian Smith
123 Oak Ave.
San Diego, CA  92123

Dear Mrs. Smith:

Thank you for your letter regarding our Hawaiian outer-island tour
packages. Currently, we offer two travel packages with no overnight
stays on Oahu.

The enclosed brochures describe these packages in more detail. A
current price sheet is also _____
enclosed. If you have any questions, or wish to make a reservation,
please feel free to call me at (800) 555-1234 during regular hours.

Best regards,



Olivia Newton

D:\WPWIN\FIG2-11.WP                    Doc 1 Pg 1 Ln 3.33" Pos 3.8"
```

To join two lines or paragraphs, position cursor at end of top line and press Delete

To split text into two lines or paragraphs, position cursor and press ↵ once or twice

FIGURE 2.11:
Joining and splitting text

SAVING YOUR CHANGES

> ### TO "QUICK-SAVE" A DOCUMENT WITHOUT CLEARING THE SCREEN,
>
> **select Save from the File menu, or press Save (F10).**

When you're editing a document, it is important to keep in mind that your changes are made to the copy of the document currently stored in the computer's memory and displayed on the screen, *but not to the copy stored on the disk*. If you turn off your computer (or if a power outage turns it off for you), your changes will not be saved on the disk, and all your work will be lost.

Therefore, it's important to save your work even after editing an existing document. In fact, it's a good idea to save your work from time to time to prevent accidental loss of your efforts. For example, if you save your document about every five minutes, and a power outage suddenly turns off your computer, the most you can lose is five minutes' worth of work.

You don't have to exit WordPerfect to save your work; you can instead use the Save key (F10) to save your current work and continue working with the same document.

NOTE NOTE *You can have Word-Perfect automatically save your work every few minutes, as you'll learn in Chapter 13.*

1. Pull down the **F**ile menu and select **S**ave, or press the Save key (**F10**).

2. If you have not already named the document, type in a valid file name.

3. Press ↵.

4. If asked about replacing the previous version of the file, select Yes (either by pressing **Y** or clicking on Yes).

The current copy of the document is saved on-disk and remains on your screen for additional editing.

When you want to save your work and exit WordPerfect or clear the screen, you can use the method described in Chapter 1.

By now, you can see some of the incredible advantages that word processors have over typewriters when it comes to typing and editing text. But the best is yet to come. In the next chapter, I'll show you how to get the most out of WordPerfect, to prepare you to use the many features in the chapters that follow.

CHAPTER 3

Getting the Most from WordPerfect

Now that you've had a chance to learn the basics of creating, editing, printing, and saving a document, you're ready to start moving into some of WordPerfect's more powerful features. As the sheer length of this book hints at, there are lots of them.

HANDS-ON
. . . .
LESSON 3

For a hands-on lesson in interacting with WordPerfect, see Lesson 3 in Part 9.

But now that your basic typing and editing skills are in shape, you'll be able to pick and choose whatever features are relevant to your work. So don't think you need to read this book from cover to cover to become a WordPerfect whiz. But even the picking and choosing will be easier if you understand two things: 1) the basic WordPerfect interface, which applies to *all* the features available to you, and 2) some general-purpose features that are useful in all kinds of work.

WHAT IS AN INTERFACE?

If you work with (or around) computers, you may have heard the term *interface*. An interface is simply the means by which a person interacts with a machine. All machines, not just computers, have some sort of interface. For example, practically all cars have the same interface—you steer with your hands, and accelerate and brake with your foot.

But besides the basic steering wheel, accelerator, and brake, cars offer many other pieces of equipment, like turn signals, headlights, and stereos. These are not so standardized, and sometimes you have to look around for them (as I'm sure you've discovered if you've ever rented or borrowed a car).

In a sense, learning to use WordPerfect is like learning to drive a new car. On the one hand, the typing aspect is pretty standard, much like a typewriter. But sometimes you have to look around for other features and figure out how to operate them. This aspect of WordPerfect will be a lot clearer if you take the time now to learn about the WordPerfect interface.

USING A MOUSE

A *mouse* is a small hand-held device that lets you interact with the WordPerfect menus. Using a mouse is optional, but can be a great tool for quickly moving around the menus without ever touching the keyboard. (It may be an indispensable tool if you're a hunt-and-peck typist.) If you've never used a mouse before, there are a few terms you need to know:

> **NOTE NOTE** *The mouse buttons are reversed on a left-handed mouse. You can use the left-handed mouse by selecting the **F**ile ➤ Set up ➤ **M**ouse ➤ **L**eft-Handed Mouse from the menus. See "Customizing the Mouse" in Chapter 13 for more information.*

◆ The *mouse pointer* is not the same as the cursor. The cursor is a small, blinking underline; the mouse pointer is a nonblinking box.

◆ In mouse terminology, the term *click* means to position the mouse pointer on a character, word, or menu option, then press and release the left mouse button.

◆ The term *right-click* means to position the mouse pointer, then press and release the right mouse button.

◆ The term *double-click* means to position the mouse pointer, then click the left mouse button twice very quickly (as fast as you can say "click-click").

◆ The term *drag* means to position the mouse pointer, then hold down the left mouse button while moving the mouse.

SUMMARY OF MOUSE TECHNIQUES

> **NOTE NOTE** *The mouse pointer may not appear on the screen until you start moving the mouse.*

You can use WordPerfect either with or without a mouse. If you do have a mouse, you must be sure to install it according to the manufacturer's instructions before you can use it with WordPerfect. Then you can use the mouse in the following ways (many of these techniques were already discussed in chapters 1 and 2):

◆ To position the cursor on any character in a document, move the mouse pointer to that character and click.

◆ To scroll through text not currently on the Edit screen, hold down the right mouse button and roll the mouse in the direction you want to scroll, as though you were trying to push the mouse pointer right off the edge of the screen. Release the mouse button when the text you want to work with is in view.

◆ To block a section of text for moving, copying, or deleting, move the mouse pointer to the start of the block, hold down the left mouse button, and drag the highlight to the end of the block. Then release the mouse button.

◆ To select an option from a menu, click the right mouse button to display the menu bar, then move the mouse pointer to the option and click the left button.

◆ As an alternative to pressing Cancel (F1) to cancel an operation or to restore accidentally deleted text, you can click the right mouse button or simultaneously click both buttons (or click the middle button if you have a three-button mouse).

◆ As an alternative to pressing ↵, such as after typing a file name, you can click the right mouse button.

You'll see more specific examples of using the mouse in the sections that follow.

USING THE PULL-DOWN MENUS

TO DISPLAY THE MENU BAR,

press Alt-= or click the right mouse button.

Chapter 1 briefly summarized the general techniques for using the pull-down menus. In this section I'll cover the broader issues of using your keyboard and mouse to select menu options, respond to prompts, and recover from errors that produce *error messages* on the screen.

THE MENU BAR

Remember that, to get to a pull-down menu, you first need to display the *menu bar,* shown in Figure 3.1. You can use any one of the following techniques to display the menu bar:

◆ Press **Alt-=** (hold down the Alt key, press the = key, then release the Alt key).

◆ Click the right mouse button.

◆ Depending on how WordPerfect is configured on your computer, you may be able to view the menu bar simply by pressing and releasing the **Alt** key. (If you're a mouse user, you might want to keep the menu bar displayed at all times.)

Notice in the menu bar that the first option, File, is highlighted. Pressing the ← and → keys moves the highlight across the various options. When the option you want is highlighted, press ↵ or ↓ to view the associated pull-down menu. Optionally, just move the mouse pointer to any option and click the left mouse button to view the menu.

PULL-DOWN MENU OPTIONS

Each pull-down menu offers its own set of options, or *commands*. As on the menu bar, one letter in each option is brighter, or colored differently, from the rest of the letters; you can type that letter to select the option (for example, you can type **S** to select **S**ave). But be aware that you can only select options in the *current* menu by typing the highlighted letter. (The current menu is whichever one the blinking cursor is on.) For example, in Figure 3.2, you could not select **L**ayout from the menu bar because the blinking cursor is in the Edit pull-down menu.

*The third option is available only if you've changed the default method of activating the mouse, by selecting **F**ile ➤ Setup ➤ **D**isplay ➤ **M**enu Options ➤ **A**lt Key Selects Pull-Down Menu ➤ **Y**es.*

To use the arrow keys on the numeric keypad, Num Lock must be off.

*You can customize the color, appearance, and action of the menus by using **F**ile ➤ Setup ➤ **D**isplay ➤ **M**enu Options (see Chapter 13).*

File **Edit Search Layout Mark Tools Font Graphics Help   (Press F3 for Help)**

Doc 1 Pg 1 Ln 1" Pos 1"

FIGURE 3.1:

The menu bar at the top of the screen

Also, as on the menu bar, you can select any option on a pull-down menu by clicking on the option with your mouse (the left button) or by using the arrow keys to position the highlight on the option and pressing ↵.

Incidentally, referring back to Figure 3.2, even though you cannot select Layout by typing **L** in that example, you can easily get to the Layout menu simply by pressing the → key a couple of times or by clicking on the Layout option with your mouse.

Bracketed Options

You may notice that some of the options on pull-down menus are inside square brackets ([ ]). These options are currently unavailable, because they are not relevant at the moment. For example, the options to move and copy text are not available if no text is blocked (as in Figure 3.2), because these work only if you've already blocked the text you want to move or copy.

Options That Lead to Submenus

Some menu options (marked with a right-pointing triangle, ➤) have *submenus* associated with them, which present still more options. When a submenu is displayed, you can press → to move the highlight into the submenu, making it the current menu. You can also leave the submenu without making a selection by

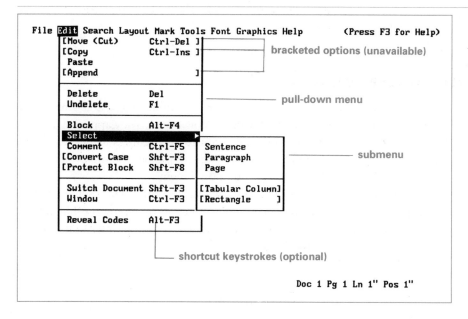

FIGURE 3.2:

A pull-down menu and submenu

pressing ← to move back to the previous menu. In Figure 3.2, the submenu for Select appears after choosing Select from the Edit pull-down menu.

Shortcut Keystrokes

Some options have a shortcut keystroke to the right. For example, Move (Cut) in Figure 3.2 shows the shortcut *Ctrl-Del*. Using the shortcut keystroke is another way to select the option, which may save you a keystroke or two. Shortcut keystrokes are often used by people who are familiar with earlier versions of WordPerfect, which offered no pull-down menus, and by "power users" who have memorized many shortcuts and have little need for the menus. I'll discuss the shortcut keystrokes in more detail later.

BACKING OUT OF PULL-DOWN MENUS

When you're first learning WordPerfect, you're likely to make menu selections that take you to features you don't understand yet. Therefore, it's good to know how to back out of the menus so that you can get back to more familiar territory. There are two main ways to back out of menu selections:

◆ To back out one step at a time, press Cancel (**F1**).

◆ To back out all the way to the Edit screen, press Exit (**F7**) or **Alt-=**, or click the right mouse button.

There are a few shortcut methods for making bigger moves through the menus. For future reference, Table 3.1 lists all the keys that you can use to navigate the pull-down menus.

FULL-SCREEN MENUS

Whereas pull-down menus temporarily cover portions of the Edit screen, full-screen menus temporarily cover the entire Edit screen. They appear when you select an option that offers too many features and settings to fit into a pull-down menu. The Print menu, shown in Figure 3.3, is one example—it appears after you select Print from the File pull-down menu.

You cannot use the arrow keys to make selections on full- screen menus. As Figure 3.3 points out, you make your selection by typing the highlighted letter or number in the option or by moving the mouse pointer to the option and clicking the left mouse button.

KEY	FUNCTION
Alt-=	Turns pull-down menus on and off
Cancel (F1)	Backs out of menu selections
→	Moves highlight to the right
←	Moves highlight to the left
↑	Moves highlight up
↓	Moves highlight down
↵	Selects highlighted option
Page Down (or gray +)	Moves highlight to last item on menu
Page Up (or gray −)	Moves highlight to first item on menu
Home →	Moves highlight to last option on menu bar
Home ←	Moves highlight to first option on menu bar
Home ↓	Moves highlight to bottom option on pull-down menu
Home ↑	Moves highlight to top option on pull-down menu

TABLE 3.1:

Keys Used with the Pull-Down Menus

```
Print

        1 - Full Document
        2 - Page
        3 - Document on Disk
        4 - Control Printer
        5 - Multiple Pages
        6 - View Document
        7 - Initialize Printer


Options

        S - Select Printer              HP LaserJet III (Additional)
        B - Binding Offset              0"
        N - Number of Copies            1
        U - Multiple Copies Generated by  Printer
        G - Graphics Quality            Draft
        T - Text Quality                High




Selection: 0    ▌
```

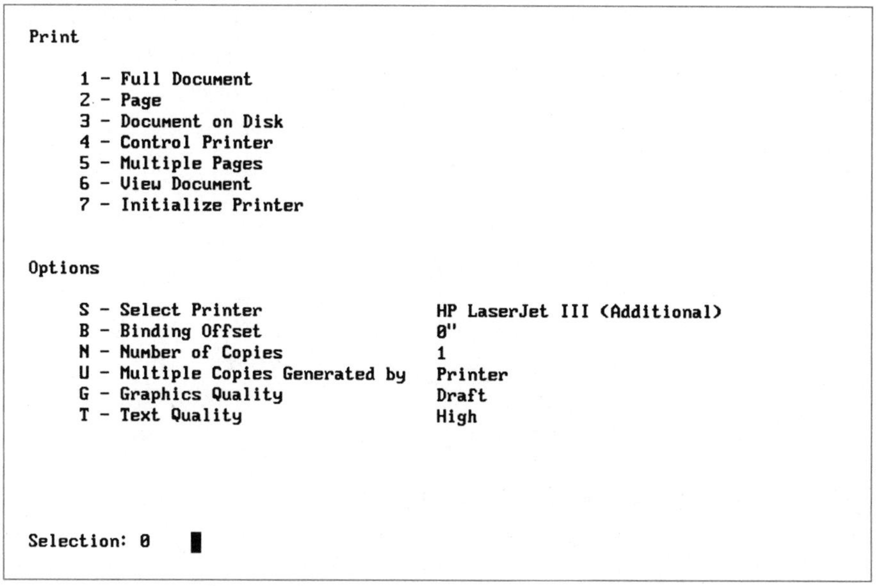

FIGURE 3.3:

The full-screen Print menu

LEAVING FULL-SCREEN MENUS

You can leave a full-screen menu after making selections or without making a selection by doing one of the following:

◆ Press Cancel (**F1**).

◆ Select option 0 (by typing **0** or by pressing ↵ if *0* is already displayed above the cursor).

◆ Click the right mouse button.

You may need to press Cancel (F1) or select 0 several times to back up through several full-screen menus. But regardless of which technique you use to leave full-screen menus, eventually you will be returned to the Edit screen.

BOTTOM MENUS

Bottom menus are used by WordPerfect when you need to see the text on the Edit screen or on a full-screen menu while making selections. Figure 3.4 shows an example of such a menu.

As with full-screen menus, you select an option from a bottom menu by typing the highlighted number or letter or by clicking on the option with your

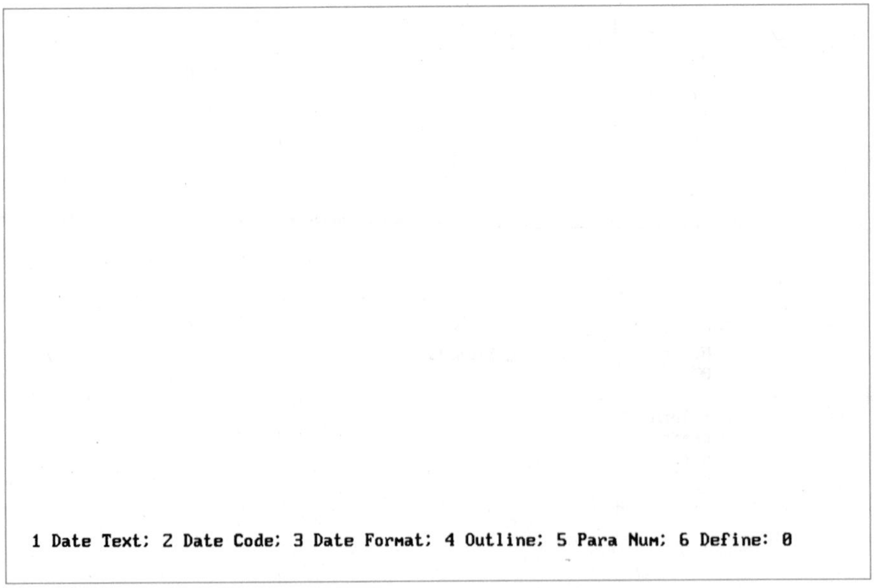

FIGURE 3.4:

An example of a menu at the bottom of the screen

```
1 Date Text; 2 Date Code; 3 Date Format; 4 Outline; 5 Para Num; 6 Define: 0
```

mouse (the arrow keys don't do anything). You can back out of a bottom menu by pressing Cancel (**F1**), Exit (**F7**), or **0**.

SCREEN MESSAGES AND PROMPTS

When WordPerfect has to tell you something (a message) or ask you something (a prompt), it does so in the lower-left corner of the screen. You already saw some examples of messages and prompts when you saved your work and exited WordPerfect in chapters 1 and 2. For example, when you opt to exit WordPerfect, you see the prompt

Save document? Yes (No)

In this type of prompt, WordPerfect asks for a Yes or No answer. You can respond by using whichever technique you feel most comfortable with:

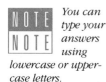

You can type your answers using lowercase or uppercase letters.

◆ Press **Y** to answer Yes, or press **N** to answer No.

◆ Click on Yes to select Yes, or click on No to select No.

◆ Press ↵ (or click the right mouse button) to accept the default answer (the one that is *not* in parentheses).

◆ Press Cancel to leave the prompt without making a choice (**F1**).

As you also saw in some previous examples, some prompts require information, but offer no alternatives to choose from. For example, when you save a new document for the first time, you see this message:

Document to be saved:

WordPerfect waits for you to type in a file name. You must press ↵ after typing the name so that WordPerfect knows when you are finished.

Incidentally, some people find it confusing trying to remember when it is and is not necessary to press ↵ in response to a screen prompt. There is, however, a consistency that should help clarify the matter: If WordPerfect is expecting a single-character entry, such as *Y* for *Yes* or *N* for *No,* there is no need to press ↵ after typing that character.

However, if what you're entering is of unknown length, like a file name or a number, you must press ↵. Otherwise, WordPerfect will just keep waiting for you to type in more text. If you want to leave such a prompt without making any selection, just press Cancel (**F1**), as with any other type of menu or prompt.

TIP
Most computer books and manuals assume that you know "enter" means "type, then press ↵." Thus a phrase like "enter a file name" actually means "type a file name, then press ↵."

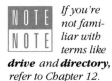

If you're not familiar with terms like **drive** *and* **directory,** *refer to Chapter 12.*

Messages (including error messages) don't require any response from you—they just stay on the screen for a few seconds, then disappear. For example, if you enter an invalid drive and directory name or press just ↵ in response to the "Document to be saved:" prompt, you'll see the message

ERROR: Invalid drive/path specification

for a few seconds, then the original prompt reappears.

The message tells you that you've made a mistake—the disk drive or directory that you want to save this document on does not exist. (Pressing ↵ alone displays this message because a "blank" *drive\directory\filename* combination is also invalid.)

When the error message disappears, you're returned to the original prompt, where you can try again with a new entry, or press Cancel (**F1**) to back out without responding to the prompt.

SHORTCUTS TO MENU SELECTIONS— THE FUNCTION KEYS

I've already briefly discussed the shortcut keys, which provide a quicker route to features than the menus do and are often preferred by more experienced users. For example, to save a file, as an alternative to pulling down the File menu and selecting Save, you can just press the shortcut key, F10.

As you've seen, shortcut keys are listed right on the pull-down menus. Your WordPerfect package also includes some keyboard templates and a sheet of color-coded key decals, designed to simplify your use of many of the shortcut keys.

If you have the template handy, notice that the features on the template are color-coded:

Red	Hold down the **Ctrl** key, press the function key, and release both keys.
Blue	Hold down the **Alt** key, press the function key, and release both keys.
Green	Hold down the **Shift** key, press the function key, and release both keys.
Black	Press the function key alone.

This book makes it easy for you to find the right shortcut key to press: Rather than saying only "press Print," I'll tell you to "press Print (Shift-F7)."

On your template, you can see that Print is shown in green, next to (or above) the F7 key. The fact that it's printed in green indicates that you must press "Green F7" (that is, Shift-F7) to access the Print menu.

Again, using the shortcut function keys is entirely optional, so if you prefer to use the pull-down menus for now, do so.

HOW TO FOLLOW THE STEPS IN THIS BOOK

For the remainder of this book, I'll present exact instructions on how to perform every operation that requires menu selections, showing both the pull-down menu approach and the shortcut-key approach. This will give you a chance to try both methods and choose which one works best for you. For brevity, I'll use the symbol ➤ to indicate selections made from the menus.

For example, when presenting the instructions to get to the WordPerfect Print menu, I might use this instruction:

1. Select **File** ➤ **P**rint (or press **Shift-F7**).

Given this instruction, you can use any of the following techniques:

◆ Click the right mouse button to bring up the menu bar, click on File, then click on Print.

◆ Press **Alt-=** to bring up the menu bar, highlight Print with the arrow keys and press ↵, then use the arrow keys to highlight Print and press ↵.

◆ Press **Alt-=** to bring up the menu bar, then press **F** to select File and **P** to select Print.

◆ Press **Shift-F7**.

In addition, you can use any combination of these alternatives. For example, you can make a couple of selections with the mouse, then a couple with the keyboard. It really doesn't matter, since these are all simply alternative ways of doing the same thing. There is no right or wrong, or best or worst, way—it's simply a matter of learning what's most convenient and comfortable for you.

VIEWING THE HIDDEN CODES

TO ACTIVATE OR DEACTIVATE THE REVEAL CODES SCREEN,

select Edit ➤ Reveal Codes, or press Alt-F3 or F11.

In Chapter 2, you edited your text in several ways: by inserting blank lines, joining two paragraphs, separating one paragraph into two, and so forth.

When you perform such operations, WordPerfect inserts *hidden codes* in your document.

The reason these codes are initially hidden is simple: WordPerfect wants your document to look normal as you type and make changes. If your Edit screen were cluttered with a bunch of strange-looking codes, your work would be much more complicated.

On the other hand, you can use the hidden codes to your advantage, particularly when you start using some more advanced WordPerfect features. For this reason, WordPerfect lets you view the codes so that you can see what's really going on behind the scenes in your document.

Viewing the hidden codes is a simple, one-step process:

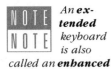

An ex-tended keyboard is also called an enhanced keyboard.

◆ Select **Edit** ➤ **R**eveal Codes, or press **Alt-F3** (or **F11** if you have an extended keyboard).

Your screen will be split in half, with the normal Edit screen on the top and the Reveal Codes screen on the bottom. The bottom half of the screen shows (roughly) the same text that the top half of the screen shows, but with the codes revealed, as in the example shown in Figure 3.5.

On the Reveal Codes screen, codes are enclosed in square brackets ([ ]) and are usually highlighted. Figure 3.5 shows soft-return codes [SRt] wherever WordPerfect has automatically word-wrapped a line and hard-return codes [HRt] wherever the author intentionally ended a line or added a blank line by pressing ↵.

```
Mrs. Adrian Smith
123 Oak Ave.
San Diego, CA  92123

Dear Mrs. Smith:

Thank you for your letter regarding our Hawaiian outer-island tour
packages. Currently, we offer two travel packages with no overnight
stays on Oahu.

The enclosed brochures describe these packages in more detail. A
                                        Doc 1 Pg 1 Ln 2" Pos 1"
[
Mrs. Adrian Smith[HRt]                                      }
123 Oak Ave.[HRt]
San Diego, CA  92123[HRt]
[HRt]
Dear Mrs. Smith:[HRt]
[HRt]
Thank you for your letter regarding our Hawaiian outer[-]island tour[SRt]
packages. Currently, we offer two travel packages with no overnight[SRt]
stays on Oahu.[HRt]
[HRt]

Press Reveal Codes to restore screen
```

FIGURE 3.5:

An example of the activated Reveal Codes screen

I'll take a moment to discuss some basic types of codes, then I'll discuss ways in which you can manipulate them.

PRACTICAL USE OF HIDDEN CODES

Every code on the Reveal Codes screen plays some role in WordPerfect. For example, a single hard-return code, [HRt], tells WordPerfect and your printer to "end the line here, and go to the next line." On the Edit screen, you see only the broken line, as in the split-paragraph example in Chapter 2. But on the Reveal Codes screen, you can actually see the [HRt] code.

If you were to move the highlight to that hidden code on the Reveal Codes screen and pressed Delete to delete it, the [HRt] code would disappear, and the line would no longer be broken, as in the example of rejoining two lines of text in Chapter 2.

Although it's possible to split or join two lines of text without using the Reveal Codes screen, you'll probably find it easier to do so with Reveal Codes turned on. In fact, when you start using the more advanced formatting features discussed in the chapters that follow, you'll probably find the Reveal Codes screen to be an indispensable aid in troubleshooting formatting problems in your document. I'll provide more specific information in future chapters, but for now, I'll discuss general techniques for using the Reveal Codes screen effectively.

About Single and Paired Codes

Most features in WordPerfect are controlled by a single code, such as [HRt] or [SRt]. As you'll see in future chapters, however, some features are controlled by *paired codes*. For example, on your Edit screen, you might see a section of text that's highlighted or colored differently. When you look at that text on the Reveal Codes screen, you might notice that the same colored text is surrounded by a pair of codes, like this:

[BOLD]This text is boldfaced**[bold]**, and this is not.

In this case WordPerfect is using paired codes to activate and deactivate a specific printer feature, boldface print. In paired codes, the starting code, which activates the feature, is shown in uppercase (e.g., [BOLD]), and the ending code, which deactivates the feature, is shown in lowercase (e.g., [bold]). Hence, when you print the sentence shown above, it appears partly boldface, partly normal:

This text is boldfaced, and this is not.

About Hard and Soft Codes

 This distinction between hard and soft codes varies slightly, but will be clarified as necessary in future chapters.

In most cases, codes are inserted in a document when you press some key (such as ↵) or select a formatting feature. In other cases, codes are inserted automatically, behind the scenes. For example, when you are typing a paragraph and type past the right margin, WordPerfect inserts a *soft-return* ([SRt]) code at the end of the uppermost line. This code tells WordPerfect and your printer to "end this line here and resume text on the next line."

Generally, codes that you insert yourself are referred to as *hard codes*, and codes that WordPerfect inserts for you are referred to as *soft codes*.

THE EFFECTS OF HIDDEN CODES ON CURSOR MOVEMENT

As you know, you can move the cursor around on your screen by using the arrow keys or mouse. Even when the hidden codes are not revealed, the cursor is still affected by them. For example, if the cursor is under a character that has a hidden code next to it, pressing ← or → may not move the cursor at all on the Edit screen, because WordPerfect has moved the hidden-code highlight behind the scenes. Depending on how many hidden codes are near the cursor, you may actually need to press ← or → a few times to get the cursor moving.

 Word-Perfect won't ask you about deleting codes if the Reveal Codes screen is already turned on, since it knows you can already see them.

Similarly, if the cursor is actually on a hidden code, but appears to be on a specific character on the Edit screen, pressing Delete will not delete the character. Instead, WordPerfect will ask whether you mean to delete the hidden code, for example,

Delete [BOLD]? No (Yes)

Selecting Yes deletes the [BOLD] code and removes the boldface. Selecting No moves you to the next character to the right without deleting the hidden code. If you get confused, just turn on the Reveal Codes screen so that you can see exactly where the cursor is before you press Delete.

POSITIONING THE CURSOR IN REVEAL CODES

 While the Reveal Codes screen is on, you can still use the mouse to scroll or position the cursor on the Edit screen, but the mouse is useless when used directly on the Reveal Codes screen.

When the Reveal Codes screen is on, you can still use the basic cursor-movement keys to move about the document. As you move the cursor around the Edit screen, the cursor on the Reveal Codes screen follows.

When the cursor lands on a hidden code rather than on some character, the entire character is highlighted on the Reveal Codes screen. For example, in Figure 3.5, the cursor is on the blank line above the salutation of the letter

(*Dear Mrs. Smith*). But on the Reveal Codes screen, you can see that the [HRt] code is highlighted.

You can delete, move, or insert codes on the Reveal Codes screen by using the same basic techniques that you use on the Edit screen. As you gain experience and read later chapters, you'll better appreciate this convenience. But for now, I'll just describe the general techniques for editing codes on the Reveal Codes screen. Feel free to refer back to this section if you later forget how to insert, delete, move, or copy codes.

Deleting one code in a paired-code set, such as [BOLD]...[bold], automatically deletes the other code. Some soft codes cannot be deleted—examples are presented in later chapters as required.

You can also use the Search feature (Chapter 9) to locate a specific code on the Reveal Codes screen.

DELETING CODES

If you are having a problem with the format of your document, sometimes simply removing the code that's activating a feature that you no longer want to use will fix the problem. Figure 3.6 shows an example from Chapter 2, where a line was split in two at the word *also* in midsentence. With Reveal Codes on, it's easy to see the hard-return code ([HRt]) that's causing the line break. To fix the problem, you'd simply remove the [HRt] code.

Deleting a hidden code is the same as deleting any other character on the screen:

1. If you have not already done so, turn on Reveal Codes (select **E**dit ➤ **R**eveal Codes, or press **Alt-F3** or **F11**).

```
stays on Oahu.

The enclosed brochures describe these packages in more detail. A
current price sheet is also_
 enclosed. If you have any questions, or wish to make a
reservation, please feel free to call me at (800) 555-1234 during
regular hours.

Best regards,



                                        Doc 1 Pg 1 Ln 3.33" Pos 3.7"
[
stays on Oahu.[HRt]
[HRt]
The enclosed brochures describe these packages in more detail. A[SRt]
current price sheet is also[HRt]
 enclosed. If you have any questions, or wish to make a[SRt]
reservation, please feel free to call me at (800) 555[-]1234 during[SRt]
regular hours.[HRt]
[HRt]
Best regards,[HRt]
[HRt]

Press Reveal Codes to restore screen
```

FIGURE 3.6:

A hard-return code ([HRt]) causing a line to break in midsentence

2. Move the cursor to the code you want to delete so that the entire code is highlighted on the Reveal Codes screen.

3. Press **Delete.**

As always, if you delete a code by accident, you can press Cancel (**F1**) and select Retrieve to undelete the code.

If you want to delete several codes, you can block the codes you want to delete, then press Delete, just as you would delete a block of text.

MOVING AND COPYING CODES

You cannot move or copy only one code in a set of paired codes, though you can move or copy the pair and all text in between.

Moving and copying codes is virtually identical to moving or copying a block of text. Here are the basic steps:

1. Move the cursor to the first code that you want to move or copy.

2. Select **E**dit ➤ **B**lock, or press Block (**Alt-F4** or **F12**).

3. Use the arrow keys to highlight all the codes (and text) that you want to move so that the cursor lands on the character *after* the last code you want to move or copy (for example, even to move the one code only, you still must press → to move the highlight to the next code).

4. Select **E**dit ➤ **M**ove (Cut) or **C**opy (or press **Ctrl-F4 B**, then **M** or **C**).

5. Move the cursor to the destination of the moved or copied codes.

6. Press ↵ to complete the job.

Shortcut for Moving a Single Code

If you simply want to move a single code (excluding a single code that's part of a paired set) from one location to another, follow these steps:

1. Delete the code from its present location by pressing **Delete.**

2. Move the cursor to the new location for the code.

3. Press Cancel (**F1**).

4. Select Restore to restore the code at the current location.

CHANGING CODES

Except in a few rare instances pointed out in later chapters, there is no means for changing an existing code in one step. You have to delete the existing code first, then go through whatever steps are required to insert the correct code.

INSERTING CODES

The only way to insert a new code is to press the keys or select the menu options that activate the feature. For example, pressing the Tab key inserts a [Tab] code, which indents your text. If you try to insert a [Tab] code by literally typing the word *[Tab],* the code is treated as plain text and is not a hidden code at all. Similarly, the only way to insert a hard-return code ([HRt]) is to press ↵.

INSERTING TEXT BETWEEN CODES

You can insert text between codes at any time. For example, if you want to add more boldface text between the [BOLD] and [bold] codes, just move the cursor anywhere between the codes, make sure you're in Insert mode, and type your new text. Of course, you can also delete any text between the paired codes and move or copy text into or out of the codes with the usual deletion and move / copy techniques.

SUMMARY OF HIDDEN CODES

Although it's not at all necessary to memorize, or even understand, the role of every code to use WordPerfect successfully, I've included a complete list for future reference in Appendix B.

ABOUT THE HOME HOME HOME KEYS

In Chapter 2, I mentioned that pressing the Home key before pressing an arrow key exaggerates the movement of the next key you press. For example, pressing Home Home ↑ moves the cursor to the top of the document. Pressing Home three times before pressing an arrow key goes a step further by moving the code highlight above or to the left of the hidden codes. In later chapters, you'll see examples of where pressing Home Home Home ↑ before entering a code is particularly handy.

 A window is any portion of the screen that provides a partial view of information. For example, with Reveal Codes on, the top window shows you text as it normally appears on the Edit screen, and the bottom window shows the same text with codes revealed.

CHANGING THE SIZE OF THE REVEAL CODES WINDOW

If you'd like to see more of your text and less of the codes (or vice versa) on your screen, you can change the size of the *window.* Here's how:

1. If you have not already done so, turn on the Reveal Codes screen (**E**dit ➤ **R**eveal Codes, or **Alt-F3** or **F11**).

2. Select **Edit** ➤ **Window**, or press **Ctrl-F3 W**.

3. Type the number of lines to display in the upper window, where 11 is the default of about one-half of the screen; 17 increases the top window to about two-thirds of the screen, and so forth.

4. Press ↵.

With Reveal Codes activated, you can display about 21 lines of text, with a maximum of 19 lines in one window and a minimum of 2 lines in the other window.

Figure 3.7 shows an example where the text window (at the top) occupies 16 lines, leaving 5 lines of text displayed in the Reveal Codes window (at the bottom). To return to the half-and-half window display, you would repeat the steps above, and enter *11* as the window size in step 3.

PREVIEWING YOUR PRINTED DOCUMENT

TO PREVIEW YOUR PRINTED DOCUMENT,

select File ➤ Print ➤ View Document, or press Shift-F7 V.

The WordPerfect Edit screen shows you *approximately* what your printed document will look like, but cannot duplicate your printer's output, such as text sizes, appearances, graphics, and fonts. The Reveal Codes screen provides a little more information about the format of the document, but this is still not an accurate representation of how the final printed document will look.

It's not necessary to print the entire document to see what the final printed document will look like. Instead, you can use the View Document screen to preview the printed document. To switch from the Edit screen to the View Document screen, follow this simple, one-step procedure:

You cannot make any changes to a document while previewing it on the View Document screen.

◆ Select **File** ➤ **Print** ➤ **View Document**, or press **Shift-F7 V**.

The techniques and codes for changing the size and appearance of text in figures 3.8 and 3.9 are covered in chapters 4 and 5.

For example, Figure 3.8 shows a portion of a sample document on both the Edit screen and Reveal Codes screen. Figure 3.9 shows the same document on the View Document screen.

Besides giving you an on-screen replica of how your final printed document will look, the View Document screen also lets you view your text at various sizes:

1 100%   Letters are shown at their actual printed size.

2 200%   Letters are displayed at twice their actual size, for a closer look.

```
July 20, 1991


Mrs. Adrian Smith
123 Oak Ave.
San Diego, CA  92123

Dear Mrs. Smith:

Thank you for your letter regarding our Hawaiian outer-island tour
packages. Currently, we offer two travel packages with no overnight
stays on Oahu.

The enclosed brochures describe these packages in more detail. A
current price sheet is also enclosed. If you have any questions, or
wish to make a reservation, please feel free to call me at (800)
                                        Doc 1 Pg 1 Ln 1" Pos 1"
{                                                    }
July 20, 1991[HRt]
[HRt]
[HRt]
Mrs. Adrian Smith[HRt]
123 Oak Ave.[HRt]

Press Reveal Codes to restore screen
```

FIGURE 3.7:

The Edit window increased to 16 lines, leaving about 5 lines for the Reveal Codes window

```
            ANSWERS TO BURNING QUESTIONS
_

WHY do fleas seem to disappear when they jump?

The much maligned flea, Ctenocephalides canis, seems to disappear before your
very eyes, and reappear several feet away, because of its tremendous jumping
power and speed:

    o  The flea can leap a distance 150 times its body length -- the
       equivalent of a human being jumping ¼ mile from a standstill.
                                        Doc 1 Pg 1 Ln 1" Pos 1"
{                                                    }
[Center][DBL UND][Font:Univers Bold Italic (Scalable) 24pt]ANSWERS TO BURNING QU
ESTIONS[Font:CG Times (Scalable) 14pt][dbl und][HRt]
[HRt]
[HRt]
[BOLD][VRY LARGE]WHY[vry large] do fleas seem to disappear when they jump?[bold]
[HRt]
[HRt]
The much maligned flea, [ITALC]Ctenocephalides canis[italc], seems to disappear
before your[SRt]
very eyes, and reappear several feet away, because of its tremendous jumping[SRt
]
Press Reveal Codes to restore screen
```

FIGURE 3.8:

Sample text on the Edit and Reveal Codes screens

3 Full Page   The entire page is shown at arm's length.

4 Facing Pages   In long documents, even-numbered pages are displayed on the left, and odd-numbered pages are displayed on the right (like two pages from a book).

To select a different size option, just type the number that precedes the size (e.g., *3* to select Full Page), or click on the option with your mouse.

While the document is displayed on the View Document screen, you can use the cursor-movement keys to scroll around and look at various parts of the document, if necessary, though the keys react more slowly than they do with the Edit screen.

When you're finished previewing the document, you can do any of the following to exit:

◆ Press Cancel (**F1**) to return to the Print menu.

◆ Press Exit (**F7**) or click the right mouse button to return to the Edit screen.

◆ Press the spacebar to back out of the menus.

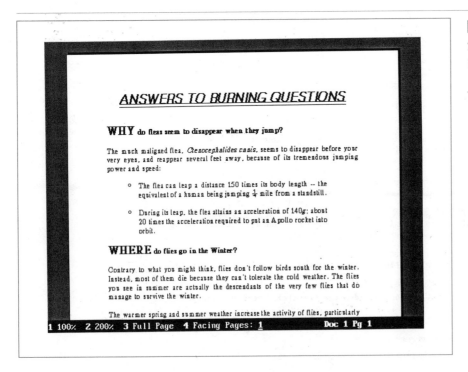

FIGURE 3.9:

The sample text on the View Document screen

GETTING HELP

> **TO GET ON-SCREEN HELP,**
>
> **press Help (F3), or select Help from the menu bar, followed by some other option.**

WordPerfect's built-in Help feature lets you see helpful advice and quick reminders on your screen without your having to refer to a book or manual. WordPerfect's Help system is *context-sensitive,* which means that, unless you're on the Edit screen, the help that appears on the screen is relevant to the task you are trying to perform at that moment.

For example, if you've already worked your way to the Print menu and then press Help (F3), you'll see information about printing rather than a general help message, as shown in Figure 3.10.

In most cases the Help screen looks very much like the screen you see when you press Help (F3), except that the message "(Press ENTER to exit Help)" appears in the lower-right corner.

You can press any highlighted letter or number (for example, *2* or *P* to get help with the Page option). When you've finished reading the Help system's information, you can press ↵ to return to the Edit screen.

*If you prefer to use the more common F1 key to activate help, you can customize your keyboard by selecting the **F**ile ➤ **S**etup ➤ **E**nvironment ➤ **A**lternate Keyboard (Chapter 13) or by using soft keyboards (Chapter 27).*

```
Print

     1 - Full Document
     2 - Page
     3 - Document on Disk
     4 - Control Printer
     5 - Multiple Pages
     6 - View Document
     7 - Initialize Printer

Options

     S - Select Printer
     B - Binding Offset
     N - Number of Copies
     U - Multiple Copies Generated by
     G - Graphics Quality
     T - Text Quality

If you run WordPerfect on Novell NetWare, you have two additional options:

     A - Banners
     O - Form Number

Selection: 0                        (Press ENTER to exit Help)
```

This message always appears on Help screens

FIGURE 3.10:

The Help screen, displayed after pressing Help (F3) at the Print screen

HELP WITH FUNCTION KEYS

If you've lost your WordPerfect template, you can view a substitute through the Help screens. Follow these simple steps:

1. Press Help (**F3**) twice.

2. If you're not using an enhanced keyboard, press **1** to view the template for the PC/XT keyboard.

3. If you need a printed copy of the template screen, hold down the **Shift** key and press **Print Screen** (abbreviated *PrtSc* on some keyboards), then release both keys. (This may not work with some printers.)

4. Press ↵ to exit help.

CAUTION *If you have a laser printer, you'll need to eject the page from the printer before you can see the printed copy of the screen. See your printer manual or Chapter 8 if you need help.*

The printed copy of the template may not look as good as the copy on the screen because of the graphics characters used to draw the lines. Sorry, there's not much you can do about that.

ACCESSING HELP FROM THE PULL-DOWN MENUS

You can also access general help (but not context-sensitive help) from the pull-down menus. Follow these steps:

1. Press **Alt-=** or click the right mouse button to access the menu bar.

2. Select **Help**.

3. Choose any one of three options:

NOTE NOTE *The mouse cannot be used to make selections within the Help system.*

   Help: displays general instructions on using the Help system.

   Index: takes you directly to the Help Index, described below.

   Template: takes you to the on-screen function-key template described earlier in "Help with Function Keys."

USING THE HELP INDEX

The Help Index is an alphabetical list of topics that you can get help with. To use it, start at the Edit screen and follow these steps:

1. Select **Help** ➤ **Index** (or press **F3** and then **A** to get to the same place). Part of the "a's" portion of the index appears on the screen, as in Figure 3.11.

2. If the topic you need help with does not appear on the first Index screen, press the first letter of the topic you need help with. For example, press **S** to look up information on Save.

3. If more than one screenful of information is available for the letter you entered, you'll see a message like "More... Press s to continue" near the bottom of the screen. If necessary, press the letter again to view additional topics.

When the topic you need help with is available on the screen, press the key(s) listed in the right column to get help with that topic. For example, if you press S until you see the Save Text option listed in the Help Index, you can then press F10 (listed in the right column next to Save Text) to get help with saving text.

When you're finished using the Help screens, press ⏎ to return to the Edit screen.

MANAGING MULTIPLE DOCUMENTS

TO SWITCH TO A SECOND DOCUMENT-EDITING AREA,

Select Edit ➤ Switch Document, or press Switch (Shift-F3).

Sometimes it's handy to work on two or more documents at a time. For example, you might want to use material from an older work in a newer one or

```
Features [A]                          WordPerfect Key   Keystrokes

Absolute Tab Settings                 Format            Shft-F8,1,8,t,1
Acceleration Factor (Mouse)           Setup             Shft-F1,1,5
Add Password                          Text In/Out       Ctrl-F5,2
Additional Printers                   Print             Shft-F7,s,2
Advance (To Position, Line, etc.)     Format            Shft-F8,4,1
Advanced Macro Commands (Macro Editor) Macro Commands   Ctrl-PgUp
Advanced Merge Codes                  Merge Codes       Shft-F9,6
Align/Decimal Character               Format            Shft-F8,4,3
Align Text on Tabs                    Tab Align         Ctrl-F6
Alphabetize Text                      Merge/Sort        Ctrl-F9,2
Alt/Ctrl Key Mapping                  Setup             Shft-F1,5
Alt-=                                 Menu Bar          Alt-=
Appearance of Printed Text            Font              Ctrl-F8
Append Text to a File (Block On)      Move              Ctrl-F4,1-3,4
Append to Clipboard (Block On)        Shell             Ctrl-F1,3
ASCII Text File                       Text In/Out       Ctrl-F5,1
Assign Keys                           Setup             Shft-F1,5
Assign Variable                       Macro Commands    Ctrl-PgUp
Attributes, Printed                   Font              Ctrl-F8
Attributes, Screen                    Setup             Shft-F1,2,1
More... Press a to continue.

Selection: 0                              (Press ENTER to exit Help)
```

FIGURE 3.11:
Part of the "a's" portion of the Help Index

have two different drafts of the same document handy. To work with two separate documents at one time, follow these steps:

1. If you haven't done so already, retrieve the first document with **File ➤ Retrieve** (**Shift-F10**).

2. Select **Edit ➤ S**witch Document or press Switch (**Shift-F3**) to switch to the other document area. Notice that the first document seems to disappear, but the right side of the status line at the bottom of the screen indicates that you are now in Doc 2, as Figure 3.12 shows.

3. Retrieve the second document with **File ➤ Retrieve** (**Shift-F10**).

4. To switch back and forth between documents, select **Edit ➤ S**witch Document, or press **Shift-F3**. The Doc number on the status line displays the current document number.

VIEWING TWO DOCUMENTS AT ONCE

Rather than switching back and forth from one document to the other, you can split the screen to view both documents at the same time. Here's how:

1. Choose either Doc 1 or Doc 2 with **Edit ➤ S**witch Document or **Shift-F3**.

2. Select **Edit ➤ W**indow (or press **Ctrl-F3 W**).

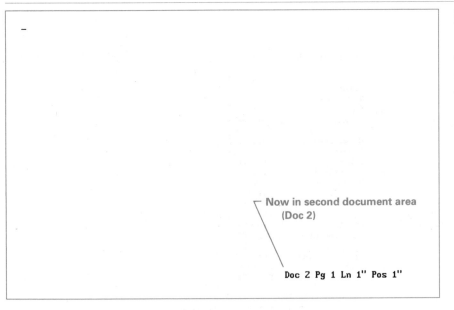

FIGURE 3.12:

The Edit screen for a second document, as indicated by Doc 2 on the status line

Now in second document area (Doc 2)

Doc 2 Pg 1 Ln 1" Pos 1"

3. Enter the number of lines that the current document should occupy on the screen—for example, *11* if you want to split the screen roughly in half.

4. Press ↵.

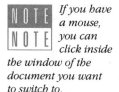

If you have a mouse, you can click inside the window of the document you want to switch to.

Doc 1 appears in the top half of the screen, Doc 2 in the bottom half. A tab ruler (described in Chapter 4) separates the two documents. Each document has its own status line, as shown in the example in Figure 3.13. To switch from one document to the other, select **Edit ➤ S**witch or press **Shift-F3**.

If you activate Reveal Codes, only one document remains on the screen (the other is temporarily hidden). Deactivating Reveal Codes redisplays the two documents.

VIEWING TWO PARTS OF THE SAME DOCUMENT

You can use File ➤ Exit (F7) to save or not save text in either window.

While you're writing or editing, sometimes it's nice to be able to see two parts of the same document—for example, text in the middle and text at the end. To do so, you can load a copy of the same document in both Doc 1 and Doc 2 and split the screen into two windows.

Make all your changes in one window. When you're finished, save only the copy of the document where you made changes, not the copy that you didn't change (it no longer matches the newer revision in the other window).

```
INSTALLING YOUR MOUSE

Your ABC Corporation "Wizard Mouse" can use any existing serial
port. If you don't have a serial port available, you can install
a new serial card in any available slot.

WARNING: BEFORE REMOVING THE COVER FROM YOUR COMPUTER BE SURE TO
TURN OFF AND UNPLUG THE COMPUTER AND ALL PERIPHERALS. IF IN A DRY
CLIMATE, REDUCE THE RISK OF STATIC SHOCK BY LIGHTLY SPRAYING THE
CARPET WITH FABRIC SOFTENER, OR PLACING A PLASTIC MAT OVER IT.
                                Doc 1 Pg 1 Ln 2.5" Pos 7.2"
```

```
INSTALLING YOUR MULTISYNC GRAPHICS ADAPTER
     Your MultiSync Graphics Adapter displays text in 1,024 x 768
resolution, far crisper and more detailed than standard EGA, VGA,
or even Super VGA. Installing the Graphics Adapter is a simple
process.

1.   Remove the cover from your main system unit. This is
     generally accomplished by removing the cover screws from the
     back of the computer, and sliding the cover back until it's
     completely free of the unit.

2.   Identify any full-size slot, and remove the cover plate from
                         Doc 2 Pg 1 Ln 1" Pos 1"
```

FIGURE 3.13:

Two documents on the Edit screen, each in a half-size window

MOVING AND COPYING TEXT BETWEEN DOCUMENTS

If you want to move or copy text from one document to another, block the text and select **E**dit ➤ **M**ove (Cut) or **C**opy, as described in Chapter 2. Figure 3.14 shows some blocked text in the Doc 1 window and a different document in the Doc 2 window, in the bottom half of the screen.

Next, select **E**dit ➤ **S**witch Document or press **Shift-F3**, and position the cursor where you want the text to appear in the other document. Then, press ↵, as usual, to complete the operation. Figure 3.15 shows an example where text from Doc 1 was successfully copied to Doc 2 by positioning the cursor at the end of the first paragraph, pressing ↵ to complete the move, then pressing ↵ again to insert a line break.

SAVING MULTIPLE DOCUMENTS

NOTE
NOTE

To unsplit the screen and place both Doc 1 and Doc 2 in full screens, enter 24 for the number of lines the document should occupy on the screen.

When you load and work with two documents, remember that those documents are treated independently. When you save a document, only the document in the current window (i.e., the document that the cursor is in) is actually saved. Therefore, be sure to save both documents after making changes.

If you attempt to exit WordPerfect when two documents are loaded, you'll be taken through the options to save (or not save) both documents before you are allowed to exit WordPerfect.

```
INSTALLING YOUR MOUSE

Your ABC Corporation "Wizard Mouse" can use any existing serial
port. If you don't have a serial port available, you can install
a new serial card in any available slot.

WARNING: BEFORE REMOVING THE COVER FROM YOUR COMPUTER BE SURE TO
TURN OFF AND UNPLUG THE COMPUTER AND ALL PERIPHERALS. IF IN A DRY
CLIMATE, REDUCE THE RISK OF STATIC SHOCK BY LIGHTLY SPRAYING THE
CARPET WITH FABRIC SOFTENER, OR PLACING A PLASTIC MAT OVER IT.
Block on                                    Doc 1 Pg 1 Ln 2.5" Pos 7.2"
[                                                             }
INSTALLING YOUR MULTISYNC GRAPHICS ADAPTER
    Your MultiSync Graphics Adapter displays text in 1,024 x 768
resolution, far crisper and more detailed than standard EGA, VGA,
or even Super VGA. Installing the Graphics Adapter is a simple
process.

1.  Remove the cover from your main system unit. This is
    generally accomplished by removing the cover screws from the
    back of the computer, and sliding the cover back until it's
    completely free of the unit.

2.  Identify any full-size slot, and remove the cover plate from
                                Doc 2 Pg 1 Ln 1" Pos 1"
```

FIGURE 3.14:

The text to be moved or copied in Doc 1 is blocked (highlighted).

USING THE APPEND OPTION TO COPY TEXT ACROSS DOCUMENTS

As an alternative to using multiple windows, you can use the Append option on the Move/Copy menu to copy text from one document to another. This comes in handy when you want to copy text from one document to several others and don't want to bother loading each document into Doc 2.

To append text from one document to any document on-disk, follow these steps:

1. Block the text that you want to move or copy to another document.

2. Select **E**dit ➤ **A**ppend ➤ To **F**ile (or press **Ctrl-F4 B A**).

3. Type the complete name of the file you want to append the text to, then press ↵.

The text remains in the current document, but a copy is added to the *bottom* of the document you named in step 3. You can later retrieve and view that document to verify that the text was appended and optionally move the appended text within that document.

```
INSTALLING YOUR MOUSE

Your ABC Corporation "Wizard Mouse" can use any existing serial
port. If you don't have a serial port available, you can install
a new serial card in any available slot.

WARNING: BEFORE REMOVING THE COVER FROM YOUR COMPUTER BE SURE TO
TURN OFF AND UNPLUG THE COMPUTER AND ALL PERIPHERALS. IF IN A DRY
CLIMATE, REDUCE THE RISK OF STATIC SHOCK BY LIGHTLY SPRAYING THE
CARPET WITH FABRIC SOFTENER, OR PLACING A PLASTIC MAT OVER IT.
                              Doc 1 Pg 1 Ln 2.5" Pos 7.2"

INSTALLING YOUR MULTISYNC GRAPHICS ADAPTER
    Your MultiSync Graphics Adapter displays text in 1,024 x 768
resolution, far crisper and more detailed than standard EGA, UGA,
or even Super UGA. Installing the Graphics Adapter is a simple
process.

WARNING: BEFORE REMOVING THE COVER FROM YOUR COMPUTER BE SURE TO
TURN OFF AND UNPLUG THE COMPUTER AND ALL PERIPHERALS. IF IN A DRY
CLIMATE, REDUCE THE RISK OF STATIC SHOCK BY LIGHTLY SPRAYING THE
CARPET WITH FABRIC SOFTENER, OR PLACING A PLASTIC MAT OVER IT.

1.   Remove the cover from your main system unit. This is
                         Doc 2 Pg 1 Ln 2" Pos 1"
```

FIGURE 3.15:
Blocked text from Figure 3.14 was copied to the document in the Doc 2 window.

USING SAVE AND RETRIEVE TO COPY TEXT ACROSS DOCUMENTS

There is another means of copying text between documents: Block the text that you want to use in other documents and save a copy of it by pressing Save (**F10**) and entering a unique file name. For example, suppose you block the "Author Description" portion of a current proposal and save it with an easily remembered file name, such as *AUTHDESC.WP*. In the future, you could easily load a copy of AUTHDESC.WP into any new proposal, as Figure 3.16 illustrates, without retyping. To do so, you would just position the cursor where the passage should appear in the new, current document and select **F**ile ➤ **R**etrieve (or press **Shift-F10**). WordPerfect would then ask the following:

Retrieve into current document? **No (Yes)**

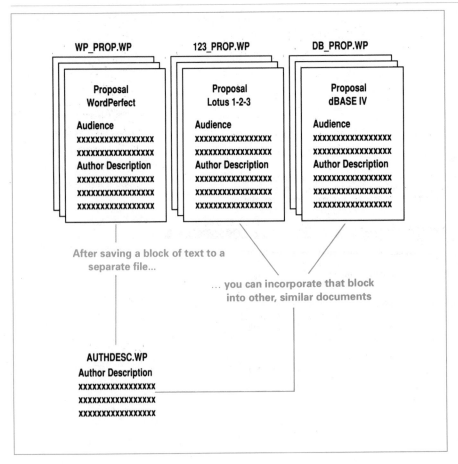

FIGURE 3.16:

Once you save an often-used block of text, you can easily retrieve a copy of it into whatever document you happen to be working on at the moment.

Boiler-plate *text is text that you use repeatedly in different documents.*

You would select Yes to copy the text into the current document.

If you have several *boilerplate* passages of text that you use repeatedly in documents, such as corporate descriptions, employee descriptions, or disclaimers, you might want to save copies of these in their own files so that you can easily pull them into whatever document you're working on at the moment.

USING DOCUMENT COMMENTS

TO INSERT A DOCUMENT COMMENT AT THE CURRENT CURSOR POSITION,

select Edit ➤ Comment ➤ Create or press Ctrl-F5 C C, type your comment, and press Exit (F7).

If you work in groups, or if you like to write notes to yourself as you write, or if you are one member of an author/editor team, you'll probably find the *document comments* feature handy in your work. This feature lets you add notes to your document that stand out clearly from the rest of the text on your screen. Figure 3.17 shows an example in which a document comment, surrounded by a box, has been used to drop a note to an author.

```
      The British Conservative Party has been in trouble as of late.
Their woes appear related to their leadership crisis.  Margaret
Thatcher has been a dynamic Prime Minister in her years in office.
However, it is this uncompromising nature of hers which has been as
a spot on an otherwise spotless career.  Lately this attitude has
cost her dearly with back benchers and cabinet members alike.  Her
"public approval rating at 24% is lower than any other Prime
Minister since the polling has been conducted."

  ┌─────────────────────────────────────────────────────────────┐
  │ Au:                                                          │
  │ Because the political climate has changed so much lately, the focus of │
  │ this article needs to be the current climate, and the factors that led up │
  │ to it. Suggest changing this material to past tense, since it's now of │
  │ historical interest.                                         │
  │                                                             │
  │ Ed.                                                         │
  └─────────────────────────────────────────────────────────────┘

      With the Conservative Party running 19 percentage points
behind Labour,1 questions have arisen as to which direction the
Tory Party should take, more precisely who shall be chosen as its
director.  However, neither will out-and-out declare their
candidacy in fear that voters would see it as back-stabbing the
A:\ENDNOTE.WP                          Doc 1 Pg 1 Ln 1" Pos 1"
```

FIGURE 3.17:

A sample document comment on the Edit screen

Another advantage of document comments is that they don't appear on the printed document. This allows you to review a clean copy of the manuscript without the distraction of the comments, then add or review comments on the screen, as required.

To add a comment to a document, follow these steps:

1. Position the cursor where you want the comment to appear.

2. Select **Edit ➤ Comment Create** (or press **Ctrl-F5 C C**). You're taken to the screen shown in Figure 3.18.

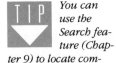

You can use the Search feature (Chapter 9) to locate comments easily.

3. Type your comment, up to 20 lines in length, using the standard editing keys to make changes and corrections.

4. When you're finished, press Exit (**F7**) to return to the Edit screen. The comment appears on the screen in a box.

CHANGING A DOCUMENT COMMENT

*You can use boldface (**F6**) and underline (**F8**) while typing a comment (see Chapter 5).*

If you need to change the text within a document comment,

1. Move the cursor just below the comment you want to change.

2. Select **Edit ➤ Comment ➤ Edit** (or press **Ctrl-F5 C E**). This takes you back to the same screen you used to create the comment.

```
Document Comment

 ┌─────────────────────────────────────────────────┐
 │ _                                               │
 │                                                 │
 │                                                 │
 │                                                 │
 │                                                 │
 │                                                 │
 │                                                 │
 │                                                 │
 │                                                 │
 └─────────────────────────────────────────────────┘


Press Exit when done
```

FIGURE 3.18:

The screen for entering a document comment

3. Make whatever changes you wish, using the same editing keys you use on the normal Edit screen, then press Exit (**F7**).

DELETING A DOCUMENT COMMENT

You can delete all the com- ments in a document in one step by using the Search and Replace feature (Chapter 9) to replace each [Comment] code with "nothing."

To delete a document comment, follow these steps:

1. Move the cursor to the vicinity of the comment you want to delete.

2. Turn on Reveal Codes (select **Edit ➤ R**eveal Codes, or press **Alt-F3** or **F11**).

3. Move the cursor to the [Comment] code (only the code appears; the text within the comment is not visible on the Reveal Codes screen).

4. Press **Delete** to delete the comment.

If you delete a comment by accident, you can use the Cancel key (F1) to un- delete it.

CONVERTING TEXT TO A COMMENT

You can convert up to 20 lines of existing text into a comment. This might come in handy if, say, you cannot decide whether or not to leave a particular passage in text, but don't want to completely delete it. Follow these steps:

1. Block the text that you want to convert to a comment (up to 20 lines).

2. Select **Edit ➤ Comment ➤ Create ➤ Y**es (or press **Ctrl-F5 C C Y**).

The blocked text is now displayed within a comment and is removed from the regular text.

CONVERTING A COMMENT TO TEXT

There is no direct way to print document comments within their boxes; you must con- vert them to text first.

If you want to convert a "commented" passage to normal text within the docu- ment, follow these steps:

1. Move the cursor just below the comment you want to convert to text.

2. Select **Edit ➤ Comment ➤ Convert to Text** (or press **Ctrl-F5 C T**).

The text within the comment is converted to normal text, and the [Comment] code is removed. If necessary, add spaces or hard returns (press ↵) to blend the text correctly with existing text.

HIDING DOCUMENT COMMENTS

If you want to hide document comments on the screen so that you can focus on editing the regular text, follow these steps:

1. Select **F**ile ➤ Se**t**up (or press **Shift-F1**). Then choose **D**isplay ➤ Edit-Screen Options.

2. Select **C**omments Display.

3. Select **N**o.

4. Press Exit (**F7**).

All document comments become invisible. To redisplay the document comments, repeat steps 1 and 2 but select **Y**es in step 3.

DATE STAMPING

> **TO INSERT THE CURRENT DATE IN YOUR DOCU-MENT WITHOUT HAVING TO TYPE IT,**
>
> **select Tools (or press Shift-F5), then choose either Date Text or Date Code.**

A simple, though handy, feature of WordPerfect is its ability to *date stamp* a document. There are obviously lots of occasions for using dates in documents, such as the date at the top of a business letter or a memo, or perhaps a date used to indicate the current revision or printing of a document.

There are actually two types of dates you can type:

Date Text: types the current date, as determined by the system clock; the date never changes.

Date Code: enters a code that appears as the current system date; the date automatically changes when the system date changes.

*The **system clock** is the calendar/clock built into most computers. If you have such a clock, you can set the correct date and time by using the DATE and TIME commands in DOS. See your DOS book or manual.*

Date Text is useful when you want to type a dated document and never want that date to change. Date Code is useful when you do want the date to change. For example, when printing multiple revisions of the same document, you might want to use the Date Code feature to always display the date of the most recent printing (Chapter 7 presents an example in a page footer). When printing a mass mailing (Chapter 16) that takes several days, you might want to use the Date Code feature to reflect accurately the date on which each letter was printed.

Regardless of whether you use Date Code or Date Text to enter the current date and time in your document, you can define a format for the date along the way.

1. Position the cursor where you want to insert a date.

2. If you want to use the current date format, select **T**ools ➤ Date **C**ode or Date **T**ext, depending on which kind of date you want to insert. Skip the remaining steps.

3. If you want to specify a new date format, select **T**ools ➤ Date **F**ormat. The screen shown in Figure 3.19 appears.

4. Design your date or time format by using the symbols listed under *Character* in the first column of the display. Note also the examples shown near the bottom of the screen and in Table 3.2.

5. Press ↵.

6. If you want to insert the date or time at the current cursor position now, select either Date **T**ext or Date **C**ode.

NOTE NOTE *The shortcut key for getting to the Date options is Shift-F5.*

When designing a date format, notice that the numbers 1 through 9 each represent a part of the date, such as the day of the month, the month as a number, the month as a name, and so forth. Number 0 represents am/pm. The percent

```
Date Format

   Character    Meaning
      1         Day of the Month
      2         Month (number)
      3         Month (word)
      4         Year (all four digits)
      5         Year (last two digits)
      6         Day of the Week (word)
      7         Hour (24-hour clock)
      8         Hour (12-hour clock)
      9         Minute
      0         am / pm
      %,$       Used before a number, will:
                   Pad numbers less than 10 with a leading zero or space
                   Abbreviate the month or day of the week

   Examples:  3 1, 4       = December 25, 1984
              %6 %3 1, 4   = Tue Dec 25, 1984
              %2/%1/5 (6)  = 01/01/85 (Tuesday)
              $2/$1/5 (%6) =  1/ 1/85 (Tue)
              8:90         = 10:55am


Date format: 3 1, 4
```

FIGURE 3.19:

Options for designing a date and time format

DATE FORMAT	SAMPLE DATE/TIME
3 1, 4	October 1, 1991
6, 3 1, 4	Tuesday, October 1, 1991
2/1/5	10/1/91
%2/%1/%5	10/01/91
$2/$1/$5	10/ 1/91
%6 - %2/%1/%5	Tue - 10/01/91
6, %3$1, 5	Tuesday, Oct 1, 91
8:9	4:30
8:90	4:30pm
7:9	16:30

TABLE 3.2:

Examples of date and time formats

symbol (%) adds a zero to any number that has fewer than two digits (e.g., 9 is displayed as *09*) and abbreviates month names (e.g., January is displayed as *Jan*). The dollar sign adds a blank space in front of any number that is less than 10 (e.g., the date 12/1/91 is displayed *as 12/ 1/91*). (See Figure 3.19 or Table 3.2 for examples.)

SELECTING A DEFAULT DATE FORMAT

Normally WordPerfect displays dates in the **3 1, 4** format (e.g., *December 25, 1991*), unless you specifically change the default format before entering the date text or date code. If you want to change the default date format for the current session and future sessions with WordPerfect, select **File ➤** Setup (or press **Shift-F1**). Then select **I**nitial Settings **➤ D**ate Format, and enter your new date format as usual. Press Exit (**F7**) twice to return to the Edit screen.

In the future, selecting **Tools ➤** Date **T**ext or **Tools ➤** Date **C**ode will display the current date in the format you specified (unless, of course, you later change the date format again).

FINDING MISSING FILES

> **TO DISPLAY THE LIST FILES SCREEN,**
>
> **select File ➤ List Files (or press F5) and press ⏎.**

Using **F**ile ➤ **R**etrieve (Shift-F10) is a quick and easy way to retrieve a document if you remember the exact location and name of the document. If you're having trouble finding a particular document or don't quite remember its name, use the List Files screen, shown in Figure 3.20.

As you may be able to tell from the figure, List Files displays the names of existing files on the current directory in alphabetical order, so you can see what's available. To get to this screen, select **F**ile ➤ List **F**iles and press ⏎, or press F5 and ⏎. To exit List Files without making a selection, press Cancel (**F1**).

Chapter 4 will hone your newfound skills by teaching you basic document formatting, such as spacing, indenting, and aligning your text.

NOTE *To learn more about the List Files screen, refer to Chapter 12.*

```
05-03-91  09:57a          Directory C:\WP51\WPFILES\*.*
Document size:    3,986   Free:  7,520,256 Used:  2,963,218      Files:      174

     .   Current   <Dir>             ..   Parent    <Dir>
TEST     .         <Dir>  04-22-91 08:04p   TEST2    .         <Dir>  04-22-91 08:04p
2NDEDIT  .LBL     29,296  04-19-91 11:33a   5-WP              39,736  09-12-90 01:22p
ACKNOW   .WP       1,848  09-13-90 02:47p   AD       .WP       2,766  09-18-90 08:23a
ALARM    .WP      14,445  12-25-90 12:12a   APPS     .TP       3,844  09-18-90 04:07p
ARTICLE  .WP         697  06-15-91 02:46p   ASHLEY   .WP      54,032  12-23-90 11:04p
ASHLEY2  .WP      52,210  01-04-91 01:19a   BBDOS5   .LBL     16,497  01-02-91 11:09a
BBDOS5   .WP       1,209  09-18-90 11:01a   BBSCHED  .WP      17,484  11-12-90 02:59p
BUCKINGH.WP        1,927  09-12-90 11:27a   CAREER   .WP       1,894  08-20-90 08:49a
CAREPACK.LBL      12,840  01-20-91 05:23a   CAREPACK .WP      12,840  01-20-91 05:22a
CBACKUPS.LBL      15,406  02-08-91 09:41a   CBSCHED  .WP      16,932  11-06-90 12:19p
CHAP5    .ALN     71,290  09-14-90 12:43p   CHAP5    .DON     46,174  09-12-90 08:23p
CHAP5    .WP      71,290  09-14-90 12:43p   CHCODES  .WP      26,238  01-11-91 07:42a
COLORS   .EPS     15,383  09-25-90 08:01p   COLORS   .WP      25,096  09-25-90 03:55p
COLUMNS  .DUN     88,049  01-21-91 04:00a   COLUMNS  .WP      19,639  12-25-90 03:01a
CRUMLISH.WP        1,665  12-01-90 02:26p   DB41-1   .WP      45,919  11-09-90 02:12p
DB41-1-B.WP       36,903  11-09-90 01:39p   DB4PRG   .LBL      6,582  09-12-90 12:05p
DBIV1-1  .WP     192,100  12-18-90 07:17p   DISKLAB  .PRM      9,788  12-31-91 04:31p
DISKLAB  .SCD      2,572  12-31-91 04:20p   DISKLABS .PRM      3,442  12-31-91 04:22p

1 Retrieve; 2 Delete; 3 Move/Rename; 4 Print; 5 Short/Long Display;
6 Look; 7 Other Directory; 8 Copy; 9 Find; N Name Search: 6
```

FIGURE 3.20:

The List Files screen

PART TWO

Formatting Your Documents

Part 2 builds upon the basic skills you learned in Part 1, giving you more control over the format and appearance of your printed documents. You'll learn to indent, align, and justify text; to embellish your document with fonts, lines, and special characters; to create tables and other multicolumn documents; and to format longer, multi-page documents. You'll also learn to take advantage of whatever features your particular printer offers. In the process, you will not only refine your word processing skills but will also start advancing into the more advanced realm of desktop publishing.

CHAPTER 4

Spacing, Aligning, and Indenting Text

any typing and writing tasks require spacing, justifying, indenting, and aligning text. As you'll discover in this chapter, WordPerfect offers much more flexibility in these areas than even the most sophisticated typewriter. As just one small example, on a typewriter, you must set your tab stops before you type. But with WordPerfect, you can change the tab stops *after* you've typed your text, and your text will adjust to the new tab stops.

HANDS-ON
....
LESSON 4

For hands-on practice in using some of the features described in this chapter, see Lesson 4 in Part 9.

CHANGING LINE SPACING

TO CHANGE THE LINE SPACING,

position the cursor and select Layout ➤ Line ➤ Line Spacing (Shift-F8 L S). Then enter a number and press ↵.

If you use a typewriter to type a document using single spacing, only to find that it should have been double-spaced, you have no choice but to retype the entire document. In WordPerfect, however, retyping isn't necessary. You can just click on a few menu options or press a shortcut key to change the line spacing to any measurement you wish. Here's how:

You can change the line spacing anywhere in your document and in as many different places as you want.

1. Move the cursor to the first character of the line where you want to change the line spacing (or to where you're about to type new text).

2. Select **Layout ➤ Line ➤ Line Spacing** from the pull-down menu (or press **Shift-F8 L S**).

3. Type the new line spacing and press ↵.

4. Press Exit (**F7**) to return to the Edit screen.

The Edit screen may not exactly reflect the line spacing you choose. For a more accurate picture, check the View Document screen.

In step 3 above, you can enter fractions. For example, *1* is single spacing, *2* is double spacing, and *1.5* or *1¹/2* is one-and-a-half spacing. Figure 4.1 shows examples of all three. You can enter virtually any value when choosing your line spacing (e.g., *3* for triple spacing, *4* for quadruple spacing, and so on).

The code on the Reveal Codes screen for a line-spacing change is [Ln Spacing:] followed by the current spacing (e.g., [Ln Spacing:2] for double spacing). When you change the line spacing, all text to the right of

---

Single spacing_____

Here is a paragraph that uses the default single spacing. To change the line spacing, position the cursor wherever you want to change the spacing (either before or after typing the text), and select Layout ▸ Line ▸ Line Spacing. Then type a number and press ↵.

Double spacing_____

Here is a paragraph that uses the double spacing (2). To select double spacing,

position the cursor wherever you want to start double spacing (either before or

after typing the text), and select Layout ▸ Line ▸ Line Spacing. Then type **2**

and press ↵.

One-and-a-half spacing _____

You can enter fractions when defining your line spacing. For example, this text

uses one-and-a-half spacing, typed as either 1.5 or 1 1/2 when defining the line

spacing. WordPerfect lets you set the line spacing to just about any number -

you're not at all limited to 1, 1.5, and 2.

FIGURE 4.1:

Single (1), one-and-a-half (1.5) and double spacing (2)

and below the cursor position is spaced accordingly, up to the next [Ln Spacing:] code in the document (if any).

TROUBLESHOOTING LINE-SPACING PROBLEMS

If WordPerfect seems to ignore your request when you change the line spacing, it's probably because a previous [Ln Spacing] code is canceling the new one. Turn on the Reveal Codes screen (press **Alt-F3** or **F11**), and check for any multiple [Ln Spacing:] codes, like those below:

[Ln Spacing:2][Ln Spacing:1]

In this example, the second code is canceling the first one, so if you want double spacing, you need to delete the [Ln Spacing:1] code.

If your printer prints at double the spacing you requested (e.g., you want single spacing, but it prints double), chances are the Auto Line-Feed or Auto LF setting on your printer is turned on. See your printer manual to learn how to turn this switch off.

CHANGING THE MARGINS

As mentioned previously, WordPerfect places a default 1-inch margin around every printed page of your document, as Figure 4.2 shows. But you can change the margins at any time, either before or after typing your document.

You don't need to change the margins to indent a block of text. You can use the Indent keys instead, as discussed a little later.

As with all formatting techniques discussed in this chapter, WordPerfect adjusts margins by inserting hidden codes at the current cursor position. Therefore, if you want to change the margins for an entire document, you should start by pressing **Home Home** ↑ to move the cursor to the top of the document, before you change the margin settings. If you only want to change the margins for a particular section of a document, move the cursor to the top of that section before changing the margins.

CHANGING THE LEFT AND RIGHT MARGINS

TO CHANGE THE LEFT AND RIGHT MARGINS,

position the cursor, select Layout ➤ Line ➤ Margins (or press Shift-F8 L M), and enter your left and right margin measurements in inches.

To change the left and right margins in a document, follow these steps:

1. Position the cursor where you want the new left and right margins to start.

2. Select Layout ➤ Line ➤ Margins (or press **Shift-F8 L M**).

3. Type a measurement for the left margin, such as *2* for 2 inches, or *1.5* or *1¹⁄2* for 1¹⁄2 inches, then press ↵.

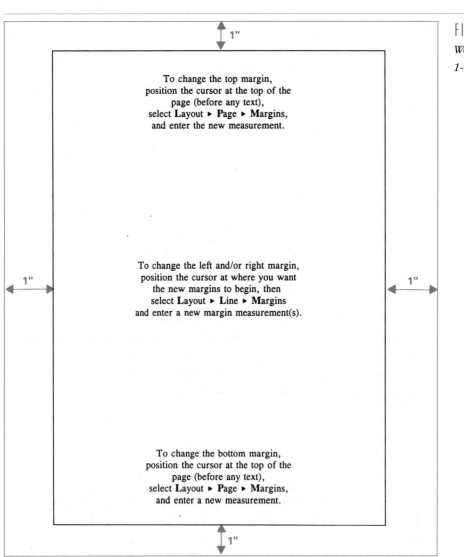

FIGURE 4.2:

WordPerfect's standard 1-inch margins

4. Type a measurement for the right margin (again using a whole number, decimal, or fraction) and press ↵.

5. Press Exit (**F7**) to return to the Edit screen.

All text below the cursor position is automatically reformatted to fit in the new margins. You may want to check the View Document screen (File ➤ Print ➤ View Document) at 100% or so to verify.

CHANGING THE TOP AND BOTTOM MARGINS

TO CHANGE THE TOP AND BOTTOM MARGINS,

1. Move the cursor to the top of the page where you want the new margins to take effect.

2. Select Layout ➤ Page ➤ Margins (or press Shift-F8 P M).

3. Enter the new margin measurements.

To change the top and bottom margins on the printed page, follow these steps:

1. Position the cursor at the top of the page where you want the new top or bottom margin spacing to start (the cursor must be placed before any text on that page.)

2. Select **L**ayout ➤ **P**age ➤ **M**argins (or press **Shift-F8 P M**).

3. Type a measurement for the top margin, such as *2* for 2 inches, or *1.5* or *1¹/₂* for 1¹/₂ inches, then press ↵.

4. Type a measurement for the bottom margin (again using a whole number, decimal, or fraction) and press ↵.

5. Press Exit (**F7**) to return to the Edit screen.

You may want to check the View Document screen at Full Page size (option 3) to verify your change.

CHANGING OR DELETING MARGIN SETTINGS

Sometimes, finding the best margins for printing a document involves a little trial and error. If you change your mind about the margin settings in a document, you can delete the hidden codes used to adjust the margins and replace them with new codes (by following the steps above to change the margins).

The Reveal Codes screen shows the left and right margin settings as the code [L/R Mar:] followed by the left and right margin measurements. The code for the top and bottom margins appears as [T/B Mar:] followed by the top and bottom margin measurements.

TROUBLESHOOTING MARGIN PROBLEMS

If you have problems printing text within the margins, it may be because the paper is simply misaligned in your printer. See Chapter 8 for some tips.

If WordPerfect seems to ignore your request for new margin settings, it may be that a previous [L/R Mar:] or [T/B Mar:] code is canceling your most recent request. For example, in the sequence of codes below, the code for using 0.75-inch left and right margins does nothing, because it's followed by a code that immediately changes the margins to 1.5 inches:

[L/R Mar:.75",.75"][L/R Mar:1.5",1.5"]Four score and

To use the 0.75-inch margins, you'd need to delete the [L/R Mar:1.5",1.5"] code on the Reveal Codes screen, as described in Chapter 3.

Also, be aware that if WordPerfect encounters a [T/B Mar:] code in your document *after* it has already started printing the page, the new top and bottom margins will not take effect until the next page. This is why it's important to change the top and bottom margins at the very top of the page where you want the new margins to take effect.

Minimum Margin Widths

The "dead zone" is at the outer edges of the page, where the printer cannot print.

Laser and other printers that feed paper from a tray do so with small wheels that pull the paper by its edges through the printer. The outer edges of the page make up what is called the "dead zone," because the printer cannot print there. (If text were printed within the dead zone, the small wheels would likely smudge the printed text.)

You cannot set the margins to a value that falls within the dead zone. For example, if you try to set the margins to 0", WordPerfect automatically increases your margin measurement to compensate for the dead zone, typically a value between 0.20 and 0.30 inches.

ALIGNING AND JUSTIFYING TEXT

**TO CHANGE THE ALIGNMENT OF
A PARAGRAPH OR BLOCK OF TEXT,**

1. **Move the cursor to the point where you want to change the alignment.**

2. **Select Layout ➤ Justify (or press Shift-F8 L J).**

3. Choose the type of alignment you want.

There are several ways to align and justify written text, as summarized below:

Left justification (produces a *ragged right margin*): Only the left margin is justified (smooth); the right margin is ragged.

Full justification (produces a *smooth right margin*): Both the left and right margins are smooth.

Center justification (produces text *centered* between the margins): Text is evenly positioned between the left and right margins.

Right justification (produces *flush-right* text): Text is smooth and flush against the right margin; the left margin is ragged.

Figure 4.3 shows examples of the various types of justification.
The basic steps for justifying text are as follows:

1. Position the cursor where you want to change justification, whether it's at the first character of existing text or where you are about to start typing new text.

2. Select **Layout** ➤ Justify (or press **Shift-F8 L J**). This displays the various justification options.

3. Select a justification style (**L**eft, **C**enter, **R**ight, or **F**ull).

4. At this point, all text to the right of and below the cursor is justified according to your selection. However, you can repeat steps 1–3 anywhere in the document to change to some other form of justification.

We'll talk about each type of justification and some shortcuts in the sections that follow.

LEFT-JUSTIFYING TEXT

*Another way to reduce rivers of white space in full justification is with **hyphenation** (Chapter 11).*

Left justification is useful for creating a typewritten look and is often used for form letters that are supposed to look as if they were typed personally. Left justification also removes the extra white space added between letters and words in full justification, thereby reducing the "rivers" of white space that often flow through text that's fully justified.

To left-justify text, follow the general steps for justifying text above, selecting Left in step 3. If you later change your mind and want to go back to full justification, move the cursor near the place where you activated left justification, turn on the Reveal Codes screen (press **Alt-F3** or **F11**), and delete the [Just:Left] code.

FULLY JUSTIFYING TEXT

Full justification is the default justification option; that is, if you do not activate any other type of justification, your text will be fully justified. However, once you do activate some other form of justification, all text beneath that place in the document takes on the justification you specify.

If you want to return to full justification elsewhere in the document, you must position the cursor where you want to reinstate full justification and follow the general steps for justifying text above, selecting Full in step 3.

If you change your mind after reactivating full justification, delete the [Just:Full] code near the place where you reactivated full justification.

Full Justification_____

Unless you tell it otherwise, WordPerfect will print paragraphs with full justification, where both the left and right margins are smooth. Full justification is one of the hallmarks of documents created with a word processor instead of a typewriter. But in order to get both the left and right margins smooth, WordPerfect needs to add space between words and letters. This, in turn, can make the text look "gappy," and even produce rivers of white space running down the page in large documents.

Left Justification_____

Left justification produces a ragged-right margin, as in this example. This is often used to create a personalized "hand-typed" look. This justification method also removes the extra gaps between words and letters, and any rivers of white running down the page, because there's no need to add spacing text to reach the right margin.

Center Justification_____

An Example of Center-Justified Text
by
N.E. Buddee

August 18, 1991

Right Justification_____

Rightly Justified, Inc.
1234 Walla Walla Lane
P.O. Box 1234
Cucamonga, CA 91234

FIGURE 4.3:

Various types of justification

CENTERING TEXT

Centering text is so common that there are actually a couple of ways to do it, either by justification, when you want to center several lines of text (such as all the text on a title page), or by alignment, when you want to center one or a few lines on a page. The result is the same: The text is centered between the margins. Choosing one technique over the other is simply a matter of deciding what's more convenient at the moment.

Centering a Short Line

TO CENTER A SHORT LINE OF TEXT,

position the cursor at the short line you want centered (or where you are about to type that line), then press Center (Shift-F6) or select Layout ➤ Align ➤ Center.

If you want to center just a single short line, such as a title, follow these steps:

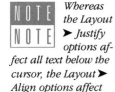

Whereas the Layout ➤ Justify options affect all text below the cursor, the Layout ➤ Align options affect only the current line.

1. Position the cursor where you are about to type the short line or at the start of the short line if you've already typed it.

2. Press Center (**Shift-F6**) or select **Layout** ➤ **Align** ➤ Center.

3. If you have not already done so, type your short text and press ↵.

4. If you have already typed (and now centered) a short line, press the **End** key, then ↓ or ↵.

Following these steps centers only the current line, rather than all text beneath the cursor. The hidden code for centering a single short line is [Center]. You can remove the code if you change your mind about centering the short line.

Centering Several Lines

Word-Perfect can also center text vertically, between the top and bottom margins, as you'll learn in Chapter 7.

If you want to center several lines of text, you may find it easier to turn on center justification above (or to the left of) the first line you want centered, by following the general steps for justifying text, selecting Center in step 3. Then, to reinstate some other form of justification, move the cursor below (or to the right of) the last centered line, and activate some other form of justification, again following the general steps.

The hidden code for activating centering for all text to the right and below is [Just:Center], which you can move or remove if you change your mind about center justification.

RIGHT-JUSTIFYING TEXT

Like centering, right justification (text is flush-right) is pretty common, so WordPerfect offers an easy way to right-justify a single line, as well as groups of lines.

Right-Justifying a Short Line

TO RIGHT-JUSTIFY A SHORT LINE OF TEXT,

position the cursor at the short line you want to right-justify (or where you are about to type that line), and press Flush Right (Alt-F6) or select Layout ➤ Align ➤ Flush Right.

If you just want to right-justify a single short line, follow these steps:

1. Position the cursor where you are about to type the short line or at the start of the short line if you've already typed it.

2. Press Flush Right (**Alt-F6**) or select **Layout** ➤ **Align** ➤ Flush Right.

3. If you have not already done so, type your text and press ↵.

4. If you have already typed (and now right-justified) a short line, press the **End** key, then ↓ or ↵.

If you change your mind about a single right-justified line of text, remove the hidden [Flsh Rgt] code at the start of that line, using the Reveal Codes screen (press **Alt-F3** or **F11**).

Right-Justifying Several Lines

If you want to right-justify several lines of text, you may find it easier to turn on right justification at the point where you want it to begin, by following the general steps for justifying text, selecting Right in step 3. This method inserts a hidden [Just:Right] code at the cursor position, right-justifying all text to the right of and below the cursor. As usual, you can move or remove the [Just:Right] code should you later change your mind about right justification.

A SHORTCUT FOR JUSTIFYING BLOCKS OF TEXT

Another quick way to center or right-justify several existing lines of text is to block them first, then select the justification. This is especially handy because the justification only affects the blocked lines. Therefore, you save time because you don't have to change the justification for any text below the lines you justified. Follow these steps:

 *Chapter 2 has a complete discussion of blocking techniques.*

1. Block the lines you want to justify with the mouse or by pressing Block (**Alt-F4** or **F12**) and highlighting the text.

2. Select **L**ayout ➤ **A**lign ➤ **C**enter (to center the lines) or **L**ayout ➤ **A**lign ➤ **F**lush Right (to right-justify the lines).

3. Press **Y** (for **Y**es) when asked whether you want to center or right-justify the lines.

INDENTING PARAGRAPHS

TO INDENT OR "OUTDENT" A PARAGRAPH,

move the cursor to the start of the paragraph you want to indent or outdent (or where you're about to type that paragraph), and press one of the following keys: Tab, Margin Release (Shift-Tab), →Indent (F4), or →Indent← (Shift-F4).

There are lots of ways to indent paragraphs, as demonstrated in Figure 4.4. All these indentations are easy to achieve with WordPerfect. Here are the general steps:

1. Move the cursor to the point at which you want to start typing your paragraph or, if you've already typed the paragraph, move the cursor to the first character in the paragraph.

2. Depending on what you want, do one of the following:

   ◆ To indent the first line of the paragraph, press **Tab**.

   ◆ To indent the entire left side of the paragraph, press →Indent (**F4**) or select **L**ayout ➤ **A**lign ➤ **I**ndent →.

   ◆ To indent both the left and right sides of the paragraph, press →Indent← (**Shift-F4**) or select **L**ayout ➤ **A**lign ➤ **I**ndent→←.

   ◆ To outdent the first line of the paragraph, press →Indent (**F4**) and press Margin Release (**Shift-Tab**), or select **L**ayout ➤ **A**lign ➤ **I**ndent and **L**ayout ➤ **A**lign ➤ **M**argin Rel←.

   ◆ To hang (outdent) the first line of a paragraph into the left margin, press Margin Release (**Shift-Tab**) or select **L**ayout ➤ **A**lign ➤ **M**argin Rel.

Regardless of how you indent or outdent a paragraph, you can change your mind and unindent or unoutdent the text.

REMOVING INDENTS AND OUTDENTS

If you change your mind about an indent or outdent in a paragraph, you can simply remove the hidden codes that are controlling the indent or outdent at the start of the paragraph.

Indenting with Tab_____

     If you just want to indent the first line of a paragraph, just press Tab before typing the first line. That's how you'd do it on a typewriter, and that's how it was done at the beginning of this paragraph. Of course, if you've already typed the entire paragraph, *then* later decide to indent the first line, just move the cursor to the start of that line and press Tab.

Indenting with →Indent (F4)_____

     If you want to indent the entire left margin, move the cursor to the beginning of the paragraph you want to indent (or where you are about to type a paragraph), and press →Indent (F4) as many times as necessary to get the level of indentation you want. The entire left margin of that paragraph will be indented, like this one (typed after pressing →Indent twice).

Indenting with →Indent← (Shift-F4) _____

     If you want to indent both the left and right margins, as when typing a long quotation, move the cursor to the beginning of the paragraph you want to indent (or where you are about to type a paragraph), and press →Indent← (Shift-F4) as many times as necessary to get the level of indentation you want.

Outdenting the First Line_____

If you want to indent all the lines *beneath* the first line in a paragraph, move the cursor to the beginning of that paragraph (or where you are about to start typing that paragraph), then press →Indent (F4) then Margin Release (Shift-Tab).

Hanging (outdenting) into the Left Margin_____

If you want to hang the first line of a paragraph out into the margin, move the cursor to the beginning of that paragraph (or where you are about to start typing that paragraph), then press Margin Release (Shift-Tab).

FIGURE 4.4:

A document with various indents and outdents

If you want to change the amount of indentation (or outdentation), change the tab stops, as described later in this chapter.

1. Move the cursor to the start of the paragraph that you want to unindent or unoutdent.

2. Select **Edit** ➤ **Reveal Codes** (or press **Alt-F3** or **F11**) to activate the Reveal Codes screen (as described in Chapter 3).

3. Delete the code controlling the indent or outdent.

The hidden codes for indentations are pretty obvious when you see them on the Reveal Codes screen and are listed below:

Tab	[Tab]
→Indent	[→Indent]
→Indent←	[→Indent←]
Margin Release	[←Mar Rel]

If your indents and outdents seem wildly out of control on the Edit screen, you may just need to "redraw" the screen (press Page Down, then Page Up). If that doesn't clear things up, you'll need to take a look at the Reveal Codes screen (Alt-F3 or F11) to see if any extraneous or missing codes are to blame.

TYPING LISTS

TO TYPE A BASIC NUMBERED (OR OTHER TYPE) OF LIST,

1. Type the number or special character that identifies the item in the list.

2. Press →Indent (F4).

3. Type the text of that item.

4. Press ↵ once or twice to start the next item in the list.

Bullets, pointing hands, check boxes, and other special characters are described in more detail in Chapter 5.

Short lists are easy to type; Figure 4.5 shows some examples. Follow these steps:

1. If you want to indent the item number or letter (or bullet, pointing hand, or check box) from the left margin, press **Tab** until you've indented far enough.

2. Type the item number, letter, bullet, pointing hand, or check box.

3. Press →Indent (**F4**), or press →Indent← (**Shift-F4**) if you want to indent the text from both sides.

4. Type the text of the item, and press ↵ (press ↵ twice if you want a blank line between items).

Numbered List_____

1. To type a numbered list, type the number (and perhaps a period) that identifies the item (e.g., 1. next to this item).

2. Press →Indent (F4) or →Indent← (Shift-F4) if you want to indent text from both sides.

3. Type the text (this part).

4. Press Enter (once or twice) and repeat the steps above for the next item in the list.

Indenting the Entire List_____

  1. If you want to indent the entire list like this...

  2. Press Tab as many times as necessary to move the cursor out to the tab stop that you want the numbers aligned on, then type the number (e.g., 2.).

  3. Then press F4 or Shift-F4 and type the text next to the number, as usual.

Changing the Tab Stops_____

 1. This list was typed exactly like the one above...

 2. But then we changed the tab stops to narrow the gap between the left margin, each number, and its text, as described later in this chapter.

Bulleted List_____

 • A bulleted list is the same as a numbered list...

 • Except that you type a bullet (a special character) rather than a number to identify each item in the list.

Check List_____
  ☐ A check list is like any other list...
  ☐ Except that each item starts with a large hollow square (another special character).
  ☐ This example is also unique in that it's single-spaced by pressing Enter only once after typing each item.

Pointing List_____
  ☞ This list is just like any of those above...
  ☞ except it uses a different special character to the left.

FIGURE 4.5:

Examples of various lists

AUTOMATIC NUMBERING

Rather than typing each number in a numbered list or each letter in a lettered list (e.g., *A., B., C.*), you can use *automatic paragraph numbering* or *outlining* (see Chapter 22). These features offer a real advantage because they automatically adjust all numbers (or letters) in the left column if you add, delete, or move items in your list.

CHANGING THE GAP

The gap between the number (or bullet or other special character) in each item in the list and the text of the item is controlled by the *tab stops*. To narrow or widen the gap, just change the tab stops, as described later in this chapter.

ABOUT TAB STOPS

WordPerfect automatically sets tab stops at every $\frac{1}{2}$ inch, starting at the left margin. Because of this, if you do not change the tab stops, all indents and outdents created with the Tab, Margin Release (Shift-Tab), →Indent (F4), and →Indent← (Shift-F4) keys will initially be in $\frac{1}{2}$-inch increments. That is, the first level of indentation will be $\frac{1}{2}$ inch from the left margin, the next level will be 1 inch from the left margin, and so forth.

VIEWING THE TAB RULER

You can turn the tab ruler on and off at any time to see your current tab stops. To do so, follow these steps:

1. Select **E**dit ➤ **W**indow or press Screen (**Ctrl-F3**) then **W**.

2. Type **23** and press ↵.

This will display a highlighted tab ruler at the bottom of the Edit screen, as shown in Figure 4.6. The triangles show you the current tab stops. A left curly brace ({) or left bracket ([) shows the left margin setting, and a right curly brace (}) or right bracket (]) shows the right margin setting. (You'll see braces if the margin falls on a tab setting and brackets if it does not.)

Turning the tab ruler off is as easy as turning it on. Just follow the steps above, except type **24** for the number of lines in the window instead of 23 in step 2.

As you'll see next, you can change the tab stops used for your indentations, either before or after you've typed your text. You can also set up different tab rulers throughout your document, which means that you can use any tab stops you want anywhere in your document; you are not confined to one particular set of tab stops.

ADJUSTING TAB ALIGNMENT

Not only can you change the position of tab stops but you can also determine how text is aligned at each tab stop. Your options are as follows:

Left (L): Text typed at the tab setting is left-aligned at the tab stop (the usual method).

Center (C): Text is centered at the tab stop.

Right (R): Text is right-justified at the tab stop.

Decimal (D): Text is aligned on a decimal point or some other character.

Dot Leader (.): Empty space to the left of the tab stop is filled with dots (used in conjunction with any setting above).

We've already talked about left, center, and right justification in relation to paragraphs and short lines of text (which are really just very short paragraphs, since you end them with a ↵ keypress, like a paragraph). In terms of tab alignment, these same concepts apply to aligning text at the tab stop (or, in other

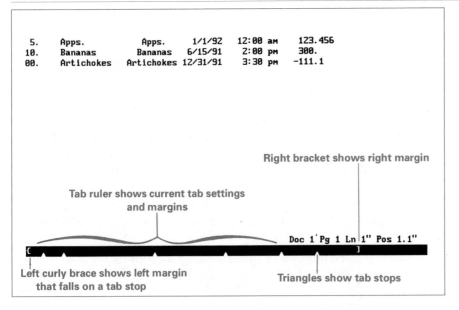

The tab ruler at the bottom of the Edit screen

5.	Apps.	Apps.	1/1/92	12:00 am	123.456
10.	Bananas	Bananas	6/15/91	2:00 pm	300.
00.	Artichokes	Artichokes	12/31/91	3:30 pm	−111.1

Right bracket shows right margin

Tab ruler shows current tab settings
and margins

Doc 1 Pg 1 Ln 1" Pos 1.1"

Left curly brace shows left margin
that falls on a tab stop

Triangles show tab stops

words, to how text is aligned within tabular columns). Figures 4.7 through 4.9 show examples of left, center, right, and decimal alignment, as well as dot leaders. Notice the tab-setting ruler, which was used to create each example. The next section explains how to display and use this ruler.

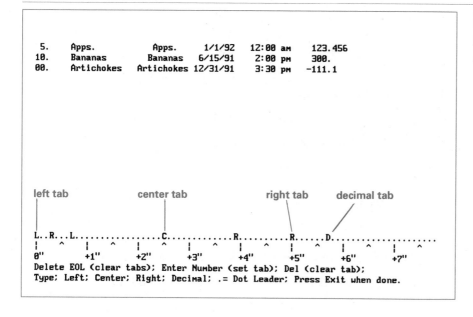

FIGURE 4.7:

Examples of various tab alignments

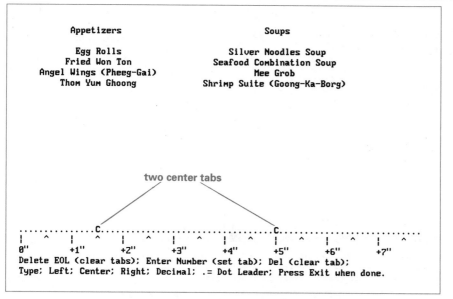

FIGURE 4.8:

An example of two center-aligned tab stops

The Tables feature is covered in Chapter 6.

In all fairness, I should warn you that using tab alignments is just one way of typing text in tabular columns. A second and often much easier method is to use the Tables feature. Nonetheless, you need to know some of the basics of using tab stops, even if it's just to control the amount of indenting and outdenting, or the "gaps" in lists. So read on, but remember that using the Tables feature is probably the best method of typing text into two or more columns.

CHANGING TAB STOPS

TO CHANGE THE TAB STOPS,

1. Move the cursor above the text where you want to change the tab.

2. Select Layout ► Line ► Tab Set (Shift-F8 L T).

3. Adjust the tab stops on the tab ruler.

To change the tab stops, follow these steps:

1. If you want to change tab stops in existing text, position the cursor at the first character (or just above) that text. Otherwise, position the cursor wherever you're about to start typing new text.

2. Select Layout ► Line ► Tab Set (or press **Shift-F8 L T**).

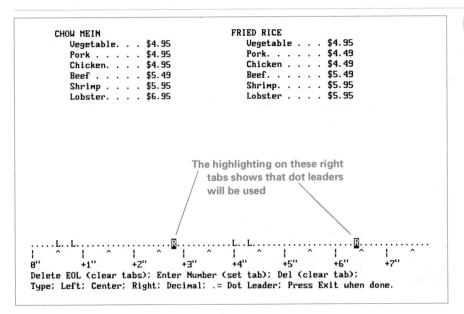

FIGURE 4.9:

An example of dot leaders

3. Adjust the tab stops as described below.

4. Press Exit (**F7**) twice to return to the Edit screen.

The current tab stops appear at the bottom of the screen, with brief reminders on how to change the stops. Figure 4.10 shows the default tab stops for Word-Perfect. Notice that the tab stops are marked in inches, with a vertical bar (┊) at every inch mark and a carat (^) at every ½-inch mark. The place marked 0" is actually the left margin, not the left edge of the page.

A careful look at Figure 4.10 shows the same text as Figure 4.9, but you'll note that the text in 4.10 is aligned differently and has a different tab line. That's because Figure 4.10 is the *before* shot, using the default tab settings of ½ inch. Figure 4.9, on the other hand, shows the text alignment and tab ruler *after* finishing the setting of the tab stops.

To modify the tab ruler, you can do any of the following (in any order you wish):

 *As you ad-just the tab ruler, your changes will be reflected in any tabbed text that is visible on the tab-setting screen.*

◆ Move the cursor along the ruler by clicking on any position where you want a tab stop to appear or by pressing the ← and → keys.

◆ Move the cursor quickly to the edges of the tab ruler by using these cursor-movement keys: **Home** ← (left edge of screen), **Home Home** ← (extreme left edge of ruler), **Home** → (right edge of screen), or **End** (extreme right edge of ruler).

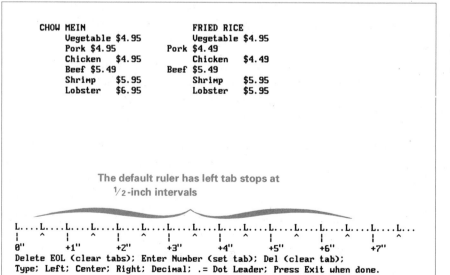

FIGURE 4.10:

Ready to change the tab stops, after selecting Layout ➤ Line ➤ Tab Set

◆ Move the cursor from tab stop to tab stop by pressing the ↑ key (next tab stop) or ↓ key (previous tab stop).

◆ Delete any existing tab stop by moving the cursor to it and pressing the **Delete** key.

◆ Delete all the tab stops to the right of the cursor by pressing **Ctrl-End**.

◆ Add a new tab stop by positioning the cursor at a specific place on the ruler and typing the appropriate letter for the type of tab stop (for example, **L** for left-aligned, **C** for centered, **R** for right-aligned, or **D** for decimal-aligned).

◆ If you know the exact measurement for the tab stop, type that number and press ↵. For example, type **0.25** and press ↵ to set a tab stop at ¼ inch, or type **5.25** and press ↵ to set a tab stop at 5¼ inch. Then type the appropriate letter for the type of tab you want.

◆ Change the type of tab stop by moving the cursor to an existing stop (such as *L*), and typing a new one (such as *C* or *D*).

◆ Add a dot leader to any tab stop by moving the cursor to that stop and typing a period (.). The tab stop is then displayed in reverse video or a different color.

◆ Add multiple tab stops at equal intervals by typing the position of the first stop, followed by a comma and the tab interval (for example, you would type **0,.5** to set tabs at every ½ inch, within the current left and right margins).

◆ To move an existing tab stop along the ruler line, position the cursor at the tab stop, then press **Ctrl-←** or **Ctrl-→** until the tab stop is where you want it.

◆ Select either relative tab measurement (where position 0" is at the left margin) or absolute measurement (where 0" is at the left edge of the page) by typing **T** (for *Type*) and selecting either **A**bsolute to Margin or **R**elative to Margin. (I will discuss this in more detail later.)

When you've finished modifying the tab ruler, press Exit (**F7**) twice to return to your document. Remember, all existing text and new text that you type below the current cursor position will adhere to the new tab stops. That is, any new or existing [Tab], [→Indent], [→Indent←], or [←Mar Rel] codes beneath the new stops will be adjusted. Text above the current cursor position will not be affected at all.

Delete EOL in the tab ruler is short for "Delete to End Of Line," but you actually press Ctrl-End to do that.

Be sure to type a leading 0 when entering fractional tab-stop measurements less than 1 inch; for example, type **0.25***, not* **.25***.*

*Lesson 4 in
Part 9 provides
some hands-on
exercises in set-
ting tabs.*

*Pressing
the
spacebar
repeatedly
accounts for the gap
between "CHOW
MEIN" and the next
[Tab] code on the
Reveal Codes screen
shown in Figure 4.11.*

USING TAB STOPS

Keep in mind that only the Tab, Margin Release (Shift-Tab), →Indent (F4), and →Indent← (Shift-F4) keys act on tab stops. The tab stop does nothing until you press one of these keys to move the cursor to it. For example, to create the two-column menu example in Figure 4.8, you would need to press Tab before typing the name of an appetizer or a soup to move the cursor to the next tab stop.

In Figure 4.11, dot leaders do not appear unless you press Tab after typing a Chow Mein or Fried Rice entry. Also, to *prevent* dot leaders from appearing between the headings "CHOW MEIN" and "FRIED RICE," **CHOW MEIN** was typed, the spacebar was pressed until the cursor was past the R tab stop, then Tab was pressed to move to the proper tab stop for aligning "FRIED RICE." The Reveal Codes screen clearly shows these extra spaces before the tab.

Effects of Insert And Typeover on Tabs

When working with text that's already tabbed into place, keep in mind these two important points:

◆ When you are in Insert mode, pressing Tab inserts another [Tab] code in the text.

◆ When you are in Typeover mode, pressing Tab simply moves the cursor to the next tab stop, without inserting a [Tab] code.

```
     CHOW MEIN              FRIED RICE
          Vegetable. . . $4.95       Vegetable . . . $4.95
          Pork . . . . . $4.95       Pork. . . . . $4.49
          Chicken. . . . $4.95       Chicken . . . . $4.49
          Beef . . . . . $5.49       Beef. . . . . . $5.49
          Shrimp . . . . $5.95       Shrimp. . . . . $5.95
          Lobster. . . . $6.95       Lobster . . . . $5.95

          Pressing the spacebar repeatedly
            made this gap; pressing Tab
          inserted dot leaders

                                         Doc 1 Pg 1 Ln 1" Pos 1"
[                                                      ]
[Tab Set:Rel; -1",-0.5",+0.5",+0.8",+2.8",+4",+4.3",+6.4"][HRt]
[Tab]CHOW MEIN              [Tab]FRIED RICE[HRt]
[Tab][Tab]Vegetable[Rgt Tab]$4.95[Tab][Tab]Vegetable[Rgt Tab]$4.95[HRt]
[Tab][Tab]Pork[Rgt Tab]$4.95[Tab][Tab]Pork[Rgt Tab]$4.49[HRt]
[Tab][Tab]Chicken[Rgt Tab]$4.95[Tab][Tab]Chicken[Rgt Tab]$4.49[HRt]
[Tab][Tab]Beef[Rgt Tab]$5.49[Tab][Tab]Beef[Rgt Tab]$5.49[HRt]
[Tab][Tab]Shrimp[Rgt Tab]$5.95[Tab][Tab]Shrimp[Rgt Tab]$5.95[HRt]
[Tab][Tab]Lobster[Rgt Tab]$6.95[Tab][Tab]Lobster[Rgt Tab]$5.95[HRt]
[HRt]
[HRt]

Press Reveal Codes to restore screen
```

FIGURE 4.11:

The menu with its final tab settings, as it appears on the Reveal Codes screen

Therefore, when you are editing existing text that's already aligned on tab stops, you can press **Insert** to go to Typeover mode. Then you can press **Tab** or **Shift-Tab** to move from column to column without inserting extra tabs and margin releases (which would move the text out of alignment). Of course, you can also use the mouse or arrow keys to position the cursor without inserting or deleting tabs or margin releases.

HIDDEN CODES FOR TAB RULERS AND TAB STOPS

Whenever you change the tab stops in a document, WordPerfect inserts a hidden [Tab Set:] code, followed by *Rel* if you used a relative left margin or *Abs* if you used an absolute left margin, and then the position of each tab stop. Like all codes, [Tab Set] codes can be moved or deleted as you see fit on the Reveal Codes screen.

Codes appearing outside of the [Tab Set] code indicate which kind of tab is controlling the position of the text. Normally when you press the Tab key, a hidden [Tab] code is inserted in the document. This is the "normal" left-aligned tab stop used by default.

When you use other types of tab stops, the hidden code inserted in the document depends on the type of tab stop the cursor lands on when you press Tab, as listed below:

Tab Stop	Hidden Code
Left	[Tab]
Right	[Rgt Tab]
Center	[Cntr Tab]
Decimal	[Dec Tab]

FIXING COMMON ALIGNMENT ERRORS

If you use the Tables feature, presented in Chapter 6, you can avoid all three common alignment errors.

Three alignment errors are common when using tab stops to align text in columns:

◆ Lines between the columns are wavy instead of straight.

◆ Columns are misaligned because of missing or extra [Tab] (or other tab alignment) codes.

◆ Columns are misaligned because text in one or more columns is wider than the column itself.

Let's look at examples of each.

Fixing Wavy Columns

Figure 4.12 shows an example of printed text that's supposed to be evenly spaced in columns, but appears "wavy" instead. This problem is often caused by using blank spaces between columns (i.e., pressing the spacebar) instead of tabs. It is especially noticeable when you're using proportionally spaced fonts (described in Chapter 5). The only solution is to go back and replace all the blank spaces with tabs (or to start all over using the Tables feature, presented in Chapter 6).

Fixing Column Misalignments

A second common error occurs when all the text lines up neatly into columns, but occasionally goes out of whack, as in Davidson's street address and phone number in Figure 4.13.

If you look at the Reveal Codes screen in Figure 4.13, you'll notice two [Tab] codes in front of Davidson's address. These push the address out to the second tab stop. The simple solution is to remove one of the [Tab] codes in front of the address.

Figure 4.14 shows another fairly common alignment problem, which at first glance looks a lot like the preceding problem. However, if you look at the Reveal Codes screen, you'll see that *every* address has only one [Tab] code in front of it.

So, if there are no extra [Tab] codes, what's causing some of the addresses in the second column to shoot over to the third column? The answer is that some of the names in the first column are too wide for that column. Because the name in the first column extends past the first tab stop, the next [Tab] code in that column forces the address out to the second tab stop.

Number	Date	Description	Deposit	Withdrawal
	8/1/91	Deposit	$1,000	
1001	8/1/91	Rent		$500.00
1002	8/1/91	Utilities		$75.00
1003	8/5/91	Water		$19
1004	8/14/91	Credit Card		$75.00
	8/15/91	Deposit	$1,000	
1005	8/16/91	Ray Co. (clothes)	$167.77	
1006	8/17/91	Dr. Dolittle	$88.00	
1007	8/20/91	WP Seminar	$250.00	

FIGURE 4.12:

Wavy columns caused by using spaces instead of tabs to separate columns

The only solution is to change the tab stops at the start of the list (but past the existing [Tab Set] code) until the first column is wide enough to accommodate the longest (widest) name. (See the section on "Refining Tab Stops.")

```
Name                         Address                        Phone No.
Adams, J.A.                  1234 Oak Tree Lane             555-0943
Baker, T.J.                  967 Veronica Eddy              555-0978
Christiansen, J.             P.O. Box 3323                  555-9080
Davidson, W.W.                                              2347 Apple
St.                          555-8979
Edwards, E.E.                5050 Penn Landing              555-9080
Fredrix, Jimi                609 Axis St.                   555-8090
Gomez, J.J.                  2434 Rigatoni St.              555-8374

                                                 Doc 1 Pg 1 Ln 1" Pos 1"
[                                                                   ]
[Tab Set:Rel; -1",-0.5",0",+2.5",+5.5"][HRt]
[BOLD]Name[Tab]Address[Tab]Phone No.[bold][HRt]
Adams, J.A.[Tab]1234 Oak Tree Lane[Tab]555[-]0943[HRt]
Baker, T.J.[Tab]967 Veronica Eddy[Tab]555[-]0978[HRt]
Christiansen, J.[Tab]P.O. Box 3323[Tab]555[-]9080[HRt]
Davidson, W.W.[Tab][Tab]2347 Apple[SRt]
St.[Tab]555[-]8979[HRt]                  Two [Tab] codes cause misalignment
Edwards, E.E.[Tab]5050 Penn Landing[Tab]555[-]9080[HRt]
Fredrix, Jimi[Tab]609 Axis St.[Tab]555[-]8090[HRt]
Gomez, J.J.[Tab]2434 Rigatoni St.[Tab]555[-]8374[HRt]

Press Reveal Codes to restore screen
```

FIGURE 4.13: *Columns out of alignment because of an extra [Tab] code*

```
Name            Address                   Phone No.
Adams, J.A.     1234 Oak Tree Lane        555-0943
Baker, T.J.     967 Veronica Eddy         555-0978
Christiansen, J.                          P.O. Box 3323555-9080
Davidson, W.W.  2347 Apple St.            555-8979
Edwards, E.E.   5050 Penn Landing         555-9080
Fredrix, Jimi   609 Axis St.              555-8090
Gomez, J.J.     2434 Rigatoni St.         555-8374
Text extends into next tab column...      ...so next tab stop is out here
                                                 Doc 1 Pg 1 Ln 1" Pos 1"
[                                                                   ]
[Tab Set:Rel; -1",-0.5",0",+1.5",+4"][HRt]
[BOLD]Name[Tab]Address[Tab]Phone No.[bold][HRt]
Adams, J.A.[Tab]1234 Oak Tree Lane[Tab]555[-]0943[HRt]
Baker, T.J.[Tab]967 Veronica Eddy[Tab]555[-]0978[HRt]
Christiansen, J.[Tab]P.O. Box 3323[Tab]555[-]9080[HRt]
Davidson, W.W.[Tab]2347 Apple St.[Tab]555[-]8979[HRt]
Edwards, E.E.[Tab]5050 Penn Landing[Tab]555[-]9080[HRt]
Fredrix, Jimi[Tab]609 Axis St.[Tab]555[-]8090[HRt]
Gomez, J.J.[Tab]2434 Rigatoni St.[Tab]555[-]8374[HRt]

                                     correct number of [Tab] codes
Press Reveal Codes to restore screen
```

FIGURE 4.14: *The first column spills into the second.*

Checking the Tab-Stop Codes

When you change the tab ruler, it's important to remember that WordPerfect does not change the existing [Tab Set] code. Instead, it inserts a *new* [Tab Set] code. When two or more [Tab Set] codes occur in succession in your document, only the tab stops in the *last* [Tab Set] code are effective.

Delete your old tab codes as soon as they are no longer needed to prevent code clutter.

If you are having a problem with tab stops, use Reveal Codes to see if there are multiple [Tab Set] codes after the problem and delete any that are no longer needed. As discussed under "Refining Tab Stops," it's a good habit to delete an old [Tab Set] code as soon as it is no longer needed, to prevent "code clutter."

Fixing Margin-Release Errors

Pressing Margin Release (Shift-Tab) when the cursor is in the middle of a line of text may cause some of your text to disappear, because the back-shifted text overwrites existing text. To remedy this, go to the Reveal Codes screen (press **Alt-F3** or **F11**) and delete the [←Mar Rel] code in the sentence.

Similarly, if you move text into the left margin inadvertently or change your mind about typing text in the left margin, use the Reveal Codes screen to delete the [←Mar Rel] code that's pushing the text into the margin.

ADJUSTING THE DISPLAY PITCH

You'll learn how to change fonts in the next chapter.

As you may have noticed, WordPerfect always displays characters at the same size (typically 0.1 inch) on the Edit screen, even if you are using different-size fonts. Normally this works just fine, since WordPerfect automatically calculates the proper place to wrap the text from line to line, whether you're using small fonts or larger ones. But if you've worked with text where columns are separated by tabs, especially with smaller fonts, you may have noticed two odd phenomena on the Edit screen:

◆ WordPerfect may move the display of text far off the right edge of the screen to accommodate the large number of text characters and tab spaces on a line.

The View Document screen shows you exactly how your text will appear when printed, proper font sizes and all, regardless of the display pitch used on the Edit screen.

◆ Text typed immediately before a tab stop may disappear from the display.

If text is disappearing under tab stops as you edit, you can switch off the Automatic Display Pitch feature and *decrease* the display pitch enough to uncover hidden text. Follow these steps:

1. With the cursor anywhere in the document, select **Layout ➤ D**ocument ➤ **D**isplay Pitch (or press **Shift-F8 D D**).

2. When the cursor jumps to the Automatic setting, turn off the Automatic Display Pitch feature by pressing **N** for **N**o.

3. When the cursor jumps to the Width setting, type a number smaller than the preset number displayed and press ↵—a decrease of 0.01 inch is often enough to fix the problem. Remember, you need a *smaller* Width setting to spread out the columns of displayed text (a larger number decreases the space between columns).

4. Press Exit (**F7**) twice to register your setting and return to the Edit screen.

Your new display pitch takes effect immediately on the Edit screen (although the characters will still appear to be the same size). If some text is still hidden, repeat the steps above, but enter an even smaller Width setting. Choosing a display pitch does not insert any codes in the document (but the new setting is saved with the document), so you can reset it as many times as needed without worrying about cursor placement or old codes. Keep in mind that this setting is only meant to make your Edit screen easier to read. It will have no effect whatsoever on printed text or text displayed on the View Document screen.

REFINING TAB STOPS

Unless you're plain lucky, it's unlikely that you'll always get your tab stops right the first time, every time. Here's how to refine your existing tab stops:

1. Activate the Reveal Codes screen (press **Alt-F3** or **F11**), then move the code highlight to the first character or code *after* the [Tab Set] code you want to change.

2. Select **L**ayout ➤ **L**ine ➤ **T**ab Set from the menus (or press **Shift-F8 L T**).

3. The current tab ruler appears, and you can make any changes you wish, using the same basic techniques you used to create the tab ruler.

4. Press Exit (**F7**) twice to return to the Edit screen.

5. To prevent code clutter, delete the previous (and now useless) [Tab Set] code by pressing ← twice and then pressing **Delete**.

As usual, you can turn off the Reveal Codes screen when you're satisfied with your final tab stops (press Alt-F3 or F11 again).

ALIGNING TEXT ON THE FLY

> **TO DECIMAL-ALIGN OR RIGHT-ALIGN TEXT WITHOUT CHANGING THE TAB RULER,**
>
> **press Tab Align (Ctrl-F6) or select Layout ➤ Align ➤ Tab Align before typing the text or number you want to align.**

As a shortcut to changing the tab settings in a document, you can press the Tab Align key (Ctrl-F6) to use a normal tab stop as a decimal-aligned, right-aligned, or dot-leader tab stop. Using this shortcut can be handy for aligning text without going through the steps required to change the tab settings; it allows you to align text in an as-needed, on-the-fly manner. Follow these steps:

1. Press Tab Align (**Ctrl-F6**) or select **L**ayout ➤ **A**lign ➤ **T**ab Align, rather than Tab, to move the cursor to the tab stop where you want to align text.

   ◆ If you want to align text on decimal points, type your number (e.g., *123.45*).

   ◆ If you want the text to be right-aligned at the tab stop, don't include the decimal point.

2. Press **Tab** or Tab Align (**Ctrl-F6**) to move to the next tab stop, or press ↵ to end the line.

In other words, text will be decimal-aligned if it includes a period or right-aligned if it does not.

Tab Align inserts a "hard tab" code in the document (discussed in more detail near the end of this chapter).

When you first select Tab Align, you'll notice the message "Align char = ." near the lower-left corner of the screen. This message reminds you that if you type a period, that character will line up on the tab stop. You can, however, specify a different alignment character, as discussed in the next section.

CHANGING THE DECIMAL ALIGNMENT CHARACTER

In general, dates, times, and numbers with equal (or no) decimal places look fine when right-aligned, as in Figure 4.15. However, if you right-align numbers with unequal decimal places, the decimal points won't line up vertically, as the left column in Figure 4.16 shows. To fix that problem, you need to decimal-align, rather than right-align, the numbers. For example, in the second column of the figure, the numbers are aligned on their decimal points.

You can change the alignment character and thousands separator to better align the British-style numbers. For example, the numbers in the third column in Figure 4.16 are aligned on the comma rather than on the decimal point. To make this change, follow these steps:

1. Move the cursor just above the numbers you want to realign on a new decimal character or to where you are about to type the numbers you want aligned.

2. Select **L**ayout ➤ **O**ther ➤ **D**ecimal/Align Character (or press **Shift-F8 O D**).

3. Type the character you want to use to align the numbers (for example, type a comma if you are using the European numbering system).

4. Type the character to use for separating thousands in the number (for example, type a period if you are using the European numbering system).

5. Press Exit (**F7**) to return to the Edit screen.

WordPerfect inserts a [Decml/Algn Char:] code at the current cursor position; all decimal-aligned numbers to the right of and beneath that position will then be aligned at whatever character you specified in step 3. This technique works both for numbers that are decimal-aligned with tab stops on the tab ruler and for numbers that are decimal-aligned on the fly with Tab Align.

To return to American-style decimal alignment, repeat steps 1–5 above wherever you want to resume that alignment style. If you want to use two

TIP

You can use any character, including the special characters discussed in Chapter 5, for decimal alignment and thousands separation.

Date	Time	Qty	Item	Amount
1/1/91	1:00	1	1.	1.00
6/15/91	11:00	10	2.	10.00
11/1/91	2:30	100	10.	100.00
12/31/91	16:00	1,000	100.	1,234.56

FIGURE 4.15:

Examples of right-aligned and decimal-aligned text

Right-Aligned	Decimal-Aligned (American)	Decimal-Aligned (European)
1.2345	1.2345	1,2345
12.345	12.345	12,345
123.45	123.45	123,45
1,234.56	1,234.56	1.234,56
12,345.6	12,345.60	12.345,60
123,456.00	12,345.00	12.345,00

FIGURE 4.16:

Right-aligned numbers, American-style numbers aligned on decimal points, and European-style numbers aligned on commas

different decimal alignment characters in side-by-side columns, you'll need to change the decimal alignment character at the start of each number. Look at Figure 4.17, which shows the Reveal Codes view of Figure 4.16. In the Reveal Codes part of the screen, you can see that the first tab stop is right-aligned [Rgt Tab], and the next two are decimal-aligned [Dec Tab].

To switch back and forth between aligning on a period and a comma in the right two columns, the decimal alignment character had to be redefined several times, as evidenced by the many [Decml/Algn Char:] codes. If your work requires many unusual alignments like this, you probably should use the Tables feature, covered in Chapter 6.

The Tables feature, discussed in Chapter 6, offers a simpler solution to using different decimal alignments in side-by-side columns.

CREATING DOT LEADERS ON THE FLY

TO CREATE DOT LEADERS WITHOUT CHANGING THE TAB STOPS,

press Flush Right (Alt-F6) twice where you want to start the dot leaders.

You can also add dot leaders to a column of text without changing the tab settings. This is particularly handy when you need a simple two-column list of items, like the menu in Figure 4.9. Simply type the text in the first column,

```
        Right-Aligned      Decimal-Aligned      Decimal-Aligned
                            (American)           (British)

            1.2345              1.2345               1,2345
           12.345              12.345               12,345
          123.45              123.45               123,45
        1,234.56            1,234.56              1.234,56
       12,345.6            12,345.60             12.345,60
      123,456.00           12,345.00             12.345,00

                                      Doc 1 Pg 1 Ln 1.33" Pos 1"
[                                                            ]
[Tab Set:Rel; -1",-0.5",0",+1.15",+3.16",+5.18"][Cntr Tab]Right[-]Aligned[Cntr T
ab]Decimal[-]Aligned[Cntr Tab]Decimal[-]Aligned[HRt]
[Cntr Tab][Cntr Tab](American)[Cntr Tab](British)[Tab Set:Rel; -1",-0.5",0",+1.5
",+3.5",+5.5"][HRt]
[HRt]
[Rgt Tab]1.2345[Dec Tab]1.2345[Decml/Algn Char:,.][Dec Tab]1,2345[HRt]
[Rgt Tab]12.345[Decml/Algn Char:,,][Dec Tab]12.345[Dec Tab][Decml/Algn Char:,,.
]12,345[HRt]
[Rgt Tab]123.45[Decml/Algn Char:,,][Dec Tab]123.45[Dec Tab][Decml/Algn Char:,,.
]123,45[HRt]

Press Reveal Codes to restore screen
```

FIGURE 4.17:

American-style decimal-aligned numbers next to British-style decimal-aligned numbers on the Edit and Reveal Codes screens

press Flush Right (**Alt-F6**) twice (or select **L**ayout ➤ **A**lign ➤ **F**lush Right twice), and then type the text in the second column. The text will be right-aligned at the right margin. (If you want to narrow the gap between the two columns, adjust the left and right margins.)

MOVING, COPYING, AND DELETING TABULAR COLUMNS

As mentioned, using the Tables feature is the easiest way to create multi-column tables. However, if you use tabs instead and then decide to move, copy, or delete a particular column, you can do so by blocking. It can be a little tricky, so I recommend saving your document before trying this technique. Here are the general steps:

*Saving your document just before trying **any** risky operation is a good idea, since you can always undo any mistake by immediately clearing the screen and retrieving the previous version without saving the current version.*

1. Quick-save your document by choosing **F**ile ➤ **S**ave (or pressing **F10**), just in case you do more harm than good.

2. Move the cursor to the top-left character in the column you want to move, copy, or delete.

3. Hold down the left mouse button or press Block (**Alt-F4** or **F12**) to activate blocking.

4. Move the cursor to the end of the column. Initially, the highlight covers text in adjacent columns, as shown in Figure 4.18.

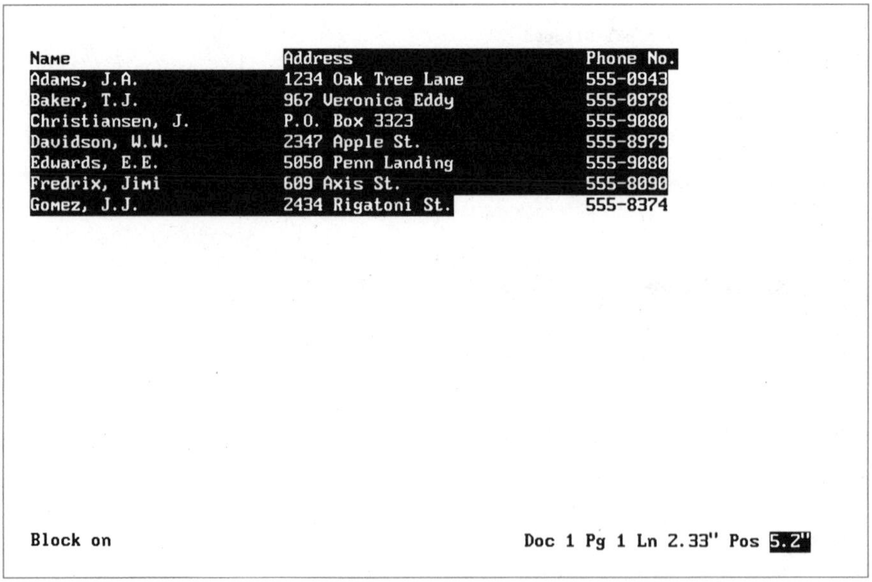

```
Name                  Address              Phone No.
Adams, J.A.           1234 Oak Tree Lane   555-0943
Baker, T.J.           967 Veronica Eddy    555-0978
Christiansen, J.      P.O. Box 3323        555-9080
Davidson, W.W.        2347 Apple St.       555-8979
Edwards, E.E.         5050 Penn Landing    555-9080
Fredrix, Jimi         609 Axis St.         555-8090
Gomez, J.J.           2434 Rigatoni St.    555-8374
```

Block on   Doc 1 Pg 1 Ln 2.33" Pos 5.2"

FIGURE 4.18:

Text from the top to the bottom of the second column is highlighted, but the highlighted area initially includes text in adjacent columns.

5. Select **Edit ➤ Se**lect **➤** Tabular **C**olumn, or press **Ctrl-F4** then **C**. Now only one column is highlighted, as shown in Figure 4.19.

6. To delete this column, choose **D**elete. Otherwise, choose **M**ove or **C**opy.

7. If you chose Move or Copy, move the cursor to where you want the top-left corner of the moved or copied column to appear.

8. Press ↵.

NOTE *You can sort text in tabular columns into alphabetical, numerical, or chronological (i.e., date) order by using the Sort feature, discussed in Chapter 17.*

You may need to adjust the tab ruler to get exactly the effect you want after deleting, moving, or copying a column, using the general technique described in "Refining Tab Stops." If you make more of a mess than an improvement, and you'd like to undo the whole operation, just follow these steps:

1. Clear the screen by selecting **File ➤ E**xit or by pressing Exit (**F7**).

2. When asked about saving the *current* copy of the file, press **N**.

3. When asked about exiting WordPerfect, press **N**.

4. Select **File ➤ R**etrieve (or press **Shift-F10**), type the file name, and press ↵ to retrieve the file in the state it was in step 1.

RELATIVE VS. ABSOLUTE TAB MEASUREMENT

As mentioned previously in this chapter, you can choose between two types of tab measurement: relative or absolute. When you use relative measurement

```
Name                    Address             Phone No.
Adams, J.A.             1234 Oak Tree Lane   555-0943
Baker, T.J.             967 Veronica Eddy    555-0978
Christiansen, J.        P.O. Box 3323        555-9080
Davidson, W.W.          2347 Apple St.       555-8979
Edwards, E.E.           5050 Penn Landing    555-9080
Fredrix, Jimi           609 Axis St.         555-8090
Gomez, J.J.             2434 Rigatoni St.    555-8374




1 Move; 2 Copy; 3 Delete; 4 Append: 0
```

FIGURE 4.19:

A single column of text is highlighted (blocked).

(the default setting in WordPerfect 5.1), tab stops are always measured from the left margin. In other words, the tab stops float with the left margin. For example, if you have relative tab stops at every $1/2$ inch and then move the left margin $1/4$ inch to the right, all tab stops also move $1/4$ inch to the right, so the first tab stop is still 1 inch from the left margin.

When you use absolute measurement, tab stops are measured from the left edge of the page, without regard to the left margin; that is, they do not float with the left margin. For example, if you have absolute tab stops at every $1/2$ inch and then move the left margin $1/4$ inch to the right, the tab stops remain unchanged. Therefore, the first tab stop will be $1/4$ inch from the left margin, the second will be $3/4$ inch from the left margin, and so forth.

From a practical standpoint, relative tab stops are probably the easiest to get along with, because the various indent keys always have the same effect, regardless of where you've set the left margin. However, when you get into more advanced work involving graphics and multicolumn layouts (Part 6), you may prefer to use the absolute tab measurements so that you know the exact location of each tab stop.

HARD VS. SOFT TABS

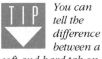

You can tell the difference between a soft and hard tab on the Reveal Codes screen by looking at the case of the letters.

One last tidbit of information about tabs is the difference between hard and soft tabs. Soft tabs are the "natural" tabs you get when you press the Tab key. Their hidden codes are displayed in mixed case on the Reveal Codes screen (e.g., [Tab], [Cntr Tab], [Rgt Tab], and [Dec Tab]). They are called soft tabs because they change automatically if you change the alignment on the tab ruler. For example, if you change a center-aligned tab stop to right-aligned, any [Cntr Tab] codes at that tab stop (and below the tab ruler) are automatically changed to [Rgt Tab] codes.

If, for whatever reason, you do not want a tab code to change when the tab ruler changes, you should press **Home Tab**, rather than Tab, when typing your document. This causes the code for that tab to be a hard tab and to appear in uppercase on the Reveal Codes screen (e.g., [TAB], [CNTR TAB], [RGT TAB], and [DEC TAB]). Soft tabs immediately adjust to any changes in the tab ruler, and hard tabs never adjust to changes in the tab ruler.

WordPerfect's justification, indentation, and alignment techniques range from simple tabs to fancy indentations and every possible kind of text alignment. (In Chapter 6, you will learn about the Tables feature, which offers a more convenient means of typing text in tabular columns.) In the next chapter, you'll learn how to use fonts in your documents and how to produce lines and special characters.

CHAPTER 5

Fonts, Lines, and Special Characters

WordPerfect lets you change the size, appearance, and typeface of printed text, and print special characters that are not available directly from your keyboard. These capabilities can make your printed documents more attractive and visually interesting. For example, Figure 5.1 shows a sample document using plain text. Figure 5.2 shows the same document "spruced up" a bit with the kind of features I'll be covering in this chapter.

LESSON 4

For a hands-on lesson in finding out your printer's capabilities, see Lesson 4 in Part 9.

WHAT CAN YOUR PRINTER DO?

Up to this point, virtually every feature of WordPerfect that I've described in the book will work like a charm, regardless of your printer. But now we've come to a place where certain features of WordPerfect aren't really WordPerfect features at all. Instead, they are *printer-specific* features that WordPerfect can use if (and *only* if) your printer is capable of producing them.

If you try using a special feature (like a specific font or typeface) that is not available on your printer, WordPerfect will ignore your request (making you

Chapter 8 shows you how to select a printer for use with WordPerfect.

feel as though you've done something wrong). So if you're not already sure of your printer's range of capabilities, you might want to complete Lesson 4 in Part 9 to try them out.

ABOUT FONTS

Unless you're already familiar with computers or typesetting, the term *font* may be new to you. A font is basically a combination of three things:

◆ A *typeface* (sometimes called a type style or a face)

Angela T. Joseph

18424 Mountain View Court Lake Meyer, Co.   93415   (319) 555-0938

OBJECTIVE   Produce word processing and desktop publishing
                     documents on a freelance basis.

EDUCATION   Bachelor of Arts, Business Administration,
                     State University of Colorado, Denver, 1980.

EXPERIENCE   Sole Proprietor, Angela T. Joseph Word
                     Processing, Sturgeon Pond, Colorado.
                                                 1985 to Present

                     Freelance secretary and home-based word
                     processing services.

                        Secretary for small office of architects
                        Freelance secretary for various offices as
                        temporary help

                     Clerk Typist II, Morgan T. Williams
                     Corporation, River Bend, Colorado
                                                 1974 to 1985

                     Clerk typist and receptionist for the
                     general business office of a consulting
                     firm.

                        Process and type forms and reports from
                        outside consultants
                        Compile and ensure accuracy of monthly
                        statistical reports
                        Perform general duties including heavy
                        typing and filing

PROFESSIONAL   Chamber of Commerce, Denver, Colorado
ORGANIZATIONS   Business & Professional Association of Lake
                     Meyer, Colorado

REFERENCES   Available upon request

FIGURE 5.1:

A plain document without fonts, lines, or special characters

- ◆ A *weight,* such as **boldface**, *italic,* or roman (regular, like this text)
- ◆ A *size,* measured in *points* or characters per inch (cpi)

TYPEFACES

Figure 5.3 shows examples of various typefaces. Different occasions call for different typefaces. For example, Courier is a typewriter font, good for printing documents that should look as if they have been manually typed. Times is a *serif* font—a serif is the little curlicue or tail at the top and bottom of each

---

Angela T. Joseph

| 18424 Mountain View Court | Lake Meyer, Colorado 93415 | (319) 555-0938 |

OBJECTIVE

Produce word processing and desktop publishing documents on a freelance basis.

EDUCATION

Bachelor of Arts, Business Administration, State University of Colorado, Denver, 1980.

EXPERIENCE

Sole Proprietor, *Angela T. Joseph Word Processing*, Sturgeon Pond, Colorado.   1985 to Present

Freelance secretary and home-based word processing services.

- ▪ Secretary for small office of architects
- ▪ Freelance secretary for various offices as temporary help

Clerk Typist II, *Morgan T. Williams Corporation*, River Bend, Colorado   1974 to 1985

Clerk typist and receptionist for the general business office of a consulting firm.

- ▪ Process and type forms and reports from outside consultants
- ▪ Compile and ensure accuracy of monthly statistical reports
- ▪ Perform general duties including heavy typing and filing

PROFESSIONAL ORGANIZATIONS

Chamber of Commerce, Denver, Colorado
Business & Professional Association of Lake Meyer, Colorado

REFERENCES

Available upon request

FIGURE 5.2:

The document in Figure 5.1 spruced up with fonts, lines, and special characters

letter. Serif fonts are often used for small- to medium-size print, because the serifs help your eyes move through the text and read more easily.

Helvetica is a sans-serif font, so called because the letters have no tails. Sans-serif fonts are mainly used for large text, from the headlines in newspapers to the messages on street signs (as a glance at any road sign will prove).

Decorative fonts, such as Cloister Black, are strictly for decoration. They are not particularly easy to read (especially in smaller sizes), but look nice and are often used to draw attention or create a mood. Examples abound all around you, from the elegant grace of a wedding invitation to the casual zaniness of a humorous greeting card. But overall, decorative fonts are best reserved for special occasions and should be used sparingly.

Chances are, if you look at the newspaper in any large city, you'll see that it uses fonts as I've discussed. The newspaper's name (e.g., *The New York Times*) might be in a decorative font like Cloister Black. But typically, headlines are in a sans-serif font like Helvetica, while text within each article is in a serif font, like Times. Individual display ads within the paper use whatever font best conveys the mood or image the company is trying to project.

 *The French word **sans** means "without," so sans serif means "without tails."*

 Chapter 8 explains how to choose various fonts for use with your printer.

 Times is commonly used in newspapers, hence its name (as in New York Times).

WEIGHTS

Figure 5.4 shows a single typeface, Times, in a variety of weights. Boldface (or bold) is a little thicker than the regular roman weight. Italic (also called

FIGURE 5.3:
Examples of different typefaces

oblique) is generally lighter and slanted. As you'll learn a little later, there are additional ways to change the appearance of text, regardless of its weight.

SIZES

Figure 5.5 shows a single typeface and style (Times Roman) in a variety of sizes. A point is roughly $1/72$ of an inch, so 72 points is about 1 inch tall, 36 points is about $1/2$ inch tall, and so forth.

Times Roman
Times Bold
Times Italic
Times Bold Italic

FIGURE 5.4:

Examples of various weights

6 points
8 points
10 points
12 points
14 points
16 points
20 points
24 points
36 points
72 points

FIGURE 5.5:

Examples of various type sizes

See Chapter 19 for more information on ITC Zapf Dingbats and other specialty fonts.

Finally, Figure 5.6 shows a variety of fonts. Each font in the figure is described in terms of typeface, weight (if any), and size: for example, Courier 10cpi, Times Roman Italic 12pt, Helvetica Bold Oblique 20pt, and so forth. (Many decorative or specialty fonts, such as Zapf Dingbats or Cloister Black, are only available in a single weight—there is no bold or italic version.)

PROPORTIONALLY SPACED VS. MONOSPACED FONTS

As mentioned earlier, some fonts are measured in points, and others are measured in characters per inch. These two systems of measurement exist because there are two different ways of spacing characters horizontally along a line:

Monospacing: Every character takes up the same space, e.g., an *i* is just as wide as a *w*.

Proportional spacing: Every character takes only the space it needs, e.g., an *i* does not take as much space as a *w*.

Courier 10cpi (pica)

Times Roman 12pt

Times Roman Italic 12pt

Palatino Bold Italic 18pt

Helvetica Bold Oblique 20pt

ITC Zapf Dingbats 20pt

✂ ✄ ☎ ✌ ✎ ① ➡ ✔ ☐ 🍒 ☆ ❄

𝕮loister 𝕭lack 36pt

Coronet/Ribbon 18pt

FIGURE 5.6:

Examples of various fonts

*A 10-cpi monospaced font is about the same size as a 12-point proportional font. The term **pitch** is sometimes used in place of cpi.*

*Actually, the point size of a character usually includes a little blank space, called **leading,** at the top.*

Figure 5.7 illustrates this with a string of the letters *i* and *w,* in a monospaced font (Courier) and a proportionally spaced font (Times). Note that the characters are the same width in the monospaced font, but unequal in the proportionally spaced font, which is why the two strings of letters are of unequal length (they both contain exactly the same number of *i* and *w* characters).

Since each character in a monospaced font takes the same space, its size can be measured horizontally, in characters per inch (abbreviated cpi). Two well-known Courier sizes are pica (10 cpi) and elite (12 cpi).

Proportionally spaced fonts cannot really be measured in this manner because the characters are different widths. Hence, these fonts are measured in terms of *height,* in points. The two different measuring systems can be a little confusing at first, but are easy to get used to with a little practice.

You might be wondering why people use both types of spacing instead of just one or the other. Well, as with everything else in fonts, different occasions call for different appearances. You might use a monospaced font to create a hand-typed official or business look in your documents, such as business letters and memos. Proportionally spaced fonts are usually preferred for other types of documents, such as newsletters, brochures, magazine articles, and books (what you are reading now is proportionally spaced).

SELECTING A FONT

TO SELECT A FONT,

1. Position the cursor where you want the new font to begin.

2. Select Font ➤ Base Font (or press Ctrl-F8 F).

3. Select the font you want.

```
iwiwiwiwiwiwiwiw
```
In a monospaced font, like Courier, every letter is the same width.

iwiwiwiwiwiwiwiw

In a proportionally spaced font, like Times, each letter uses only the space it needs.

FIGURE 5.7:

The difference between monospaced and proportionally spaced fonts

Fortunately, selecting and using fonts in WordPerfect is much simpler than learning all the terminology. Here's how you choose a font:

1. Move the cursor to the start of the text you want to be in the new font, either before existing text or where you want to start typing new text.

2. Select Font ➤ Base Font (or press **Ctrl-F8 F**). A menu like the one shown in Figure 5.8 appears (though the list of available fonts depends on your printer and current font collection). The current font has an asterisk (*) next to it and is highlighted with a colored or reverse-video bar.

3. You can scroll the highlight through the list of fonts by using the ↑ or ↓ keys, or by holding down the left mouse button.

4. Highlight the font you want, then choose **S**elect (or double-click on the font name with your mouse).

5. If your printer has scalable fonts (described in the next section), you'll be prompted to enter a point size. Type a point size and press ↵.

You'll return to the Edit screen, and all text to the right of and below the cursor will have changed to the new font. This may not be obvious, however, since the Edit screen doesn't show the actual fonts or point sizes you've selected. (But if you look very carefully, you might notice that word wrap has changed to accommodate your new font, especially if the new font is much larger or

```
Base Font

   Courier
   Courier Bold
   Courier Bold Oblique
   Courier Oblique
   Helvetica
   Helvetica Bold
   Helvetica Bold Oblique
   Helvetica Narrow
   Helvetica Narrow Bold
   Helvetica Narrow Bold Oblique
   Helvetica Narrow Oblique
 * Helvetica Oblique
   ITC Avant Garde Gothic Book
   ITC Avant Garde Gothic Book Oblique
   ITC Avant Garde Gothic Demi
   ITC Avant Garde Gothic Demi Oblique
   ITC Bookman Demi
   ITC Bookman Demi Italic
   ITC Bookman Light
   ITC Bookman Light Italic
   ITC Zapf Chancery Medium Italic

1 Select; N Name search: 1
```

FIGURE 5.8:

The Base Fonts menu for a printer with scalable fonts

smaller than the old one.) Again, as with many features that affect the appearance of your document, you'll need to go to the View Document screen (press **Shift-F7 V**) to see your changes. If you need to change the font elsewhere, simply position the cursor and repeat the steps above.

SCALABLE VS. NONSCALABLE FONTS

Scalable fonts are also called outline fonts.

Notice that the sample list of fonts shown in Figure 5.8 does not include point sizes with the fonts. Instead, you'll be prompted for the point size after you select the font you want to use (see step 5 in the preceding section). The point-size prompt appears only for printers that offer scalable fonts, such as those in the Hewlett-Packard LaserJet III series and PostScript printers like those in the Apple LaserWriter series. The beauty of scalable fonts is that you can specify any point size, even in increments (such as 10.5 points), after selecting your basic typeface.

By contrast, nonscalable fonts, such as those used with the Hewlett-Packard LaserJet II series and many other printers, combine the typeface and size in one selection. Figure 5.9 shows a sample list of fonts for a Hewlett-Packard LaserJet II printer.

Notice that each typeface is available in several sizes and that the size is included with each font name. The obvious disadvantage of this method is that you are limited to the sizes available. For example, in Figure 5.9 the Times

```
Base Font

* Courier 10cpi
  Courier 10cpi Bold
  Line Draw 10cpi (Full)
  Line Printer 16.67cpi
  TmsRmn 10pt (AC)
  TmsRmn 10pt Bold (AC)
  TmsRmn 10pt Italic (AC)
  TmsRmn 12pt (AC)
  TmsRmn 12pt Bold (AC)
  TmsRmn 12pt Italic (AC)
  TmsRmn 24pt Bold (AC)
  TmsRmn 30pt Bold (AC)




1 Select; N Name search: 1
```

FIGURE 5.9:

The Base Fonts menu, with examples of nonscalable fonts

Roman (TmsRmn) font is available in only 10-, 12-, 24-, and 30-point sizes—there is no way to get a 10.5- or 11-point size in that typeface.

EXPANDING YOUR FONT COLLECTION

Regardless of whether your printer offers scalable fonts, you can always add to your collection of fonts at any time. Bitstream Corporation offers scalable fonts (of sorts) that help overcome the disadvantages of printers that do not directly offer such fonts. See Chapter 8 for information on expanding your collection of fonts.

But do keep in mind that WordPerfect cannot create fonts for you—it can only use whatever fonts you have purchased (from your local computer store) and installed for use with your printer.

TROUBLESHOOTING FONT SELECTIONS

The quickest way to see the View Document screen is to press Shift-F7 then V. Press Exit (F7) to return to the Edit screen.

Any time you change the font in a document, the change is visible on the View Document screen (but not on the Edit screen). If a font change is not reflected on your View Document screen, it may be that an older font-change code is disabling the new one. (It's also possible that your computer monitor is not able to display the font, but this is less often the case.)

The hidden code for a font change is [Font:]; the name of the font selected follows the colon. Remember that a [Font:] code changes the font of all text to the right of and below the code, up to the next [Font:] code, if any. Hence, if two font codes are placed side by side like this:

You can also move or copy a [Font:] code by using the general method described in Chapter 3.

[Font:Times Roman 12pt][Font:Courier 10cpi]

and you want to use the Times font rather than the Courier font, you must go to the Reveal Codes screen and delete the unwanted [Font:] code (or codes).

WHY IS THE CURRENT FONT CALLED THE BASE FONT?

You may wonder why WordPerfect often refers to the current font as the *base* font. The answer to the mystery lies in the manner in which we generally use fonts. In general, you select a base (or basic) font for a passage of text. Occasionally, you use slight variations, such as boldface or italic, without changing the typeface or size. Sometimes, you just change the size—for example, when you want to type a small subscript or superscript.

For this reason, WordPerfect lets you choose a base font, such as Times Roman 12-point, and then make adjustments to the appearance and size without changing the font at all. The beauty of this approach is that, if you later change your mind and decide to go to an 11-point font, you only need to change the base font. Boldface, italic, subscripts, and superscripts will all be in place, but will now be based on the 11-point base-font size rather than the old 12-point size. This brings us to the next two topics of this chapter: changing the appearance and changing the size of the base font.

CHANGING TYPE SIZE

TO CHANGE THE SIZE OF TEXT,

1. Position the cursor where you're about to type or block any existing text.

2. Select Font (or press Ctrl-F8 S).

3. Choose any size.

If you want to change the size of the current (base) font, it's not necessary to select a different font. You can just select a size in relation to the current size. As mentioned, the advantage of changing just the size rather than selecting a whole new base font is that, if you later change the base font, all the changes in size will still be in place and proportioned to the new base font. Figure 5.10 shows the relative sizes available to you, using Times Roman 16-point as the base-font size.

Each size is a percentage of the base-font size, as shown in Table 5.1.

FIGURE 5.10:

Examples of sizes in relation to a 16-point font

Base Font: Times Roman 16pt

This ends with ^{superscript size}

This ends with _{subscript size}

This is Fine size

This is Small size

This is Large size

This is Very Large size

This is Extra Large

SIZE	PERCENTAGE OF BASE-FONT SIZE
Fine	60
Small	80
Large	120
Very Large	150
Extra Large	200
Superscript	60 (raised)
Subscript	60 (lowered)

TABLE 5.1:

Ratio of Print Sizes to Base Font

If your printer has scalable fonts, WordPerfect mathematically calculates the type size to use when you change the size, since "anything goes" with scalable fonts. So, for example, if you start with a 16-point Times Roman base font, then choose Very Large, which is 150 percent of the base font, WordPerfect will calculate a font size of 24 points for the new size (16 times 150 percent). However, if your printer does not offer scalable fonts, WordPerfect chooses an available font that is closest to the size you've requested. Hence, if your printer has a limited selection of fonts, the sizes may not match the percentages listed in the table.

When you change the font size, your text will usually appear on the Edit screen in a different color (on color screens) or with different highlighting (on monochrome screens) to help you distinguish it from normal text. For instance, a color monitor might show the Large size in red on a black background, the Very Large size in turquoise on a black background, and the Superscript size in magenta on a white background. As usual, be sure to check the View Document screen for a true picture of your fonts.

You can change the size of the current font either before or after typing the text, as discussed in the sections that follow.

 *You can customize the appearance of different font sizes on your Edit screen, as discussed in Chapter 13.*

CHANGING THE SIZE BEFORE YOU TYPE

To change the current font size before you type text, follow these steps:

1. Position the cursor wherever you are about to type your new text.

2. Select **F**ont from the menus (or press **Ctrl-F8 S**).

3. Choose one of the sizes, such as **F**ine, **S**mall, or **V**ery Large.

4. Type the text you want in the newly selected size.

5. Press → before typing additional text that should use the original base-font size.

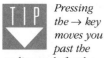

Pressing the → key moves you past the ending code for the newly selected size, so you can resume typing in the original size.

CHANGING THE SIZE OF EXISTING TEXT

If you've already typed your text, changing its size is as simple as blocking the text and selecting a new size. Here are the exact steps:

1. Move the cursor to the first character that you want to change the size of.

2. Block the text you want to change, either by using the Block (**Alt-F4** or **F12**) and cursor-movement keys or by dragging the mouse with the left button pressed down.

3. When the text is blocked and "Block on" is blinking, select F**o**nt (or press **Ctrl-F8 S**).

4. Choose a size.

The size change will be apparent on your View Document screen. But remember, the *actual* size is determined by the fonts available in your printer.

CODES FOR SIZE CHANGES

Changes you make to font size by using either technique above are controlled by paired codes on the Reveal Codes screen. The code that starts the size change is in uppercase, and the code that ends the size change (and returns to the base-font size) is in lowercase, as listed in Table 5.2.

Remember that only text between the starting and ending codes will be in the specified size. Text after the ending code will be in the original base-font size.

CHANGING SIZE RATIOS

The ratios of sizes to the base font listed in Table 5.1 are not etched in granite; they are simply the defaults that WordPerfect uses for convenience. In some situations, you may want to specify a different ratio—for example, to make your superscripts and subscripts a little smaller or to make your extra-large sizes a little larger.

You can do so quite easily with a little customization, by selecting F**i**le ➤ Se**t**up ➤ **I**nitial Settings ➤ **P**rint Options ➤ **S**ize Attribute Ratios (or by pressing **Shift-F1 I P S**) and changing the size ratios on the menu that appears. Keep in mind, however, that if your printer does not have scalable fonts, the size ratios that WordPerfect actually uses when printing your document will be whatever available size best matches the ratio you provide.

SIZE	STARTING CODE	ENDING CODE
Fine	[FINE]	[fine]
Small	[SMALL]	[small]
Large	[LARGE]	[large]
Very Large	[VRY LARGE]	[vry large]
Extra Large	[EXT LARGE]	[ext large]
Superscript	[SUPRSCPT]	[suprscpt]
Subscript	[SUBSCPT]	[subscpt]

TABLE 5.2:

Paired Codes for Print Sizes

Chapter 13 discusses customizing Word-Perfect in detail.

Also be aware that, like all customization features, changing the print size ratios affects the entire current document and all future documents (until you change the size ratios again).

CHANGING THE APPEARANCE OF TEXT

TO CHANGE THE APPEARANCE OF TEXT,

position the cursor where you're about to type, or highlight existing text, then select Font ➤ Appearance (or press Shift-F8 A) and any available appearance.

Just as you can change the size of the base font without selecting a new font, you can change its appearance. This is particularly useful for occasional boldfaced, italicized, and underlined text.

Even though your list of available fonts may include only the basic weights (roman, bold, and italic), you can embellish the current font with a variety of additional appearances or combinations of appearances, as shown in Figure 5.11.

Be aware, however, that not all printers support the full range of available appearances. For example, Outline appearance is available only on PostScript printers and Hewlett-Packard LaserJet III printers. Similarly, Redline and Shadow tend to look a little different with various printers. Again, experimentation is your best bet for learning the full range of appearances available with your printer.

The steps for changing the appearance of text are virtually identical to those for changing the size. Remember that the look of the appearances on your Edit screen will vary according to the monitor you are using and the customization you've selected for your screen display (Chapter 13). As always, previewing your document on the View Document screen is important for seeing the exact effects of changing the appearance of your text.

CHANGING TEXT APPEARANCE BEFORE YOU TYPE

To change the appearance of text before you type it, follow these steps:

1. Position the cursor wherever you are about to type your new text.

2. Select F**o**nt ➤ **A**ppearance (or press **Ctrl-F8 A**).

Normal
Bold
<u>Underline</u>
<u>Double Underline</u>
Italic
Outline
Shadow
SMALL CAP
Redline
~~Strikeout~~
Shadow and Outline
ITALIC, SMALL CAP, UNDERLINE
Shadow, Double Underline

FIGURE 5.11:

Examples of text and combined-text appearances

3. Select the appearance you want from the list of options.

4. Type the text you want in the new appearance.

5. Press → before typing additional text that should use the original appearance.

CHANGING THE APPEARANCE OF EXISTING TEXT

If you've already typed your text, changing its appearance is like changing its size—you block the text and select a new appearance:

1. Move the cursor to the first character whose appearance you want to change.

2. Block the text whose appearance you want to change, either by using the Block (**Alt-F4** or **F12**) and cursor-movement keys or by dragging the mouse with the left button depressed.

3. When the text is blocked and "Block on" is blinking, select Font ➤ Appearance (or press **Ctrl-F8 A**).

4. Select the appearance you want from the list of options.

The Bold (F6) and Underline (F8) keys are shortcuts for using these common text appearances.

The appearance change is usually indicated in some way on your Edit screen (for instance, most monitors display bold text in brighter print) and will be readily apparent on your View Document screen. Remember that not all appearances are available on all printers. WordPerfect may ignore a requested appearance if it's not available on your printer (likewise, you won't see it on the View Document screen).

CODES FOR APPEARANCES

Changes to the appearance of text are also controlled by paired codes on the Reveal Codes screen, as listed in Table 5.3.

Remember that only the text between the starting and ending codes will be in the specified appearance. Text after the ending code will be in the original appearance defined by the base font.

UNDOING SIZE AND APPEARANCE CHANGES

If you change the size or appearance of text and then decide to undo that change, just delete the code:

1. Move the cursor to the first or last character that needs to be changed back to normal text.

APPEARANCE	STARTING CODE	ENDING CODE
Bold	[BOLD]	[bold]
Underline	[UND]	[und]
Double Underline	[DBL UND]	[dbl und]
Italic	[ITALC]	[italc]
Outline	[OUTLN]	[outln]
Shadow	[SHADW]	[shadw]
Small Cap	[SM CAP]	[sm cap]
Redline	[REDLN]	[redln]
Strikeout	[STKOUT]	[stkout]

TABLE 5.3:

Paired Codes for Text Appearances

2. Turn on the Reveal Codes screen by using the Reveal Codes key (**Alt-F3** or **F11**) or by selecting **Edit** ➤ **Reveal Codes**.

3. Move the Reveal Codes highlight to the starting or ending code for the size or appearance you want to eliminate.

4. Press **Delete** to delete the code.

CHANGING SIZES AND APPEARANCES GLOBALLY

The term globally means "throughout the entire document."

Because sizes and appearances are controlled by paired, rather than single, hidden codes, you cannot use the Search and Replace feature (Chapter 9) to globally change all the codes in a document. For example, you can't directly change all the underlines to italics or all the Very Large sizes to Extra Large in a single step.

However, you're not entirely out of luck. If you use the Styles feature (Chapter 14) to define fonts, sizes, and appearances, you can easily change any of these throughout an entire document. And if you choose not to use styles, WordPerfect has a macro that is specifically designed to change paired codes (it's stored in the MACROS keyboard, discussed in Chapter 27).

TROUBLESHOOTING SIZE AND APPEARANCE PROBLEMS

Sometimes it's the little things in word processing that drive you batty. For example, suppose you type and underline some text, as shown below:

"Whoops," she cried.

Then you decide that you don't want to underline the comma and quotation marks, only the word *Whoops*.

There are a couple of ways to fix this problem. But your best starting point is to move the cursor to the general vicinity of the word, then turn on Reveal Codes. This gives you a bird's-eye view of the problem:

[UND]"Whoops," [und] she cried.

It's obvious that the problem is that the comma and quotation mark are inside the paired [UND] and [und] codes. One way to fix the problem is simply to delete the existing [UND] and [und] codes, block only the word *Whoops*, and then turn underlining back on. Or you could leave the codes in place, delete the comma and quotation mark, then retype them outside the [UND] and [und] codes. Either way, you want to end up with this arrangement:

"[UND]Whoops[und]," she cried

The printed text should look like this:

"<u>Whoops</u>," she cried

Word-Perfect does not allow you to move or copy paired codes.

You might think that a third method for fixing this problem would be simply to move the [UND] and [und] codes into their correct positions. But oddly, WordPerfect offers no way to move or copy paired codes, so this is not an option.

If WordPerfect seems to ignore a request, it's probably because of the common problem of "competing" codes. For example, suppose you have a line of text set in Extra Large size, then you reblock that text and set it in Large size, but nothing seems to change on your Edit or View Document screens. Look at the Reveal Codes screen—chances are that the old [EXT LARGE] and [ext Large] codes are canceling the newer [LARGE] and [large] codes, like this:

[LARGE][EXT LARGE]Sample text[ext large][large]

The solution is simply to delete the unwanted [EXT LARGE] codes, by highlighting either [EXT LARGE] or [ext large] and pressing Delete.

COMBINING SIZES AND APPEARANCES

You can combine a size and any number of appearances to your heart's content to get any look you want. For example, you can have an extra large, bold, italic, and redlined title or an italic superscript. Figure 5.12 shows some examples.

A behind-the-scenes look at a couple of the examples will show how they were created. The "e = mc^2" example looks like this on the Reveal Codes screen:

[Font:CG Times Italic (Scalable) 16 pt] Italic sentence with [BOLD]e=mc[SUPRSCPT]2[suprscpt][bold] in bold with superscript.

Notice that the starting and ending codes for each size and appearance correspond directly to how the example is printed.

The "Chapter 1" example looks like this on the Reveal Codes screen:

[SMALL] Chapter [small][HRT]
[EXT LARGE][REDLN] 1 [redln][ext large] [Font: Univers Bold Italic (Scalable) 16pt][SM CAP]Getting Started[sm cap]

> **NOTE NOTE NOTE** *The "Chapter 1" example requires a printer that prints redline with a grayed background.*

If you want to combine a size and one or more appearances *before* typing your text, just follow these steps:

1. Position the cursor where you are about to type.

2. Select F**o**nt (or press **Ctrl-F8 S**) and choose your size.

3. Select F**o**nt ➤ **A**ppearance (or press **Ctrl-F8 A**) and any appearance. Repeat this step as necessary to get the combination of appearances you want.

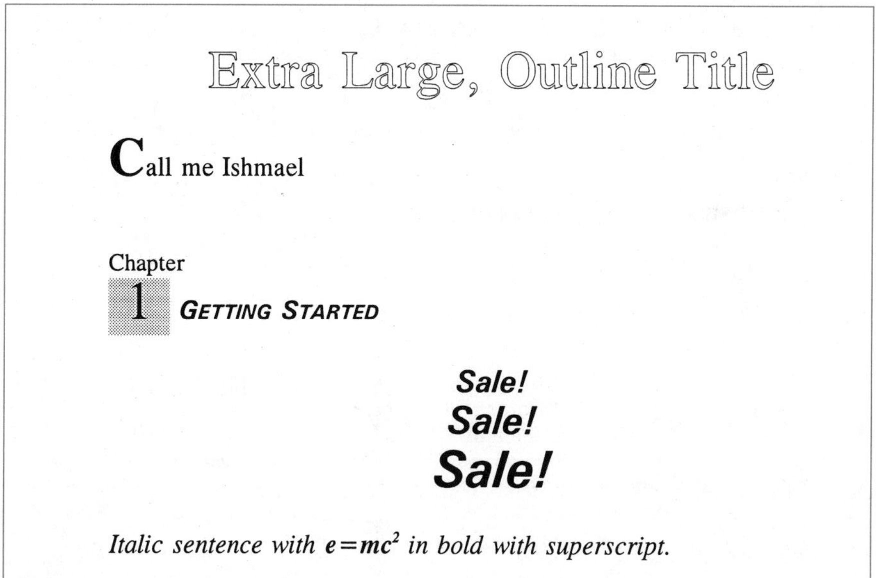

Extra Large, Outline Title

Call me Ishmael

Chapter
1 ***GETTING STARTED***

Sale!
Sale!
Sale!

*Italic sentence with **e=mc²** in bold with superscript.*

FIGURE 5.12:

Examples of combined sizes and appearances

4. Type your text.

5. When you're finished typing the text, press the **End** key to move past all the closing codes before typing normal text.

Combining sizes and appearances in text you've already typed is the same as using any single size or appearance, except you have to repeat the process of blocking, applying the appearance for each new attribute you want to add:

1. Block the text.

2. Select F**o**nt (or press **Ctrl-F8 S**), then choose a size.

3. Block the text again.

4. Select F**o**nt ➤ **A**ppearance (or press **Ctrl-F8 A**), then choose an appearance.

5. Repeat steps 3 and 4 for each appearance you want to add.

UNDERLINING BLANK SPACES AND TABS

TO CHANGE THE UNDERLINE METHOD,

position the cursor and select Layout ➤ Other ➤ Underline (or press Shift-F8 O U).

NOTE *The underline styles described here also affect text that you've underlined with the Underline key (F8).*

The Underline and Double Underline features normally underline words and blank spaces, but not tabs, between words. But you can choose whether or not to have WordPerfect underline spaces and tabs. Figure 5.13 shows examples of your options.

To control the underlining method, follow these steps:

1. Move the cursor to the first character or blank space where you want to change the underlining method.

2. Select L**a**yout ➤ **O**ther ➤ Underline (or press **Shift-F8 O U**).

<u>Name</u>	<u>Address</u>	<u>City, State Zip</u>	underlined words and spaces, but not tabs (default)
<u>Name</u>	<u>Address</u>	<u>City, State Zip</u>	underlined words only
<u>Name</u>	<u>Address</u>	<u>City, State Zip</u>	underlined words, spaces, and tabs

FIGURE 5.13:

Optional underlining methods

3. Select **Y**es if you want to underline blank spaces, or **N**o if you do not.

4. Select **Y**es if you want to underline tabs, or **N**o if you do not.

5. Press Exit (**F7**) to return to the Edit screen.

All underlined and double-underlined text to the right of and below the cursor will have the new underlining. To change the underlining elsewhere, simply repeat the steps above in the appropriate section of the document. Check your View Document screen to see the effect of your underlining selections.

SPECIAL TECHNIQUES FOR REDLINE AND STRIKEOUT

Redline and strikeout are often used to denote changes in contracts and other legal documents. Redline indicates suggested additions to the original document, and strikeout indicates suggested deletions, as shown in the example in Figure 5.14.

On some printers, WordPerfect prints redline text as a grayed shade (like Figure 5.14). On other printers, redline text is printed with a shaded background or with dots beneath the characters. On color printers, redline text is printed in red. To change the appearance of redline text, follow these steps:

1. Select **L**ayout ➤ **D**ocument ➤ **R**edline Method (or press **Shift-F8 D R**). Your choices are as follows:

Printer Dependent	Redline is printed as dictated by your particular printer.
Left	Redline text is marked by a character of your choosing in the left margin.
Alternating	Redline text is marked by a character in the left margin on even-numbered pages and a character in the right margin on odd- numbered pages.

THE PURCHASE PRICE INCLUDES: All tacked down carpeting, ~~all existing window treatments,~~ all existing window and door screens, all built-in appliances, television antennas, garage door opener and controllers, all ~~fixtures,~~ shrubs, trees and items permanently attached to the real property, all window treatments excluding the wooden louvers in the dining room, and all fixtures excluding chandelier in the dining room. Pool and spa equipment, if any, is also to be included.

FIGURE 5.14:

Redline and strikeout in a sample document

2. If you select Left or Alternating, you'll be asked to define a character to print in the margins. You can type any single character on your keyboard or enter any valid special character for your printer by using the Compose feature (described a little later in this chapter).

3. Press Exit (**F7**) after making your choice.

REMOVING REDLINE MARKINGS AND STRIKEOUT TEXT

You can remove all the redline markings and strikeout text from a document with a single command. This is useful for printing a final draft of the document, *after* you are certain that you no longer need the redline markings or the text that has been struck out. Follow these steps:

1. Select **M**ark ➤ **G**enerate ➤ **R**emove Redline Markings and Strikeout Text from Document (or press **Alt-F5 G R**).

2. Select **Y**es.

There is an important distinction between redline markings and the redline text itself. You can delete the markings and leave the text intact.

The previously struck-out text is deleted, and the redlined text has the redlines removed. If you want to keep the original copy of the document with redlines and strikeout still intact, be sure to save this copy of the document with a new file name.

COMPARING DOCUMENTS WITH REDLINE AND STRIKEOUT

If you have two slightly different versions of the same document, you can compare the two to assess their differences. This is especially useful, for example, if you are working with someone else who has made changes to a copy of your document (or you've just made changes on your own document), and you want to see exactly what changes were made. Here's how:

1. Retrieve the most recent version of the document by selecting **F**ile ➤ **R**etrieve or pressing Retrieve (**Shift-F10**).

2. Select **M**ark ➤ **G**enerate ➤ **C**ompare Screen and Disk Documents and Add Redline and Strikeout (or press **Alt-F5 G C**).

3. As prompted, enter the file name of the *older* version of the document, and press ↵.

WordPerfect compares the documents phrase by phrase, placing redline markings and strikeout codes in the document that's currently on the screen. Redline marks text that is in the newer (on-screen) document but not in the older (on-disk) document. Strikeout marks text that is in the older (on-disk) document but not in the newer (on-screen) document.

If any text in the newer document has been moved in relation to the older document, WordPerfect inserts "THE FOLLOWING TEXT WAS MOVED" above the moved text and "THE PRECEDING TEXT WAS MOVED" below the moved text.

If you want to preserve the document with its redline and strikeout codes, remember to save the document that's currently on your screen with a new name.

PRINTING SPECIAL CHARACTERS

TO TYPE A SPECIAL CHARACTER,

1. Select Font ➤ Characters (or press Ctrl-2 or Ctrl-V).

2. Type the code for the special character.

3. Press ⏎.

Your keyboard lets you type all the letters, numbers, and punctuation marks needed for most documents. But many situations call for special characters, such as bullets, copyright marks like © and ™, foreign currency signs like £, and the ↑, ↓, →, ←, and ⏎ characters used in this book.

WordPerfect offers literally thousands of such special characters and a single, simple approach to typing them, using the Compose feature. Here's how to use it:

1. Position the cursor where you want to type a special character that's not available on your keyboard.

2. Select Font ➤ Characters, or press **Ctrl-2** or **Ctrl-V** as a shortcut.

3. The prompt "Key =" appears near the lower-left corner of your screen (unless you typed Ctrl-2 in the previous step; in this case, you won't get a prompt but should still type the code as described in the next step).

4. Type the code that represents the character you want to type; for example, *4,0* for a bullet.

5. Press ⏎.

The codes for commonly used special characters are listed in Figure 5.15. You'll find some handy shortcuts for a number of special characters in figures 5.17 and 5.18 later in the chapter.

The special character you requested will appear on the Edit screen (if your monitor can display it and your printer can print it). On the Reveal Codes screen, the special characters look the same as on the Edit screen, until you

Sometimes your Edit screen won't be able to display certain special characters, even if your printer can print them. Check the View Document screen if you're in doubt.

If you need to type complex mathematical equations, see Chapter 21.

The first two pages of CHARACTR. DOC display regular characters that you can type directly at your keyboard, so you can ignore them.

You can also use styles (Chapter 14) or macros (Chapter 15) to create your own shortcuts for typing commonly used special characters.

place the Reveal Codes screen highlight directly on that code. At that point, the special character and the codes you used to type it appear, as in the example below, where the 4,0 code is used to type a bullet:

[•:4,0]

The real trick, of course, is knowing what code to type to get the special character you want. For easy reference, Figure 5.15 categorizes some of the more commonly used special characters, along with their codes. And, as discussed in a moment, WordPerfect offers alternative "shortcut" codes for entering some of the more commonly used special characters.

WordPerfect offers over 1400 special characters for many different applications, including foreign language characters, mathematical equations, scientific symbols, and more. There is also a Greek alphabet (both ancient and modern), as well as Hebrew, Russian, and Japanese.

If you have a graphics printer, you'll be able to print all the special characters that WordPerfect offers. If you don't have a graphics printer, you'll probably still be able print quite a few of these symbols.

To see the complete set of special characters available to you, just print a copy of the CHARACTR.DOC file that came with your WordPerfect package. During the installation procedure, this document is copied automatically to the WordPerfect directory on your hard disk. To print it, select **F**ile ➤ **P**rint ➤ **D**ocument on Disk (or press **Shift-F7 D**), and then type the file name **CHARACTR.DOC** and press ↵. It may take a while—the document is over thirty pages long.

Figure 5.16 shows part of a page from the CHARACTR.DOC document, printed with a laser printer. The left column of the printout displays the codes you'll use to type each special character (as explained later). The special character and a description of the character follow each pair of numbers. If there is only a blank space between the pair of numbers and the description, your printer cannot print that character.

SHORTCUTS FOR TYPING SPECIAL CHARACTERS

Obviously, you can't memorize the code numbers for thousands of special characters. After all, how meaningful is *4,0*? Fortunately, WordPerfect lets you use shortcut characters that are easier to remember than the numbers to type some of the more commonly used special characters. Figure 5.17 lists these characters and the optional codes to type them.

Use the shortcut characters presented in Figure 5.17 just as you would use the numeric codes, as summarized below:

1. Move the cursor to where you want to type the new character.

Bullets/List Items

●	4,0	Bullet
○	4,1	Hollow Bullet
■	4,2	Square Bullet
•	4,3	Small Bullet
○	4,37	Large Hollow Bullet
□	4,38	Large Hollow Square
●	4,44	Large Bullet
○	4,45	Small Hollow Bullet
■	4,46	Large Square Bullet
■	4,47	Small Square Bullet
□	4,48	Hollow Square Bullet
□	4,49	Small Hollow Square
☞	5,21	Right Pointing Index
☜	5,22	Left Pointing Index
✓	5,23	Check Mark
☐	5,24	Empty Ballot Box
☒	5,25	Marked Ballot Box

Currency

£	4,11	Pound/Sterling
¥	4,12	Yen
Pt	4,13	Pesetas
ƒ	4,14	Florin/Guilder
¢	4,19	Cent
¤	4,24	General Currency
$	4,57	Milreis/Escudo
₣	4,58	Francs
₢	4,59	Cruzado
₠	4,60	European Currency
₤	4,61	Lire

Foreign Language

¡	4,7	Inverted Exclamation
¿	4,8	Inverted Question Mark

Graphic

♥	5,0	Heart
♦	5,1	Diamond
♣	5,2	Club
♠	5,3	Spade
♂	5,4	Male
♀	5,5	Female
☿	5,6	Compass
☺	5,7	Happy Face

☻	5,8	Dark Happy Face
☹	5,26	Sad Face
☎	5,30	Telephone
☻	5,31	Clock
⌛	5,32	Hourglass

Fractions

½	4,17	1/2
¼	4,18	1/4
¾	4,25	3/4
⅓	4,64	1/3
⅔	4,65	2/3
⅛	14,66	1/8
⅜	4,67	3/8
⅝	4,68	5/8
⅞	4,69	7/8

General

¶	4,5	Paragraph Sign
§	4,6	Section Sign
®	4,22	Registered Trademark
©	4,23	Copyright
'	4,27	Left Single Quote
'	4,28	Right Single Quote
'	4,29	Inverted Single
"	4,30	Left Double Quote
"	4,31	Right Double Quote
"	4,32	Inverted Double Quote
–	4,33	En Dash (width of n)
—	4,34	Em Dash (width of m)
†	4,39	Dagger
‡	4,40	Double Dagger
™	4,41	Trademark
℠	4,42	Servicemark
℞	4,43	Prescription (Rx)
…	4,56	Em Leader (Ellipsis)
℅	4,73	Care of
‰	4,75	Per Thousand
№	4,76	Number (No.)
°	6,36	Degree
★	6,112	Solid Star
◀	6,28	**Solid Triangle Left**
▲	6,29	**Solid Triangle Up**
▼	6,30	**Solid Triangle Down**

FIGURE 5.15:

Examples of special characters not found on the keyboard

FIGURE 5.15:

Examples of special characters not found on the keyboard (cont.)

Keyboard/Computer

↵	5,20	Enter
→	6,21	Right Arrow
←	6,22	Left Arrow
↑	6,23	Up Arrow
↓	6,24	Down Arrow
↔	6,25	Left and Right Arrow
▶	6,27	Solid Triangle Right

Math

√	5,14	Bent Radical
−	6,0	Minus
±	6,1	Plus or Minus
≤	6,2	Less Than/Equal
≥	6,3	Greater Than/Equal

∝	6,4	Proportional
÷	6,8	Division
|	6,9	Absolute Value
Σ	6,18	Summation
∞	6,19	Infinity
∫	6,40	Integral

Music

♪	5,9	Eighth Note
♫	5,10	Sixteenth Notes
♯	5,27	Sharp
♭	5,28	Flat
♮	5,29	Natural

FIGURE 5.16:

A partial page from the CHARACTR.DOC document

```
Typographic Symbols
Charset: 4
Contains: Common typographic symbols not found
         in ASCII.

4,0  • Bullet
4,1  o Hollow Bullet
4,2  ■ Square Bullet
4,3  · Small Bullet
4,4  ⁎ Base Asterisk
4,5  ¶ Paragraph Sign
4,6  § Section Sign
4,7  ¡ Inverted Exclamation Point
4,8  ¿ Inverted Question Mark
4,9  « Left Double Guillemet
4,10 » Right Double Guillemet
4,11 £ Pound/Sterling
4,12 ¥ Yen
4,13 ₧ Pesetas
4,14 ƒ Florin/Guilder
4,15 ª Feminine Spanish Ordinal
4,16 º Masculine Spanish Ordinal
4,17 ½ 1/2
4,18 ¼ 1/4
4,19 ¢ Cent
```

2. Select Font ➤ Characters, or press the **Ctrl-V** or **Ctrl-2** shortcut key.

3. Type the two characters shown in the "Shortcut" column of Figure 5.17. Do not type a space or comma between the characters, and do not press ↵. For example, type ** to get the medium-filled bullet shown in the "Bullets and Fractions" section of the figure.

SIZING SPECIAL CHARACTERS

The base font determines the size of special characters. For example, the first set of list items in Figure 5.18 uses special character 5,21 to put a pointing hand at the start of each item in a list. The hands are the same size as the current (base) font.

Beneath that set, each pointing hand was increased to the Large size. To change the size of a special character, follow these steps:

1. Move the cursor to the special character you want to resize.

FIGURE 5.17:

Shortcut symbols for commonly used special characters

Character	Shortcut	Code
Bullets and Fractions		
●	*.	[4,3]
●	**	[4,0]
○	*o	[4,45]
○	*O	[4,1]
½	/2	[4,17]
¼	/4	[4,18]
Currency Symbols		
¢	c/	[4,19]
ƒ	f-	[4,14]
£	L-	[4,11]
¤	ox	[4,24]
Pt	Pt	[4,13]
¥	Y=	[4,12]
Math/Scientific Symbols		
±	+-	[6,1]
≤	<=	[6,2]
≠	/=	[6,99]
≡	==	[6,14]
≥	>=	[6,3]
≈	~~	[6,13]

Character	Shortcut	Code
Foreign Language		
¡	!!	[4,7]
¿	??	[4,8]
æ	ae	[1,37]
Æ	AE	[1,36]
å	ao	[1,35]
ij	ij	[1,139]
IJ	IJ	[1,138]
œ	oe	[1,167]
Œ	OE	[1,166]
ß	ss	[1,23]
Other Typographic		
«	<<	[4,9]
»	>>	[4,10]
©	co	[4,23]
—	m-	[4,34]
—	--	[4,34]
–	n-	[4,33]
¶	P|	[4,5]
®	ro	[4,22]
℞	rx	[4,43]
SM	sm	[4,42]
TM	tm	[4,41]

2. Block that character either by pressing Block (**Alt-F4** or **F12**) and pressing → once or by dragging with the mouse one character to the right.

3. Select F**o**nt (or press **Ctrl-F8 S**).

4. Choose the size you want.

☞   Complete the order form

☞   Include your check or money order

☞   And mail it today!

☞ Complete the order form

☞ Include your check or money order

☞ And mail it today!

☞ Complete the order form

☞ Include your check or money order

☞ And mail it today!

In the third set of pointing hands in Figure 5.18, the hands line up better with the text to the right. That's because the Advance feature (described in Chapter 20) was used to print each hand 8 points lower than the text next to it—a good trick to know if you're going to be combining text sizes!

You can also change the size of a special character by changing the base font just to the left of the character. For example, the happy face in Figure 5.18 is special character 5,7 printed at 144 points (though reduced to fit into this book).

PRINTING TWO CHARACTERS IN ONE SPACE

If you look at all the characters in the printed CHARACTR.DOC file, you'll see many accented characters, which you can use to type words like *résumé* and *après ski*. However, if your printer cannot print such a character directly, you can still type it by placing the letter and accent mark in the same space. You use the *Overstrike* feature to do this. Follow these steps:

1. Move the cursor to where you want to type the double character.

2. Select **Layout** ➤ **Other** ➤ **Overstrike** ➤ **Create** (or press **Shift-F8 O O C**).

3. Type the pair of characters (for example, *e'* for an accented letter *e*).

4. Press ↵.

5. Press Exit (**F7**) to return to the Edit screen.

The overstruck characters appear inside the [Ovrstk:] code on the Reveal Codes screen.

Changing an Overstrike Character

If you need to change an overstrike character, follow these steps:

1. Turn on Reveal Codes (press **Alt-F3** or **F11**) and move the highlight to the [Ovrstk] code that displays your overstrike characters.

2. Select **Layout** ➤ **Other** ➤ **Overstrike** ➤ **Edit** (or press **Shift-F8 O O E**).

3. Edit the existing characters or type the new pair.

4. Press ↵.

5. Press Exit (**F7**) to return to the Edit screen.

A diacritical mark is a type of overstrike used to represent certain phonetic values, such as the acute and grave accents used in French.

Typing Diacritical Marks

There are also many *diacritical marks* available in the CHARACTR.DOC file. As with other special characters, WordPerfect offers shortcuts for typing some of the more commonly used diacriticals, so you don't need to use the Overstrike feature at all. To use the shortcut, press Ctrl-V or Ctrl-2, then type the diacritical, followed by the character. Figure 5.19 shows some examples. For example, pressing Ctrl-V and typing *'i* produces an accented *i* (special character 1,49).

DRAWING LINES

Multi-column layouts, like the one used in Figure 5.20, are covered in Chapter 20.

Lines are a great way to spruce up a document, as in the sample document shown in Figure 5.20. (You'll learn to create complex documents like this in Part 6 of this book—for now just notice the various types of lines.)

There are actually several ways to add lines to a document:

◆ The *Underline* and *Double Underline* appearances described earlier can be used to underline individual words.

◆ *Line Draw* can be used to draw a variety of line styles and can be used with any printer (but can be awkward when used with proportional fonts). The double underline beneath the headline in Figure 5.20 was created by using Line Draw.

◆ *Graphic lines* work only with graphics printers, but are independent of the current font; you can control the thickness, shading, and exact position of the line. The vertical lines separating the columns in Figure 5.20 are graphic lines.

FIGURE 5.19:

Sample diacritical marks

Diacritical	Mark	Shortcut	Code
Acute	í	'i	[1,49]
Caron	ž	vz	[1,207]
Cedilla	ç	,c	[1,39]
Centered Dot	ŀ	:l	[1,151]
Circumflex	â	^a	[1,29]
Crossbar	ŧ	-t	[1,187]
Dot Above	ċ	.c	[1,103]
Grave	è	'e	[1,47]
Macron	ū	_u	[1,193]
Ogonek	ą	;a	[1,95]
Ring Above	å	@a	[1,35]
Slash	ø	/o	[1,81]
Stroke	ł	\l	[1,153]
Tilde	ñ	~n	[1,57]
Umlaut	ü	"u	[1,71]

◆ The *Tables* (Chapter 6) and *Graphics* (Chapter 19) features, which also require a graphics printer, are ideal tools for drawing boxes around text. As an example, the Graphics feature was used to draw the box surrounding the text in the middle of the document in Figure 5.20.

The differences between Line Draw and graphic lines are discussed in more detail below.

The Vacationer

Vol. 1 No. 1   Travel fun for everyone   January 1991

Newsletter debut

by Joan Smith

We're pleased to bring this first issue of our newsletter, *The Vacationer*, to our many loyal customers. The newsletter was inspired by your ideas and questions. You've asked us where to find the best travel fares, where to go for the person who has been everywhere, what to eat and how to eat it when visiting faraway countries. We've responded by creating this newsletter.

Here we'll bring you the latest news about great deals on vacations in exotic corners of our planet, fun places for inexpensive weekend getaways, and out-of-the-way spots you might never have thought to ask us about. We'll include handy vacation planning tips and introduce you to exciting foods, puzzling customs, and important laws you'll encounter during sojourns to foreign lands. So relax, enjoy, and travel with us as we bring you a new issue every quarter of the year...   ✿

Celebrate with us

by Jill Evans

In honor of our newsletter's maiden voyage, we'd like to invite you to an Open House at 7:00pm on January 11, 1991, at our offices. Feel free to dress casually, or make an appearance in your most fashionable travel togs.   ✿

Join us at our
Open House
August 11, 1991
7:00 PM

Tropical travel

by Elizabeth Olson

Travel to tropical islands is on the increase. Just look at the graph showing our clients' recent tropical trips and you'll see how dramatic the numbers really are. There's a good reason for these increases -- tropical vacations are great fun, especially when the wind and snow are swirling at your doorstep in the

USING LINE DRAW

> **TO USE THE LINE DRAW FEATURE TO DRAW
> LINES INTERACTIVELY,**
>
> **1. Select Tools ➤ Line Draw (or press Ctrl-F3 L).**
>
> **2. Select a line style.**
>
> **3. Use the cursor-movement keys to draw lines.**
>
> **4. Press Exit (F7) when finished.**

Line Draw is a tool for drawing lines interactively on your Edit screen. It uses characters based on the current font and hence does not require a graphics printer. The one problem with Line Draw, however, is that it can be difficult to use with proportionally spaced fonts. Your best bet is to use it with mono-spaced fonts like Courier, which is available on most printers.

To use Line Draw, follow these steps:

1. Position the cursor where you want to start drawing a line or box.

2. Select **Tools ➤ Line Draw** (or press **Ctrl-F3 L**).

3. Select one of the characters shown: the single line (choose *1*), the double line (choose *2*), or the asterisk (choose *3*). Or, if you want to substitute a different character for the asterisk in option 3, you can select **C**hange and one of the additional options shown. (At this point, you can also select **O**ther and type yet another character, including any special character you type with Compose, Ctrl-2).

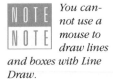
You cannot use a mouse to draw lines and boxes with Line Draw.

4. Use any cursor-movement keys (e.g. →, ←, ↑, and ↓) to draw the lines. For example, repeatedly pressing → draws the line toward the right. Pressing Home → extends the line all the way to the right margin. You can also press Repeat (**Esc**), type the number of times you want to repeat the line-draw character, then press an arrow key to draw the line in that direction (see Chapter 2 for a discussion of Repeat).

5. If you need to erase some lines, press **E** to select Erase and use the arrow keys to move the cursor over existing lines to erase them.

6. If you need to move the cursor to some new place on the screen without drawing a line, press **M** to select Move and move the cursor with the arrow keys. (To resume drawing lines, repeat step 3 above.)

7. When you've finished drawing, press Exit (**F7**) to return to your document.

Depending on what character you use to draw the line, you may notice a small arrow at the end of the line. This arrow will not appear in the printed document. Instead, it simply indicates the direction that you are going at the moment and also marks the end of a line. Any arrows that remain at the ends of lines will appear as half-space lines in the printed document, not as arrows.

Nonetheless, you can avoid the little arrow by pressing **End** when you've finished drawing a line (but before returning to the Edit screen) or by moving the cursor to the arrow and pressing **Delete** after you've returned to the Edit screen.

DRAWING GRAPHIC LINES

TO DRAW A GRAPHIC LINE,

1. Position the cursor.

2. Select Graphic ➤ Line (or press Alt-F9 L).

3. Select either Create Horizontal (Horizontal) or Create Vertical (Vertical).

4. Define the line from the options that appear.

Graphic lines are independent of the current font, so they don't pose any problems when used with proportionally spaced fonts. However, you need a graphics printer to print graphic lines, and you cannot interactively draw graphic lines on your screen.

Unlike the Line Draw feature, which lets you see what you've drawn on the Edit screen, graphic lines won't be visible until you view them on the View Document screen or print them. At first, this will be a bit awkward as you try to position your lines "just so," but don't let that deter you from using this feature.

Drawing Horizontal Graphic Lines

To draw a horizontal graphic line in a document, follow these steps:

1. Move the cursor to the approximate location for the line (by typing any text that should print on the same line as the graphic line or by pressing ↵, **Tab**, or the spacebar as necessary).

2. Select **Graphics ➤ Line ➤ Create Horizontal** (or press **Alt-F9 L H**).

3. Select **Horizontal Position, then one of the following options:

Left	The line extends from the left margin to the current cursor position (or as determined by the line length below).

Right	The line extends from the right margin to the current cursor position (or as determined by the line length below).
Center	The line is centered between the margins (its length is determined below).
Full	The line extends from the left margin to the right margin (this is the default horizontal position).
Set Position	None of the above; you enter the starting point, in inches, from the left edge of the page. For example, entering *2* starts the line 2 inches from the left edge of the paper (1 inch from the left margin).

4. If you want to control the vertical positioning of the line, select **V**ertical Position, then one of these options:

Set Position	Select this option, then type the distance from the top of the page to the top of the line and press ↵. For example, entering *2* draws the line 2 inches from the top of the page (1 inch below the top margin).
Baseline	Places the bottom of the graphic line even with the baseline (bottom) of the current line of text (this is the default vertical position).

5. Optionally, select **L**ength of Line, then type the length in inches (e.g., *3.5* for a 3½ inch line). Press ↵.

6. Optionally, select **W**idth of Line, type in a width (thickness) in the range 0.001 inches to 54 inches, and press ↵.

7. Optionally, select **G**ray Shading and enter a value between 0 (no shading, pure white) and 100 (pitch black), then press ↵.

8. Press Exit (**F7**) to return to your document.

Though Word-Perfect allows you to define a line up to 54 inches wide, be aware that such a line would be six pages thick!

Drawing Vertical Lines

Multi-column layouts are described in detail in Chapter 20.

The steps for creating a vertical line are about the same as those for creating a horizontal line. You can position the cursor where you want the line to appear or type in an exact measurement. If you want to place a line between columns created with the multicolumn layout features, first place the cursor anywhere within a column (the cursor must be below or to the right of the hidden [Col On] code that activates the columns). Then follow these steps:

1. Select **G**raphics ➤ **L**ine ➤ Create **V**ertical (or press **Alt-F9 L V**).

2. Select **H**orizontal Position, then one of the options below:

Left	The line is printed at the left margin (this is the default horizontal position).
Right	The line is printed at the right margin.
Between Columns	Prompts with "Place line to the right of column:". Type a column number and press ↵ to position the line between that column and the one to its right, where *1* is the leftmost column.
Set Position	Type the distance between the left edge of the page and the line and press ↵ (e.g., *2* places the line 2 inches from the left side of the page).

3. Select **V**ertical Position, then one of these options:

Full Page	The line runs the full length of the page, from top margin to bottom margin (this is the default vertical position).
Top	The line runs from the top margin to the cursor position (or as determined by the line length below).
Bottom	The line runs from the bottom margin to the cursor position (or as determined by the line length below).
Set Position	Enter the distance, in inches, from the top of the page to the top of the line and press ↵ (e.g., *2* starts the line 2 inches from the top of the page).

4. Optionally, select **L**ength of Line, type in the length of the line in inches (for example, *4½* or *4.5), and then press ↵.*

5. Optionally, select **W**idth of line, type in a width (thickness) in the range 0.001 inches to 54 inches, and press ↵ (see Figure 5.21).

6. Optionally, select **G**ray Shading and enter a value between 0 (for no shading, pure white) and 100 (pitch black), and press ↵.

7. Press Exit (**F7**) to return to your document.

You'll see more examples of graphic lines in Part 6—all of them were created using the steps described in this section.

CHANGING AND DELETING GRAPHIC LINES

Whenever you add a graphic line to a document, WordPerfect places a hidden code in the document: [VLine:] for vertical lines and [HLine:] for horizontal lines. The code includes the measurements that define the line. If you want to change or delete a graphic line, follow these steps:

1. Move the cursor near the place where you created the line.

2. Turn on Reveal Codes by pressing **Alt-F3** or **F11**.

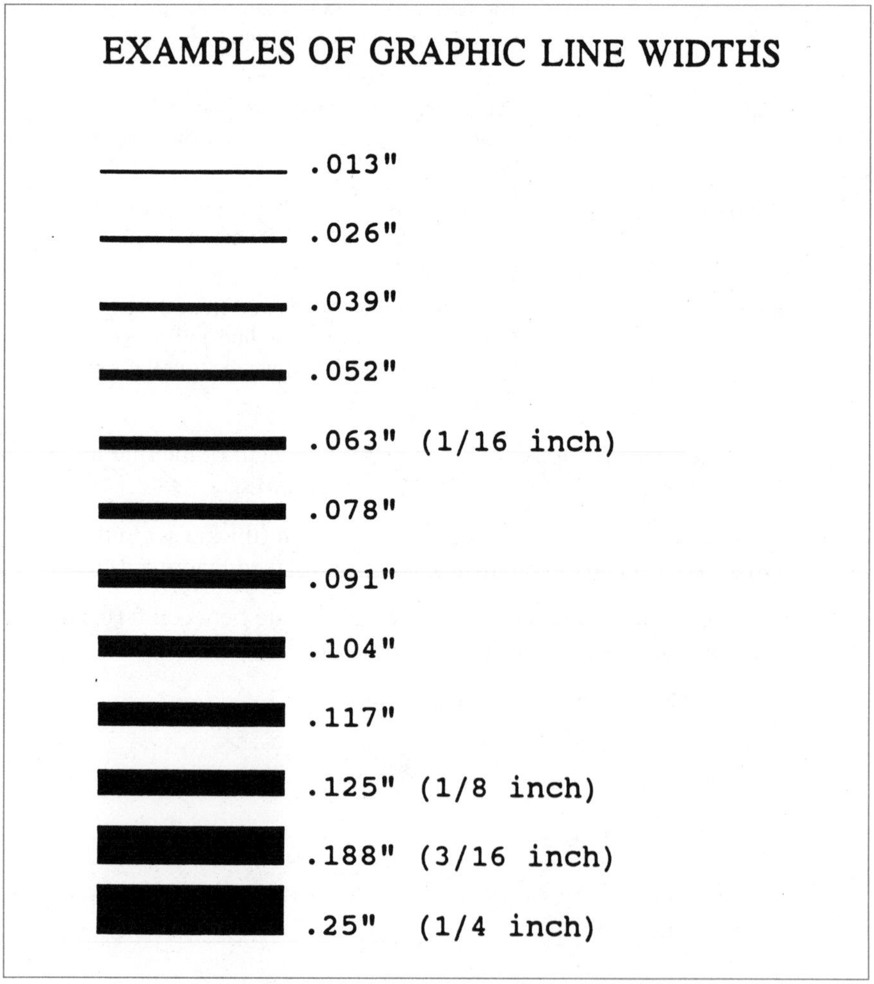

EXAMPLES OF GRAPHIC LINE WIDTHS

———————— .013"

———————— .026"

———————— .039"

———————— .052"

———————— .063" (1/16 inch)

———————— .078"

———————— .091"

———————— .104"

———————— .117"

———————— .125" (1/8 inch)

———————— .188" (3/16 inch)

———————— .25" (1/4 inch)

FIGURE 5.21:

Examples of various graphic line widths

3. If you want to delete the line, move the highlight to the [VLine:] or [HLine:] code that defines the line, and then press **Delete** to delete it. (You can skip the remaining steps.)

4. If you want to change the line, move the cursor to the right of or below the [Vline:] or [Hline:] code that defines the line.

5. Select **G**raphics ➤ Line (or press **Alt-F9 L**).

6. Select either Edit H**o**rizontal or Edit V**e**rtical, depending on which type of line you are changing.

7. Make any required changes by using the options on the menu.

8. Press Exit (**F7**) to return to your document.

COLORING YOUR TEXT

TO CHANGE THE PRINT COLOR OF TEXT,

1. Position the cursor.

2. Select Font ➤ Print Color (or press Ctrl-F8 C).

3. Choose the color you want to print in.

If you are one of the fortunate few who owns a color printer, you can easily control the color of your printed text. But even if you don't own a color printer, your local print shop can probably print documents in color for you. Use the techniques presented here to choose print colors, then refer to Chapter 8 and Part 6 for information on preparing your document for professional typesetting.

If you have a color monitor, you can preview colors on the View Document screen by pressing **Shift-F7 V**.

SELECTING A COLOR BEFORE YOU TYPE

Changing printer colors has no effect on the colors displayed on your Edit screen. If you want to change the colors on the Edit screen, see Chapter 13.

To type text that will be printed in a particular color, follow these steps:

1. Move the cursor where you want to type colored text.

2. Select F**o**nt ➤ Print **C**olor (or press **Ctrl-F8 C**). The Print Color menu appears (Figure 5.22).

3. Select a color by typing or clicking its highlighted number or letter, or select Other to create a new color (described below). The color selected will be reflected in the percentages listed next to Current Color on the Print Color menu.

4. Press Exit (**F7**) to return to the Edit screen.

5. Type all the text that should appear in the new color.

6. To switch back to black letters (or another color), select F**o**nt ➤ Print **C**olor (or press **Ctrl-F8 C**), then choose Blac**k** (or whatever other color you want).

7. Press Exit (**F7**) again.

COLORING A BLOCK OF EXISTING TEXT

Even though you cannot use the Block key (Alt-F4 or F12) or the mouse to highlight a block of text that you want to print in color, you can still color a block of existing text by following these steps:

1. Move the cursor to the first character that should be printed in a different color.

2. Select F**o**nt ➤ Print **C**olor (or press **Ctrl-F8 C**).

3. Select the color you want.

4. Press Exit (**F7**).

5. Move the cursor to the blank space (or character) *after* the last character to be printed in the color you last chose.

6. Select F**o**nt ➤ Print **C**olor (or press **Ctrl-F8 C**).

```
Print Color


                       Primary Color Mixture
                       Red      Green     Blue

          1 - Black    0%       0%        0%
          2 - White    100%     100%      100%
          3 - Red      67%      0%        0%
          4 - Green    0%       67%       0%
          5 - Blue     0%       0%        67%
          6 - Yellow   67%      67%       0%
          7 - Magenta  67%      0%        67%
          8 - Cyan     0%       67%       67%
          9 - Orange   67%      25%       0%
          A - Gray     50%      50%       50%
          N - Brown    67%      33%       0%
          O - Other

          Current Color  0%     0%        0%




Selection: 0
```

7. Select the color for the text to the right of and below the cursor.

8. Press Exit (**F7**).

CHANGING AND DELETING A COLOR

To delete a print color, move the cursor to the general area of the color change, turn on Reveal Codes (press Alt-F3 or F11), then delete the hidden [Color:] code that's activating the color. To change the print color, first delete the existing [Color:] code, then repeat the steps to activate a new color.

CREATING YOUR OWN PRINT COLORS

NOTE
NOTE

Be aware that not all color printers let you change intensity percentages to create your own colors. If your color printer seems to be ignoring your shade changes, check your printer manual for limitations and capabilities.

If none of the available print colors is exactly what you're looking for, you can create your own color. Most printed colors (other than black) are a combination of intensities of the primary colors red, green, and blue. You can create your own color by changing the mix of primary colors. Follow these steps:

1. Move the cursor wherever you want to start the new color.

2. Select **F**ont ➤ Print **C**olor ➤ **O**ther (or press **Ctrl-F8 C O**).

3. Enter a percentage for each primary color (the percentages listed with the available colors provide examples), pressing ↵ after typing each percentage.

4. Press Exit (**F7**) to return to the Edit screen.

All text to the right of and below the cursor will be printed in the specified color.

PRINTING SHADES OF GRAY

If your laser printer can print shades of gray, you can use the Print Color options to define a shade of gray for printed text. Basically, white is an equal mix of 100%, 100%, 100% of the three primary colors. An equal mix of 95%, 95%, 95% is a light gray. An equal mix of 90%, 90%, 90% is a little darker, and so forth. Figure 5.23 shows examples of gray shades, but you'll probably need to experiment with your own printer to see exactly what shades (if any) the various color combinations produce.

In the next chapter, you'll learn about WordPerfect's most powerful (and remarkably easy to use) tool for organizing text into columns, the Tables feature. As you'll see, this feature is also great for inserting horizontal and vertical lines in your text.

USING PRINT COLOR COMBINATIONS TO PRINT SHADES OF GRAY

90%, 90%, 90%	Very light
80%, 80%, 80%	A little darker
70%, 70%, 70%	Darker still
60%, 60%, 60%	Still getting darker
50%, 50%, 50%	Middle gray
40%, 40%, 40%	Darker gray
30%, 30%, 30%	Approaching black
0%, 0%, 0%	Black

FIGURE 5.23:

Examples of using custom print colors to print shades of gray

CHAPTER 6

Creating Tables

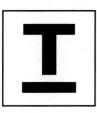 he WordPerfect Tables feature lets you type text into columns that you can later widen, narrow, or rearrange without ever changing a tab stop. It can be used to type *any* kind of document that involves columns, be it a simple list of names and addresses, a financial statement, an itinerary, or whatever.

LESSON 5

For a hands-on lesson in creating a table, see Lesson 5 in Part 9.

About the only type of column that the Tables feature is *not* particularly good for is the newspaper style, where you read down one column and then resume reading at the top of the next one (as in newsletters). It is also not very good for very long documents requiring multiple columns of text. For these jobs, multicolumn layouts (Chapter 20) are preferred.

USING THE TABLES FEATURE

If you don't have a graphics printer, WordPerfect won't print the lines in a table.

The Tables feature can be used to type any short passage or document that requires multiple columns. It is especially useful for creating small tables, like the example shown in Figure 6.1.

But this feature is great for creating *any* short multicolumn document, even if you don't want to draw lines in the document. Figures 6.2 through 6.4 show how you might use the Tables feature to create an itinerary with parallel columns. In Figure 6.2 you can see the first draft of the itinerary, with the Tables feature used to organize some of the text into columns.

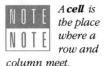

*A **cell** is the place where a row and column meet.*

At any time, you can widen or narrow columns and join and split cells to get exactly the appearance you want. Text within each cell will automatically wrap to fit within that cell, and you can see your changes right on the screen as you make them. For example, Figure 6.3 shows the sample itinerary after column widths within the table have been adjusted to better accommodate the text inside the cells.

When everything looks good, you can easily change or remove any of the lines to get exactly the look you want. For example, Figure 6.4 shows the complete printed itinerary after removing most of the lines from the table. This

Destination	Arrives	Ticket Price
Oceanside	8:30 am	$12.50
San Clemente	9:00 am	$17.50
Santa Ana	10:00 am	$37.50
Anaheim	10:30 am	$40.00
Los Angeles	11:45 am	$55.00
Malibu	1:00 pm	$70.00

FIGURE 6.1:

A sample table created with the Tables feature

DATE LINE TOURS
TOUR ITINERARY

NAME OF TOUR: EUROPEAN ESCAPADE/TWA

DAY	DATE	ITINERARY	TIME	HOTELS
1st Thur	6/10	Leave Los Angeles Arrive New York	12 noon 5:30pm	Grand Hotel
2nd Fri	6/11	Leave New York Arrive Rome	10:35am 5:00pm	Hotel Tritone
5th Mon	6/14	Naples		Hotel Gioto

Doc 1 Pg 1 Ln 1.5" Pos 2.5"

FIGURE 6.2:

The first draft of an itinerary on the Edit screen

```
              DATE LINE TOURS
              TOUR ITINERARY

       NAME OF TOUR:  EUROPEAN ESCAPADE/TWA


 ┌──────┬──────┬───────────────┬──────────┬───────────────┐
 │DAY   │DATE  │ITINERARY      │TIME      │HOTELS         │
 ├──────┼──────┼───────────────┼──────────┼───────────────┤
 │1st   │6/10  │Leave Los Angeles│12 noon │               │
 │Thur  │      │Arrive New York│5:30pm    │Grand Hotel    │
 │      │      │               │          │               │
 │      │      │               │          │               │
 │2nd   │6/11  │Leave New York │10:35am   │               │
 │Fri   │      │Arrive Rome    │5:00pm    │Hotel Tritone  │
 │      │      │               │          │               │
 │5th   │6/14  │Naples         │          │Hotel Gioto    │
 │Mon   │      │               │          │               │
 │      │      │               │          │               │
 └──────┴──────┴───────────────┴──────────┴───────────────┘
                              Doc 1 Pg 1 Ln 1" Pos 1.1"
```

FIGURE 6.3:

The second draft of the itinerary, after changing some column widths

```
                    DATE LINE TOURS
                    TOUR ITINERARY

                NAME OF TOUR:  EUROPEAN ESCAPADE/TWA


        DAY       DATE      ITINERARY          TIME         HOTELS
        ───────────────────────────────────────────────────────────
        1st       6/10      Leave Los Angeles  12 noon
        Thur                Arrive New York    5:30pm       Grand Hotel

        2nd       6/11      Leave New York     10:35am
        Fri                 Arrive Rome        5:00pm       Hotel Tritone

        5th       6/14      Naples                          Hotel Gioto
        Mon

        6th       6/15      Pompeii tour
        Tue

        7th       6/16      Pozzuoli tour
        Wed

        8th       6/17      Island of Ischia                Isla Hotel
        Thur                (Boat Tour)

        9th       6/18      Sorrento
        Fri

        10th      6/19      Leave Rome         1:15pm
        Sat                 Arrive New York    4:20pm

        11th      6/20      Leave New York     7:30pm
        Sun       6/27      Arrive Los Angeles 10:30pm
```

FIGURE 6.4:

The sample itinerary, with most of the lines removed

presents text neatly placed into columns without an abundance of lines.

In a nutshell, Tables lets you easily create and refine *any* multicolumn document. Later in this chapter, I'll show you some innovative and productive ways of using Tables to create some truly dazzling documents.

TABLES TERMINOLOGY

Knowing a cell's address is most important when you are using the Math feature, described in Chapter 18.

The Tables feature has some terminology of its own. Basically, a table consists of rows and columns. The place where a row and column meet is a *cell*. Each cell has an *address* that indicates its position in the table. Whenever the cursor is inside the table, the current cell's address appears on the status line as you move the cursor from cell to cell (see Figure 6.5).

The columns are labeled alphabetically from left to right, and the rows are numbered from top to bottom, so the cell in the upper-left corner is always cell A1, the cell to the right of that is cell B1, and so forth. Beneath cell A1 are cells A2, A3, etc.

CREATING A TABLE

TO CREATE A TABLE,

1. Position the cursor where you want the table to begin.

2. Select Layout ➤ Tables ➤ Create (Alt-F7 T C).

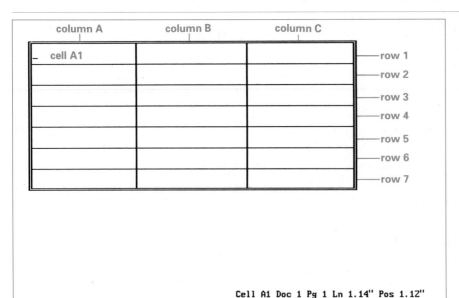

FIGURE 6.5:

Columns, rows, and a cell in a table

> **3. Adjust the table as necessary.**
>
> **4. Press Exit (F7) to return to the Edit screen.**
>
> **5. Type the text for each cell in your table.**

To work with tables, you must first create an empty table, which you can fill with information. Follow these steps:

1. Move the cursor to where you want to place the table in your document.

2. Select **L**ayout ➤ **T**ables ➤ Create, or press **Alt-F7 T C**.

3. You'll see the prompt

    Number of Columns: 3

4. Type the number of columns you want in your table (though you can add and delete columns later, if you wish), and then press ↵. (Or just press ↵ to accept the suggested number, *3*.)

5. Next you'll see the prompt

    Number of Rows: 1

    Type in the number of rows you want (you can change your mind later), and press ↵ (or just press ↵ if you want only one row).

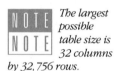 *The largest possible table size is 32 columns by 32,756 rows.*

WordPerfect creates an empty table with the number of rows and columns you specified.

WORKING WITH A TABLE

Once you create a table, there are two ways to work with it. One way is in *Table Edit mode,* where you work on the table as a whole, or on entire rows and columns. (The other way is in normal Edit mode, where you work on the text within the table.) For example, in Table Edit mode, you can change the widths of columns, add, delete, move, or copy rows and columns, and so forth.

When you first create a table, you are automatically placed in Table Edit mode. A menu of table editing options appears at the bottom of the screen, and the current cell (i.e., the cell that the cursor is in at the moment) is totally highlighted, as shown in Figure 6.6.

When you want to work with text in the table (i.e., the *contents* of individual cells), you have to exit the Table Edit mode and return to the normal Edit screen. At that point, you type and edit text as you normally would.

A large part of using Tables effectively is simply knowing when, and how, to switch from the normal Edit screen into Table Edit mode:

◆ If you're in Table Edit mode but want to work on the text within individual table cells, press Exit (**F7**) or click the right mouse button to leave the Table Edit mode.

◆ To enter Table Edit mode and work on the table as a whole, or to work on entire rows and columns or groups of cells, move the cursor into any cell of the table and select **L**ayout ➤ **T**ables ➤ **E**dit, or press Columns/Table (**Alt-F7**).

MOVING THROUGH A TABLE

One of the first things you'll need to know about using tables is how to move the cursor to a specific cell.

*BIOS is an acronym for **Basic Input Output System.***

WordPerfect offers many keyboard shortcuts for moving through a table, as listed in Table 6.1. Note that the Alt key combinations require an enhanced keyboard (more specifically, a keyboard with an enhanced BIOS that's enabled). If you don't have an enhanced keyboard, you can remap your current keyboard to act like one (see Chapter 27). If you have an enhanced keyboard, but the Alt key combinations don't work, it may be that the SWITCHES

```
Table Edit:  Press Exit when done        Cell A1 Doc 1 Pg 1 Ln 1.14" Pos 1.12"

Ctrl-Arrows Column Widths; Ins Insert; Del Delete; Move Move/Copy;
1 Size; 2 Format; 3 Lines; 4 Header; 5 Math; 6 Options; 7 Join; 8 Split: 0
```

TO MOVE	IN TABLE EDIT MODE	ON EDIT SCREEN
One cell right	Tab *or* → *or* Ctrl-Home → *or* Alt-→	Tab *or* → * *or* Ctrl-Home → *or* Alt-→
One cell left	Shift-Tab *or* ← *or* Ctrl-Home ← *or* Alt-←	Shift-Tab *or* ← * *or* Ctrl-Home ← *or* Alt-←
One cell up	↑ *or* Ctrl-Home ↑ *or* Alt-↑	↑ * *or* Alt-↑
One cell down	↓ *or* Ctrl-Home ↓ *or* Alt-↓	↓ * *or* Alt-↓
To top cell in column	Home ↑ *or* Ctrl-Home Home ↑ *or* Alt-Home ↑	Ctrl-Home Home ↑ *or* Alt-Home ↑
To bottom cell in column	Home ↓ *or* Ctrl-Home Home ↓ *or* Alt-Home ↓	Ctrl-Home Home ↓ *or* Alt-Home ↓
To first cell in row	Home ← *or* Home Home ← *or* Ctrl-Home Home ← *or* Alt-Home ←	Home Home Home ← *or* Ctrl-Home Home ← *or* Alt-Home ←
To last cell in row	End *or* Home → *or* Home Home → *or* Ctrl-Home Home → *or* Alt-Home →	Home Home Home → *or* Ctrl-Home Home → *or* Alt-Home →
To first cell in table	Home Home ↑ *or* Ctrl-Home Home Home ↑ *or* Alt-Home Home ↑	Ctrl-Home Home Home ↑ *or* Alt-Home Home ↑
To last cell in table	Home Home ↓ *or* Ctrl-Home Home Home ↓ *or* Alt-Home Home ↓	Ctrl-Home Home Home ↓ *or* Alt-Home Home ↓
To specific cell	Ctrl-Home *address* ↵	

* The ←, →, ↑, and ↓ keys move through existing text within a cell before moving to the next cell.

TABLE 6.1:

Cursor-Movement Key Operations in Tables

command in your DOS CONFIG.SYS file has disabled the enhanced BIOS (see your DOS manual).

In Table Edit mode, you can move to a specific cell by using the Goto (Ctrl-Home) key. For example, to move the cursor to cell C5, press **Ctrl-Home**, type **C5**, and press ↵.

If you prefer to use a mouse, moving from place to place is quite simple; it works the same whether you are in Table Edit mode or on the normal Edit screen:

1. Move the mouse pointer to the cell where you want the cursor.

2. Click the left mouse button.

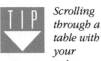

Scrolling through a table with your mouse can take a while to register on your monitor. You're probably better off using the keyboard.

If the table is too big to fit on the Edit screen, you can scroll through it with your mouse. Just click the left mouse button, then press the right mouse button as you drag the mouse in the direction you want to scroll. This technique does not work in Table Edit mode, so you should stick with the keyboard for making bigger moves.

TYPING AND EDITING TEXT IN A TABLE

TO TYPE OR EDIT TEXT IN A TABLE,

you must first leave Table Edit mode by pressing Exit (F7) or clicking the right mouse button.

Once you've created an empty table, it's easy to type and edit text in it:

1. Move the cursor to whatever cell in which you want to type text or change existing text.

2. If you are in Table Edit mode (where the entire current cell is highlighted), press Exit (**F7**) or click the right mouse button to leave Table Edit mode.

3. Type your text as you normally would, or use any WordPerfect editing technique to make changes.

You can also use WordPerfect formatting features when typing or changing text in a cell. For example, you can press Center (Shift-F6) to center text in a cell, or press Bold (F6) or Underline (F8). However, since Tab and Margin Release (Shift-Tab) are used to move from cell to cell, you can't use these keys to indent and outdent within a cell. But you can press Home Tab to indent or Home Shift-Tab to outdent. You can also change the tab ruler while in any cell. Doing so affects all indents and outdents in the current cell and all cells to the right and below.

If the text you type is too wide for the cell, WordPerfect will word-wrap the text as though the cell were a page and will expand the height of the entire row to accommodate the text in that cell. (You can later widen or narrow the cell to change the word wrap within the cell.)

If you are accustomed to ending a paragraph by pressing ↵, be aware that you'll probably inadvertently press ↵ after filling a cell. There's no harm in doing so, but it causes the row to expand in height to accommodate the new line created; you probably will not want this extra blank line across the row. If you press ↵ by mistake, just press Backspace. You can also flip on the Reveal Codes screen (press Alt-F3 or F11, or select **E**dit ➤ **R**eveal Codes) to locate and delete any extra [HRt] codes.

CHANGING A TABLE'S STRUCTURE

TO WORK WITH CELLS, COLUMNS, ROWS, OR THE TABLE STRUCTURE AS A WHOLE,

move the cursor into the table, and go into Table Edit mode by selecting Layout ➤ Tables ➤ Edit (or by pressing Alt-F7).

You can modify an existing table in almost any way imaginable, even if you've already entered text in the table. The sections that follow will describe the many ways to alter a table.

RESIZING COLUMNS

TO CHANGE A COLUMN WIDTH IN TABLE EDIT MODE,

position the highlight in any cell of the column you want to change, then press Ctrl-→ to widen the cell or Ctrl-← to narrow it.

Perhaps the single most important advantage of the Tables feature in comparison to tab stops is that it lets you change the width of columns interactively. To change the width of a column, follow these steps:

1. If you are not already in Table Edit mode, move the cursor anywhere into the table and select **L**ayout ➤ **T**ables ➤ **E**dit or press Columns/ Table (**Alt-F7**)—the Table Edit menu will appear.

2. Move the cursor to the column that you want to resize.

3. Hold down the Ctrl key and then press ← to narrow or → to widen the column to your liking.

4. Release the Ctrl key when you're finished.

NOTE *If you have more than one table on the screen, make sure you move the cursor into the one you want to work with in normal Edit mode before entering Table Edit mode.*

You cannot widen a table beyond the width of the page. Therefore, if a table already extends to the right margin, and you widen a column that has other columns to the right of it, these columns will shrink accordingly. Once the table has reached the right margin, and the columns to the right have shrunk to the minimum width of one space, pressing Ctrl-→ has no effect.

Figure 6.7 shows a small sample table before and after sizing the columns. As you can see, widening and narrowing columns helps you control word wrap within each column, the row height, and the distance between the text in the columns.

FIGURE 6.7:

A sample table before and after changing column widths

Original table, before sizing columns...

Item No.	Description	Size	Qty	Price
BW-111	Boy's Bermuda Short	22	1	$29.95
BW-204	Boy's Tank Top	12	1	$19.95
BW-607	Boy's Polo Shirt	12	1	$24.95

The same table as above after sizing the columns to better fit the text within each column...

Item No.	Description	Size	Qty	Price
BW-111	Boy's Bermuda Short	22	1	$29.95
BW-204	Boy's Tank Top	12	1	$19.95
BW-607	Boy's Polo Shirt	12	1	$24.95

And finally, the same table after realigning text to give it a more polished look...

Item No.	Description	Size	Qty	Price
BW-111	Boy's Bermuda Short	22	1	$29.95
BW-204	Boy's Tank Top	12	1	$19.95
BW-607	Boy's Polo Shirt	12	1	$24.95

This convenient feature takes the guesswork out of figuring out tab stops and column widths before typing text into columns. Instead, you can just figure out how many columns you need, type text into each column, then easily adjust the column widths to best fit the text within each column. As you'll see, you can also align text within columns, use shading and text appearances, and change lines to further improve the appearance of your tables, as in the bottom example in Figure 6.7.

Sizing Columns to a Specific Width

If you want to set a column or group of columns to a known width, such as 2.5 inches, follow these steps:

1. If you haven't already done so, switch to Table Edit mode.

2. If you want to set the width of more than one column, press Block (**Alt-F4** or **F12**) and use the → and ← keys to highlight the columns for which you want to set the width.

3. Select **F**ormat ➤ **C**olumn ➤ **W**idth.

4. Type in the column width (e.g., *2.5* or *2¹/2* for 2¹/2 inches, or *90p* for 90 points), and press ↵.

JOINING CELLS

TO JOIN TWO OR MORE CELLS IN TABLE EDIT MODE,

block the cells you want to join, then select Join ➤ Yes from the Table Edit menu.

To *join* cells means to remove the boundaries (lines) between them. You can join any number of adjacent cells into a single cell. Follow these steps:

1. If you are not already in Table Edit mode, move the cursor into the table, and select **L**ayout ➤ **T**ables ➤ **E**dit or press Columns/Table (**Alt-F7**).

2. Move the cursor to one of the cells you want to join, and press Block (**Alt-F4** or **F12**).

3. Extend the highlight over the cells you want to join, either by using the cursor-movement keys or by clicking your mouse in the cell where highlighting should extend.

4. Select **J**oin.

5. When prompted, select **Yes**.

I'll explain how to center text within a cell later in this chapter.

Figure 6.8 shows an example of cells in the top row of a table before, during, and after the joining of the cells and the centering of the text within the cell; in this figure, shading indicates blocked (highlighted) cells. This, of course, is just one example; you can join *any* group of adjacent cells in a table (you'll see additional examples later in the chapter).

FIGURE 6.8:

Joining cells to create a table title

Train Schedule		
Destination	Arrives	Price
Oceanside	8:30 am	$12.50
San Clemente	9:00 am	$17.50
Santa Ana	10:00 am	$37.50

Step 1: In Table Edit mode, move highlight to one of the cells to be joined (cell A1 in this example).

Train Schedule		
Destination	Arrives	Price
Oceanside	8:30 am	$12.50
San Clemente	9:00 am	$17.50
Santa Ana	10:00 am	$37.50

Step 2: Press Block (Alt-F4 or F12) and use your cursor-movement keys or mouse to block (highlight) the cells to be joined (all the cells in the top row in this example).

Train Schedule		
Destination	Arrives	Price
Oceanside	8:30 am	$12.50
San Clemente	9:00 am	$17.50
Santa Ana	10:00 am	$37.50

Step 3: Select Join ▸ Yes from the Table Edit menu to join the blocked cells, as shown.

Train Schedule		
Destination	Arrives	Price
Oceanside	8:30 am	$12.50
San Clemente	9:00 am	$17.50
Santa Ana	10:00 am	$37.50

Step 4: Optionally, select Format ▸ Cell ▸ Justify ▸ Center from the Table Edit menu if you want to center text in the current cell.

Incidentally, if you join cells that already contain text, the text in those cells will be separated by tabs ([TAB] codes), which you can remove on the Reveal Codes screen if you wish, after exiting Table Edit mode.

SPLITTING CELLS

Splitting cells is the opposite of joining them. Rather than removing the boundaries between cells, splitting adds them. This feature can be used to resplit cells you've joined, in case you change your mind after the fact, or to split a cell so that you can type text in two or more rows or columns within the cell. The basic steps for splitting cells are almost the same as for joining them:

1. If you are not already in Table Edit mode, move the cursor into the table and select **L**ayout ➤ **T**ables ➤ **E**dit, or press Columns/Table (**Alt-F7**).

2. Move the cursor to the cell you want to split. If you want to split several cells into even more cells, block these cells by pressing the Block key (**Alt-F4** or **F12**).

3. Select S**p**lit from the Table Edit menu.

4. Select either **R**ows or **C**olumns, depending on whether you want to split the cell into rows or columns.

5. WordPerfect will prompt you with a number indicating how many cells are in the adjacent row or column. Press ↵ to accept this number, or type in a new number and press ↵.

If you are using the Split option to undo the effects of a previous joining, WordPerfect will place the cell boundaries so that they line up with existing boundaries. If you split a single cell into two or more cells, WordPerfect will create equal-size rows or columns within the cell. Figure 6.9 shows an example of a single cell before and after being split into three columns.

CHANGING THE LINES IN A TABLE

TO ALTER OR REMOVE THE LINES IN A TABLE WHILE IN TABLE EDIT MODE,

1. Block the cells whose lines you want to change.

2. Select Lines.

3. Indicate which lines you want to alter.

4. Select the new line style.

You can change or remove the lines in any single cell or group of highlighted cells. Follow these steps:

1. If you are not already in Table Edit mode, move the cursor into the table and select **L**ayout ➤ **T**ables ➤ **E**dit, or press Columns/Table (**Alt-F7**).

2. If you want to change the lines for a single cell, move the cursor to that cell.

3. If you want to change the lines surrounding multiple cells (or the whole table), move the cursor to the upper-left corner of those cells, and then use the Block key (**Alt-F4** or **F12**) to highlight the cells whose lines you want to change.

4. Select **L**ines from the Table Edit menu. You'll see a menu that lets you choose specific lines to alter:

   Left: changes the line at the left edge of the cell or highlighted block.

   Right: changes the line at the right edge of the cell or highlighted block.

   Top: changes the line at the top of the cell or highlighted block.

   Bottom: changes the line at the bottom of the cell or highlighted block.

   Inside: changes lines inside the highlighted block.

   Outside: changes lines along the outside border of the highlighted block.

   All: changes all four lines around a cell or all the lines inside and along the outside border of the highlighted block.

A table with three columns, and two rows...

The same table as above after splitting cell B1 (center of top row) into three columns...

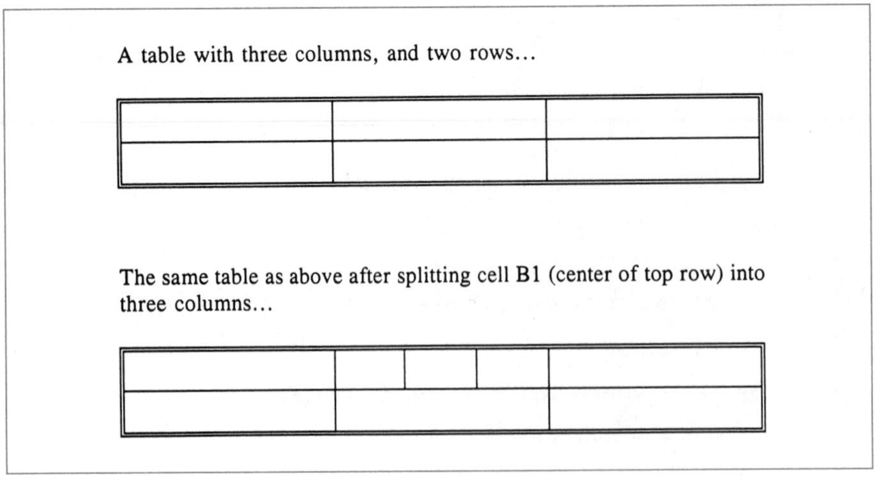

FIGURE 6.9:

A single cell before and after being split into three columns

Shade: activates or deactivates shading within the cell or all cells within the highlight (discussed in the next section).

If you select Shade, a different menu appears, as described later.

5. Select an option from the next menu. The various line styles are illustrated in Figure 6.10. (Notice the combined use of single lines at the left and top of a cell and thick lines at the right and bottom of a cell to create a "drop-shadow" appearance.)

As an example of changing the lines in a table, Figure 6.11 shows you the steps required to remove all the lines from a sample table and to place single lines around the outside border. Note, however, that after removing all the lines (step 2) the document appears to have been created by using tab stops only—which shows how the Tables feature can be used to create multicolumn tables without table lines, and without the hassle of setting tab stops on the tab ruler.

The dot leaders in Figure 6.11 were created by pressing Flush Right (Alt-F6) after typing the text that precedes the dots.

If you change the line style in such a manner that some lines don't join one another at the corner, the line ends with a small arrow on the Edit screen. The arrow itself never prints; it simply indicates where the line will be extended half a space when you print the document.

Changing the line style can be a tad tricky. For example, look at cells A1 and A2, where A2 is beneath cell A1, and a single line separates the two cells. Is that single line on the bottom of cell A1 or the top of cell A2? The answer to this question is relevant because, if cell A1 has a single line at the bottom, and cell A2 has a double line at the top, all three lines will be printed, causing an extra thick line to appear, as Figure 6.12 shows.

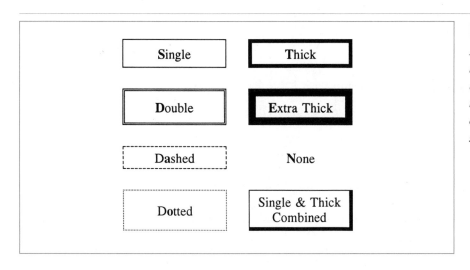

FIGURE 6.10:

Examples of various line styles, and a combination of single and thick lines in a single cell to create a "drop-shadow" appearance

There are two ways to avoid this problem. One is to be aware of how WordPerfect sets up the lines between interior cells when you first create a table, as listed below:

Top border   Single line

Left border   Single line

Step 1: The entire table is created, and all cells are blocked (highlighted) by using the Block key (Alt-F4 or F12) and pressing Home Home ↓ in the Table Edit mode.

Table of Contents	
Introduction	1
Experimental Design . .	3
Results	4
Conclusion	6

Step 2: All lines are removed from the table by selecting Lines ▸ All ▸ None from the Table Edit menu.

Table of Contents	
Introduction	1
Experimental Design . .	3
Results	4
Conclusion	6

Step 3: The entire table is reblocked by using the Block (Alt-F4 or F12) and Home Home ↑ keys while still in Table Edit mode.

Table of Contents	
Introduction	1
Experimental Design . .	3
Results	4
Conclusion	6

Step 4: A single line is drawn around the table after selecting Lines ▸ Outside ▸ Single from the Table Edit menu.

Table of Contents	
Introduction	1
Experimental Design . .	3
Results	4
Conclusion	6

Step 5: For the finale, the lines at the right and bottom of the table are changed to Thick, giving a drop-shadow appearance. To get some extra space at the bottom of the table, the Table Edit mode is exited, the cursor is moved past the number 6 at the bottom of the table, and ↵ is pressed to heighten that row.

Table of Contents	
Introduction	1
Experimental Design . .	3
Results	4
Conclusion	6

Right border   None

Bottom border   None

The outermost cells in a table obviously **have double lines at one or two borders when you first create the table.**

In other words, you can change the top or left line on an interior cell without worrying about doubling up the lines. However, if you want to change the right line on a particular cell, you should move one cell to the right and change that cell's left line. Or, if you want to change the bottom line of a cell, you should move to the cell beneath that one and change its top line.

Another way to deal with this is to first move to the cell whose border you want to change, then change whatever line you want to None. If nothing happens, it's because the line is actually being controlled by the adjacent cell. So, to change the line correctly, you need to first move to that adjacent cell, and then change the appropriate line.

The line style for the top, left, bottom, **and right edges of the current cell also appears just above the menu after you select** *Lines from the Table Edit menu.*

SHADING CELLS

TO SHADE CELLS WHILE IN TABLE EDIT MODE,

block the cells you want to shade, then select Lines ➤ Shade ➤ On.

Shading can enhance the appearance of a cell to call attention to it. Shading is also an alternative to using lines to separate cells, rows, or columns. Figure 6.13 shows an example where every other row is shaded.

To shade a cell, or group of cells, follow these steps:

1. If you are not already in Table Edit mode, move the cursor into the table and select **L**ayout ➤ **T**ables ➤ **E**dit, or press Columns/Table (**Alt-F7**).

We changed the bottom line of this cell to Double...

...but since this cell already had a single line at top, the lines combine.

Changing the top line of this cell to Double presents no problem because the cell above has no line at its bottom.

FIGURE 6.12:

Doubling of lines at the bottom of the top cell

2. Move the highlight to the cell you want to shade or to the cell in the upper-left corner of the group of cells you want to shade.

3. If you want to shade more than a single cell, press Block (**Alt-F4** or **F12**) and highlight the group of cells you want to shade by using your cursor-movement keys or mouse.

4. Select **L**ines from the Table Edit menu.

5. Select **S**hade.

6. Select **O**n to activate shading (or **Off** if you want to remove shading).

By default, the cells are shaded at 10 percent of black. But you can lighten or darken the shading by selecting **O**ptions ➤ **G**ray Shading from the Table Edit menu, as discussed later in this chapter.

To see the shading, leave Table Edit mode by pressing Exit (F7), then look at your table on the View Document screen (press Shift-F7 V).

INSERTING ROWS AND COLUMNS

TO INSERT A ROW OR COLUMN WHILE IN TABLE EDIT MODE,

position the cursor and press Insert.

If you want to add new columns or rows to the right or bottom of the table, see "Changing Table Size" later in this chapter.

You can insert new rows or columns in a table at any time. This is handy if you accidentally skip a row when typing your text, or if you need to add another row or column between existing ones. Follow these steps:

1. If you are not already in Table Edit mode, move the cursor into the table, and select **L**ayout ➤ **T**ables ➤ **E**dit or press Columns/Table (**Alt-F7**).

Milk	A	B₁	B₂	B₆	B₁₂
		Vitamin (mg)			
Whole	307	.093	.395	.102	.871
Lowfat (2%)	500	.095	.403	.105	.888
Skim	500	.088	.343	.098	.926
Buttermilk	81	.083	.377	.083	.537
Condensed	1004	.275	1.27	.156	1.36
Evaporated	306	.059	.398	.063	.205
Chocolate	302	.092	.405	.1	.835

FIGURE 6.13:
Shading used as an alternative to lines

 *New rows are added above the current row, and new columns are added to the left of the current column.*

2. Move the highlight to where you want to insert a new row or column.

3. Press **Insert**. The following options appear:

   Insert: **1** Rows; **2** Columns: 0

4. Select either **R**ows (to insert rows) or **C**olumns (to insert columns).

5. If you want to insert one row or column, just press ↵. Otherwise, type the number of rows or columns to add and press ↵.

The new rows or columns are inserted, and you're back in Table Edit mode.

When you insert rows, the rows at the bottom of the table are moved down to make room. However, if you insert a column in a table that's already as wide as the page, WordPerfect will split the current column into two columns. You can then resize the columns as necessary by using the Ctrl-← and Ctrl-→ keys in Table Edit mode.

If you have an enhanced keyboard, you can use a shortcut technique to insert a row. Rather than going to the Table Edit mode, just stay on the normal Edit screen. Then move the cursor to the row you want to insert, and press **Ctrl-Insert**.

Incidentally, you can use blank rows and columns to add space between rows and columns if you wish. For example, Figure 6.14 shows a document with a blank column separating the two columns of text and a blank row separating each section of text. Figure 6.15 shows the same document with the lines removed. The blank column and blank rows become extra blank space in the finished document.

DELETING ROWS AND COLUMNS

TO DELETE A ROW OR COLUMN WHILE IN TABLE EDIT MODE,

position the cursor and press Delete.

You can delete an entire row or column as easily as you can insert one. Follow these steps:

1. If you are not already in Table Edit mode, move the cursor into the table and select **L**ayout ➤ **T**ables ➤ **E**dit, or press Columns/Table (**Alt-F7**).

2. Move the highlight to the row or column that you want to delete.

3. Press **Delete**.

4. Select either **R**ows (to delete rows) or **C**olumns (to delete columns).

5. To delete one row or column, press ↵. Otherwise, indicate the number of rows or columns to delete and then press ↵.

Be careful when deleting multiple rows and columns. If you delete multiple rows, remember that the current row and rows beneath it are deleted. If you delete multiple columns, the current column and columns to the right are deleted.

MINUTES OF SCHEDULED REGULAR MEETING

**Conservation Commission
San Fernando, California**

7:00 p.m.   Conference Room 5
Monday, February 25, 1992   Community Building

CALL MEETING TO ORDER/ROLL CALL	Meeting was called to order at 7:00 p.m. by President Jones. Present: Commissioners Abbott, Bates, Carter, Smith. Absent: Dory, Edwards. Excused: Fox.
APPROVAL OF MINUTES	It was MSP (Bates/Carter) to approve the minutes of February 12, 1990.
NEW BUSINESS	Guest speaker Dave Garcia, City of Los Angeles Park & Recreation Dept., updated the Commission on the proposed renovation of Swift Park. The estimated cost for the first phase of the project is $2.9 million, to include enhancement of the existing parking lot.

COMMITTEE REPORTS	See attached reports.
	     Abbott - Parks and Recreation
	     Bates - Road Repair
	     Carter - Environmental Task Force

OLD BUSINESS	Abbott handed out sample letters to elected officials for the letter-writing campaign. Bates reported on the meeting he attended with the Condo Association.
STAFF REPORT	Mr. Smith reported that the next meeting of the Planning Group will include a public hearing on the proposed freeway.
ADJOURNMENT	The meeting was adjourned at 8:00 p.m. to the next meeting of Monday, March 25, 1991.

One way to exercise caution is to block exactly the rows or columns you want to delete. In Table Edit mode, press Block (**Alt-F4** or **F12**) and use your cursor-movement keys or mouse to highlight the rows or columns you want to delete. Then press **Delete**, and select either **R**ows or **C**olumns. WordPerfect will delete only the highlighted rows or columns.

If you make a mistake or change your mind about deleting rows or columns, you can undelete rows or columns by pressing Cancel (**F1**) and

 You can only restore the most recent row or column deletion; you cannot restore any previous deletions.

MINITES OF SCHEDULED REGULAR MEETING

Conservation Commission
San Fernando, California

7:00 p.m.   Conference Room 5
Monday, February 25, 1992   Community Building

CALL MEETING TO ORDER/ROLL CALL	Meeting was called to order at 7:00 p.m. by President Jones. Present: Commissioners Abbott, Bates, Carter, Smith. Absent: Dory, Edwards. Excused: Fox.
APPROVAL OF MINUTES	It was MSP (Bates/Carter) to approve the minutes of February 12, 1990.
NEW BUSINESS	Guest speaker Dave Garcia, City of Los Angeles Park & Recreation Dept., updated the Commission on the proposed renovation of Swift Park. The estimated cost for the first phase of the project is $2.9 million, to include enhancement of the existing parking lot.
COMMITTEE REPORTS	See attached reports. Abbott - Parks and Recreation Bates - Road Repair Carter - Environmental Task Force
OLD BUSINESS	Abbott handed out sample letters to elected officials for the letter-writing campaign. Bates reported on the meeting he attended with the Condo Association.
STAFF REPORT	Mr. Smith reported that the next meeting of the Planning Group will include a public hearing on the proposed freeway.
ADJOURNMENT	The meeting was adjourned at 8:00 p.m. to the next meeting of Monday, March 25, 1991.

FIGURE 6.15:

The document shown in Figure 6.14 with the lines removed from the table

answering Yes to the "Undelete?" prompt that appears. However, the width or placement of the undeleted row or column may differ from the original, particularly if you've moved the cursor. Therefore, you should still be careful when deleting.

If you have an enhanced keyboard, you can use a shortcut technique to delete a row. Rather than going to Table Edit mode, just stay on the normal Edit screen. Then move the cursor to the row you want to delete, and press **Ctrl-Delete**. WordPerfect will ask

Delete Row? No (Yes)

Press **Y** to select Yes.

Note that these commands delete an entire row or an entire column. If you simply want to delete the text within a row or column, you should do so at the normal Edit screen. Move the cursor to the cell that contains the text you want to delete, and use the standard deletion keys to delete text.

EMPTYING CELLS

> **TO DELETE THE CONTENTS OF CELLS WITHOUT CHANGING THE SIZE OF THE TABLE,**
>
> **leave Table Edit mode, block the cells you want to erase, and press Delete.**

If you want to delete text from several cells, leaving the cells empty, do so from the normal Edit screen (not from Table Edit mode). Move the cursor to one corner of the cells you want to empty, then use the Block key (**Alt-F4** or **F12**, or **E**dit ➤ **B**lock) and cursor-movement keys, or drag the mouse, to highlight all the cells you want to erase. Then press **Delete** and select **Yes** when asked for confirmation. The contents of the highlighted cells are deleted, but the empty cells remain in the table.

CHANGING TABLE SIZE

If you run out of room in a table and need to add new rows at the bottom of the table or new columns to the right of the table, follow these steps:

1. If you are not already in Table Edit mode, move the cursor into the table, and select **L**ayout ➤ **T**ables ➤ **E**dit or press Columns/Table (**Alt-F7**).

2. Select **S**ize.

3. Select either **R**ows or **C**olumns, depending on which you want to add.

4. A prompt appears, showing the number of rows or columns currently in the table.

5. Type the number of rows or columns that the table should contain. For example, if the prompt shows that there are currently 15 rows in the table, and you want to add five rows, type *20*.

6. Press ↵.

If you ***decrease*** *the number shown in the prompt, Word-Perfect will delete rows or columns to size the table accordingly. You can't correct this mistake with the Cancel key!*

If you increase the number of columns in a table that is already as wide as the margins allow, columns to the left of the new column will be resized to make room for the new columns. As always, you can resize the columns with the Ctrl-← and Ctrl-→ keys in Table Edit mode.

MOVING AND COPYING IN TABLES

There are two basic ways to move or copy information in a table in Table Edit mode: The first way is to move or copy entire rows or columns, which often changes the actual structure of the table. For example, when you copy an entire row, the copied row is added to the table, hence the table becomes one row larger. The second way is to move or copy text (the contents of cells) only. This type of move is called a *block* move and does not change the structure of the table. For example, when you block copy the contents of one row to another, the contents of these rows will match; however, WordPerfect does not add a new row to the table. Figure 6.16 illustrates the difference.

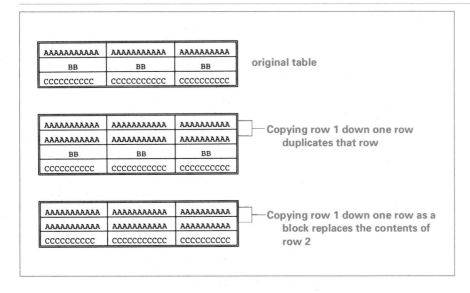

FIGURE 6.16:

Copying a row vs. copying a block

You use regular moves when you want to copy an entire row or column and block moves when you want to move or copy only some of the cells in a row or column to existing rows or columns. Note that you cannot transpose rows or columns while moving or copying; that is, you cannot copy a row to a column or vice versa. The two different types of moving and copying are discussed in separate sections that follow.

Moving or Copying a Row or Column

To move or copy a row or column in a table, follow these steps:

1. If you are not already in Table Edit mode, move the cursor into the table, and select **L**ayout ➤ **T**ables ➤ **E**dit or press Columns/Table (**Alt-F7**).

2. Move the highlight to the row or column that you want to move or copy.

3. If you want to move or copy more than a single row or column, press Block (**Alt-F4** or **F12**) and highlight the rows or columns you want to move or copy.

4. Press Move (**Ctrl-F4**) or click on Move in the Table Edit menu.

5. Select either **R**ow (to move or copy rows) or **C**olumn (to move or copy columns).

6. Select either **M**ove or **C**opy. (If you select Move, the row or column temporarily disappears.) Note the message "Move cursor; press Enter to retrieve" on the status line.

7. Move the highlight to the row or column you want to copy to (a moved or copied row will be positioned above, and a moved or copied column will be positioned to the left of, the highlight in this step).

8. Press ↵.

Because WordPerfect always moves or copies to the row above, or to the column to the left of, the current one, you cannot directly move or copy to the last column or last row of a table. (For example, if you select the last column of a table as the place to copy a column, the copied column will be one column to the left of the last column.)

To get around this, you need to move or copy the row or column as close to the last row or column as you can get. Then you can move the last column one column to the left, or move the last row one row up, to get things positioned the way you want them.

Moving or Copying a Block

When moving or copying a block (i.e., the contents of cells) in a table, you must make sure that there is a sufficient number of rows and columns to accept the moved or copied data. For example, you cannot move or copy three rows into only one row. (If you try to do this, WordPerfect will only move as much of your text as will fit into available rows and columns.) If necessary, add some new rows or columns first.

Follow these steps to move or copy a block:

 The steps for moving or copying a block are almost the same as for moving or copying a row or column. Only step 5 differs.

1. If you are not already in Table Edit mode, move the cursor into the table, and select **L**ayout ➤ **T**ables ➤ **E**dit or press Columns/Table (**Alt-F7**).

2. Move the cursor to the cell, row, column, or corner of a group of cells that you want to move or copy.

3. If you want to move or copy more than one cell, press Block (**Alt-F4** or **F12**), then highlight the cells you want to move or copy with your cursor-movement keys or mouse.

4. Press Move (**Ctrl-F4**), or click on Move in the Table Edit menu.

5. Select **B**lock.

6. Select either **M**ove or **C**opy (if you select Move, your text will disappear temporarily). Note the message "Move cursor; press Enter to retrieve" on the status line.

 If you move or copy data to cells that already contain text, the existing text will be replaced by the text you are moving or copying.

7. Move the highlight to where you want to move or copy data (or if you are moving or copying multiple cells, to the upper-left corner of the destination cells).

8. Press ↵.

You can also move or copy the contents of cells when you are at the normal Edit screen, rather than in Table Edit mode.

1. If you are in Table Edit mode, press Exit (**F7**) or click the right mouse button to leave that mode.

2. Block the text that you want to move or copy (press **Alt-F4** or **F12**, or drag your mouse).

3. Select **E**dit from the pull-down menu, or press **Ctrl-F4 B**.

4. Select **M**ove or **C**opy. You'll see the message "Move cursor; press Enter to retrieve" on the status line.

5. Move the cursor to the destination cell.

6. Press ↵.

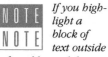 *If you high-light a block of text outside of a table, and then move or copy that text into a table cell, the entire block is placed in a single cell.*

You can use the general technique above to copy text within a table out of the table, to copy text outside of a table into the table, or to copy text from one part of a table to another.

Repeating a Table Header on Multiple Pages

A *header* is a row or group of rows in a table that is repeated on each page where the table is printed. This is very useful when your table spans several pages of text and you want a table title or column titles to appear at the top of the table on each printed page. You can use any number of rows at the top of the table for a header. Here's how to do it:

1. If you are not already in Table Edit mode, move the cursor into the table, and select **L**ayout ➤ **T**ables ➤ **E**dit or press Columns/Table (**Alt-F7**).

2. Select **H**eader.

3. Type the number of rows to repeat on each page, counting from the top of the table (e.g., *2* to repeat the first two rows).

4. Press ↵.

The heading rows won't be repeated on the Edit or Table Edit screens, but you will see an asterisk next to the cell address on the status line when your cursor lands in a cell in a heading row. For example, you'll see a message on the status line like this one:

Cell A1* Doc 1 Pg 1 Ln 1.14" Pos 1.12"

As usual, you'll need to visit the View Document screen (press **Shift-F7 V**) if you want to see the heading rows repeated on subsequent pages of a multipage table.

If you change your mind about the headers, just select Header from the Table Edit menu, type **0**, and press ↵.

FORMATTING TEXT IN A TABLE

TO CHANGE THE SIZE OR APPEARANCE OF ALL THE TEXT IN ONE OR MORE CELLS,

1. Go to Table Edit mode.

2. Select a cell, block a group of cells, or select any cell in a column.

3. Select Format, then either Cell or Column, then Size or Appearance.

Formatting helps you improve the appearance of text within the table. You can format a single cell, a group of cells, a column, or several columns in a single operation. Several formatting techniques were used to create the table shown in Figure 6.17:

◆ The top title is in large size, boldfaced, and italicized.

◆ The column titles are boldfaced.

◆ The row titles are italicized.

◆ All numbers are right-aligned in their columns.

The many formatting options and features are accessible when you select **Format** from the Table Edit menu. Here's how to get started on formatting text in a cell or column:

1. If you are not already in Table Edit mode, move the cursor into the table, and select **Layout ➤ Tables ➤ Edit** or press Columns/Table (**Alt-F7**).

2. Select the cells you want to format.

◆ If you want to change the format of a single cell or column, move the highlight to that cell or column.

COMPARATIVE OPERATING EXPENSES			
Division	**1990**	**1991**	**% Change**
North	1,980,870	2,780,870	40.4%
South	987,750	760,080	-23.1%
East	986,500	1,100,000	11.5%
West	1,275,000	987,000	-22.6%
Total	5,230,120	5,627,950	7.6%

FIGURE 6.17:
A formatted table

◆ If you want to change the format of a group of cells, use the Block key (**Alt-F4** or **F12**) to highlight those individual cells.

◆ If you want to change the format of several columns, move the cursor to the leftmost column that you want to format, then press Block (**Alt-F4** or **F12**), and press → until all the columns that you want to format are highlighted.

3. Select **F**ormat. You'll see the options below:

Format: **1 C**ell; **2** Column; **3** Row Height

The Type and Lock options are math-related; they are covered in Chapter 18.

◆ If you are formatting a single cell or group of highlighted cells, select **C**ell, and you'll see these options:

1 Type; **2 A**ttributes; **3 J**ustify; **4 V**ertical Alignment; **5 L**ock

◆ If you are formatting a column or a group of highlighted columns, select Co**l**umn, and you'll see these options:

1 Width; **2 A**ttributes; **3 J**ustify; **4 # D**igits

The sections that follow describe these options.

ATTRIBUTES

Selecting Attributes presents these options:

The Reset option is only available if you are formatting cells.

1 Size; **2 A**ppearance; **3 N**ormal; **4 R**eset

Size   If you select Size, you'll see these options (which are illustrated in Chapter 5):

1 Suprscpt; **2 S**ubscpt; **3 F**ine; **4 S**mall; **5 L**arge; **6 V**ry Large; **7 E**xt Large

Your Edit screen may show a different color or highlighting for the resized text, but the text won't appear in its new size unless you print the document or view it on the View Document screen.

Selecting an option from this menu changes the size of the text in the specified cell or column. Text outside the cells or columns remains unchanged. However, be aware that the actual printed size is determined entirely by your printer, not by WordPerfect (see Chapter 5).

If you select a large size, the height of the entire row in the table is expanded to accommodate the large size. If you select a small size for all the cells across a row, the height of the row is *not* decreased. (But you can use the Row Height feature, discussed later, to change the height of the row if you wish.)

If you want to change the size of *part* of the text in a cell, do so while typing, or after blocking, text in the cell (*not* in Table Edit mode) with the F**o**nt menu option or Font key (Ctrl-F8 S).

Appearance Selecting Appearance takes you to the appearance options, as shown below:

1 Bold **2 U**nd**l**n **3 D**b**l** Und **4 I**talc **5 O**ut**l**n **6 S**h**a**dw **7 S**m **C**ap
8 Red**l**n **9 S**tkout

On the At-tributes menu, Normal removes all print at-tributes from the cell; Reset resets the cell or cells to the current column settings.

These print appearances are described in Chapter 5. Be aware that these options are cumulative. For example, if you assign the Outline appearance to some cells and then assign the Bold appearance to any of the same cells, the result is Bold and Outline combined. To undo the appearance attributes of a cell or column, you must select F**o**rmat ➤ **C**ell *or* C**o**lumn ➤ **A**ttributes ➤ **N**or-mal. Again, you'll need to go to the View Document screen to see the actual appearance change, although your Edit screen may show a different color or highlighting for the new appearance.

If you want to change the appearance of only part of the text in a cell (for example, double-underline a single word), do so while typing, or after blocking, the text on the Edit screen (*not* while in Table edit mode). Select F**o**nt ➤ **A**ppearance (or press **Ctrl-F8 A**) to change the appearance.

In Table Edit mode, you can boldface or underline all the text in a cell simply by moving to that cell and pressing Bold (F6) or Underline (F8).

Normal The Normal option removes all size and appearance options from the specified cells or columns. Use this option when you decide to reverse size or appearance changes and have the text print normally.

Reset The Reset option is available only when you are formatting cells. Use this option to reset the size and appearance of the cell or highlighted cells to match the size and appearance of the rest of the column.

JUSTIFY

The Justify option lets you determine how text in a cell or column is justified. When you select this option, you'll see the following menu:

1 Left; **2 C**enter; **3 R**ight; **4 F**ull; **5 D**ecimal Align; **6 R**eset

The Reset option ap-pears only when you are formatting cells.

Figure 6.18 shows examples of the various types of column and cell jus-tification. The Left, Center, Right, and Full options behave the same way they do when you justify paragraphs (discussed in Chapter 4). The Decimal Align option is used to align numbers on a specific character (typically the decimal point), as in the tabular columns described in Chapter 4.

For the most part, you'll probably use center alignment for column titles, left alignment for text, and right alignment for numbers, dates, times, and so forth. However, if you want to display numbers with decimal points (especially when some numbers have more digits than others to the right of the decimal point), or if you want to display negative numbers in parentheses (as described briefly later on in this chapter and in Chapter 18), you'll probably want to use decimal alignment so that the numbers align on the decimal point.

If you use a non-American numbering system that aligns numbers on something other than a period, such as the comma in European format (e.g., *123.456,78*), change the alignment character anywhere above and to the left of (or even outside of and above) the decimal-aligned column. Do so at the regular Edit screen, not in Table Edit mode, by selecting **L**ayout ➤ **O**ther ➤ **D**ecimal/Align Character or by pressing **Shift-F8 O D**. (See "Changing the Decimal Alignment Character" in Chapter 4.)

If you want to justify only a portion of the text in a cell, do so while typing text into the cell or editing text (not in Table Edit mode). For example, you can press Center (Shift-F6) to center part of the text in a cell.

To correctly decimal-align numbers with more than two decimal places or with negative numbers displayed in parentheses, you must change the # Digits setting of that column by selecting **Format** ➤ **Co**l**umn** ➤ **#D**igits *on the Table Edit screen.*

An example of this can be found later in the chapter, in Figure 6.28. The words in the calendar are centered, but the numbers are not.

DIGITS

The # Digits option is available when you are formatting columns. It lets you determine how many decimal places are displayed to the right of the decimal point. If left unchanged, WordPerfect uses two decimal places.

If your numbers have more than two decimal places of accuracy in a column, and they are decimal-aligned, you should select the # Digits option and indicate the correct number of decimal places to show for each number. Otherwise, the numbers will not wrap correctly in their cells. If you are

The # Digits option is also very useful when doing math in tables, as discussed in Chapter 18.

Left	Full	Center	Right	Decimal
ABC Corp.	ABC Corp.	ABC Corp.	100.00	.123
Acme Rentals	Acme Rentals	Acme Rentals	1,000.00	123.45
Digital, Inc.	Digital, Inc.	Digital, Inc.	10,000.00	(1,234.56)
SYBEX, Inc.	SYBEX, Inc.	SYBEX, Inc.	100,000.00	99,999.99
Ann Nye Chiropractic	A n n N y e Chiropractic	Ann Nye Chiropractic	900,000.00	0.001

FIGURE 6.18:

Examples of types of column justification

displaying negative numbers in parentheses, add an extra digit in # Digits for the closing parenthesis.

To display negative results of math calculations using parentheses instead of leading minus signs, select Options ▶ Display Negative Results from the Table Edit menu, then type 2 and press ↵.

VERTICAL ALIGNMENT

The Vertical Alignment option is available only when you've opted to format a cell (or a block of highlighted cells). It's generally used to control how text is vertically aligned in a cell that is several lines tall. When you select Vertical Alignment, you'll see the following options:

1 Top; **2 B**ottom; **3 C**enter

Figure 6.19 shows how you could use these options to control vertical alignment in a table. When you select an option, you will not see any change on the Edit screen. But you can preview the effects on the View Document screen if you wish.

WIDTH

If you are formatting columns, selecting Format also displays the Width option on a menu. If you select this option, you'll see the following prompt:

Column width:

This is followed by the current width of the column.

You can type in a new width in inches (e.g., *1.5* for 1.5 inches wide) and then press ↵. WordPerfect will adjust the widths of other columns if necessary, as when you widen and narrow columns with the Ctrl-→ and Ctrl-← keys.

Top Vertical Alignment	This cell contains enough text to extend through three lines
Center Vertical Alignment	This cell contains enough text to extend through three lines
Bottom Vertical Alignment	This cell contains enough text to extend through three lines

FIGURE 6.19:

Examples of vertical alignments in cells

You'll probably find that changing column widths interactively with the Ctrl-→ and Ctrl-← keys is easier than using this menu option. But if you want several columns to have the same width, you can block all these columns, then select **F**ormat ➤ Co**l**umn ➤ **W**idth from the Table Edit menu to set the widths of all these columns.

ROW HEIGHT

The Format menu also offers a Row Height option. This option affects the row that the cursor is currently in or any number of rows that you have highlighted as a block.

If you want to decrease or increase the distance between rows in a table, use the Options menus described later in this chapter, rather than the Row Height option.

Normally, WordPerfect determines the height of a row based on the height of the text printed in that row and the space allotted between rows (as set on the Options menus, discussed below). After you select Format and Row Height from the Table Edit menu, you'll see the following menu:

Single line: **1 F**ixed; **2 A**uto; Multi-line: **3 F**ixed; **4 A**uto

By default, all rows are defined as Multi-line Auto (option 4). This means that a single row can contain multiple lines of word-wrapped text, and that WordPerfect will determine the height of each line automatically.

Changing the setting to Single Line means that cells in that row can no longer support multiple lines of text. Any text that would normally word-wrap within a cell is simply cut off and becomes invisible. (However, WordPerfect "remembers" the wrapped text, so if you change the setting back to Multi-line, that wrapped text reappears in the cell.)

If you change the height method from Auto to Fixed, WordPerfect will display a prompt requesting the new row height, along with the current row height. You can type in a new row height and press ↵.

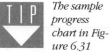
The sample progress chart in Figure 6.31 shows a practical example of changing the row height.

Note that if you use the Single-line Fixed option and the row height you specify is not tall enough to display the text within the row, that text will not appear on the View Document screen and will not be printed. You'll only want to use this option to increase the row height.

If you assign the Multi-line Fixed option to a row, then all the lines of text within a cell in that row must fit within the row height you specify. Any lines of text that do not fit within the fixed row height you determine will not be visible. Once again, this option is best used for increasing the row height.

TROUBLESHOOTING FORMAT PROBLEMS

If you change the format of a group of cells or a column, and some (or all) cells ignore the change, it's probably due to the way WordPerfect prioritizes formatting changes (not a malfunction). Here's how these priorities work:

◆ Formatting codes entered *outside* of Table Edit mode, such as when you are entering or editing text in the table, get highest priority.

◆ Formatting options activated in Table Edit mode after selecting **F**ormat ➤ **C**ell get second priority and override only those selections made by selecting **F**ormat ➤ Co**l**umn.

◆ Formatting options activated by selecting **F**ormat ➤ Co**l**umn get lowest priority and override neither of the above.

For example, if you center text in a cell using the Center key (Shift-F6) while typing text in a cell, that text will always be centered, regardless of formatting selections made in Table Edit mode. To uncenter text in that cell, you'd have to turn on the Reveal Codes screen and remove the [Center] code from the cell.

Similarly, if you use **F**ormat ➤ **C**ell to format a particular cell, then use **F**ormat ➤ Co**l**umn to reformat that entire column, the previous **F**ormat ➤ **C**ell selections remain in effect. To reset the cells to match the format of the column, rehighlight the "faulty" cells, select **F**ormat ➤ **C**ell, select either **A**ttributes or **J**ustify, and then select **R**eset to undo the previous selections.

You can use this built-in prioritization to your advantage. For example, each column in Figure 6.18 has a different type of alignment, and each was aligned using **F**ormat ➤ Co**l**umn ➤ **J**ustify in Table Edit mode. But the title (top) cell of each column contains centered text. That's because all the cells in the top row were highlighted, hence they all share center alignment of text, overriding the alignment assigned to the column as a whole.

USING FONTS IN A TABLE

Fonts are discussed in Chapter 5.

Changes to the base font in a table act like changes to the base font on the normal Edit screen; that is, all text (in all cells) to the right of and below a font change (i.e., a hidden [Font] code) is changed to the selected font. As always, you'll need to go to the View Document screen or print your table to see the effect of your font changes.

If you want to set the font for the entire table, do so on the normal Edit screen, outside of Table Edit mode. Move the cursor outside of and just above the start of the table (so that the cursor is on, or to the left of, the [Tbl Def] code that starts the table), and select your font by choosing **F**ont ➤ Base **F**ont (or pressing **Ctrl-F8 F**).

To change the font for text in a given cell, move the cursor to the first character of text in that cell (on the Edit screen, not in Table Edit mode), and select **F**ont ➤ Base **F**ont (or press **Ctrl-F8 F**). All cells to the right of and below the cursor position will be affected. Then, if necessary, change the font at the beginning of any cell to the right of or below the current one to initiate a different font.

POLISHING THE APPEARANCE OF A TABLE

Whenever you are in Table Edit mode, you can select Options to bring up the Table Options menu, shown in Figure 6.20. This menu helps you refine the appearance of your tables, as discussed in the sections that follow. After making your selections, press Exit (**F7**) to leave this menu and return to Table Edit mode.

NOTE *Options you select from the Table Options menu will apply to the entire table (but won't affect any other tables in your document).*

Spacing Between Text and Lines The Spacing Between Text and Lines option lets you control the distance between the lines that surround the cells and the text within the cells. Figure 6.21 shows examples of spacing between text and lines, using both left-aligned and right-aligned text examples.

This option is especially useful when you want to print your table without any lines and need to control the line spacing and the spacing between the columns. For example, the bottom half of Figure 6.21 shows a table printed with lines removed and the default spacing settings, and the same table after reducing the Top spacing option from the default of 0.1 inch (see Figure 6.20) to 0.028 inches.

```
Table Options

    1 - Spacing Between Text and Lines
            Left                    0.083"
            Right                   0.083"
            Top                     0.1"
            Bottom                  0"

    2 - Display Negative Results     1
            1 = with minus signs
            2 = with parentheses

    3 - Position of Table            Left

    4 - Gray Shading (% of black)    10%




Selection: 0
```

FIGURE 6.20:

The Table Options menu, with the default settings

Display Negative Results The Display Negative Results option lets you determine whether table calculations that result in negative numbers are displayed with a leading minus sign or in parentheses. Select this option, choose **1** to display negative results with the usual leading minus sign or choose **2** to display negative results in parentheses, then press ↵. See Chapter 18 for more details.

FIGURE 6.21:

Examples of spacing between text and lines

Examples of Spacing Between Text and Lines (Left-justified text)

Default spacing between text and lines

Spacing: Left=0, Right=0, Top=0, Bottom=0

Spacing: Left=.1, Right=.1, Top=.07, Bottom=.03

Spacing: Left=.25, Right=.25, Top=.25, Bottom=.25

Examples of Spacing Between Text and Lines (Right-justified text)

Default spacing between text and lines

Spacing: Left=0, Right=0, Top=0, Bottom=0

Spacing: Left=.1, Right=.1, Top=.07, Bottom=.03

Spacing: Left=.25, Right=.25, Top=.25, Bottom=.25

Table with default Spacing Between Text and Lines, and no lines...

```
Wanda Carneros        (123)555-0123
Tersha d'Elgin        (818)555-0987
Victoria Dumplin      (313)555-0385
Ambrose Pushnik       (714)555-5739
Frankly Unctuous      (414)555-0312
```

Same table as above after changing the Spacing Between Text and Lines at the Top to 0.028...

```
Wanda Carneros        (123)555-0123
Tersha d'Elgin        (818)555-0987
Victoria Dumplin      (313)555-0385
Ambrose Pushnik       (714)555-5739
Frankly Unctuous      (414)555-0312
```

Position of Table If your table is narrower than the width of the margins on the page, you can select the Position of Table option to determine how your table is positioned between the margins. When you select this option, you can choose from the selections summarized below:

Left	The left edge of the table is aligned at the left margin.
Right	The right edge of the table is aligned at the right margin.
Center	The table is centered between the two margins.
Full	The table is sized to fit between the margins.
Set Position	Lets you align the left edge of the table a specific distance from the left edge of the page. For example, if you enter .5, the left edge of the table is printed 0.5 inches from the left edge of the page.

NOTE *See "Making More Room in a Table" later in this chapter for information on creating and printing wide tables.*

If you use the Set Position option, be careful to leave enough room for the table to be printed. For example, if there are 6.5 inches of space between the margins on your page, and your table is 5 inches wide, you have 1.5 inches of "play" between the table and the margins. If, however, you set the position of the left edge of the table to 2 inches, the rightmost 0.5 inch of the table will simply not be printed.

The Left, Center, and Right options only affect tables that are narrower than the distance between the margins. Since WordPerfect automatically creates tables to fill the space between the margins, you must narrow one or more columns before any of these options will have an effect.

Gray Shading The Gray Shading option lets you determine the darkness of the shading in table cells where shading is turned on by using **Lines ➤ S**hade ➤ **O**n (see "Shading Cells" earlier in this chapter). By default, WordPerfect uses a light shading, 10 percent of black.

After selecting this option, enter a value between 0 (no shading) and 100 (100 percent shading, which is black) and press ↵. You can then press Exit (**F7**) to return to Table Edit mode.

MANAGING TABLES

The remainder of this chapter discusses general topics concerning tables and how you use tables in combination with other features of WordPerfect. Chapter references to these related features are also provided.

HIDDEN CODES FOR TABLES

When you create a table, WordPerfect stores several hidden codes in the document, starting with [Tbl Def:] and ending with [Tbl Off]. Between these, the [Row] codes mark the beginning of a new row in the table, and the contents of a cell are preceded by the [Cell] code. All these codes, of course, are visible on the Reveal Codes screen.

Graphic boxes are covered in Chapter 19.

A cell cannot contain another table; that is, it cannot contain [Tbl Def:] and [Tbl Off] codes. But it can contain a code to display a graphic box that contains a table. So technically, it is possible to display a table within a table (though you may be hard-pressed to think of a practical application for this).

MOVING AND COPYING TABLES

Moving and copying within a document is covered in Chapter 2. Moving and copying between documents is covered in Chapter 3.

If you ever need to move or copy a table in a document, leave Table Edit mode, and turn on the Reveal Codes screen (press **Alt-F3** or **F11**). Then block the entire table (press **Alt-F4** or **F12**), including the [Table Def:] and [Tbl Off] codes that mark the beginning and end of the table. You can then move or copy the table as you would any other block of text, by selecting **E**dit ➤ **M**ove (**Ctrl-F4 B M**) or **E**dit ➤ **C**opy (**Ctrl-F4 B C**).

MOVING AND COPYING TEXT BETWEEN TABLES

If your document contains two or more tables, you can copy and move text between them quite easily. Move the cursor into the table that contains the text you want to copy or move, and go into Table Edit mode (select **L**ayout ➤ **T**ables ➤ **E**dit or press **Alt-F7**). Then block and copy or move the text in the first table, like this:

1. Block the text that you want to move or copy.

2. Press Move (**Ctrl-F4**), or click on Move on the Table Edit menu.

3. Select **B**lock.

4. Select **M**ove or **C**opy.

5. Press Exit (**F7**) to return to the Edit screen.

Now move the cursor into the cell in the other table where you want to copy or move the text to (i.e., the destination cell). Then go into Table Edit mode (select **L**ayout ➤ **T**ables ➤ **E**dit or press **Alt-F7**), and complete the move/copy, like this:

1. Press Move (**Ctrl-F4**), or click on Move on the Table Edit menu.

2. Select **R**etrieve.

3. Select **B**lock.

4. Press Exit (**F7**) to return to the Edit screen.

DELETING A TABLE

To delete an entire table, including all of its contents, follow the same techniques described above to block [Tbl Def:], [Tbl Off], and all the codes between. Then press **Delete** (Del), and press **Y** when asked for permission to delete the table.

CONVERTING A TABLE TO TEXT

You can use the Tables feature to organize your text, and then convert the table to standard text if you wish. This is sometimes handy when exporting a document to another word processor or typesetting machine that cannot interpret WordPerfect codes.

To convert a table to text, go into Reveal Codes (**Alt-F3** or **F11**), then delete the [Tbl Def:] code at the top of the table. WordPerfect immediately converts [Cell] codes to [Tab] codes, and the spacing of the table depends on the current tab settings. Most likely, you will need to change the tab settings above the text to get it properly aligned and to get exactly the spacing you want.

Changing tab settings is covered in Chapter 4.

Figure 6.22 shows an example where text was initially entered in a table. The middle example shows the table just after the [Tbl Def:] code was removed. The phone numbers are out of alignment because the current tab stops weren't properly set. The bottom example shows the table after the tab stops were changed to better align the text.

CONVERTING TEXT TO A TABLE

If you currently have text that is organized into columns with [Tab] codes and want to convert it to a table, follow these steps:

1. Move the cursor to the first character of text that you want to put into a table.

2. Turn on the Reveal Codes screen by selecting **E**dit ➤ **R**eveal Codes or by pressing **Alt-F3** or **F11**.

3. Select **E**dit ➤ **B**lock, or press Block (**Alt-F4** or **F12**).

4. Move the cursor to the [HRt] code after the last character of text that you want to put into the table. Make sure all of the text is highlighted

(on the upper screen) and that only the single, last [Hrt] code is highlighted (on the lower screen).

5. Select **L**ayout ➤ **T**ables ➤ **C**reate, or press **Alt-F7 T C**. You'll see this prompt:

   Create table from: **1** Tabular Column; **2** Parallel Column: **0**

6. If you are creating the table from text organized with tabs, select the first option. If you've defined parallel columns, select the second option.

NOTE *Tabs are covered in Chapter 4, parallel columns in Chapter 20.*

The table will be created and you'll be in Table Edit mode, where you can make changes if you wish.

The procedure can be tricky if you did not modify the tab ruler before initially typing your columnar table, because WordPerfect interprets each [Tab] (or similar) code as a cell when converting text to a table. For example,

A sample table...

Wanda Carneros	(123)555-0123
Tersha d'Elgin	(818)555-0987
Victoria Dumplin	(313)555-0385
Ambrose Pushnik	(714)555-5739
Frankly Unctuous	(414)555-0312

Same table as above after removing the [Tbl Def] code...

Wanda Carneros (123)555-0123
Tersha d'Elgin (818)555-0987
Victoria Dumplin (313)555-0385
Ambrose Pushnik (714)555-5739
Frankly Unctuous (414)555-0312

Same as above after changing the tab stops...

Wanda Carneros (123)555-0123
Tersha d'Elgin (818)555-0987
Victoria Dumplin (313)555-0385
Ambrose Pushnik (714)555-5739
Frankly Unctuous (414)555-0312

FIGURE 6.22: *Converting a table to text*

Figure 6.23 shows text on the Edit screen neatly arranged into columns. However, the original tab ruler was used, so in some cases it requires two or more [Tab] codes to move text over to the appropriate tab stop (as you can see on the Reveal Codes screen).

If you were to then highlight that block of text and create a table, you'd end up with a pretty messy table, as shown in Figure 6.24.

Rather than trying to fix the table, you'll probably find it easier to convert such a table back to text by deleting the [Tbl Def:] code that defines the table. Then remove any multiple [Tab] codes (on the Reveal Codes screen) so that only one [Tab] code separates each column. Next, move to the top of the columns and adjust the tabs (select **L**ayout ➤ **L**ine ➤ **T**ab Set or press **Shift-F8 L T**) so that the text is neatly aligned, as in Figure 6.25.

Now you can reblock the text you want to move into a table, and create a table. The result is a much neater and more manageable table, as shown in Figure 6.26.

MAKING MORE ROOM IN A TABLE

One of the most common problems with tables is simply not having enough space on the page to get all the information you need into the table. There

```
Item No.  Description           Size Qty  Price
BW-111    Boy's Bermuda Short   22   1    $29.95
BW-204    Boy's Tank Top        12   1    $19.95
BW-607    Boy's Polo Shirt      12   1    $24.95




                                    Doc 1 Pg 1 Ln 1" Pos 1"
[                                              }              
[Item No.[Tab]Description[Tab][Tab][Tab]Size[Tab]Qty[Tab]Price[HRt]
BW[-]111[Tab]Boy's Bermuda Short[Tab][Tab]22[Tab]1[Tab]$29.95[HRt]
BW[-]204[Tab]Boy's Tank Top[Tab][Tab][Tab]12[Tab]1[Tab]$19.95[HRt]
BW[-]607[Tab]Boy's Polo Shirt[Tab][Tab]12[Tab]1[Tab]$24.95[HRt]
[HRt]




Press Reveal Codes to restore screen
```

FIGURE 6.23:

Columns typed using the initial ½-inch tab stops

The results of convert-ing the text shown in Figure 6.23 to a table

```
It  Description        Siz  Qty  Price
em                     e
No
.

BW  Boy's Bermuda      22   1    $29.95
-   Short
11
1
                                      Doc 1 Pg 1 Ln 1" Pos 1"
{                                                    }
[HRt]
[Tbl Def:I;7,0.5",1.5",0.5",0.5",0.5",0.5",2.5"]
[Row][Cell]It[DSRt]
em[SRt]
No[DSRt]
.[Cell]Description[Cell][Cell][Cell]Siz[DSRt]
e[Cell]Qty[Cell]Price
[Row][Cell]BW[DSRt]
[-]
11[DSRt]

Press Reveal Codes to restore screen
```

The text shown in Fig-ure 6.23 after removing multiple [Tab] codes and adjusting the tab ruler

```
Item No.  Description        Size   Qty   Price
BW-111    Boy's Bermuda Short 22    1     $29.95
BW-204    Boy's Tank Top      12    1     $19.95
BW-607    Boy's Polo Shirt    12    1     $24.95




                                      Doc 1 Pg 1 Ln 1" Pos 1"
{                                                    ]
[Tab Set:Rel; -1",-0.5",0",+0.908",+3",+3.72",+4.45",+5.45"]Item No.[Tab]Descrip
tion[Tab]Size[Tab]Qty[Tab]Price[HRt]
BW[-]111[Tab]Boy's Bermuda Short[Tab]22[Tab]1[Tab]$29.95[HRt]
BW[-]204[Tab]Boy's Tank Top[Tab]12[Tab]1[Tab]$19.95[HRt]
BW[-]607[Tab]Boy's Polo Shirt[Tab]12[Tab]1[Tab]$24.95[HRt]




Press Reveal Codes to restore screen
```

are four ways to solve this problem, and you can choose any one, or any combination:

◆ Change the base font to a smaller point size (see Chapter 5) just to the left of the [Table Def] code. The entire table will use the base font, so more characters can fit into each cell.

◆ If your printer can do it, print the table sideways on the page by changing the paper size/type code to landscape format (Chapter 7). After you've changed the paper size, you can add more columns to the new page width or widen existing columns.

◆ Reduce the left and right spacing between text and lines on the Table Options menu (described earlier in this chapter).

◆ Reduce the left and right margins just above the table so that the table is printed within the narrower margins.

Of the four options, printing the table sideways on the page, in landscape format, gives you the greatest overall width without reducing the type size.

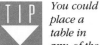

*You could place a table in **any** of the graphic boxes shown in Figure 6.27, as you'll learn in Chapter 19.*

WRAPPING TEXT AROUND A TABLE

If you want to print a table so that text wraps around it, or if you want to display two or more tables side by side, you must place the table in a graphic

---

Item No.	Description	Size	Qty	Price
BW-111	Boy's Bermuda Short	22	1	$29.95
BW-204	Boy's Tank Top	12	1	$19.95
BW-607	Boy's Polo Shirt	12	1	$24.95

```
                                          Doc 1 Pg 1 Ln 1" Pos 1"
[                                                                    ]
[Tab Set:Rel; -1",-0.5",0",+0.908",+3",+3.72",+4.45",+5.45"][HRt]
[Tbl Def:I;5,1.01",2.72",0.727",0.999",1.05"]
[Row][Cell]Item No.[Cell]Description[Cell]Size[Cell]Qty[Cell]Price
[Row][Cell]BW-]111[Cell]Boy's Bermuda Short[Cell]22[Cell]1[Cell]$29.95
[Row][Cell]BW-]204[Cell]Boy's Tank Top[Cell]12[Cell]1[Cell]$19.95
[Row][Cell]BW-]607[Cell]Boy's Polo Shirt[Cell]12[Cell]1[Cell]$24.95
[Tbl Off][HRt]



Press Reveal Codes to restore screen
```

FIGURE 6.26:

The results of converting the text shown in Figure 6.25 to a table

box. For example, the table in the lower-right corner of Figure 6.27 is in a page-anchored graphic box, so text and columns outside the box flow around it.

In Part 6, you'll learn how to create more complex documents like the one shown in Figure 6.27.

FIGURE 6.27:

A table in a graphic box in the lower-right corner of a sample document

Examples of Graphic Boxes

CHECK BOX
We start with a small graphic image that is anchored to this paragraph (the box's hidden code is just before the first character of this paragraph.

The box is sized small, and the text of the paragraph wraps around it.

DIPLOMA
Another case for anchoring a figure to a paragraph is when you want a figure to closely follow its callout in text.

For example, Figure 1 shows a diploma. To keep that figure near, but below, it's anchored to the top of the next paragraph. Its width is the full width of this column.

Figure 1.

Because the box is as wide as this column, no text wraps around the side of the box.

TEXT BOX
The text box in the center of the page is anchored to the page. Its hidden code is at the top of the page. All text wraps around it. Page anchoring is the only way to create boxes that cross columns.

TABLE BOX
The Table box in the lower right corner of the page is

WordPerfect has lots of tools for aligning graphic boxes in columns

also anchored to the page (bottom right corner). Page anchoring was required here because we needed the table to be wider than one column.

FOOTER
The star symbol at the lower left corner of the page is actually in a footer. It's character-anchored, because that's the

only anchor type allowed in headers and footers.

IN-LINE GRAPHIC
Next we have a small graphic mouse ✎ in text. The mouse graphic is in a character anchored User Box, and is sized small enough to fit on a line of text.

Small character-anchored graphics like that can be used as icons in text, margins, or in margin notes -- or perhaps for amusing pictures in children's books.

COLUMNS & LINES
The columns in this example are newspaper columns with a distance of .4" between them. Chapter 20 discusses multi-column layouts in detail.

The lines are all graphic lines with the Graphics ▶ Line menu options.

The table below shows the Column (horizontal) and Vertical position, as the length, of each vertical line.

Line	1st	2nd	3rd	4th
Column	1	2	1	2
Vertical	1.51	1.51	6.35	6.35
Length	2.63	2.63	3.45	2.08

PREVENTING PAGE BREAKS

If you want to ensure that a small table is never split across two pages in your document, your best bet is to place the table in a graphic box (see Chapter 19) and reference the table by its number. This is the most common method used in larger documents; for example, the text may refer the reader to "Table 2.1," and Table 2.1 is placed as close to the reference as possible, without being split across two pages.

REFERENCING TABLES AUTOMATICALLY

 *You'll learn about automatic referencing in Chapter 23.*

The other advantage of placing tables in graphic boxes is that you can use *automatic referencing*: If you add or delete a table, all the table numbers are automatically adjusted, as are the references in text to those tables. So you don't need to manually renumber all the tables and the references to them.

SORTING OR ALPHABETIZING TEXT IN A TABLE

If you want to sort (or alphabetize) the contents of a table, use the sorting and selecting options discussed in Chapter 17.

CREATING ADVANCED DOCUMENTS

The Tables feature is a great tool for typing text into tables, but as you've seen, it's also a great tool for typing any kind of multicolumn text, such as the sample itinerary shown earlier in this chapter. With a little ingenuity, you can use the Tables feature to create some extraordinary documents, such as those normally produced by graphic arts departments. The next few sections present some examples that you can use as "food for thought," if you're so motivated, in creating your own advanced documents.

CALENDAR

The school lunch calendar shown in Figure 6.28 was created using Tables. All the cells in the top row are joined (**Join ➤ Yes** on the Table Edit menu), and the month name (November) is centered and displayed in a 30-point font with small caps. Each day name is centered and italicized in its cell.

Within each day, the day number is presented in a 20-point bold, italic, Univers font (similar to Helvetica). Pressing ↵ after typing the day number moves the cursor down a line. Then you can type in the two lines of text in each cell, using the Center key (Shift-F6) to center each line and ↵ to end the first line.

ORG CHART

Tables are a great way to create org (organizational) charts, like the one shown in Figure 6.29. Figure 6.30 shows the org chart after joining and filling cells, but before removing any lines.

Notice in the bottom row of the org chart that you need to join a pair of cells to create one box. This is necessary to get the centered vertical line to come out of the top of the box. You also need at least one blank cell separating each box. The drop-shadow appearance of the topmost cell was created by setting the top and left lines to Single, and the right and bottom lines to Thick.

PROGRESS CHART

Figure 6.31 shows a progress chart created with the Tables feature. The chart is printed sideways on the page (landscape format), as discussed in Chapter 7. Figure 6.32 shows the chart before removing any lines from the table.

NOVEMBER						
Sun	Mon	Tue	Wed	Thu	Fri	Sat
				1 Hot dogs n' bananas	**2** Peaches in spinach	**3**
4	**5** Ice cream pasta	**6** Vermicious Knids	**7** Homemade Wangdoodle	**8** Liver and Jujubes	**9** Sweet n' Sour sundae	**10**
11	**12** Deep fried loquat	**13** Pepperoni in potatoes	**14** Macaroni n' liverwurst	**15** Marshmallows in pea soup	**16** Cosmic Sustenance	**17**
18	**19** Day-old nachos	**20** M&M's in Brie cheese	**21** Mushrooms in caramel sauce	**22** MSG-caked doughnuts	**23** Cream puff on a stick	**24**
25	**26** Peanut butter n' bacon bits	**27** Steamed head cheese	**28** Big Hunk omelette	**29** Wholly Macaroni	**30** Cajun-style caviar	

FIGURE 6.28:

A sample calendar created with the Tables feature

Two basic tricks were used to create the progress chart. First, every other row, starting at the second row, was narrowed to 0.1" inch by selecting **F**ormat ➤ **R**ow Height ➤ **F**ixed on the Table Edit menu. This was necessary to reduce the gap between the bars in the chart.

To draw the bars, I first used **O**ptions ➤ **G**ray Shading from the Table Edit menu to set the gray shade to 100 percent (pure black), then used blocking and **L**ines ➤ **S**hade ➤ **O**n to draw the bars.

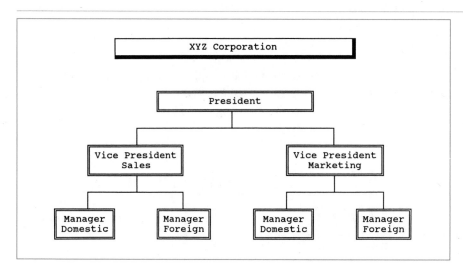

FIGURE 6.29:

A sample org chart

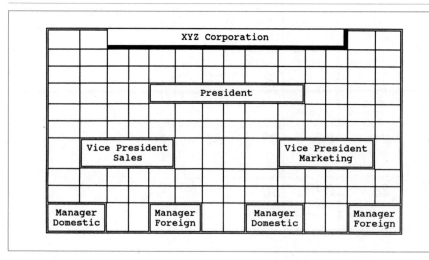

FIGURE 6.30:

The org chart before removing table lines

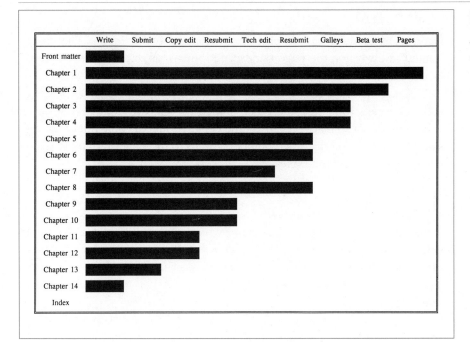

FIGURE 6.31:

A sample progress chart created with Tables

	Write	Submit	Copy edit	Resubmit	Tech edit	Resubmit	Galleys	Beta test	Pages	
Front matter	■									
Chapter 1										
Chapter 2										
Chapter 3										
Chapter 4										
Chapter 5										
Chapter 6										
Chapter 7										
Chapter 8										
Chapter 9										
Chapter 10										
Chapter 11										
Chapter 12										
Chapter 13										
Chapter 14										
Index										

FIGURE 6.32:

The progress chart before removing table lines

PLAY-OFF CHART

Figure 6.33 shows a sample play-off chart created with Tables. The chart is printed sideways on the page (landscape format), as discussed in Chapter 7. Figure 6.34 shows the chart before removing any table lines.

The general design of the play-off chart is fairly simple; each box is actually two cells (one atop the other) joined by selecting **J**oin ➤ **Y**es on the Table Edit menu so that you can get the centered line to come out of the right side of the box. You need two empty columns to the right of a box to get the lines needed to join the boxes.

FILL-IN FORMS

Tables are also great for creating your own company fill-in forms, like the invoice shown in Figure 6.35. This invoice is actually a collection of three tables on a single page, as you can see in Figure 6.36. That figure shows the invoice after joining cells and filling them with text, but before shading cells and removing table lines.

Actually, one of the trickiest parts of creating this form was getting the company name and address to align next to the table. To accomplish that, the text

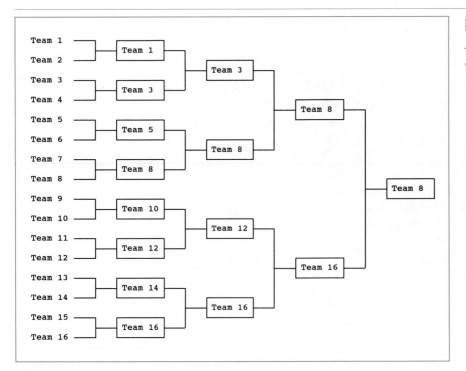

FIGURE 6.33:

A sample play-off chart created with Tables

was put in a User box (Chapter 19) that was anchored to the upper-right corner of the page, with Wrap Text Around Box set to No.

TEXT FRAMES

Figure 6.37 shows an example from the menu of a Mexican fast-food stand—framed text with the lines running into the title. Figure 6.38 shows the menu before removing table lines and changing the fonts.

Notice how the table started out as three columns (across the bottom row). To get the run-in line effect, I had to split the top two rows into three columns each, then join the vertical pair of cells in the middle. Then I typed the title into this joined cell (e.g., "Burritos") and centered it vertically within its cell (**F**ormat ➤ **C**ell ➤ **V**ertical Alignment ➤ **C**enter from the Table Edit menu). You may need to experiment with the column widths to get the run-in lines the desired distance from the text.

Team 1				
	Team 1			
Team 2				
		Team 3		
Team 3				
	Team 3			
Team 4				
			Team 8	
Team 5				
	Team 5			
Team 6				
		Team 8		
Team 7				
	Team 8			
Team 8				
				Team 8
Team 9				
	Team 10			
Team 10				
		Team 12		
Team 11				
	Team 12			
Team 12				
			Team 16	
Team 13				
	Team 14			
Team 14				
		Team 16		
Team 15				
	Team 16			
Team 16				

FIGURE 6.34: *The play-off chart before removing any table lines*

I typed the dot leaders in the lower cells by pressing Flush Right (Alt-F6) twice. I typed the indents by pressing Home Tab (described earlier in this chapter).

The Tables feature is so powerful, and so useful, that it's practically a product in itself. And we haven't even touched on its math capabilities (Chapter 18), which are perfect for typing financial reports, invoices, and more.

A sample fill-in form created with Tables

In Chapter 7, you'll learn about some general techniques for formatting pages and entire documents, including numbering pages, printing headers and footers on every page, printing on nonstandard paper sizes (such as labels and envelopes), and much more.

The fill-in form before removing lines from the three tables

Burritos		Tacos	
Carne Asada	**$2.40**	**Folded:**	
Machaca	**$2.10**	**1 Beef**	**$1.60**
Chorizo	**$2.10**	**1 Chicken**	**$1.60**
Mixed	**$2.10**	**1 Carne Asada** . . .	**$2.00**
Beef	**$2.00**	**Rolled:**	
Chicken	**$2.00**	**1 Rolled Taco**	**$ .50**
Bean	**$1.60**	**w/ Guacamole**	**$ .60**
		3 Plain w/ Cheese	**$1.30**
		w/ Guacamole	**$1.80**

A sample menu

Burritos			Tacos	
Carne Asada	$2.40		Folded:	
Machaca	$2.10		1 Beef	$1.60
Chorizo	$2.10		1 Chicken	$1.60
Mixed	$2.10		1 Carne Asada . . .	$2.00
Beef	$2.00		Rolled:	
Chicken	$2.00		1 Rolled Taco . . .	$ .50
Bean	$1.60		w/ Guacamole .	$ .60
			3 Plain w/ Cheese .	$1.30
			w/ Guacamole .	$1.80

The sample menu before removing table lines and changing fonts

CHAPTER 7

Formatting Your Pages

hapter 4 introduced several features that control the general appearance of text on a page, including indenting and aligning text, and setting margins. This chapter discusses additional ways to format your printed pages, particularly when you have documents that are more than a page or two in length. Topics include creating title pages, numbering pages, controlling how and when WordPerfect starts printing on a new page, protecting certain blocks of text from being split across two pages, and using nonstandard paper sizes like envelopes, mailing labels, and more.

VERTICAL CENTERING

TO VERTICALLY CENTER ALL THE TEXT ON A PAGE,

1. Move the cursor to the top of the page.

2. Select Layout ➤ Page ➤ Center Page ➤ Yes (or press Shift-F8 P C Y).

> ### 3. Press Exit (F7). If necessary, move the cursor to the end of the page and insert a hard page break (Ctrl-↵).

Title pages and some other documents often require that text be centered both horizontally (from left to right) and vertically (from top to bottom) on the page. Figure 7.1 shows an example in which the text on a title page is centered both horizontally and vertically.

To center text vertically on the page, you can use the Center Page option on the Format: Page menu. Follow these steps:

You've already seen how to center-justify text horizontally in Chapter 4.

1. Move the cursor to the top of the page where you want to center text vertically (the cursor must precede all text on that page).

2. Select **Layout ➤ P**age (or press **Shift-F8 P**), which takes you to the Format: Page menu shown in Figure 7.2.

3. Select **C**enter Page (top to bottom).

4. Select **Y**es.

5. Press Exit (**F7**).

Vertical centering affects all the text on the current page only; it is typically used to center all the text on a title page (though it can be used to center text on any single page that would look better with identical top and bottom margins, such as very brief letters, memos, invitations, and so forth).

To prevent text beyond the title page from being vertically centered, add a hard page break (discussed under "Starting Text on a New Page" below) just below the last line of text on the title page.

As with most page-formatting features, vertical centering will not be obvious on your Edit screen. To see it, you'll need to switch to the View Document screen (**Shift-F8 V**) or print your document.

UNCENTERING A CENTERED PAGE

If you change your mind about centering the text on a page, move the cursor to the top of the page, turn on the Reveal Codes screen (press **Alt-F3** or **F11**), and delete the [Center Pg] code that's centering the text.

STARTING TEXT ON A NEW PAGE

TO INSERT A HARD PAGE BREAK,

position the cursor and press Ctrl-↵.

A sample page with text centered horizontally and vertically

```
                    ALL-AMERICAN LIFE


        A Flexible Premium Life Insurance Policy




                    Issued by:


        PREMIUM LIFE INSURANCE COMPANY
           1234 Avenue of the Americas
              New York, NY   10019
                 (800)555-1234




        Supplement Dated August 30, 1990

                      to

        Prospectus Dated June 1, 1990
```

WordPerfect breaks a long document into separate pages automatically. That is, as you type beyond the length of a page, WordPerfect inserts a *soft page break,* which appears on the screen as a long dashed line. It's called a soft page break because WordPerfect can automatically adjust it as you add and delete text in your document. For example, if you add another paragraph to a page that is already filled with text, WordPerfect will automatically move some of the text on the current page down to the next page.

For the most part, you should allow WordPerfect to handle page breaks automatically—this gives you the most flexibility for adding and deleting text in a long document. However, in some situations, you may want to force WordPerfect to start a new page at a certain point in your document. For example, if your document starts with a title page, any text that you type beneath the title page should start on a new page.

To force WordPerfect to start printing on a new page, you need to insert a *hard page break:*

1. Position the cursor where you want to end the current page.

2. Press **Ctrl-⏎**.

You will see a long string of equal signs indicating where the page will break, as in the example in Figure 7.3. As you move the cursor above or below the hard page break, using the usual arrow keys, the status line will show the page number that the cursor is on.

```
Format: Page

    1 - Center Page (top to bottom)      No

    2 - Force Odd/Even Page

    3 - Headers

    4 - Footers

    5 - Margins - Top                     1"
                  Bottom                  1"

    6 - Page Numbering

    7 - Paper Size                        8.5" x 11"
                  Type                    Standard

    8 - Suppress (this page only)




Selection: 0
```

FIGURE 7.2:

The Format: Page menu

On the Reveal Codes screen, a soft page break appears as [SPg], and a hard page break appears as [HPg]. You never need to delete a soft page break.

DELETING A HARD PAGE BREAK

If you change your mind about a hard page break, you can delete the [HPg] code that's forcing the page break from the Reveal Codes screen.

OTHER LINE AND PAGE BREAK CODES

While I'm on the subject of codes, I might as well briefly mention a few of the more obscure codes that you might discover on the Reveal Codes screen. WordPerfect automatically takes care of creating these codes and converting them into other types of codes when necessary, so you needn't be too concerned about them. The codes are the following:

[DSRt]: A *deletable soft return* is inserted when automatic hyphenation is turned off and WordPerfect needs to break a word that's wider than the margins (or column). You'll learn about hyphenation in Chapter 11.

[HRt-SPg]: This code will appear if a soft-page code [SPg] was originally a hard-return code [HRt].

[Dorm HRt]: A *dormant hard return* is created automatically when a hard-return [HRt] code appears alone on a line at the top of a page that is started by a soft page break [SPg]. WordPerfect creates this

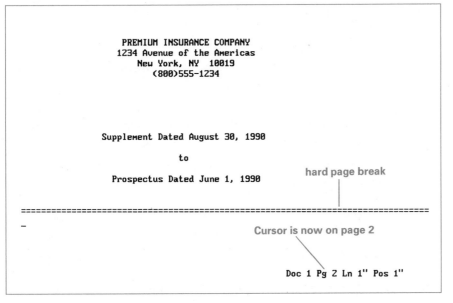

FIGURE 7.3:

A hard page break at the bottom of a title page

PREMIUM INSURANCE COMPANY
1234 Avenue of the Americas
New York, NY 10019
(800)555-1234

Supplement Dated August 30, 1990

to

Prospectus Dated June 1, 1990

hard page break

Cursor is now on page 2

Doc 1 Pg 2 Ln 1" Pos 1"

code to prevent unwanted blank lines at the top of a page and will change the code back to [HRt] if it moves from the top of the page as a result of text being added or removed above it.

AUTOMATIC PAGE NUMBERING

TO ACTIVATE AUTOMATIC PAGE NUMBERING,

position the cursor at the top of the page where page numbers should begin printing, then select Layout ➤ Page ➤ Page Numbering ➤ Page Number Position (or press Shift-F8 P N P), and any one of the nine suggested positions.

You'll need to print the document or go to the View Document screen to see the page numbers.

You never need to type page numbers in a WordPerfect document because WordPerfect can number the pages for you automatically. The beauty of automatic page numbering is that no matter how much text you add, change, or delete in a document, the page numbers will always be in proper sequence and in the right place on each printed page.

As you may have guessed by now, WordPerfect uses hidden codes to control page numbering. Therefore, before selecting the menu options to display the page numbers, be sure to position the cursor at the top of the first page (before any text on that page) where you want page numbering to start.

POSITIONING THE PAGE NUMBERS

You can also place page numbers in headers or footers, as described a little later in this chapter.

You can have WordPerfect display page numbers anywhere in your printed document. To print page numbers, follow these steps:

1. Move the cursor to the top of the page (before any text) where you want page numbers to start. For example, to start numbering from the first page of a document, press **Home Home ↑**.

2. Select **Layout ➤ Page ➤ Page Numbering** (or press **Shift-F8 P N**).

3. Select Page Number **P**osition.

4. Select an option in the range 1 to 9 from the screen that appears (Figure 7.4) by typing the option number.

5. Press Exit (**F7**).

When you select Page Numbering, the options shown in Figure 7.4 appear on your screen. Options 1, 2, 3, 5, 6, and 7 let you place the number in the same place on each printed page. For example, if you select 1 (by typing the number *1*), the page number will appear in the upper-left corner of each printed page. If you select 6 (by typing the number *6*), the page number will be centered at the bottom of each page.

Options 4 and 8 are for placing page numbers on alternating pages. These are used in documents that are bound like a book. If you select option 4, the page number appears in the upper-left corner of even-numbered pages and in the upper-right corner of odd-numbered pages. If you select 8, the page number appears in the lower-left corner of even-numbered pages and in the lower-right corner of odd-numbered pages. Option 9 (**N**o Page Numbers) omits page numbers for the current page and all pages that follow.

RESTARTING THE PAGE-NUMBERING SEQUENCE

Normally WordPerfect automatically keeps track of page numbers based on the order in which they will be printed, with the first page being page 1. However, you might need a different starting page number.

Front matter *is any material that precedes the main text of a book.*

For example, if your document begins with a title page and other front matter, you don't normally number those pages. Instead, page 1 is probably the first page of body text (e.g., the first page of Chapter 1), even though that page is not actually the first page that's printed.

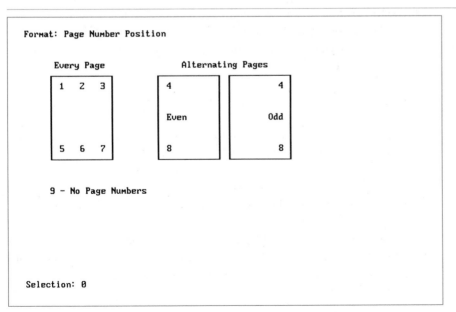

```
Format: Page Number Position


    Every Page               Alternating Pages

    ┌─────────────┐      ┌─────────────┐  ┌─────────────┐
    │ 1   2   3   │      │ 4           │  │           4 │
    │             │      │             │  │             │
    │             │      │ Even        │  │        Odd  │
    │             │      │             │  │             │
    │ 5   6   7   │      │ 8           │  │           8 │
    └─────────────┘      └─────────────┘  └─────────────┘


    9 - No Page Numbers






  Selection: 0
```

Options for placing page numbers on printed pages

Therefore, if you turn on page numbering on the third page of the document, its page number will still be 3. (In other words, WordPerfect knows that this is the third printed page, even though you did not print page numbers on any of the preceding pages.) To get around this problem, you need to restart the page number sequence. Here's how:

1. Move the cursor to the top of the page where you want to change the page-numbering sequence (before any text on that page).

2. Select **Layout** ➤ **Page** ➤ Page **Numbering** ➤ **New** Page Number (or press **Shift-F8 P N N**).

3. Type the new page number for the current page and press ↵.

4. Press Exit (**F7**).

Page numbering will start at whatever number you entered in step 3, and all subsequent pages will be numbered accordingly (assuming, of course, that you also remember to turn on page numbering so that the page numbers are printed).

Using Roman Numerals for Page Numbers

If you want to see an example of Roman-numbered pages, look through the first few pages of this book.

You can number your WordPerfect documents with Roman numerals (e.g., *i, ii, iii*) instead of the usual Arabic numbers (e.g., *1, 2, 3*). Just follow the steps described in the preceding section "Restarting the Page-Numbering Sequence," but type the starting Roman numeral page number in step 3 above.

For example, if you enter *i* as the starting page number for a page, Word-Perfect will automatically number that page as *i* and the pages that follow as *ii, iii, iv, v,* and so forth.

CHANGING THE APPEARANCE OF PAGE NUMBERS

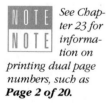

See Chapter 23 for information on printing dual page numbers, such as **Page 2 of 20.**

You can change the style of page numbers to include other characters. For example, you can print page numbers in the format *Page 1* or *-1-*. To do this, you need to press **Ctrl-B**, which shows up as ∧*B* on the Edit and Reveal Codes screens, to indicate exactly where you want the page number to appear. That is, the first example would be represented as *Page ∧B,* and the second would be *-∧B-.*

Be sure to include blank spaces if required. For example, if you type *Page* and then press Ctrl-B (without pressing the spacebar to separate the two), your page-numbering style will appear as *Page∧B* on the Page Numbering screen and *Page1* on the first printed page or the View Document screen.

The maximum length of the text and page number is 30 characters. You can include special characters entered with Compose (Ctrl-2), as described in Chapter 5.

The steps to follow are listed below (assuming that you've already specified that page numbers should be printed, as discussed earlier):

1. Position the cursor at the top of the page where you want the new page-numbering style to start (before any text on that page).

2. Select **L**ayout ➤ **P**age ➤ Page **N**umbering ➤ Page Number **S**tyle (or press **Shift-F8 P N S**).

3. Type in your page-numbering style, remembering to press Ctrl-B where you want the actual page number to appear—for example, *-^B-* or *Page ^B*, where the *^B* is typed by pressing Ctrl-B.

4. Press ↵.

5. Press Exit (**F7**).

 If you forget to include Ctrl-B in your page-numbering style, WordPerfect adds it to the end of your text automatically, without inserting a blank space.

WordPerfect will add a hidden [Pg Num Style:] code to your document at the cursor position. As usual, if you change your mind about the new page-numbering style, or you end up with competing codes, you can use the Reveal Codes screen to delete the hidden code.

PRINTING A PAGE NUMBER IN TEXT

If you want to print the current page number somewhere within the body of your text (as opposed to above or below the text), press Ctrl-B wherever you want the page number to appear. For example, suppose you want to include the line

This page (24) intentionally left blank

in a document, but want to ensure that the page number shown in parentheses was indeed the current page number, regardless of any later editing.

To do so, position the cursor wherever you want that line of text to appear, type *This page (*, press Ctrl-B, and type *) intentionally left blank.*

You can also insert the page number at the current cursor position by selecting **L**ayout ➤ **P**age ➤ Page **N**umbering ➤ **I**nsert Page Number (or by pressing **Shift-F8 P N I**). Whichever method you choose, WordPerfect displays *^B* on the Edit screen as the page number (again, just switch to the View Document screen to see the actual page number).

HIDING THE PAGE NUMBER ON A PAGE

In some situations, you might not want to print the page number on a specific page in a document. For example, you might want to omit the number from a page that shows a full-page illustration. To hide the page number on a particular page, without disrupting the page-numbering sequence, follow these steps:

1. Move the cursor to the top of the page where you want to hide the page number (before any text on that page).

2. Select **L**ayout ➤ **P**age ➤ **Su**ppress (this page only), or press **Shift-F8 P U**.

3. Select Suppress **P**age Numbering.

4. Select **Y**es.

5. Press Exit (**F7**).

The page number will be deleted from the current page, but subsequent pages will be numbered in correct sequence.

PRINTING PAGE HEADERS AND FOOTERS

TO PRINT A PAGE HEADER OR FOOTER ON PRINTED PAGES IN A DOCUMENT,

1. **Position the cursor at the top of the page where you want the headers or footers to start.**

2. **Select Layout ➤ Page (or press Shift-F8 P).**

3. **Choose either Headers or Footers, either A or B, and the frequency of the header or footer.**

4. **Create the header or footer. Press Exit (F7) twice when you're finished to return to the Edit screen.**

NOTE NOTE *You will see page headers and footers when you print the document and on the View Document screen, but not on the normal Edit screen. The hidden codes are [Header A:], [Header B:], [Footer A:], and [Footer B:].*

With WordPerfect, you can define a *page header,* which is printed automatically at the top of printed pages, and a *page footer,* which is printed automatically at the bottom of printed pages. If you've ever had to type a document where you needed to include a header and footer on every page, you're sure to love this feature, because you only have to type the header or footer once. From that point on, WordPerfect will print it on every page (or alternating pages, if you request it), regardless of whether you add or delete paragraphs.

To add an extra blank line after a graphic line, as in Figure 7.5, create the graphic line, then press ↵ once for each line you want. If you want to use a graphic box in a header or footer, anchor the box to a character (Chapter 19).

Page headers and footers can be any length, but generally one or two lines are sufficient, since you'll rarely need to repeat several lines of text on every page in a document. You can also include page numbers, the current date, lines, special characters, graphic boxes, and other formatting features in a header or footer. Figure 7.5 shows an example where the header has a graphic line at the bottom, and the footer has one at the top, to better set off the header and footer from the rest of the text.

You might want to print different headers and footers on alternating pages. For example, you might want to print Header A on even-numbered pages and Header B on odd-numbered pages. This is the standard format used in books and other documents. Figure 7.6 shows two pages from a sample document with this header format.

CREATING A PAGE HEADER

*Alternating right and left page headers are sometimes called the **recto head** and **verso head** in publishing. **Recto** means "right," **verso** means "left."*

The steps for adding a page header to a document are listed below:

1. Move the cursor to the top of the page where you want the header to start printing (before any text on that page).

2. Select **L**ayout ➤ **P**age ➤ **H**eaders, or press **Shift-F8 P H**.

3. Select Header **A**.

4. Select Every **P**age to print the header on every page, or **O**dd Pages to print the header on odd-numbered pages only, or E**v**en Pages to print the header on even-numbered pages only.

5. You will see a blank Edit screen with the message

   Header A: Press Exit when done

6. Type the header, which can contain up to a page of text. You can design your page header by using any of the techniques available at the Edit screen, including the Center (Shift-F6) and Flush Right (Alt-F6) keys to align text, Line Draw (**T**ools ➤ **L**ine Draw or Ctrl-F3 L), graphic lines (**G**raphics ➤ **L**ine or Alt-F9 L), Compose (Ctrl-2) for special characters, and any size, appearance, or base-font options on the F**o**nt pull-down menu (Ctrl-F8). If you want to include a page number, position the cursor where you want the page number to appear and press **Ctrl-B**.

7. If you want to print more than one blank line beneath the header, press ↵ once for each additional blank line.

8. Press Exit (**F7**) when you've finished typing the header.

If you print A and B on every page, they may print over one another, unless you align text in each header.

If you want to create a second header, select **H**eaders again and select Header **B**. Repeat the steps for selecting a position for the header (e.g., odd-numbered pages or even-numbered pages). Then type the second header, and press Exit (**F7**). When you've finished typing your header (or headers), press Exit (**F7**) to return to the Edit screen.

Thatcher History   First Draft

    The British Conservative Party has been in trouble as of late. Their woes appear related to their leadership crisis. Margaret Thatcher has been a dynamic Prime Minister in her years in office. However, it is this uncompromising nature of hers which has been as a spot on an otherwise spotless career. Lately this attitude has cost her dearly with back benchers and cabinet members alike. Her "public approval rating at 24% is lower than any other Prime Minister since the polling has been conducted."

    With the Conservative Party running 19 percentage points behind Labour, questions have arisen as to which direction the Tory Party should take, more precisely who shall be chosen as its director. However, neither will out-and-out declare their candidacy in fear that voters would see it as back-stabbing the "Iron Lady." They too fear a confrontation with Thatcher herself. "When Maggy bites she finds it a bit rough to let go."

    In estimating these possible candidates chances of gaining the Tory leadership, it is first important to demonstrate there is a crisis which would, or rather could, dictate a change in leadership. Thus, it must be shown that Margaret Thatcher does not have a monopoly on Tory future leadership. One member of Parliament was quoted as saying, "In '84 she could have pushed

---

Date Printed: August 16, 1991   Page: 6
File Name: Thatcher.wp

FIGURE 7.5:

A sample page header and footer with graphic lines

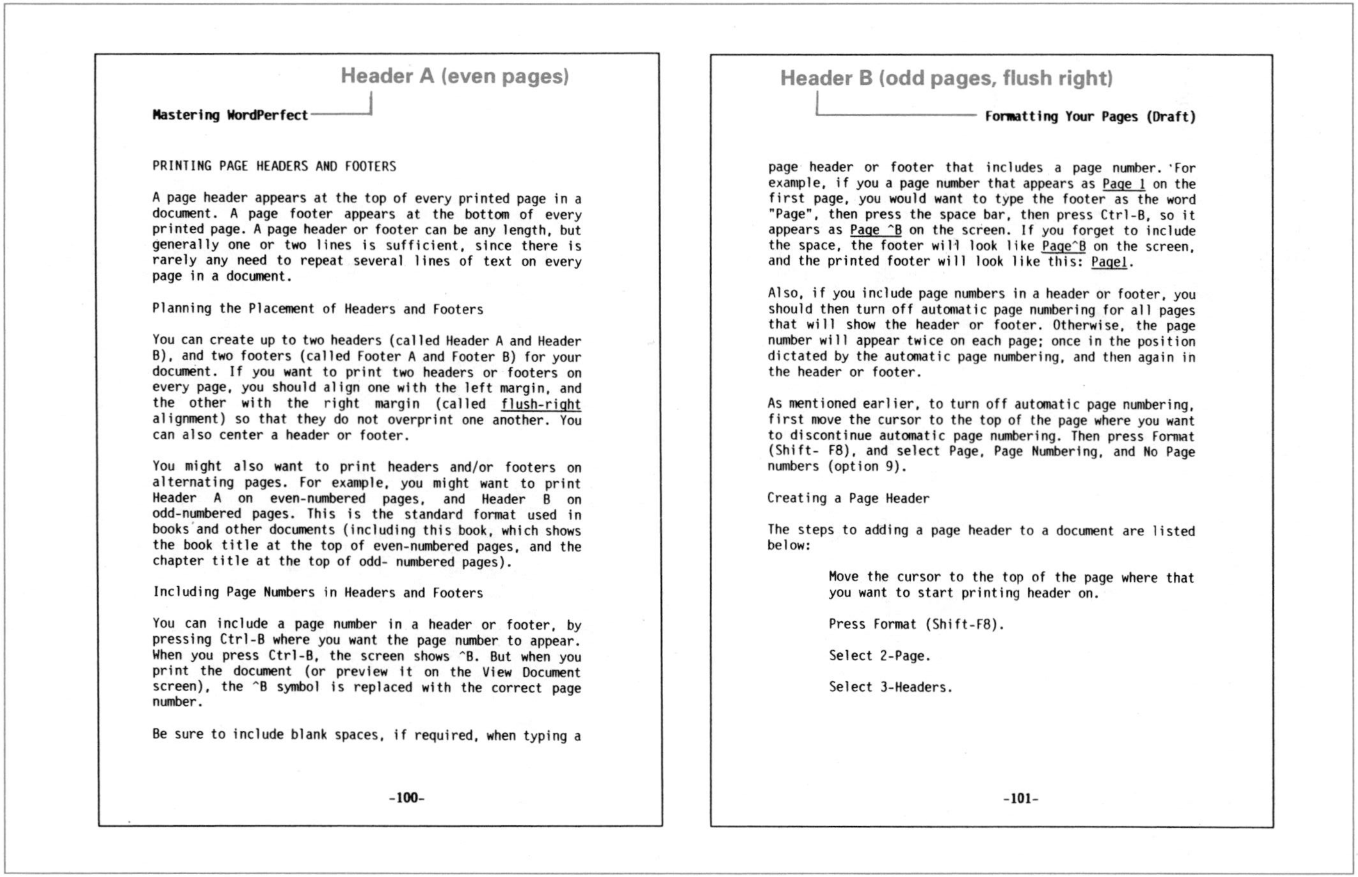

Header A (even pages)

Mastering WordPerfect

PRINTING PAGE HEADERS AND FOOTERS

A page header appears at the top of every printed page in a document. A page footer appears at the bottom of every printed page. A page header or footer can be any length, but generally one or two lines is sufficient, since there is rarely any need to repeat several lines of text on every page in a document.

Planning the Placement of Headers and Footers

You can create up to two headers (called Header A and Header B), and two footers (called Footer A and Footer B) for your document. If you want to print two headers or footers on every page, you should align one with the left margin, and the other with the right margin (called flush-right alignment) so that they do not overprint one another. You can also center a header or footer.

You might also want to print headers and/or footers on alternating pages. For example, you might want to print Header A on even-numbered pages, and Header B on odd-numbered pages. This is the standard format used in books and other documents (including this book), which shows the book title at the top of even-numbered pages, and the chapter title at the top of odd-numbered pages).

Including Page Numbers in Headers and Footers

You can include a page number in a header or footer, by pressing Ctrl-B where you want the page number to appear. When you press Ctrl-B, the screen shows ^B. But when you print the document (or preview it on the View Document screen), the ^B symbol is replaced with the correct page number.

Be sure to include blank spaces, if required, when typing a

-100-

Header B (odd pages, flush right)

Formatting Your Pages (Draft)

page header or footer that includes a page number. For example, if you a page number that appears as Page 1 on the first page, you would want to type the footer as the word "Page", then press the space bar, then press Ctrl-B, so it appears as Page ^B on the screen. If you forget to include the space, the footer will look like Page^B on the screen, and the printed footer will look like this: Page1.

Also, if you include page numbers in a header or footer, you should then turn off automatic page numbering for all pages that will show the header or footer. Otherwise, the page number will appear twice on each page; once in the position dictated by the automatic page numbering, and then again in the header or footer.

As mentioned earlier, to turn off automatic page numbering, first move the cursor to the top of the page where you want to discontinue automatic page numbering. Then press Format (Shift-F8), and select Page, Page Numbering, and No Page Numbers (option 9).

Creating a Page Header

The steps to adding a page header to a document are listed below:

Move the cursor to the top of the page where that you want to start printing header on.

Press Format (Shift-F8).

Select 2-Page.

Select 3-Headers.

-101-

FIGURE 7.6:

Two different headers, one for even-numbered pages and one for odd-numbered pages

CREATING A PAGE FOOTER

The steps for creating page footers are almost identical to those for creating page headers; the only real difference is that you choose *Footers* instead of *Headers* on the Format: Page menu.

1. Move the cursor to the top of the page where you want the footer to start printing (before any text on that page).

2. Select **L**ayout ➤ **P**age ➤ **F**ooters, or press **Shift-F8 P F**.

3. Select Footer **A**.

4. Select Every **P**age to print the footer on every page, or **O**dd Pages to print the footer on odd-numbered pages only, or E**v**en Pages to print the footer on even-numbered pages only.

5. You will see a blank Edit screen with the message

   Footer A: Press Exit when done

6. If you want to print more than one blank line between your text and the page footer, press ↵ once for each blank line you want printed.

7. Type your footer, using any of the Edit screen techniques described under page headers to format the text. As with headers, footers can contain up to a page of text.

8. Press Exit (**F7**) when you've finished typing the footer.

If you want to create a second footer, select **F**ooters again and select Footer **B**. Repeat the steps for selecting a position for the footer (e.g., odd-numbered pages or even-numbered pages), and create your second footer. As mentioned earlier, if you want both Footer A and Footer B to be printed on every page, be sure to align the text in each footer so that they don't overwrite one another. When you've finished typing your footer or footers, press Exit (**F7**) to return to the Edit screen menu.

There's really no need to create two separate headers or footers to be printed on every page, unless you want to suppress only one of the headers or footers on certain pages.

CHANGING AN EXISTING HEADER OR FOOTER

NOTE NOTE

When you edit a header or footer, WordPerfect searches backward from the current cursor position and lets you edit whichever header or footer it finds first.

If you want to change an existing header or footer without retyping it, follow these steps:

1. Position the cursor just to the right of the header or footer you want to change (turning on Reveal Codes by pressing **Alt-F3** or **F11** will help you do this more easily).

2. Select **L**ayout ➤ **P**age, or press **Shift-F8 P**.

3. Select either **H**eaders (to change an existing header) or **F**ooters (to change an existing footer).

4. Select the header or footer you want to change (either **A** or **B**).

5. Select **E**dit.

At this point, the existing header or footer appears on an otherwise blank Edit screen. You can use all the usual WordPerfect editing techniques to change the header or footer, including turning on Reveal Codes to view blank lines beneath a header (these appear as [HRt] on the Reveal Codes screen). When you've finished making your changes, press Exit (**F7**) to return to the menu. Then press Exit again to return to the Edit screen.

INCLUDING PAGE NUMBERS IN HEADERS AND FOOTERS

As mentioned, you can include a page number in a header or footer by pressing Ctrl-B where you want the page number to appear. First, you need to go through the steps to create or edit the header or footer, as described above. When you get to the screen for editing the header or footer, press Ctrl-B where you want the page number to appear. Although the screen will show ^*B*, this symbol will be replaced by the correct page number when you print the document or preview it on the View Document screen.

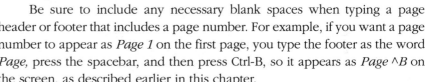
Any changes you make by selecting Layout ➤ *Page* ➤ *Page Numbering* ➤ *New Page Number will also affect page numbers that appear in headers and footers.*

Be sure to include any necessary blank spaces when typing a page header or footer that includes a page number. For example, if you want a page number to appear as *Page 1* on the first page, you type the footer as the word *Page,* press the spacebar, and then press Ctrl-B, so it appears as *Page ^B* on the screen, as described earlier in this chapter.

Also, if you include page numbers in a header or footer, you should turn off automatic page numbering for all pages that will show the header or footer. Otherwise, the page number will appear twice on each page: once in the position dictated by the automatic page numbering and then again in the header or footer.

INCLUDING THE DATE AND TIME IN A HEADER OR FOOTER

If you plan to print multiple revisions of a document under development, it's a good idea to *date stamp* each printed copy, so you can see at a glance how recent it is. Figure 7.5 showed an example where the page footer included the date of the current printing.

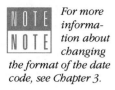

For more informa- tion about changing the format of the date code, see Chapter 3.

To include the current date or time in a header or footer, go through the usual steps to create or edit the header or footer. Then position the cursor wherever you want the date or time to be displayed in the header or footer, select **T**ools ➤ Date **F**ormat (or press **Shift-F5 F**), and define a format for the date or time. Then select **D**ate ➤ **C**ode to insert the date or time in the header or footer.

HIDING HEADERS AND FOOTERS ON A PAGE

You can hide the headers or footers on any single page in your document. For example, you may want to omit headers and footers from pages that have full-page graphs or from blank pages that you've intentionally included for back-to-back printing or binding. To omit all, or some, headers and footers on a single page, follow these steps:

1. Move the cursor to the upper-left corner of the page where you want to hide headers or footers.

2. Select **L**ayout ➤ **P**age ➤ **Su**ppress (this page only), or press **Shift-F8 P U**.

At this point, a menu of options appears on your screen, as shown in Figure 7.7. As you can see, the menu lets you suppress all page numbering,

```
Format: Suppress (this page only)

    1 - Suppress All Page Numbering, Headers and Footers

    2 - Suppress Headers and Footers

    3 - Print Page Number at Bottom Center   No

    4 - Suppress Page Numbering              No

    5 - Suppress Header A                     No

    6 - Suppress Header B                     No

    7 - Suppress Footer A                     No

    8 - Suppress Footer B                     No




Selection: 0
```

FIGURE 7.7:

Options for suppressing features on the current page

headers, and footers; just headers and footers; just page numbers; or individual headers and footers. You can select any option in the usual manner, by pressing the boldfaced number or letter for the option. You can change the options with Yes/No alternatives to Yes or No by selecting the option, and pressing **Y** for Yes or **N** for No, or by clicking on the alternative you want.

After you've defined the features you want to suppress on the current page, press Exit (**F7**) to return to the Edit screen.

DISCONTINUING HEADERS AND FOOTERS

*Discontinuing headers and footers does not discontinue automatic page numbering (if you've chosen to number your pages automatically, instead of in a header or footer). To discontinue automatic page numbering, select **L**ayout ➤ **P**age ➤ **P**age **N**umbering ➤ Page Number **P**osition ➤ **N**o Page Numbers (or press **Shift-F8 P P N**).*

In the preceding section, you learned how to temporarily suppress headers and footers on a specific page. You can also turn off, or discontinue, headers and footers to suppress them on the current page and all pages that follow. Follow these steps:

1. Move the cursor to the top-left corner of the page where you want to discontinue a page header or footer (or anywhere beneath the first line of the preceding page).

2. Select **L**ayout ➤ **P**age, or press **Shift-F8 P**.

3. Select **H**eaders to discontinue page headers, or select **F**ooters to discontinue page footers.

4. Select the header or footer that you want to discontinue (**A** or **B**).

5. Select **D**iscontinue.

6. Repeat steps 3, 4, and 5 for each header and footer that you want to discontinue.

7. Press Exit (**F7**) to return to the Edit screen.

TROUBLESHOOTING HEADER AND FOOTER PROBLEMS

Headers and footers can be a bit troublesome when you're first trying to get the hang of them, so let's look at some common problems and their solutions.

Refining the Position of Headers and Footers

Neither headers nor footers are ever printed within the top and bottom margins. Instead, the first line of the header is always printed as the first line below the top margin, and the bottom line of the footer is always printed as the last line above the bottom margin. WordPerfect automatically leaves one blank line between the text and the header or footer, but you can press ↵ to add more blank space after typing a header or before typing a footer.

If you want to print your document with headers or footers so that they appear to be within the 1-inch margins at the top and bottom of the page, you must change those margins. For example, suppose you want the header to be printed 0.5 inches from the top of the page and the footer to be printed 0.5 inches from the bottom of the page. You must change the top and bottom margins to 0.5 inches by using the techniques described in Chapter 4 for changing margins (that is, select **L**ayout ➤ **P**age ➤ **M**argins, or press **Shift-F8 P M**, and type the new margin settings). Make sure the [T/B margin] code that defines the new top and bottom margins precedes the codes that define the header and footer.

Disappearing Headers and Footers

When WordPerfect prints a page, it first plans the page by observing the formatting codes at the top of that page. If any text on that page precedes a [Header] or [Footer] code, the code is ignored until the next page is about to be printed.

Techniques for moving codes from one place to another are covered in Chapter 3.

Therefore, if you place [Header] and [Footer] codes in or after the first line of text on a page, or they get moved away from the top of the page when you insert new text, the headers and footers will not be printed until the next page. If this is a problem, you can use the Reveal Codes screen to move the [Header] and [Footer] codes to the top of the page where you want the headers and footers to begin.

FORMATTING FOR BINDING

When writing a manuscript with lengthy chapters or sections, you may find it easier to store each chapter or section in a separate file. The Styles (Chapter 14) and Master Document (Chapter 24) features can help you better manage large documents.

In many situations, you will want to ensure that a particular page is printed as an odd-numbered page. For example, for documents containing chapters, it's common practice to start each new chapter on an odd-numbered page. If you are printing a brochure with a mail-in coupon attached, you might want to ensure that the coupon is printed as an odd-numbered page, so it won't be on the back of another page.

If you are certain that you want a particular page to be printed as an odd- or even-numbered page, you can inform WordPerfect of this by following these steps:

1. Move the cursor to the top of the page that should have an odd or even page number.

2. Select **L**ayout ➤ **P**age ➤ **F**orce Odd/Even Page, or press **Shift-F8 P O**.

3. Select either **O**dd or **E**ven.

4. Press Exit (**F7**).

On the Edit screen, you may see that WordPerfect has inserted a soft page break (if necessary) to ensure that the page begins on either a new odd- or even-numbered page. If you look at the page on the Reveal Codes screen, you'll see the [Force:Odd] or [Force:Even] code at the top of the page. You may also see the Soft Page Break code [SPg], indicating the location of the soft page break.

ENSURING A NEW ODD-NUMBERED PAGE

When copying back to back, you always need to place an even number of pages in the copy machine (for example, insert four, not three, pages into the machine). Therefore, you may need to add a blank piece of paper after your stand-alone coupon if it is currently the last (odd-numbered) page of your document.

Keep in mind that forcing text to be printed on an odd-numbered page does not guarantee that the text will be printed on a *new* page. Instead, it only guarantees that the text will start on a new page if the page currently being printed is even-numbered. If you need to ensure that text starts on a new odd-numbered page (like a chapter heading or a full-page coupon), you should first insert a hard page break at the top of the page (by pressing **Ctrl-↵**). Then, insert the [Force:Odd] code at the top of that page, using the steps listed above.

When you print the document, if the page before the new odd-numbered page is itself an odd-numbered page, WordPerfect will print a blank, even-numbered page and then the new odd-numbered page. If you then copy the pages back to back on a copy machine (including the blank even-numbered page), the stand-alone odd-numbered page will appear on a page by itself, and it won't be attached to the back of an even-numbered page.

KEEPING TEXT TOGETHER

WordPerfect offers two techniques to ensure that a block of text stays together on one page: *Block Protect* and *Conditional End of Page*. Block Protect is generally used to prevent passages of text, such as a quotation, sidebar, or columnar table, from being split across two pages. Conditional End of Page is generally used to keep section headings and the text that follows from being split across two or more pages.

USING BLOCK PROTECT TO KEEP TEXT TOGETHER

The Block Protect feature is best used when you want to keep a block of text (which can include hidden formatting codes) together on a page. These are the general steps for protecting a block:

1. Move the cursor to the upper-left corner of the block you want to protect.

2. Use the Block (**Alt-F4** or **F12**) and cursor-movement keys, or your mouse, to block the text you want to keep together.

3. Select **E**dit ➤ Pro**t**ect Block or press Format (**Shift-F8**).

4. If you pressed the Format key in step 3, you'll be asked to verify Block Protect. Press **Y** for Yes.

When you print the document (or preview it on the View Document screen), WordPerfect will calculate the number of lines available on the current page before printing the protected block. If there isn't enough room to print the protected block, it will skip to the next page before printing it.

A disadvantage of this technique for protecting a block is that the page preceding the protected block may end with too many blank lines, since WordPerfect skipped to the next page prematurely to prevent splitting the protected block of text.

Graphic boxes offer a better solution to this problem, particularly if you're concerned about splitting a table. If you place a table in a graphic box (and the table can fit on one page), WordPerfect will not break the table across two pages and will not leave a gap at the end of the page preceding the table. See Chapter 19 for more information on graphic boxes.

 *You can move or copy existing text or tables to graphic boxes.*

Removing Block Protection

If you protect a block, then change your mind and decide to unprotect it, use the same general technique that you'd use to turn off any other formatting feature: Delete the hidden code that is activating that feature.

1. Move the cursor to the upper-left corner of the protected block.

2. Activate Reveal Codes by selecting **E**dit ➤ **R**eveal Codes or by pressing **Alt-F3** or **F11**.

3. Move the Reveal Codes highlight to the [Block Prot:On] code and press **Delete**.

USING CONDITIONAL END OF PAGE TO KEEP LINES TOGETHER

You may also want to keep certain lines of text together on a page in a document. For example, if your document uses section headings, you might want to ensure that the heading does not end up at the bottom of one page, with its related paragraph at the top of the next page.

You can define a *conditional end of page* to prevent two or more specific lines of text from being broken across two pages. To do this, you need to count the number of lines that must be kept together, including any blank lines. For example, if you have a heading, followed by a blank line, followed by the first line of text of the paragraph beneath that heading, as in Figure 7.8, you specify three lines for a conditional page break to prevent the heading and paragraph from being split across two pages.

When you've determined how many lines of text need to be kept together on the page, follow these steps to insert the conditional end of page:

1. Move the cursor to the line *above* the lines that you want to keep together (even if that line contains text).

2. Select **Layout** ➤ **O**ther ➤ **C**onditional End of Page, or press **Shift-F8 O C**.

3. Type the number of lines below the cursor that should be kept together (for example, *3*), and press ↵.

4. Press Exit (**F7**) to return to the Edit screen.

These commands insert a hidden code indicating how many lines beneath the code's position are to be kept on a single page. For example, if you specify three lines, the inserted code is [Cndl EOP:3].

When WordPerfect encounters this code in a document, it counts the number of blank lines available on the page currently being printed. If there isn't enough space to print the number of lines that must be kept together (three in this example), it skips to the next page before printing the lines.

Many people ask why WordPerfect has both Block Protect and Conditional End of Page. After all, they seem to serve the same purpose. But there is a subtle difference. Block Protect works by placing a [Block Prot:On] code at the top, and [Block Prot:Off] at the bottom, of the protected block. Any changes that you make to the protected block, including the addition or deletion of lines, will still keep the entire block protected.

On the other hand, Conditional End of Page inserts only one hidden code, [Cndl EOP:*n*] into a document, which tells WordPerfect to skip to the next page if there is not enough space to print at least *n* lines. Whether the

Soon you'll learn about widow and orphan protection, yet another technique for keeping lines of a paragraph together.

Work Avoidance

Sometimes work itself can be a form of work avoidance. Recently, while writing an article that absolutely had to be done by 3:00, I suddenly had the urge to vacuum my closet. While waving the vacuum nozzle around without paying attention, I (or rather, the vacuum cleaner) sucked some ties off my tie rack. They came out of the vacuum cleaner hose looking like little silk prunes. So now there was another job to do -- iron some ties.

FIGURE 7.8:

A sample heading followed by a blank line and paragraph of text. Conditional End of Page can prevent the heading from ending up alone at the bottom of a page.

text beneath the [Cndl EOP:] code grows or shrinks is irrelevant, because the idea is simply to keep a few lines from being split, not a whole body of text.

Removing a Conditional End of Page

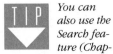

You can also use the Search feature (Chapter 9) to move the cursor to specific codes.

If you change your mind about using Conditional End of Page in a document, move the cursor wherever it was when you selected the commands to insert the conditional end of page. Then open the Reveal Codes screen and delete the [Cndl EOP:] code that's keeping the lines together.

PREVENTING WIDOWS AND ORPHANS

In WordPerfect terminology, a *widow* is the first line of a paragraph, printed on the last line of a page. An *orphan*, on the other hand, is the last line of a paragraph, printed on the first line of a new page. Figure 7.9 shows an example of a page with both a widow and an orphan.

You can have WordPerfect automatically prevent widows and orphans in a printed document. To avoid a widow, WordPerfect will move the first line of a paragraph to the top of the next page. To avoid an orphan, WordPerfect will move the next-to-last line of a paragraph to the top of the next page.

Follow these steps to invoke widow/orphan protection:

1. Move the cursor to the top of the document (or to the place where you want to begin protecting against widows and orphans).

2. Select **Layout** ➤ **Line** ➤ **W**idow/Orphan Protection, or press **Shift-F8 L W**.

3. Select **Yes**.

4. Press Exit (**F7**) to return to the Edit screen.

All text to the right of and below the cursor in the current document will be reformatted to prevent widows and orphans. For example, Figure 7.10 shows the same page as Figure 7.9, but printed with widow/orphan protection. Two lines from the paragraph at the end of the previous page are now printed at the top of the current page. The first line of the last paragraph is no longer on this page; instead, it's printed as the first line on the next page (not shown).

Disabling Widow/Orphan Protection

To disable widow/orphan protection at a particular place in your document (so that later pages are not protected), move the cursor to where you want to turn off widow/orphan protection. Then repeat the steps described above, but select **N**o rather than Yes in the third step.

If you want to disable widow/orphan protection altogether, first position the cursor where you initiated widow/orphan protection, then use the Reveal Codes screen to locate and delete the [W/O On] code.

A page with both a widow and an orphan

LASERS AND MASERS

orphan

problem". However, lasers are now in widespread use.

HOME APPLICATIONS

Though many people aren't aware of it, most American households now use laser technology to listen to music. The modern CD player, which has virtually replaced the phonograph, uses a laser beam to read music from the compact disk.

COMPUTER APPLICATIONS

The precision of lasers has played two major roles in the computer industry. CD ROM (an acronym for Compact Disk Read-Only Memory) allows a single compact disk to store as much information as hundreds of floppy disks.

Laser printers have brought the precision of high-priced typesetting machines to the desktop. Coupled with a new breed of desktop publishing software, the laser printer lets businesses produce their own presentation-quality reports, graphics, and transparencies.

MANUFACTURING APPLICATIONS

Manufacturers use lasers for a wide variety of applications, including precise drilling in extremely hard materials, precision cutting of soft materials, and welding.

INTERESTING FACTS

In September of 1964, the highest musical note in history was produced by striking a sapphire crystal with a laser beam -- 60,000 vibrations per second!

The FBI can now examine fingerprints left 40 years ago, thanks

2

widow

KEEPING WORDS TOGETHER ON A LINE

You can also prevent a particular pair of words from being separated onto two lines by inserting a *hard space* between the words. For example, when printing a document that contains phone numbers with area codes, like *(415) 555-8233,* you might want to prevent WordPerfect from putting the area code on one line and the rest of the phone number on the next line or page.

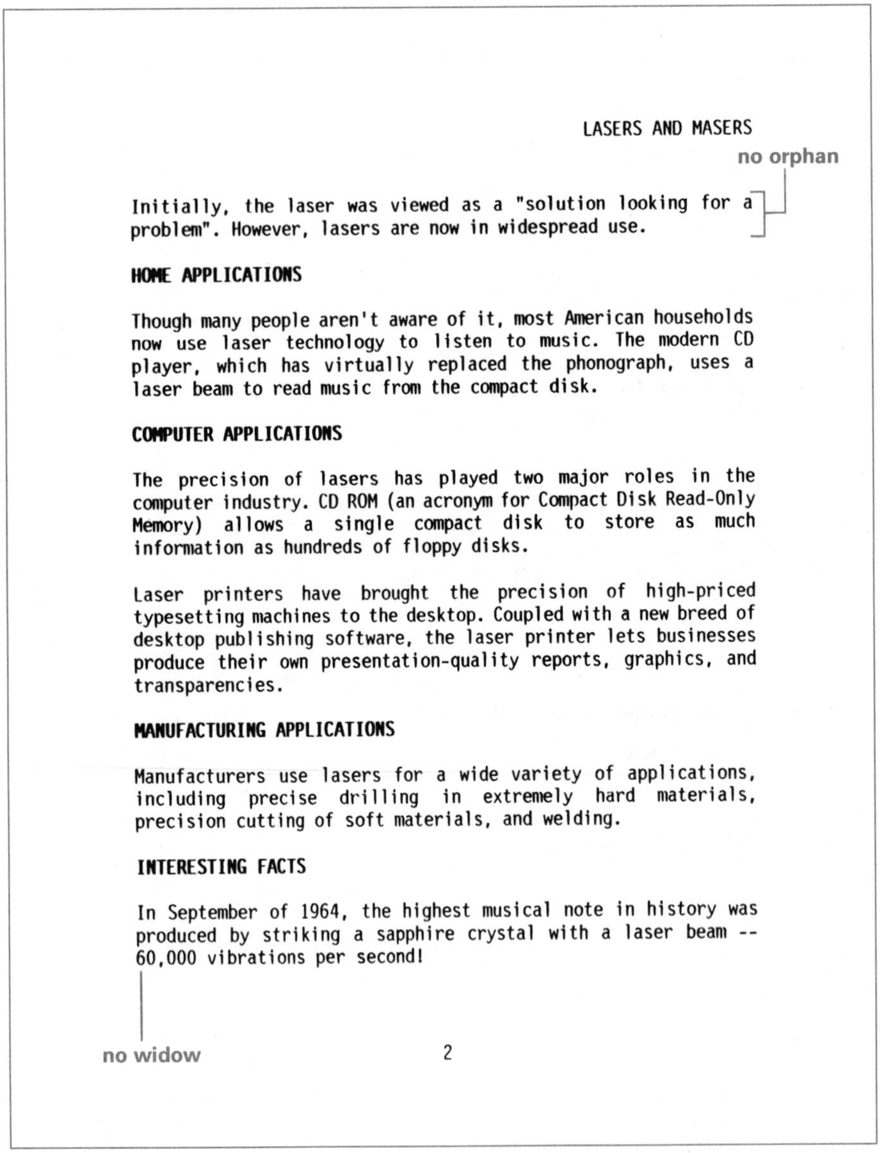

FIGURE 7.10:

A page printed with widow/orphan protection

LASERS AND MASERS

no orphan

Initially, the laser was viewed as a "solution looking for a problem". However, lasers are now in widespread use.

HOME APPLICATIONS

Though many people aren't aware of it, most American households now use laser technology to listen to music. The modern CD player, which has virtually replaced the phonograph, uses a laser beam to read music from the compact disk.

COMPUTER APPLICATIONS

The precision of lasers has played two major roles in the computer industry. CD ROM (an acronym for Compact Disk Read-Only Memory) allows a single compact disk to store as much information as hundreds of floppy disks.

Laser printers have brought the precision of high-priced typesetting machines to the desktop. Coupled with a new breed of desktop publishing software, the laser printer lets businesses produce their own presentation-quality reports, graphics, and transparencies.

MANUFACTURING APPLICATIONS

Manufacturers use lasers for a wide variety of applications, including precise drilling in extremely hard materials, precision cutting of soft materials, and welding.

INTERESTING FACTS

In September of 1964, the highest musical note in history was produced by striking a sapphire crystal with a laser beam -- 60,000 vibrations per second!

no widow   2

To insert a hard space between two words while typing them, press **Home**, then the spacebar, rather than just pressing the spacebar alone. The space looks like any other normal blank space on the Edit screen. However, on the Reveal Codes screen, it appears as a pair of brackets with a space in between ([ ]).

If you want to insert a hard space between two words that are already separated by a normal space, move the cursor between the two words, press **Home**, then press the spacebar to insert the hard space. Then press the **Delete** key to delete the regular space.

PRINTING ON NONSTANDARD PAGE SIZES

TO PRINT ON PAPER OTHER THAN THE STANDARD 8.5" x 11" SIZE,

1. **Position the cursor at the top of the page where the new paper size should begin.**

2. **Select Layout ➤ Page ➤ Paper Size (or press Shift-F8 P S) and the paper size you want to use.**

3. **Press Exit (F7).**

> **TIP** *You can preview the effects of selecting nonstandard page sizes on the View Document screen.*

By default, WordPerfect assumes that you will print your document on the *standard* page size, which is 8.5" × 11" in the United States. But many documents call for other page sizes, such as legal documents that must be printed on 8.5" × 14" paper or labels that are only a few inches wide and high. Many preprinted forms, such as invoices and packing slips, also require unusual paper sizes.

Whether you can print text on nonstandard page sizes depends largely on your printer. For example, most laser printers require a special sheet feeder for legal-size paper. On many dot-matrix and other tractor-fed printers, you can only print sideways on the page if the platen is wide enough to accommodate 11-inch wide paper.

If you have any problems using the techniques described in this section, you should study printing in general (see Chapter 8) and perhaps learn more about your particular printer by referring to its manual.

SELECTING A PAPER SIZE

Whenever you install a printer for use with WordPerfect, the installation program creates a *printer resource file* (which has the file-name extension .PRS), containing information and options for that printer. Included in this file are some paper sizes and types commonly used with that printer. To use one of these predefined paper sizes, follow these steps:

Installing a printer for use with Word-Perfect is covered in Appendix A.

1. Move the cursor to the top of the first page that will be printed on the page with the new size (before any text on that page).

2. Select **L**ayout ➤ **P**age ➤ Paper **S**ize, or press **Shift-F8 P S**.

3. The currently available paper sizes appear on the screen, as in the example in Figure 7.11 (though the paper sizes displayed depend on your printer and the paper sizes you've created).

If you don't see the paper size you need, you can add it (as described later in this chapter).

4. Select the paper size you want, either by using the arrow keys to move the highlight to the size you want and pressing **S** to choose **S**elect or by double-clicking on the paper size with your mouse.

5. Press Exit (**F7**) to return to your document.

WordPerfect puts a hidden [Paper Sz/Typ] code at the cursor position, indicating the size of paper to be used for printing. As with most page-formatting codes, only text to the right of and below the cursor position will be printed on the paper with the new size. Hence, if any text precedes the [Paper Sz/Typ] code on the page, the code will be ignored until the next printed page.

As usual, if you change your mind about the currently selected page size, you can return to the normal page size by deleting the hidden [Paper Sz/Typ]

```
Format: Paper Size/Type

                                                Font  Double
Paper type and Orientation    Paper Size   Prompt Loc  Type  Sided Labels

1" x 4"                       8.5" x 11"    No   Contin Port  No    2 x 10
Envelope - Wide              9.5" x 4"     No   Manual Land  No
Legal                        8.5" x 14"    No   Contin Port  No
Legal - Dup Long             8.5" x 14"    No   Contin Port  Yes
Legal - Dup Long - Wide      14" x 8.5"    No   Contin Land  Yes
Legal - Dup Short            8.5" x 14"    No   Contin Port  Yes
Legal - Dup Short - Wide     14" x 8.5"    No   Contin Land  Yes
Legal - Wide                 14" x 8.5"    No   Contin Land  No
Standard                     8.5" x 11"    No   Contin Port  No
Standard - Dup Long          8.5" x 11"    No   Contin Port  Yes
Standard - Dup Long - Wide   11" x 8.5"    No   Contin Land  Yes
Standard - Dup Short         8.5" x 11"    No   Contin Port  Yes
Standard - Dup Short - Wide  11" x 8.5"    No   Contin Land  Yes
Standard - Wide              11" x 8.5"    No   Contin Land  No
[ALL OTHERS]                 Width ≤ 8.5"  Yes  Manual      No




1 Select; 2 Add (Create); 3 Copy; 4 Delete; 5 Edit; N Name Search: 1
```

FIGURE 7.11:

Some typically available paper sizes

code. If you need to change a selected page size, be sure to delete the existing [Paper Sz/Typ] code so that it does not override the new code.

In the following sections, we'll talk about printing on some common paper sizes. Remember that if a particular paper size is not currently available for your printer, you can probably just add that paper size, as discussed later in this chapter.

PRINTING SIDEWAYS ON THE PAGE

In some situations you might want to print a document sideways. Sideways printing is often called *landscape* printing, because the text or graphic is printed horizontally across the page (the way landscapes in art are usually painted). The normal printing used with most documents is called *portrait* printing, because the text is printed vertically (the way portraits are usually painted).

Printing in landscape mode is useful for many types of documents, particularly large, lengthy tables. Figure 7.12 shows a printed table at arm's length in portrait mode and in landscape mode. As you can see by the number of rows and the amount of white space on the pages, the landscape mode offers much better use of the available space on the page. How you go about printing sideways on a page depends on what kind of printer you have, as the following sections explain.

Printing Sideways with a Laser Printer

*Options on the Paper Size/Type screen that end with **Wide** show **Land** (for Landscape font) in the Font Type column, because they print characters sideways on the page (see Figure 7.11).*

To print sideways on a standard-size page with a laser printer, you must first select the 11" × 8.5" paper size (often titled *Standard - Wide* on the Paper Size/Type menu). Follow the steps above to select this paper size.

When it's time to actually print the document, just use the usual techniques (select **File ➤ Print ➤ Full** Document or press **Shift-F7 F**). You do not need to change the direction of the paper in the printer—the laser printer will automatically print sideways on the page, even though the page is fed into the printer normally.

Printing Sideways with a Nonlaser Printer

See your printer manual for information about printing in landscape mode.

If you want to print sideways on a regular (nonlaser) printer, you must first inform WordPerfect that you will be printing on this size of paper, by following the steps above to select the 11" × 8.5" paper size.

When you're ready to actually print the document, you will probably need to feed the paper into the printer sideways, as shown in Figure 7.13. The platen (the paper roller) must be wide enough to accommodate the page. For example, you can only print sideways on an 8.5" × 11" page if your printer can accept 11-inch-wide paper.

Once you've selected the paper size and placed the paper properly in the printer, you can go ahead and print the document (select **F**ile ➤ **P**rint ➤ **F**ull Document or press **Shift-F7 F**). If WordPerfect expects manually fed pages at this point, you'll need to insert the paper a page at a time (as described under "Location" and "Prompt to Load" in "Adding a Paper Size" later in this chapter).

PRINTING ON LETTERHEAD

Most businesses use letterhead stock to print letters. Typically, only the first page of a multipage letter is printed on letterhead; any pages that follow are

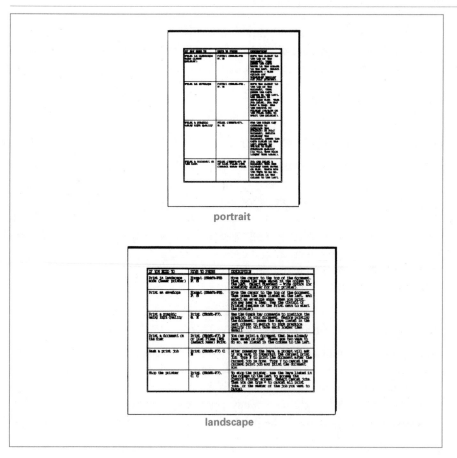

portrait

landscape

FIGURE 7.12:

A large table printed in portrait and landscape mode

printed on plain sheets. Therefore, there's no need to adjust the margins to print beneath the letterhead. Instead, you just need to make sure that the first line of the letter on the first page will be printed beneath the letterhead. To do so, first measure the distance from the top of the page to where you want the first line of the letter to be printed, as shown in Figure 7.14.

When you're ready to create your letter, start with a clear Edit screen and look at the Ln (line) measurement in the lower-right corner of your screen. Press ↵ until that measurement is set about where you want to print the first line, as in Figure 7.15. Then just type your entire letter (and save it in case you want to use it again).

When you're ready to print your letter, put the letterhead page into the printer. If you are using a printer that is fed from a tray, put as many blank letterhead bond pages into the bin as necessary to print all the pages after the first. Then put the letterhead page on top of those pages. If you're using a tractor-fed printer, put the letterhead page into the printer, positioning the top of the page just slightly above the print head.

 *With a tractor-fed printer, you might have to move or remove the tractors to insert the paper; consult your printer manual.*

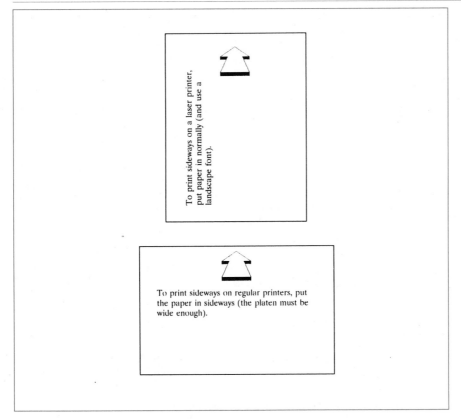

FIGURE 7.13:

Landscape printing with laser and nonlaser printers

To print sideways on a laser printer, put paper in normally (and use a landscape font).

To print sideways on regular printers, put the paper in sideways (the platen must be wide enough).

Then print as you normally would (select **File** ➤ **P**rint ➤ **F**ull Document or press **Shift-F8 F**). That's about all there is to it, though there may be one additional catch if you are using a tractor-fed printer that is not giving you ample time to load additional pages after the first printed page. You may want to use (or create) a paper size that pauses before printing each page, so you have time to individually load each sheet. To do so, you'll need to set the location of paper to Manual, as described in "Adding a Paper Size" later in this chapter.

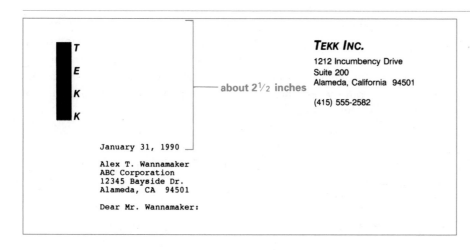

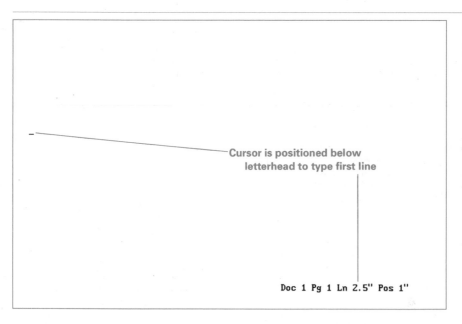

PRINTING ON ENVELOPES

Check your printer manual for additional information on how to load envelopes into your particular printer.

To print on legal-size (9.5" × 4") envelopes, you need a laser printer that can handle envelopes or a dot-matrix or other type of printer that can handle 9.5-inch-wide paper. Then you have to select the paper size for printing on envelopes, as discussed earlier in "Selecting a Paper Size." The size to select (or create, if it's not already available) is 9.5" × 4", often named *Envelope - Wide* with printers that have predefined this size for you.

After you've selected that paper size, be sure to reduce the top and left margins to about 0.3" each if you want to type a return address on the envelope. You may also want to adjust the tab ruler so that there is only one tab stop, at about the 3.25" mark.

Now type the return address (if any), then press ↵ about seven times to add some blank lines. Finally, type the recipient's name and address, remembering to tab to about the 3.5" mark before typing each line. Figure 7.16 shows an example of an envelope on the Edit and Reveal Codes screens. Figure 7.17 shows the sample envelope after printing. You can preview the printed envelope on the View Document screen and make adjustments on the Edit screen if necessary, before printing the envelope.

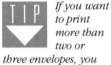

If you want to print more than two or three envelopes, you should look into the Merge feature (Chapter 16).

If you want to type multiple envelopes before printing them, add a hard page break (by pressing Ctrl-↵) before typing each envelope; this ensures that the previous, complete envelope is ejected from the printer before text for the next envelope is printed. If your printer cannot handle a stack of envelopes,

```
Ino Ramirez
1234 Calle Fuerte
Rancho Santa Fe, CA  92067




                          Wilson Dendrobium
                          Attaboy, Inc.
                          P.O. Box 7784
C:\ENVELOPE.WP                               Doc 1 Pg 1 Ln 1" Pos 1"
   ▲   {                                                      }  ▲
[Paper Sz/Typ:9.5" x 4",Envelope][T/B Mar:0.3",1"][L/R Mar:0.3",1"][Tab Set:Rel:
 +3.5"]Ino Ramirez[HRt]
1234 Calle Fuerte[HRt]
Rancho Santa Fe, CA  92067[HRt]
[HRt]
[HRt]
[HRt]
[HRt]
[HRt]
[Tab]Wilson Dendrobium[HRt]

Press Reveal Codes to restore screen
```

FIGURE 7.16:

An example of an envelope on the Edit and Reveal Codes screens

make sure your envelope paper size's paper location is set to Manual so that you have time to feed each envelope individually. (See the sections on adding or changing a paper size below.)

PRINTING ON LABELS

Most printers can print directly on labels. With laser printers, you need to purchase special sheet-fed labels that are specifically designed to tolerate the high heat generated by laser printers. Avery offers a wide variety of laser-printer labels. Figure 7.18 shows an example of some printed sheet labels (though the sheets are generally 11 inches long and can accommodate six or seven rows of labels).

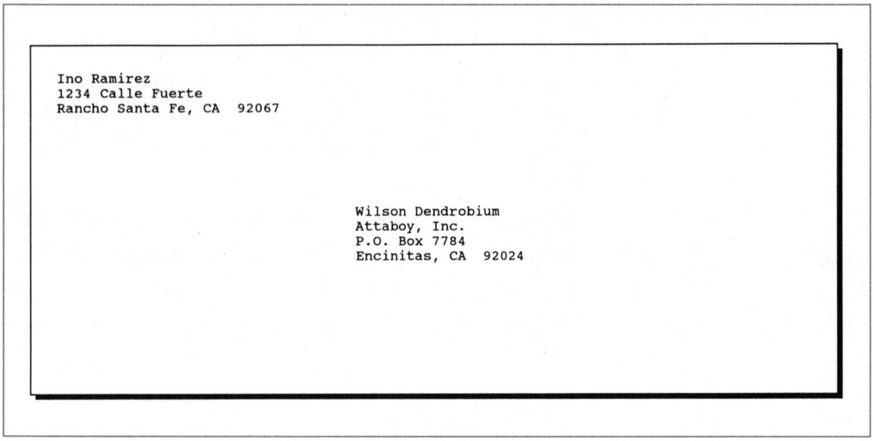

FIGURE 7.17:

A sample printed envelope

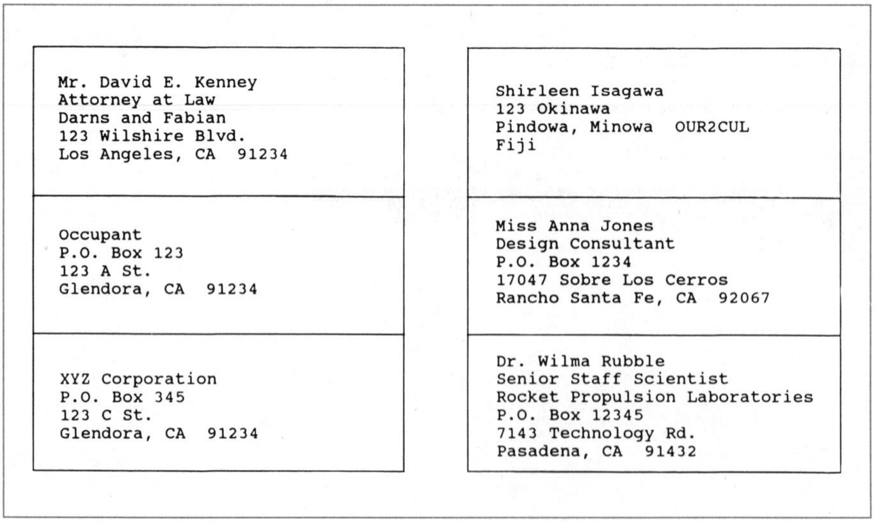

```
Ino Ramirez
1234 Calle Fuerte
Rancho Santa Fe, CA  92067




                    Wilson Dendrobium
                    Attaboy, Inc.
                    P.O. Box 7784
                    Encinitas, CA  92024
```

FIGURE 7.18:

An example of printed sheet-fed labels

```
Mr. David E. Kenney          Shirleen Isagawa
Attorney at Law              123 Okinawa
Darns and Fabian             Pindowa, Minowa  OUR2CUL
123 Wilshire Blvd.           Fiji
Los Angeles, CA  91234


Occupant                     Miss Anna Jones
P.O. Box 123                 Design Consultant
123 A St.                    P.O. Box 1234
Glendora, CA  91234          17047 Sobre Los Cerros
                             Rancho Santa Fe, CA  92067


XYZ Corporation              Dr. Wilma Rubble
P.O. Box 345                 Senior Staff Scientist
123 C St.                    Rocket Propulsion Laboratories
Glendora, CA  91234          P.O. Box 12345
                             7143 Technology Rd.
                             Pasadena, CA  91432
```

Dot-matrix and similar printers use tractor-fed labels. These are often single-column labels, on long continuous rolls (or connected sheets) of paper, with holes on both edges for feeding through the printer tractor. Figure 7.19 shows an example of some printed tractor-fed labels.

Both types of labels are generally available at any office-supply or computer-supply store.

To print on labels, you must first select the appropriate label size at the top of the document (select **Layout** ➤ **P**age ➤ Paper **S**ize options or press **Shift-F8 P S**). If the label size you want is not listed, you'll need to create that label size first (see "Creating a Paper Size for Labels" later in this chapter), then select that paper size.

Once you've selected the paper size for printing on labels, you can think of each label as a "page" of text, because typing on individual labels is pretty much the same as typing on individual pages. Here are some tips:

◆ If you want to center text horizontally on each label, select (just once) **Layout** ➤ **J**ustify ➤ **C**enter (or press **Shift-F8 L J C**) before typing the first label. If you want to center only a few lines in each label, use the Center key (**Shift-F6**) instead.

◆ If you want to center text vertically on each label, select **Layout** ➤ **P**age ➤ **C**enter Page ➤ **Y**es (or press **Shift-F8 P C Y**) at the top of each label.

> **NOTE NOTE**
>
> *The last column of the Paper Size/Type menu, Labels, displays the number of columns and rows of labels per page, if the paper size is indeed designed to print labels.*

HANDS-ON
· · · · · · · · · · · ·
LESSON 9

Hands-On Lesson 9 in Part 9 has a hands-on example of printing labels.

Darns and Fabian **123 Wilshire Blvd.** **Los Angeles, CA 91234**	
Shirleen Isagawa **123 Okinawa** **Pindowa, Minowa OUR2CUL** **Fiji**	
Occupant **P.O. Box 123** **123 A St.** **Glendora, CA 91234**	
Miss Anna Jones **Design Consultant**	

FIGURE 7.19:

An example of printed tractor-fed labels

Because Word-Perfect treats each label as a separate page, selecting File ➤ Print ➤ Page prints a single label only (whichever label the cursor is on at the moment).

◆ When you've finished typing one label and are ready to type the next one, insert a hard page break (press **Ctrl-↵**) to move to the next "page" (label).

◆ To see how your labels will look when printed, switch to the View Document screen (select **F**ile ➤ **P**rint ➤ **V**iew Document or press **Shift-F7 V**).

Figure 7.20 shows some sample names and addresses typed on the Edit screen for printing on labels. On the Reveal Codes screen, notice that the [Paper Sz/Type] code for labels is the first code in the document. Each label starts with a [Center Pg] code to vertically center text on the page, and each label ends with a hard page break ([HPg]), typed by pressing Ctrl-↵. This is the exact (top portion of the) Edit screen used to print the labels shown in Figure 7.18.

After typing your label text, load your labels into the printer. If you are using a dot-matrix printer, align the paper so that the print head is positioned where you want to start printing the first label. Then print as you normally would. If you have problems aligning text in each label, it may be that you've simply misaligned the labels in your dot-matrix printer, or you may need to modify (edit) the label's paper size, as described later in this chapter.

```
Mr. David_E. Kenney
Attorney at Law
Darns and Fabian
123 Wilshire Blvd.
Los Angeles, CA  91234
=================================================================
Shirleen Isagawa
123 Okinawa
Pindowa, Minowa  OUR2CUL
Fiji
=================================================================
                                      Doc 1 Pg 1 Ln 1" Pos 1"
     ▲   {    ▲    ▲ ▲    ▲    ▲    ▲    ▲              }
[Paper Sz/Typ:8.5" x 11",Address labels - Avery 5162,4" x 1.5"][Center Pg]Mr. Da
vid E. Kenney[HRt]
Attorney at Law[HRt]
Darns and Fabian[HRt]
123 Wilshire Blvd.[HRt]
Los Angeles, CA  91234[HPg]
[Center Pg]Shirleen Isagawa[HRt]
123 Okinawa[HRt]
Pindowa, Minowa  OUR2CUL[HRt]
Fiji[HPg]

Press Reveal Codes to restore screen
```

FIGURE 7.20:

Sample labels on the Edit and Reveal Codes screens

ADDING A PAPER SIZE

TO ADD (CREATE) A NEW PAPER OR LABEL SIZE,

select Layout ➤ Page ➤ Paper Size ➤ Add (or press Shift-F8 P S A), then select the options that define your page or label size.

Use this same feature to create a paper size for printing on labels.

If you've installed Word-Perfect for use with multiple printers, be sure to select the appropriate printer before defining a page size, using File ➤ Print ➤ Select Printer or Shift-F7 S (Chapter 8).

If the paper size you need is not available on the Paper Size/Type menu, you can add your own paper size. You only need to define a new paper size once. In the future, you can select that size whenever you want, using options on the Format menu (as explained later). Before defining the paper size, of course, you must measure the width and length of the paper, or each label on the paper. Then follow these steps to create your paper size:

1. Select **L**ayout ➤ **P**age ➤ Paper **S**ize, or press **Shift-F8 P S**.

2. Select **A**dd (Create).

3. Select a general paper type from the options shown in Figure 7.21. (This selection is just part of the name used to describe the paper size. You can select **O**ther from this menu and enter any name you want, such as *Address labels,* rather than selecting one of the suggested names.)

4. The Edit Paper Definition menu (Figure 7.22) appears next. Here you will define more information about your paper, as described in the sections that follow.

MAKING SENSE OF THE OPTIONS ON THE PAPER DEFINITION MENU

The Edit Paper Definition menu has options for changing paper size and type, and a number of other options.

*If you define a paper size that's wider than it is tall, WordPerfect automatically adds **Wide** to the paper-type name.*

Paper Size When you select the Paper Size option, you'll see a menu that lists many common paper sizes, including standard (8.5" × 11"), legal (8.5" × 14"), envelope (9.5" × 4"), some landscape (sideways) versions of these, and a few others. If the paper size you want is not displayed, you can select **O**ther and enter your own width and height measurements.

Paper Type The Paper Type option takes you back to the Paper Type menu shown in Figure 7.21. You don't need this option unless you want to change your original selection from that menu. Again, you're only defining the *name*

```
Format: Paper Type

        1 - Standard

        2 - Bond

        3 - Letterhead

        4 - Labels

        5 - Envelope

        6 - Transparency

        7 - Cardstock

        8 - [ALL OTHERS]

        9 - Other




Selection: 1
```

FIGURE 7.21:

Paper-type names for adding a new paper size

```
Format: Edit Paper Definition

        Filename                HPLASIII.PRS

        1 - Paper Size          8.5" x 11"

        2 - Paper Type          Letterhead

        3 - Font Type           Portrait

        4 - Prompt to Load      No

        5 - Location            Continuous

        6 - Double Sided Printing   No

        7 - Binding Edge        Left

        8 - Labels              No

        9 - Text Adjustment - Top   0"
                         Side   0"

Selection: 0
```

FIGURE 7.22:

The menu for defining a paper size

of the paper size here; this option has no effect on how WordPerfect or your printer operates.

Font Type Selecting the Font Type option gives you two choices: **P**ortrait and **L**andscape. Portrait is the normal mode, in which text is printed across the page, top to bottom. Landscape fonts print sideways on the page, even though the page is inserted normally into the printer.

If your paper is wider than it is tall, and you're using a laser printer, WordPerfect automatically sets this option to Landscape. Chances are you will not need to change this setting.

Prompt to Load The Prompt to Load option lets you determine whether WordPerfect will beep and wait before printing a document. If this option is set to **N**o, WordPerfect starts printing immediately after you select **F**ile ➤ **P**rint ➤ **F**ull Document (or press Shift-F7 F) or some other option that prints a document.

If you set this option to **Y**es, WordPerfect will beep and pause before printing the first page of your document. This is useful if you are defining a nonstandard paper size, and you want WordPerfect to remind you to insert that paper size before printing.

If you do set Prompt to Load to Yes, here's what happens when you print a document by selecting **F**ile ➤ **P**rint ➤ **F**ull Document (or any other printing option): First, WordPerfect displays the message "Press Shft F7,4 to resume printing", and the printer does nothing. Pressing **Shift-F7 4** (or selecting **F**ile ➤ **P**rint ➤ **C**ontrol Printer) will take you to the Control Printer screen, where you'll see instructions under the *Action:* heading. (Basically, these instructions tell you to insert a sheet of paper, then press **G** to select Go.)

When you press G, printing begins, and WordPerfect prints the entire document. It does *not* prompt you to load additional sheets unless you've also selected Manual as the location for the paper (described below).

Location The Location option lets you define where and how the paper is loaded into the printer. When you select this option, you are given three options:

Continuous	Select this option if the paper is fed continuously through a tractor or from the standard bin (sheet feeder) on a laser printer.

Bin Number   Select this option if the paper is fed from a bin other than the standard bin. For example, if your printer lets you feed standard-size paper from one bin and legal-size from another, select this option, type the bin number for the paper size you are currently defining, and then press ↵.

Manual   Select this option if you want to feed sheets one at a time and have WordPerfect pause after printing each page.

If you select Continuous or Bin Number, then print using that paper size, WordPerfect prints normally, in the sense that, after you select **F**ile ➤ **P**rint **F**ull Document (or any other printing commands), WordPerfect just starts printing immediately.

If you choose Manual and later print a document using that paper size, here's what happens instead:

Different printers may react slightly differently to the Location and Prompt to Load settings.

◆ If you set Prompt to Load to No, neither the printer nor the screen do anything right away. The printer waits for you to insert a sheet of paper before it starts printing (some printers may flash a message, such as "LOAD LETTER", while waiting for you to insert a sheet of paper). After printing a page, WordPerfect again waits for you to insert the next page before resuming printing.

◆ If you set Prompt to Load to Yes, basically the same as above happens, except that after you insert a page into the printer, WordPerfect displays the message "Press Shft F7,4 to resume printing" before actually printing the page. You must individually feed each sheet to the printer, then go to the Control Printer screen (select **F**ile ➤ **P**rint ➤ **C**ontrol Printer, or press **Shift-F7 C**) and press **G** (for Go) to print each page.

There's really no need to select both Manual location and Prompt to Load, since the Manual location waits for each sheet to be fed before prompting you to load the sheet.

See Chapter 8 for help with printing on both sides of the paper with a nonduplex (regular) printer.

Double Sided Printing If you have a duplex printer (a printer that can print on both sides of the page), like the LaserJet IID or IIID, you can select the Double Sided Printing option to activate that capability for the page size you are currently defining. If you select this option, but your printer cannot print on both sides of the page, the selection will be ignored.

Binding Edge You can select the Binding Edge option to determine how the pages are printed:

Top   Pages will be printed for binding at the top.

Left   Pages will be printed for binding at the left side.

The amount of space allowed for binding is determined by the Binding Offset selection on the Print menu (select **F**ile ➤ **P**rint ➤ **B**inding Offset or press Shift-F7 B). See "Printing for Binding" in Chapter 8.

    If you have a duplex printer and have set Double Sided Printing to Yes, this option has a more pronounced effect. With Top selected as the binding edge in double-sided printing, every other page is printed upside down so that the pages read normally when bound at the top. With Left selected as the binding edge, the binding edge is at the right margin on even-numbered pages and at the left margin on odd-numbered pages.

If you have a duplex printer, its manual may provide additional examples of double-sided printing and binding.

Labels Select the Labels option, then **Y**es, only if the paper size you are defining is for printing on labels (see the next section, "Creating a Paper Size for Labels").

Text Adjustment The Text Adjustment option lets you handle situations in which different types of paper are loaded into the printer differently. For example, if you set the margins to 1 inch all the way around a page, but then find that some of the margins are not exactly 1 inch, you can adjust the overall placement of text on the page with this option.

    Suppose you consistently load paper into your printer with the left edge of the page as far to the left as it can go in the printer, but when printing pages with a 1-inch left margin specified, you still end up with only a 0.75-inch left margin. To shift all the text 0.25 inches to the right on the page, select the Text Adjustment option, select **R**ight, and enter ¼ (or .25) and press ↵. Your 1-inch margins will be correct in future printings.

    You can use the Text Adjustment option to move the text up, down, to the left, or to the right. If you change your mind about the text adjustment, and you want to reset the adjustment to 0 inches, just choose the Text Adjustment option again and type **0** for the up, down, left, or right adjustment.

    When you've finished defining your paper size, press Exit (**F7**) to return to the Paper Size/Type options. Your new paper size will be included in the list of available paper sizes. To use your new size, select it as you would any other paper size on the list, as described earlier in this chapter.

*Don't use the text adjustment feature to try to **create** margins on your pages. Use it only to make adjustments when WordPerfect's margin measurements don't come out right on your printed pages.*

CREATING A PAPER SIZE FOR LABELS

There are two ways to create labels. One is with the handy Labels *macro,* which can handle many commonly used predefined label sizes. The other involves going through the same techniques described under "Adding a Paper Size" above. This method may be required if the labels you're using are not included in the options that appear when you use the Labels macro.

Using the Labels Macro to Create a Label Size

If you are (or will be) using standard sheet labels, there's a quick and easy way to create label formats: Just use the LABELS.WPM macro that came with your WordPerfect package. This macro presents a menu of predefined label sizes for you to choose from, as shown in Figure 7.23.

Look in the left-hand columns of this menu for the part number and manufacturer's name for the label format you'll be using. If you don't see the exact part number and name, you can choose a format that's close to what you need by checking the columns for Sizes (H x W), number of Labels per Sheet, and RowxColumn. If one of the label sizes shown in Figure 7.23 looks like it will do the trick, follow these steps to use the LABELS.WPM macro:

1. Start from the Edit screen (clear or otherwise).

Predefined label sizes

```
                        Label Page/Size Definitions
 Labels        Sizes        Labels per.  Labels        Sizes        Labels per.
               H x W        Sheet RowxCol              H x W        Sheet RowxCol

 5096 Avery  3 1/2" diskette   9   3 x 3   5160 Avery  1" x 2 5/8"     30  10 x 3
 5161 Avery  1" x 4"          20  10 x 2   5162 Avery  1 1/3" x 4"     14   7 x 2
 5163 Avery  2" x 4"          10   5 x 2   5164 Avery  3 1/3" x 4"      6   3 x 2
 5165 Avery  8 1/2" x 11"      1   1 x 1   5196 Avery  2 3/4" x 2 3/4"  9   3 x 3
 5197 Avery  1 1/2" x 4"      12   6 x 2   5198 Avery  1 5/8" x 3 1/2" 12   6 x 2
 5199 Avery  1 5/6" x 3 1/16" 10   5 x 2   5260 Avery  1" x 2 5/8"     30  10 x 3
 5261 Avery  1" x 4"          20  10 x 2   5262 Avery  1 1/3" x 4"     14   7 x 2
 5266 Avery  2/3" x 3 7/16"   30  15 x 2   5267 Avery  1/2" x 1 3/4"   80  20 x 4
 5293 Avery  1 2/3" round     12   4 x 6   5294 Avery  2 1/2" round     9   3 x 3
 5295 Avery  3 1/3" round      6   3 x 2   5660 Avery  1" x 2 5/6"     30  10 x 3
 5662 Avery  1 1/3" x 4 1/4"  14   7 x 2   5663 Avery  2" x 4 1/4"     10   5 x 2
 7701 3M     11" x 8 7/16"     1   1 x 1   7709 3M     3 1/3" x 2 5/6"  9   3 x 3
 7712 3M     2 1/2" x 2 5/6"  12   4 x 3   7721 3M     1 1/2" x 2 5/6" 21   7 x 3
 7730 3M     1" x 2 5/8"      30  10 x 3   7733 3M     1" x 2 5/6"     33  11 x 3

 1 Select; 2 Name Search; 3 Mark (*): 1
```

If you see the message "ERROR: File not found" when trying to run the macro, you'll need to locate and install the LABELS.WPM macro that came with your package (see Appendix A).

If you use a variety of label sizes in your work, you can create several sizes at once. Mark each label size with an asterisk, then press ↵ and press **Y** *when prompted.*

If you choose **S***elect, the paper size/type for the label will automatically be inserted in the document's initial codes (described later in this chapter).*

2. If you've installed multiple printers, select **F**ile ➤ **P**rint ➤ **S**elect Printer (or press **Shift-F7 S**), choose the printer you want, then press Exit (**F7**) to return to the Edit screen (see Chapter 8).

3. Select **T**ools ➤ **M**acro ➤ E**x**ecute, or press Macro (**Alt-F10**).

4. Type **LABELS** and press ↵.

5. Use the ↑ and ↓ keys to move the cursor through the options on the screen.

6. When the option or options you want are highlighted, press ↵.

7. Select one of these options:

    Continuous: Labels are fed automatically and continuously from a tractor feed or paper tray.

    Bin Number: Labels are fed automatically from a bin other than the standard bin.

    Manual: Each sheet of labels must be fed individually, and therefore WordPerfect must pause after printing each sheet.

8. If you selected **M**anual above, you'll see the "Prompt to Load" prompt. Press **Y** if you want WordPerfect to beep and wait before printing labels, or press **N** if you don't want it to beep and wait.

9. If you selected **B**in Number above, type the bin number you want to use (but do not press ↵ after typing the number).

10. You'll be returned to the Paper Size/Type menu, with the new label size highlighted and ready for selection. You can press **S** to select the new label size right now, or press **E** to exit without selecting the new paper size.

In the future, you need not bother with using the Labels macro. Just select **L**ayout ➤ **P**age ➤ Paper **S**ize (or press **Shift-F8 P S**) to get to the Paper Size/Type menu, and your new label size will be included in the list of available paper sizes. You can select it as you would any other paper size in the list. (If you've installed multiple printers, remember that a new paper size is stored with the currently selected printer only.)

Note that the Labels macro assigns the label *size* as the name. For example, Avery 5197 labels are specifically designed as 5 1/4" disk labels, but are named 1 1/2 " × 4". This can be confusing if you have lots of different label sizes. To change the name (starting at the Edit screen), select **L**ayout ➤ **P**age ➤ Paper **S**ize (or press **Shift-F8 P S**), and move the highlight to the label size whose name you want to change. Then select **E**dit ➤ Paper **T**ype ➤ **O**ther, type in a new name for the labels (such as *5¼″ disk labels*), then press ↵. Finally, press Exit (**F7**) until you return to the Edit screen.

Defining Your Own Label Size

Some companies include specific instructions for using their labels with Word-Perfect right in the box.

If your label size is not one that's included in the Labels macro listing, or if you can't find the Labels macro for any reason, you can always create your label size manually. To define your own size, you first need to know the exact measurements of your labels. Typically, these measurements are printed on the box containing the labels. But if the measurements are not handy, you can break out your trusty ruler and measure the labels yourself. Most important, you need to know the label height and width. Figure 7.24 shows the measurements that WordPerfect will ask you about.

Note that the exact steps for defining *sheet* labels (those that are on separate sheets), and for defining *tractor-fed* labels (those on a continuous roll, used with nonlaser printers), vary slightly. You may need to make some adjustments to print properly on tractor-fed labels. But regardless of which type of label you're using, the basic steps are similar to creating (adding) any other paper size:

1. Start at the WordPerfect Edit screen (at the top of the document if you already have labels on-screen).

2. If you've installed multiple printers, select **File ➤ Print ➤ S**elect Printer (or press **Shift-F7 S**) and the printer of your choosing. Then press Exit (**F7**) to get back to the Edit screen.

3. Select **Layout ➤ P**age **➤** Paper Size **➤ A**dd (or press **Shift-F8 P S A**).

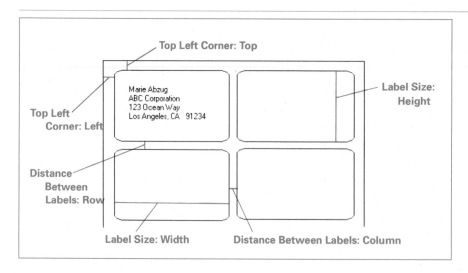

Label measurements on sample labels

4. Select **L**abels.

5. Select Paper **S**ize. If you are defining a paper size to print sheet (laser printer) labels, select Standard (8.5 × 11) as the paper size—the size of the entire sheet of labels. If you are defining a paper size for trac-tor-fed labels, select **O**ther and enter the combined width of the labels (and any space between them) as the Width and the height of a single label as the Height. For example, if you want to print on two-across labels on a dot-matrix printer, where each label is 4" wide and 1 $^{15}/_{16}$" tall, with $^1/_{16}$" space between each row of labels, enter *8* (or *8.5"*) as the page width and *2* as the page height.

6. Select Paper **T**ype ➤ **O**ther, type a name of your choosing for the label size (for example, *Address Labels* or *3.5" Disk Labels*), then press ↵.

7. If you want WordPerfect to beep to remind you to load tractor-fed labels into the printer before it starts printing them, select **P**rompt to Load ➤ **Y**es.

8. If you want WordPerfect to pause to allow you to feed sheets of labels individually into your laser printer, select **L**ocation ➤ **M**anual.

9. Select La**b**els ➤ **Y**es. The screen shown in Figure 7.25 appears. Use Fig-ure 7.24 and the sections that follow to define the size of your labels.

Label Size Select Label **S**ize, then type in the width of a single label and press ↵. Next, enter the height of a single label and press ↵. If you are

```
Format: Labels

    1 - Label Size
                 Width          2.63"
                 Height         1"

    2 - Number of Labels
                 Columns        3
                 Rows           10

    3 - Top Left Corner
                 Top            0.5"
                 Left           0.188"

    4 - Distance Between Labels
                 Column         0.125"
                 Row            0"

    5 - Label Margins
                 Left           0.103"
                 Right          0.063"
                 Top            0"
                 Bottom         0"

Selection: 0
```

FIGURE 7.25:

Options for defining a label format

defining tractor-fed labels, include the distance between labels in the label width and height. For example, if labels are 2 $^{15}\!/_{16}$" tall with $^{1}\!/_{16}$" in between each row, define the label height as 3".

Number of Labels Select **N**umber of Labels, then type the number of labels across the page (for columns) and press ↵. Next, if you are using sheet labels, enter the number of labels down one column on a sheet (for rows). If you are using continuous (tractor-fed) labels, enter **1** as the number of rows. Press ↵ after typing your entry.

Top Left Corner Select Top Left **C**orner, then enter the measurement from the top and press ↵. As Figure 7.24 shows, this is the distance from the top of the page to the top of the first label. Next, you'll be prompted to enter the measurement for the distance from the left edge of the page to the first label. Again, type your measurement, and press ↵. If you are using tractor-fed labels, you can set both of these measurements to 0 inches. But, before printing labels, you'll need to position the first label in the printer so that the print head is exactly where you want to print the first character of the label.

Distance Between Labels The distance between labels is difficult to measure exactly, but it is typically 0 inches (no space), $^{1}\!/_{16}$ inch, $^{1}\!/_{8}$ inch, or perhaps 0.25 ($^{1}\!/_{4}$) inch. Type in the distance between columns (the physical space between adjacent labels) and press ↵. If you are using tractor-fed labels, this distance should be entered as 0 regardless of the actual distance between two or more labels. Next, type in the distance between two rows or, if you are using tractor-fed labels, type 0 (you've already accounted for the distance between labels in your height measurement; e.g., when you typed 3" for 2 $^{15}\!/_{16}$" labels with $^{1}\!/_{16}$" between labels). Press ↵ after typing your entry.

Label Margins The Label **M**argins option specifies the margins used on a single label. Typically, you do not want the contents of mailing labels to be word-wrapped, so you should leave all these selections set to zero.

However, if you want to ensure that text on each label is not too close to the left edge of the label, you might want to specify a small left margin, of about 0.25" or so. Or, if you will be printing on labels that already have your company logo and return address printed at the top, you can specify a top margin equal to the height of that preprinted return address. This way, text will always print below the return address.

Similarly, when printing 3$^{1}\!/_{2}$" disk labels, leaving a top margin of about 0.68 inches prevents text from being printed on the area of the label that wraps to the back of the disk, and also helps you to vertically center text on the front of the label.

When printing tractor-fed labels, remember that the left-right position of the tractors and the vertical position of the print head on the first label before printing will greatly affect how text is printed on each label. WordPerfect doesn't know how you've aligned the labels in your printer; it just starts printing at the current print-head position. See Chapter 16 for additional information.

After defining your label format, press Exit (**F7**) twice to return to the Paper Size/Type menu. If you want to put your new label format to work now, choose **S**elect. Otherwise, press Exit to get back to the Edit screen. You can use your new label format (with the current printer) at any time in the future simply by positioning the cursor at the top of the document and selecting **L**ayout ➤ **P**age ➤ Paper **S**ize (or by pressing **Shift-F8 P S**) and the name of your new label format.

CHANGING A PAPER SIZE DEFINITION

If you define and use a paper (or label) size and find that it needs some fine-tuning, follow these steps to make changes:

1. If the document you're using at the moment uses the paper size you're about to change, delete the existing [Paper Sz/Typ] code on the Reveal Codes screen (to prevent code clutter or confusion).

2. Select **L**ayout ➤ **P**age ➤ Paper **S**ize/Type, or press **Shift-F8 P S**.

3. Move the highlight to the paper size you want to change.

4. Select **E**dit.

5. Make your selections from the Edit Paper Definition menu (just as when you initially created the paper or label size).

6. Press Exit (**F7**) until you return to the Paper Size/Type menu.

7. If you want to use the newly modified paper size now, choose **S**elect, then Exit (**F7**) to return to the Edit screen. (If you don't want to use the newly edited paper size, just press Exit until you get back to the Edit screen).

DELETING, COPYING, AND FINDING PAPER SIZES

If you look at the bottom of the Paper Size/Type menu, you'll see that the menu also includes these options:

Delete   Deletes the currently highlighted paper size definition. If you delete one by accident, press Cancel (**F1**) to bring it back.

Copy   Makes an exact copy of the currently highlighted paper size definition. The copy can be used as the starting point for creating a similar paper size.

Name Search	Lets you search for a paper size definition by name. Select this option, type the first character (or characters) of the name of the paper size you want, then press ↵. Then choose **S**elect to select the currently highlighted paper size, or use the arrow keys to move to another paper size before choosing **S**elect.

The "All Others" Paper Size

The ALL OTHERS paper size that appears on the Paper Size/Type menu, and elsewhere, is confusing for many people. Basically, it's a catchall category for invalid paper sizes. For example, suppose a friend creates some disk labels, using a paper size for printing on Avery 5197 (5¼" disk) labels. He gives you a copy of the document, and you use the usual File ➤ Retrieve command (Shift-F10) to retrieve the file.

If you do not have the Avery 5197 label size defined for your printer, WordPerfect automatically assigns the ALL OTHERS paper size to that document. Typically, the paper size is simply the standard 8.5" × 11" page. (The easiest way to solve this problem is to delete the old [Paper Sz/Typ] code and run the Labels macro, described earlier in this chapter, to set up this label size for your printer and select it for use with this document.)

You can change the ALL OTHERS size if you want (though offhand I can't think of any practical reasons for doing so, since it is just a catchall for invalid paper sizes). To change the ALL OTHERS paper size, select **L**ayout ➤ **P**age ➤ Paper **S**ize (or press **Shift-F8 P S**), highlight [ALL OTHERS], and select **E**dit. A brief summary of options, similar to those for creating normal paper sizes, appears. Make your selections as usual.

PROTECTING YOUR FORMATTING CODES

As I've mentioned repeatedly throughout this chapter, many formatting codes must be at the top of the page where you want them to take effect, before any text on that page.

Selecting an Initial Format

If you want to use a certain format throughout a document, such as printing every page in landscape mode, you can place the formatting codes in an area typically called Document Initial Codes (so called because it contains codes used to format the entire document). Placing formatting codes in the initial codes area offers two advantages:

◆ Because the codes are outside of and before all the text in the document, you need not be concerned about inadvertently inserting text before the codes, or inadvertently moving the codes to another place in the document.

◆ When you use **File ➤ R**etrieve (Shift-F10) or **File ➤ L**ist **F**iles (F5) to combine documents, only the Document Initial Codes for the first document are retained. The initial codes from subsequently retrieved files are ignored, giving all the combined files the same set of initial formatting codes.

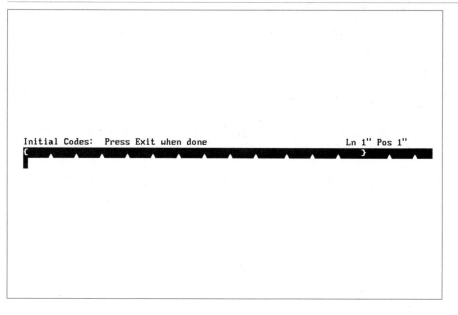

You'll learn more about combining documents in Chapter 12.

To place formatting codes in the Document Initial Codes area, follow these steps:

1. Select **L**ayout ➤ **D**ocument ➤ Initial **C**odes, or press **Shift-F8 D C**. A small Edit and Reveal Codes screen appears, with the prompt "Initial Codes: Press Exit when done", as in Figure 7.26.

2. Choose your formatting options from the **File ➤ P**age (**Shift-F8 P**) or **File ➤ L**ine (**Shift-F8 L**) menus. (A particular request will be ignored if that option is not allowed in Document Initial Codes.)

FIGURE 7.26:

The Edit and Reveal Codes screen for Document Initial Codes

```
Initial Codes:  Press Exit when done                    Ln 1" Pos 1"
```

3. Press Exit (**F7**) twice to return to the normal Edit screen.

The codes will not appear in the document but will affect all the text (up to a competing formatting code) in the document. Check the View Document screen if necessary to make certain.

If you later change your mind about the Document Initial Codes, use the same basic steps (select **L**ayout ➤ **D**ocument ➤ Initial **C**odes or press **Shift-F8 D C**) to return to the Initial Codes Edit screen and make new selections, or delete old ones, as necessary. You can delete any code by highlighting it and pressing Delete.

If you forget to exit from the Initial Codes screen before typing text, simply block all the text that you typed accidentally. Then select **E**dit ➤ **M**ove (Cut) or press **Ctrl-F4 B M**. Press **E**xit (F7) twice to leave the Initial Codes screen. Finally, position the cursor where you want to insert the text in the actual document, and press ↵ to retrieve the text.

SELECTING AN INITIAL BASE FONT

You can also select an initial base font for the document by using a similar technique. As with formatting codes, the selected font affects all the starting text in the document (up to the next [Font] code—it is ignored if the document is combined with another document that uses a different font).

To change the initial base font of a document, follow these steps:

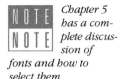

Chapter 5 has a complete discussion of fonts and how to select them.

1. Select **L**ayout ➤ **D**ocument ➤ Initial Base **F**ont, or press **Shift-F8 D F**.

2. Use the ↑ and ↓ keys to highlight the font you want and press ↵, or double-click on the font using your mouse.

3. If you've chosen a scalable font, type the point size and press ↵.

4. Press Exit (**F7**) to return to the Edit screen.

If you want to change the initial base font again in the future, follow the same steps.

In the next chapter, you'll learn how to gain more control over your printer and learn more about its capabilities.

CHAPTER 8

Mastering Your Printer

his chapter is about using your printer effectively. After all, the goal of any word processing project is to produce a neatly printed *hard copy* (paper copy) of your document. So here I'll talk about keeping text aligned on pages, printing multiple copies, printing specific pages from a document, expanding your font collection, and basic troubleshooting.

KEEPING PAGES ALIGNED WHEN PRINTING

TO ENSURE THAT TEXT IS ALIGNED PROPERLY WHEN PRINTING WITH DOT-MATRIX OR DAISY-WHEEL PRINTERS,

align a page perforation just above the print head before turning on the printer.

 If you have a printer that prints from sheets in a tray or requires you to load sheets individually, you can skip this section.

If your printer uses continuous form (also called tractor-fed) paper, your first step in printing a document should be to avoid the common text-over-the-page-break syndrome. That occurs when text that's supposed to be together on a page is split across two pages, as in Figure 8.1 (the grayed area represents printed text, the white area represents margins). You can easily avoid this problem once you understand how tractor-feed printers work.

Your computer and WordPerfect assume that when you first turn on the printer, a page perforation is just above the print head so that the printer is ready to print the first page. This place is called the *top of form,* and your computer keeps track of it by counting how many lines are printed.

If you turn on your computer with the print head somewhere near the middle of the page, you've inadvertently chosen *that* position as the top of the page. Hence, when you print, the top of your text will start printing in the middle of the page, and you'll end up with the situation shown in Figure 8.1.

But even if you *do* turn on your printer with the page perforation properly aligned, you may still end up with this problem. WordPerfect knows the paper has been moved when *it* moves the paper, but does not know the paper has been moved when *you* move it. So, if you manually crank a sheet of paper through the printer after you've turned it on, future printed pages will be misaligned.

The general rules of thumb to follow are these:

◆ If your pages are misaligned, turn off the printer and manually crank the paper through until there's a page perforation just above the print head, then turn the printer back on.

◆ Once the paper is aligned properly and the printer is turned on, do not crank paper manually through the printer. Instead, use the printer's *form-feed* or *line-feed* button (see your printer manual for more information).

Pages may also be mis-aligned if you're using the wrong size paper. This is discussed in "Selecting a Paper Size" in Chapter 7.

Not only does manually cranking the paper through a printer mess up the page alignment, it can also damage your printer.

STARTING PRINTING

TO PRINT A COPY OF THE DOCUMENT CURRENTLY BEING EDITED,

select File ➤ Print ➤ Full Document (or press Shift-F7 F).

You've already learned how to start printing a document by selecting **F**ile ➤ **P**rint ➤ **F**ull Document; you'll learn some new ways to print a document in this chapter. Regardless of which techniques you use, a couple of general points are worth keeping in mind about printing.

First, be aware that WordPerfect may not start printing your document right away. That's because it makes a special copy of the text to be printed before it starts printing. (After printing is complete, WordPerfect automatically deletes this copy.) This process may take a minute or more depending on your

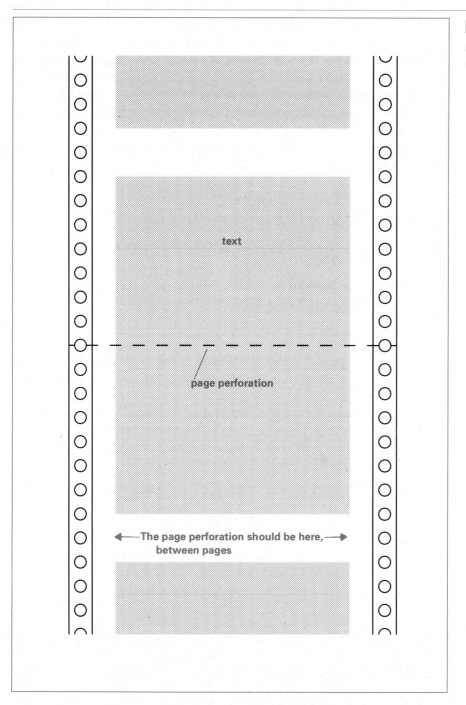

computer, your printer, and the size of your document. So if you start printing and nothing happens immediately, be patient.

On the other hand, if the printer doesn't start printing for a long time, or if you hear a beep and see the message "Print Shft F7,4 to resume printing", you should check the Control Printer screen (discussed in more detail later) by selecting **F**ile ➤ **P**rint ➤ **C**ontrol Printer (or by pressing **Shift-F7 C**).

WordPerfect uses a technique called *background printing* to print your documents. This means that once you tell WordPerfect to start printing something, it performs that job "in the background" so that you can continue editing other documents or select other documents to print.

CHOOSING FROM MULTIPLE PRINTERS

IF YOU'VE INSTALLED MULTIPLE PRINTERS FOR USE WITH WORDPERFECT,

select **File** ➤ **Print** ➤ **Select Printer (or press Shift-F7 S) to choose one to work with.**

NOTE
NOTE
If you want to install additional printers for use with WordPerfect, see Appendix A.

WordPerfect lets you install as many printers as you wish. You can even install printers that you don't own (such as a PostScript printer) to develop a document that you'll be typesetting later.

Keep in mind that every installed printer has its own set of fonts and its own set of paper sizes. Therefore, before you even start typing a document, you should probably select the printer you plan to use to print that document. Here's how:

NOTE
NOTE
Selecting File ➤ Setup ➤ Initial Settings ➤ Format Retrieved Documents for Default Printer (Shift-F1 I F) controls whether WordPerfect will use the default printer to format documents or will try to use the printer that was in use when you saved the document (Chapter 13).

1. Select **F**ile ➤ **P**rint ➤ **S**elect Printer (or press **Shift-F7 S**).

2. A list of available, installed printers appears, as in the example shown in Figure 8.2 (your screen will show the printers available to you).

3. Use the ↑ and ↓ keys to highlight the printer you want, or double-click on the printer you want to use, then choose **S**elect.

You'll be returned to the main Print menu. You can press Exit (**F7**) to return to the Edit screen.

When you save a document, WordPerfect also saves the name of the printer that was selected at that time. If in the future, you retrieve that document with a different printer in use, you may see the message "Formatting while retrieving" near the lower-left corner of the screen. WordPerfect is choosing whatever fonts and paper sizes in the currently selected printer best match the ones you chose when first developing the document with a different printer selected.

If you later look at the document on the Reveal Codes screen, you'll see that many of the [Font] codes now include an asterisk (*), indicating that Word-Perfect will use the available font shown, rather than the one you originally selected.

To revert to your original font selections, reuse the same printer: Select **F**ile ➤ **P**rint ➤ **S**elect Printer (or press **Shift-F7 S**), then choose the printer originally used to create the document.

PRINTING THE DOCUMENT ON THE SCREEN

NOTE NOTE
*Any chan-ges you make to the current document while it is being printed will **not** be incorporated in the current printing.*

I've already covered the steps required to print the document currently on your screen. You start by selecting **F**ile ➤ **P**rint or pressing Shift-F7 to get to the Print menu, shown in Figure 8.3. As you'll see, most printing techniques start with the same steps: **F**ile ➤ **P**rint. Choose **F**ull Document when you want to print the entire document that's currently on your screen and then return to the Edit screen.

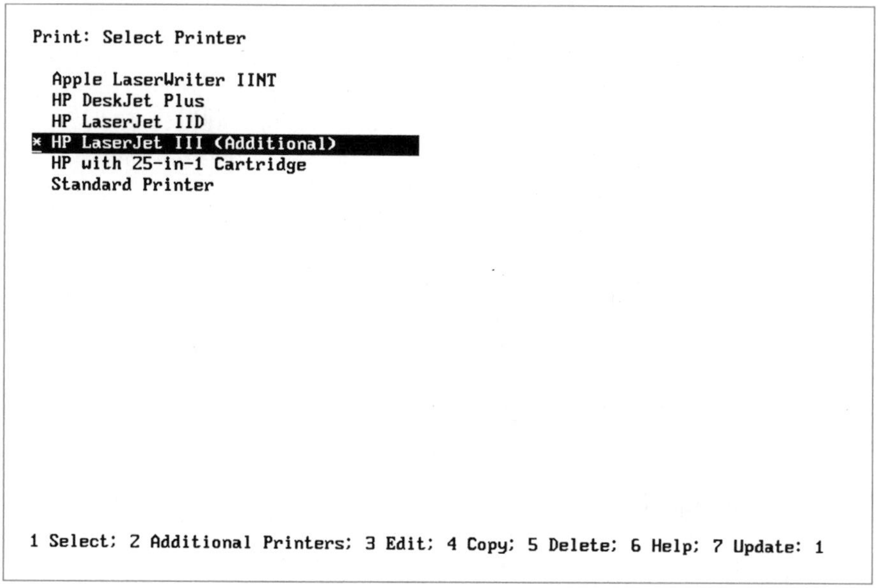

```
Print: Select Printer

    Apple LaserWriter IINT
    HP DeskJet Plus
    HP LaserJet IID
  * HP LaserJet III (Additional)
    HP with 25-in-1 Cartridge
    Standard Printer
```

FIGURE 8.2:
The list of available, installed printers

```
 1 Select; 2 Additional Printers; 3 Edit; 4 Copy; 5 Delete; 6 Help; 7 Update: 1
```

PRINTING A PAGE

Sometimes after typing a long document, you discover a mistake on a particular page. To save time and paper, you can simply correct the error and reprint that page only. (This assumes, of course, that your changes do not alter the number of lines on the page.) To print a particular page in your document, follow these steps:

1. Move the cursor to the page of the document where you want to make the correction.

2. Make your correction.

3. Select File ➤ Print ➤ **P**age (or press **Shift-F7 P**).

After the page is printed, compare it to the previous copy of the page to make sure that the new copy starts and ends with the same word. If not, you'll need to reprint all pages that follow the page you just printed.

PRINTING A BLOCK

You can print any highlighted block of text in your document by highlighting the block with the Block key (**Alt-F4** or **F12**) or your mouse, and selecting File ➤ **P**rint or pressing **Shift-F7**. When the screen asks "Print block? **N**o (**Y**es)", select Yes.

```
Print

        1 - Full Document
        2 - Page
        3 - Document on Disk
        4 - Control Printer
        5 - Multiple Pages
        6 - View Document
        7 - Initialize Printer


Options

        S - Select Printer              HP LaserJet III (Additional)
        B - Binding Offset              0"
        N - Number of Copies            1
        U - Multiple Copies Generated by   Printer
        G - Graphics Quality            Draft
        T - Text Quality                High




Selection: 0
```

FIGURE 8.3:

The Print menu

PRINTING A DOCUMENT STORED ON-DISK

TO PRINT A DOCUMENT THAT IS STORED ON THE DISK,

select File ➤ Print ➤ Document on Disk (or press Shift-F7 D), and enter the name of the file you want to print.

It's not necessary to retrieve a saved document onto the Edit screen to print it. You can print a document directly from disk, so long as you know its file name. Follow these steps:

1. Select **F**ile ➤ **P**rint ➤ **D**ocument on Disk (or press **Shift-F7 D**).

2. Type the complete file name of the document you want to print, then press ⏎.

3. When WordPerfect displays "Page(s): (All)", you can press ⏎ to print the entire document or specify pages to print (as discussed in the next section).

The List Files feature, discussed in Chapter 12, provides an easier way to print documents from the disk.

WordPerfect will begin printing the document you've named, unless you've made a mistake. For example, if you mistyped the file name or typed the name of a file that is not available on the current disk and directory, the lower-left corner of the screen will briefly show the message "ERROR: File not found". You'll have to try again by typing the file name correctly and pressing ⏎, or cancel the operation by pressing Cancel (F1).

If the document was formatted for a printer other than the currently selected printer, you'll see the message "Document not formatted for current printer. Continue? **N**o (**Y**es)". If you select Yes, WordPerfect will print the document, using the currently selected printer. However, the document will be printed with whatever fonts most closely match your originally selected fonts. If you don't want to print the document using the current printer, press **N** to select No. Then select the printer you want (select **F**ile ➤ **P**rint ➤ **S**elect Printer or press **Shift-F7 S**), and then select **F**ile ➤ **P**rint ➤ **D**ocument on Disk (or press **Shift-F7 D**) to print the document.

PRINTING SPECIFIC PAGES

> **TO PRINT SELECTED PAGES FROM A DOCUMENT,**
>
> **select File ➤ Print ➤ Multiple Pages (or press Shift-F7 M) and enter the page, or range of pages, you want to print.**

You can print specific pages or groups of pages from any document, whether you select **F**ile ➤ **P**rint ➤ **M**ultiple Pages (Shift-F7 M) or **F**ile ➤ **P**rint ➤ **D**ocument on Disk (Shift-F7 D). To do so, you need to tell WordPerfect exactly which pages to print using page numbers and punctuation, as discussed below.

To print a specific page, simply enter the page number after selecting the **M**ultiple Pages option or **D**ocument on Disk option. You can combine the page selection styles if you wish. For example, entering *5, 7, 9, 15-20* prints pages 5, 7, and 9, and then pages 15 through 20. Entering *1-3 7-9* prints pages 1 through 3, then pages 7 through 9. Entering *-10 90-* prints the first 10 pages of the document, then skips to page 90 and prints the rest of the document (that is, page 90 and all pages that follow).

You can also enter *O* (for Odd) to print odd-numbered pages (for example, the first, third, and fifth) and *E* for even-numbered pages (for example, the second, fourth, and sixth). Be aware, however, that these are *physical* pages and don't necessarily adhere to page numbering you've defined with Layout ➤ Page ➤ Page Numbering ➤ New Page Number. To ensure that odd-numbered and even-numbered pages are printed in proper sequence when using this feature, you should also use Layout ➤ Page ➤ Force Odd/Even in the document to make sure that a page-numbering change also forces an odd/even page break when required.

A docu-ment sum-mary con-tains the file's name, type, and creation date. You can add more infor-mation, such as the subject of your file and an abstract of its contents.

You can also use *LO* (logical odd) and *LE* (logical even) to print odd and even, *logical pages,* which are labels on a sheet. The sheet of paper is always considered a physical page, whereas each label on a sheet is a logical page. Logical pages are numbered from left to right starting at the top of the sheet. So if you print the LO labels, WordPerfect will print the first, third, fifth, and following odd labels. If you print the LE labels, WordPerfect will print the second, fourth, sixth, and following even labels.

You may also enter *s* or *S* to print the document summary (Chapter 12). The *S* or *s* must precede any other page numbers. Examples of pages to print are presented in Table 8.1.

ENTRY	WHAT IS PRINTED
5	Page 5 only
5,7	Pages 5 and 7, but no pages in between
5 7	Same as above (a blank space can be used in lieu of a comma)
5-	Page 5 and all pages that follow
5-7	Pages 5 through 7
-7	From the beginning of the document to page 7
S1-5	Document summary, followed by pages 1 through 5
S-	Document summary and entire document
S,5,7	Document summary, page 5, and page 7
O	All odd-numbered pages
E1-4	Even-numbered pages from 1 to 4 (pages 2 and 4)
LE	All even-numbered logical pages (e.g., labels 2, 4, 6, 8, etc.) when a label paper size is in use

TABLE 8.1:

Examples of Entries Used to Specify Multiple-Page Printing

The complete procedure for printing specific pages from a document is summarized in the steps below:

1. If you want to print certain pages from the document currently on your screen, select **F**ile ➤ **P**rint ➤ **M**ultiple Pages (or press **Shift-F7 M**). If you want to print selected pages from a document stored on-disk, select **F**ile ➤ **P**rint ➤ **D**ocument on Disk (or press **Shift-F7 D**), and enter the complete file name of the document you want to print (press ↵).

2. When prompted, type in the numbers of the pages you want to print.

3. Press ↵.

These steps assume that the pages in your document are numbered consecutively. However, if your document has several pages numbered *1*, you can still use the same general technique, but you'll need to provide section numbers with the page numbers, as described next.

PRINTING PAGES FROM SECTIONS

If your document is divided into sections or chapters, you may have numbered the first page of each section or chapter *page 1*. In addition, you may have numbered introductory pages with Roman numerals like *i, ii, iii* (discussed in Chapter 7). For example, suppose you've created a document consisting of a preface and three chapters, with the range of page numbers shown below:

Preface	i-ix
Chapter 1	1-15
Chapter 2	1-10
Chapter 3	1-20

To print specific pages from such a document, you can indicate a section by typing the section number, followed by a colon, followed by page numbers. For example, typing *2:10-15* will print pages 10 through 15 from Chapter 2. To print page 15 from Chapter 1, you would specify page *1:15*. To print pages i through iii of the preface, you would specify *i-iii*.

PRINTING BACK TO BACK WITH NONDUPLEX PRINTERS

Printing back to back with duplex printers like the Laser-Jet IID and IIID is simply a matter of choosing a back-to-back paper size. See Chapter 7.

On most laser (and other sheet-fed) printers, you can print back to back simply by printing all the even-numbered pages, flipping the pages over, putting them back into the printer, and then printing the odd-numbered pages on the front of each even-numbered page. When creating the document, however, be sure that you force an odd/even page break wherever you use Layout ➤ Page ➤ Page Numbering ➤ New Page Number to start a new page number. Then you can follow these steps to print the document:

See your printer manual for instructions on changing the collation.

1. If possible, change your print collation so that the printer collates backward (i.e., pages come out faceup with the first printed page at the bottom of the stack).

2. With the document you want to print already on the Edit screen, select **File** ➤ **Print** ➤ **Multiple Pages** (or press **Shift-F7 M**).

3. Type **E** (for Even) and press ↵.

4. When the print job is finished, if you couldn't collate backward in step 1, reshuffle so that page 2 is on the bottom, page 4 is on top of that,

and so forth, until the last page is on top. (You may also want to wait a few minutes for the paper to dry out, and help uncurl it if possible, so it will feed better going back through the printer.)

5. Flip over the whole stack so that the back of page 2 is on top of the stack, and put the stack back into the printer.

6. Select **F**ile ➤ **P**rint ➤ **M**ultiple Pages (or press **Shift-F7 M**).

7. Type **O** for Odd and press ↵.

As long as no paper jams cause problems on the paper's second pass through the printer, your back-to-back document should be complete.

PRINTING BACKWARD—LAST PAGE FIRST

Some sheet-feed printers *always* print pages face up, so the first printed page ends up at the bottom of the stack. Consequently, you must manually recollate all the pages top to bottom.

As an alternative, you can just print the entire document backward (from last page to first) so that the first pages (which get printed last) end up on the top of the stack, and all the pages that follow are in proper sequence.

| NOTE | *Macros are intro-duced in Chapter 15.* |

Unfortunately, there's no simple way to do this in WordPerfect, but the macro shown in Figure 8.4 can handle the job quite easily. It works by moving the cursor to the end of the document, printing that page, then moving the cursor up a page, printing that page, and so forth. It stops when it gets to page 1.

To use the macro (after creating it), select **T**ools ➤ Macro ➤ **Ex**ecute (or press **Alt-F10**), type the macro name (such as *BACKPRIN*), then press ↵. Just make sure your printer is ready, and the macro will do the rest. (You'll hear two beeps when the macro is finished, indicating that you can use the keyboard again.)

PRINTING MULTIPLE COPIES

TO PRINT MULTIPLE COPIES OF A WORDPER-FECT DOCUMENT,

1. Select **F**ile ➤ **P**rint ➤ **N**umber of Copies (or press **Shift-F7 N**).

2. Type the number of copies to print.

3. Press ↵.

You can tell WordPerfect to print multiple copies of any document by following these steps:

1. Select **F**ile ➤ **P**rint ➤ **N**umber of Copies (or press **Shift-F7 N**).

2. Type the number of copies you want to print and press ↵.

3. Select **F**ull Document, or **D**ocument on Disk, or **P**age, as described in preceding sections.

N O T E
N O T E

See Chapter 13 for more information on changing the default for print copies.

It's important to remember that once you change the number of copies to print, that setting stays in effect for the remainder of the current session. Therefore, if you will be printing other documents in the same session, be sure to change the number of copies, as required, for each document that you print. You can also change the default number of copies to print for all future sessions with WordPerfect (this holds true for print quality and binding offset, discussed later in this chapter).

Some printers can print multiple copies by themselves; WordPerfect merely has to tell the printer how many copies to print. Other printers, however, do not have this capability, so WordPerfect must tell the printer to print one copy several times (that is, after the printer prints one copy, WordPerfect tells it to print the next copy).

Printing multiple copies is slightly faster if the printer handles the job by itself. To use this method with your own printer, select **F**ile ➤ **P**rint ➤ **Mu**ltiple Copies Generated by (or press **Shift-F7 U**). Then select **P**rinter. If your printer

```
Macro: Action

     File          BACKPRIN.WPM

     Description

     {;}------------------------- Backprn.wpm
     ·····Prints·pages·in·backward·order.~
     {DISPLAY OFF}
     {Home}{Home}{Down}
     {WHILE}{SYSTEM}Page~>1~
        {Print}P
        {Page Up}
     {END WHILE}
     {Print}P
     {BELL}{BELL}




Ctrl-PgUp for macro commands;   Press Exit when done
```

FIGURE 8.4:

A macro that prints pages backward, from the last page to page #1, as displayed on the Macro Edit screen

cannot print multiple copies by itself, your selection will be ignored and Word-Perfect will handle the multiple copies.

Incidentally, using the printer to print multiple copies may change how the printed pages are collated. If you set Multiple Copies Generated By to *WordPerfect* (the default setting), and you print two copies of a five-page document, WordPerfect will print the entire first copy, then the entire second copy. But if you set Multiple Copies Printed by to *Printer,* WordPerfect may print two copies of page 1, then two copies of page 2, and so forth.

SELECTING A PRINT QUALITY

TO CHOOSE A PRINT QUALITY,

select File ➤ Print (or press Shift-F7), then select either Graphics Quality or Text Quality.

NOTE NOTE *You'll learn how to use graphics in a document in Chapter 19.*

The Print menu offers two options for controlling print quality: Text Quality and Graphics Quality. Both options offer the following four settings:

Do **N**ot Print   Text or graphics are not printed at all.

Draft   Uses the high-speed, draft-quality print mode (if your printer has it).

Medium   Uses the medium-speed, medium-quality print mode (if your printer has it).

High   Uses the slow, high-quality print mode (if your printer has it).

NOTE NOTE *You may not be able to see any difference between text qualities on a laser printer, since it will always produce fairly high quality output.*

If your printer has only two print qualities, such as draft and high, then medium print quality will probably be the same as high quality. Usually, you will use draft or medium quality when you want a quick printing or a draft copy of your document. When ready to print the final document, you can use the high-quality mode, which will take longer.

To change the quality of text or graphics for a document, follow these steps:

1. Retrieve the document onto an empty Edit screen by selecting **F**ile ➤ **R**etrieve (or pressing **Shift-F10**).

2. Select **F**ile ➤ **P**rint (or press **Shift-F7**).

3. Select **T**ext Quality or **G**raphics Quality, depending on which you want to change.

4. Select one of the options from the menu.

5. Repeat steps 3 and 4 if you want to change both the text and graphics quality.

Now you can select Full Document to print the document currently on your Edit screen, or you can select Document on Disk to print a document stored on-disk.

The Do Not Print options are useful when you are printing a document that combines text and graphics. If you just want to review a printed copy of the text in a document, you can set the graphics quality to Do Not Print so that you don't have to wait for all the graphics to be printed.

These options can also come in handy if you run out of memory while trying to print a document that combines text and graphics. First, print the text only. Then run the same pages through the printer again, printing only the graphics.

Figure 8.5 shows examples of draft- and high-quality text from a dot-matrix printer, and draft-, medium-, and high-quality graphics from a laser printer.

When you save a document, WordPerfect saves the text and graphics qualities you've selected with the document. If you print a document from disk, it will be printed with the stored print quality, regardless of the current settings on the Print menu. Therefore, to change the print quality of a document stored on-disk, you must first retrieve that document onto the Edit screen and then change the print quality before printing the document.

EXITING WHILE PRINTING

You can exit Word-Perfect while the printer is running if WordPerfect has already sent all its text to the printer buffer. The Control Printer screen can help you see whether all text has been sent.

About the only thing you can't do while WordPerfect is printing is exit Word-Perfect. If you attempt to exit WordPerfect while documents are still being printed, you'll see the message "Cancel all print jobs? **N**o (**Y**es)". If you choose Yes, WordPerfect will stop sending data to the printer; you'll be returned to the DOS command prompt. If you choose No, printing will resume normally and you'll be returned to the blank Edit screen.

You can exit WordPerfect temporarily to run another program or enter a DOS command. However, doing so will stop the printer (once the printer's buffer is empty), and printing will not resume until you return to WordPerfect.

If you are using version 5 of DOS and the Task Swapper is active, you can (usually) flip back to the DOS Shell or to another running program by pressing **Alt-Tab** (or **Alt-Esc** or **Ctrl-Esc**). To return to WordPerfect, press Alt-Tab repeatedly until WordPerfect appears at the top of the screen, or double-click on its name in the Task Swapper window.

If you are using any version of DOS, you can temporarily exit to DOS during a print job by selecting **File ➤ G**o to DOS or pressing **Ctrl-F1**. If you just want to enter a single DOS command, select DOS **C**ommand, type your DOS command, and press ↵. If you want to enter a few commands, select **G**o to DOS. You'll see the DOS command prompt; you can then enter whatever commands you wish. Type **EXIT** and press ↵ to return to WordPerfect.

 Do not load any memory-resident (TSR) programs while temporarily in DOS. Otherwise, you may not be able to return to WordPerfect.

Draft quality

High quality

Medium quality

This is dot matrix low quality.

This is dot matrix high quality.

FIGURE 8.5:

Examples of draft-, medium-, and high-quality printing

TESTING YOUR PRINTER'S CAPABILITIES

> **TO SEE HOW YOUR PRINTER HANDLES THE SAMPLE PRINTED DOCUMENT,**
>
> **1.** Select **File ➤ Print ➤ Document on Disk** (or press **Shift-F7 D**).
>
> **2.** Type **PRINTER.TST** as the name of the file to print.
>
> **3.** Press ↵ twice.

Your WordPerfect program includes a document named PRINTER.TST that demonstrates a wide range of your printer's current capabilities. (The word *current* is important here because, as you'll learn in a moment, you can expand the capabilities of many printers through the addition of extra fonts.) You can also use this document to test your printer's print qualities.

If your computer has a hard disk, the PRINTER.TST file is copied to your \WP51 directory by default during the WordPerfect installation process. If you use floppies, you can find the file on the installed WordPerfect 1 disk. Follow these steps to print the PRINTER.TST file:

1. If you have multiple printers, select **File ➤ Print ➤ S**elect Printer (or press **Shift-F7 S**) to choose whatever printer you want to test.

2. Optionally, select **G**raphics Quality or **T**ext quality, and whichever qualities you want to test.

3. **S**elect **D**ocument on Disk, type **PRINTER.TST**, and press ↵ twice to print all pages.

Before printing Figure 8.6, I set the graphics quality to high by using File ➤ Print (Shift-F7), then choosing Graphics Quality ➤ High.

Figure 8.6 shows how the document looks when printed on a LaserJet III printer, which handles a wide range of fonts, text sizes, and text appearances, and has full graphics capability. Comparing your printed copy to Figure 8.6 will help you see the capabilities and limitations of your own printer.

CONTROLLING PRINT JOBS

> **TO CANCEL, RUSH, OR PAUSE A PRINT JOB,**
>
> first get to the Control Printer screen by selecting **File ➤ Print ➤ Control Printer** (press **Shift-F7 C**).

Whenever you tell WordPerfect to print a document, it treats your request as a *print job*. Rather than forcing you to wait for your entire document to be printed before you can resume your work, WordPerfect starts your print request and then returns control to you so that you can edit another document or select other documents for printing.

WordPerfect 5.1 Printer Test

WordPerfect 5.1 has many new features such as labels, spreadsheet imports, tab sets relative to margins, pull-down menus, mouse support, and more advanced macro and merge functions. WordPerfect 5.1 also supplements your printer's available characters by graphically printing over 1,500 international, legal, math, scientific, and typographical characters.

Japanese ざ   Copyright ©   Hand ☞   Greek Δ

Equations can be created using WordPerfect's <u>Equation</u> feature.

$$\int_0^\infty x^{n-1}e^{-x}dx = \int_0^1 \left(\log\frac{1}{x}\right)dx = \frac{1}{n}\prod_{m=1}^\infty \frac{\left(1+\frac{1}{m}\right)}{1+\frac{n}{m}} = \Gamma(n) , \; n \neq 0, -1, -2, -3, \ldots$$

The <u>Tables</u> feature in WordPerfect 5.1 creates, formats, and edits tables easily. The Tables Options[1] can be used to improve the appearance of the table.

Print Attributes	567,845.56	Centered	Right Aligned
	67,887.47	Shadow	SMALL CAPS
	635,733.03	Redline	~~Strikeout~~

Fine, Small, Normal, Large, Very Large, Extra Large, Superscript, and Subscript are some of the printing features that have made **WordPerfect the world's number one word processor.**

1   You can create ruled and numbered paper by using <u>User Boxes</u>

2   with numbers and graphic lines as borders. Text size and *appearance*

3   may be changed without affecting the numbers or lines.

4

5   <u>Integrating Text and Graphics</u>

6   Graphic images can be scaled, rotated, and moved. You can indicate the style of the border and include a caption. MOUSE   The graphic image can be placed anywhere on the page, inserted in a line, tied to a paragraph, or included in a header or footer.

7

8

---

[1]Although only double and single lines are used in this table, many other border styles are available including dashed lines, dotted lines, thick lines, extra thick lines, and no lines at all.

This document printed in WordPerfect 5.1 · April 18, 1991 11:39 pm.

FIGURE 8.6:
The PRINTER.TST file printed on a LaserJet III

You can also print several files by marking their names on the List Files screen. See Chapter 12 for more information.

This comes in handy when you're printing many lengthy documents, because you can easily stack up a series of print jobs. For example, if you need to print several chapters from a book, you can repeatedly use the Document on Disk option of the Print command to specify several chapters to print. Then you can resume working on another document (or go to lunch) while WordPerfect prints all your documents.

Of course, WordPerfect lets you change your mind about printing a document or any series of documents. You can also stop the printer, or pause it, in case you need to start over (or change the printer ribbon). To do any of these things, you need to access the Control Printer screen. Follow these steps:

Graphics printing is fastest when the Control Printer screen is displayed, because WordPerfect doesn't need to check constantly to see whether editing activities need attention.

1. Select **File** ➤ **P**rint or press **Shift-F7**.

2. Select **C**ontrol Printer.

Figure 8.7 shows the Control Printer screen with some documents already stacked up for printing.

The screen is divided into three sections: the current job, the job list, and menu options. Each of these is discussed in the following sections.

THE CURRENT JOB

The Current Job portion of the Control Printer screen describes the document currently being printed. It shows the number of the current print job, the bin

```
Print: Control Printer

Current Job

Job Number: 4                        Page Number:  1
Status:     Printing                 Current Copy: 1 by Printer
Message:    None
Paper:      Standard 8.5" x 11"
Location:   Continuous feed
Action:     None


Job List

Job  Document            Destination   Print Options
  4  C:\WP51\PRINTER.TST COM 1         Graphics=High
  5  C:\...\CHAP5.WP      COM 1         Text=Medium
  6  C:\...\FAX.WP        COM 1         Graphics=Draft

Additional Jobs Not Shown: 0



1 Cancel Job(s); 2 Rush Job; 3 Display Jobs; 4 Go (start printer); 5 Stop: 0
```

FIGURE 8.7:

The Control Printer screen

location (e.g., Continuous or Manual) in use, the page number currently being printed, and the number of the current copy. More important, however, this part of the screen also displays messages and actions to take when problems arise, as described below.

Whenever you encounter a printing problem, you should check the Message line on the Control Printer screen to determine the problem.

Message The Message line provides information on what's happening with the printer. If WordPerfect is busy printing, the line shows the message "Printing". If there is a problem (such as the printer isn't plugged in, isn't properly connected to the computer, or isn't online), the Status line shows "Printer not accepting characters".

Action The Action line suggests what action to take in case of a problem. If there is no problem, the Action line displays "None". If the printer is not connected properly, is not turned on, or is not online, the Action line displays "Check cable, make sure printer is turned ON".

If you are manually feeding sheets of paper to the printer, the Message line shows

Manual sheet feeding is determined by the Location option when defining or changing a paper size. See Chapter 7.

Insert paper
Press "G" to continue

When you've placed the page in the printer, just type the letter *G* to start printing.

THE JOB LIST

The Job List portion of the screen lists all the jobs that are currently stacked up for printing. Each entry in this list includes a job number (which Word-Perfect assigns automatically), the name of the document being printed, where the print job is being sent, and any special options you selected from the Print menu.

The Job List displays only the next three print jobs that are waiting to be printed. If additional jobs are waiting, the Additional Jobs Not Shown line shows you how many others there are. To view all the print jobs, including those not currently shown on the screen, select the **D**isplay Jobs option from the menu at the bottom of the screen. Press any key to return to the Control Printer screen after viewing the additional print jobs.

The following sections describe how to control the printer and print jobs in more detail.

SLAMMING ON THE BRAKES

Sometimes a page gets mangled while printing, or a label peels off and sticks to the platen, and yet the printer keeps trying to print. To immediately stop all printing, follow these steps:

1. Turn off the printer, or press the Online button to take it offline.

2. Select **File ➤ P**rint or press **Shift-F7**.

3. Select **C**ontrol Printer **➤ C**ancel Job(s).

4. Type an asterisk (*) to cancel all print jobs.

5. Select **Y**es.

6. Select **C**ancel to cancel all printing immediately.

7. Select **Y**es if asked whether you're sure.

8. Press Exit (**F7**) to return to the Edit screen.

At this point, you are back to square one. There are no print jobs waiting to be printed and you can deal with whatever situation caused you to slam on the brakes. You'll need to reset the printer, by turning it off then back on (if you have not done so already) or by pressing the reset button (if any). If you're using a dot-matrix printer, remember to align the top of the first page just above the print head before turning on the printer.

To resume printing, you'll need to go through the Print menu. If you don't want to start printing the document from page 1, use the Multiple Pages option on the Print menu to specify which pages to print.

CANCELING A SPECIFIC PRINT JOB

You can also cancel print jobs without resetting the printer. You might want to do this if you discover that a particular document is not printing with the right format, or if you discover an error in a document and want to fix it. To cancel a specific print job, follow these steps:

1. Select **File ➤ P**rint **➤ C**ontrol Printer (or press **Shift-F7 C**).

2. Select **C**ancel Job(s).

3. To cancel the current job only, press ↵. Optionally, type the number of the job you want to cancel and then press ↵.

If you canceled the current print job, printing may not stop immediately, because your printer buffer already contains additional pages to be printed.

When the buffer is empty, WordPerfect will advance the paper to the top of the next page and begin the next print job.

PAUSING THE PRINTER

If you just want to pause the printer temporarily while a document is being printed (to change the ribbon or to make some other adjustment to your printer, for example), follow these steps:

1. Select **F**ile ➤ **P**rint (or press **Shift-F7**). Then choose **C**ontrol Printer ➤ **S**top and wait for the current page to finish printing.

2. You'll see the message "Adjust paper (press FORM FEED or advance paper to top of page)" and the instructions "Press 'G' to Restart, 'C' to cancel" on the Control Printer screen.

3. Adjust the printer as necessary, then realign the top of the page (on a sheet-feed printer, use the form feed or FF button; on a dot-matrix printer, turn off the printer, scroll the top of a page perforation up to the print head, then turn on the printer again).

4. When you are ready to resume printing, select **G**o.

5. When prompted, type the number of the page where you want to resume printing, and press ↵.

You may need to take the printer off-line before pressing the form-feed button to eject a page. See your printer manual.

WordPerfect will start printing again, from the top of the page you specified in step 5.

PRINTING ONE PAGE AT A TIME

When using a printer that requires manual feeding or a paper size defined for manual feeding (Chapter 7), WordPerfect will beep and wait after you tell it to print something. The beep is your cue to insert the page to print on. Follow these steps when you hear the beep:

Turning the platen manually while the printer is on can damage some printers!

1. If you're using a dot-matrix printer, turn off the printer.

2. Insert the page on which you want to print, making sure to align the top of the page just above the print head.

3. If you're using a dot-matrix printer, turn the printer back on and make sure it's online.

4. Select **F**ile ➤ **P**rint ➤ **C**ontrol Printer (or press **Shift-F7 C**).

5. Note the message next to the Action prompt on your screen, as shown in Figure 8.8.

6. When you are ready to print, press **G** (for Go), as instructed on the screen.

7. If there are additional pages to be printed, you'll hear a beep before the next page is printed and the printer will stop. Insert another page, and press **G** again.

RUSHING A PRINT JOB

Suppose you stack up several lengthy print jobs but suddenly need to print a quick memo or letter. You need not cancel your existing print jobs. Instead, you can just rush the job that needs to be handled to the front of the line. Follow these steps:

1. Select **File** ➤ **Print** ➤ **Control Printer** (or press **Shift-F7 C**).

2. If you cannot see all print jobs on the job list, select **D**isplay Jobs.

3. Note the number of the last print job in the list—this is the one you've just told WordPerfect to print.

4. Select **R**ush Job.

5. Type the number of the job to rush if it's not the suggested number, and press ↵.

```
Print: Control Printer

Current Job

Job Number: 10                      Page Number:  1
Status:     Printing                Current Copy: 1 by Printer
Message:    None
Paper:      Transparencies - Avery 5182 8.5" x 11"
Location:   Manual feed
Action:     Insert paper
            Press "G" to continue          ——— instructions

Job List

Job  Document             Destination    Print Options
10   C:\WP51\PRINTER.TST  LPT 1          Graphics=High



Additional Jobs Not Shown: 0



1 Cancel Job(s); 2 Rush Job; 3 Display Jobs; 4 Go (start printer); 5 Stop: 0
```

FIGURE 8.8:
The instructions to start printing are on the screen.

6. If you want to print the rush job after the current job is finished, select **N**o when asked about interrupting the current print job. To print the rush job immediately, select **Y**es.

In the last step, if you opt to interrupt the current print job and print the rush job immediately, the Action line on the Control Printer screen will display the message

Press R to rush job immediately

You should ignore this message and allow WordPerfect to continue printing the current page. When the current page is finished printing, WordPerfect will print your rush job. After completing the rush job, it will resume printing where it left off in the preceding print job.

If, on the other hand, you *do* press R a second time, WordPerfect will immediately stop printing the current page of the current document, and print your rush job. However, it will not be able to resume printing the current job normally when your print job is finished. You must cancel the print job that your rush job has interrupted.

PRINTING FOR BINDING

NOTE
NOTE

The binding offset will be placed at the top of the page when you select a paper size that calls for binding at the top (Chapter 7).

If your document will be printed (or copied) back to back and then bound like a book, you might want to leave some extra space for the right margin of even-numbered pages and the left margin of odd-numbered pages, as the example in Figure 8.9 shows. This will prevent text from running into the binding when the document is bound.

Follow these steps to add space for binding (assuming the document you want to print is on the Edit screen):

1. Select **File ➤ P**rint **➤ B**inding Offset (or press **Shift-F7 B**).

2. Type in the extra space you want to allot for binding (for example, 1/2 or .5 to leave an extra half-inch of space), then press ↵.

3. Press Exit (**F7**) to return to the Edit screen.

You will not see any obvious change on your Edit screen. However, you can preview the printed document on-screen by selecting **File ➤ P**rint (or pressing Shift-F7), then **V**iew Document **➤ 4** Facing Pages.

Changing the binding offset alone may not be sufficient for printing your document because it may decrease the right margin too far. You can even out the margins by cutting the desired binding offset in half and adding that value to both the left and right margins for the document.

For example, suppose you want a 0.5-inch binding offset and 1-inch margins on both sides of each printed page. The magic number for evening the margins is half of the desired binding offset (in this case, 0.25 inches). When you've determined the magic number, follow these steps:

1. Select **File ➤ Print ➤ B**inding Offset (or press **Shift-F7 B**).

2. Enter the magic number (one-half of the desired binding offset; in this example, the number is 0.25), and then press ↵.

3. Press Exit (**F7**) to return to your document.

4. Press **Home Home** ↑ to move the cursor to the top of the document.

5. Select **L**ayout (or press **Shift-F8**) then choose **L**ine ➤ **M**argins.

6. Add the magic number to the left margin setting (for example, if you want a 1-inch margin with a 0.5-inch binding offset, type *1.25*). Then press ↵.

7. Repeat step 6 for the right margin.

8. Press Exit (**F7**).

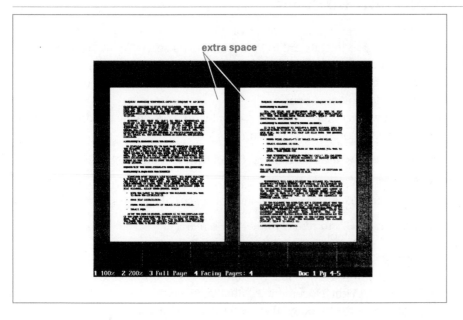

FIGURE 8.9:

Extra margin space allotted for binding

You may want to view facing pages on the View Document screen again, just to make sure that all is well. If you save the document after making these changes, the new binding offset is also saved with the document. Therefore, if you print the document from the disk (rather than from the screen), your binding offset will still be correct. On the other hand, if you want to change the binding offset of a file on-disk, you must first open that file, and make the change while the document is on the Edit screen.

PRINTING TO DISK

TO PRINT A FILE TO DISK,

**select File ➤ Print ➤ Select Printer ➤ Edit ➤ Port ➤
Other (or press Shift-F7 S E P O), and enter a path
and file name for the print file.**

You can print a copy of your document directly to a disk in a format that can later be printed directly from DOS. This is handy if you want to print your document with a computer that does not have WordPerfect installed on it or with typesetting equipment.

For example, suppose your home computer has WordPerfect installed on it, but has no printer or just a so-so printer. However, your office has a computer that uses DOS and has a laser printer connected to it, but does not have WordPerfect installed on it.

To print your documents with the office printer, you first need to install the WordPerfect office printer files on your home computer, just as if that printer were attached to your home computer (you need only do this once). You can then create, edit, and save your documents in the usual manner. You might also want to format and label a floppy disk for storing the printed copy of your file (I'll refer to this disk as the *transfer* disk).

When you want to print a copy of your document to disk, so you can later print it on the office printer, follow these steps:

1. If you have not done so already, retrieve the file you want to print at the office by selecting **File ➤ R**etrieve (or pressing **Shift-F10**).

2. Select **File ➤ P**rint ➤ **S**elect Printer (or press **Shift-F7 S**), then move the highlight to the name of the office printer (the printer you'll actually use to print the document).

3. Select **E**dit ➤ **P**ort ➤ **O**ther.

*If you just want to save a plain ASCII-text copy of your document, perhaps for use with a simple text editor, select **F**ile ➤ Text **O**ut ➤ DOS **T**ext (or press **Ctrl-F5 T S**) instead.*

4. Type the path and name for the file you'll use to store the "printed" document (e.g., MYDOC.PRN or A:\TRANSFER.PRN).

5. Press ↵ twice to return to the Select Printer menu.

6. Choose **S**elect.

You use DOS, not Word-Perfect, to format floppy disks.

7. If you named a floppy drive in step 4 above (e.g., *A:* or *B:*), insert a formatted disk in that drive.

8. Check the **T**ext Quality and **G**raphics quality options and make changes, if necessary.

9. Select **F**ull Document (or whatever print option you prefer) to begin printing.

You'll probably hear some whirring and buzzing, and see the drive light go on as WordPerfect prints your document to the disk. It may take a few seconds, or a few minutes. If you specified the hard-disk drive in step 4, be sure to copy the file named in step 4 to a floppy disk so that you can take that file to your office. You can use DOS, or **File** ➤ List **Files** (**F5**), discussed in Chapter 12, to make the copy.

To print the document on your office laser printer, follow these steps:

1. Get to the DOS command prompt (e.g., *C:>*).

2. Insert the transfer disk in drive A.

*To resume normal printing to a printer after printing to a disk, be sure to change the port back to its original setting: Select **F**ile ➤ **P**rint (or press **Shift-F7**), then choose **S**elect Printer ➤ **E**dit ➤ **P**ort. Reset the port, typically LPT 1 for parallel printers and COM 1 for serial printers. Then press Exit (**F7**), choose **S**elect, and press Exit again.*

3. At the DOS command prompt, type **COPY** *filename* **/B PRN,** where *filename* is the path and name of the print file. For example, if you used A:\TRANSFER.PRN in step 4 above, and the disk you created in that step is now in drive A of the office computer, the actual command is **COPY A:\TRANSFER.PRN /B PRN**.

4. Press ↵. It may take a couple of minutes for the document to start printing.

Whenever you print a document on the home computer using the name of the printer from the office, the printout will go to the file that you specified as the port. You don't have to change the port again unless you want to print to a different file name in the future, or you want to resume printing to a real printer port.

Incidentally, if you are using this technique to print your document on a typesetting machine, you use the same first set of steps listed above for sending printed output to a file instead of a printer port. The only difference is that you'll probably want to select a PostScript printer, such as the Apple Laser-Writer, after choosing **File** ➤ **Print** ➤ **S**elect Printer.

MAXIMIZING PRINTER SPEED

If you're not familiar with all this technical printer terminology, don't worry about it. Printing to the hardware port only increases print speed by a tiny amount, which won't be noticeable in most situations.

If you are not sharing printers with others on a network, and you are not using any third-party print spoolers, you can maximize printer performance by sending text directly to the printer port rather than through the traditional PC BIOS:

1. Select **F**ile ➤ **P**rint ➤ **S**elect Printer (or press **Shift-F7 S**).

2. Highlight the printer you want to use.

3. Select **E**dit ➤ Print to **H**ardware port ➤ **Y**es.

If you find that printing is disabled or impaired, repeat steps 1 and 2 and select **N**o in step 3 to go back to the traditional PC BIOS method. Optionally, if you can find information about your printer's Interrupt Request Level (IRQ) and Base Address, you may be able to set the Print to Hardware Port to Yes, but also select **A**dvanced Setup from that same menu to specify the appropriate IRQ and Base Address.

SELECTING A SHEET FEEDER

Whenever you use Print Screen or Shift-Print Screen to print a "screen dump," you should press the form-feed button on your printer to eject the printed page.

If your printer uses an oversize or multiple-bin paper feeder (excluding the regular paper bin or sheet feeder that came with your printer), you may need to inform WordPerfect that this new feeder is in use. To do so, select **F**ile ➤ **P**rint (or press **Shift-F7**). Then choose **S**elect Printer ➤ *highlight a printer* ➤ **E**dit ➤ **S**heet Feeder.

Select a sheet feeder from the list of available options (or **N**one to use your regular, original sheet feeder). You'll see some helps and hints about using the feeder, like in the example shown in Figure 8.10. You may want to jot these down, or press **Print Screen** (or Shift-Print Screen) to print a copy of the page, then press Exit (F7) until you return to the normal Edit screen.

Because custom sheet feeders can generally hold many types of paper (legal, letter, envelopes, and more), you'll want to change some of your existing paper size definitions to use the new sheet feeder:

1. Select **L**ayout (or press **Shift-F8**).

2. Choose **P**age ➤ Paper **S**ize, and highlight (or create) any paper size, as discussed in Chapter 7.

3. Select **E**dit ➤ **L**ocation ➤ **B**in Number, and enter the appropriate bin number for the paper size you're changing (or creating).

EXPANDING YOUR FONT COLLECTION

TO INSTALL NEWLY ACQUIRED CARTRIDGE OR SOFT FONTS FOR USE WITH WORDPERFECT,

select File ➤ Print ➤ Select Printer ➤ Edit ➤ Cartridges/Fonts/Print Wheels (or press Shift-F7 S E C).

Chapter 5 explains how to determine which fonts are currently available to you.

Many printers require that you turn off the printer or take it offline before plugging in a cartridge. See your printer manual for instructions.

It's important to understand that WordPerfect cannot actually *create* a font. WordPerfect can only *use* a font that your printer supports; there are several kinds:

Built-in fonts   Built-in (also called *resident*) fonts are built into your printer. If you have not installed any other fonts for use with WordPerfect, only the built-in fonts are available.

Cartridge fonts   You can add fonts to your printer with cartridges that you purchase separately.

Soft fonts   Soft fonts are stored on your computer's hard disk and are *downloaded* (sent) to the printer as needed. Like cartridge fonts, soft fonts must be purchased separately. You must also copy the soft fonts onto your computer's hard disk and install them for use with WordPerfect before you can use them, as discussed later in this chapter.

```
 Sheet Feeder Helps and Hints:   BDT LaserFeeder 890 (SF)

 Note: Be sure to use the Paper Size/Type option on the Page Format
       menu to indicate the location of available forms.

 Bin 1 is the first letter size bin.
 Bin 2 is the second letter size bin.
 Bin 3 is the third letter size bin.
 Bin 4 is the envelope bin.
 Bin 5 is the manual feed slot.




 Press Exit when done                 (Use Cursor Keys for more text)
```

FIGURE 8.10:

Sample helps and hints after selecting a custom sheet feeder

PRINTERS AND FONTS

The range of fonts you can choose from is entirely dependent on your printer. There are four basic categories of printers; each supports different types of fonts.

Daisy-wheel printers: To change fonts on a daisy-wheel printer, you need to change the printing wheel (see your printer manual for instructions).

Dot-matrix printers: Some dot-matrix printers come with several built-in fonts and also let you add fonts with cartridges.

LaserJet and compatible printers: LaserJet and compatible laser printers offer very few built-in fonts, but you can expand your collection of fonts with cartridge fonts or soft fonts (or both).

PostScript printers: PostScript printers usually come with about 35 built-in, scalable typefaces. In addition, you can purchase soft fonts, though not all soft fonts for PostScript printers are supported by WordPerfect.

Soft fonts can consume a lot of disk space, so you might want to stick with cartridges if your hard disk lacks ample free space.

If you have a laser printer that supports both cartridges and soft fonts and are considering buying your first set of fonts, consider a few points: First, cartridge fonts are generally much more expensive than soft fonts and offer a limited selection. However, they are printed faster than soft fonts, because they need not be downloaded from the disk to the printer. On the other hand, soft fonts are less expensive than cartridge fonts and provide more flexibility in the long run, because you do not need to switch cartridges to change fonts.

If you have a laser printer and a hard disk, you might want to consider purchasing the Bitstream Starter Set, which includes three useful typefaces. The starter kit is practically free to registered owners of WordPerfect ($29.95 was the charge at the time this book was written). In addition, the Starter Set includes a program to help you add other Bitstream fonts that you might later decide to purchase (there are over 200 fonts to choose from).

The number to call for ordering your Bitstream Starter Set and descriptions of other font products you can order for use with WordPerfect are included in the documentation that came with your WordPerfect package. Remember, the Bitstream fonts can be used only with laser printers.

INSTALLING FONTS

Information about the fonts supported by your printer is stored in a Word-Perfect file with the extension .ALL. For example, information about

Hewlett-Packard fonts is stored in a file named *WPHP1.ALL*. Information about PostScript fonts is stored in a file named *WPPS1.ALL*. When you installed your printer, WordPerfect copied the appropriate .ALL file to your hard disk, or to the PTR Program disk if you installed WordPerfect for use with floppies.

When you install fonts, you will see all the fonts supported by your printer; these are listed in the .ALL file. As you select the fonts you own, Word-Perfect will copy the names of selected fonts to your printer resource file (.PRS). In the future, when you select fonts for use in a document, only the fonts specified during the installation process will appear as valid options. This prevents you from inadvertently selecting fonts that you do not really own and have not specifically installed.

In other words, the .ALL file contains data for all Word-Perfect-supported printers; the .PRS file contains data for your particular printer, paper sizes, and fonts.

Installing a Font Cartridge

Some font cartridges are available directly from your printer manufacturer; cartridges are also available from third-party vendors. For example, Hewlett-Packard offers a wide variety of cartridges for all their laser printers. Pacific Data Products, a separate company, also offers cartridges for use with LaserJet printers.

*Laser printer cartridges that are used to **emulate** (act like) other printers need not be installed for use with Word-Perfect. Only font cartridges need to be installed.*

Before you buy a font cartridge from a third-party vendor, make sure that it's compatible with WordPerfect 5.1. (Compatible products are usually listed right on the cartridge packaging.) The manual that comes with a third-party cartridge should include specific instructions for updating the WordPerfect .ALL file. You should follow those instructions first, before proceeding with the steps below.

If you have a font cartridge that you want to use with WordPerfect, fol-low these steps to install the cartridge:

1. If you do not have a hard disk, put the installed WordPerfect *Printer (All) Files* disk in drive B.

2. Starting from the WordPerfect Edit screen, select **File** ➤ **Print** ➤ **S**elect Printer (or press **Shift-F7 S**).

3. If several printer names are shown, use the ↑ or ↓ key to move the highlight to the name of the printer for which you are installing fonts. If you are using a mouse, you can just click once on the name of the printer you want.

4. Select **E**dit ➤ Cartridges/Fonts/Print Wheels.

These steps will bring you to the screen for installing cartridges and fonts, as-suming that the .ALL file is available. If you see the message "Printer file not found", insert the *Printer (All) Files* disk in drive B (or A if you have a hard disk), then type the name of the drive containing that disk (A: or B:) and press ↵. If the error persists, you'll need to reinstall the printer.

The options shown on this screen depend on the printer you are using. If you have a printer that supports cartridge fonts but not soft fonts, this screen will display only the options Built-In and Cartridges. If your printer supports built-in, cartridge, and soft fonts, you'll see all three options on your screen, as shown in Figure 8.11.

If you are installing a cartridge, select **C**artridges. You'll see the list of cartridges that WordPerfect supports—an example is shown in Figure 8.12 (though your screen may show completely different options, depending on the printer you are using). You can use the ↑, ↓, Page Up, and Page Down keys to scroll through the entire list, or press and hold the left mouse button as you drag it up or down through the list.

NOTE NOTE *The term* **slot** *refers to the place on the printer where you plug in the cartridge.*

In the upper-right corner of the screen, notice that the Quantity indicator shows the total number of font cartridges in the printer and the number available for installation. If you have more cartridges than slots and have already installed the maximum number of cartridges, you must unselect one of your installed cartridges by moving the highlight to one of the cartridges that is already marked with an asterisk (*), then typing an asterisk. Then you can install a different cartridge for the slot you've made available.

```
Select Printer: Cartridges/Fonts/Print Wheels

Font Category                        Quantity        Available

Built-In
Cartridges                               2               2
Soft Fonts                            2048 K          1991 K




NOTE: Most fonts listed under the Font Category (with the exception of Built-In)
are optional and must be purchased separately from your dealer or manufacturer.
If you have fonts not listed, they may be supported on an additional printer
diskette.  For more information call WP at (801) 225-5000.

If soft fonts are marked '*', you must run the Initialize Printer option in WP
each time you turn on your printer.  Doing so deletes all soft fonts in printer
memory and downloads those marked with '*'.

If soft fonts are not located in the same directory as your printer files, you
must specify a Path for Downloadable Fonts in the Select Printer: Edit menu.

1 Select; 2 Change Quantity; N Name search: 1
```

FIGURE 8.11:

The screen for installing optional fonts

Remember, you may need to do this often if you use a wide variety of cartridge fonts (which is one of the disadvantages of cartridge fonts; you don't have to be concerned about available slots with soft fonts).

Follow these steps to proceed:

1. Use the cursor-movement keys to move the highlight to the name of the cartridge you are installing (press **Page Up** and **Page Down** to scroll through additional options, if any), or click on the name with your mouse.

2. Type an asterisk (*) when the highlight is on the correct name for your cartridge.

3. Press Exit (**F7**) until you return to the Edit screen.

Now you can select any fonts available on that cartridge with Font ➤ Base Font (**Ctrl-F8 F**), described in Chapter 5.

Installing Soft Fonts

Installing soft fonts is a two- or three-step process.

1. You must copy the fonts from the disks they are delivered on to a directory on your hard disk. Typically, the soft-font kit will include a program to simplify this process for you. It's important that all fonts be

NOTE *Before purchasing a set of third-party soft fonts, make sure they're compatible with WordPerfect 5.1.*

```
Select Printer: Cartridges                    Quantity
                                     Total:      2
                                 Available:      2

                                          Quantity Used

   HP A Courier 1                              1
   HP B Tms Proportional 1                     1
   HP Bar Codes & More                         1
   HP C International 1                         1
   HP D Prestige Elite                         1
   HP E Letter Gothic                          1
   HP F Tms Proportional 2                     1
   HP Forms Etc.                               1
   HP G Legal Elite                            1
   HP Global Text                              1
   HP Great Start                              1
   HP H Legal Courier                          1
   HP J Math Elite                             1
   HP K Math Tms                               1
   HP L Courier P&L                            1
   HP M Prestige Elite P&L                     1

Mark:  * Present when print job begins      Press Exit to save
                                          Press Cancel to cancel
```

FIGURE 8.12:
An example of cartridge selections

copied to the same directory. (This chapter assumes that all fonts are stored in a directory named *C:\FONTS.*)

2. If you are using a third-party font, such as Bitstream, or the Adobe fonts designed for PostScript printers, you may first need to define your fonts, and then add them to the WordPerfect .ALL file for later selection. The soft-font package will provide instructions for doing so, if necessary.

3. Finally, you must inform WordPerfect that these fonts are now available for use.

Assuming you've completed the first two steps listed above, and you stored the soft fonts in the C:\FONTS directory, here are the details for completing the third step above:

1. Starting from the WordPerfect Edit screen, select **File ➤ Print ➤ S**elect Printer (or press **Shift-F7 S**).

2. Highlight the name of the printer for which you are installing fonts, and then select **E**dit.

3. Select **C**artridges/Fonts/Print Wheels.

These steps will bring you to the screen for installing cartridges and fonts (Figure 8.12). If you see the message "Printer file not found" instead, insert the *Printer (All) Files* disk in drive B (or A if you have a hard disk) and then type the name of the drive containing the printer disk (A: or B:) and press ↵. If you see the same error message, you may need to reinstall the printer, as described in Appendix A.

Defining Printer Memory Notice the Quantity and Available options to the right of the Soft Fonts option. The Quantity option lists the default amount of printer memory available for soft fonts. For example, many LaserJet printers come with half a megabyte (512K) of printer memory, 350K of which is available for soft fonts.

If you added memory to your laser printer when you purchased it, you should increase Quantity accordingly. For example, if you added a megabyte (about 1000K) of printer memory, bringing your total printer memory up to 1.5MB, you would select Change Quantity, type in *1350* for the amount of memory available for soft fonts (adding the extra megabyte), and then press ↵.

Telling WordPerfect Which Fonts You Have Now you are ready to tell WordPerfect which soft fonts you have purchased and copied to your hard disk. Follow these steps:

1. Move the highlight to the Soft Fonts (or Downloadable Fonts) option and press ↵.

2. Depending on your printer, you may see a screen of font groups identified by the manufacturer's part number—for example, (AC) and (AD) are part-number groups for Hewlett-Packard soft fonts, and (FW) is a part-number group for Bitstream fonts. Select the part-number group that identifies your cartridge.

3. A list of all the *possible* fonts to choose from (including many that you may not have already purchased) appears. Figure 8.13 shows an example, but your screen may show other options; the options available depend on your printer.

Select only soft fonts that you have already purchased and copied to your disk.

The example lists the Helvetica fonts from the Hewlett-Packard AC set. But the list of soft fonts for most printers is quite long. You can scroll through the entire list by using the ↓, ↑, Page Down, and Page Up keys or by holding the left mouse button as you drag up or down.

Use the arrow keys or mouse to scroll through the fonts. As you scroll, you may notice that some fonts are categorized as *(Landscape)* or *(Land)*. You can select these fonts for printing in landscape mode on LaserJet and

```
Select Printer: Soft Fonts                    Quantity
                                      Total:   2048 K
                                  Available:   1991 K

HP AC TmsRmn/Helv US (P/L)                     Quantity Used

   (AC) Helv  6pt                                  8 K
   (AC) Helv  6pt Bold                             8 K
   (AC) Helv  6pt Italic                           8 K
   (AC) Helv  8pt                                  9 K
   (AC) Helv  8pt Bold                            11 K
   (AC) Helv  8pt Italic                          10 K
   (AC) Helv  10pt                                13 K
   (AC) Helv  10pt Bold                           13 K
   (AC) Helv  10pt Italic                         14 K
   (AC) Helv  12pt                                15 K
   (AC) Helv  12pt Bold                           16 K
   (AC) Helv  12pt Italic                         16 K
   (AC) Helv  14pt                                18 K
   (AC) Helv  14pt Bold                           19 K
   (AC) Helv  14pt Italic                         20 K
   (AC) Helv  18pt Bold                           29 K

Mark:  * Present when print job begins        Press Exit to save
       + Can be loaded/unloaded during job    Press Cancel to cancel
```

FIGURE 8.13:

A partial list of available soft fonts

compatible printers. Fonts that are not marked as *(Land),* or are marked as *(Port),* are for printing in normal portrait mode.

To tell WordPerfect that you have installed a soft font on your disk, move the cursor to the appropriate font and then type either **+** or *****. Typing ***** tells WordPerfect that the font will already have been downloaded when printing begins. This requires an extra step (called *printer initialization*) before printing documents that use the font. You can only use the ***** to mark as many fonts as your printer can hold in memory. The Available memory indicator near the top of the screen informs you of how much memory remains.

Typing **+** tells WordPerfect that the selected font will not be available when printing starts, and hence WordPerfect should copy the font to the printer before attempting to use it. This is the easiest way to use soft fonts, but it does slow down printing a bit.

Some printers let you mark fonts with both an asterisk and a plus sign (***+**), which makes fonts "swappable." Such fonts are swapped out of printer memory, if necessary, to make room for additional fonts, then swapped back into the printer when the print job is complete. Figure 8.14 shows an example of soft fonts marked with both an asterisk and a plus sign.

If you mark a font with **+**, *****, or both by mistake, or you change your mind, move the highlight to that selection and type **+** or ***** again to remove the mark. Then you must complete two more steps:

1. Mark all fonts that you have copied to your hard disk and want to use in the future with *****, **+**, or both (***+**).

You cannot use either * or + to mark a font that requires more memory than your printer has.

There's no harm in marking fonts with both * and + on any printer, but remember that all fonts marked with * must be predownloaded by selecting File ➤ Print ➤ Initialize Printer to work properly.

```
Select Printer: Soft Fonts                    Quantity
                                   Total:     2048 K
                               Available:     1960 K

FW HP LaserJet IID                                      Quantity Used

  + (FW) Cloister Black 24pt (HP Roman 8)                    81 K
  + (FW) Cloister Black 36pt (HP Roman 8)                   169 K
  + (FW) Dutch Bold 10pt (HP Roman 8)                        22 K
 *+ (FW) Dutch Bold 12pt (HP Roman 8)                        29 K
  + (FW) Dutch Bold 14pt (HP Roman 8)                        36 K
  + (FW) Dutch Bold 20pt (HP Roman 8)                        66 K
  + (FW) Dutch Bold 24pt (HP Roman 8)                        91 K
  + (FW) Dutch Bold Italic 10pt (HP Roman 8)                 23 K
 *+ (FW) Dutch Bold Italic 12pt (HP Roman 8)                 29 K
  + (FW) Dutch Bold Italic 14pt (HP Roman 8)                 37 K
  + (FW) Dutch Bold Italic 20pt (HP Roman 8)                 67 K
  + (FW) Dutch Bold Italic 24pt (HP Roman 8)                 95 K
  + (FW) Dutch Italic 10pt (HP Roman 8)                      23 K
 *+ (FW) Dutch Italic 12pt (HP Roman 8)                      30 K
  + (FW) Dutch Italic 14pt (HP Roman 8)                      39 K
  + (FW) Dutch Italic 20pt (HP Roman 8)                      70 K

Mark:  * Present when print job begins         Press Exit to save
       + Can be loaded/unloaded during job    Press Cancel to cancel
```

FIGURE 8.14:

Examples of some soft fonts marked with +, others marked with *+

2. When you've finished marking your available soft fonts, press Exit (**F7**) until you see the Select Printer Edit screen, shown in Figure 8.15 (though specific selections shown in this figure will probably be different on your computer).

Identifying the Fonts Directory Next you need to tell WordPerfect where to find your soft fonts. If you've been following along, you should now be at the screen shown in Figure 8.15. (If you've already exited to the Edit screen, select **F**ile ➤ **P**rint ➤ **S**elect Printer ➤ **E**dit or press **Shift-F7 S E**.) Then follow these steps to specify your fonts directory:

1. Select Path for **D**ownloadable Fonts and Printer Command Files.

2. Type the name of the directory where your soft fonts are stored (earlier examples used C:\FONTS).

3. Press ↵.

4. Press Exit (**F7**) until you return to the Edit screen.

In the future, you can choose any of your newly installed soft fonts just as you did in Chapter 5, by selecting **F**ont ➤ Base F**o**nt (or by pressing **Ctrl-F8 F**). However, don't forget that you'll need to complete one extra step if you choose a font marked only with an asterisk in the preceding section. This step is explained below in "Downloading Soft Fonts You Marked with an Asterisk."

CAUTION

You must enter a valid drive and directory name in step 2; otherwise, WordPerfect rejects your entry with "ERROR: Invalid drive/path specification".

```
Select Printer: Edit

        Filename                HPLASIID.PRS

    1 - Name                    HP LaserJet IID

    2 - Port                    LPT1:

    3 - Sheet Feeder            BDT LaserFeeder 890 (SF)

    4 - Cartridges/Fonts/Print Wheels

    5 - Initial Base Font       Courier 10cpi

    6 - Path for Downloadable   C:\FONTS
          Fonts and Printer
          Command Files

    7 - Print to Hardware Port  Yes




Selection: 0
```

FIGURE 8.15:

The screen for changing printer options

CHOOSING AN INITIAL BASE FONT FOR A PRINTER

Typically, WordPerfect uses a basic "typewriter" font (typically 10 cpi) if you choose to print a document without specifically selecting a different font within that document. If you'd like to change this assumption, you can change the Initial Base Font for that particular printer. Follow these steps:

1. Select **File ➤ P**rint ➤ **S**elect Printer from the Edit screen (or press **Shift-F7 S**).

2. Highlight the printer whose initial base font you want to change.

3. Select **E**dit ➤ **I**nitial Base **F**ont.

4. Highlight the new base font, then choose **S**elect or press ⏎.

5. Press Exit (**F7**) until you return to the Edit screen.

Remember that the selection you make here is used only if you do not override the selection by changing the base font within the document (by selecting **F**ont ➤ Base **F**ont or pressing Ctrl-F8 F) or the initial base font for this particular document (by selecting **L**ayout ➤ **D**ocument ➤ Initial Base **F**ont or by pressing Shift-F8 D F).

DOWNLOADING SOFT FONTS YOU MARKED WITH AN ASTERISK

If you marked any soft fonts with only an asterisk (*), you must download them to your printer before using them to print a document. Otherwise, WordPerfect will substitute a font that has already been downloaded or a built-in font. Follow these steps:

1. Starting at the Edit screen, select **F**ile ➤ **P**rint ➤ **I**nitialize Printer, or press **Shift-F7 I**.

2. When prompted, select **Y**es.

The downloading is treated like any other print job, so you can monitor it from the Control Printer screen. Once downloading is complete, the fonts will reside in the printer until you either turn off the printer or select **F**ile ➤ **P**rint ➤ **I**nitialize Printer (Shift-F7 I) again. Therefore, any print jobs using those fonts will be completed quite quickly, because you don't need to wait for WordPerfect to re-download each font in the document every time you print the document.

MAKING SOFT FONTS
OPERATE AT BUILT-IN FONT SPEEDS

This "trick" is strictly for convenience and is not at all required to use soft fonts effectively. So please don't feel intimidated if you're unfamiliar with DOS commands.

One trick I've come up with to avoid the long wait for soft fonts to load is to automatically load a selected few every morning, when I first start my computer. The wait is just as long, but not nearly so annoying when it takes place first thing in the morning when all the equipment (and myself) are just warming up.

Once the start-up procedure is finished, the downloaded fonts are available for the rest of the day (or at least until I turn off the printer), at built-in font speeds, so I *never* have to wait for those fonts to be downloaded when I use them in a document.

The basic idea is to mark your most frequently used soft fonts with * or *+, as described earlier, within the limitations of your printer's memory. Don't use *all* your printer's memory; you need to save some for printing graphics (I use about half my printer's 4MB memory for soft fonts).

See Chapter 15 for more information on macros.

Next, create a macro that initializes the printer, like the example shown in Figure 8.16. Use the Macro Editor, and be sure to store the macro in the directory where WordPerfect normally expects to find macros (as defined by selecting **File ➤** Se**t**up **➤** Location of Files or by pressing **Shift-F1 L**).

Next, modify the AUTOEXEC.BAT file that DOS reads whenever you first start or reboot your computer. You must use either a plain text editor or DOS

```
  Macro: Action

     File            LOADFONT.WPM

     Description


    ┌─────────────────────────────────────────────────────┐
    │{;}--------------------------- LoadFont.wpm           │
    │         ----------------Initialize·the·printer~      │
    │{;}Select·printer·to·initialize~                      │
    │{Print}snHP·LaserJet·IID{Enter}s                      │
    │iy               {;}Initialize·printer...~            │
    │{Print}c         {;}Show·Printer·Control·Screen~      │
    │                                                      │
    │{;}Keep·Printer·Control·screen·visible·during·download~│
    │{WHILE}{SYSTEM}Print~&128~                            │
    │   {WAIT}20~                                          │
    │{END·WHILE}                                           │
    │                                                      │
    │{Exit}           {;}Exit·Printer·Control~             │
    │{Exit}ny         {;}Exit·WordPerfect~                 │
    └─────────────────────────────────────────────────────┘


  Ctrl-PgUp for macro commands;  Press Exit when done
```

FIGURE 8.16:

A macro to initialize the printer by downloading soft fonts, displayed on the Macro Edit screen

*DOS commands and file names can be typed in uppercase, lowercase, or a mixture. All are equivalent. For example, **c:\wp51\wp /m-loadfont** is the same as **C:\WP51\WP /M-LoadFont**.*

The difference between formatted files and DOS text (ASCII) files is discussed in more detail in Chapter 25.

text in WordPerfect. To use DOS text in WordPerfect, select **File** ➤ **Text In** ➤ DOS Text (CR/LF to **H**rt) (or press **Ctrl-F5 T R**), type **C:\AUTOEXEC.BAT**, and press ↵.

Next, add a command that loads WordPerfect and the LoadFont macro automatically, like this:

C:\WP51\WP /M-LoadFont

The C:\WP51\WP command starts WordPerfect. The /M-LoadFont command tells WordPerfect to automatically load and execute the LoadFont macro. In Figure 8.17, this is the second-to-last command in a sample AUTOEXEC.BAT file in DOS 5.

In this arrangement, WordPerfect and the LoadFont macro are executed after most of the other commands in AUTOEXEC.BAT. The {Exit}ny command in the last line of the LoadFont macro exits WordPerfect, then automatically returns control to AUTOEXEC.BAT. So the last command in AUTOEXEC.BAT is LOADHIGH DOSSHELL, which leaves me conveniently placed at the DOS 5 Shell. But of course, all my soft fonts are downloaded to the printer, so I can use them at will without waiting.

If you used WordPerfect to edit AUTOEXEC.BAT, you *must* remember to save it by selecting **File** ➤ **Text O**ut ➤ DOS **T**ext (or by pressing **Ctrl-F5 T S**) and typing the complete path and file name (e.g., C:\AUTOEXEC.BAT). Then clear

```
rem ***************************** AUTOEXEC.BAT (DOS 5 and 386)
rem ********* load memory resident programs in upper memory.
loadhigh c:\dos\mode com1:9600,n,8,1,b
loadhigh c:\dos\mode lpt1:,,b
loadhigh d:\mouse1\mouse
loadhigh c:\dos\print.exe /d:lpt1
loadhigh c:\dos\doskey
loadhigh c:\dos\fastopen.exe c:=10 d:=10 e:=10 f:=10

c:\dos\mirror c: /tc /td /te /tf
PATH h:\temps;c:\wp51;c:\dos;e:\windows;e:\toolbook;f:\fontware
prompt $p$g

rem *************** Directory for backups on ramdrive
md h:\temps
set temp=h:\temps

rem *************** Install custom DOS 5 macros
call c:\dos\macros

rem *************** Load WP soft fonts, activate the DOS 5 Shell.
c:\wp51\wp /m-loadfont
loadhigh dosshell
```

FIGURE 8.17:

A sample DOS 5 AUTOEXEC.BAT file with a command to load WordPerfect and execute the macro that downloads soft fonts

the screen (select **File** ➤ **Exit** ➤ **No** ➤ **No** or press **F7 N N**), so you don't inadvertently save a WordPerfect-formatted copy over the plain ASCII copy.

If you want your boot-up procedure to take you into WordPerfect and leave you there (with your soft fonts already downloaded), the C:\WP51\WP /M-LoadFont command must be the *last* command in AUTOEXEC.BAT. Also, you'll want to remove {Exit}ny from the end of the LoadFont macro, so it does not exit WordPerfect after initializing the printer.

CONVERTING THIRD-PARTY 5.0 FONTS TO 5.1 FONTS

If you've recently upgraded from WordPerfect 5.0 to 5.1, you should install your printers as though you were doing so for the first time. However, you may be left without third-party fonts, such as Bitstream fonts, in 5.1. To use third-party fonts that you created in WordPerfect 5.0 in WordPerfect 5.1, you'll need to convert them to 5.1 format.

First, make backup copies of all your existing 5.0 and 5.1 .ALL and .PRS files (in case you make a mistake along the way). Then follow these steps, starting at the DOS command prompt, at the WordPerfect 5.1 directory (typically C:\WP51):

1. Type **PTR** and press ↵ to run the WordPerfect 5.1 printer program.

2. Press Retrieve (**Shift-F10**) and type the location and name of the WordPerfect 5.0 printer .ALL file that you want to convert (e.g., C:\WP50\ WPRINT1.ALL). Press ↵. Notice the warning on the screen about inconsistencies between 5.0 fonts and 5.1 fonts.

3. Highlight the name of the printer you are working with, and press ↵ to select it.

4. Select Fonts from the next menu to appear, by highlighting it and pressing ↵.

5. Move the highlight to the Cartridge or Soft fonts area of the screen (depending on which type of font you are converting), and select **1** Add.

6. Press **Ctrl-↵**, then type a name (such as *3RDPARTY*) and press ↵.

7. Select **2** Soft (KB). Your screen should now look like Figure 8.18.

8. Move the highlight to the name of the printer you are working with and press ↵. You'll see a list of all the fonts for that printer.

9. Mark with an asterisk every third-party soft font that you want to convert to 5.1 format.

10. When you've finished marking all the fonts that you want to convert, select **4** Copy.

11. Highlight the name you entered in step 6 (e.g., *3RDPARTY*) and press ↵.

12. Press Exit (**F7**) to return to the previous screen.

13. Move the highlight to the name of the font library you just created (e.g., *3RDPARTY*) and select **4** Copy.

14. Enter the name of the WordPerfect 5.1 .ALL file that you want to copy these converted fonts to (e.g., C:\WP51\WPHP1.ALL) and press ↵.

15. Press Exit (F7) three times, then select **N**o twice to leave the Word-Perfect 5.0 .ALL file, but stay in the PTR program.

16. Retrieve the .ALL file you just copied fonts to (e.g., C:\WP51\WPHP1.ALL) by pressing Retrieve (**Shift-F10**) and entering the complete path and file name.

17. Highlight the name of your printer and press ↵.

18. Select Fonts by highlighting it and pressing ↵.

19. Highlight the name you gave to the converted font library (e.g., *3RDPARTY*) and type an asterisk (*) to mark it.

20. Press Exit (**F7**) three times, and press **Y** when asked about saving the current file and replacing the existing one, then exit the Printer Program.

```
File: c:\wp50\wprint1.all

                    Printer: HP LaserJet+, 500+
                        Font Libraries
  ┌────────────────────────────────────────────────────────┐
  │ Built-In                                                │
  │   ×HP LASERJET+, 500+                                   │
  │ Cartridge Slot                                          │
  │   ×HP LASERJET+, 500+                                   │
  │ Soft Fonts (Kb)                                         │
  │   ×3RDPARTY                                             │
  │   ×HP LASERJET+, 500+                                   │
  │                                                          │
  │                                                          │
  │                                                          │
  │                                                          │
  │                                                          │
  │                                                          │
  │                                                          │
  └────────────────────────────────────────────────────────┘
  1 Add; 2 Delete; 3 Rename; 4 Copy; 5 Update Flag;
  × Select; Backspace Unmark; Enter Look or Edit; A - Z Name Search;
```

FIGURE 8.18:

Preparing to convert third-party 5.0 soft fonts to 5.1

Now you can install the third-party fonts for use with WordPerfect 5.1, as described under "Installing Fonts" earlier in this chapter.

TROUBLESHOOTING PRINTER PROBLEMS

In this section, I'll look at some common printer problems and give some suggestions for diagnosing and solving them.

THE PRINTER DOES NOT PRINT AT ALL

If the printer totally ignores your print request, ask yourself the following:

◆ Is the printer turned on and online?

◆ Is the printer cable properly connected at both ends?

◆ Is the printer waiting for you to insert paper? (Insert paper through the manual feed to find out.)

◆ Are instructions waiting at the Control Printer screen? (Select **File** ➤ **Print** ➤ Control Printer, or press **Shift-F7 C** to find out.)

◆ Is the appropriate printer selected? (Select **File** ➤ **Print** ➤ **S**elect Printer, or press **Shift-F7 S** to find out).

◆ Is the proper printer port selected? (Select **File** ➤ **P**rint or press **Shift-F7**, then choose **S**elect Printer ➤ **E**dit ➤ **P**ort to find out.)

◆ Does the printer work with other programs? If not, are you sure the printer has been properly installed according to the manufacturer's instructions?

TEXT DOES NOT ALIGN PROPERLY ON THE PAGE

If your printer prints, but the text is poorly aligned on the page, ask yourself the following:

◆ If you're using a dot-matrix printer, did you properly align the paper while the printer was off (as described near the beginning of this chapter)?

◆ Does your printer have buttons of its own for controlling page length, line length, number of lines per inch, and automatic line-feed? If so, are they set correctly?

◆ Did you select the correct printer name? (Select **File** ➤ **Print** ➤ Select Printer or press **Shift-F7 S** to find out.)

THE WRONG FONT APPEARS ON THE PRINTOUT

If the wrong font appears on your printout, ask yourself the following:

◆ Are you using the same printer to print the document that you used when creating the document? (Select **F**ile ➤ **P**rint ➤ **S**elect Printer or press **Shift-F7 S** to find out.) WordPerfect can only use whatever fonts the current printer has available.

◆ Did you use a soft font marked with an asterisk during font installation but have not yet downloaded by selecting **F**ile ➤ **P**rint ➤ Initialize Printer (or by pressing **Shift-F7 I**)?

◆ If you're using downloadable soft fonts, is WordPerfect looking for them in the correct directory? (Select **F**ile ➤ **P**rint or press **Shift-F7**, then choose **S**elect Printer ➤ **E**dit ➤ Path for **D**ownloadable Fonts and Printer Files to find out.)

◆ If you're using cartridge fonts, have you installed them for use with Word-Perfect yet? (See "Installing a Font Cartridge" earlier in this chapter.)

◆ Is a message waiting at the Control Printer screen that will provide further information? (Select **F**ile ➤ **P**rint ➤ **C**ontrol Printer or press **Shift-F7 C** to find out.)

This chapter completes Part 2, where you've covered a lot more of the meat of WordPerfect, giving you more control over the "day-to-day stuff" of using WordPerfect. Starting in Part 3, you'll learn about many techniques to make all that day-to-day stuff a bit easier, especially when you start getting into larger jobs.

PART THREE

Tools to Simplify Your Work

Now that you've reached this part of the book, your word processing skills should be well honed, and your documents should have a more polished appearance. Here you'll learn to simplify your work and increase your productivity with features designed to do just that. You'll learn about searching and replacing, checking your spelling, and using the Thesaurus and automatic hyphenation. You'll also learn about tools that help you manage your documents, and how to customize Word-Perfect to better suit your own word processing needs.

CHAPTER 9

Searching and Replacing

**D**id you ever type a lengthy report, only to notice you'd gotten an important detail wrong over and over? Maybe you used the word "Corp." instead of "Inc." in a company name, or used first names instead of last names.

One of the most powerful features of a word processor is its ability to search rapidly through a document to locate specific text, and optionally, to replace that text with something else. This chapter covers WordPerfect's powerful Search and Replace feature, which you'll undoubtedly find to be one of your most indispensable word processing tools.

THE SEARCH FEATURE

TO SEARCH FOR TEXT IN A DOCUMENT,

1. Select Search ➤ Forward (or press F2).

2. Type the text you want to search for (if you want to search backward, press ↑).

3. Press Search (F2) to begin the search.

The Search feature lets you to locate a specific sequence of characters anywhere in your document. You tell WordPerfect what you're looking for, and WordPerfect finds it, moving the cursor immediately past the last character in the sequence. To search for something, follow these steps:

1. Position the cursor where you want to begin the search (e.g., at the top of the document if you want to search the entire document).

2. Select **S**earch ➤ **F**orward, or press Search (F2). You'll see the Search prompt in the lower-left corner of your screen:

    –> Srch:

3. Type the characters you want to search for. You can type almost anything at the Search prompt: single characters, words, partial sentences, even special codes (Bold, Underline, Tab, Enter, Center, etc.)—up to 59 characters. What you type at the prompt is often referred to as the *search string,* because it's a string of characters.

4. Press the Search key (**F2**) to start the search.

You can also start the search by pressing the Escape key instead of Search (F2).

Once the search starts, WordPerfect scans your document from the cursor position downward. If it encounters a matching piece of text, it stops searching and places the cursor just to the right of the matching text. If WordPerfect cannot find the text you're looking for, it displays "* Not found *" for a few seconds at the bottom of the screen and returns the cursor to its original position.

It's useful to know that WordPerfect always remembers a previous search. For example, suppose you search for the word *horse* and the cursor lands at that word. If this is not the particular instance of *horse* you're looking for, you can just press Search (F2) twice to find the next occurrence of the word (optionally, select **S**earch ➤ **N**ext). Or, to search backward for the previous occurrence, select **S**earch ➤ **P**revious, or press Shift-F2, then F2.

To return the cursor to its original position after a successful search, press **Ctrl-Home Ctrl-Home** *.*

Of course, if you don't want to repeat your previous search, you can just type your new search text after selecting ➤ **S**earch ➤ **F**orward or after pressing Search (F2).

A common mistake made by WordPerfect beginners (and many old pros) is pressing ↵, rather than Search (F2), to start a search. In WordPerfect's Search feature, ↵ is considered a character, one you may want to search for in your documents. Pressing ↵ enters its code, [HRt], along with any other search text. So remember, to start a search, press Search (F2) rather than ↵ after typing your search string.

If you do press ↵ by mistake, just press **Backspace** *to delete the [HRt] code.*

Searching Backward

Normally Search searches from the cursor down (forward) to the end of a document. However, sometimes you want to search from the cursor position backward, toward the beginning of your document. Follow these steps:

1. Position the cursor where you want to begin your backward search.

2. Select **S**earch ➤ **B**ackward or press Backward Search (**Shift-F2**). The following prompt appears (notice that the arrow points to the left):

   <- Srch:

3. Type the characters or enter the codes you want to search for, just as in a forward search.

4. Press Search (**F2**) to start the search.

There's a third technique for deciding the direction in which you want to search. After you press F2 and the –> Srch: prompt appears, you can press ↑ to reverse the direction of the search (the prompt's arrow points to the left) or ↓ to search forward again.

If you decide to search backward after starting a forward search with F2, just press ↑ to change the direction of the search.

EDITING THE SEARCH TEXT

As mentioned, WordPerfect always remembers the previous search string. When you begin a search and that "remembered" search string appears, you can do one of three things with it:

◆ Leave the search text as is to repeat the previous search, by pressing Search (F2).

◆ Enter new search text, simply by typing it (the old search text disappears immediately as soon as you start typing).

◆ Edit the previous search text with the usual cursor-movement keys.

If you choose the third option, it's important to start out by pressing a cursor-movement key (such as →, ←, or Delete) so that the existing search string is not erased. Here are the editing keys you can use, which work virtually the same as they do in normal text editing:

Delete	Deletes the character the cursor is on
Backspace	Deletes the character to the left of the cursor
Ctrl-End	Deletes from the cursor position to the end of the search text
→, ←, Home ←, Home →, and End	Move the cursor around the search string

| Insert | Toggles between Insert mode and Typeover mode |
| Cancel (F1) | Cancels any editing changes and exits Search |

Some of the standard editing keys are unavailable for editing a search string. These include Ctrl-→ and Ctrl-← for moving right and left a word at a time, and Ctrl-Backspace for deleting a word.

Editing the search string comes in handy when you're searching for text that's subtly different from what you had listed before. You simply use the editing keys to change the search string, and then press F2 to start the search.

CASE SENSITIVITY IN SEARCHING

Normally, you wouldn't consider the difference between the words *Little* and *little* to be anything big. But Search is a little picky about case. If you tell it to locate *little,* it will find *Little,* as well as *little,* but if you tell it to locate *Little,* it won't find *little.* Here are the basic rules for uppercase and lowercase letters in WordPerfect search strings:

◆ Search matches all lowercase characters in the search string with either uppercase or lowercase characters in the document.

◆ Search matches uppercase characters in the search string with only uppercase characters in the document.

For example, if you want to find the word *nirvana* and don't care what case it is, enter *nirvana* as the search text. If you want to find *Nirvana*—perhaps in a specific spot where you know it's the start of a sentence—enter *Nirvana* as the search text.

SEARCHING FOR WORDS

The Search feature cannot distinguish letter combinations from words. For example, if you tell it to search for the word *go,* it looks for the letters *g-o.* Therefore, it will find words like *gotten,* a*go*raphobia, Spa*go,* *Go*dzilla, and others.

If you want to search specifically for a word, you also need to search for the spaces surrounding the word. For example, to search for the word *go* (not the letters *g* and *o*), you press Search (F2), press the spacebar, type *go,* press the spacebar again, then press Search (F2) to begin the search. WordPerfect looks for a space, followed by *go,* followed by another space.

Of course, it won't find *go,* (*go* followed by a comma) or *go.* (*go* followed by a period), because that's not the same as space-*go*-space. However, it will find these if you search for a space followed by *go* (without the additional space at the end). But of course, then it will also find *goofy, gone, gory,* and any other word beginning with *go,* since you're searching for a space followed by the letters *g* and *o.*

The bottom line is simply that spaces are characters, just like any letter, number, or punctuation mark. Therefore, you can use spaces in your search string to specify exactly what you're looking for.

SEARCHING FOR SPECIAL CHARACTERS

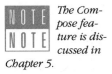

The Compose feature is discussed in Chapter 5.

You can also search for any special characters entered with Compose (Ctrl-V or Ctrl-2). You simply go through the usual Compose sequences to type the special character you're looking for at the –> Srch: prompt. For example, to search for a bullet you typed using special character 4,0, you start the search, press Ctrl-V, type *4,0,* and press ↵. The bullet appears as the search string. You can then type additional characters, or press Search (F2) to begin the search.

USING WILDCARDS IN A SEARCH STRING

WHEREVER YOU WANT TO USE A WILDCARD IN YOUR SEARCH STRING,

press Ctrl-V Ctrl-X. It appears as ^X (Control X).

What if you're not quite sure how you spelled a word in a document or you're afraid it's spelled two different ways? This need not stymie your search efforts. WordPerfect lets you insert a *wildcard* character in the search string to represent any character. The wildcard character is ^X (pronounced "Control X"); to insert it in a search string, you must first press Ctrl-V and then press Ctrl-X. It cannot serve as the first character in the search string.

For example, let's say you know you mentioned Carl Yastrzemski somewhere in your document, but you can never remember if the first *s* in his name should really be a *z.* At the Search prompt, you type *Ya,* press Ctrl-V Ctrl-X, and type *trzemski.* The prompt looks like this:

-> Srch: Ya**^X**trzemski

Assuming you spelled the rest of the name correctly, this search string will bring you to the right spot in your document.

SEARCHING FOR CODES

> **TO PUT FORMATTING CODES IN THE SEARCH STRING,**
>
> **press the shortcut keys you use to create that code on the Edit screen.**

In addition to locating text in your document, you can also locate special characters and codes. In fact, nearly anything you type can be located in a document by searching for it.

As an example, consider [HRt], the special WordPerfect hard-return code inserted in your documents whenever you press ↵. You can search for a hard return just as you'd search for any word in a document—simply by pressing ↵ at the Search prompt to place the [HRt] code in the search string.

To search for special characters, follow these steps:

1. Press Search (**F2**) or select **S**earch ➤ **F**orward. (You could also search backward, as you've learned.)

2. Press the keys that will produce the codes and characters you want to search for. Figure 9.1 shows the [Center] code that appears in a search string for a centered line, after you press Shift-F6 at the –> Srch: prompt.

3. Press Search (**F2**) to start the search.

You can search for the special codes alone, or you can mix them with text. It all depends on what you're looking for. To search for hidden codes, press the same shortcut key (or keys) you'd use to actually insert those codes in a document. For example, to search for a centered line, start the search as usual, by selecting **S**earch ➤ **F**orward or pressing Search (F2), then pressing Center (Shift-F6). This inserts a [Center] code in the search string. Now you can add more codes, then press Search (F2) to start the search. .

Here's how to search for some other special codes:

Soft page break ([SPg])	Press **Ctrl-V** followed by **Ctrl-K** as the search string.
Soft return ([SRt])	Press **Ctrl-M** as the search string.
Combined hard return and soft page break ([HRt-SPg])	Just search for an [HRt] code, by pressing ↵ as the search string.

CAUTION *To search for a code, such as [HRt], you must press the appropriate key (↵ in this case). If you simply type the characters in [HRt] as the text to search for, WordPerfect will not match them to a [HRt] code.*

NOTE *The pull-down menus do not operate when the Search prompt is displayed, so you must use the shortcut keys to search for special codes.*

SEARCHING FOR PAIRED CODES

To use paired codes in the search string, press the appropriate key once for the beginning code and again for the ending code. For example, to search for

[BOLD]Getting Started**[bold]**

press Search (F2), press Bold (F6), type *Getting Started,* then press Bold (F6) again. Press Search (F2) to start the search.

If you want to search for only the closing code in a paired-code set, press the appropriate keys twice, then erase the opening code. For example, to search for a [bold] closing code, press Search (F2), and press Bold (F6) twice. This gives you the following:

[BOLD][bold]

Next, press ←, then Backspace to remove the first code, leaving you with

[bold]

Then, press Search (F2) to start the search as usual.

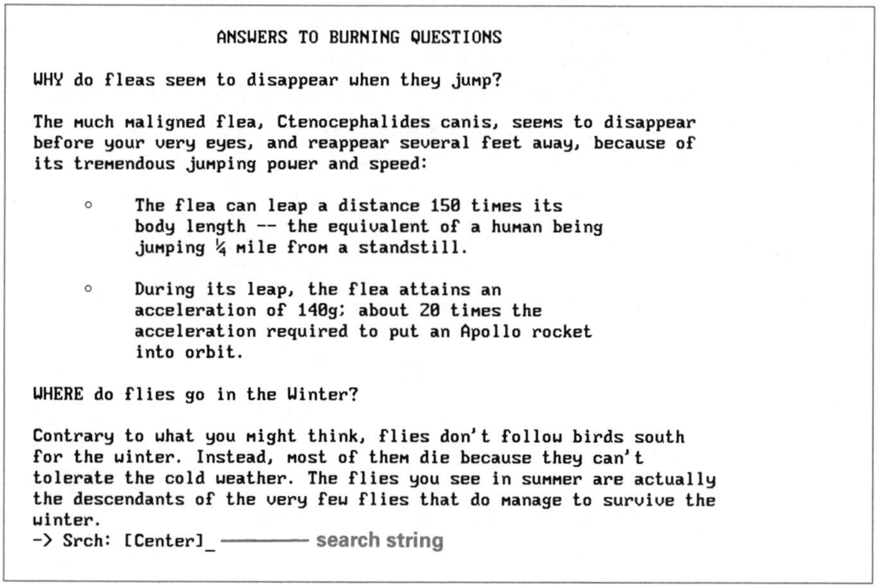

```
                ANSWERS TO BURNING QUESTIONS

WHY do fleas seem to disappear when they jump?

The much maligned flea, Ctenocephalides canis, seems to disappear
before your very eyes, and reappear several feet away, because of
its tremendous jumping power and speed:

     o     The flea can leap a distance 150 times its
           body length -- the equivalent of a human being
           jumping ¼ mile from a standstill.

     o     During its leap, the flea attains an
           acceleration of 140g; about 20 times the
           acceleration required to put an Apollo rocket
           into orbit.

WHERE do flies go in the Winter?

Contrary to what you might think, flies don't follow birds south
for the winter. Instead, most of them die because they can't
tolerate the cold weather. The flies you see in summer are actually
the descendants of the very few flies that do manage to survive the
winter.
-> Srch: [Center]_ ————— search string
```

FIGURE 9.1:

The code for centered text as the search string

SEARCHING FOR FONTS AND STYLES

Chapter 26 presents examples of macros that can locate a specific font and can even change a font throughout a document.

Like all formatting features, fonts (Chapter 5) and styles (Chapter 14) are controlled by codes, which you can search for like any other code. For example, to create the search string [Font], which searches for a font, press Search (F2), press Font (Ctrl-F8), then select Base **F**ont. To produce a [Style On] search string, which searches for a style, press Search (F2), press Style (Alt-F8), then select Style **O**n.

When you perform the search, WordPerfect finds the nearest [Font] or [Style On] code. However, it won't let you search for a specific font (such as Courier 10-point) or a specific style.

EXTENDED SEARCHING

TO EXTEND SEARCHING TO INCLUDE HEADERS, FOOTERS, CAPTIONS, AND SO FORTH,

begin the search with Search ➤ Extended, or press Home, then Search (F2).

*An extended search searches through **all** the text in your document, including everything that will be printed as the final result, not just what is on the Edit screen.*

Normally, the Search feature only looks for text and special codes in the main body (including tables) of your document. It won't find text listed in headers, footers, footnotes, endnotes, graphic-box captions, or text boxes. To locate that text, you must perform an *extended search*.

The extended search works the same as a regular search. To perform an extended search, just press **Home**, then Search (**F2**), and proceed as usual. Or, select **S**earch ➤ **E**xtended, select the direction in which you want to perform the search (**F**orward or **B**ackward), and then proceed with the search normally.

To continue an extended search, press **Home**, then Search (**F2**) or Backward Search (**Shift-F2**). Or, select **S**earch ➤ **E**xtended, then **N**ext or **P**revious.

SEARCHING FOR A PAGE

If you are using Roman page numbering (Chapter 7), you should still type an Arabic-style number when using the Go To feature. For example, type 6, not vi, to go to page 6.

To quickly move the cursor to a particular page in your document, use the Go To feature, rather than Search: Select **S**earch ➤ **G**o To or press **Ctrl-Home**, then type the page number and press ↵.

USING SEARCH TO BLOCK TEXT

The Search feature plays an interesting and helpful role in blocking text. In Block mode, WordPerfect uses the Search feature to extend the block. This lets you extend the block to a specific word or phrase, rather than just a single character.

To use Search while blocking, start the block as you normally would, by selecting **E**dit ➤ **B**lock, by pressing the Block key (Alt-F4 or F12), or by holding down the left mouse button and dragging. While "Block on" is flashing, perform your search as you normally would, with the Search (F2) or Backward Search (Shift-F2) keys or by choosing the pull-down menu options.

Whether the search is forward or backward, the cursor will land immediately *past* (to the right of) the first occurrence of the search string. Thus, if you use this technique for a backward search, the characters in the search string will *not* be highlighted as part of the block.

USING SEARCH TO FIND BOOKMARKS

When WordPerfect loads a document, it places the cursor at the very top of the first page. However, you may not have been at the top the last time you finished working with the document, especially if it's a long document that you've been working on over a number of days.

You can press Home Home ↓ to get quickly to the end of the document. But suppose you were last working on text in the middle of a document? Or what if you wanted to go back to a few spots in the text where you weren't quite finished? How can you get there?

Two amper-sands (&&) make a good book-mark, because they are rarely used together in normal text.

The solution is to use an old word-processing device called a *bookmark*. A bookmark is simply a special character, pair of characters, symbol, or unique word you place in the text where you were last working. It's like an actual bookmark—you use it to keep your place. To locate your place again, you can use the Search feature and enter your bookmark as the search string.

For example, suppose you are working in your document and suddenly remember that you need to move some text from another place in the document to where you are now. You can type two ampersands to mark your current spot, then go looking for the text you want to move to that spot (of course, you can use the Search feature to look for this text). When you find the text you want to move, you can block it as usual, start the Move operation (select **E**dit ➤ **M**ove (Cut) or press Ctrl-F4 B M), then press Search (F2) or Backward Search (Shift-F2) and type in the && search string. The cursor will jump immediately to the destination, so you don't have to search around for it. You can press ↵ to complete the move.

Block and Move operations are dis-cussed in Chapter 2.

Just remember to erase your bookmarks (&&) as soon as you've finished using them. Otherwise, you'll end up with a lot of && characters throughout your document.

THE REPLACE FEATURE

TO REPLACE TEXT THROUGHOUT A DOCUMENT,

1. Select Search ➤ Replace or press Replace (Alt-F2).

2. Choose Yes or No to indicate whether you want to confirm each replacement.

3. Enter the text or codes you want to search for, then press F2.

4. Enter the text or codes you want to replace the first ones with, then press F2.

*The term **global** refers to any operation that affects an entire document or an entire block within the document.*

Replace is a powerful WordPerfect operation that lets you select any sequence of characters or codes and globally change it to something else. With one command you can change every *aunt* in your document to *uncle,* every *red* to *blue,* every *night* to *day.* As you'll see, you can also use Replace to make changes selectively rather than globally. Changing references to a location in a report, renaming characters in a play, even changing the format of a document can be done easily with the Replace feature.

The steps for using Replace are as follows:

1. To play it safe, save the entire document with **F**ile ➤ **S**ave or Save (**F10**). As you'll see, there is some risk of getting more than you bargained for when using Replace. Saving the document before you begin ensures that you'll be able to retrieve the original if the operation doesn't go as planned.

Like Search, Replace begins from the current cursor position, not the top of the document.

2. Move the cursor to wherever you want to begin the Replace operation (e.g., to the top of the document if you want to search and replace throughout the entire document).

3. Select **S**earch ➤ **R**eplace, or press Replace (**Alt-F2**).

4. Select **Y**es or **N**o to indicate whether you wish to confirm each replacement before it takes place or prefer to have the replacements made automatically (more on this in a moment).

5. Optionally, reset the direction of the Replace operation with ↑ or ↓.

All the techniques described earlier for creating a search string can be used while entering the search string to be used in a Replace operation.

6. Enter the search string at the Search prompt. This is the sequence of text or codes whose occurrences you want to change.

7. Press Search (**F2**).

8. Enter the *replacement string*—the text that will replace the search string at every occurrence.

9. Press Search (**F2**) to carry out the Replace operation. If you selected **Y**es in step 4 (and the search string does exist in the text), press Y or N to indicate whether each particular occurrence of the search string should be replaced.

While Replace is working, the message "* Please wait *" appears at the bottom of the screen. If any text was replaced, the cursor will be positioned immediately after the first character of replaced text. If the search string wasn't found and no text was replaced, the cursor will remain at its current position. Unlike the Search feature, Replace doesn't display a "* Not Found *" message.

 You cannot undo a Replace operation, so remember to save your work first.

You cannot undo a Replace operation. If you save your document for safety as suggested earlier, then goof with Replace, you can simply clear the screen and re-retrieve the copy of the document you just saved, without saving the current version.

What kind of mistake might you make with the Replace feature? Let's say you typed someone's name as *Simms* throughout a document, and you later learn that the person's name is spelled *Sims*. You could tell WordPerfect to replace *mm* with *m* at every occurrence, without confirmation. This will certainly do the job of changing *Simms* to *Sims,* but it will also change *hammer* to *hamer, summer* to *sumer,* and so on—not what you want, and potentially a real mess for your document.

You can stop the replacement operation by pressing Cancel (F1) anytime before completing step 9 above, and whenever you are prompted to confirm a replacement.

If you saved your document before the replacement operation, you can just exit the fouled-up document without saving, clear the screen, and retrieve the saved version from disk to try again. (This is also a good illustration of why it's important to make your search string as specific as possible in a Replace operation. Specifying *Simms* as the search string and *Sims* as the replacement string will avoid this problem altogether.)

Replace also has an extended capability, just like the Search feature does. When you press the Home key before activating the Replace feature (that is, press Home Alt-F2), the Replace operation will scan a document's headers, footers, captions, and so forth, as well as the main body of text. Alternatively, you can select **S**earch ➤ **E**xtended ➤ **R**eplace.

When all text replacements have been made, the cursor will be positioned after the first character of the last text replacement made. You can press Ctrl-Home twice to return the cursor to its original position before Replace was started.

Confirming Each Replacement

The first prompt to appear when you begin a Replace operation asks "With confirm?", like this:

w/Confirm? No (Yes)

If you select No, the default, WordPerfect replaces every occurrence of the search string (starting at the current cursor position) with the replacement string, without checking with you first. If you select Yes, WordPerfect stops before making the replacement and asks

Confirm? No (Yes)

If you select No, that one instance is not replaced. If you select Yes, that instance is replaced. Either way, WordPerfect then goes on to the next matching search string and asks for permission again. It continues in this way until all matches have been found.

If you are at all doubtful about the outcome of a Replace operation, it's probably a good idea to use Confirm.

REPLACING TEXT

To save time and typing, use abbreviations throughout your document, then use Replace to expand the abbreviations into complete words! Just be sure that you use your abbreviations consistently.

Most often you'll use the Replace feature to change one word to another, often to fix a mistake. For example, if you find that you've inadvertently misspelled "Avco Corporation" as "Arco Corporation" in a document, you can use Replace to change every occurrence of Arco to Avco.

Besides fixing mistakes, Replace can also save you time. For example, suppose you have to type a long company name, like *Dendrobium Pharmaceuticals, Inc.,* throughout a document. To save some work, you can just type *XX* wherever you want that long company name to appear. Then, when you're finished, you can use Replace to change every occurrence of XX to Dendrobium Pharmaceuticals, Inc.

REPLACING CODES

As with the Search feature, you can use Replace to scan for special formatting codes. With Replace, you can both scan for the special codes and replace them with other codes. (This technique works only for single, not paired, codes.)

For example, there are two common techniques for formatting paragraphs: You can type two hard returns at the end of a paragraph, or you can end a paragraph with a single hard return and start the next paragraph with a tab. Neither one is incorrect, they're just different.

You may need to manually delete the Tab in the first paragraph after completing the replacement.

As an example, let's suppose you type a document using a single Return and Tab to separate paragraphs, then decide to use the double Returns, without Tabs, instead. Here's how you can use Replace to make the change:

1. Move the cursor to the top of the document (Home Home ↑).

2. Select **S**earch ➤ **R**eplace, or press Replace (Alt-F2).

3. Select **N**o when asked about Confirm.

4. Press ⏎, then Tab. This makes the search string *[HRt][Tab]*.

5. Press Search (F2).

6. Press ⏎ twice. This makes the replacement string *[HRt][HRt]*.

7. Press Search (F2) to perform the replacement.

Using the Styles feature (Chapter 14) is the best way to get around the limitations of Replace in globally changing formatting codes.

As with Search, there are limitations in replacing formatting codes. For example, you can search for a generic [Ln Spacing] code, but you cannot change all the single-spacing codes, [Ln Spacing:1], to double-spacing codes, [Ln Spacing:2].

USING REPLACE IN PART OF A DOCUMENT

To limit a Replace operation to a specific part of your document, follow these steps:

1. Block the text where you want to perform the search, using **E**dit ➤ **B**lock, the Block (**Alt-F4** or **F12**) key, or your mouse.

2. Select **S**earch ➤ **R**eplace or press Replace (**Alt-F2**).

3. Choose either **Y**es or **N**o for Confirm, then follow the usual steps for entering the text to search for and the text to replace it with.

4. Press Search (**F2**).

Only text within the highlighted block will be searched for and replaced. Any text outside the highlighted block will be ignored.

REPLACING CASE-SENSITIVE TEXT

Like Search, Replace observes differences between upper- and lowercase. Replace locates matching words based on the same rules that Search follows, but in making the replacement, it attempts to match the case of the text being replaced.

◆ Replace matches lowercase characters in the search string with either uppercase or lowercase characters in the document.

◆ Replace matches uppercase characters in the search string with only uppercase characters in the document.

Based on the case of the replacement string and the case of the search string, WordPerfect guesses what case is needed in the replacement itself. In general, it replaces a capitalized word in the document with a capitalized version of the replacement. If a character in the replacement must always be uppercase, be sure to type it uppercase in the replacement string.

For example, suppose you're replacing *circle* with *square*. You enter *circle* as the search string, and Replace finds *Circle* (with an initial capital letter) in the text. It will replace *Circle* with *Square* (note the initial capital).

Note that if Replace found *CIRCLE* (all caps), it would also replace it with *Square*—only the initial capital letter would be retained. Any other words in the replacement text remain lowercase when the search string is all lowercase.

Any capital letters in the replacement text will always remain capitalized. For example, if you are replacing *circle* with *SQUARE,* then all replacement text will be capitalized in the document. That is, any instance of *circle,* with any mixture of upper- and lowercase letters, will always be replaced with *SQUARE.*

USING REPLACE TO DELETE TEXT

Replace can be used when you need to delete identical text repeatedly throughout your document. The procedure is simple; just don't supply a replacement string. The steps are as follows:

1. To play it safe, save your document by selecting **File** ➤ **S**ave or pressing Save (**F10**).

2. Select **S**earch ➤ **R**eplace, or press Replace (**Alt-F2**).

3. Select either **Y**es or **N**o for confirmation.

4. Type the text you want to delete.

5. Press Search (**F2**).

6. Instead of entering a replacement string, press Search (**F2**) again. This causes Replace to change existing text to *nothing* (which is the same as deleting it).

NOTE
NOTE

When you delete the starting or ending code of a paired code, the other code is automatically deleted. Hence, replacing all the [Und] codes with nothing deletes all the [UND] and [und] codes.

It's generally a good idea to use confirmation when deleting text with the Replace feature. The only exception is when you're sure the search text is unique. Also, be doubly certain to save your text before you use Replace to delete text. There is no way to re-search and re-replace text that's been deleted. Once it's gone, it's gone! Even the Cancel key (F1) can't get it back.

A common use of Replace is to delete formatting codes. For example, you can strip out all the underlined text in your document simply by searching for the underline code, [UND], entered by pressing Underline (F8), and replacing it with nothing.

EXTENDED REPLACING

Replace generally works only on text in the main body of your document. If you want to extend the Replace operation to include headers, footers, endnotes, footnotes, graphic-box captions, and text boxes, press Home before pressing Replace (Alt-F2), or select **S**earch ➤ **E**xtended ➤ **R**eplace. Then proceed as you normally would.

REPLACING PAIRED CODES

You can't use the Replace feature to change paired codes. For example, you can't change all italics to underline or all boldface to Large text. Similarly, you cannot change a specific font, such as Courier to Times Roman, because Replace can only find "generic" [Font] codes.

The way to avoid this problem in the first place is to use styles (Chapter 14) rather than actual codes in your document. But if it's too late for that, you can use a handy macro WordPerfect provides to find and replace paired codes. In addition, Chapter 26 of this book provides macros that can find and replace fonts throughout your document.

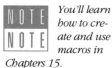

You'll learn how to create and use macros in Chapters 15.

A Macro to Change Paired Codes

*A **soft keyboard** is a set of redefined keys and key combinations that perform different actions from the ones originally assigned by WordPerfect.*

WordPerfect's macro to change paired codes is stored in the MACROS keyboard (see Chapter 27). You can transform this into a generic macro that you can use now, without a soft keyboard, by following these steps:

1. At the Edit screen, select **F**ile ➤ Se**t**up ➤ **K**eyboard Layout (or press **Shift-F1 K**).

2. Highlight MACROS and select **E**dit.

3. Highlight the second line (press **Alt-R**) and select **S**ave.

4. Type in a valid file name, such as *CHPAIRS.WPM,* and press ↵.

5. If prompted to replace the existing macro, select **Y**es.

6. Press Exit (**F7**) twice to return to the Edit screen.

From now on, whenever you want to use that macro, follow these steps:

1. Move the cursor to where you want to begin changing paired codes.

2. Press **Alt-F10** and type **CHPAIRS** (or whatever name you typed in step 4 above), then press ↵.

3. If you want to confirm each replacement before it takes place, press **Y** to select Yes. If you want the replacements to take effect without your confirmation, press **N** for No.

4. The prompt "Delete original attribute? (Y/N) Yes" appears. If you want to delete the original attribute, press **Y**. If you want to add another attribute to the existing attribute, press **N**. If you want to change the existing attribute, press ⏎.

5. At the "Convert From" prompt, select **S**ize or **A**ppearance, whichever one you want to change. Then select the specific size or appearance from the menu that appears.

6. At the "Convert To" prompt, select **S**ize or **A**ppearance, then select the size or appearance that you want to change to (or add to the existing size or appearance).

The macro will do its job and keep you informed of its progress. When it's finished, you'll be returned to the Edit screen.

In the next chapter, you'll learn how to polish your finished documents by checking your spelling. You'll also learn to use the WordPerfect Thesaurus.

CHAPTER 10

Checking Your Spelling
and Finding the Right Word

nless you happen to be some kind of "human dictionary," you'll probably need to correct misspellings in your documents and go to the dictionary to find correct spellings. Let's face it, even human dictionaries make mistakes now and again. But with the help of WordPerfect, you can probably put away your dictionary once and for all and find the right spellings just by pressing a few keys.

Have you ever found yourself smack-dab in the middle of writing a sentence, only to discover that you're suddenly at a loss for words, or you've already overused a word like "exciting" and want to try something spicier like "delightful," "electrifying," "exhilarating," "inspiring," or "thrilling"? Even if you have the vocabulary of a verbal genius, you'll appreciate the convenience of having an online thesaurus that can not only suggest the right word to use, but type it in for you as well.

This chapter discusses the Speller and the Thesaurus, two very handy tools for checking your spelling and finding just the right word for any occasion.

ABOUT THE SPELLER

WordPerfect's Speller checks your document for misspelled words, double words, numbers embedded in words, and certain types of capitalization errors and typos. You can use the Speller to scan a single word, a page, a document, or a block of text from your current document.

Before learning the functions of the Speller in detail, you should know a few things about what it can and cannot do. The Speller works by simple comparison. It checks words in your document against its own dictionary of about 115,000 words. If it can't find a word in its dictionary, it offers suggestions on correct spelling, providing a list of alternatives from which to choose. Even though the Speller can do this, keep in mind that it's still up to you to choose the correct word.

The English language includes nearly half a million words, with new ones being added almost daily. Even more words exist when you count last names, names of businesses, technical terms used in certain professions, and other proper nouns that don't appear in dictionaries. You can add these words, such as your last name, your hometown, and other correctly spelled but uncommon words, to a *supplemental dictionary.* The Speller will then check for words there as well as in its own dictionary.

You can add proper nouns and technical terms to the Speller's supplemental dictionary.

Keep in mind that the Speller does not check context. Even though you may have spelled a word correctly, it may not be the word you intended to type. Common mistakes like typing *the* instead of *they* or *he* instead of *the* are not caught by the Speller, because *the* and *he* are not incorrectly spelled words—they're just the wrong words for the occasion. Until a contextual speller comes along, it's up to you to spot these kinds of errors. (Grammar checkers can catch some mistakes like these.)

Likewise, the Speller cannot check grammar. Hence, it will not catch homonym mistakes. Common foul-ups include using *it's* instead of *its* or switching *their, there,* and *they're.*

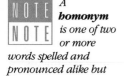

*A **homonym** is one of two or more words spelled and pronounced alike but different in meaning.*

The Speller will also check for some mistakes in the use of upper- and lowercase letters. If only the first two letters of a word are capitalized (for example, *THere*), or if the first letter is lowercase and the second letter is uppercase (such as *yOur*), WordPerfect will point out the irregular use of case. I'll discuss this topic in more detail later in the chapter.

USING THE SPELLER

TO START THE SPELLER,

select Tools ➤ Spell or press Ctrl-F2, and choose an option from the Speller menu that appears.

If you are running Word-Perfect on a computer with no hard disk, put the Speller disk in drive A.

To use the Speller, follow these steps:

1. Select **T**ools ➤ S**p**ell, or press Spell (**Ctrl-F2**). The Speller menu (Figure 10.1) appears at the bottom of the screen.

2. Select one of the following options from the menu:

*I'll discuss the **L**ook Up, **N**ew Sup. Dictionary, and **C**ount options a little later in this chapter.*

Word	Checks only the spelling of the word at the cursor position
Page	Checks the spelling of the current page only
Document	Checks the spelling of the entire document
Look Up	Looks up the spelling of a specific word
New Sup. Dictionary	Adds and looks up words from a different supplemental dictionary.
Count	Counts the number of words in the document

3. If the Speller finds a word likely to be misspelled, it highlights that word and presents a different menu of options (Figure 10.2). You can select any of the following options:

Letter: If you see the correctly spelled word, type its letter to select it (e.g., typing *A* in Figure 10.2 would replace *truely* with *truly*).

Skip Once: ignores the misspelling, this time only.

Skip: ignores the misspelling here and throughout the rest of the document.

Add: ignores the misspelling here and throughout this and all future documents by adding the word to the supplemental dictionary.

Edit: lets you edit the word, using the standard WordPerfect editing keys. Press Exit (F7) when finished editing.

Look Up: lets you look up a different word and (optionally) replace the word with a looked-up word.

Ignore Numbers: lets you ignore words that contain numbers.

4. When the Speller has finished its job, it displays a total word count. You can then press any key to return to the Edit screen.

As we'll discuss in the following sections, the Speller does more than look for misspelled words. It also looks for embedded numbers, irregular use of case, and double words.

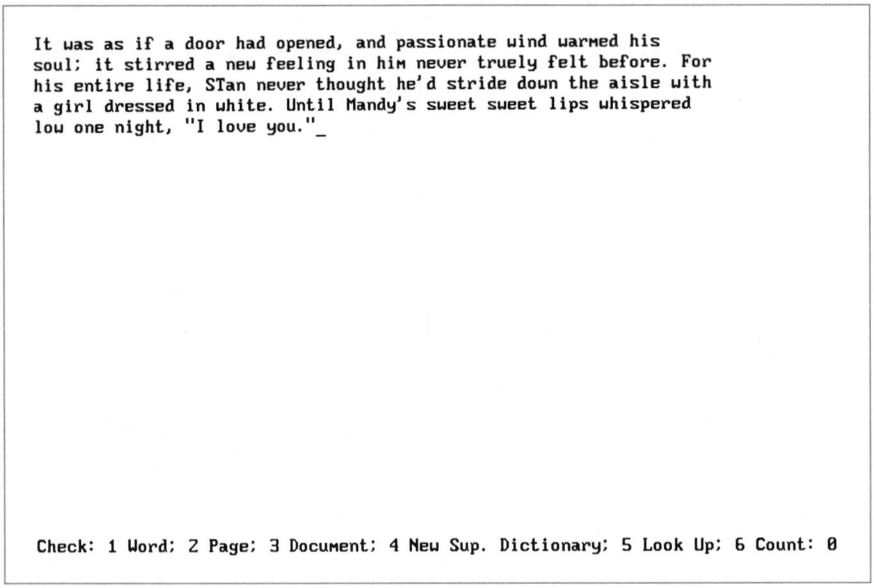

```
It was as if a door had opened, and passionate wind warmed his
soul; it stirred a new feeling in him never truely felt before. For
his entire life, STan never thought he'd stride down the aisle with
a girl dressed in white. Until Mandy's sweet sweet lips whispered
low one night, "I love you."_
```

```
Check: 1 Word; 2 Page; 3 Document; 4 New Sup. Dictionary; 5 Look Up; 6 Count: 0
```

FIGURE 10.1:

The Speller menu appears at the bottom of the screen after you select Tools ➤ Spell or press Ctrl-F2.

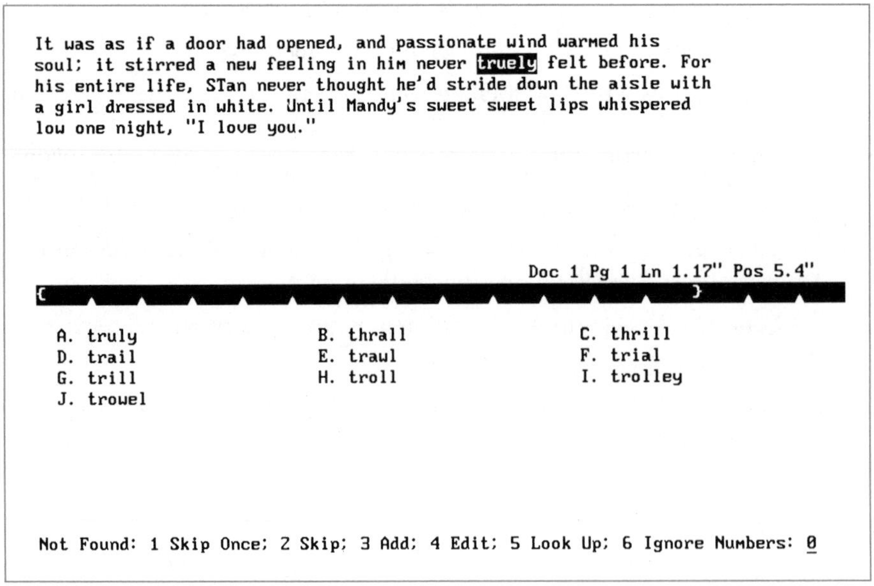

```
It was as if a door had opened, and passionate wind warmed his
soul; it stirred a new feeling in him never truely felt before. For
his entire life, STan never thought he'd stride down the aisle with
a girl dressed in white. Until Mandy's sweet sweet lips whispered
low one night, "I love you."
```

```
                                    Doc 1 Pg 1 Ln 1.17" Pos 5.4"
```

```
  A. truly          B. thrall         C. thrill
  D. trail          E. traul          F. trial
  G. trill          H. troll          I. trolley
  J. trowel
```

```
Not Found: 1 Skip Once; 2 Skip; 3 Add; 4 Edit; 5 Look Up; 6 Ignore Numbers: 0
```

FIGURE 10.2:

The Speller has found a word likely to be misspelled.

CHECKING WORDS WITH NUMBERS

The Speller stops at words that have numbers embedded in them, like *123 Oak Tree Lane, Shift-F1,* and *WordPerfect5.1.* It treats these as it does any other misspelling and presents suggestions for correct spelling. If you want the Speller to ignore embedded numbers throughout the rest of the document, select Ignore Numbers (**6**) when it finds the first embedded number.

CHECKING IRREGULAR CASE

While scanning your document, the Speller also checks for irregular use of upper- and lowercase letters in the first three characters of words. This feature can help you find common typos that result from

♦ holding the Shift key down a bit too long, causing the first two letters to be capitalized (as in *THe*),

♦ pressing the Shift key a little too late, causing the second letter to be capitalized (as in *tHe*), and

♦ pressing the Shift key inadvertently (as in *thE*).

WordPerfect can find and correct five types of capitalization errors, summarized below, where *U* indicates uppercase, and *l* indicates lowercase:

♦ UUl is changed to Ull (e.g., *THis* becomes *This*).

♦ lUl is changed to Ull (e.g., *tHis* becomes *This*).

♦ lUU is changed to UUU (e.g., *tHIS* becomes *THIS*).

♦ llU is changed to lll (e.g., *thIs* becomes *this*).

♦ lU is changed to Ul in two-letter words (e.g., *iS* becomes *Is*).

The capitalization of the entire word is based on the first three characters only. For example, the variations of *apple* shown below would be replaced as follows:

WORD	REPLACEMENT
aPple	Apple (matches lUl pattern)
apPle	apple (matches llU pattern)
APple	Apple (matches UUl pattern)
APPLE	APPLE (no change)

Once WordPerfect locates an irregular use of case, it presents the following options, as shown in the example in Figure 10.3:

Irregular Case: 1 2 Skip; **3** Replace; **4** Edit; **5** Disable Case Checking

You can add your own words to the WordPerfect diction-ary, as you'll learn later.

If you select Skip (by pressing *1* or *2*), the word is ignored. If you select Replace (*3*), WordPerfect corrects the word. If you select Edit (*4*), you can change the word in any manner you like, using the usual editing keys, then pressing Exit (F7) or ⏎. If you select Disable Case Checking (*5*), case checking is disabled for the current word and the remainder of the spelling check.

CHECKING DOUBLE WORDS

The Speller also points out double words, such as *the the,* while scanning your document. When it encounters double words, it highlights both words and presents these options, as shown in Figure 10.4.:

Double Word: 1 2 Skip; **3** Delete 2nd; **4** Edit; **5** Disable Double Word Checking

If you select Skip (by pressing *1* or *2*), the double word is ignored. If you select Delete 2nd (*3*), WordPerfect deletes the second occurrence of the word. If you select Edit (*4*), you can change the text in any manner you like,

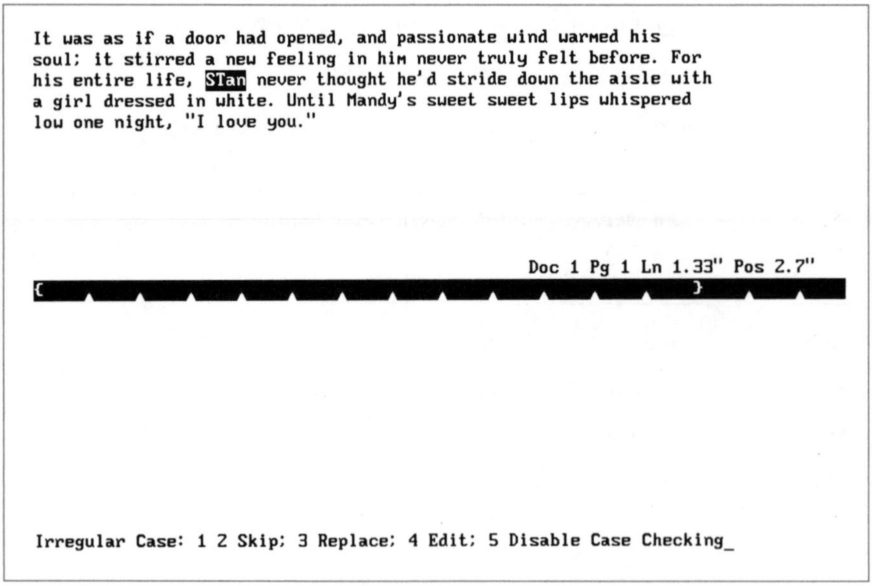

```
It was as if a door had opened, and passionate wind warmed his
soul; it stirred a new feeling in him never truly felt before. For
his entire life, Stan never thought he'd stride down the aisle with
a girl dressed in white. Until Mandy's sweet sweet lips whispered
low one night, "I love you."




                                    Doc 1 Pg 1 Ln 1.33" Pos 2.7"




Irregular Case: 1 2 Skip; 3 Replace; 4 Edit; 5 Disable Case Checking_
```

FIGURE 10.3:

The Speller has found irregular use of upper- and lowercase letters.

using the usual editing keys, then pressing Exit (F7) or ↵ to continue spell-checking. To stop checking for double words, select Disable Double Word Checking (5).

CANCELING THE SPELLER

You can cancel the Speller at any time by pressing the Cancel key (F1). After you press Cancel, you will be given a count of all words checked so far and will be returned to the document. This is handy when you find a passage in the middle of a document that needs more work, and you want to stop spell-checking right there and fix the passage.

WHEN TO USE THE SPELLER

Remember, everything described above takes place in your entire document when you select **T**ools ➤ Sp**e**ll ➤ **D**ocument (or press Ctrl-F2 D)—and it only takes a few seconds or minutes. So it's a good idea to use the Speller to check the entire document just before printing a final copy of the document and saving it. That way, you won't waste paper by having to reprint an entire document just to correct some misspelled words.

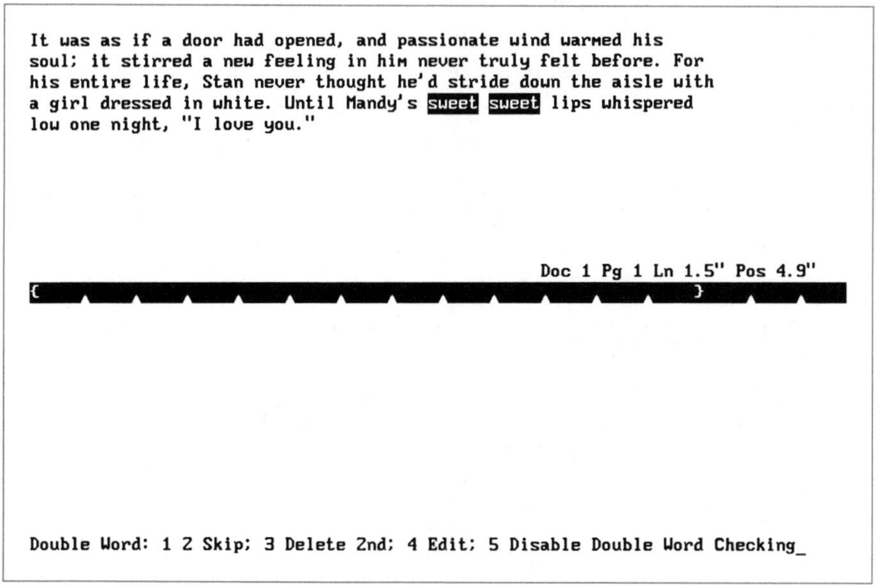

```
It was as if a door had opened, and passionate wind warmed his
soul; it stirred a new feeling in him never truly felt before. For
his entire life, Stan never thought he'd stride down the aisle with
a girl dressed in white. Until Mandy's sweet sweet lips whispered
low one night, "I love you."




                                        Doc 1 Pg 1 Ln 1.5" Pos 4.9"
{                                                   }



Double Word: 1 2 Skip; 3 Delete 2nd; 4 Edit; 5 Disable Double Word Checking_
```

FIGURE 10.4:

The Speller has found double words.

USING THE SPELLER TO LOOK UP A WORD

Though the Look Up feature is handy, it's probably easier to check all the spelling in the document just before printing, using Tools ➤ Spell ➤ Document (or Ctrl-F2 D).

You can also use the Speller like an electronic dictionary, to look up the spelling of a word *before* you type it. This feature is called Look Up; there are two ways to access it:

♦ From the Edit screen, select **Tools** ➤ Spell ➤ **L**ook Up (or press **Ctrl-F2 L**)

♦ When the Speller finds a suspect word, select **5** Look Up.

Either way, you'll see the prompt

Word or word pattern:

This type of lookup is called a "phonetic" lookup, because it uses the sound of the word, rather than the exact spelling, to find the word.

near the lower-left corner of the screen.

To look up a word, type it at the prompt and then press ↵. The Speller will display words similar in pronunciation or construction to that word (including the word itself, if the Speller can find it in the dictionary).

For example, suppose you want to use the word *quick* but forget how it is spelled. You can type the following at the "Word or word pattern:" prompt:

kwik

Press ↵ after typing the word. The Speller searches for that word and all similar words, as shown in Figure 10.5.

As you can see, the word *quick* doesn't appear on the first screen. If you press ↵, however, a second screen will be displayed. (The suggested words are all listed alphabetically, as stored in the Speller's dictionary.) On that screen, the word *quick* will be visible. Since it's the final screen, the "Word or word pattern:" prompt again returns, allowing you to enter another word to look up.

USING WILDCARDS WITH LOOK UP

You can also look up words by using the ? and * wildcards. These wildcards are used to replace a single letter or group of letters within a word. The Speller will then scan the dictionary and look for any words that match the letters and wildcards you've specified.

The ? wildcard stands for a single character in a word. For example, when you specify *?ing*, the Speller will display all four-letter words in its dictionary that end in *-ing*, as shown in Figure 10.6.

The * wildcard stands for a group of any number of letters (from no letters to all the letters in the word). For example, specifying **ing* displays all

WordPerfect Corporation offers a product called "Rhymer," which is specifically designed to find rhyming words.

words (of any length) that end in *-ing*. This can be a real boon to poets yearning for the perfect rhyme.

The * wildcard can appear anywhere in a word. And you can use both ? and * together to create a specific search, for example,

i?p*

```
It was as if a door had opened, and passionate wind warmed his
soul; it stirred a new feeling in him never truly felt before. For
his entire life, Stan never thought he'd stride down the aisle with
a girl dressed in white. Until Mandy's sweet sweet lips whispered
low one night, "I love you."




                                       Doc 1 Pg 1 Ln 1.5" Pos 5.5"
[▲     ▲     ▲     ▲     ▲     ▲     ▲     ▲     }      ▲      ▲   ▲

    A. cache          B. cake           C. calk
    D. caulk          E. chalk          F. check
    G. cheek          H. cheeks         I. cheque
    J. chic           K. chick          L. chock
    M. choice         N. choke          O. chuck
    P. coach          Q. coax           R. cock
    S. coke           T. cook           U. cooks
    V. couch          W. kayak          X. kayaks


Press any key to continue_
```

FIGURE 10.5:

The Look Up command displays a list of words similar to "kwik."

```
It was as if a door had opened, and passionate wind warmed his
soul; it stirred a new feeling in him never truly felt before. For
his entire life, Stan never thought he'd stride down the aisle with
a girl dressed in white. Until Mandy's sweet sweet lips whispered
low one night, "I love you."




                                       Doc 1 Pg 1 Ln 1.5" Pos 5.5"
[▲     ▲     ▲     ▲     ▲     ▲     ▲     ▲     }      ▲      ▲   ▲

    A. ding            B. king           C. ling
    D. ming            E. ping           F. ring
    G. sing            H. wing           I. xing
    J. zing



Word or word pattern: _
```

FIGURE 10.6:

The Look Up command displays a list of four-letter words ending in "-ing."

If you list only an asterisk at the Look Up prompt, the Speller will display every word in its dictionary. If this happens, just press Cancel (F1) to return to the "Word or word pattern:" prompt.

This combination will find any word that starts with *i,* has a *p* in its third position, and ends with any combination of characters. Figure 10.7 shows the results.

As before, if there are more matching words to be viewed, simply press ↵ to see them, or press Cancel (F1) to return to the "Word or word pattern:" prompt at any time. To return all the way to the Edit screen, press Cancel (F1) until the Speller disappears from the screen.

PERFORMING A WORD COUNT

*Though the Speller always performs a word count whenever you proof a document, using the Count feature is much faster if you **only** need to know the number of words in your document.*

The Count feature is a useful tool for writers who are paid by the word, people who write to spec (i.e., writing just enough text to fit within a particular space), and students who need to write essays of a particular length. Though WordPerfect always displays a word count after spell-checking your document, you can have it quickly *just* count the words, without spell-checking. Follow these steps:

1. Select **T**ools ➤ Sp**e**ll or press Spell (**Ctrl-F2**).

2. Select **C**ount. The message "* Please wait *" is displayed while the Speller counts words.

3. You'll eventually see the word count at the bottom of the screen.

```
It was as if a door had opened, and passionate wind warmed his
soul; it stirred a new feeling in him never truly felt before. For
his entire life, Stan never thought he'd stride down the aisle with
a girl dressed in white. Until Mandy's sweet sweet lips whispered
low one night, "I love you."




                                   Doc 1 Pg 1 Ln 1.5" Pos 5.5"
[                                                              }

  A. imp             B. impact          C. impacted
  D. impacting       E. impaction       F. impacts
  G. impair          H. impaired        I. impairing
  J. impairment      K. impairments     L. impairs
  M. impala          N. impalas         O. impale
  P. impaled         Q. impalement      R. impalements
  S. impaler         T. impalers        U. impales
  V. impaling        W. impalpability   X. impalpable


Press any key to continue_
```

FIGURE 10.7:

The results of the Look Up command trying to match "i?p"*

Count always moves the cursor to the end of the document. To return to your previous position, press Ctrl-Home twice.

4. Press any key to return to the Speller menu, then press Cancel (**F1**) or Exit (**F7**) to leave the Speller menu and return to your document.

WordPerfect counts the following as part of a word:

◆ a–z

◆ A–Z

◆ International alphabetical characters

◆ Apostrophe (')

◆ Hard hyphen (Home hyphen)

The numerical digits 0–9 are also valid characters; however, WordPerfect does not count "words" that consist entirely of numbers (e.g., *999* is not a word). Therefore, the Speller will count 5 words in the following:

Please call (800) 555-0102 for an appointment.

CHECKING A BLOCK OF TEXT

Aside from proofing a single word or page, or an entire document, the Speller can also examine a selected block of text for misspelled words. Follow these steps:

1. Block the text that you want to check the spelling of or count words in by selecting **E**dit ➤ **B**lock (or pressing **Alt-F4** or **F12**) and using the cursor-movement keys, or by using your mouse.

2. Select **T**ools ➤ Sp**e**ll or press Spell (**Ctrl-F2**).

The Speller immediately proofs that block and provides a total word count for the block when it's finished.

REFINING THE SPELLER

*If you create your own main dictionary, its file name must follow the general pattern WP{WP}**xx**.LEX.*

The main Speller dictionary is stored in a file named WP{WP}*xx*.LEX, where *xx* is the abbreviation for the language of your version of WordPerfect. For example, WP{WP}US.LEX is the name of the main dictionary for the United States; WP{WP}FR.LEX is the name of the French main dictionary.

When the Speller finds a misspelled word, and you select Add to add that word to the dictionary, the word automatically goes into a separate, *supplemental* dictionary, with the file name WP{WP}*xx*.SUP, where *xx* is the abbreviation for the language. WordPerfect uses both dictionaries when checking the spelling of a document.

There's rarely a need to tamper with either dictionary directly, because WordPerfect automatically handles both quite efficiently. However, in the event that you accidentally add a misspelled word to the supplemental dictionary or want to create a unique supplemental dictionary of specialized terms, such as technical, legal, or medical terms that you use frequently in your work, you can do so with the Speller Utility.

The Speller Utility is a separate program that comes with your Word-Perfect package, but is accessed directly from DOS (not from WordPerfect). Typically it's stored on-disk with the file name SPELL.EXE in the same directory where WordPerfect is installed (usually C:\WP51) during the Installation procedure.

If you cannot find the SPELL.EXE file on your hard disk, you may need to perform a custom installation and install the Utility files, as discussed in Appendix A.

If you're using a computer with no hard disk, you must exit WordPerfect to get to the DOS command prompt, then insert the disk you labeled "Utilities" in drive A and the disk you labeled "Speller" in drive B. Then type **A:** and press ↵ to switch to drive A, and enter **SPELL B:** to start the Speller Utility.

> ☐ N O T E
> ☐ N O T E
>
> *You can determine, and option-ally change, the directory location of dictionaries by selecting* **F**ile ➤ Set up ➤ **L**oca-tion of Files ➤ **T**hesaurus/Spell/Hyphen-ation *(or by pressing* **Shift-F1 L T**). *If you change the location, you must move the dic-tionary files to that new directory location.*

RUNNING THE SPELLER UTILITY

To run the Speller Utility, follow these steps:

1. First exit WordPerfect (if it's running) to get to the DOS command prompt.

2. Go to the WordPerfect directory (typically by typing **CD \WP51** and pressing ↵).

3. Type **SPELL** and press ↵.

The Speller Utility menu appears, as shown in Figure 10.8.

Some options on the Speller Utility menu are available for both main and supplemental dictionaries (options 0, 1, 2, 3, 4, 7, and 8) and others for the main dictionary only (options 5, 6, 9, and A). In addition, option B is used only with supplemental dictionaries, and option C requires a main dictionary, an algorithmic dictionary, and a supplemental dictionary. The following sections describe how to use these various options.

SELECTING A DICTIONARY TO WORK WITH

Whenever you're using the Speller Utility, you should include the path (e.g., C:\MYFILES\MYWORDS .SUP) if the file you're working with is not in the current directory.

The first step in using the Speller Utility is to choose the dictionary you want to work with by selecting option **1** - Change/Create Dictionary. You see three options:

0 - Cancel - do not change dictionary
1 - Change/Create main dictionary
2 - Change/Create supplemental dictionary

Selecting option 1 presents the screen shown in Figure 10.9. Selecting option 2 presents a similar screen, except that it shows the name of the supplemental dictionary instead of the main dictionary. The name of the default main dictionary (e.g., WP{WP}US.LEX) or supplemental dictionary (e.g., WP{WP}US.SUP) is displayed, and you can press ↵ to use that dictionary. Optionally, you can enter a new dictionary name, including the path, if the dictionary is not in the current directory, then press ↵.

The name of the current dictionary is always displayed in the upper-right corner of the Speller Utility screen.

If the dictionary name you enter does not exist, you'll be asked whether it should be created. Select **N**o if you simply misspelled the dictionary name, or **Y**es if you do want to create a new dictionary.

```
Spell -- WordPerfect Speller Utility                    WP{WP}US.LEX

0 - Exit
1 - Change/Create Dictionary
2 - Add Words to Dictionary
3 - Delete Words from Dictionary
4 - Optimize Dictionary
5 - Display Common Word List
6 - Check Location of a Word
7 - Look Up
8 - Phonetic Look Up
9 - Convert 4.2 Dictionary to 5.1
A - Combine Other 5.0 or 5.1 Dictionary
B - Compress/Expand Supplemental Dictionary
C - Extract Added Words from Wordlist-based Dictionary

Selection: _
```

FIGURE 10.8:

The Speller Utility menu

ADDING WORDS TO THE DICTIONARIES

To keep the Speller running at top speed, avoid adding infrequently used words to the common word list.

When you select **2** - Add Words to Dictionary from the Speller Utility menu in Figure 10.8, you'll see the options shown in Figure 10.10. As the menu indicates, you can enter words by typing them at the keyboard or by reading them from a file (discussed in a moment).

```
  Spell -- Change Dictionary                           WP{WP}US.LEX

  0 - Cancel - do not change dictionary
  1 - Change/Create main dictionary
  2 - Change/Create supplemental dictionary

  Selection: 1

  You may now safely exchange diskettes in any drive.


  Name of dictionary to use: WP{WP}US.LEX
```

FIGURE 10.9:

The screen for selecting a dictionary to work with

```
  Spell -- Add Words                                   WP{WP}US.LEX

  0 - Cancel - do not add words
  1 - Add to common word list (from keyboard)
  2 - Add to common word list (from a file)
  3 - Add to main word list (from keyboard)
  4 - Add to main word list (from a file)
  5 - Exit

  Selection: _
```

FIGURE 10.10:

The options for adding words to the current dictionary

You can add words to the common word list or the main word list. The common word list contains frequently used words, like *the, that,* and so forth. When checking your spelling, the Speller first checks the common word list in the main dictionary. If the word is not on that list, it checks the main list. If the word still can't be found, the Speller checks the supplemental dictionary. This allows the Speller to run at top speed, since the common word list is considerably smaller than the main list.

Only the main dictionary is divided into common and main word lists. If you are currently working with a supplemental dictionary, options 1 and 2 (Add to common word list) are not functional.

*The hyphens you add to words here are really just **hyphenation indicators,** which Word-Perfect will use only to hyphenate the word, if necessary, when you activate automatic hyphenation.*

Because the automatic hyphenation feature (Chapter 11) uses the same main dictionary as the Speller, you should include hyphens when adding words to the main dictionary. For example, if you want to add the word *pipelining* (a computer term) to the current main dictionary, you can enter it as

pipe-lining

You can include as many hyphens as you wish. If you don't include any hyphens, the automatic hyphenator will not hyphenate the word.

Adding Words from the Keyboard

Pressing ↵ after typing a word will end your entry, but if you accidentally press ↵ instead of the spacebar, you can just select the Add Words option again and pick up where you left off.

If you select one of the options marked *(from keyboard),* you can type in the words you wish to add to the specified dictionary, separating them with spaces. Remember to include hyphens in the words.

When you're finished specifying the words you want to add to the dictionary, select option 5. This will update the current dictionary. Be forewarned that updating the main dictionary can take twenty minutes or more. If you change your mind about adding the words, or you don't have twenty minutes to spare, you can press 0 to cancel your additions and return immediately to the Speller Utility menu.

Adding Words from a File

A quick way to add many words to a dictionary is to first create a list of the words you want to add. You do this in WordPerfect, not the Speller Utility. (If you happen to be in the Speller Utility at the moment, exit by selecting option 0 until you get to the DOS command prompt, then run WordPerfect as usual.)

When typing your list of words to add to a Speller dictionary, include hyphens and separate each word with a hard return (by pressing ↵). Figure 10.11 shows an example.

Before saving your word list, you might want to use the Speller to check the spelling (select **T**ools ➤ Sp**e**ll ➤ **D**ocument or press Ctrl-F2 D). Any words that the Speller does not catch as misspelled words are already in the dictionary; therefore, you should remove those words from the list to avoid replacing them in the dictionary (and save yourself the trouble of hyphenating them). Also, because adding these words to the dictionary will be faster if the words are in alphabetical order, you might want to "line sort" the entire list first, as discussed in Chapter 17.

Finally, save the entire list and exit WordPerfect by selecting **File ➤ Ex**it (Shift-F7). For simplicity, save your list on the same drive and in the same directory where the dictionary files are stored. For example, enter the name of the file as C:\WP51\MYLIST.WP when prompted for a file name.

Now you can run the Speller Utility, choose the dictionary where words will be added (using option 1), select option 2 - Add Words to Dictionary, then select one of the *(from a file)* options. Enter the name of the file (including the directory if it's not the same as the current directory) containing the words you want to add, and press ↵. Finally, be sure to select option 5 (Exit) to actually add the words to the dictionary. You can then use the Look Up option (option 7) to look up any words to verify the addition if you wish.

```
Catt-leya
Cym-bidium
Den-drobium
Epi-dendrum
Laelia
Mil-tonia
Odon-to-glossum
Oncidium
Paphio-pedilium
Phala-enopsis
Vanda
Zygo-petalum
_
```

C:\WP51\WPFILES\ORCHIDS3.WP   Doc 1 Pg 1 Ln 3" Pos 1"

FIGURE 10.11:

A list of words to be added to a dictionary

WHY BOTHER WITH ALL OF THIS?

You may be thinking that everything I've discussed so far is an awfully complicated way to go about adding words to the dictionary. After all, simply selecting option 3 (Add) when you're spell-checking a document does all this for you automatically. You are absolutely correct in your thinking.

Word-Perfect only uses the main dictionary, not supplemental dictionaries, for hyphenation.

But one slight advantage of manually adding words to the main dictionary in this manner is that you can add hyphens to the main dictionary used by the automatic hyphenator. Another advantage is that you can create specialized supplemental dictionaries that you use with some documents but not with others. This might come in handy if you work with highly technical or foreign-language manuscripts, because a smaller, specialized supplemental dictionary will be slightly faster than a larger, more general one, particularly on a slow computer.

To create a specialized supplemental dictionary, start by creating and saving your list of specialized terms in WordPerfect, as discussed earlier under "Adding Words from a File." Then exit WordPerfect and run the Speller Utility.

*Unlike the main dictionary, file names of supplemental dictionaries need not follow the WP{WP}**xx**.SUP pattern—you can use any valid DOS file name. Just be sure to store the names in the same directory that contains your other supplemental dictionaries.*

In the Speller Utility, select option 1 - Change/Create Dictionary on the main Utility menu, then select option 2 - *Change/Create supplemental dictionary* to create a new supplemental dictionary with a unique name in the same directory where the other dictionary files are stored (e.g., C:\WP51\MYDICT.SUP). Then select option 2 - Add Words to Dictionary on the Utility menu to add the words from your word-list file to this new dictionary and exit the Speller Utility.

To have WordPerfect use this new supplemental dictionary when you run the Speller, first select **T**ools ➤ Sp**e**ll ➤ **N**ew Sup. Dictionary (or press **Ctrl-F2 N**), and enter the name of the specialized dictionary. Then select **D**ocument or any other option from the Speller menu.

Be aware that you can use only one main dictionary and one supplemental dictionary when spell-checking a document. If you want to combine two or more specialized dictionaries into one, you can join several word lists in WordPerfect (by using **F**ile ➤ **R**etrieve or Shift-F10), then add those combined word lists to any dictionary you choose by means of the Speller Utility. Or you can just select any dictionary you want to work with in the Speller Utility and add words from any word list to the current dictionary.

Remember, words added to the Speller dictionary with the Add option in Word-Perfect are added to the current supplemental dictionary, not the main dictionary.

DELETING WORDS FROM A DICTIONARY

If you accidentally add a misspelled word to one of the Speller dictionaries, you'll probably want to delete it so that the Speller catches the misspelling in the future. You can do so by selecting the Delete Words from Dictionary option (option 3) from the Speller Utility menu. WordPerfect presents options for deleting words from either the common word list (available for the main dictionary only) or the main word list (available for both main and supplemental dictionaries). You can specify the words either by typing them directly from the keyboard or by entering the name of a file that contains the words to be deleted.

The Delete Words options work exactly the same as the Add Words options explained above, except that the specified words will be deleted rather than added. Type **5** after deleting a word or words (or **0** to cancel the deletion). Then you have to wait for the updating process again, which, as mentioned, can take twenty minutes or more. Again, if you are deleting words from a list in a file, the process will be faster if the words are in alphabetical order; therefore, you might want to "line sort" the entire list first, as discussed in Chapter 17.

USING THE THESAURUS

TO USE THE THESAURUS,

position the cursor on the word you want to check, and select Tools ➤ Thesaurus or press Alt-F1.

WordPerfect's Thesaurus helps you out when you are at a loss for words. It can help you find a more precise or expressive synonym for a word, such as *enormous* instead of just *big*. It can also help you find an antonym. For example, when you need a word that means the opposite of *arrogant,* but just can't quite think of the right word, you can look up *arrogant* and discover antonyms like *polite* and *humble*.

Selecting the best word can add spice to your writing. For example, suppose you're writing about a mountain-climbing adventure and write the sentence *We climbed the big hill.* With the help of the Thesaurus, you can find more exciting words, changing that rather dull sentence to something a bit more dramatic, such as *We scaled the towering peak.*

To use the Thesaurus, follow these steps:

1. Place the cursor on the word for which you want a synonym or antonym.

2. Select **Tools ➤ Th**esaurus, or press Thesaurus (**Alt-F1**). Suggested synonyms and antonyms are displayed, as shown in Figure 10.12.

3. If you don't see exactly the word you want, you can type the highlighted letter next to any word shown to see synonyms and antonyms for that word.

If you decide not to replace the highlighted word in your document, just press Cancel (F1) to return to the Edit screen without making any changes.

4. When you see the word you want, select **1** Replace Word, then press the highlighted letter next to the word you want. This will replace the highlighted word in your document with the word you selected.

The Thesaurus occupies the lower three-quarters of the display. The synonym listing is divided into three columns, with four menu items on the bottom of the screen. Each of the columns can list synonyms for one word. Definitions from one column will scroll into the next column if it is empty. If the next column is full and there are more synonyms, you can use the ↑ and ↓ keys to scroll through the column.

Each column is divided into sections, each section starting with a different number and containing a group of words related to one another in concept (since synonyms can have slightly different meanings). Additional sections may contain uses of the word as an adjective (*a*), a noun (*n*), or a verb (*v*). If the word has any antonyms, that group will be marked by *(ant)*. The last section, which has *(ant)* in its heading, is the antonym list.

Only one of the columns is active at any time. The active column shows highlighted letters next to each word; inactive columns show only bullets next to each word. You can switch between columns with the ← and → keys. The four menu commands at the bottom of the screen are summarized below and described in more detail later in the chapter.

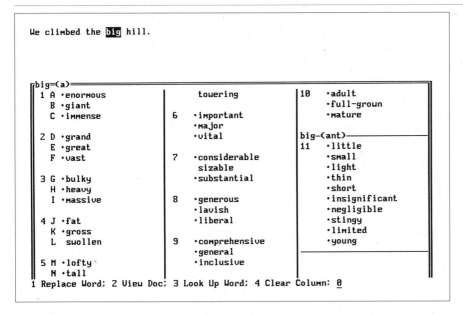

FIGURE 10.12:

The Thesaurus screen for the word "big"

1 Replace Word	Replaces the word in the document with one of the alternate words displayed on the screen. After selecting this option, type the letter next to the word that you want to select.
2 View Doc	Lets you scroll the upper portion of the screen and review the text surrounding the word, in case you need to see the context in which the word is used.
3 Look Up Word	Lets you enter any word to look up. Select this option, type in any word, and press ↵.
4 Clear Column	Erases the currently selected column of alternate words from the screen.

The Thesaurus contains about 10,000 headwords.

If you press the letter assigned to a word and that word has a bullet by it, then synonyms for that word will be listed in their own column. The bullet indicates that the word is a *headword,* a word for which the Thesaurus has a synonym list. For example, Figure 10.13 shows the screen after pressing F to select *vast* from the screen shown in Figure 10.12.

You can press Cancel (**F1**), Exit (**F7**), or **0** to exit the Thesaurus.

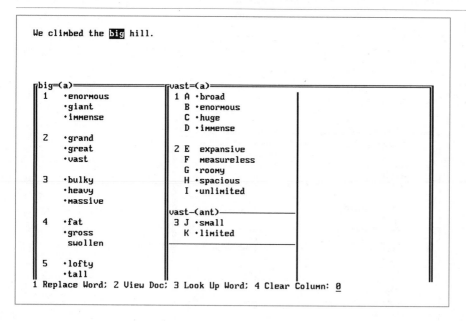

FIGURE 10.13:

The synonyms for "vast" appear after selecting option F from the screen shown in Figure 10.12.

OTHER THESAURUS FEATURES

Learning to use the Thesaurus is much like learning to use the Speller: A little practice goes a long way. I hope the steps above have helped you get a start. The Thesaurus includes some other handy features, summarized in the sections that follow.

VIEWING THE CONTEXT OF A WORD

When you activate the Thesaurus, it temporarily covers about three-fourths of your document on the screen. If you need to see more of your document, select **2** View Doc. The cursor will jump up to the top of the screen, and you will be able to scroll through your text using the ↑, ↓, ←, and → keys. This can help you see the full context where your word is used (you cannot make any changes to your text in this mode, however).

After viewing your text, press Exit (F7) or ↵ to return to the Thesaurus portion of the screen.

FINDING THE RIGHT WORD

You can also use the Thesaurus to find the right word before you type it. To do so, you must first position the cursor so that it isn't on a word or between any two words. Typically, the easiest way to do this is to move the cursor to the bottom of the document, by pressing Home Home ↓. If necessary, press ↵ to move down to a blank line.

Select **T**ools ➤ **Th**esaurus, or press Thesaurus (Alt-F1), and you'll see an empty Thesaurus screen with the prompt "Word:" in the lower-left corner of the screen, as in Figure 10.14.

Type in a word and press ↵. As usual, the Thesaurus screen will show synonyms and antonyms, and you can type the letter next to any bulleted word to determine more synonyms for that word. Use the usual techniques to explore synonyms and antonyms.

When you find the word you want, you can just press Cancel (F1) if you want to leave without changing your Edit screen. Then, you can press Ctrl-Home twice to move the cursor back to its previous place in the document if you wish.

As an alternative, you can select **1** Replace Word, and then type the letter of the word you want to select from the Thesaurus screen. That word will be inserted at the current cursor position.

N O T E
N O T E
You can move the word by using the usual techniques for moving a block, as described in Chapter 2.

CLEARING A CLUTTERED THESAURUS SCREEN

As you repeatedly select bulleted words from the Thesaurus screen to view other related words, WordPerfect fills up the columns on the screen. When the columns are filled, you may need to scroll up and down with the ↑ and ↓ keys to view all the words that are available.

As an alternative, you can also clear any column on your screen if you no longer need it to find alternative words. Just use the ← or → keys to move the highlighted letters to the column you no longer need, then select **4** Clear Column from the menu. The contents of that column will be cleared, and any columns to the right will shift to the left to fill in the cleared space.

In the next chapter, you'll learn about how to hyphenate words.

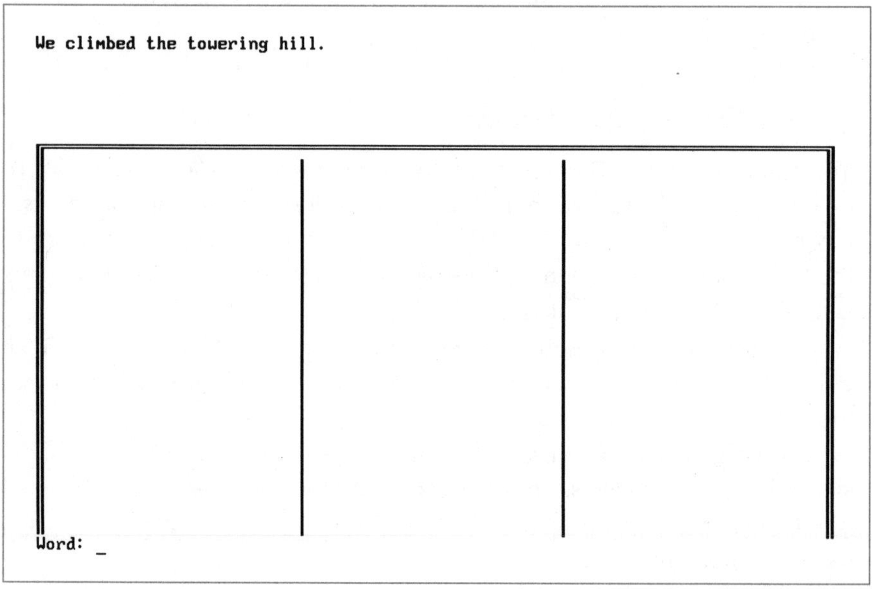

FIGURE 10.14:

The Thesaurus screen, with the cursor not positioned on a word

CHAPTER 11

Hyphenating Text

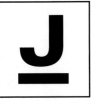

Just as WordPerfect can use a dictionary to check your spelling, it can also use a dictionary to hyphenate words. The main purpose of hyphenation is to tighten loose lines that contain too much white space. For example, the first paragraph in Figure 11.1 has a very loose line because of some lengthy words at the ends of lines. The figure shows how much tighter that same paragraph looks with some hyphens added.

There are several ways to hyphenate words with WordPerfect, ranging from the fully manual method, where you insert your own hyphens, to the fully automatic method, where WordPerfect handles hyphenation for you. I'll discuss all the possibilities in the sections that follow.

USING AUTOMATIC HYPHENATION

TO ACTIVATE AUTOMATIC HYPHENATION, position the cursor where you want to start hyphenating and select Layout ➤ Line ➤ Hyphenation ➤ Yes, or press Shift-F8 L Y Y.

If your computer does not have a hard disk, refer to the section titled "Hyphenation Options for Floppy-Disk Users" later in this chapter.

Unlike the Speller and Thesaurus, automatic hyphenation is a formatting feature that is activated at the current cursor position. That is, only text below the current cursor position will be hyphenated after you activate automatic hyphenation. Therefore, if you want to use hyphenation throughout your entire document, you must position the cursor at the top of the document before turning on automatic hyphenation.

To activate automatic hyphenation, follow these steps:

1. Move the cursor to where you want to start using automatic hyphenation or to the beginning of the document (press **Home Home Home** ↑).

2. Select **Layout** ➤ **Line** or press **Shift-F8 L**.

3. Select **H**yphenation.

4. Select **Y**es.

5. Press Exit (**F7**) to return to the Edit screen.

As you type new text or move the cursor through existing text below the cursor, WordPerfect will check for long words at the ends of lines. When it encounters a line where the spacing could be improved by hyphenation, one of two things will occur:

◆ WordPerfect will hyphenate the word without asking for your help.

Very long words like supercalifragilisticexpialidocious, of Mary Poppins fame, cause very loose lines (too much white space) if left unhyphenated, particularly when squeezed into tight margins.

Very long words like supercalifragilisticexpialidocious, of Mary Poppins fame, cause very loose lines (too much white space) if left unhyphenated, particularly when squeezed into tight margins.

FIGURE 11.1:

A paragraph with and without hyphenation

◆ In some circumstances (discussed later), if WordPerfect is not certain how to hyphenate the word, you'll hear a beep and be asked to select a position for the hyphen.

You might want to buy one of those handy little books containing lists of words that are divided and spelled correctly. Proper word division can be tricky, so you'll want to be sure you are hyphenating correctly.

WordPerfect uses the Speller dictionary. If the word that needs to be hyphenated is in the dictionary, WordPerfect will hyphenate according to the dictionary. If WordPerfect cannot find the word, then it will either leave the word unhyphenated or ask you to help it hyphenate the word.

For example, if you type Mary Poppins's *supercalifragilisticexpialidocious* near the end of a line, WordPerfect won't find that word in its dictionary (because it's not a bona-fide word). Therefore, you'll hear a beep and see a message like this one at the bottom of your screen:

Position hyphen; Press ESC supercalifragilistic-expialidocious

At this point, you have three options:

◆ To insert the hyphen where WordPerfect suggests (between the letters *c* and *e* in this example), press the Escape key.

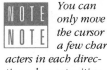

You can only move the cursor a few characters in each direction when repositioning the hyphen.

◆ If the suggested hyphenation point is not acceptable, press ← or → to reposition the hyphen, and then press **Esc**.

◆ If you prefer that the word not be hyphenated at all, press Cancel (**F1**).

CHANGING AN AUTOMATIC HYPHEN

Let's suppose WordPerfect automatically hyphenates a word in your document. Then, while scrolling through the document, you find that you don't like the way WordPerfect hyphenated the word. If automatic hyphenation is still turned on, you can follow these steps to change the position of the hyphen:

1. Move the cursor to the hyphen that WordPerfect placed in the word (at the end of the line).

2. Press the **Delete** key.

3. You'll hear a beep and see a message at the bottom of the screen asking you to position the hyphen.

Your choices are now the same as before: Use the ← and → keys to move the hyphen to where you want it to break the word, then press the Escape key. Or, if you prefer that WordPerfect not hyphenate the word, press the Cancel (F1) key instead.

TURNING OFF AUTOMATIC HYPHENATION

> **TO DEACTIVATE AUTOMATIC HYPHENATION,**
>
> **position the cursor where you want to stop hyphenating, and select Layout ➤ Line ➤ Hyphenation ➤ No or press Shift-F8 L Y N.**

You can use Search and Replace (Chapter 9) to help locate and remove [Hyph On] codes.

When you turn on automatic hyphenation, WordPerfect inserts a [Hyph On] code at the current cursor position. All text beneath that position is subject to automatic hyphenation, either to the end of the document or to the place where WordPerfect encounters a [Hyph Off] code.

Therefore, you have two choices for turning off automatic hyphenation:

◆ Remove the [Hyph On] code on the Reveal Codes screen (press **Alt-F3** or **F11** to activate this screen).

◆ Insert a [Hyph Off] code where you want to end automatic hyphenation, by positioning the cursor and selecting **L**ayout ➤ **L**ine ➤ **H**yphenation ➤ **N**o (or pressing **Shift-F8 L Y N**).

The first method, removing the [Hyph On] code, deactivates automatic hyphenation below the cursor, but does not remove existing hyphens. However, as you add and change text, WordPerfect will no longer hyphenate words.

Only text that is between a [Hyph On] and [Hyph Off] code is automatically hyphenated.

The latter technique keeps automatic hyphenation active above the cursor, but turns it off for text below the cursor. Use this method when you want WordPerfect to hyphenate some sections of your text, but not others. You can have as many [Hyph On] and [Hyph Off] codes in your document as you please, and you can place any amount of text—from a few lines to many pages—between any pair of [Hyph On] and [Hyph Off] codes.

HYPHENATING TEXT MANUALLY

> **TO ADD A NORMAL HYPHEN TO YOUR TEXT,**
>
> **just type the hyphen. Optionally, use a hard hyphen (press Home hyphen), which is never used to break text, or a soft hyphen (press Ctrl-hyphen), which is used to break text only if necessary.**

You can hyphenate words without the aid of WordPerfect's automatic hyphenation at any time. However, an understanding of several characters—*hyphen characters, soft hyphens, hard hyphens,* and *dashes*—is helpful.

HYPHEN CHARACTERS

A hyphen character is really a normal hyphen, which you use to divide compound words like *thirty-three* and compound names like *Livingston-Gladstone.* It is used to break a word at the end of a line only when it's convenient to do so.

For example, if the name Livingston-Gladstone appears in the beginning or middle of a line, the hyphen appears as normal. However, if that name comes at the end of a line, WordPerfect may put *Livingston-* at the end of the first line and *Gladstone* at the start of the next line.

Because the hyphen character is really just a normal hyphen, no special techniques are required to type it. For example, to type *Livingston-Gladstone,* you type *Livingston,* then type the hyphen, then type *Gladstone,* just as on a typewriter. On the Reveal Codes screen, however, the hyphen character appears between square brackets, like this: [-].

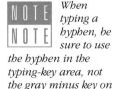 *When typing a hyphen, be sure to use the hyphen in the typing-key area, not the gray minus key on the numeric keypad.*

SOFT HYPHENS

When you use automatic hyphenation, WordPerfect inserts *soft hyphens* in hyphenated words. They are called soft hyphens because they disappear automatically when no longer needed. For example, this happens if the word *instructions* is hyphenated at the end of a line, and then you remove a word from that line, making it shorter. If there's enough room on the shorter line to display *instructions* without hyphenating it, WordPerfect simply removes the soft hyphen.

If you are typing a paragraph without the aid of automatic hyphenation and decide you want to hyphenate a long word at the beginning of a line (so that part of it moves up onto the line above), follow these steps:

1. Make sure you are in Insert mode (if "Typeover" appears in the lower-left corner of the screen, press the **Insert** key).

2. Position the cursor where you want to insert a soft hyphen in the word.

3. Press **Ctrl-hyphen** (hold down the Ctrl key and type a hyphen). Note that the hyphen appears *only* on the Reveal Codes screen.

To see if WordPerfect will use the soft hyphen to break the long word, press ↑ or ↓ to reformat the paragraph. If WordPerfect can use the soft hyphen to better format the line above, it will do so. If WordPerfect can't use the soft hyphen now, it will keep it in the word for possible use later. On the Reveal Codes screen, you'll see the soft hyphen displayed as a highlighted (bright) hyphen.

HARD HYPHENS

A *hard hyphen* is something like a normal hyphen character: It is always shown in your text; it never disappears. However, unlike the hyphen character, a hard hyphen is not used to break a compound word at the end of a long line. A hard hyphen is often used when typing short formulas, like 10 − 5 = 5, phone numbers like *555-1234,* or hyphenated words that should be kept together.

Using the hard hyphen makes WordPerfect treat the hyphenated words as one word, as though the hyphen were some other character, like a letter or number. For example, if the formula 10 − 5 = 5 or the phone number 555-1234 falls at the end of a line, WordPerfect will *not* split the two words at the end of the line. Instead, it will wrap the entire formula or paired words to the next line.

To insert a hard hyphen in a word, press the **Home** key, then the hyphen. It looks like a normal hyphen on the Edit screen and the Reveal Codes screen as well.

DASHES

NOTE NOTE *Dashes are treated like any other normal character in automatic hyphenation.*

A dash is two hyphens—sometimes used as a punctuation mark to connect two sentences. If you do not want WordPerfect to use the first of the hyphens in the dash as the hyphen at the end of a line, type the first hyphen as a hard hyphen character and the second as a hyphen character. To type the dash, press and release the **Home** key, then type two hyphens. On the Reveal Codes screen, the dash will appear as -[-].

BREAKING WORDS WITHOUT HYPHENS

It's also possible to break words at the ends of lines without inserting hyphens. This is handy when you want to use a character other than a hyphen to break long words, such as a slash (/), an en dash, or an em dash. For example, if you create your own compound word, such as *Cattleya/Cymbidium/ Dendrobium,* and that word comes at the end of a line, you might want to have WordPerfect break it onto two lines at a slash, without inserting a hyphen.

The character used to tell WordPerfect where to break a word at the end of a line (without hyphenating) has the rather poetic name of *invisible soft return*. You type this character by pressing Home, then ↵. The character is indeed invisible on the Edit screen and on the printed document, but it appears as [ISRt] on the Reveal Codes screen.

To use an invisible soft return, let's assume you type a word like *Cattleya/Cymbidium/Dendrobium* in your document while automatic hyphenation is turned on. Then WordPerfect inserts a hyphen, placing *Cattleya/-* on the first line and *Cymbidium/Dendrobium* on the next line. To delete the hyphen and just break the words at the slash, follow these steps:

1. Move the cursor to the hyphen.

2. Press the **Home** key and then press the ↵ key.

3. Press the **Delete** key to delete the hyphen.

4. If the new break is not satisfactory, move the cursor to the right of any other slash, and press **Home** ↵. You can press Home ↵ after each slash if you want to have WordPerfect use whichever slash is best.

You can also type the invisible soft return whenever you're prompted to press Esc during automatic hyphenation. When you get the prompt, move the cursor to where you want the word to break (to the right of a slash, for example) and press Home ↵ instead of Escape.

DELETABLE SOFT RETURNS

There is another, rather odd, code that WordPerfect sometimes uses to break long words, called the *deletable soft return*. WordPerfect inserts this code automatically when you type long words into very narrow columns when automatic hyphenation is turned off. It is invisible on the Edit screen, but appears as [DSRt] on the Reveal Codes screen.

Multi-column layouts are covered in Chapter 20.

This code tells WordPerfect to split the word without hyphenating it. You never type this code yourself and really don't need to be concerned with it until you start working with very narrow columns of text.

For future reference, Table 11.1 summarizes the various hidden codes that you can use to handle breaks at the ends of lines. The table also lists how each type of hyphen appears on the Reveal Codes screen.

HYPHEN	DESCRIPTION	KEYSTROKE	CODE
Hyphen character	Permanent hyphen that may be used to break two words at the end of a line	-	[-]
Soft hyphen	Temporary hyphen used to break a word when necessary (the kind used in automatic hyphenation)	Ctrl-hyphen	- (highlighted)
Hard hyphen	Permanent hyphen that is not used to break a word at the end of line	Home -	-
Dash	Two hyphens, never separated at the end of a line	Home --	-[-]
Invisible soft return	Breaks words at a certain place without showing a hyphen	Home ↵	[ISRt]

TABLE 11.1:

A Summary of Hyphens and Dashes

WHAT TO DO WHEN A WORD REFUSES TO BE HYPHENATED

IF A LONG WORD REFUSES TO BE HYPHENATED,

check for and remove the [/] character in front of that word on the Reveal Codes screen.

NOTE
NOTE

As discussed in Chapter 10, new words that you add to the Speller dictionary without hyphen indicators may not be hyphenated—more on this in a moment.

If you are deep in the throes of hyphenation and find that a word you expect to be hyphenated isn't, it may be that the word is marked for no hyphenation. This occurs when you press Cancel (F1) in response to WordPerfect's request to position the hyphen in a word that needs to be hyphenated.

If you are certain that a word needs to be hyphenated but it refuses to be, follow these steps to correct the situation:

1. Move the cursor to the first character in the word that refuses to be hyphenated.

2. Select **Edit** ➤ **R**eveal Codes, or press Reveal Codes (**Alt-F3** or **F11**).

3. Check to see whether the word is preceded by or contains the [/] code (which tells WordPerfect never to hyphenate the word).

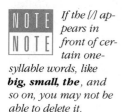

*If the [/] appears in front of certain one-syllable words, like **big, small, the**, and so on, you may not be able to delete it.*

4. Move the code highlight to the [/] code by using the arrow keys.

5. Press the **Delete** key.

6. At this point, WordPerfect may beep and ask you to position the hyphen in the word. Position the hyphen by using the ← and → keys, and then press the **Escape** key.

7. Press Reveal Codes (**Alt-F3** or **F11**) again to return to the Edit screen.

PREVENTING A WORD FROM BEING HYPHENATED

If WordPerfect's automatic hyphenation helps to hyphenate a word, and you decide that you don't want to hyphenate that particular word, follow these steps to prevent hyphenation:

1. Move the cursor to the first character of the word that you do not want WordPerfect to hyphenate.

2. Press **Home**.

3. Press / (a forward slash).

4. Move the cursor to the hyphen that WordPerfect placed in the word.

5. Press **Delete** to delete the hyphen.

If you press Reveal Codes (Alt-F3 or F11) after performing the steps above, you'll see that the word begins with the [/] code. This code prevents the word from being hyphenated. If you later change your mind and decide that you do want to hyphenate the word after all, you'll need to remove the [/] code from the front of the word, using the Delete key on the Reveal Codes screen.

REFINING AUTOMATIC HYPHENATION

TO CUSTOMIZE SOME FEATURES OF HYPHENATION,

select File ➤ Setup ➤ Environment, or press Shift-F1 E.

In most cases, WordPerfect's automatic hyphenation will be sufficient for your needs, but there are several ways to refine and customize the automatic hyphenation techniques. These are entirely optional, so if you are doing well with what you've learned so far, feel free to skip the rest of this chapter.

SELECTING A HYPHENATION DICTIONARY

When automatic hyphenation is on and WordPerfect decides to hyphenate a word, it looks into either an internal or external hyphenation dictionary. The internal dictionary is built into WordPerfect and is always available. The external dictionary is much larger than the internal one and is stored either on your hard disk or Speller disk.

 The hyphenation dictionary is stored in two separate files named WP{WP}US.LEX (also used for the Speller) and WP{WP}US.HYC.

The external dictionary provides many more hyphenation possibilities than the internal dictionary and will also prompt you less often during automatic hyphenation. If your computer has a hard disk, and you've installed WordPerfect according to the usual procedure, you'll probably want to use the external dictionary. If you don't have a hard disk, or you don't want to store the large hyphenation files on your hard disk, you might prefer to use the smaller, internal dictionary.

You can choose either dictionary by following these steps:

1. Select **File** ➤ Setup or press Setup (**Shift-F1**).

2. Select **E**nvironment.

3. Select **H**yphenation.

4. Select **E**xternal Dictionary/Rules if you want to use the external dictionary, or select **I**nternal Rules if you want to use the internal dictionary.

5. Press Exit (**F7**).

Your selection will affect the current WordPerfect session, as well as all future sessions. If, at some time in the future, you want to use a different dictionary, just repeat the steps above.

HYPHENATION OPTIONS FOR FLOPPY-DISK USERS

If your computer does not have a hard disk, you should either avoid using automatic hyphenation or use automatic hyphenation with the internal dictionary only, until you've finished typing and editing your document.

If you want to check all hyphenation using the more complete external dictionary, first move the cursor to the top of the document, then remove the disk in drive B and replace it with the Speller disk. Finally, follow the steps below to activate automatic hyphenation with the external dictionary and hyphenate the entire document:

1. Select **File** ➤ Setup or press Setup (**Shift-F1**).

2. Select **E**nvironment.

3. Select **H**yphenation.

4. Select **E**xternal Dictionary/Rules.

5. Press Exit (**F7**).

6. Select **L**ayout ➤ **L**ine Hyphenation ➤ **Y**es (or press **Shift-F8 L Y Y**).

7. Press Exit (**F7**) to return to your document.

8. Press **Home Home** ↓ to move to the bottom of the document.

Moving to the bottom of the document will start the automatic hyphenation process, and you'll be prompted for any hyphenation where WordPerfect needs your help. When the cursor gets to the bottom of the document, remove the Speller disk from drive B and replace the disk that was originally there. Then save your document by pressing the Save key (F10) or by exiting Word-Perfect (F7).

SELECTING THE FREQUENCY OF HYPHENATION PROMPTS

During automatic hyphenation, WordPerfect usually asks you to position the hyphen only when it cannot find the current word in one of its dictionaries. This is the most convenient way to use automatic hyphenation, because Word-Perfect will usually be able to hyphenate long words without your help.

There are actually three different settings to choose from for determining when WordPerfect asks you for help in positioning the hyphen in a word that needs to be broken:

Never: WordPerfect never prompts you to position the hyphen and always hyphenates according to the current hyphenation dictionary. If a word that needs to be hyphenated is not in the dictionary, it will be word-wrapped to the next line without hyphenation.

When Required: This is the normal setting; WordPerfect only asks for help in positioning the cursor when it cannot find that word in the current dictionary.

Always: WordPerfect stops and ask you for help in positioning the cursor every time it finds a word that needs to be hyphenated (this can be pretty tedious but gives you practice using the feature).

To select one of the options listed above, follow these steps:

1. Select **F**ile ➤ Se**t**up or press Setup (**Shift-F1**).

2. Select **E**nvironment ➤ **P**rompt for Hyphenation.

3. Select **N**ever, **W**hen Required (the usual technique) or **A**lways.

4. Press Exit (**F7**) to return to your document.

Your selection will affect automatic hyphenation in the current document and all future documents as well (until you repeat the steps above and select a different option).

DISABLING THE HYPHENATION BEEP

Normally, WordPerfect beeps when it needs help with hyphenating a word. If you would prefer that it not beep, follow these steps:

1. Select **F**ile ➤ Se**t**up ➤ **E**nvironment ➤ **B**eep options (or press **Shift-F1 E E**).

2. Select Beep on **Hy**phenation ➤ **N**o (or **Y**es if you want to reactivate beeping).

3. Press Exit (**F7**).

Changing the Beep option to No deactivates beeping for the current session and all future sessions, until you repeat these steps to reactivate it.

USING HYPHENATION ZONES

TO CHANGE THE HYPHENATION ZONES,

select Layout ➤ Line ➤ Hyphenation Zone (or press Shift-F8 L Z) and either decrease the zones (for more hyphens and tighter text) or increase them (for fewer hyphens and looser text).

When you use automatic hyphenation, WordPerfect decides whether or not to break a word at the end of a line by using *hyphenation zones*. You might think of a hyphenation zone as the place on a standard typewriter where the bell sounds to indicate that you are nearing the end of a line as you type. Of course, WordPerfect doesn't sound a bell because it hyphenates automatically.

WordPerfect's hyphenation zones are not visible on your screen. WordPerfect uses two zones, one on each side of the right margin, to control hyphenation. Figure 11.2 shows how these zones would look if they were visible on your screen.

WordPerfect uses the following rules to decide whether or not to hyphenate a word (when automatic hyphenation is on, or when you insert your own hyphen or soft hyphen):

◆ If the last word on a line starts before the left edge of or within the hyphenation zone and extends past the right edge of the hyphenation zone, it will be hyphenated.

◆ If the last word on the line starts before the left edge of or within the hyphenation zone and is narrower than the zone, it is wrapped to the next line without hyphenation.

The sample paragraphs in Figure 11.2 illustrate this. At the end of the first line in the first paragraph, there is not enough room for the word *the* before the right margin. But the word is narrower than the hyphenation zones, so it is wrapped to the next line. In the second paragraph, the long word *philanthropic* is hyphenated, because it begins before the left hyphenation zone and would extend past the right hyphenation zone if it weren't hyphenated.

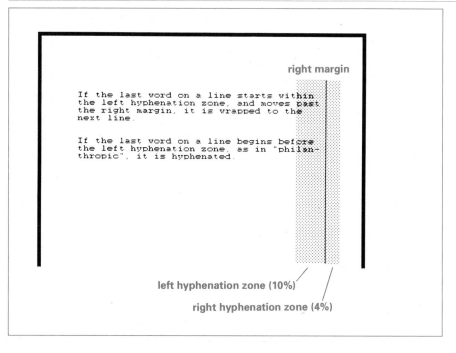

FIGURE 11.2:

WordPerfect hyphenation zones

CHANGING THE HYPHENATION ZONES

The hyphenation zones are measured as percentages of the line length. By default, WordPerfect uses a left hyphenation zone of 10 percent and a right hyphenation zone of 4 percent. Hence, when you are printing on standard 8.5" × 11" paper, with 1-inch margins at the left and right and a standard print size of 10 characters to the inch, the length of each line is 6.5 inches. Therefore, a left hyphenation zone of 10 percent is 0.65 inches, and a right hyphenation zone of 4 percent is about 0.26 inches.

These preselected hyphenation zones provide a sort of happy medium between how tight the text is in justified paragraphs (or how much space is at the end of ragged-right lines) and the amount of hyphenation required. But you can change the sizes of the hyphenation zones to tighten the text further, or loosen it a bit.

Basically, it works like this: Smaller hyphenation zones produce tighter text, but you'll pay the price of having to hyphenate more words. Larger hyphenation zones require less hyphenation but produce looser text.

The decision on whether to use wide or narrow hyphenation zones is entirely up to you. You can leave them as preset by WordPerfect or change them. If you decide to change them, remember that, like all formatting codes, new hyphenation measurements affect only text that is to the right of and below the cursor position.

Follow these steps to change the hyphenation zones:

1. Move the cursor to where you want new hyphenation zones to take effect (e.g., to the top of the document if you want the entire document to use the new hyphenation zones).

2. Select **Layout** ➤ **Line** ➤ Hyphenation **Z**one (or press **Shift-F8 L Z**).

3. Type in a new left hyphenation zone as a percentage (e.g., *5* for 5 percent) and press ↵, or just press ↵ to leave the current setting unchanged.

4. Type in a new right hyphenation zone as a percentage (e.g., *2* for 2 percent) and press ↵, or just press ↵ to leave the current setting unchanged. (The right zone should always be smaller than or equal to the left zone.)

5. Press Exit (**F7**) to return to the Edit screen.

If help with automatic or manual hyphenation is turned on (as described above), any new text that you type will trigger hyphen help, using the new hyphenation zones. If you scroll through existing text beneath the cursor position, WordPerfect will adjust the existing text to comply with the new hyphenation zone settings.

REMOVING NEW HYPHENATION ZONE SETTINGS

If you alter the hyphenation zone settings in your document and then change your mind and want to use the preset hyphenation zones, you'll need to remove the [HZone:] code from your document on the Reveal Codes screen. If you then scroll through existing text beneath the current cursor position, WordPerfect will readjust the hyphenation to the original settings, again prompting you (when necessary) to help with any revised hyphenation (assuming that you've activated manual or automatic hyphenation help).

In the next chapter you'll learn how to keep better track of your files and also how to search for missing ones. As you'll see, you can use these file management techniques to move, copy, rename, and delete files, as well as create and change directories.

CHAPTER 12

Managing Your Files

As you know, WordPerfect stores your saved documents in files on-disk. As you create and save documents, your collection of files can become quite large. Managing that collection of files can be a job in itself. For example, you might need to delete old files to make room for new ones. Or you might need to look for a file that you know you saved, but whose name you have forgotten.

NOTE NOTE *If you are not already familiar with basic DOS concepts, you might want to refer to your DOS manual or **The ABC's of DOS 5,** by Alan Miller, SYBEX, 1991.*

These kinds of jobs fall into the category of file management, which is what this chapter is all about. You should already be familiar with basic DOS terminology; the terms *file, drive,* and *directory* are summarized below for quick review:

Drive: short for *disk drive*, where all files are stored. The first floppy drive is named *A:,* the second (if any) is named *B:*. Hard drives are named *C:, D:,* and so forth. A disk drive is like a file cabinet.

Directory: a portion of a drive where numerous files are stored. For example, your WordPerfect 5.1 program, and its various related files, may be stored on C:\WP51 (the directory named *WP51* on hard-disk-drive C). A directory is like a single drawer within a file cabinet.

File: a single document or single program. File names can be up to eight characters long and optionally can be followed by a period (dot) and an extension up to three characters long. A file is like a single manila folder in a file drawer.

HAND-OUT.WP is spoken as "handout dot wp."

Often, the drive and directory location of a file are referred to as the *path,* since they tell the computer the route to take to find a particular file. For example, the path and file name C:\WP51\MYFILES\HANDOUT.WP says, "Go to drive C:, then to the directory named WP51, then to the directory below named *MYFILES,* and there you can locate a file named *HANDOUT.WP.*"

SAVING DOCUMENTS

As discussed in chapters 1 and 2, it's important to remember that while you are creating or editing a document, your work is stored in RAM (random access memory) only. If you turn off the power, or a power failure turns it off for you, your current work will be lost. That's because your work is not "permanent" until you save a copy to the disk. You can save your work at any time by selecting **F**ile ➤ **S**ave or by pressing the Save key (F10) and responding to the prompts that appear. In the sections that follow, I'll look at some additional options and techniques you can use while saving files.

ABOUT DRIVES, DIRECTORIES, AND FILE NAMES

Whenever you opt to save a file, you will see this prompt:

Document to be saved:

Later in this chapter, you'll learn how to create directories using WordPerfect.

You have the full range of flexibility that DOS offers at this point to determine the name and location of your file. Here's how it works:

◆ If you enter only the file name (e.g., *MYDOC.WP*), the file is stored on the default drive and directory for WordPerfect documents (which, in turn, is determined by the Location of Files options covered in Chapter 13).

◆ If you enter a subdirectory name and file name (e.g., *WPFILES\MYDOC.WP*), the file is stored on the named subdirectory of the current directory, with the file name you provided (assuming that subdirectory exists). For example, if the current directory is C:\WP51, and there is also a C:\WP51\WPFILES directory, the example name will work. If there is no WPFILES directory beneath the current directory, the entry is rejected with the message "ERROR: Invalid drive/path".

◆ If you enter a drive name (other than the default drive) but no directory name, the file is saved on the root directory of that drive. For example, if you save the file as *A:MYDOC.WP,* the file is saved in the root directory of the disk currently in disk-drive A.

◆ If you enter a complete drive and path, such as *C:\WP51\WPFILES\ MYDOC.WP,* the file is saved to that drive and directory only if they already exist. If C:\WP51\WPFILES (in this example) does not exist, WordPerfect returns the error message "ERROR: Invalid drive/path".

*You can save multiple drafts of the same document simply by changing the file name slightly with each save (e.g., **DRAFT1.WP, DRAFT2.WP, DRAFT3.WP,** and so forth).*

Once you save a file, WordPerfect remembers its name and location. So, when you resave the same file in the future, it displays that location and name, as in the example below:

Document to be saved: C:\WP51\MYDOC.WP

You can press ↵ to reuse that name, in which case WordPerfect will ask for permission before overwriting the existing copy on-disk. Optionally, you can change the name or location. Doing so leaves the original file intact and unchanged, and stores the latest copy of the file at the name and location you specify.

TIMED AND ORIGINAL BACKUPS

As added protection against power outages and other mishaps, you can have WordPerfect automatically save your work at timed intervals. You can set the timing interval through the WordPerfect customization feature, covered in Chapter 13. You may also want to look into original document backup in that chapter, which lets you store both a new and a previously saved copy of a file on-disk.

PASSWORD-PROTECTING FILES

TO ADD, CHANGE, OR DELETE A PASSWORD FOR A DOCUMENT,

1. Select File ➤ Password (or press Ctrl-F5 P).

2. Select Add/Change to add or change a password, or Remove to remove a password.

3. Save the file.

If you share a computer with others, and you want to prevent them from viewing, printing, or modifying a document, you can assign it a password of up to 23 characters. Only people who know the password will be able to gain access to the document.

There's one catch, though. If you forget the password, even *you* won't be able to access the document. So once you think up a password, write it down and store it in a safe place. Then follow these steps to use the password to "lock" your document:

Use the same password in all your documents to avoid confusion later.

1. Select **F**ile ➤ Pass**w**ord ➤ **A**dd/Change, or press **Ctrl-F5 P A**.

2. At the "Enter Password:" prompt, type the password (it will not appear on the screen), then press ↵.

3. At the "Re-Enter Password:" prompt, type the password again (just to be sure you typed it correctly the first time), and press ↵.

If you type the same password both times, WordPerfect will accept it. Otherwise, you'll hear a beep and have to start over at step 2. When you've successfully typed your password, you'll be returned to the Edit screen.

Now you must save the file in the usual manner, with either **F**ile ➤ E**x**it (F7) or **F**ile ➤ **S**ave (F10). In the future, whenever you retrieve that document, you'll first see the message "Enter Password", followed by the name of the document you are retrieving. You must type the correct password (it won't appear on the screen as you type), and then press ↵.

If you type the wrong password, you'll see the message "ERROR: File is locked" and will need to start over, or press Cancel (F1) to give up.

You must know the password before you can change or delete it, because you first must be able to retrieve the document!

If you decide to change the password in the future, retrieve the document to the Edit screen. Then select **F**ile ➤ Pass**w**ord ➤ **A**dd/Change (or press **Ctrl-F5 P A**), type the new password, then press ↵. Optionally, if you prefer to delete the password at that point so that anyone can retrieve it, select **F**ile ➤ Password ➤ **R**emove (or press **Ctrl-F5 P R**). Always remember to resave the document after changing or deleting the password.

Incidentally, password-protecting a file does not prevent other users from *deleting* that file. For that kind of protection, you should always keep an extra copy of your document on a floppy disk, in a safe place. Or, refer to the ATTRIB command in your DOS book or manual, which offers techniques for protecting (and in DOS 5, hiding) files.

SAVING DOS TEXT FILES

*Never try to edit a program file— such files usually have the extension .COM, .EXE, or .BIN—with Word-Perfect. If you load one by accident, clear the screen **without** saving the file.*

If you want to use WordPerfect to edit DOS text files (or ASCII files), you must remember to save those files by selecting **F**ile ➤ Text **O**ut ➤ DOS **T**ext (or pressing **Ctrl-F5 T S**). Otherwise, WordPerfect will save the file as a word

See Chapter 25 for more information on DOS text files and interacting with other programs.

processing document, making it totally unreadable by DOS and most other programs outside of WordPerfect. As soon as you finish saving the file in text format, clear it from the Edit screen by selecting **File ➤ Exit No No** (or by pressing **F7 N N**). Otherwise, you run the risk of inadvertently resaving the file as a document.

Note that it's impossible to tell whether a DOS text file has been corrupted by word processing codes simply by viewing that file through the word processor. Instead, you should use the TYPE command in DOS to view the file. If the file is uncorrupted, you won't see any strange graphics characters or hear any beeps. If the file is corrupted, it will look quite messy.

If you think the DOS text file was corrupted by WordPerfect, retrieve the file to the Edit screen, then save it and clear the screen as described at the beginning of this section. Again, be sure that you don't attempt to retrieve or edit program files (which have extensions such as .COM, .EXE, and .BIN).

RETRIEVING DOCUMENTS

As you learned in Chapter 2, you can retrieve a document by selecting **File ➤ Retrieve** or pressing Retrieve (Shift-F10) and entering the name of the document you want to work with. If the file name you enter cannot be found, you'll see the message "ERROR: File not found". There are three possible reasons for this:

◆ You misspelled the file name or forgot to add the extension (e.g., *MYDOC* instead of *MYDOC.WP*).

◆ You spelled the file name correctly, but the file is not on the current drive\directory or disk. Press List (**F5**) to view and optionally change the current drive and directory, as discussed later in this chapter.

◆ You (or somebody else) deleted the file you're looking for.

The List Files feature (F5), discussed in the next section, can help you determine which of the above is the problem.

COMBINING DOCUMENTS

If you already have a document on the screen, you can combine the on-screen document with another one by selecting **File ➤ Retrieve** (or pressing Shift-F10). This inserts the retrieved file in the current document at the current cursor position. For example, if your cursor is at the beginning of the on-screen document when you retrieve another document, the entire retrieved document will be placed at the beginning, before the existing text. Likewise, if your cursor is in the middle of the on-screen document when you retrieve another document, you'll end up with the first part of your original document, all of the retrieved document, then the remainder of the original document.

Note that if you already have a current document on-screen and use List (F5) to retrieve another, you'll see the message

Retrieve into current document? No (Yes)

If you select **Y**es, the document you are retrieving will be retrieved to the Edit screen and will be combined with the existing document at the current cursor position. If you select **N**o, the file will not be retrieved, and you will be returned to the Edit screen. There you can save the current document and clear the screen or switch to the Doc 2 screen, if you wish, before retrieving the previous document.

RETRIEVING PASSWORD-PROTECTED FILES

If the file you are retrieving has been saved with a password, you'll see the message

Enter password

followed by the location and name of the file in parentheses. You must type the correct password (it will not appear on the screen as you type) and press ↵ to retrieve the file.

COPYING A BLOCK SEVERAL TIMES

Blocking techniques are described in Chapter 2.

Here's a neat trick for copying the same block repeatedly, whether throughout the same document or throughout several documents. Block and copy or move the text once as usual. For additional copies, move the cursor to wherever you want the next copy to appear, select **F**ile ➤ **R**etrieve or press Retrieve (Shift-F10), then just press ↵ instead of entering a file name. You can do so as many times as you wish, to make as many copies as you wish.

If you get an "incom- patible file format" error message, refer to Chapter 25 for more information.

RETRIEVING EARLIER VERSIONS AND NON-WORDPERFECT DOCUMENTS

If you retrieve a document that was created and saved with an earlier version of WordPerfect (such as 4.2 or 5.0), WordPerfect automatically converts the document to 5.1 format. If you retrieve a document that was not created in WordPerfect, WordPerfect will try to convert the file. However, if it cannot, you'll likely get an error message, such as "ERROR: Incompatible file format", and no retrieved document.

ORGANIZING YOUR FILES WITH DOCUMENT SUMMARIES

> **TO ADD A DOCUMENT SUMMARY TO THE CURRENT DOCUMENT,**
>
> **1. Select Layout ➤ Document ➤ Summary (or press Shift-F8 D S).**
>
> **2. Fill in whatever prompts you want.**
>
> **3. Press Exit (F7).**

The file name assigned to a document when you save it is limited to the eight-character name, followed by the optional dot (.) and three-character extension. This really limits how descriptive the file name can be.

One way to work around this restriction is to add a *summary* to your document. That way, if you lose track of which files are which, you can just view your document summaries along with the file names (you'll see how later in this chapter).

To create a document summary for a particular document, you must first retrieve that document to the Edit screen. Then you must get to the Document Summary screen (Figure 12.1). Once you're there, you can just "fill in the blanks" as you like. There are no rules, and you can leave any option blank. However, the Document Name and Document Type options are the most useful, because as you'll see later, they're readily visible when you search through files on the List Files screen.

Figure 12.2 shows a sample completed Document Summary screen, just as a general example.

To add a document summary to the current document, follow these steps:

1. Select **L**ayout ➤ **D**ocument ➤ **S**ummary (or press **Shift-F8 D S**). The Document Summary screen appears.

2. Select any option you want (details provided below).

3. Type whatever you want for that option, and press ↵.

4. Press Exit (**F7**) to return to the Edit screen.

The document summary is saved the next time you save the document.

```
Document Summary

        Revision Date  06-15-91 02:31p

   1 - Creation Date  04-23-91 02:30p

   2 - Document Name
       Document Type

   3 - Author
       Typist

   4 - Subject

   5 - Account

   6 - Keywords

   7 - Abstract




Selection: 0                 (Retrieve to capture; Del to remove summary)
```

```
Document Summary

        Revision Date  06-15-91 02:31p

   1 - Creation Date  04-23-91 02:30p

   2 - Document Name  SuperLearning in PreSchool
       Document Type  1st Draft

   3 - Author         Marsha Koblentz
       Typist         Mike Koblentz

   4 - Subject

   5 - Account        PreSchooler Magazine

   6 - Keywords       SuperLearning, PreSchool, Toddlers

   7 - Abstract       Article for September '91 PreSchooler Magazine.
                      Due 7/1/91.


Selection: 0                 (Retrieve to capture; Del to remove summary)
```

USING RETRIEVE TO BUILD DOCUMENT SUMMARIES

Once you're at the Document Summary screen, you can use the Retrieve key (Shift-F10) as a shortcut to retrieve information from the document itself or to repeat information from a previous document summary in the same editing session. You'll see the prompt

Capture Document Summary Fields? No (Yes)

Selecting Yes fills in a few of the fields, as summarized in the next section.

DOCUMENT SUMMARY CATEGORIES

Here is a brief description of each category that appears on the Document Summary screen:

Even if you use long document names for your WordPerfect documents, they still retain their standard DOS file names. You can only use the long document names from within Word-Perfect.

Revision Date	The date and time the document was last changed and saved. You cannot change this entry.
Creation **D**ate	The date and time the document was created; remains constant unless you select this option and change the date or time.
Document **N**ame/ Document Type	Document Name lets you add a longer name, up to 68 characters long, to override the eight-character file-name limit of DOS. You can search through these long names by using the WordPerfect List Files option (discussed below). The document type can be 20 characters long, can contain whatever text or numbers you wish (e.g., *DRAFT, FINAL, TYPE-47*), and also appears on the List Files screen.
Author/ Typist	You can enter an author's name and typist's name (up to 60 characters each) for this entry. If you press Retrieve (Shift-F10), the Author and Typist entries from the previous document (if any) are entered on this screen.
Subject	Type a subject of your choosing. If your document contains the abbreviation *RE:*, with text to the right of these letters, pressing Retrieve copies the first 39 characters to the right of RE: to the Document Summary screen.
A**c**count	Type an account name of your choosing, if it will help you identify the document.
Keywords	Enter a list of any keywords (separated by spaces) that might later help you locate the document or a group of documents on the same subject. For example, you could later isolate all documents having the keyword "Saturn" when looking for documents on that topic.

Abstract   The abstract can contain up to 780 characters that
                             summarize the contents of the document. Pressing Retrieve
                             copies the first 400 characters of the document to the
                             Document Summary screen.

See "View-
ing a File's
Document
Summary"
and "Searching the
Contents of Files" later
in this chapter for tips
on using document
summaries.

The document summary can also help you find a file later. For example, if you
forget the file name of a document, you can look for it by document name,
type, or keywords. You'll learn how a bit later in this chapter.

DELETING DOCUMENT SUMMARIES

If you want to delete a document summary (but not the file itself), press
Delete while the Document Summary screen for the document is displayed,
then press **Y** when prompted "Delete Document Summary? **N**o (**Y**es)".

PRINTING DOCUMENT SUMMARIES

If you want
to print
only *the*
document
summary, type ***S***
rather than ***S-*** *in*
step 2.

If you want to print the document summary along with the rest of the document, follow these steps:

1. With the document on your screen, select **File ➤ Print ➤ Multiple
    Pages** (or press **Shift-F7 M**); if the document is not on your screen,
    select **File ➤ Print ➤ Document on Disk** (or press **Shift-F7 D**).

2. At the "Page(s):" prompt, type **S-** (the letter *s* followed by a hyphen).
    See "Printing Specific Pages" in Chapter 8 for more information.

3. Press ↵.

If you want to print a quick copy of the contents of the Document Summary
screen while it's on your screen, just press Print (Shift-F7).

You can
also view,
print, and
save docu-
ment summaries by
using the Look option
on the List Files
screen, described later
in this chapter.

If you want to save a copy of the document summary that's currently on
your screen (perhaps to print it later), press Save (F10), type a file name, and
press ↵. Be aware that the file name you enter will contain *only* the document
summary (stored as a regular document) and will not contain any text of the
document whose summary you are saving. Therefore, be sure to use a unique
file name if you decide to save only a copy of the document summary to disk.

CUSTOMIZING DOCUMENT SUMMARIES

Chapter 13 covers some ways in which you can customize document summaries, such as making the Document Summary screen appear automatically
when you save a document, changing the characters used to retrieve a subject
from RE: to whatever you want, and more.

USING THE LIST FILES SCREEN

TO GET TO THE LIST FILES SCREEN,

select File ➤ List Files or press List (F5).

The List Files screen in WordPerfect lists the names of files in a particular directory (or on a floppy disk). It also has options for managing those files, including copying, deleting, retrieving, and searching for files. All these features can make it much easier to manage your WordPerfect documents and other files as well.

To access the List Files screen from the Edit screen, follow these steps:

1. Select **F**ile ➤ List **F**iles or press List (**F5**).

2. The prompt displays a *file specifier,* such as C:\WP51*.*. You can change the file specifier, or just press ↵ to select the one that's displayed.

NOTE *I'll talk about changing the file specifier a little later in this chapter.*

You'll be taken to the List Files screen, an example of which is shown in Figure 12.3.

The screen is divided into three parts:

◆ General information, near the top of the screen

```
06-15-91  02:46p           Directory C:\WP51\*.*
Document size:        0   Free:  5,484,544 Used:   8,908,079     Files:      153

   .   Current  <Dir>              ..    Parent   <Dir>
MACROS   .        <Dir>  02-08-91 11:36a  STYLES  .       <Dir>  02-08-91 12:16p
WPFILES .        <Dir>  01-24-90 11:20p  AD      .WP      2,766  09-18-90 08:23a
ALARM   .WP     14,445  12-25-90 12:12a  APLASII0.PRS    52,346  11-12-90 04:38p
APLASIIN.P18    52,346  06-15-90 03:14p  APLASIIN.PRS    52,408  04-16-91 04:04p
APLASPLU.P18    47,148  02-01-90 03:42p  APLASPLU.PRS    47,148  02-01-90 03:42p
APPLLASE.P18    27,213  10-26-89 08:30p  APPLLASE.PRS    27,213  10-26-89 08:30p
ARTICLE .WP      1,136  06-15-91 02:46p  ASHLEY  .WP     54,032  12-23-90 11:04p
ASHLEYZ .WP     52,210  01-04-91 01:19a  ATI     .VRS    29,944  12-31-90 12:00p
BUCKINGH.WP      1,927  09-12-90 11:27a  CAREER  .WP      1,894  08-20-90 08:49a
CAREPACK.LBL    12,840  01-20-91 05:23a  CAREPACK.WP     12,840  01-20-91 05:22a
CHANGE  .PS        256  02-09-90 04:22p  CHAP_1  .WP     61,230  04-10-91 10:09p
CHAP_2  .WP     42,525  03-29-91 11:39a  CHAP_3  .WP     80,246  04-12-91 03:25p
CHAP_4  .WP     48,419  04-10-91 09:43a  CHAP_5  .WP     71,290  04-14-90 12:43p
CHARACTR.DOC    47,078  04-04-91 02:59a  CHARMAP .TST    42,620  12-31-90 12:00p
CHCODES .TXT    15,833  01-11-91 06:54a  CHCODES .WP     26,238  01-11-91 07:42a
CHFONT  .TXT     3,041  01-14-91 03:30a  COLORS  .EPS    15,383  09-25-90 08:01p
COLORS  .WP     25,096  09-25-90 03:55p  COLUMNS .WP     19,639  12-25-90 03:01a
CONVERT .EXE   109,591  12-31-90 12:00p  CRUMLISH.WP      1,665  12-01-90 02:26p

1 Retrieve; 2 Delete; 3 Move/Rename; 4 Print; 5 Short/Long Display;
6 Look; 7 Other Directory; 8 Copy; 9 Find; N Name Search: 6
```

FIGURE 12.3:

A sample List Files screen

◆ The list of files, in the middle of the screen

◆ Menu options (commands), at the bottom of the screen

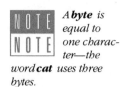 *A **byte** is equal to one charac- ter—the word **cat** uses three bytes.*

General information includes the current date and time, the name of the direc- tory you're viewing, the size of the document currently being edited, the amount of free space left on the disk in bytes, the amount of space used by the files in the directory, and the number of files in the directory.

File and subdirectory names are listed in alphabetical order. Subdirec- tories appear first, marked as *<Dir>,* and are followed by the names of all the files, or only those you've specified with wildcards in the file specifier (de- scribed in more detail later).

List Files displays three items of information for each file:

◆ The file name and extension

◆ The file's size in bytes

◆ The date and time the file was last saved to disk

The top two items on the list—even with an empty disk or subdirectory—will always be Current and Parent, preceded by a period and a double period, respectively. These two items represent the current directory and the *parent* directory (the directory above the current directory). They can be used for navigating between subdirectories and disk drives.

Only 38 files (two columns of 19) can be shown at once. If you see a downward-pointing arrow at the bottom of the vertical line separating the two columns of files (as in Figure 12.3) or an upward-pointing arrow at the top, then the listing contains more files than can be displayed on the screen at once. You can scroll with the usual cursor-movement keys or by pressing and holding the left mouse button to display files that do not fit on the initial List Files screen. At the bottom of the List Files screen are the ten options to help you manage your files.

PRINTING THE FILE LIST

To print a copy of the List Files screen, including any files that may not cur- rently be visible on the screen, press Print (Shift-F7).

VIEWING LONG NAMES

The standard two-column file listing is known as the Short Display. You can switch this to Long Display, which includes *only* WordPerfect 5.1 document files along with the more descriptive information from your document summaries. To switch to the Long Display, select **S**hort/Long Display ➤ **L**ong Display from the menu at the bottom of the List Files screen. Figure 12.4 shows an example of a Long Display screen.

Besides providing additional information, the Long Display has another potential advantage over Short Display: Because you see only WordPerfect document files, it makes document management easier. You don't have to go through a cluttered listing of macro files, graphic files, printer files, and others just to root out the documents you want to work with.

If you activate Long Display, it will appear from then on when you use List Files in the current work session. To switch back to Short Display, select **S**hort/Long Display ➤ **S**hort Display from the menu at the bottom of the List Files screen.

 *Short Display is always active when you first start WordPerfect.*

SELECTING FILES ON THE LIST FILES SCREEN

You move the highlight through the file list by using the usual WordPerfect cursor-movement keys (↑, ↓, →, ←) or the mouse. Some of the keys that produce more extreme cursor movements can be very handy in long file listings. The gray − (or Home ↑) key moves up a screen, Page Up moves up a page, gray - (or Home ↓) moves down a screen, and Page Down (PgDn) moves down a page. Also, Home Home ↑ and Home Home ↓ can be used to move quickly to the top and bottom of the list of files.

```
06-15-91  03:22p            Directory C:\WP51\*.*
Document size:      0  Free:  5,464,064 Used:  8,925,919     Files:      31
Descriptive Name              Type    Filename      Size    Revision Date

Current Directory                       .          <Dir>
Parent Directory                        ..         <Dir>
                                        MACROS  .   <Dir>   02-08-91 11:36a
                                        STYLES  .   <Dir>   02-08-91 12:16p
                                        WPFILES .   <Dir>   01-24-90 11:20p
Captured video image of Ashley Cropped  ASHLEY2 .WP 52,633  06-15-91 02:50p
Captured video image of Ashley Uncropped ASHLEY .WP 54,122  06-15-91 02:50p
Career goals                            CAREER  .WP  1,858  06-15-91 02:55p
Help Wanted Ad                          AD      .WP  3,078  06-15-91 02:48p
Instructions for alarm system           ALARM   .WP 12,171  06-15-91 02:49p
Mastering WP                  Draft     CHAP_4  .WP 48,419  06-15-91 03:06p
Mastering WP                  Draft     CHAP_3  .WP 80,221  06-15-91 03:22p
Mastering WP                  Draft     CHAP_5  .WP 71,340  06-15-91 03:07p
Mastering WP                  Draft     CHAP_1  .WP 61,230  06-15-91 03:04p
Mastering WP                  Draft     CHAP_2  .WP 42,525  06-15-91 03:05p
                                        SMITH   .WP  1,042  04-02-91 12:46p
SuperLearning in PreSchool    1st Draft ARTICLE .WP  1,136  06-15-91 02:46p
                                        WP      .LRS 24,396 12-31-90 12:00p

1 Retrieve; 2 Delete; 3 Move/Rename; 4 Print; 5 Short/Long Display;
6 Look; 7 Other Directory; 8 Copy; 9 Find; N Name Search: 6
```

FIGURE 12.4:

An example of Long Display, showing longer file names from Document Summary screens

It doesn't matter which file is high-lighted when you select Short/Long Display, Other Directory, Find, or Name Search.

You move the highlight bar around to *select* the file on which to perform the next command. Most of the commands at the bottom of the List Files screen are performed only on files selected by the highlight or on a group of files marked with asterisks (*), as will be discussed in a moment.

LOOKING UP A FILE NAME

A List Files screen may contain dozens, even hundreds, of files, depending on how many files are in the current directory. If you know the name of a file you want to highlight, you don't need to scroll through the list by using the cursor-movement keys. Instead, use Name Search:

Name Search is used with several other WordPerfect screens where you can choose one item from a potentially long list.

1. Select **N**ame Search from the List Files screen.

2. Type in the first letter of the file's name.

3. You can type in additional letters if you wish; each new letter will bring you closer to your destination.

4. When the highlight is on the file you want, press ↵ or an arrow key to exit Name Search mode.

RETRIEVING A DOCUMENT FROM THE LIST FILES SCREEN

*Whereas many programs let you retrieve a file by high-lighting its name and pressing ↵, using this technique on the List Files screen selects the **L**ook option, which lets you only view the con-tents of the file, not change its contents.*

To use List Files to retrieve a file onto the Edit screen, move the highlight to the name of the file you want to retrieve, then select **R**etrieve from the List Files menu. From here, retrieving is exactly as described under retrieving files earlier in this chapter. For example, if there is already a document on the Edit screen, you'll be asked about retrieving this document into the existing one and will be given a chance to answer Yes or No.

VIEWING A FILE'S CONTENTS

List Files lets you take a quick look at a file's contents, including the document summary, before taking action on it—printing, retrieving, or whatever. The steps to follow are easy:

1. Move the highlight to the name of the file whose contents you want to view.

2. Select **L**ook (or just press ↵) to view the contents of the document. Figure 12.5 shows an example of a document on the Look screen.

3. You can scroll through the document with the cursor-movement keys or Search (F2), but you cannot make changes.

4. Optionally, select **N**ext Doc to view the next file on the List Files screen, or select **P**rev Doc to view the previous file.

5. When you're finished viewing file contents, press Exit (**F7**) to return to the List Files screen.

Selecting Look does not retrieve the document, but instead activates a special file-viewing screen. Note that this is a single-spaced, text-only peek at the file's contents.

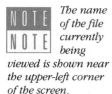

The name of the file currently being viewed is shown near the upper-left corner of the screen.

VIEWING A FILE'S DOCUMENT SUMMARY

If the document you choose to view with Look has a document summary, you'll first see the document summary, as in the example shown in Figure 12.6. If you want to view the text of the document rather than the summary, select **L**ook at Text from the menu. (To switch back to the summary, select **L**ook at Document Summary.)

If the document you view happens to be a macro, you'll see the macro description (if any) followed by gibberish, which is the actual macro. Despite the gibberish, this is a handy way to see the description of a perhaps long-forgotten macro.

You'll also notice two other menu options in Figure 12.6: **P**rint Summ and **S**ave to File. You can select **P**rint Summ to print just the document summary. After the summary prints, you'll be returned to the List Files screen.

If you want to save just the document summary (not the actual document itself) to a new WordPerfect file, you can choose **S**ave to File. Type a file name for the summary and press ↵. If the file already exists, you'll see this prompt:

File already exists: 1 Replace **2 A**ppend

```
File: C:\WP51\SAMPLE.WP              WP5.1      Revised: 06-15-91 03:24p


                    ANSWERS TO BURNING QUESTIONS

WHY do fleas seem to disappear when they jump?

The much maligned flea, Ctenocephalides canis, seems to disappear
before your very eyes, and reappear several feet away, because of
its tremendous jumping power and speed:

        o       The flea can leap a distance 150 times its
                body length -- the equivalent of a human being
                jumping ¼ mile from a standstill.

        o       During its leap, the flea attains an
                acceleration of 140g; about 20 times the
                acceleration required to put an Apollo rocket
                into orbit.

WHERE do flies go in the Winter?

Contrary to what you might think, flies don't follow birds south

Look: 1 Next Doc; 2 Prev Doc: 0
```

FIGURE·12.5:

The Look screen for a sample document file

Select Replace to replace the file with the current document summary, select Append to add the document summary to an existing file, or press Cancel (F1) to prevent the summary from being saved. You'll be returned to the List Files screen after the summary is saved. The Save to File feature can be handy when you want to create a file of document summaries only, perhaps for printing out later and filing in a notebook for reference.

WORKING WITH GROUPS OF FILES

For added convenience, List Files lets you mark a group of files and manipulate them all at the same time. You mark each file in the group by highlighting it and typing an asterisk (*). An asterisk then appears next to the file name, letting you know that the file is marked.

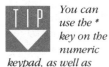

*You can use the * key on the numeric keypad, as well as Shift-8, to type the asterisk.*

The * key acts as a *toggle.* Pressing * when a marked file is highlighted unmarks the file. To mark all the files on the List Files screen (including those that do not fit on the current display), press Mark Text (**Alt-F5**) or **Home** then *. To unmark all the files, press Mark Text or Home * again.

You can continue marking files until you've selected all those you want to treat as a group. Figure 12.7 shows a List Files screen with several files marked. Once you've marked a group of files, you can delete, move, rename, print, or copy them all in a single step, as discussed in the sections that follow.

```
File: C:\WP51\ARTICLE.WP              WP5.1     Revised: 06-15-91 03:30p
Name: SuperLearning in PreSchool      1st Draft Created: 04-23-91 02:30p

Subject

Account    PreSchooler Magazine

Keywords   SuperLearning, PreSchool, Toddlers

Author     Marsha Koblentz
Typist     Mike Koblentz
Abstract
  Article for Sptember '91 PreSchooler Magazine.
  Due 7/1/91




Look Doc Summ: 1 Next; 2 Prev; 3 Look at text; 4 Print Summ; 5 Save to File: 0
```

FIGURE 12.6:

The Look screen of a file with a document summary

DELETING FILES

Once you delete a file, you cannot simply undelete it. You'll need to use the UNDELETE command in DOS 5, or some other undelete program, to undelete an accidentally deleted file. But you must do so before saving any new files.

If a directory is cluttered with outdated drafts or other files you don't need anymore, List Files is a great way to clean house. To delete a file from the disk, follow these steps:

1. Highlight the name of the file you want to delete, or mark every file you want to delete with an asterisk (*).

2. Choose **D**elete from the List Files menu line, or press **Delete**.

3. If any files are marked, you'll be prompted for permission to delete all the marked files. Select **Y**es to delete all marked files or **N**o to delete just the currently highlighted file.

4. If no files are marked with *, or you answered No in step 3, you'll be prompted for permission to delete the currently highlighted file. Select **Y**es or **N**o.

MOVING OR RENAMING A SINGLE FILE

If no files are currently selected with *, you can move or rename the currently highlighted file by following these steps:

1. Move the highlight to the file you want to rename or move.

2. Select **M**ove/Rename.

```
06-15-91  03:30p              Directory C:\WP51\*.*
Document size:       0  Free:  5,421,056 Used:     428,286      Marked:      11

.    Current   <Dir>               ..   Parent   <Dir>
MACROS  .       <Dir> 02-08-91 11:36a   STYLES  .       <Dir> 02-08-91 12:16p
WPFILES .       <Dir> 01-24-90 11:20p   AD      .WP    3,078  06-15-91 02:48p
ALARM   .WP   12,171  06-15-91 02:49p   APLASII0.PRS  52,346  11-12-90 04:38p
APLASIIN.P18  52,346  06-15-90 03:14p   APLASIIN.PRS  52,408  04-16-91 04:04p
APLASPLU.P18  47,148  02-01-90 03:42p   APLASPLU.PRS  47,148  02-01-90 03:42p
APPLLASE.P18  27,213  10-26-89 08:30p   APPLLASE.PRS  27,213  10-26-89 08:30p
*ARTICLE .WP    1,020  06-15-91 03:30p  *ASHLEY  .WP   54,122  06-15-91 02:50p
*ASHLEYZ .WP   52,633  06-15-91 02:50p   ATI     .URS  29,944  12-31-90 12:00p
*BUCKINGH.WP    2,266  06-15-91 02:56p  *CAREER  .WP    1,858  06-15-91 02:55p
 CAREPACK.LBL  12,652  06-15-91 03:08p  *CAREPACK.WP   12,652  06-15-91 03:18p
 CHANGE  .PS      256  02-09-90 04:22p  *CHAP_1  .WP   61,230  06-15-91 03:04p
*CHAP_2  .WP   42,525  06-15-91 03:05p  *CHAP_3  .WP   80,221  06-15-91 03:22p
*CHAP_4  .WP   48,419  06-15-91 03:06p  *CHAP_5  .WP   71,340  06-15-91 03:07p
 CHARACTR.DOC  47,256  06-15-91 02:57p   CHARMAP .TST  43,320  06-15-91 03:03p
 CHCODES .TXT  15,833  01-11-91 06:54a   CHCODES .WP   26,492  06-15-91 03:18p
 CHFONT  .TXT   3,041  01-14-91 03:30a   COLORS  .EPS  15,383  09-25-90 08:01p
 COLORS  .WP   22,547  06-15-91 03:17p   COLUMNS .WP   19,780  06-15-91 03:19p
 CONVERT .EXE 109,591  12-31-90 12:00p   CRUMLISH.WP    1,665  06-15-91 03:19p

1 Retrieve; 2 Delete; 3 Move/Rename; 4 Print; 5 Short/Long Display;
6 Look; 7 Other Directory; 8 Copy; 9 Find; N Name Search: 6
```

FIGURE 12.7:

A List Files screen with files marked for group selection

3. The current location and name of the file appears. Now you can do any of the following:

- ◆ Change the file name to rename the file without moving it
- ◆ Change only the drive or directory of the file to move the file to a new location without renaming it
- ◆ Change the location and name of the file to both move and rename it

4. Press ↵ after making your changes.

MOVING ONE OR MORE FILES

You can move a single file or group of files to another drive or directory, using the Move/Rename options on the File List screen. Follow these steps:

If you mark a group of files, you must move them to another drive or directory name, not a file name.

1. Move the highlight to the name of the file you want to move or rename, or mark each file you want to move or rename with an asterisk (*).

2. Choose **M**ove/Rename from the List Files menu.

3. If multiple files are marked with *, you'll see this prompt:

Move marked files? No (Yes)

Select **Y**es to move all the marked files, or select **N**o to move just the currently highlighted file.

4. If no files are marked with *, or you answered No in step 3, only the highlighted file will be moved or renamed. You'll see this prompt:

Move this file to:

If you have marked multiple files and answered Yes in step 3, you'll see this prompt:

Move marked files to:

5. Type the destination for the moved file or group of files (e.g., *A:* to move the highlighted file to the disk in drive A), then press ↵.

COPYING FILES

By selecting Copy from the List Files menu line, you can make a duplicate of the highlighted file (with a different file name), copying it to another location on the disk or to another disk. Unlike moving, the original file remains in place when you use Copy; otherwise, the steps are nearly identical. Follow these steps to copy the highlighted file:

1. Move the highlight to the name of the file you want to copy, or mark each file you want to copy with an asterisk (*).

2. Choose **C**opy from the List Files menu.

3. If multiple files are marked with *, you'll be asked whether or not to copy the marked files. Select **Y**es to copy all the marked files, or select **N**o to copy just the currently highlighted file.

4. You'll then be asked where you want to copy the files to.

5. Type the destination for the copied file or group of files (e.g., *A:* to copy the highlighted file to the disk in drive A), then press ↵.

> **NOTE** *If you're not sure what a formatted disk is, refer to your DOS book or manual.*

You can use the steps above to copy any set of files from your hard disk to any formatted disk in one of your floppy drives. It's a good idea to do so just in case you accidentally erase the copies from your hard disk or your hard disk crashes; that way, you'll still have the copies to work with.

If you want to copy files *from* a floppy to your hard disk, press List (F5), specify **A:** as the current drive and directory, then press ↵. Next, mark with an asterisk every file you want to copy from the disk in drive A to your hard disk. Finally, select **C**opy and specify **C:\WP51** (or whatever destination you choose) as the place to copy these files to.

PRINTING A DOCUMENT FROM LIST FILES

> **NOTE** *See Chapter 8 for comprehensive information on printing with WordPerfect.*

You can choose any file or group of files to print from the List Files screen. This operation is similar to selecting the Document on Disk option on the Print menu (**File ➤ Print ➤ Document** on Disk or **Shift-F7 D**), but you have the advantage of seeing all the file names at once and marking with asterisks the ones you want to print. The basic procedure is the following:

1. On the List Files screen, mark with asterisks the files you want to print (or, if you want to print only a single file, move the highlight to it).

2. Select **P**rint from the List Files menu.

3. If several files are marked with *, you'll see the message

   Print marked files? No (Yes)

   Select **Y**es to print the marked files or **N**o to print just the currently highlighted file.

4. If no files are marked with *, or you answered No in step 3, you'll see this prompt:

Print *filename*? **No (Yes)**

where *filename* is the name of the file to be printed.

5. If you select Yes in response to either prompt in step 3 or 4, you'll see

Page(s): (All)

6. Press ↵ to print the entire document, or refer to Chapter 8 for information on specifying the range of pages to print.

7. If the document to be printed was not created with the currently selected printer, you'll see this prompt:

Document not formatted for current printer. Continue? **No (Yes)**

If you select **Y**es, WordPerfect will print the document using whatever fonts in the current printer match the fonts selected in the document (but it will *not* change the font selections within the document). If you select **N**o, the file will not be printed.

Remember, all files on the disk or directory are displayed by List Files, but you can print only WordPerfect document files. If the file you choose to print isn't a WordPerfect document file, List Files displays the message

ERROR: Incompatible file format

and cancels the operation.

NOTE NOTE NOTE *"Printing Specific Pages" in Chapter 8 describes the various ways to specify the pages to print.*

SEARCHING THE CONTENTS OF FILES

If you forget the name of a file but remember something about its contents (such as the addressee of a business letter), you can have WordPerfect search the contents of documents for a specific word or phrase. This will narrow down the file list considerably, and if your search is specific enough, it might pinpoint the exact file you're looking for. To narrow the list in this way, select the **F**ind option from the List Files menu. You'll see the following options:

1 Name; **2 D**oc Summary; **3** First **Pg**; **4 E**ntire Doc; **5 C**onditions; **6 U**ndo: **0**

Each option is summarized below:

Name   Searches only short file names

Doc Summary	Searches only the document summaries
First **Pg**	Searches only the first page of each document
Entire Doc	Searches every page of every document
Conditions	Lets you refine the search further (see below)
Undo	Restores the original file listing

 Word-Perfect can undo the three most recent Find operations, as you'll see later.

If you choose any of the first four options, you'll see the prompt:

Word pattern:

Type the text (up to 39 characters) you want to search for, then press ↵. Word-Perfect tells you how many files it has searched and then reorganizes the List Files screen to display only the files containing the text you asked for. You can select the Find option again, perhaps with more specific word patterns, to narrow the list even further.

ENTERING THE WORD PATTERN

When entering your word pattern, you can type letters in uppercase, lower-case, or any mixture of the two—all are treated the same. So, for example, typing *PRIMordial* is the same as typing *Primordial* or *primordial*. If your search text consists of only one word, just type it at the "Word pattern:" prompt and press ↵. To search for multiple words, you must enclose them in quotation marks; for example:

Word Pattern: "Cream of Primordial Soup"

The ? and * wildcards can help you find various word combinations. As in DOS, the ? represents a single character or letter in a word, and the * represents multiple letters. So if you select **E**ntire Doc, and at the "Word pattern:" prompt enter

T?P*

WordPerfect will show you only files containing words starting with *T*, with any second character, with *P* as the third letter, and ending in any combination of characters. This would include words such as *tap, type,* and *topographical.* The name of any document in the file listing containing any of those words would be displayed after the search was over.

You can also impose more complex, specific conditions on your search from the "Word pattern:" prompt. These conditions are determined by the following *logical operators:*

OPERATOR	**SYMBOL**
AND	; (or space)
OR	, (comma)
NOT	- (hyphen)

For example, to locate documents containing both the words *computer* and *debt,* you can specify the following word patterns:

computer;debt

or

computer debt

Similarly, to find documents with both *computer* and *more productive,* you can use

computer "more productive"

or

computer;"more productive"

To find documents that contain either *New York* or *New Jersey,* you can use the following:

"New York","New Jersey"

And to find documents that contain *New York,* but not *New Jersey,* you can use this:

"New York"-"New Jersey"

If you need to find documents containing a hyphen (-), place the phrase containing the hyphen in quotation marks, as in "two-bit".

FASTER FILE SEARCHES

The Doc Summary and First Pg options on the Find menu line are ideal when searching for text that you know will be near the beginning of a document, such as the word *memo,* a subject, a title, or a company name. That's because they're quicker than Entire Doc, which must scan the entire document before moving on to the next file.

SEARCHING FROM THE CONDITIONS MENU

Selecting the Conditions option from the Find menu line brings up a full-screen menu of options that offers an alternative way of defining the search, with a little more flexibility. The Conditions menu is shown in Figure 12.8.

The Revision **D**ate option on the Conditions menu lets you locate files based on the date when they were last saved. If you select Revision Date, then specify a *From* and *To* range (earliest to latest date), the Find command will show you only files satisfying that range. You should type dates in *mm/dd/yy* format, as in *04/27/91* for April 27, 1991.

The **T**ext option works like the Doc Summary, First Pg, and Entire Doc options on the Find menu line, where you search for one or more keywords in specific parts of the document. Only one of these must be filled in, but you could fill in two or all three of them to get very specific. If you fill in more than one of these entries, all search conditions must be met by a file for it to remain in the narrowed-down listing.

The last option on the Conditions menu, Document **S**ummary, allows you to search for specific text or keyword patterns in various parts of each file's document summary (if any). For example, you can use Document Summary to locate all documents typed by a certain typist or written by a particular author.

After entering the search conditions, you select **P**erform Search to activate the Find operation. **R**eset Conditions is used to remove any changes made in this menu so that you can start from scratch.

Press Exit (F7) or Cancel (F1) to return to the List Files screen from the Conditions menu.

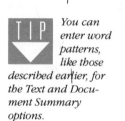

You can enter word patterns, like those described earlier, for the Text and Document Summary options.

RESTORING THE ORIGINAL FILE LIST

To restore the file list to its original state, before you last used Find, select **F**ind again and then select **U**ndo, or press F5 then ⏎. All the file names that were there prior to the Find operation will once again be displayed on the screen. You can undo the three most recent Find operations.

CHANGING THE FILE SPECIFIER

WordPerfect, like DOS, offers two wildcard characters for displaying file names:

?   Matches any single character

*   Matches any group of characters

As mentioned near the beginning of the chapter, when you first select **File ➤ List** Files or press List (F5), you'll see a file specifier, like this:

C:\WP51*.*

where *.* means "any file name, followed by any extension." Hence, List Files initially displays the name of every file in the current (default) directory.

If you want to narrow the display of file names, change the file specifier. For example, to display only file names with the .WP extension, change the file specifier from *.* to *.WP. You can use the usual editing keys (→, ←, End, Delete) to make the change, either

◆ immediately after selecting **File ➤ List** Files (or pressing F5) to get to the List Files screen, or

◆ after pressing F5 while on the List Files screen.

```
Find: Conditions                              Files Selected:    149

     1 - Perform Search
     2 - Reset Conditions

     3 - Revision Date - From
                          To

     4 - Text - Document Summary
                First Page
                Entire Document

     5 - Document Summary
         Creation Date - From
                          To
         Document Name
         Document Type
         Author
         Typist
         Subject
         Account
         Keywords
         Abstract

Selection: 1
```

FIGURE 12.8:

The Conditions menu

Suppose you've named some files *QTR1.WP, QTR2.WP,* and so forth. Using the file pattern QTR?.WP limits the List Files display to file names that begin with *QTR,* followed by any single character, followed by the extension .WP.

To change the file specifier, even while the List Files screen is displayed, you just press the List Files key (F5) again. You'll see the current drive, directory, and file specifier near the bottom of the screen, like the example below:

Dir C:\WP51*.*

To change the file specifier only, press End to move the cursor to the end of the line. Then press Backspace three times to delete *.* (only), then type **QTR?.WP**, so the specifier looks like this:

Dir C:\WP51\QTR?.WP

Then press ↵ to view only file names that match QTR?.WP.

This simple technique can be a real time-saver. For example, after limiting the file display to QTR?.WP files, you can immediately mark each of those files with an asterisk just by pressing Home * or Alt-F5 (rather than marking each one individually), then copy them to a backup disk in drive A.

Similarly, if you are going to use Find on the List Files screen to search through documents, you can save a lot of time by first narrowing the screen to "likely candidates," such as *.WP files, before beginning the Find operation.

CHANGING DIRECTORIES

*The normal directory for saving and restoring files is determined on the Location of Files screen, discussed in Chapter 13 (select **F**ile ➤ Set up ➤ **L**ocation of Files or press **Shift-F1 L**).*

Normally the job of creating and changing directories is relegated to the MKDIR (MD) and CHDIR (CD) commands in DOS, or the DOS 4 or 5 Shell. But you can do both without ever leaving the List Files screen in WordPerfect. There are two ways to change directories in WordPerfect:

◆ You *temporarily* change directories when you want to search other directories for a specific file, but want to continue using your normal directory for storing and retrieving document files. This is a common technique for searching for a file that's not in the current directory, because you've either purposely or inadvertently stored it in some directory other than the current one.

◆ You change the *default* (or current) directory when you want to use a different directory for storing and retrieving files for a while. For example, if you are writing a book and storing all the files for that book in a unique directory, you probably want to make the book's directory the default directory to simplify saving and retrieving files for the book during the current session.

Not knowing where files are being stored is the main reason for complaints by many beginning WordPerfect users that "the computer" is losing their files!

It's important to know which directory is the current (default) directory. Otherwise, you may lose track of where you're storing files, making it harder to find them in the future. You can always determine the current directory simply by pressing List (F5), looking at the displayed file specifier, then pressing Cancel (F1) to return to the Edit screen.

CHANGING DIRECTORIES TEMPORARILY

If you want to change the current directory temporarily to some other directory, you can do so in either of two ways:

◆ At the Edit screen, select **File ➤ List Files**, or press List (**F5**), then change the file specifier to the directory you want to use for viewing file names.

◆ At the List Files screen, press List (**F5**), then change the name of the directory to the directory you want to use for viewing file names.

Directories are indicated by **<Dir>** *in* place of a file size on the List Files screen; they are at the top of the list of file names.

To prevent WordPerfect from interpreting a nonexistent directory name as a file name, it's a good idea to end the directory specification with a closing backslash. For example, to switch to C:\WP51\MYFILES, enter *C:\WP51\MYFILES* as the directory to search, not *C:\WP51\MYFILES*. If you enter a nonexistent directory name, you'll briefly see the message "ERROR: Invalid drive/directory specification" and be returned to wherever you started from; the current directory will be unchanged.

As a shortcut for the techniques above, you can do either of the following from the List Files screen:

◆ To move up one level, to the *parent* directory, move the highlight to the ..Parent option in the upper-right corner of the screen, and press ↵ twice.

◆ To move down one level, to a *child* directory (a subdirectory beneath the current directory), move the highlight to that directory name, and press ↵ twice.

CHANGING THE CURRENT DIRECTORY

If you want to use some directory other than your normal directory for saving and retrieving WordPerfect documents, you can do either of the following:

◆ At the Edit screen, select **File ➤ List Files**, or press List (**F5**). Then type = and the name of the directory you want to use for saving and retrieving files.

◆ At the List Files screen, select **O**ther Directory, then type the name of the directory you want to use for storing and retrieving files.

The directory name you specify remains the current directory for saving and retrieving files until you change it again by using either of the techniques above or until you exit WordPerfect.

If you enter the name of a nonexistent directory using either technique above, you'll be asked whether you want to create that new directory. Select No, unless you want to create a new directory with that name, as described in the next section.

CREATING A NEW DIRECTORY

To create a new directory, use either of the techniques listed above for changing the current default directory. When you enter the new directory name, you'll see this prompt:

Create *directory*? **No (Yes)**

where *directory* is the name of the new directory you're about to create. To create the directory, select **Y**es. WordPerfect will create a new, empty directory, but will not take you to it. You can use the new directory as you would any other.

This chapter has shown you the many ways to manage files stored on-disk. As you've seen, your options are nearly limitless, and you will do much of your basic file management on the List Files screen.

Chapter 13 covers some optional techniques that let you customize many elements of the WordPerfect package to suit your own tastes and work habits.

CHAPTER 13

Customizing WordPerfect

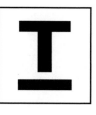**T**his chapter describes WordPerfect's many *customization* features. With these features, you are free to make changes to almost any aspect of WordPerfect, tailoring it to your tastes, work habits, and office requirements.

Everything in this chapter is completely optional, and your eventual use of it, if any, will be entirely up to you. You might just want to glance through the chapter at first to see what customization options are available. Then, should you decide to customize a feature, you can return to this chapter to see how to do so.

THE SETUP OPTIONS

TO GET TO THE MENUS FOR CUSTOMIZING WORDPERFECT,

> select File ➤ Setup, or press Setup (Shift-F1).

 *The Keyboard Layout option on the Setup menu lets you choose a **soft keyboard**. See Chapter 27 for information on this topic.*

WordPerfect's customization features are on the Setup submenu (if you go through the pull-down menus), which is shown in Figure 13.1, and the full-screen menu shown in Figure 13.2 (if you use the shortcut key). Both menus offer the same options, so as usual you should feel free to use whichever method is most comfortable. To get to the Setup menu, select **F**ile ➤ Setup, or press Setup (**Shift-F1**).

From this point on, any changes you make will take effect as soon as you return to the Edit screen. Furthermore, your changes will affect not only the current WordPerfect session, but all future sessions as well. Of course, no setting change is irreversible; you can always go back and make a different choice or restore the original setting.

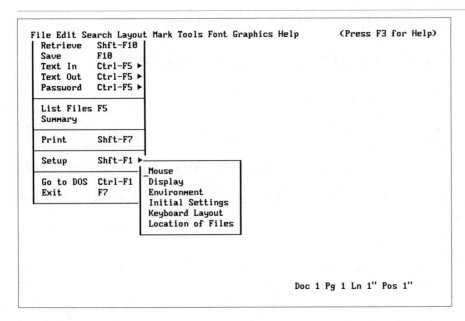

FIGURE 13.1:

The Setup submenu

```
File Edit Search Layout Mark Tools Font Graphics Help        (Press F3 for Help)
  Retrieve     Shft-F10
  Save         F10
  Text In      Ctrl-F5 ▶
  Text Out     Ctrl-F5 ▶
  Password     Ctrl-F5 ▶

  List Files F5
  Summary

  Print        Shft-F7

  Setup        Shft-F1 ▶┌─────────────────┐
                        │ Mouse           │
  Go to DOS  Ctrl-F1    │ Display         │
  Exit         F7       │ Environment     │
                        │ Initial Settings│
                        │ Keyboard Layout │
                        │ Location of Files│
                        └─────────────────┘



                              Doc 1 Pg 1 Ln 1" Pos 1"
```

FIGURE 13.2:

The Setup full-page menu

```
Setup

    1 - Mouse

    2 - Display

    3 - Environment

    4 - Initial Settings

    5 - Keyboard Layout

    6 - Location of Files








  Selection: 0
```

Moreover, for many features, you can temporarily override the Setup options, for just the current document or the current WordPerfect session. For example, you can alter the initial settings for the printer (described later) to handle the majority of situations, then use the Print menu (File ➤ Print or Shift-F7) to change them for just the current document. This way, you can have your cake and eat it too.

CUSTOMIZING THE MOUSE

TO CHANGE THE MOUSE DEFAULTS,

select File ➤ Setup ➤ Mouse, or press Shift-F1 M.

If you have a mouse, you can make it more comfortable to use by adjusting the mouse defaults. Also, if you start using a mouse after installing WordPerfect or if you change mouse types, you must tell WordPerfect what kind of mouse you're using and where it is attached to your computer.

Some mice also require you to run a *device driver* (a type of program), often named *MOUSE.COM,* before the mouse is active. Typically, this requires a change to your computer's CONFIG.SYS or AUTOEXEC.BAT file. See your mouse documentation for further information.

Here are the steps for customizing mouse operation:

1. Select File ➤ Setup ➤ Mouse (or press **Shift-F1 M**). The Mouse menu appears, as shown in Figure 13.3.

2. Make your selections as summarized below, then press Exit (**F7**) to return to the Edit screen.

Here are the selections you can make:

Type: presents a list of available mice, from which you select your own mouse type. If your mouse is already working, there's no need to use this option.

Port: allows you to specify COM1–COM4 as the serial port through which the mouse is attached to your computer. If your mouse is already working properly with WordPerfect, you can skip this option.

Double Click Interval: lets you increase or decrease the amount of time that defines a double click; entered in hundredths of a second.

Sub-Menu Delay Time: sets the amount of time, in hundredths of a second, before a submenu is displayed when you highlight a menu

---

NOTE NOTE *The term **default** refers to a predefined setting, which is in place automatically. In WordPerfect, you can override or change most defaults.*

NOTE NOTE *You don't need to select a serial port if you are using a bus-type mouse.*

option offering a submenu. The smaller the delay time, the more responsive the menus are to the mouse.

Acceleration Factor: lets you adjust the responsiveness of the mouse pointer to mouse movements. The higher the number, the farther the pointer will move with a given mouse movement.

Left-Handed Mouse: reverses the functions of the left and right mouse buttons.

Assisted Mouse Pointer Movement: When reset to Yes, the mouse pointer automatically moves to the first option when you display the menu bar or a bottom menu. You can then select the first option by clicking the left mouse button (without having to move the mouse first).

MODIFYING THE SCREEN DISPLAY

TO CUSTOMIZE THE SCREEN DISPLAY,

select File ➤ Setup ➤ Display, or press Shift-F1 D.

WordPerfect's Display menu, shown in Figure 13.4, offers you several ways to adjust the screen display. Although you can go to the Display menu just to spruce up the screen—especially if you have a color monitor—some of the Display options can make your work a little easier or can display your document so that it more closely resembles the printed version.

```
Setup: Mouse

    1 - Type                           Mouse Driver (MOUSE.COM)

    2 - Port

    3 - Double Click Interval (1 = .01 sec) 70

    4 - Submenu Delay Time (1 = .01 sec)   15

    5 - Acceleration Factor               24

    6 - Left-Handed Mouse                 No

    7 - Assisted Mouse Pointer Movement   No




Selection: 0
```

FIGURE 13.3:

The Mouse menu

To reach and use the Display menu, follow these steps:

1. Select **F**ile ➤ Se**t**up ➤ **D**isplay (or press **Shift-F1 D**).

2. Make your selections from the Display menu, then press Exit (**F7**) to get back to the Edit screen.

The sections that follow describe the many ways to customize your screen display.

CHANGING MONOCHROME-SCREEN TEXT ATTRIBUTES

If you have a monochrome (noncolor) screen, it probably shows boldface and underline accurately, shows a marked block in reverse video (highlighted), and shows all other text attributes (italics, different type sizes, and so on) as normal text. Thus, to remind yourself of where these attributes appear in your document, you must use Reveal Codes (select **E**dit ➤ **R**eveal Codes, or press Alt-F3 or F11), check the View Document screen (select **F**ile ➤ **P**rint ➤ **V**iew Document, or press Shift-F7 V), or print the document.

 *Text appearance is covered in Chapter 5.*

Selecting Colors/Fonts/Attributes from the Display menu gives you an opportunity to change this sometimes inconvenient state of affairs. It brings up the Attributes menu, shown in Figure 13.5. This menu lets you set one or more of four properties—Blink, Bold, Blocked (highlighted), or Underline— for the display of any text attribute. To change a setting, use the arrow keys

---

```
Setup: Display

     1 - Colors/Fonts/Attributes

     2 - Graphics Screen Type      UGA 640x480 16 Color

     3 - Text Screen Type          Auto Selected

     4 - Menu Options

     5 - Uiew Document Options

     6 - Edit-Screen Options













Selection: 0
```

FIGURE 13.4:

The Display menu

to move to the display property you want to set for a given attribute, and press Y to turn the property on. For example, to have Strikeout appear on the Edit screen as blocked text, move the cursor down to the Strikeout attribute, then to the right (under the Blocked property), and press Y. If you want to make Strikeout stand out even more, you can turn on blinking by moving the cursor to the left (under the Blink property) and again pressing Y.

To turn off a property that's set for an attribute, move the cursor to the *Y* (which tells you that a property is set) and press N. WordPerfect will not let you set a combination of display properties that your screen cannot produce; switching on a property will automatically switch off any properties that are incompatible with it.

Press Exit (F7) twice to return to the Edit screen from the Attributes menu. If you've reset the display for attributes that happen to be in the text on your screen, you'll notice that your new settings have already taken effect.

CHANGING THE SCREEN COLORS

You can change the colors on the screen if you have a color monitor. To do so, select Colors/Fonts/Attributes from the Display menu. If you have a CGA (Color Graphics Adapter), an MCGA (Memory Controller Gate Array), or similar color adapter, you'll see two options:

1 - **S**creen Colors
2 - **F**ast Text

```
Setup: Attributes

Attribute            Blink  Bold  Blocked  Underline  Normal  Sample
Normal               N      N     N        N          Y       Sample
Blocked              N      N     Y        N          N       Sample
Underline            N      N     N        Y          N       Sample
Strikeout            N      N     N        N          Y       Sample
Bold                 N      Y     N        N          Y       Sample
Double Underline     N      N     N        N          Y       Sample
Redline              N      Y     Y        N          N       Sample
Shadow               N      N     Y        N          N       Sample
Italics              N      N     N        N          Y       Sample
Small Caps           N      N     N        N          Y       Sample
Outline              N      N     N        N          Y       Sample
Subscript            N      N     N        N          Y       Sample
Superscript          N      N     N        N          Y       Sample
Fine Print           N      N     N        N          Y       Sample
Small Print          N      N     N        N          Y       Sample
Large Print          N      N     N        N          Y       Sample
Very Large Print     N      N     N        N          Y       Sample
Extra Large Print    N      N     Y        N          N       Sample
Bold & Underline     N      Y     N        Y          N       Sample
Other Combinations   N      Y     Y        N          N       Sample

Switch documents; Move to copy settings      Doc 1
```

FIGURE 13.5:

The Attributes menu for a monohrome monitor

The Screen Colors option lets you select a foreground and background color for each attribute in the menu, as described below for changing colors on an EGA (Enhanced Graphics Adapter) or a VGA (Video Graphics Array) adapter.

You can also set the Fast Text option to Yes to speed up the text display; however, if this change causes your screen to display a lot of "snow" when you scroll through your document, you should change it back to No to eliminate the snow.

If you have an EGA or a VGA adapter, selecting Colors/Fonts/Attributes shows the Screen Colors option, as well as a set of font options that you can use for displaying foreground text on your screen. These fonts are Italics, Underline, Small Caps, 512 Characters (this increases the number of displayable characters from 256 to 512), and Normal. For example, if you select the Italics font, any text on your screen that is marked for printing in italics will actually be displayed in italics on your screen. Note that if you select any font other than Normal, you will be limited to eight foreground colors for your text, instead of the usual sixteen.

If you select a font at this point and then change the screen colors, the screen colors you select will affect only that screen font.

To change the screen colors, select the Screen Colors option. You'll see a menu similar to Figure 13.6. Various attributes are listed down the left side of the screen. You'll also see a column for setting the foreground color and a column for the background color. Letters at the top of the screen provide a legend of various colors.

Most EGA and VGA monitors can display foreground text in a normal font and one additional screen font.

```
Setup: Colors          A B C D E F G H I J K L M N O P
                       A   C D E F G H I J K L M N O P
Attribute              Foreground  Background  Sample
Normal                     H           B       Sample
Blocked                    H           E       Sample
Underline                  B           H       Sample
Strikeout                  A           D       Sample
Bold                       P           B       Sample
Double Underline           B           D       Sample
Redline                    E           H       Sample
Shadow                     B           H       Sample
Italics                    O           B       Sample
Small Caps                 E           D       Sample
Outline                    F           D       Sample
Subscript                  E           H       Sample
Superscript                F           H       Sample
Fine Print                 A           F       Sample
Small Print                H           F       Sample
Large Print                E           A       Sample
Very Large Print           D           A       Sample
Extra Large Print          H           A       Sample
Bold & Underline           P           H       Sample
Other Combinations         A           G       Sample

Switch documents; Move to copy settings      Doc 1
```

FIGURE 13.6:

The Screen Colors menu for setting the Normal font colors on an EGA or a VGA monitor

If you select a font other than Normal, the Screen Colors menu will also include a Font column, to the left of the Foreground column. If you type Y in that column, the attribute will appear in the selected font.

Using the arrow keys, you can move the cursor to the foreground or background color for any attribute, such as Normal, Blocked, Underline, Strikeout, or Bold. Then type the appropriate code for the color you want. For example, if you want your normal text to print as yellow letters on a black background, change the foreground color for Normal to *O* and the background color to *A*. The sample in the rightmost column shows you how the screen will look as you change colors.

After changing the color combinations to your liking, press Exit (F7) twice to return to the Edit screen. The screen colors will then take effect immediately.

Coloring Doc 1 and Doc 2 Screens

A "Doc 1" or "Doc 2" indicator appears at the bottom of the Colors/Fonts/Attributes screen to remind you which screen you're coloring. See Chapter 3 for more on editing multiple documents.

Regardless of whether you are using a monochrome or color monitor, the screen colors or attributes you define are initially for the Doc 1 screen only. If you want to color the Doc 2 screen, press Switch (Shift-F3) while you're at the Colors/Fonts/Attributes screen, and choose your colors. If you want to copy the colors from the Doc 1 screen to the Doc 2 screen, press Switch to switch to Doc 2, then press Move (Ctrl-F4) and select Yes to copy the Doc 1 colors to the Doc 2 screen. Make any additional changes you might want to the Doc 2 screen, then press Exit (F7) twice to return to the Edit screen.

RESETTING THE GRAPHICS SCREEN TYPE

If Auto-Select doesn't seem to work, and you're not sure what type of display card or monitor you have, you'll need to check your computer documentation or ask your dealer.

WordPerfect automatically detects the kind of graphics screen you are using— that is, it detects your monitor type or the special driver software that enables your monitor to show graphics, such as those displayed on the View Document screen and in the Equations Editor.

If you upgrade to a new monitor or are having a problem using graphics screens, you can select the Graphics Screen Type option to specify a different screen driver. You'll see a list of screen types. Use the arrow keys or your mouse to highlight the one that seems to best describe your own monitor and choose Select. Or choose Auto-Select to have WordPerfect make a "best guess" for you.

If you select your own driver, you also may be given a list of optional modes that the screen type offers. Once again, you can select a mode, or choose Auto-Select to have WordPerfect make a selection for you. Press Exit (F7) to return to the Edit screen.

RESETTING THE TEXT SCREEN TYPE

The text screen displays nongraphical text; the normal Edit screen and full-screen menus are text screens. Some screens let you display more than the usual 25 lines. If you have such a screen, you can activate its special features by selecting Text Screen Type from the Display menu.

When you select this option, you'll see a list of available text screen drivers. Use your arrow keys or the mouse to highlight the driver you want, then choose Select. Or choose Auto-Select to have WordPerfect make a best guess based on your equipment.

If you select your own driver, you'll be given options that are relevant to that screen, such as 43 or 50 lines of text (which lets you see more lines in your document but makes the print quite small). You'll then see some helps and hints relevant to that text screen type. Press Exit (F7) after reading the screen. Press Exit after selecting your text screen type.

CUSTOMIZING THE MENUS

Selecting Menu Options from the Display menu brings up the screen shown in Figure 13.7. From this screen, you can adjust the action and colors of Word-Perfect menus.

Notice that some of these options display bold or another attribute as their selection. These refer to the colors or properties associated with these

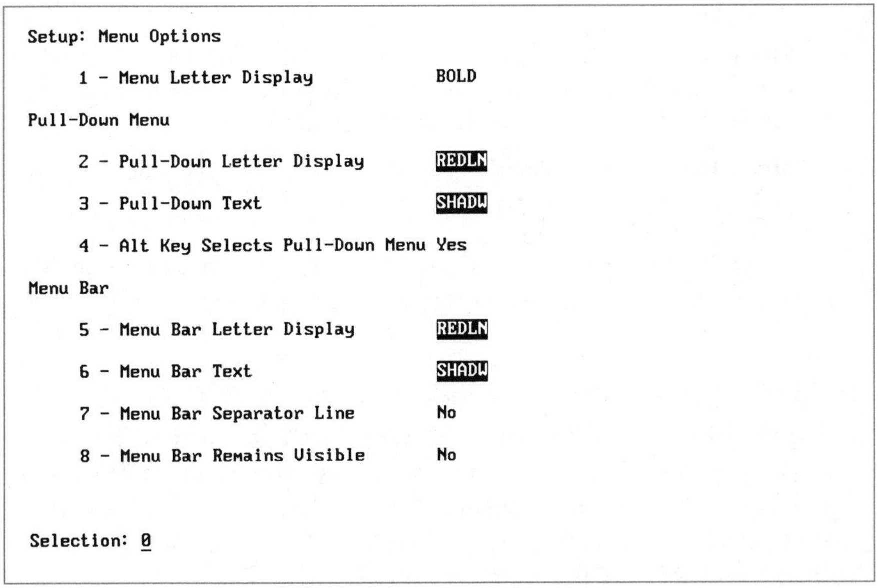

```
Setup: Menu Options

     1 - Menu Letter Display          BOLD

Pull-Down Menu

     2 - Pull-Down Letter Display     REDLN

     3 - Pull-Down Text               SHADW

     4 - Alt Key Selects Pull-Down Menu  Yes

Menu Bar

     5 - Menu Bar Letter Display      REDLN

     6 - Menu Bar Text                SHADW

     7 - Menu Bar Separator Line      No

     8 - Menu Bar Remains Visible     No


Selection: 0
```

FIGURE 13.7:

The Menu Options screen

It's a good idea to make your menu letters stand out with bold or color so that you can easily identify which letter to type when choosing menu options.

attributes, as defined with the Colors/Fonts/Attributes option discussed previously. For example, if you define the color of bold print as bright white on blue, then options displayed as *BOLD* will be bright white on blue. If you define the color of extra-large print as yellow on black, then change the Menu Letter Display option to Extra Large, the menu letters will be displayed as yellow on black (not as an extra-large size).

The options on this menu are summarized below:

Menu Letter Display: changes the color of the highlighted letter used to select options on full-screen and bottom menus (but not the menu bar or pull-down menus). For example, this option colors the *V* in View Document on the Print screen.

Pull-Down Letter Display: changes the color of the mnemonic selection letters on the pull-down menus (but has no effect on the menu bar itself). For example, this affects the selection letters on the pull-down menu that appears after you select **F**ile from the menu bar.

Pull-Down Text: changes the color of nonhighlighted text on the pull-down menus.

Alt Key Selects Pull-Down Menu: changes the key that displays the menu bar from Alt-= to Alt alone. If you change the option to Yes, you need only press and release the Alt key to access the menu bar.

Menu Bar Letter Display: changes the color of the highlighted letter that selects an option from the menu bar.

Menu Bar Text: changes the color of the nonhighlighted text on the menu bar.

Menu Bar Separator Line: adds a double line between the menu bar and the document if you set the option to Yes. Note that this separator line will hide a second line of your document.

Menu Bar Remains Visible: keeps the menu bar visible at all times if you set the option to Yes.

As usual, you can press Exit (F7) to return to the Edit screen after making your selections. Your menu changes should be immediately apparent.

CUSTOMIZING THE VIEW DOCUMENT SCREEN

If you have a color monitor but not a color printer, you may prefer to have View Document display your document in black and white, so it will more closely resemble the printed version. The options affecting the View Document screen are available when you select View Document Options from the Display menu; they are shown in Figure 13.8.

You can make the following selections from the View Document Options menu:

Text in Black & White: Yes displays text on the View Document screen as black print on a white background. No restores color text display.

Graphics in Black & White: Yes displays graphics on the View Document screen in black and white. No restores color graphics display.

Bold Displayed with Color: No displays boldfaced characters in your document as boldfaced black characters, rather than in the color used for bold on your Edit screen. Press Y for Yes if you later decide to restore the color display of boldface.

NOTE
NOTE
Some of the options for customizing the Edit screen affect only specific features, such as merges or multicolumn layouts.

Press Exit (F7) to return to the Edit screen after modifying the View Document display. You will notice your changes the next time you select View Document.

CUSTOMIZING THE EDIT SCREEN

Selecting Edit-Screen Options from the Display menu brings up a menu of miscellaneous options that affect the display on your Edit screen, as shown in Figure 13.9.

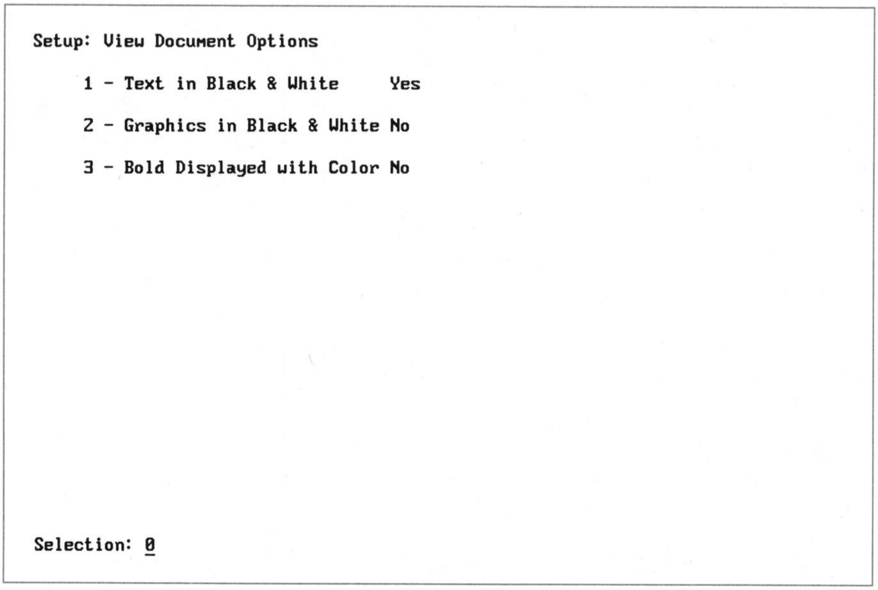

```
Setup: View Document Options

    1 - Text in Black & White      Yes

    2 - Graphics in Black & White No

    3 - Bold Displayed with Color No













Selection: 0
```

FIGURE 13.8:

The View Document Options menu

Here are your choices:

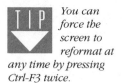

You can force the screen to reformat at any time by pressing Ctrl-F3 twice.

Automatically Format and Rewrite: Select No to reformat your text only as you scroll through it; this can be useful when working with narrow columns (where frequent screen reformatting can be distracting), because it prevents WordPerfect from reformatting your paragraphs with every cursor movement as you edit. Selecting Yes restores automatic reformatting, where text is formatted and rewritten as you edit it.

Comments Display: Selecting No hides the display of document comments. Whether displayed or not, document comments are never printed. Selecting Yes reinstates the display of document comments.

Filename on the Status Line: Selecting No hides the file name of the current document on the bottom line of the screen, creating a somewhat less cluttered (though less informative) screen display. Selecting Yes restores the display of the file name.

See Chapter 5 for information on the Compose feature.

Hard Return Display Character: Type any character or any Compose (Ctrl-2) character to have that character represent each hard return on your Edit screen; the character will never be printed. Press the spacebar as the hard-return character if you decide you no longer want hard returns displayed as characters.

Merge Codes Display: Select No to hide the display of merge codes on your Edit screen. Select Yes to reinstate their display (see Chapter 16).

```
Setup: Edit-Screen Options

     1 - Automatically Format and Rewrite      Yes

     2 - Comments Display                       Yes

     3 - Filename on the Status Line            Yes

     4 - Hard Return Display Character

     5 - Merge Codes Display                    Yes

     6 - Reveal Codes Window Size               10

     7 - Side-by-side Columns Display           No




  Selection: 0
```

FIGURE 13.9:

The Edit-Screen Options menu

Reveal Codes Window Size: Type the number of screen lines you want to devote to the Reveal Codes screen when it is displayed, and then press ↵. To restore the default of ten lines (on most monitors), you must return to this option and enter **10.**

Side-by-side Columns Display: Select No to have columns displayed on separate pages rather than side by side; this speeds up scrolling somewhat and makes editing easier in multicolumn layouts. Selecting Yes restores side-by-side column display (see Chapter 20).

Press Exit (F7) to return to the Edit screen from the Edit-Screen Options menu.

SETTING ENVIRONMENT FEATURES

TO CHANGE THE WORDPERFECT ENVIRONMENT DEFAULTS,

select File ➤ Setup ➤ Environment, or press Shift-F1 E.

Selecting Environment from the Setup menu gives you the opportunity to change the status of certain background operations. These are really miscellaneous settings, so I will discuss them separately in the sections that follow. To get started using these options, follow these steps:

1. Select **File** ➤ Se**t**up (or press **Shift-F1**).

2. Select **E**nvironment. The Environment menu appears, as shown in Figure 13.10.

AUTOMATIC BACKUPS

By now you should understand the importance of saving your work regularly with Save (select **F**ile ➤ **S**ave or press F10). This practice will minimize your loss of work in case of a power failure or other mishap that shuts down your computer without giving you a chance to exit WordPerfect normally. But WordPerfect offers two additional safety valves through the Backup menu (Figure 13.11), which you reach by selecting Backup Options from the Environment menu.

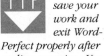 *Always save your work and exit Word-Perfect properly after ending a session. Use the timed backups only to recover from emergencies.*

Timed Document Backup

By default, WordPerfect backs up your document automatically every 30 minutes, using the file name WP{WP}.BK1 (or .BK2 for the document in the

Doc 2 window). These backup files are automatically deleted when you exit WordPerfect normally, but remain on-disk if a power failure or static electricity ends your WordPerfect work session unexpectedly. They are also saved if a computer problem forces you to reboot (Ctrl-Alt-Del) without exiting Word-Perfect properly.

```
Setup: Environment

    1 - Backup Options

    2 - Beep Options

    3 - Cursor Speed                    50 cps

    4 - Document Management/Summary

    5 - Fast Save (unformatted)         Yes

    6 - Hyphenation                     External Dictionary/Rules

    7 - Prompt for Hyphenation          When Required

    8 - Units of Measure

    9 - Alternate Keyboard              No
        (F1 - Help, Esc - Cancel, F3 - Repeat)




Selection: 0
```

FIGURE 13.10:

The Environment menu

```
Setup: Backup

    Timed backup files are deleted when you exit WP normally.  If you
    have a power or machine failure, you will find the backup file in the
    backup directory indicated in Setup: Location of Files.

        Backup Directory

    1 - Timed Document Backup           Yes
        Minutes Between Backups         30


    Original backup will save the original document with a .BK! extension
    whenever you replace it during a Save or Exit.

    2 - Original Document Backup            No








Selection: 0
```

FIGURE 13.11:

The Backup menu

After selecting Timed Document Backup, you can press N if you decide you don't want automatic timed backups (though there's very little benefit to canceling them—you just eliminate the slight interruption caused when WordPerfect performs the backup and save some disk space). If you have set this option to Yes, you can also enter a different backup interval, in minutes, and press ↵. Since automatic backups cause only the slightest inconvenience, you may want to make them more frequent—perhaps every 10 minutes.

If you've switched off Timed Document Backup and decide you want to reinstate it, select it, press Y for Yes, and, if necessary, change the displayed backup interval.

When you start WordPerfect, it looks for the WP{WP}.BK1 and WP{WP}.BK2 files and, if it finds one or both, displays this message:

Are other copies of WordPerfect currently running? (Y/N)

Unless you are running WordPerfect on a shared network system or on a multitasking operating system (such as DOS 5 or Windows), the answer to this question is No (press N). If you're not on a shared system and you get this message, you either failed to exit WordPerfect properly the last time you used it or a power outage terminated WordPerfect before you could exit properly. Hence, the backup files from the previous WordPerfect session are still stored on the disk. If either of those backup files exists when you start WordPerfect, you'll see this message:

Old document *n* backup file exits. 1 Rename; 2 D**elete:**

The *n* is either the number 1 or 2, depending on whether WordPerfect discovers the backup file for Doc 1 or Doc 2. If you want to save the backup file, so you can later retrieve it, choose **R**ename, type any file name, then press ↵. After renaming the files, you can retrieve them normally and resume your work. If you select **D**elete, the backup file will be deleted.

If you want to retrieve a timed backup file for some reason, you can use the Rename feature in List Files (Chapter 12) to rename the backup file, then retrieve it as you would any other file.

Original Document Backup

Selecting Original Document Backup from the Backup menu and pressing Y for Yes saves a backup copy of any document replaced by either of these Save commands:

◆ **File ➤ S**ave or F10 to save and continue

◆ **File ➤ Ex**it or F7 to save and exit

NOTE NOTE *A network timed-backup file is named* **WPxxx}.BK1** *(or .BK2), where* **xxx** *is the user's ID.*

 If you want to run multiple copies of WordPerfect 5.1, you'll need to select Yes and enter a unique directory for the backup files for each copy.

NOTE NOTE *The timed backup files are stored in the backup directory named in the Location of Files option (discussed below) or in the same directory as WP.EXE (typically C:\WP51) if no directory is specified.*

The backup copy will be stored in the same directory with your document file and will have the same file name as the document being replaced, but with the extension .BK!. For example, if you're replacing a file named *MEMO.WP,* the backup file will be named *MEMO.BK!.*

If you use one of the Save commands to replace a document and then realize you still need the original version, you can retrieve the .BK! file to a clear screen the same way you retrieve any document (select **F**ile ➤ **R**etrieve or press Shift-F10) and resave it under any name.

Press Exit (F7) to return to the Edit screen from the Backup menu.

Controlling the Warning Beeps

Hyphena-tion is dis-cussed in Chapter 11.

By default, the only time WordPerfect beeps at you is when the Hyphenation feature is active and it needs you to place a hyphen in a word. By selecting Beep Options from the Environment menu, you can deactivate this warning beep or set others, as shown in Figure 13.12.

You can choose any of these options for warning beeps:

Beep on Error: Yes has WordPerfect sound a warning tone when-ever it encounters an error. No turns this beep off if it is already set.

Beep on Hyphenation: No deactivates the beep that notifies you when WordPerfect needs help positioning the hyphen in a word. Yes reinstates this warning tone if you've switched it off.

```
Setup: Beep Options

    1 - Beep on Error            No

    2 - Beep on Hyphenation      Yes

    3 - Beep on Search Failure   No

















Selection: 0
```

FIGURE 13.12:

The Beep Options menu

Beep on Search Failure: Yes has WordPerfect warn you when a search operation does not locate the search string. No turns off this warning beep.

Press Exit (F7) to return to the Edit screen from the Beep Options menu. Your new settings take effect immediately.

ADJUSTING THE SPEED OF CURSOR MOVEMENT

The Cursor Speed option on the Environment menu lets you change the speed at which the cursor moves through the document when you press and hold down any key that moves the cursor (spacebar, Backspace, Delete, and the cursor-movement keys). The cursor speed is originally set at 50 characters per second (cps). When you select Cursor Speed, you'll see the following settings:

Characters Per Second: 1 15; **2** 20; **3** 30; **4** 40; **5** 50; **6** Normal: **0**

Each of the first five settings provides the cursor speed indicated, in characters per second. The Normal setting is worth some special mention: It is not, as you might expect, the default cursor speed of 50 cps. (You'll notice, in fact, that 50 cps, the WordPerfect default, is one of the specific Cursor Speed settings.) Instead, Normal refers to the speed considered by WordPerfect to be normal for your computer—usually a pretty slow speed.

After setting the cursor speed, press Exit (F7) to return to the Edit screen.

AUTOMATING THE DOCUMENT SUMMARY

NOTE NOTE *Document summaries are covered in Chapter 12.*

If creating a document summary is something you regularly do when you create a document—or if you'd like it to be—you can make life a little easier by having WordPerfect prompt you to create one and by specifying defaults for some of the entries on the Document Summary screen. To set this in motion, select Document Management/Summary from the Environment menu. You'll see the menu shown in Figure 13.13.

Here are your choices:

Create Summary on Save/Exit: causes WordPerfect to prompt you to create a document summary when saving a document that doesn't already have one. Press Y for Yes to switch this feature on, or press N for No if this feature is on and you want to deactivate it.

Subject Search Text: lets you change the preselected characters WordPerfect uses to search on the first page of the document for the document summary's suggested Subject entry. The default is *RE:*, which means that WordPerfect searches for *RE:* in the document and pulls the word or phrase immediately following it into the Subject entry. Type up to 39 characters for Subject Search Text and press ↵.

Long Document Names: causes WordPerfect to prompt you for a long document name when you save a document that does not already have one. The name, which can be up to 68 characters long, will appear on the List Files screen (Chapter 12) to help you identify the contents of the document. Press Y for Yes to activate this prompt, or press N for No to switch it off.

Default Document Type: sets the default for Document Type in the document summary for all future documents. Type up to 20 characters and press ↵. The first three characters will also be suggested as the file-name extension when you name the file (so, for example, the Document Type "Letter" will make .LET the default file-name extension).

Press Exit (F7) to return to the Edit screen when you're finished automating your document summaries. You will notice your new settings at work the next time you create a document summary or save a new document (depending on the settings you made).

FAST SAVE

Switched on by default, Fast Save saves your documents a little faster by not reformatting them. The amount of time saved is slight. Printing a fast-saved document from disk takes a little longer because WordPerfect must format

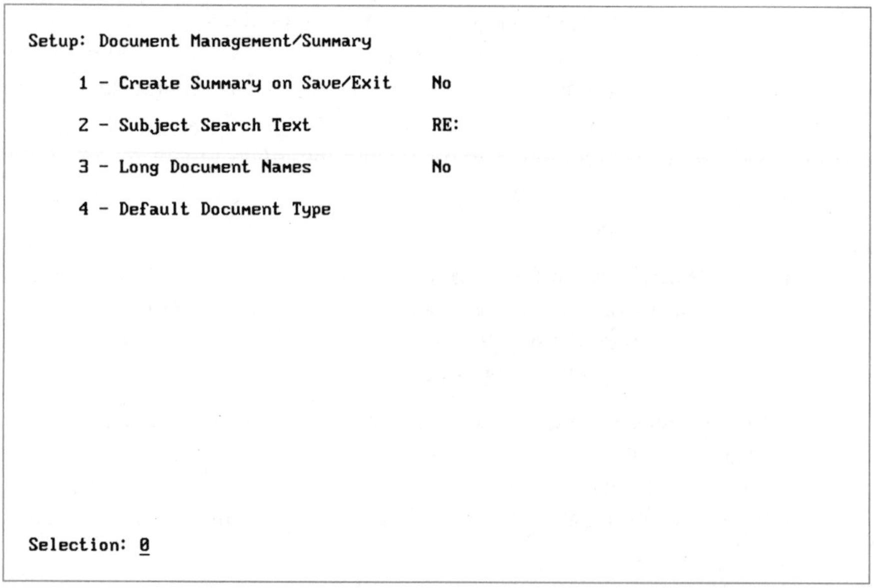

```
Setup: Document Management/Summary

    1 - Create Summary on Save/Exit     No

    2 - Subject Search Text             RE:

    3 - Long Document Names             No

    4 - Default Document Type




















Selection: 0
```

FIGURE 13.13:

The Document Management/Summary menu

the document before sending it to the printer.

*You can print a document from disk by selecting **F**ile ➤ **P**rint ➤ **D**ocument on Disk or by pressing **Shift-F7 D** (see Chapter 8).*

Even if the fast-saved document was saved with a different printer selected from the one you've currently chosen, you can use the currently selected printer to print the document from disk (by pressing Y for Yes at the confirmation prompt), but you may get unexpected results, such as strange font choices. In this case it's usually better to retrieve the document first (to reformat it using the current printer selection), and then print it from the screen (select **F**ile ➤ **P**rint ➤ **F**ull Document or press Shift-F7 F).

To change the status of Fast Save, select Fast Save (unformatted) from the Environment menu. Press N for No to turn off Fast Save, for slightly slower saves but slightly faster printing from disk. Press Y for Yes if Fast Save is switched off and you want it restored. After making your selection, press Exit (F7) to return to the Edit screen.

CHANGING THE HYPHENATION RULES

Removing the .LEX file disables the Speller.

When the automatic hyphenation feature is active, WordPerfect normally bases its hyphenation decisions on the contents of two disk files: the WP{WP}US.HYC and WP{WP}US.LEX files for American English, or WP{WP}UK.HYC and WP{WP}UK.LEX for British English. If you don't have a hard disk, or you don't want to store these two files on your hard disk, you can still use hyphenation capabilities by switching to the internal rules.

To do so, select Hyphenation from the Environment menu, where you will see the following options:

Hyphenation: **1** External Dictionary/Rules; **2** Internal Rules: **1**

Automatic hyphenation is covered in detail in Chapter 11.

The External Dictionary/Rules option tells WordPerfect to hyphenate words based on the hyphenation files (dictionaries) described above. The Internal Rules option tells WordPerfect to hyphenate words based on a set of general rules concerning syllabication in English. These rules, while helpful, will produce some errors and therefore are not as efficient as the .HYC and .LEX files. If you've been working with the internal rules but have reinstalled the .HYC and .LEX files, select External Dictionary/Rules to activate the more reliable hyphenation system. When you've made your selection, press Exit (F7) to return to the Edit screen.

RESETTING THE HYPHENATION PROMPT OPTION

The Prompt for Hyphenation option tells WordPerfect when (or if) you would like to be prompted when it needs help hyphenating a word. See Chapter 11 for information.

Changing the Default Unit of Measurement

WordPerfect is preset to display measurements, such as those on the status line. It assumes that your measurement entries, such as those for new margin settings, are in inches as well. If you'd rather work with another unit of measure, you can simply tell WordPerfect your preferred unit; all affected displays will be changed immediately, and WordPerfect will expect the measurements you enter from then on to be in the selected unit.

To change the default unit of measurement, select Units of Measure from the Environment menu. The Units of Measure menu appears, as shown in Figure 13.14.

Though you'll most likely want to change the default unit across the board, WordPerfect lets you select the unit of measurement for two components separately. *Display and Entry of Numbers for Margins, Tabs, etc.* refers to the unit of measure used for typing in numbers and displaying them everywhere but the status line. Status Line Display refers only to the units displayed on the status line, in the Ln (line) and Pos (position) entries, which tell you the location of the cursor on the page.

When you select either Display and Entry of Numbers or Status Line Display from the Units of Measure menu, the cursor moves to the corresponding entry near the top of the screen. Referring to the legend near the bottom of the menu, type the character representing the new unit. Your choices are as follows:

" Inches, displayed with the inch symbol

i Inches, displayed with the letter *i*

```
Setup: Units of Measure

    1 - Display and Entry of Numbers          "
            for Margins, Tabs, etc.

    2 - Status Line Display                   "


Legend:

    " = inches
    i = inches
    c = centimeters
    p = points
    u = 1200ths of an inch
    u = WordPerfect 4.2 Units (Lines/Columns)











Selection: 0
```

FIGURE 13.14:

The Units of Measure menu

c   Centimeters

p   Points (a typesetting unit in which 72 points equals 1 inch)

w $\frac{1}{1200}$ of an inch

u   WordPerfect 4.2 units, based on the number of lines and columns on a page

Remember to set the same unit for both Status Line Display and Display and Entry of Numbers if you want a consistent measurement and display system for all of your work. Press Exit (F7) to return to the Edit screen from the Units of Measure menu. Your new settings take effect immediately.

If you ever need to enter a measurement in a unit that's not your current default, you don't need to change the default unit. Instead, you can type the measurement followed by the symbol representing the alternate unit (as summarized in the table above).

For example, if you are preparing a document for typesetting and need to set the left and right margins to 90 points, but you are working with inches in WordPerfect, you can select **L**ayout ➤ **L**ine ➤ **M**argins (or press Shift-F8 L M), then type *90p* and press ↵ for both the Left and Right settings. WordPerfect automatically converts your entries to 1.25 inches.

CHANGING HELP AND OTHER KEYS

Chapter 27 discusses other ways to customize your keyboard.

Most DOS programs use the F1 key for Help and the Escape key for Cancel. Although WordPerfect does not follow this standard, it does let you change the keyboard to match the standard: Select **A**lternate Keyboard from the Environment menu, then choose **Y**es which reassigns the following keys as indicated:

F1   Calls up context-sensitive help, or the opening Help screen if no menu or option is selected

Esc   Becomes the Cancel key for backing out of menus without making a selection, as well as for undeleting text

F3   Becomes the Repeat key (the role previously played by Esc)

CUSTOMIZING THE EDITING DEFAULTS

TO CHANGE THE BASIC EDITING AND FORMATTING DEFAULTS,

select File ➤ Setup ➤ Initial Settings, or press Shift-F1 I.

You can establish new default format settings for your documents and change the operation of several other WordPerfect editing features from the Initial Settings menu (Figure 13.15). Follow these steps to reach it:

1. Select **F**ile ➤ Se**t**up, or press Setup (**Shift-F1**).

2. Select **I**nitial Settings.

The following sections describe the options available on the Initial Settings menu.

REDEFINING THE DELIMITERS FOR MERGE FILES

NOTE *Merges are covered in Chapter 16, DOS text files in Chapter 25.*

If you are planning to merge data stored in DOS text files into a WordPerfect document, WordPerfect needs to know how to recognize the beginning and end of each field and record. By default, WordPerfect assumes that fields are

---

```
Setup: Initial Settings

      1 - Merge

      2 - Date Format                    3 1, 4
                                         May 6, 1991
      3 - Equations

      4 - Format Retrieved Documents     No
             for Default Printer

      5 - Initial Codes

      6 - Repeat Value                   8

      7 - Table of Authorities

      8 - Print Options




   Selection: 0
```

FIGURE 13.15:
The Initial Settings menu

separated by commas and that each record ends with a carriage return (⏎). Selecting Merge from the Initial Settings menu lets you redefine these characters to reflect the structure of the text file.

When you select Merge, the following options appear:

1 Field Delimiters -   Begin
                                 End
2 Record Delimiters - Begin
                                 End

Select Field Delimiters if you want to redefine the characters that begin and end fields. Select Record Delimiters to redefine the characters that begin and end records. See Chapter 25 for additional information.

CHANGING THE DEFAULT DATE FORMAT

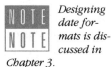

Designing date formats is discussed in Chapter 3.

By selecting Date Format from the Initial Settings menu, you can control the default date and time format used with the Date Text or Date Code options (introduced in Chapter 3). Initially, the default format is *3 1, 4* (e.g., *December 25, 1991*). When you select this option, you'll see the same menu used to define the date format for the current work session, as shown in Figure 13.16.

When you design a date format, the new format becomes the default format for all future Date Text or Date Code entries. Of course, you can override

FIGURE 13.16:

The Date Format menu

```
Date Format

     Character   Meaning
         1       Day of the Month
         2       Month (number)
         3       Month (word)
         4       Year (all four digits)
         5       Year (last two digits)
         6       Day of the Week (word)
         7       Hour (24-hour clock)
         8       Hour (12-hour clock)
         9       Minute
         0       am / pm
         %,$     Used before a number, will:
                    Pad numbers less than 10 with a leading zero or space
                    Abbreviate the month or day of the week

     Examples:   3 1, 4       = December 25, 1984
                 %6 %3 1, 4   = Tue Dec 25, 1984
                 %2/%1/5 (6)  = 01/01/85 (Tuesday)
                 $2/$1/5 (%6) =  1/ 1/85 (Tue)
                 8:90         = 10:55am


Date format: 3 1, 4
```

this default for any current WordPerfect session by selecting **T**ools ➤ Date Format (**Shift-F5 F**).

SETTING THE DEFAULT EQUATION STYLE

If you are using WordPerfect's Equations feature (Chapter 21), you can select Equations from the Initial Settings menu to change some settings that affect how you set up your equations and how WordPerfect prints them. After selecting Equations, you'll see the menu shown in Figure 13.17. All of the options on this menu are described in Chapter 21.

FORMATTING DOCUMENTS FOR THE DEFAULT PRINTER

If the original printer is not available for selection, WordPerfect adjusts the incoming document to the current printer, as if you had selected Yes.

The Format Retrieved Documents for Default Printer option gives you two choices, which affect WordPerfect's retrieval of documents that use paper sizes and fonts for a printer other than the currently selected printer. If you select Yes, the current printer remains selected, and fonts and paper sizes in the incoming document are modified to best match those available in the current printer. If you select No, WordPerfect automatically selects whatever printer was used to create the current document (if it's available) and leaves fonts and paper sizes unchanged.

```
Setup: Equation Options

      1 - Print as Graphics     Yes

      2 - Graphical Font Size  Default

      3 - Horizontal Alignment Center

      4 - Vertical Alignment    Center

      5 - Keyboard for Editing




















Selection: 0
```

FIGURE 13.17:

The Equation Options menu

CHANGING THE INITIAL CODE DEFAULTS

WordPerfect Corporation has chosen the most common document format as the default for each document you create: All documents, unless you specify otherwise, are single-spaced and fully justified, with 1-inch margins on all four sides.

But as stated earlier, defaults are simply suggested values that Word-Perfect uses if you do not request some other option. If you find that the margins, spacing, or justification need changing in nearly every document you create, it may be easier to change the default settings. For example, if you use left justification in most documents, you can change the default justification to Left. In the future, all documents will be left-justified automatically (unless, of course, you change the justification for a specific document with **Layout ➤ Line ➤ J**ustification).

To change a default setting, follow these steps:

 *The Initial Codes screen looks and works a lot like the Reveal Codes screen.*

1. Display the Initial Settings menu by selecting **F**ile ➤ Setup ➤ **I**nitial Settings (or by pressing **Shift-F1 I**).

2. Select Initial **C**odes. The Initial Codes screen appears, as shown in Figure 13.18.

3. Select the normal menu options or press the shortcut keys to insert the formatting codes you want to have in effect for every document.

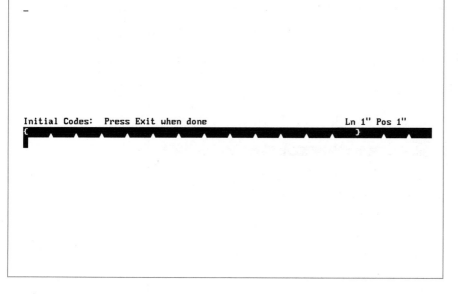

FIGURE 13.18:

The Initial Codes screen, with no new formats set

Initial Codes: Press Exit when done   Ln 1" Pos 1"

Not all formatting options can be defined in Initial Codes, and any text you type will be ignored. If a particular option seems to be ignored, try placing it at the top of the document rather than in the Initial Codes area.

For example, to change from full justification to left justification, select **L**ayout ➤ **L**ine ➤ **J**ustification (or press Shift-F8 L J) to get started, then select an option. You can then choose other formatting options if you wish. Figure 13.19 shows an Initial Codes screen with left justification and line spacing of 2.5 set as the new defaults. When you've finished entering the new defaults, press Exit (F7) twice to return to the Edit screen.

Your new settings will affect only documents that you create in the future. They will not change the format of the document currently on the Edit screen or of previously saved documents that you retrieve for editing.

Moreover, the codes you enter on this screen are automatically stored as the initial codes in every new document you create. For example, even when you first start WordPerfect and are in a blank document, selecting **L**ayout ➤ **D**ocument ➤ Initial **C**odes (Shift-F8 D C) displays the default codes. You can delete any of these codes for the current document only, or press Exit (F7) to leave them unchanged.

Remember that the formatting codes in the document are saved as part of the document. Hence, they will be in effect even if you retrieve the document on a computer with different default settings.

Keep in mind that any settings in Document Initial Codes (Chapter 7) for the current document (only) take precedence over the settings in Initial Codes. In turn, the format settings at specific locations in a document override both Initial Codes and Document Initial Codes.

FIGURE 13.19:

The Initial Codes screen, with new format defaults set

```
  ─




















Initial Codes:   Press Exit when done                        Ln 1" Pos 1"
[
[Ln Spacing:2.5][Just:Left]
```

MODIFYING THE REPEAT VALUE OF THE ESCAPE KEY

If you've switched to the alternate keyboard, as described earlier under "Changing Help and Other Keys," the Repeat Value option affects the F3 key rather than the Escape key.

Pressing Escape at the Edit screen causes the next action you take to be repeated eight times by default. If you want a specific action to be repeated a different number of times, you press Escape, type the number of repetitions, and then take the given action. But if you find yourself consistently repeating actions a certain number of times other than eight, you can make that number the default repeat value. To do so, select Repeat Value from the Initial Settings menu, type the desired number of repetitions, press ↵, then press Exit (F7) to return to the Edit screen.

You'll see the new setting in action the next time you press Escape at the Edit screen. Of course, you can still repeat a single action any number of times by pressing Escape, typing the number of repetitions, and performing the action.

CHANGING THE TABLE OF AUTHORITIES DEFAULTS

The Table of Authorities feature is discussed in Chapter 23.

If you often use WordPerfect's Table of Authorities feature and must reset the format every time in order to follow the conventions of your law firm, you'll be glad to know that you can reset certain formats permanently. See Chapter 23 for more information on this topic.

CHANGING THE PRINTER DEFAULTS

You can change the default settings that WordPerfect uses to print your documents. Of course, you can change most of these settings directly at the Print menu for a specific document (even if you change the defaults from Initial Settings), but you may prefer to change the overall defaults so that you don't always have to remember to change settings on the Print menu in the future.

To change the defaults used for printing, select Print Options from the Initial Settings menu. You'll see the screen shown in Figure 13.20.

Changing any of these options makes them defaults for future documents, rather than just the current document. The first four options on the menu are described in Chapter 8. The redline method is described in Chapter 5, as is the last option, which lets you customize how WordPerfect defines the various size options in relation to the current font.

ORGANIZING YOUR FILES

**TO CHANGE THE DEFAULT LOCATIONS OF
VARIOUS TYPES OF WORDPERFECT FILES,**

**select File ➤ Setup ➤ Location of Files, or press
Shift-F1 L.**

NOTE NOTE *Actually,
the Style
Library
Filename
option expects you to
enter a file name, but
all other entries must
be directory locations.*

As you may know, DOS lets you divide your hard disk into separate drives, directories, and subdirectories. In a sense, each directory on a drive is its own file cabinet and contains its own set of files. Storing files in separate directories helps keep information organized and prevents individual directories from becoming cluttered with too many file names.

With the Location of Files menu, you can specify a directory location for each of several categories of WordPerfect files so that WordPerfect always knows where to store files as they are created and where to look for them when they are needed.

Follow these steps to display and work with the Location of Files menu:

1. Select **F**ile ➤ Se**t**up (or press **Shift-F1**).

2. Select **L**ocation of Files. The Location of Files menu appears, as shown in Figure 13.21. Note that WordPerfect inserted C:\WP51 (or the name of your own WordPerfect directory) as the location for most files when you installed the program.

```
Setup: Print Options

    1 - Binding Offset               0"

    2 - Number of Copies             1
        Multiple Copies Generated by Printer

    3 - Graphics Quality             Draft

    4 - Text Quality                 High

    5 - Redline Method               Printer Dependent

    6 - Size Attribute Ratios - Fine 60%
        (% of Normal)        Small   90%
                             Large   120%
                        Very Large   150%
                       Extra Large   200%
                     Super/Subscript 60%




Selection: 0
```

FIGURE 13.20:

The Print Options menu

3. Select the category of files whose directory location you want to set.

4. Type the drive or directory location for that category of files, using proper DOS conventions (e.g., *C:\WP51\DOCS*), and press ↵. (For best results, include both the drive letter and directory name.)

The default style-library file is automatically retrieved when you create a new document.

5. Optionally, you can choose the Style Files option (see Chapter 14), type a directory name for style files, and press ↵. Then you can type a default style-library file name (or complete path name, including the file name) and press ↵.

6. Select another category of files and enter its location, or press Exit (F7) to return to the Edit screen.

Note that any directory you list on the Location of Files menu must already exist; WordPerfect will not create it for you. If you list a nonexistent subdirectory as a file location, WordPerfect will display the following error message:

ERROR: Invalid drive/path specification

*You can use List Files (**F**ile ▶ List **F**iles or F5), described in Chapter 12, to create a new directory.*

You will not be permitted to leave the screen until you change all invalid directory names to valid names.

Also, once you select a new location for a certain type of file, such as a macro, be sure to move all your existing files of that type to the new location. You can use the Move option on the List Files screen to do so.

```
Setup: Location of Files

      1 - Backup Files

      2 - Keyboard/Macro Files        C:\WP51

      3 - Thesaurus/Spell/Hyphenation
                          Main         C:\WP51
                          Supplementary C:\WP51

      4 - Printer Files               C:\WP51

      5 - Style Files                 C:\WP51
                Library Filename      LIBRARY.STY

      6 - Graphic Files               C:\WP51

      7 - Documents                   C:\WP51

      8 - Spreadsheet Files




Selection: 0
```

FIGURE 13.21:

The Location of Files menu, with default file locations displayed

MAXIMIZING COMPUTER SPEED

If you are responsible for configuring systems, you should keep in mind that if the WordPerfect 5.1 directory (typically C:\WP51) is in the PATH statement in the AUTOEXEC.BAT file, DOS must search every file in that directory before searching other directories listed after it. For example, suppose your AUTO-EXEC.BAT file contains this command:

PATH C:\WP51;C:\DOS;E:\WINDOWS;D:\123

If the WP51 directory contains hundreds, or thousands, of files, access to programs in the DOS, Windows, and 1-2-3 directories will be slowed dramatically.

To regain some speed, either move the C:\WP51 directory to the end of the PATH statement or store only the WordPerfect program files in the C:\WP51 directory, and use the Location of Files option to select other directories for storing WordPerfect documents, macros, keyboard files, and so forth.

This concludes Part 3 of this book. In the next part, you'll start to learn about additional tools that save time and effort by automating portions of your work.

PART FOUR

Automating Your Work

In this part you'll learn about two important features of Word-Perfect that not only simplify your work but can also help automate portions of it. The first tool, Styles, lets you predefine the appearance of certain elements of your documents. Not only does this feature save time and ensure consistency, it also lets you easily redesign an entire document with just a few keystrokes. The second tool, Macros, lets you automate complex tasks, reducing them to just a couple of keystrokes.

CHAPTER 14

Using Styles to Simplify Your Work

HANDS-ON
....
LESSON 6

For a hands-on lesson in creating and using styles, see Lesson 6 in Part 9.

I f you look at just about any document that's longer than a page or two, particularly a professionally published document, you'll notice that it consists of certain design elements, or *styles*. For example, as you flip though this book, you'll see that every chapter contains a chapter title, several main section headings (called A heads), subsection headings (B heads), sub-subsection headings (C heads), margin notes, body text (like this paragraph), and more.

The fonts used to print these elements are used consistently throughout the book. For example, all the margin notes are printed in the same small size and typeface. This consistent use of design makes it easier for the reader to scan the material and find needed information.

WHAT IS A STYLE?

Virtually any size of document can benefit from consistent use of styles. For example, Figure 14.1 shows a sample newsletter that uses three basic design

You'll learn to create documents like the one in Figure 14.1 in Part 6 of this book, but you can start using styles with any document right now.

Chapter 5 discusses fonts and special characters, which you'll probably want to use when creating styles.

With the aid of the Master Document feature, you can easily change a style throughout many separate documents at once. Be sure to read Part 7 if you work with large documents.

elements (styles) to print each article: a headline (or article title), a byline (the author's name), and body text (which ends with a small graphic to indicate the end of each article).

The WordPerfect Styles feature lets you predefine the appearance and format of various elements of your document. For example, you could create these three styles before creating the newsletter in Figure 14.1:

◆ Headline (style of each article title)

◆ Byline (style for printing the author name)

◆ Body (style for the article text and closing graphic)

When you're about to type the headline, byline, or article text, you simply press a few keys to activate the appropriate style, rather than pressing all the keys required to select the font and change the print size or print attribute. This saves you a lot of time and guarantees that the elements are used consistently throughout the document.

But the real advantage of styles is this: If you change your mind about the appearance of a style, you only need to change the style once—you need not change it repeatedly throughout the document. Suppose you decide to change the font of all the headings for the newsletter in Figure 14.1. With styles already set up, you only need to change the font in the Headline style one time, not repeatedly throughout the document. All the headlines in the document are instantly converted to the new style. Figure 14.2 shows this idea in action. It's exactly the same newsletter as the one in Figure 14.1, but the font of the Headline style has been changed from Times to Univers. Now all the headlines are printed in the new font, and because a style was used for the headlines, they could be changed all at once, in just a few seconds.

Needless to say, if your document has several dozen, or several hundred, headings in it, you can save yourself from a great deal of boring, repetitive work. This is especially true when you remember the many limitations of the Search and Replace feature (Chapter 9) for locating and changing fonts, paired codes, and other specific formatting codes.

After you've worked up a nice set of styles for a document, you can save those styles and reuse them in other documents, without re-creating them from scratch. This can be very handy for creating a monthly newsletter or a monthly report to management, or if you need to create a large book, report, or dissertation consisting of several sections or chapters that must follow specific formatting guidelines.

Styles are easy to create, easy to use, and easy to change. So even if your particular documents only use a handful of simple styles, like boldface, italics, and extra-large size, you'll probably find it worthwhile to use styles.

body

The Vacationer

Vol. 1 No. 1   Travel fun for everyone   January 1991

Celebrate with us —— headline
by Jill Evans —————— byline

In honor of our newsletter's maiden voyage, we'd like to invite you to an Open House at 7:00pm on January 11, 1991, at our offices. Please dress casually or come in your most fashionable travel togs. ✿

Tropical travel —— headline
by Elizabeth Olson —— byline

Travel to tropical islands is on the increase. Just look at the graph showing our clients' recent tropical trips and you'll see how dramatic the numbers really are. There's a good reason for these increases -- tropical vacations are great fun, especially when the wind and snow are swirling at your doorstep! ✿

Vacation Trips to Paradise
(booked by our office)

Newsletter debut —— headline
by Joan Smith —————— byline

We're pleased to bring this first issue of our newsletter, *The Vacationer*, to our many loyal customers. The newsletter was inspired by your ideas and questions. You've asked us where to find the best travel fares, where to go for the person who has been everywhere, what to eat and how to eat it when visiting faraway countries. We've responded by creating this newsletter.

Here we'll bring you the latest news about great deals on vacations in exotic corners of our planet, fun places for inexpensive weekend getaways, and out-of-the-way spots you might never have thought to ask us about. We'll include handy vacation planning tips and introduce you to exciting foods, puzzling customs, and important laws you'll encounter during sojourns to foreign lands. So relax, enjoy, and travel with us as we bring you a new issue every quarter of the year... ✿

Inside...

Newsletter debut 1
Celebrate with us 1
Tropical travel 1
New employees 2
Travel calendar 3

body   body

FIGURE 14.1:

A sample newsletter with three consistently used styles: Headline, Byline, and Body

The Vacationer

Vol. 1 No. 1   Travel fun for everyone   January 1991

Newsletter debut
by Joan Smith

We're pleased to bring this first issue of our newsletter, *The Vacationer*, to our many loyal customers. The newsletter was inspired by your ideas and questions. You've asked us where to find the best travel fares, where to go for the person who has been everywhere, what to eat and how to eat it when visiting faraway countries. We've responded by creating this newsletter.

Here we'll bring you the latest news about great deals on vacations in exotic corners of our planet, fun places for inexpensive weekend getaways, and out-of-the-way spots you might never have thought to ask us about. We'll include handy vacation planning tips and introduce you to exciting foods, puzzling customs, and important laws you'll encounter during sojourns to foreign lands. So relax, enjoy, and travel with us as we bring you a new issue every quarter of the year...   ☼

Celebrate with us
by Jill Evans

In honor of our newsletter's maiden voyage, we'd like to invite you to an Open House at 7:00pm on January 11, 1991, at our offices. Please dress casually or come in your most fashionable travel togs.   ☼

Tropical travel
by Elizabeth Olson

Travel to tropical islands is on the increase. Just look at the graph showing our clients' recent tropical trips and you'll see how dramatic the

numbers really are. There's a good reason for these increases -- tropical vacations are great fun, especially when the wind and snow are swirling at your doorstep!   ☼

Inside...

PAIRED, OPEN, AND OUTLINE STYLES

Before learning how to work with styles in WordPerfect, you need to get a bit of terminology under your belt. There are three types of styles: *paired, open,* and *outline.*

◆ A paired style is used to switch a specific format on and off; for example, to format a heading or a table caption. It behaves like the paired codes of "regular" print attributes, such as the [BOLD] and [bold] codes that activate and deactivate boldface for the words between the codes.

◆ An open style is switched on once and applies indefinitely, except where explicitly overridden with another style or specific formatting codes. This kind of style acts like any other single code, such as [Ln Spacing], affecting all text below the position of the code (up to the next overriding code, if any).

◆ An outline style is used only with the Outline feature to apply styles to outlines. This specialized category of style is covered in Chapter 22.

CREATING A NEW STYLE

TO CREATE A NEW STYLE,

1. Select Layout ➤ Styles ➤ Create (or press Alt-F8 C).

2. Enter a style Name and optionally a Description.

3. Select a Type, and optionally select Enter to specify a role for the ↵ key to play.

4. Choose Codes and enter your formatting codes.

5. Press Exit (F7) after entering your formatting codes.

NOTE
NOTE
Since an open style generally affects all text below the cursor, a single document will generally use only one open style, though it may use several paired styles.

To create a style, you first must consider whether it should be a paired style, which is used for headings or small blocks of text, or an open style, which affects the entire document. Then you must think about what features you want it to activate, such as a particular font or appearance, or a formatting code. A style can also contain text, which is typed automatically as soon as you activate the style.

To create a style, follow these steps:

1. Select **L**ayout ➤ **S**tyles, or press Style (**Alt-F8**). This displays the list of available styles, as shown in Figure 14.3 (your list will probably be different).

2. Select **C**reate, which takes you to the screen for defining a style (Figure 14.4).

3. Select **N**ame, then type a descriptive name of your choosing, up to 12 characters long (including blank spaces if you want them), and press ↵.

4. If you want to create an open style, select **T**ype, and then select Open. Otherwise, leave this option unchanged to create a paired style.

5. Optionally, select **D**escription and type a description up to 54 characters long, which will be displayed along with the list of available styles (see the Description column in Figure 14.3). Press ↵.

6. Select **C**odes. If you are creating a paired style, you will see the screen in Figure 14.5. If you are creating an open style, the comment box in the middle of the screen is not displayed.

7. Use the pull-down menus or shortcut keys to select formatting features for the style. The hidden code for each format you select appears in the Reveal Codes (bottom) window of the screen. You may also type any text that you want the style to insert for you automatically.

8. If you are creating an open style, skip steps 9 and 10.

9. If you are creating a paired style and want it to end by doing something more than simply terminating the codes it uses, press ↓ to move the cursor beneath the comment box.

10. Again, use the menus or shortcut keys to select formatting features, fonts, etc., or type the text that you want the style to insert for you.

11. Press Exit (**F7**) after defining your formatting codes and text.

12. If you are defining a paired style, you can alter the function of the ↵ key (as described below) by selecting **E**nter and an option from the menu that follows.

13. Press Exit (**F7**) again to return to the list of available styles.

Your newly created style will be added to the list of available styles and will be saved for future use (in the current document only) when you save the

---

NOTE *Word-Perfect assigns a number to a style if you don't name it. The first style will be named **1**, the next will be named **2**, and so forth.*

NOTE *Any codes above the [Comment] box are automatically deactivated when you leave the style, so it's not necessary to turn off codes that are activated above the comment. The only exceptions are Page Format codes (selected from the Layout ➤ Page menu), which are not deactivated.*

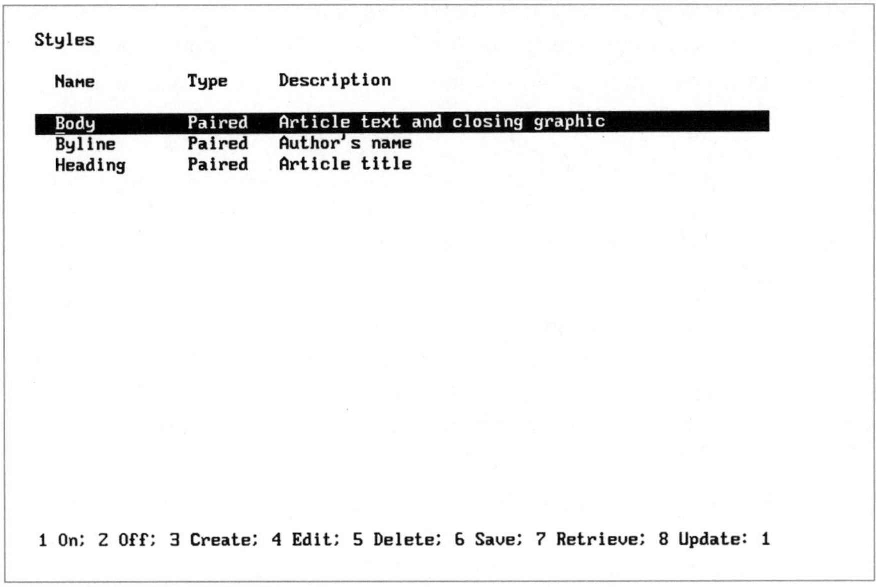

```
Styles

   Name        Type      Description

   Body        Paired    Article text and closing graphic
   Byline      Paired    Author's name
   Heading     Paired    Article title













 1 On; 2 Off; 3 Create; 4 Edit; 5 Delete; 6 Save; 7 Retrieve; 8 Update: 1
```

FIGURE 14.3:

A sample list of available styles

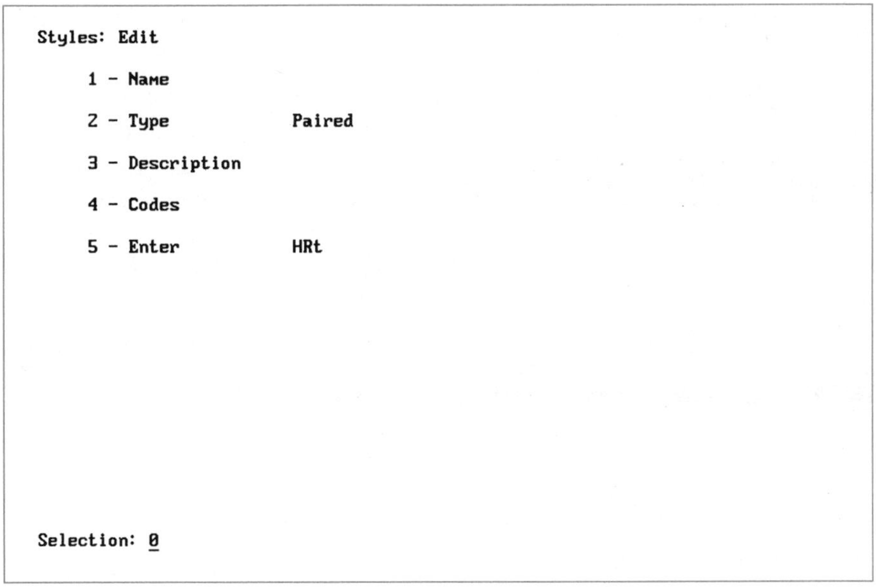

```
Styles: Edit

      1 - Name

      2 - Type          Paired

      3 - Description

      4 - Codes

      5 - Enter          HRt













 Selection: 0
```

FIGURE 14.4:

The screen for defining a style

document. In a moment, I'll talk about ways to use the style to make it accessible to multiple documents. First, though, I'll discuss the Enter option, which is used to change the role of the ↵ key.

Defining the Enter Key for Paired Styles

If you are creating a paired style, you might want to think about how you want the ↵ key to behave while the cursor is within the paired style. Your options are the following:

Hrt: ↵ works normally, inserting a hard-return [HRt] code. Use this option for paired codes that will be used to format text that's more than a single paragraph long or will contain hard returns. When using the style, you must press → to move the cursor past the [Style Off] code to end the style.

Off: ↵ terminates the style and activates any features defined in the [Style Off] code; best used with styles that define headings and other short lines of text that do not contain hard returns.

Off/On: ↵ turns off the style, activating the codes in the [Style Off] code, and then immediately reactivates the style. This is useful with a style that types a list or formats a series of paragraphs. When using the style you must press → to move the cursor past the [Style Off] code to end the style.

```
 ┌──────────────────────────────────────────────────────────────────┐
 │ Place Style On Codes above, and Style Off Codes below.           │
 └──────────────────────────────────────────────────────────────────┘




Style:  Press Exit when done                    Doc 1 Pg 1 Ln 1" Pos 1"
{                                                               }
[Comment]
```

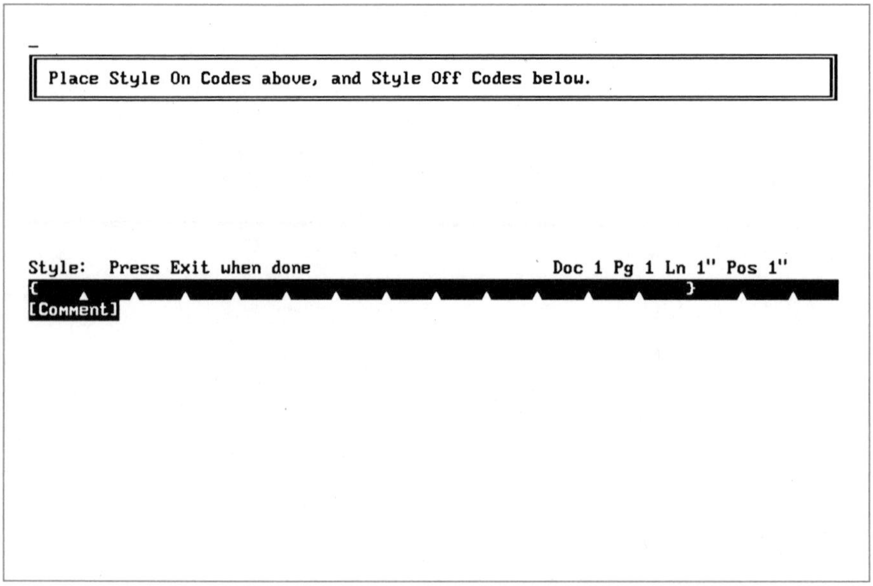

FIGURE 14.5:

The empty screen for creating a paired style

CREATING A STYLE FROM EXISTING CODES

TO COPY EXISTING CODES INTO A STYLE,

1. **Block the codes on the Reveal Codes screen.**

2. **Select Layout ➤ Styles ➤ Create ➤ Codes, or press Alt-F8 C C.**

3. **Press Exit (F7) to insert the codes automatically and return to the previous menu.**

4. **Enter a name and any other options you want for the new style.**

This method copies only hidden codes to the style, never any text.

If you've already formatted some text in a document (without using styles) and now want to use those formatting codes as a general style, you can easily do so. This is handy when you want to repeat the codes elsewhere in the same document or save them for use in other documents. Follow these steps:

1. Position the cursor near the codes you want to save as a style.

2. Select **Edit ➤ R**eveal Codes or press Reveal Codes (**Alt-F3** or **F11**) to make sure you can see the codes accurately.

3. Position the highlight on the first code to be used in the style.

4. Block all the codes to be used in the style by using the Block key (**Alt-F4** or **F12**) or your mouse. Be sure that the highlight extends past the last code you want to include in the style.

5. Select **L**ayout ➤ **S**tyles or press Style *(Alt-F8)* to display the Styles menu.

6. Select **C**reate to create a new style.

7. Select **C**odes. The lower window will show that the codes you blocked are now in the style.

8. Press Exit (**F7**) to insert the codes automatically and return to the Styles menu.

At the Styles menu, you can then select Name, Type, Description, or Enter to further define your new style. You can also select Codes to further refine the codes in your new style, or add text to it. Once you've finished defining your new style, press Exit (F7) until you return to the Edit screen, then use the style normally, as discussed in the following sections.

USING STYLES

> **TO USE AN EXISTING STYLE,**
>
> **1. Position the cursor where you're about to start typing new text, or block existing text.**
>
> **2. Select Layout ➤ Styles (or press Alt-F8).**
>
> **3. Highlight the name of the style you want to activate.**
>
> **4. Press ↵.**

Once you've created a style, using it is no different from using any other Word-Perfect feature: You can activate the style before you start typing new text, or you can block existing text and then turn on the style.

ACTIVATING A STYLE BEFORE YOU TYPE

You can activate a style before typing the text you want formatted. Just start at the Edit screen and follow these steps:

1. Position the cursor where you're about to type text that uses the style.

2. Select **L**ayout ➤ **S**tyles, or press Style (**Alt-F8**).

3. Use the arrow keys or the mouse to move the cursor to the style you want to use, then select **On**. (This is the default selection, so you can just press ↵ instead.)

4. Type your text. If you've activated an open style, skip the next step, since open styles can't be deactivated (you normally won't want to deactivate an open style anyway).

5. When you want to resume typing "unstyled" text, press → once to move the cursor beyond the [Style Off] code, or select **L**ayout ➤ **S**tyles (**Alt-F8**) and select **Off**. Alternatively, if you set the role of the Enter key to Off or Off/On, you can just press ↵ to move past the [Style Off] code and resume typing normal text.

If you want to turn off an open style, you must either select a different open style that cancels the codes in the style, or insert the equivalent codes on the Edit screen in the normal manner.

You can verify that the style has been activated by previewing your text on the View Document screen.

ACTIVATING A STYLE FOR EXISTING TEXT

If you've already typed some text, you can reformat it later with an existing style. Just follow these steps, starting at the Edit screen:

1. If you're activating an open style, move the cursor just before the text that should be formatted with the new style, or to the beginning of the document if you want to format all the text. If you're activating a paired style, block the text that you want to format.

2. Select **L**ayout ➤ **S**tyles, or press Style (**Alt-F8**).

3. Move the highlight bar to the style you want to use, then press ↵ to select the style.

After activating a style, you are returned to your document, and the codes and text from your style are in effect. You can verify this on the Reveal Codes or View Document screen.

HIDDEN CODES FOR STYLES

Whenever you format text with a paired style, WordPerfect inserts [Style On] codes where you activate the feature and [Style Off] codes where you deactivate it. The name of the style is included in the code. For example, Figure 14.6 shows a portion of the sample newsletter from Figure 14.2 on both the Edit and Reveal Codes screens. As you can see, the title "Celebrate with us" is formatted with a style named *Headline,* the line "by Jill Evans" is formatted with a style named *Byline,* and the text of the article is formatted with a style named *Body.*

When you move the highlight directly onto a [Style On] or [Style Off] code, the code expands, and you can see the actual formatting codes within the style, including any codes that were automatically determined by Word-Perfect in the [Style Off] code when you first created the style.

Open styles are activated with an [Open Style] code, which includes the name of the style. There is no closing code for an open style, since an open style is designed to format all text below the code.

CHANGING A STYLE

TO ALTER AN EXISTING STYLE,

1. Select Layout ➤ Styles (or press Alt-F8).

2. Highlight the name of the style you want to edit.

3. Select Edit, and choose whichever element of the style you want to change.

You can edit the codes in WordPerfect's prepackaged styles the same way you edit a style you created yourself.

If you decide that a style is not doing exactly what you want, you can edit the style by using the same basic techniques you used to create it.

1. Select **L**ayout ➤ **S**tyles, or press Style (**Alt-F8**).

2. Highlight the name of the style you want to change.

3. Select **E**dit. The Styles Edit screen for the selected style appears—it's the same screen you worked with when you created the style.

4. You can change the style's name, type, and description, and the function of the ↵ key, using techniques you learned for creating a style. To change the formatting codes within the style, select **C**odes. You'll be taken to the screen for entering and changing formatting codes.

5. Insert and delete codes and text for the style by using the usual Word-Perfect editing techniques. If you're editing a paired style, remember that actions to be performed when the style is activated go before the [Comment] code, and actions to be performed when the style is deactivated go after the [Comment] code.

6. Press Exit (**F7**) three times to return to the Edit screen.

```
Celebrate with us
by Jill Evans

In honor of our newsletter's maiden voyage,
we'd like to invite you to an Open House at
7:00pm on January 11, 1991, at our offices.
Please dress casually or come in your most
fashionable travel togs.


Tropical travel
                                    Col 1 Doc 1 Pg 1 Ln 6.72" Pos 1"
```
```
{                              }        {
[Style On:Headline]Celebrate with us[Style Off:Headline][HRt]
[Style On:Byline]by Jill Evans[Style Off:Byline][HRt]
[HRt]
[Style On:Body]In honor of our newsletter's maiden voyage,[SRt]
we'd like to invite you to an Open House at[SRt]
7:00pm on January 11, 1991, at our offices.[SRt]
Please dress casually or come in your most[SRt]
fashionable travel togs.[Style Off:Body][HRt]
[HRt]
[Style On:Headline]Tropical travel[Style Off:Headline][HRt]

Press Reveal Codes to restore screen
```

FIGURE 14.6:

[Style On] and [Style Off] codes on the Reveal Codes screen

If the style has been used anywhere in the current document, the text affected by it will be reformatted automatically to reflect the changes you have made.

REMOVING A STYLE FROM TEXT

If you apply the wrong style to part of your document, or if you decide that one section doesn't require special formatting after all, you can delete the style without going to the Styles menu and without affecting the use of the same style elsewhere in the document. To do so, simply go to the Reveal Codes screen, move the cursor to the [Style On] or [Open Style] code that's activating the style you want to deactivate, then press Delete to delete the code.

For a paired style, both the [Style On] code and the [Style Off] code are deleted automatically, regardless of which one was highlighted when you pressed Delete. Note that any text that was part of the style itself (*not* text you typed between the two style codes) is deleted along with the style's formats.

HANDS-ON
LESSON 6

See Lesson 6 in Part 9 for a hands-on exercise in creating similar styles.

SAMPLE STYLES AS FOOD FOR THOUGHT

Take a look at some sample styles now, referring back to Figure 14.2, to give you some food for thought when creating your own styles. Each style in this section was created using the general steps described at the outset of this chapter, and each can be used either before typing text or after blocking existing text.

EXAMPLES OF PAIRED STYLES

A paired style is used to format a short passage of text, for example, to define the font and text appearances of titles, headings, margin notes, footnotes, lists, and other elements of text that are used consistently throughout a document. Using paired styles is also a good means of storing frequently used special symbols, such as bullets or "graphic" quotation marks, since a style name is easier to remember than a Ctrl-V code. In short, a paired style can be used for any element in a document that has a beginning and an end. Sample paired styles are discussed in the following sections.

The codes in styles appear only in the Reveal Codes window, at the bottom of the screen.

A Paired Style to Format Headlines

Figure 14.7 shows a paired style named *Headline* that was used to format the headlines (article titles) in the sample newsletter in Figure 14.2.

Here are the codes used in the style:

*Condition-
al End of
Page is
covered in
Chapter 7.*

[Cndl EOP:4][HRt]: This code was inserted in the style by selecting **L**ayout (Shift-F8), then **O**ther ➤ **C**onditional End of Page, entering *4*, and pressing ↵ twice. The conditional end of page keeps the article title, byline, and first line of text together (preventing them from being split across two pages or two columns).

[Font: Univers Bold Italic (Scalable) 16pt]: This code was inserted by selecting F**o**nt ➤ Base F**o**nt (Ctrl-F8 F) and choosing the font and point size for printing article titles.

*Normally,
you do not
need to
bother with
inserting closing codes
in styles. Exceptions to
this rule include Table
of Contents and List
features, and Block
Protect. For these fea-
tures, you must first
move the highlight to
the [Comment] code in
the style, press Block
(Alt-F4 or F12), then
press → before select-
ing the feature.*

[Mark: ToC,1][End Mark: ToC,1]: This code pair is entirely optional and was entered by blocking the [Comment] code (placing the cursor on the code and pressing Alt-F4 then →), then selecting **M**ark ➤ Table of **C**ontents, and entering *1* as the Table of Contents level. This makes it easy to automatically generate a table of contents when the newsletter is finished. (See Chapter 23 for additional information.)

After creating the style and exiting the screen, you can set the Enter option to either HRt or Off, depending on whether you want to be able to turn off the style by pressing → or ↵.

A Paired Style to Format Bylines

The paired style for formatting bylines is shown in Figure 14.8, again on the screen for editing the codes in a style.

FIGURE 14.7:

A sample paired style to format article titles in the newsletter in Figure 14.2

```
                                                              Doc 1 Pg 1 Ln 1" Pos 1"

Place Style On Codes above, and Style Off Codes below.




Style:   Press Exit when done
[
[Cndl EOP:4][HRt]
[Font:Univers Bold Italic (Scalable) 16pt][Mark:ToC,1][Comment][End Mark:ToC,1]
```

This simple style uses these two formatting features:

[LARGE]: This code was entered by selecting Font ➤ Large (Ctrl-F8 S L) to format the byline using the same typeface as body text, but slightly larger.

[ITALC]: This code, entered by selecting Font ➤ Appearance ➤ Italics (Ctrl-F8 A I), displays the byline in italic style.

Note that, even though [LARGE] and [ITALC] are paired codes, it's not necessary to place the closing codes (e.g., [Large] and [Italc]) to the right of [Comment], since paired codes do this automatically. Again, after saving the codes, you can select either HRt or Off as the role of the Enter key, depending on whether you'd prefer to end the style by pressing → or ↵.

A Paired Style to Format Body Text

The style for formatting the body of text in each article is shown in Figure 14.9. This style has no codes in front of the [Comment] code and the following codes to the right of the [Comment] code:

[Flsh Rgt]: This code, entered by selecting **L**ayout ➤ **A**lign ➤ **F**lush Right (or pressing Alt-F6), moves the cursor to the right margin (or right edge of the column).

[*:5,6]: This code, entered by pressing Ctrl-V 5 6 and pressing ↵, is the Compose character (Chapter 5) for the little sunshine graphic used at the end of each article.

After saving the codes for this particular style, by pressing Exit (F7), you'll want to be sure the Enter option is set to HRt so that ↵ behaves normally

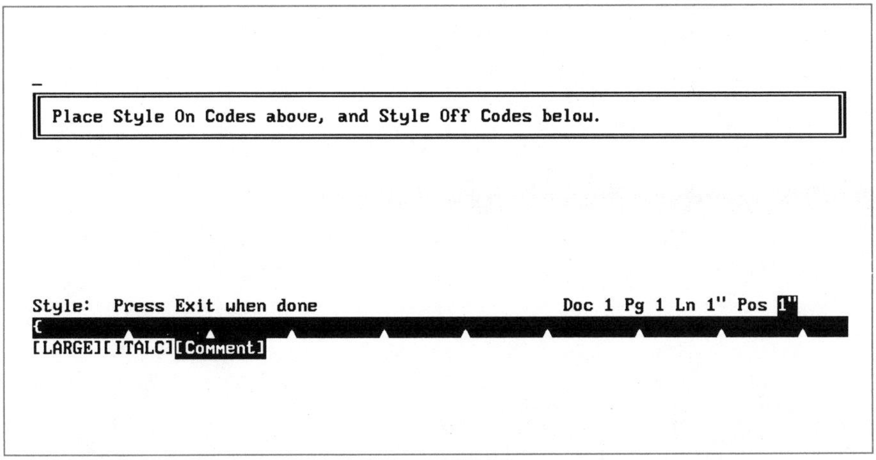

Both the Byline and Body Text styles in these examples use the default base font for the overall document or the base font specified just above the first article title. They could, however, contain their own [Font] code to specify any font you wish.

FIGURE 14.8:

A sample style for formatting bylines

```
 ┌─────────────────────────────────────────────────────────┐
 │ │ Place Style On Codes above, and Style Off Codes below. │
 └─────────────────────────────────────────────────────────┘



 Style:  Press Exit when done              Doc 1 Pg 1 Ln 1" Pos 1
 [LARGE][ITALC][Comment]
```

and does not turn off the style. This prevents the ⏎ entered between multiple paragraphs typed in this style from turning off the style.

EXAMPLES OF OPEN STYLES

If you try out any of these open styles, remember that most of the features they use appear only on the View Document screen and the printed copy of the document.

An open style is generally used to set the format of an entire document, such as margins, paper size and type, columns, and so forth. For example, you can use an open style to predefine a commonly used combination of paper size, margins, and spacing. That way, when you need to create a document with that particular paper format, you simply need to select the appropriate style rather than bothering to select all the formatting codes.

With some ingenuity and experience, you can also create advanced styles that use more sophisticated WordPerfect features. In all these examples, keep in mind that you could place the same codes at the top of any document, without using a style, and come up with the same results. But ease of use is the clear advantage gained by placing the codes in a style. You can easily activate the style in each new document you create, rather than going through the steps required to enter each code independently.

An Open Style to Format a Brochure

Figure 14.10 shows an example of a style that prints text sideways on the page and divides it into three columns, making it easy to create three-fold brochures.

FIGURE 14.9:

A paired style to format body text

Here is a list of the various codes placed in the style and what they do:

[Paper Sz/Typ:11" x 8.5", Standard][T/B Mar:0.5",0.5"]: These codes were inserted by choosing options from the **L**ayout ➤ **P**age menu (Shift-F8 P) to select landscape (sideways) printing and top and bottom margins of ½ inch.

[L/R Mar:0.5",0.5"][Just:Left]: These codes were inserted by choosing options from the **L**ayout ➤ **L**ine menu (Shift-F8 L) to change the left and right margins, and set justification to Left.

[Col Def:Newspaper...][Col On]: These codes were inserted by choosing **L**ayout ➤ **C**olumns (Alt-F7 C) and defining three columns across the page (Chapter 20).

[VLine:Column 1...]: These codes were inserted by choosing **G**raphics ➤ **L**ine ➤ Create **V**ertical (Alt-F9 L V) and positioning the graphic line between columns.

See Chapter 20 for more information on creating multicolumn documents.

Figure 14.11 shows how the style, when used alone and viewed on the View Document screen, prints lines between columns on a sheet of paper. Figure 14.12 shows an example where the style was used to format a three-fold brochure, complete with text and graphics.

An Open Style to Print a Letterhead

If you have a laser (or other high-quality printer), you can design and develop your own letterhead with WordPerfect, then place it in a style. When you need to type on letterhead, just select the letterhead style and type your letter. Then insert a plain sheet of paper in the printer, and print your document. You'll

---

FIGURE 14.10:

An open style for typing brochures

```
−




Style:   Press Exit when done              Col 1 Doc 1 Pg 1 Ln 0.5" Pos 0.5"
{                        }   {                        }   {
[Paper Sz/Typ:11" x 8.5",Standard][T/B Mar:0.5",0.5"][L/R Mar:0.5",0.5"][Just:Le
ft][Col Def:Newspaper;3;0.5",3.5";4",7";7.5",10.5"][Col On][VLine:Column 1,Full
Page,7.5",0.013",100%][VLine:Column 2,Full Page,7.5",0.013",100%]█
```

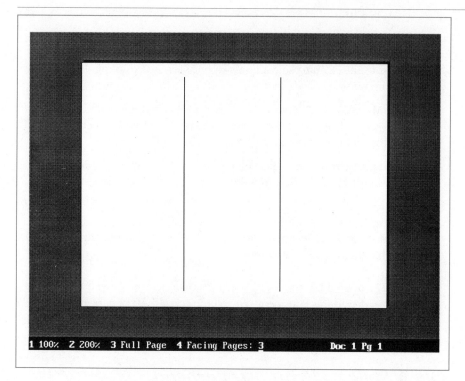

1 100%   2 200%   3 Full Page   4 Facing Pages: 3   Doc 1 Pg 1

FIGURE 14.11:

An example of an open style used to format a blank page into three columns

Charters	Hot Air Balloons		Seasonal		CALENDAR OF EVENTS
	Paddle Boats				
	Helicopters	Spring	MARCH		
			Run for Fun		
Cultural Events	Paramount		Heart Builders		Weekend Activities for Visitors
	Square				
	Fifth Opera		APRIL		
	Stage		Jenson County Golf		
	Scott Balk Center		Tournament		
	Symphonic Arts		Governor's Cup Sailing		
	Jackson Center				
	Center for the		MAY		
	Arts		County Trail Run		
	Bates Assembly		10K for Health		
Entertainment	Laffs on Us	Summer	JUNE		
	Jamison Theater		Quarterhorse		
	Cross Center		Racing		
	Auditorium Five		City Marathon		
	Theater for Art				
	Public Dance		JULY		
			Fiesta		
Museums	Orl Southwest		Riverfest		
& Galleries	Gallery				
	Geoffrey Gallery		AUGUST		
	Santa Fe Style		Symphony Outdoor Series		
	Dillman Museum				
	Art in Sound	Fall	SEPTEMBER		
			Riverfront School Festival		
			OCTOBER		
			Pumpkin Pick		
			City Hall Masquerade		
					City of Metropolis
		Winter	DECEMBER		Chamber of Commerce
			Capital Christmas		345 Main Street
			Santa's Visit		Metropolis, AZ 12345
			New Year's Gala		(999) 555-3452

FIGURE 14.12:

The open style used in Figure 14.11, as the basic format for typing a three-fold brochure

see that both your letterhead and the letter will be printed for you. Figure 14.13 shows a sample letterhead that was created by selecting a letterhead style and printing the document on plain paper.

Figure 14.14 shows the style editing screen for the open style used to create the letterhead.

Here's how each code in the style works:

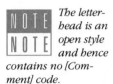

The letterhead is an open style and hence contains no [Comment] code.

[T/B Mar:0.5",1"]: entered with **L**ayout ➤ **P**age ➤ **M**argins (Shift-F8 P M); sets the top margin to ½ inch.

[Usr Box:1;GLOBE2-M.WPG;]: entered with **G**raphics ➤ **U**ser Box ➤ **C**reate (Alt-F9 U C); contains the WordPerfect GLOBE2-M image with a width of 1.5 inches, page-anchored to the top-left corner of the page; and **W**rap Text Around Box set to No.

[Font…]: Each font code was entered with **F**ont ➤ Base F**o**nt (Ctrl-F8 F).

[Flsh Rgt]: Each flush-right code was entered by pressing Flush Right (Alt-F6).

[Ln Height:0.026"]: entered with **L**ayout ➤ **L**ine ➤ Line **H**eight ➤ **F**ixed (Shift-F8 L H F), and set at 0.026". This sets the height of the gap between the two horizontal lines that appear below the company address.

[HLine:…]: Both horizontal lines were entered with **G**raphics ➤ **L**ine ➤ Create **H**orizontal (Alt-F9 L H). The top line is 0.013" wide, the bottom one is 0.026" wide, and a blank line ([HRt]) separates the two lines.

MegaCorp Int'l.

1234 Xanadu Lane
Ponto, CA 92007
(619)555-0123

FIGURE 14.13:

A sample letterhead created and printed with WordPerfect

[Ln Height:Auto]: entered with Layout ➤ Line ➤ Line Height ➤ **A**uto (Shift-F8 L H A) to resume automatic line height for text that will follow in the letter.

An Open Style to Frame Text

The graphic frame can only be printed by a printer that prints graphics.

An open style to frame text prints a solid border around each printed page of a document. Figure 14.15 shows a sample page on the View Document screen, where you can easily see both the edge of the paper and the printed frame.

This style uses an empty Figure box (Chapter 19) in a page header to print the frame around each page. To get the frame to print on every page, it must be treated as a page header. This makes it a slightly tricky style to create because it consists of a graphic box inside a page header inside a style. Figure 14.16 shows the style as it appears on the screen for editing style codes.

If you'd like to try it out, follow these steps to create the style:

1. Starting at a blank Edit screen, select **L**ayout ➤ **S**tyles ↵ **C**reate (or press **Alt-F8 C**).

2. Select **N**ame, enter a name (such as *Full Frame*), and press ↵.

3. Select **T**ype ➤ **O**pen.

4. Select **D**escription and type a description, such as *Print a frame around text on each page,* then press ↵.

5. Select **C**odes.

```
                              MegaCorp Int'l.
                              1234 Xanadu Lane
  —                           Ponto, CA 92007
                                (619)555-0123




Style:   Press Exit when done                 Doc 1 Pg 1 Ln 1" Pos 1"
[                                              ]
[T/B Mar:0.5",1"][Usr Box:1;GLOBE2-M.WPG;][Font:×Univers Bold Italic (Scalable)
24pt][Flsh Rgt]MegaCorp Int'l.[HRt]
[Font:×Univers Italic (Scalable) 12pt][Flsh Rgt]1234 Xanadu Lane[HRt]
[Flsh Rgt]Ponto, CA 92007[HRt]
[Flsh Rgt](619)555[-]0123[HRt]
[Ln Height:0.026"][HLine:Full,Baseline,6.5",0.013",100%][HRt]
[HRt]
[HLine:Full,Baseline,6.5",0.026",100%][HRt]
[Ln Height:Auto]
```

FIGURE 14.14:
An open style for printing a sample letterhead

6. From the pull-down menus, select **L**ayout ➤ **P**age (or press **Shift-F8 P**). Then choose **H**eaders ➤ Header **A** ➤ Every **P**age. Press Exit (**F7**).

7. Using the pull-down menus again, select **G**raphics (or press **Alt-F9**). Then choose **F**igure ➤ **C**reate ➤ **A**nchor Type ➤ **P**age, then press ↵ to accept page 0.

8. Select **H**orizontal Position ➤ **M**argins ➤ **F**ull.

9. Select **S**ize ➤ Set **B**oth, and enter the width as 6.5 inches and the height as 8.5 inches (press ↵ after each entry).

10. Select **W**rap Text Around Box ➤ **N**o.

11. Press Exit (**F7**) until you return to the style-code editing screen.

Increasing the default 1-inch margins in steps 12 and 13 ensures some extra space between the inside of your page border and any text you type on the page.

12. From the menus, select **L**ayout ➤ **P**age ➤ **M**argins (or press **Shift-F8 P M**), and enter top and bottom margins of your choosing (the example uses 1.25" and 1.5"). Press ↵ to return to the Format menu.

13. Select **L**ine ➤ **M**argins and enter left and right margins of your choosing (the example uses 1.5" and 1.5"). Press Exit (**F7**) until you return to the Styles: Edit menu.

14. Press Exit (**F7**) to return to the Edit screen.

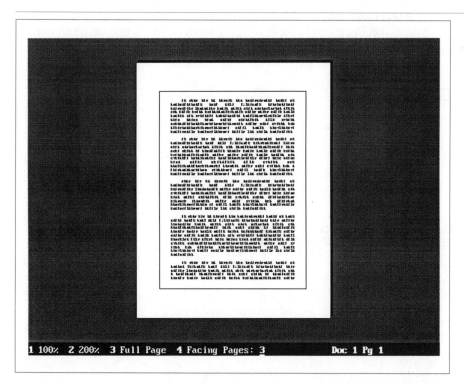

FIGURE 14.15:
A frame printed around text with an open style

To test your new style, make sure the cursor is at the top of the first page, then use **Layout** ➤ **S**tyles (or press Alt-F8), highlight the new style, and press ↵, as described earlier. Type in some text, and use the View Document screen's full-page view (press Shift-F7 V 3) to view your page. If you want to use the style in a variety of documents, be sure to save it in a style library, as discussed later in "Saving a Set of Styles."

A REPEATING STYLE TO TYPE A LIST

A *repeating* style is just a paired style with the Enter option set to Off/On. Figure 14.17 shows an example of a style that helps you type a bulleted list without manually typing the special bullet codes, indents, and extra space between list entries.

Here is a list of the codes that were entered in the style and what they do:

[Tab]: entered by pressing Tab; indents the bullet one tab stop.

[•:4,3]: entered by pressing Ctrl-V 4 3 ↵; this inserts the bullet automatically.

[→Indent]: entered by pressing →Indent (F4); indents the text to the right of the bullet.

[HRt][HRt]: entered by moving the cursor to the right of the [Comment] code, then pressing ↵ twice; inserts a blank line between each item in the bulleted list.

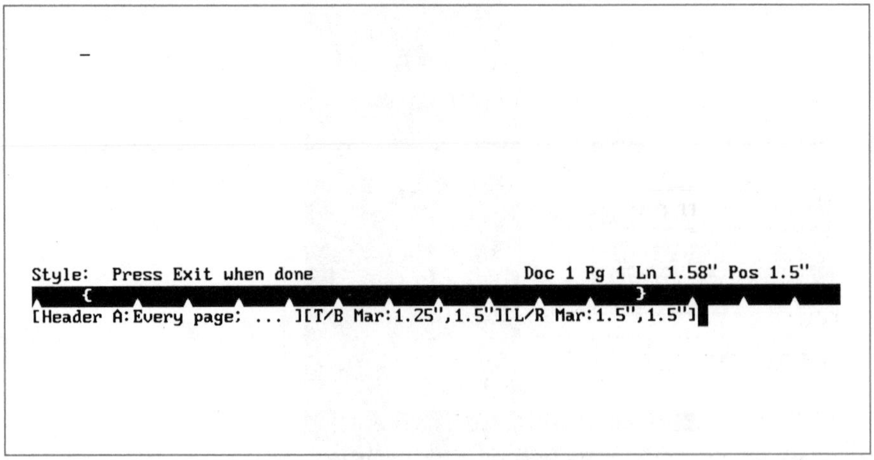

```
─




Style:  Press Exit when done                Doc 1 Pg 1 Ln 1.58" Pos 1.5"
        {                                                   }
[Header A:Every page;  ... ][T/B Mar:1.25",1.5"][L/R Mar:1.5",1.5"]
```

FIGURE 14.16:

A style for printing a frame around text on every page

After entering and saving the codes for this style, you choose the Enter option, and change it to Off/On. Press Exit (F7) to return to the Edit screen when you're finished creating the style. After you activate the style, it types the bullet and indent for the first item automatically. You type the text for the bulleted list, and press ↵. A blank line, the bullet, and the indent for the next item in the list appear automatically. Repeat this until you've typed each item in the bulleted list (do not press ↵ after typing the last item in the list). Then press → to move the cursor past the [Style Off] code, and resume typing normal text.

SAVING A SET OF STYLES

TO USE A STYLE IN MORE THAN ONE DOCUMENT, you must first save the style in a library by selecting Layout ➤ Styles ➤ Save or by pressing Alt-F8 S.

When you create a style or several styles, then save the overall document, the styles are saved with that document and can only be used in that document. However, you can build up a collection of "generic" styles for use in several documents by saving your styles in a separate *style library,* which will be available to all documents.

For example, if you print a monthly newsletter, you can create a collection of styles called NEWSLET.STY for formatting the newsletter. If you also happen to be working on a book, you can create another style library named BOOK.STY, that contains styles relevant to the book.

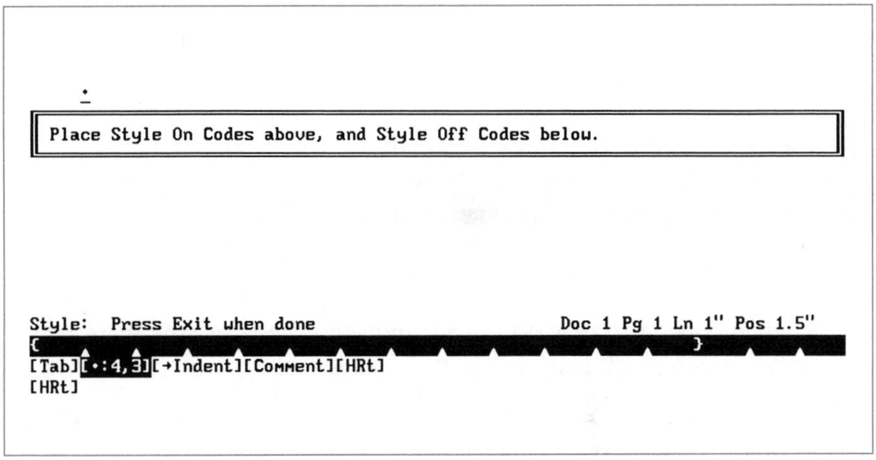

```
                       ⋮

 ┌───────────────────────────────────────────────────────┐
 │ Place Style On Codes above, and Style Off Codes below. │
 └───────────────────────────────────────────────────────┘




Style:   Press Exit when done                 Doc 1 Pg 1 Ln 1" Pos 1.5"
[
[Tab][•:4,3][→Indent][Comment][HRt]
[HRt]
```

FIGURE 14.17:

A style to format a bulleted list

When you first install WordPerfect, it automatically displays its own sample style library, named LIBRARY.STY. This library contains seven sample styles, described a little later in the chapter. To create and save your own style library, follow these steps:

1. From the Edit screen, select **L**ayout ➤ **S**tyles or press Style (**Alt-F8**).

2. Optionally, delete any styles that you do not want to save in the current library (such as some of the examples provided by WordPerfect), by highlighting the name of the unwanted style and selecting **D**elete ➤ **I**ncluding Codes.

3. Select **S**ave. The following prompt appears:

   Filename:

4. Type a file name for the current set of styles, and press ↵. Include the path if you don't want to store them in the usual style file directory. If you want to *replace* a style library, you must use the same name as the existing style-library file.

5. If you are replacing an existing library, you'll be asked to verify the replacement. Select **Y**es to replace the library with the new list of styles, or select **N**o to enter a different file name.

WordPerfect saves the styles in the current listing as a file and leaves you at the Styles menu with the same styles available. Be sure to save or replace a style library whenever you add, change, or delete any styles within that library; otherwise, the saved library will no longer match the library in the current document.

RETRIEVING A STYLE LIBRARY

TO USE A STYLE IN THE CURRENT DOCUMENT THAT YOU'VE PREVIOUSLY SAVED IN A STYLE LIBRARY,

select Layout ➤ Styles ➤ Retrieve (or press Alt-F8 R), and enter the file name of the library containing the style or styles you want to use.

When you're in a new document, and you want to use the styles you've previously saved in a library, follow these steps:

1. Starting at the Edit screen, select **L**ayout ➤ **S**tyles or press Style (**Alt-F8**) to view the current style library.

2. Optionally, delete any styles from the current library that you do not want to use in the current document, by moving the highlight to the name of any unwanted style and selecting **D**elete ➤ **I**ncluding Codes.

3. Select **R**etrieve. You see the following prompt:

Filename:

In place of step 4, you can press List (F5) and enter a drive/path to view existing file names. Then highlight the style file you want and select Retrieve.

4. Type the file name of the style library you want to use, including any necessary path information, and press ↵.

5. If any of the styles in the current style library has the same name as a style in the library you are retrieving, WordPerfect will ask

Style(s) already exist. Replace? No (Yes)

Because styles in a retrieved style library are combined with existing styles, you can easily use styles from several separate libraries in any single document.

6. If you want to replace the current styles with the incoming styles, select **Y**es. Otherwise, select **N**o to avoid replacing any existing styles (this way, the unique styles will be combined with the existing styles, but the existing styles won't be changed).

The styles in the retrieved file will appear in your Styles menu, along with any that were already listed. The listing is alphabetized automatically. If you save the current document, all the styles in it at that point are saved with it.

DELETING A STYLE FROM A LIBRARY

If a particular style library contains a style that you don't really want, you can easily delete the style. Here's how:

1. Select **L**ayout ➤ **S**tyles or press Style (**Alt-F8**) to get to the list of available styles.

2. Move the highlight to the name of the style that you want to delete.

3. Select **D**elete from the menu, or press **Delete**. You'll see the options shown below:

Delete Styles: 1 Leaving Codes; 2 Including Codes; 3 Definition Only: 0

These options are summarized below:

Leaving Codes: deletes the style from the library. However, any hidden codes that were contained in the style remain in the current document, replacing the [Style On], [Style Off], and [Open Style] codes that were deleted.

Including Codes: deletes the style from the library and also deletes the hidden codes from the document that were contained within the [Style On], [Style Off], and [Open Style] codes.

If you want to build a new style library from scratch, first delete all the styles in the current library by choosing the Including Codes option.

Definition Only: deletes the style from the menu of style names, but has no effect on the document itself. You can use this option to help you determine which styles are actually used in your document. To do this, delete the name of every style in the list of available styles, then return to the Edit screen and scroll through the entire document (e.g., press Home Home Home ↑, then Home Home ↓). WordPerfect will automatically re-create the list of styles, using only the names of styles actually used in the current document.

The style is deleted from the list of available styles immediately. Don't forget to save the entire library again (using **L**ayout ➤ **S**tyles ➤ **S**ave or Alt-F8 S) if you want to update the copy of the library on-disk as well as the copy in the current document.

GENERAL TIPS FOR USING STYLES

Learning to use styles effectively is largely a matter of recognizing when you will be using a format repeatedly throughout a document or several documents, and having the foresight to predefine that format as a style to save time and effort down the road. The sections that follow contain some tips that will help you as you gain experience and learn to use styles to your advantage.

MANAGING YOUR STYLE LIBRARIES

If you work on lots of different kinds of documents and need to create numerous style libraries, there are several things you can do to keep your libraries organized:

◆ Assign the same file-name extension, such as *.STY,* to all style libraries, so you can easily recognize them by name.

◆ Store all your style libraries in the same directory. You can select **F**iles ➤ **S**etup ➤ **L**ocation of Files or press Shift-F1 L to specify a directory. Be sure to move any existing style libraries to that directory if you change the location.

◆ Create a library of general-purpose styles, and make this the default library that appears automatically when you first run WordPerfect. After you create, name, and save this library, make it the default library by selecting **F**ile ➤ **S**etup ➤ **L**ocation of Files (or pressing Shift-F1 L) and specifying its name at the second prompt, "Library Filename".

◆ Because styles are stored with individual documents, as well as in style libraries, it's often difficult to keep track of the most recent version of a style that's been modified. If you type the date of the most recent revision to a style as part of the style's description, you'll find it easier to know which version of a style is available in the current document.

◆ If you are using the default style library, and you want to make sure the styles in the current document are up to date, select **L**ayout ➤ **S**tyles ➤ **U**pdate or press Alt-F8 U. All the styles from the default library on-disk will be read into the current document, without asking you for permission to replace existing styles that have the same name.

The default style library is the one whose name is listed on the Location of Files menu.

SEARCHING FOR STYLES

When using the Search and Replace feature (Chapter 9), you can search for the generic style codes, such as [Style On], [Style Off], and [Open Style]. But you cannot search for a specific, named style. This can be inconvenient, but Chapter 26 presents a macro that can locate a specific style.

GRAPHICS IMAGES IN STYLES

If you include a graphic image in a style, you must specify Graphic on Disk as the graphic type. Consequently, you can only print that document on a computer that also has a copy of the graphic image (that image must be stored on the same drive and directory as was specified when you created the graphic). For more information, see Chapter 19.

NESTING STYLES

You can nest styles while using them, but you cannot use a style as part of another style while creating or editing a style's codes.

Nesting is a technique where you use one paired code or paired style as part of another. You may have already used nesting if you applied both bold and underline to some text before you typed it. If you nest paired styles, the result is the same as nesting any other paired style: The formats are combined (provided that one does not cancel the other). For example, if Style ABC formats text for boldface, and Style XYZ formats text for italics, then the codes and text

[Style On:ABC][Style On:XYZ]Hello**[Style Off:ABC][Style Off:XYZ]**

print the word *Hello* in boldface and italics.

STYLES VS. MACROS

A macro records keystrokes and plays them back just as they were recorded. As you'll learn in Chapter 15, you can activate a macro with a simple combination keystroke (for example, Alt-H), which requires fewer keystrokes than selecting a style. However, styles are far easier to change than codes in a macro.

If you want the editing convenience of styles, along with the keystroke convenience of macros, create the style first, then create a macro to activate the style. See Chapter 15 for more information.

OVERCOMING STYLE LIMITATIONS

Not all codes work with or can be used in styles. Such codes are simply ignored when you try to enter them in a style. For example, you cannot place [Col On] and [Col Off] codes in a style to manage columns.

One way around this is to create a macro that inserts the codes that the style cannot, and also activates the style so that you still get the best of both worlds—the keystroke savings of macros with the editing ease of styles. Another way to overcome style limitations is to place the code you want in the document, via the regular Edit screen, then move or copy the code into a style. This works well for many codes that you would normally access by selecting **M**ark ➤ **D**efine, which is bracketed on the pull-down menus, has no effect when you press the shortcut keys, and is therefore unavailable while you're on the code-editing screen for a style.

EXPLORING WORDPERFECT'S SAMPLE STYLES

As mentioned earlier, WordPerfect comes with seven sample styles for you to explore. If you haven't already changed the default style library, you can view the style names by selecting **L**ayout ➤ **S**tyle or pressing Alt-F8. Figure 14.18 shows them listed on the screen.

To view the codes within any style, simply select **L**ayout ➤ **S**tyles (or press Alt-F8), highlight the name of the style, and select **E**dit ➤ **C**odes. After looking at the codes, press Exit (F7) twice to return to the style list. Descriptions of each style follow:

Bibliography: hangs (outdents) the first line of a paragraph and ends each paragraph with two hard returns. To try it, activate the style, and type several brief paragraphs (slightly wider than the screen), pressing ↵ after typing each one. Press → to move out of the style.

You can use the Document, Right Par, and Technical styles in conjunction with automatic outlining and numbering (see Chapter 22).

Doc Init: automatically puts in the codes needed to generate a table of contents from [Mark: Toc] codes within the document, when placed near the top of the document. It also turns on automatic paragraph numbering and outlining. (See Part 7 for more information about automatic referencing.)

Document: An outline style designed for use immediately after selecting Doc Init and pressing →. This style inserts a table-of-contents entry, aligns outline numbers on the decimal point, centers very large, bold text, and turns on kerning.

Pleading: An open style that places line numbers and a graphic line in the left margin. Activate this style near the top of an empty Edit screen, and switch to View Document to view the result.

Right Par: An outline style that right-aligns the outline numbers. For example, if you type a list of ten items in legal format, the number *1* preceding the first item and the *0* in the number *10* preceding the last item line up with one another.

Tech Init: An open style that defines the numbering style for a technical outline and turns on automatic outlining.

Technical: An outline style, designed for use immediately after selecting Tech Init above, to type the technical outline. The technical outline style has one line or paragraph of numbered text in very large, bold type and another line or paragraph of unnumbered text in normal type.

```
Styles

   Name         Type      Description

   Bibliogrphy  Paired    Bibliography
   Doc Init     Paired    Initialize Document Style
   Document     Outline   Document Style
   Pleading     Open      Header for numbered pleading paper
   Right Par    Outline   Right-Aligned Paragraph Numbers
   Tech Init    Open      Initialize Technical Style
   Technical    Outline   Technical Document Style
```

```
 1 On; 2 Off; 3 Create; 4 Edit; 5 Delete; 6 Save; 7 Retrieve; 8 Update: 1
```

FIGURE 14.18:

A list of the sample styles that come with WordPerfect

In this chapter you've learned about the Styles feature, which can make some of your bigger projects more manageable, lend consistency to the appearance of your documents, and save you considerable time.

In the next chapter, you'll learn about another timesaving feature: Macros.

CHAPTER 15

Saving Time with Macros

acros help you automate some of your more mundane, repetitive word processing tasks by letting you record all the necessary keystrokes to perform those tasks, then "play back" those keystrokes at any time with just a few keypresses.

HANDS-ON
....
LESSON 8

*To create some
macros that can
simplify your
work right now,
see Lesson 8 in
Part 9.*

Though the term "macro" sounds somewhat mysterious, macros are easy to use and have something for everyone. If you know how to perform a task in WordPerfect, you can probably just as easily create a macro to perform it for you more quickly and easily in the future. Anytime you find yourself typing the same text or selecting the same series of menu options over and over, remember that you can just record those keystrokes in a macro, and play them back as often as you wish with just a couple of keypresses.

WHAT IS A MACRO?

Macro is the opposite of micro (small). In a sense, a macro is a "large keystroke," because a single macro keystroke can perform many keystrokes. For example, if you have to type your company name many times, in many documents, you might want to record those keystrokes in a macro.

In the future, whenever you need to type your company name, you don't need to type it over again. Instead, just run the macro and let it do the typing. Once you create a macro, you can reuse it as many times as you wish. Options for creating (defining) a macro, as well as for executing (running) a macro, are both available by selecting **T**ools ➤ **Ma**cro (Figure 15.1) or by pressing the shortcut key Macro Define (**Ctrl-F10**) or Macro (**Alt-F10**), as described below.

CREATING A MACRO

TO RECORD KEYSTROKES IN A MACRO,

1. Select Tools ➤ Macro ➤ Define (or press Ctrl-F10).

2. Enter a name and optional description for the macro.

3. Type the keystrokes you want to record.

4. When you're finished recording, select Tools ➤ Macro ➤ Define or press Ctrl-F10 again.

Creating a macro is easy; just follow these steps:

1. Select **T**ools ➤ **Ma**cro ➤ **D**efine (or press **Ctrl-F10**), and enter a name from one to eight characters in length (no spaces or punctuation), or press an Alt-key combination (the difference is described in "Naming a Macro").

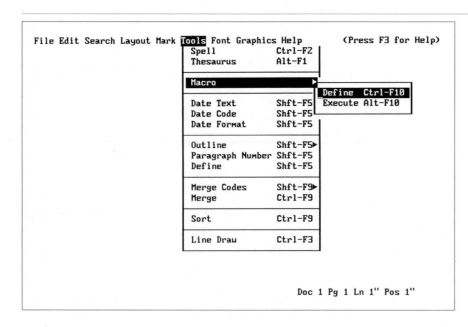

FIGURE 15.1:

Options for creating and running macros on the Macro submenu

2. If a macro with the name you've entered already exists, you'll be prompted to replace, edit, or change the description of the existing macro (described under "Editing a Macro" later in this chapter). Choose an option.

3. At the "Description" prompt, enter a plain-English description up to 39 characters long, and press ↵.

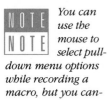

You can use the mouse to select pull-down menu options while recording a macro, but you cannot use it to position the cursor in your document (use the cursor keys instead).

4. The blinking "Macro Def" indicator in the lower-left corner of the screen indicates that keystrokes are now being recorded. Type whatever keystrokes you want to record, including any menu selections and shortcut keypresses.

5. When you've finished recording keystrokes, select **T**ools ➤ **M**acro ➤ **D**efine, or press **Ctrl-F10** again.

Before I talk about how to run (play back) your macro, I'll discuss some of the options you'll come across while creating the macro.

NAMING A MACRO

The first prompt you see when creating a new macro is "Define macro:", in which WordPerfect requests a name for the macro. You can assign two types of names to a macro at this point:

◆ Alt-*letter* macros

◆ Named macros

Alt-*letter* macros are assigned to the various Alt-letter key combinations on the keyboard, such as *Alt-A, Alt-B,* and so on. When asked for the macro's name in the macro-definition process, you press the Alt-*letter* key combination you want assigned to that macro. For example, to name a macro *Alt-H,* you hold down the Alt key, type the letter **H** (upper- or lowercase), then release both keys.

The longer macro names, from one to eight characters in length, are actually file names. The type of name you assign to a macro determines how you later run the macros:

◆ If you assign an Alt-*letter* name to a macro, you can run the macro in the future simply by holding down the Alt key and typing that letter (e.g., press Alt-H to run the macro you named Alt-H).

◆ If you assign a file name to a macro (e.g., *HEADING*), you can run the macro by selecting **T**ools ➤ Ma**c**ro ➤ E**x**ecute (or pressing Alt-F10), typing the macro name (e.g., *HEADING*), and pressing ↵.

The beauty of Alt-*letter* names is that you can execute the macro with just a couple of keystrokes. But of course, you can only have 26 such macros (Alt-A through Alt-Z) and it's sometimes difficult to remember what the single letter of the Alt-*letter* macro name stands for. Therefore, if you build up a large collection of macros, you might want to assign Alt-*letter* names to your most frequently used macros (because they're so easy to run).

The drive\directory where macros are stored is defined on the Location of Files menu, described under "Organizing Your Macros" later in this chapter.

All macros are stored on-disk as files with the extension .WPM (which WordPerfect adds automatically). Hence, if you name your macro *BULLET,* it is stored on-disk as BULLET.WPM. If you press Alt-B to name your macro, WordPerfect automatically stores the macro in a file named *ALTB.WPM*. In the future, pressing Alt-B automatically tells WordPerfect to find the ALTB.WPM file on-disk and to play back the macro within that file.

DESCRIBING A MACRO

The second prompt you'll see when creating a macro is "Description:", in which WordPerfect asks you to type a brief description of the macro. You can enter a short phrase or sentence, up to 39 characters long, describing your macro (for example, "Quick Save," "Mark page and copy," or "Change italic to underline").

Although the description is entirely optional, it can be useful. For example, if you create a macro, then don't use it for several weeks or months, you might forget its purpose. If you enter a description for the macro, you can find out what the macro does simply by viewing its description.

There are two ways to review a macro's description. The first way is as follows:

◆ Press Macro Define (**Ctrl-F10**).

◆ Enter the name of the macro (or press its Alt-*letter* combination) and press ↵.

◆ Select **D**escription from the menu that appears.

◆ After viewing the description, press **F7** twice to return to the Edit screen.

The second way is to go to the List Files screen (**F**ile ➤ List **F**iles, or F5), get to the macros directory, then highlight the file name of the macro. You'll see

See Chapter 12 for more information on

List Files.

the date and time the macro was created or last edited, along with the file name. To view the macro description, highlight the macro file name and press ↵ or press **L** (for Look), or double-click on the file name with your mouse. The macro description appears near the top of the Look screen.

RECORDING KEYSTROKES

If your macro is designed to select an option from a menu that's subject to change, such as the list of styles or fonts, use the Name Search feature to position the highlight. See "Designing Macros That Activate Styles" later in this chapter.

After entering your macro name and description, you'll see "Macro Def" flashing in the lower-left corner of your screen. This is the time to start typing the keystrokes you want to record. The keystrokes can be typing keys, cursor movements (but not with the mouse), pull-down menu selections, shortcut function-key presses—anything you can normally do in WordPerfect.

The "Macro Def" message (short for *Macro Define*) may temporarily disappear when some menu or other message overwrites it, but it will reappear as soon as the menu or other message is cleared from the screen. While you are recording keystrokes, don't forget that they are also being played out on your Edit screen and are therefore affecting your document now. (Be sure to have a backup of your document available, just in case you make a mistake when defining your macro.)

When you've finished recording your keystrokes, press Macro Define (Ctrl-F10). WordPerfect stops recording keystrokes and saves the macro. The "Macro Def" message stops blinking, and everything returns to normal. You can play back your macro right now or at any time in the future (discussed below in "Running a Macro").

CANCELING KEYSTROKE RECORDING

If you start recording a series of keystrokes, then make a mistake and want to start all over, you can't just press Cancel or Esc, as these keystrokes would just be recorded like any other. Instead, you have to stop recording keystrokes and start over from scratch: Select **T**ools ➤ **Ma**cro ➤ **D**efine or press Ctrl-F10, then start all over, as described in "Replacing an Existing Macro" later in this chapter.

RUNNING A MACRO

TO RUN A MACRO,

press its Alt-*letter* name, or, if you've given it a longer name, select Tools ➤ Macro ➤ Execute (or

> **press Alt-F10), type the macro name, and press ↵.**

Running a macro is even easier than creating one:

1. If the macro will be working on a particular section of text (such as italicizing a word), position the cursor where you want the macro to start taking action.

2. If you gave the macro an Alt-*letter* name, press that combination now, then skip all the remaining steps (the macro will run immediately).

3. If you assigned a longer name to the macro, select **T**ools ➤ **M**acro ➤ Ex**e**cute, or press Macro (**Alt-F10**). You'll see this prompt:

Macro:

> **N O T E** *If you want to watch Word-Perfect play back a macro keystroke by keystroke, see "Watching Macros Play Back Keystrokes" below.*

4. Type the name you assigned to the macro when you created it, and press ↵.

WordPerfect replays all the keys you recorded when you defined the macro, then returns you to the Edit screen. What you'll see at the Edit screen are the *results* of the keys being played back, not the actual keystrokes.

STOPPING A RUNNING MACRO

> **N O T E** *The "Please Wait" message appears in the lower-left corner of the screen while a macro is running.*

If you start a macro and want to stop it dead in its tracks (perhaps because you've run the wrong macro or didn't properly position the cursor before running it), press Cancel (F1). This will leave you at whatever point the macro was when you canceled it—maybe on the Edit screen, or maybe at a menu or prompt. Since the macro probably will play back some keystrokes before you cancel it, you might want to take a quick look at your Edit screen to see what changes have been made and make any necessary corrections.

You may want to try creating some macros on your own now. As mentioned earlier, if you want to get some hands-on experience (as well as some suggestions for) creating and using some practical macros, refer to Lesson 8 in Part 9 near the back of this book. Macros are one area where a little experience is a very enlightening teacher.

REPLACING AN EXISTING MACRO

Remember that macros are very literal—they record your keystrokes exactly. For example, suppose that while recording keystrokes you mistype a word, backspace over the mistake to correct it, then continue recording keystrokes.

When you play back that macro, it too will misspell the same word, backspace over the mistake, and type the correction.

This is harmless, but you may get tired of seeing the macro make and correct the same mistake over and over again. There are two possible ways to fix this problem: either replace the faulty macro by starting over and re-creating it from scratch, or edit the macro to remove the mistake.

The first method is generally the easiest for small macros. Follow the same basic steps you used to create the first macro:

It is usually easier to re-create a faulty macro than to edit it, if it is small.

1. Select **T**ools ➤ **M**acro ➤ **D**efine, or press **Ctrl-F10**.

2. At the "Define macro:" prompt, type the name of the macro you want to replace (this can be an Alt-*letter* keypress or a longer name), and press ↵.

3. Enter the same Alt-*letter* combination or longer name you originally as-signed to the macro. WordPerfect presents the following options:

   FILENAME.WPM Already Exists: **1 R**eplace; **2 E**dit; **3 D**escription

4. Select the **R**eplace option to replace the faulty macro.

5. Select **Y**es when asked to confirm the replacement.

6. Type the keystrokes you want to record, from scratch, remembering to select **T**ools ➤ **M**acro ➤ **D**efine or press **Ctrl-F10** after recording all the macro's keystrokes.

The macro you create completely replaces the previous macro.

As an alternative to replacing an existing macro, you can use the Macro Editor, described later in this chapter, to make changes and corrections.

ORGANIZING YOUR MACROS

TO ORGANIZE ALL YOUR MACROS INTO A SEPARATE DIRECTORY,

1. Select **File ➤ Setup ➤ Location of Files ➤ Key-board/Macro Files (or press Shift-F1 L K)**.

2. Enter a valid drive and directory name.

3. Press ↵.

4. Press Exit (F7).

As mentioned, all macros are stored on-disk as files. This makes it easy for you to run any existing macro, regardless of the document you happen to be working on at the moment.

You can choose where to store macro files by selecting the Location of Files option (**F**ile ➤ Se**t**up ➤ **L**ocation of Files ➤ **K**eyboard/Macro Files). To prevent cluttering the C:\WP51 directory, you might want to store all your macros (and keyboard files, discussed in Chapter 27) in a separate directory, such as C:\WP51\MACROS.

If you change the location of your keyboard or macro files, remember that you should immediately move all those files (i.e., *.WPM and *.WPK) to the new directory. You can use the List Files screen (**F**iles ➤ List **F**iles, or F5) to do so.

If several persons share a computer, each one may want to create their own Alt-M or Alt-J macro, which can cause "macro warfare" among them. If you want to create your own unique set of macros that nobody else can change or replace, you should use a soft keyboard (see Chapter 27).

> **T I P**
>
> *When recording and playing back a macro, you can temporarily override the default location for macro files by typing the complete drive\ directory\file name (e.g., C:\WP51\MY-STUFF\MYMACRO) when prompted for a macro name. This only works for macros with file names, not the Alt-letter macros.*

CREATING AN IMMEDIATE MACRO

TO CREATE AN IMMEDIATE, TEMPORARY MACRO,

follow the same steps as for creating any other macro, but press ↵ when prompted for a name, when both creating and running the macro.

Some macros are handy for typing repetitive information in the current document, but not particularly worth saving for use in other documents. You can create such a macro, called an "immediate" macro, by following these steps:

1. Select **T**ools ➤ **M**acro ➤ **D**efine, or press **Ctrl-F10**.

2. Press ↵ instead of entering a macro name.

3. Type the keystrokes you want to record.

4. Press **Ctrl-F10**.

To play back your immediate macro, select **T**ools ➤ **M**acro ➤ **E**xecute (or press **Alt-F10**) and press ↵ rather than entering a macro name. Remember that this macro is temporary and will vanish once you exit WordPerfect.

CREATING A TEMPORARY ALT-NUMBER MACRO

TO CREATE A TEMPORARY ALT-*NUMBER* MACRO,

1. Press Macro Commands (Ctrl-Page Up).

2. Type a number between 0 and 9 and press ↵.

3. Type up to 79 characters and spaces and press ↵.

WordPerfect lets you create another kind of temporary macro, which you run by pressing any of the ten Alt-*number* combinations, Alt-0 through Alt-9. Like the immediate macros described earlier, these are available only during the current work session. However, these macros aren't quite as flexible, because they can contain only a limited number of characters and cannot contain menu selections or ↵ keypresses.

The biggest benefits of Alt-*number* macros are that you can define up to ten of them, and you can speed up repetitive typing of finger-twisting words and phrases like "Dendrobium Pharmaceuticals" or the typing of bullets and other Compose characters.

To create a temporary macro, follow these steps:

1. This step is optional. If you want to create the macro from existing text, block up to 128 characters of text (including spaces and any characters created by the Compose feature) by selecting **E**dit ➤ **B**lock or pressing **Alt-F4** or **F12**. Count the characters in the block carefully; any extras will just be ignored. In step 4, blocked text automatically becomes the value for the temporary macro.

2. Press Macro Commands (**Ctrl-Page Up**). You will see the following prompt in the lower-left corner of your screen:

Variable:

3. Type the number that, in combination with Alt, will invoke the temporary macro. You can use any of the ten number keys from 0 through 9 (if Num Lock is on, you can use the numeric keypad). Press ↵. You'll see this prompt:

Value:

WordPerfect is asking for the text that it will type automatically whenever you run the temporary macro.

4. If you skipped step 1, type up to 79 characters, including Compose (Ctrl-2) and spaces, and press ⏎.

When you want to play back your temporary macro, move your cursor to where the macro should start typing the automatic text, and hold down the Alt key while typing the number you assigned to the macro. For example, if you typed the number *1* in step 3 above, press Alt-1 to run the macro.

Temporary macros can be very convenient for typing repeated words and phrases, but you should remember that such macros disappear at the end of your WordPerfect session and can contain only characters and spaces.

Temporary macros are convenient for typing repeated words and phrases.

CONTROLLING HOW MACROS RUN

> **TO MAKE A MACRO DISPLAY ITS KEYSTROKES OR PAUSE FOR INPUT DURING EXECUTION,**
>
> **press Macro Commands (Ctrl-Page Up) while recording the macro keystrokes, then choose Display or Pause (depending on what you want the macro to do).**

Normally when you run a macro, WordPerfect executes every keystroke from beginning to end, very quickly, showing you only the results of the completed keystrokes. As the following sections discuss, there are several ways to customize how WordPerfect plays back your recorded keystrokes.

WATCHING MACROS PLAY BACK KEYSTROKES

When you run a macro, you see the results of the completed macro, not the keystroke-by-keystroke playback. If you are trying to fix a macro that isn't producing the results you want, or if you are using your macro to teach less-experienced users, you may want to see each keystroke as it's played back. There are two ways to accomplish this:

1. Follow steps 1–4 in "Creating a Macro" to name, describe, and start recording macro keystrokes.

2. When WordPerfect starts recording keystrokes (as indicated by the blinking "Macro Def" indicator), press Macro Commands (**Ctrl-Page Up**). You'll see the following options:

1 Pause; 2 Display; 3 Assign; 4 Comment

You can turn Display on or off at any time while recording key-strokes, to selectively choose when the run-ning macro does and does not show in-dividual keystrokes as they're played back.

If you want to slow down a macro so that you can better see each step as it's played back, insert a {SPEED} or {STEP} command by using the Macro Editor.

If you are at a menu choice, you see only the first two options.

3. Select **D**isplay. You'll see this prompt:

   Display Execution? No (Yes)

4. Select **Y**es to have keystrokes that follow be displayed when the macro is executed. (Optionally, select **N**o if you don't want the macro to display keystrokes that follow.)

5. Resume typing the keystrokes you want to record.

6. Select **T**ools ➤ **M**acro ➤ **D**efine or press Macro Define (**Ctrl-F10**) when you've finished recording keystrokes.

If you've already recorded your macro keystrokes without completing these steps, but want the macro to display each keystroke as it's played back, you need to use the Macro Editor to remove the {DISPLAY OFF} command at the beginning of the macro.

MAKING A MACRO PAUSE FOR AN ENTRY

As you know, once you start a macro it plays back *all* of its keystrokes very quickly. However, you might want a macro that pauses for an entry. For ex-ample, you could create a macro that types your company name and address, but pauses to allow you to type in a specific department name. Or, you could create a macro that lists only files with the .WP extension on the List Files screen, waits for you to move the highlight to a file name and press ↵, then retrieves that file onto the Edit screen.

To make a macro pause, follow these steps:

1. Follow steps 1–4 in "Creating a Macro" to name, describe, and start recording macro keystrokes.

2. Type the keystrokes of the macro in the usual way, up until the point where you want the macro to wait for an entry.

3. Press the Macro Commands key (**Ctrl-Page Up**). You'll see these options:

   1 Pause; 2 Display; 3 Assign; 4 Comment

   or

1 Pause; 2 Display

4. Select **P**ause.

5. Press ↵. (This *won't* create a blank line; it just ends the Pause command.)

6. Continue pressing the keys you want to be in the macro after the pause. (You can add additional pauses as needed while recording more keystrokes.)

7. When you've finished recording the macro, select **T**ools ➤ **M**acro ➤ **D**efine, or press **Ctrl-F10**.

You run a macro that contains a pause the same way you run any other macro. When the macro reaches the point where you entered the pause, it will stop and wait for you to take action. Type in your entry, and then press ↵ to end the pause and to play back the rest of the keystrokes.

If you've already recorded your macro, and you want to modify it so that it pauses for your keystroke rather than typing a previously recorded keystroke, you need to insert a {PAUSE} command at the appropriate point in the macro by using the Macro Editor (described later).

Figure 15.2 shows a sample macro that was originally recorded by going to the List Files screen, displaying file names with the extension .WP only, pressing ↓ to highlight the first file name, then selecting **R**etrieve to retrieve that file.

NOTE

*WordPerfect also offers the {PAUSE}key~ command, which waits for whatever key you specify (rather than ↵); the {CHAR} command, which waits for a single character (like **Y**es/**N**o answers); and more.*

```
Macro: Action

      File              ALTF.WPM

      Description       Display .WP files, retrieve first one

  ┌────────────────────────────────────────────────────────────────┐
  │{DISPLAY OFF}{List}{End}{Backspace}WP{Enter}                      │
  │{Down}r                                                           │
  │                                                                  │
  │                                                                  │
  │                                                                  │
  │                                                                  │
  │                                                                  │
  │                                                                  │
  │                                                                  │
  │                                                                  │
  │                                                                  │
  └────────────────────────────────────────────────────────────────┘

Ctrl-PgUp for macro commands;   Press Exit when done
```

FIGURE 15.2:

A sample macro to select the first file from the List Files screen

Figure 15.3 shows the same macro, after editing the description and macro with the Macro Editor. Notice that the {Down} arrow keypress from the original macro has been removed and replaced with a {PAUSE} command. The PAUSE command makes the macro wait for you to highlight a specific file and press ↵ before it selects the Retrieve command that brings the file onto the Edit screen. The {DISPLAY OFF} command has also been removed to make the macro's actions visible while it's running.

CHAINING MACROS

If you often find yourself running the same two (or more) macros in succession, you can save some time and effort by *chaining* them. As the name implies, chaining links two or more macros together, like links in a chain. As soon as one macro has finished running, the next one begins.

To create a new macro that performs some keystrokes, then passes control over to another macro, follow these steps:

1. Start recording your new macro as you normally would.

2. Type all the keystrokes you want the current macro to play back.

3. Press Macro (**Alt-F10**), then press the other macro's Alt-*letter* name, or type its longer file name and press ↵. (The other macro is *not* executed at this time.)

```
Macro: Action

    File            ALTF.WPM

    Description     Display .WP files, retrieve any one

    ┌─────────────────────────────────────────────────┐
    │ {List}{End}{Backspace}WP{Enter}                 │
    │ {PAUSE}r                                        │
    │                                                 │
    │                                                 │
    │                                                 │
    │                                                 │
    │                                                 │
    │                                                 │
    │                                                 │
    │                                                 │
    │                                                 │
    │                                                 │
    └─────────────────────────────────────────────────┘

Ctrl-PgUp for macro commands; Press Exit when done
```

FIGURE 15.3:

A macro to display .WP files, wait for a ↵ keypress, then retrieve the selected file to the Edit screen

4. Optionally, you can continue recording keystrokes in the current macro.

5. Select **T**ools ➤ **M**acro ➤ **D**efine or press Macro Define (**Ctrl-F10**) to stop recording keystrokes.

If you've already created a macro and you want it to chain to another macro, you can use the Macro Editor described later to insert a {CHAIN}-macroname~ command in the macro.

You run a chained macro the same way you run any other macro. In a macro that contains a chained macro, all the keystrokes in the current macro are executed before the chained macro. To have keystrokes executed *after* running the chained macro, you must use nesting.

If you want to chain multiple macros, you must do so in succession. For example, if you want to chain macros named *PART1, PART2,* and *PART3* (in that order), first create the macro named PART3. Then, create PART2, and end it by running PART3 (see step 3). Finally, create PART1, and end it by running PART2 (again, see step 3). When you execute PART1, it runs PART2; PART2, in turn, runs PART3.

NESTING MACROS

The technique of running one macro within another macro is known as nesting. To understand the difference between chaining and nesting, consider this example: Suppose you have two macros, named *ALT-A* and *ALT-B*. If ALT-B is chained to ALT-A and you run ALT-A, ALT-A completes all the actions in its job, passes control to ALT-B, ALT-B does its own job, and all macro execution stops. (You're returned to the Edit screen.) If, on the other hand, ALT-B is nested in ALT-A, and you run ALT-A, ALT-A does a portion of its job, and passes control to ALT-B, which does its job. But then, ALT-B passes control back to ALT-A, which picks up where it left off, and finishes its own job. Figure 15.4 illustrates these differences.

The technique for creating a macro that nests another macro is basically the same as for chaining another macro, except that the macro you want to nest must have an Alt-*letter* name. Follow these steps:

1. Start creating the macro as usual.

2. Type whatever keystrokes you want to record in the current macro.

3. When you get to the place where you want the nested macro to be executed, press its Alt-*letter* name. That macro is executed on the screen.

4. Continue typing the keystrokes that you want to be played back in the macro you are creating right now.

5. You can repeat steps 3 and 4 as many times as you wish, to nest as many macros as you wish.

6. When you've finished recording keystrokes in the current macro, stop recording (select **T**ools ➤ **M**acros ➤ **D**efine or press **Ctrl-F10**).

When you run the macro you've just recorded, it will execute the keystrokes you recorded in step 2, execute the entire macro you specified in step 3, then continue executing the keystrokes you recorded in step 4.

If you've already created a macro, and you would like to change it so that it calls another macro in a nested manner, you can use the Macro Editor to insert a {NEST}*macroname~* command in it, as discussed later in this chapter and in Chapter 26.

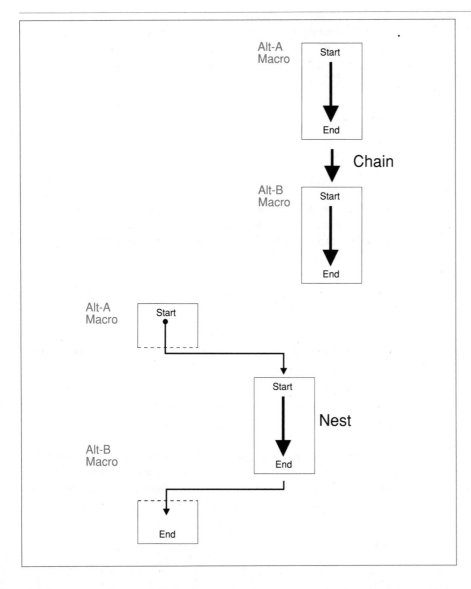

FIGURE 15.4:

How two sample macros named ALT-A and ALT-B are executed when chained and when nested

RUNNING A MACRO SEVERAL TIMES

Suppose you create a macro that performs a single job, such as changing italic text to underlined text, or recalculating all the formulas in a single table. Later, you decide you want to run that macro many times in a document so that it changes all the italics to underlines or recalculates all the tables in a document.

There are more sophisticated ways to control how many times a macro is executed, using the advanced macro commands {WHILE}, {FOR}, and {ON}, discussed in Chapter 26.

An easy way to do so is to use the Repeat (Esc) key. For example, suppose your macro to change italics to underlines is named ALT-U, and you estimate that there are at least 50 italics in the current document. You could press Escape to get the "Repeat=" prompt, then type *50,* and press Alt-U. Your macro will be executed 50 times.

Another way to make a macro run repeatedly is to chain it to itself by placing the {CHAIN}*macroname~* command at the end of the macro, where *macroname* is the name of the macro. For example, using {CHAIN}AltZ.wpm~ as the last command in a macro you start by pressing Alt-Z will make the macro repeat itself indefinitely. To stop the macro after it starts running, press Cancel (F1).

EDITING A MACRO

TO EDIT A MACRO,

select Tools ➤ Macro ➤ Define (or press Ctrl-F10), enter the name of the macro you want to edit, then select Edit. Optionally, press Home and Ctrl-F10, edit the description or leave it unchanged, and press ↵.

Rather than replacing a macro, as described earlier in this chapter, you can just change an existing macro with the Macro Editor. But before you try to use the Editor, you need to understand a little bit about what's really "inside" a macro.

WHAT'S INSIDE A MACRO?

When you record keystrokes in a macro, WordPerfect actually divides your recorded keystrokes into two types of actions: *keystrokes* and *commands*. If you type text, such as your name and address, WordPerfect stores exactly those keystrokes in the macro and plays them back when you run the macro.

However, if you enter keystrokes that invoke a command, WordPerfect simply records the command rather than the keystrokes. For example, if you press Alt-= and select Layout, or press Shift-F8, to get to the Format menu, Word-Perfect doesn't record those exact keystrokes. Instead, it converts them to the command *{Format},* which simply tells the macro to "get to the Format menu" when it's played back. This helps WordPerfect to produce smaller, faster-running macros.

A third type of element, called a *macro programming command,* can be used in a macro.

◆ Macro programming commands are displayed like other commands on the macro editing screen, but in all uppercase letters, e.g., *{DISPLAY OFF}.*

◆ Most macro programming commands can be entered only from within the Macro Editor; they cannot be recorded at the Edit screen.

As you'll see in a moment, the Macro Editor lets you change any of the elements of a macro.

USING THE MACRO EDITOR

If you press and release the Home key before pressing Ctrl-F10 in step 1, you'll be given the option to edit the description, then be taken directly to the Editor in step 3.

If you want to edit the macro's description as well as its content, select Description instead of Edit. After you edit the description and press ↵, you'll be brought to the Macro Editor.

If you decide to change, rather than replace, an existing macro, follow these steps to bring the macro into the Macro Editor:

1. From the Edit screen, select **T**ools ➤ **M**acro ➤ **D**efine, or press Macro Define (**Ctrl-F10**), as though you were creating a new macro.

2. At the "Define Macro:" prompt, press the Alt-*letter* combination, or type the name of the macro you want to edit and press ↵.

3. You'll see the following message and options displayed at the bottom of the screen:

   FILENAME.WPM Already Exists: **1 R**eplace; **2 E**dit; **3 D**escription

4. Select **E**dit.

The Macro Editor screen appears; Figure 15.5 shows an example (the Alt-W macro created in Lesson 8 to transpose two words).

Once you get to the Macro Editor, the basic cursor-movement and editing keys—↑, ↓, →, ←, Page Up, Page Down, End, Backspace, and Delete—

perform normally. You can also press Tab to indent and ↵ to end a line to "tidy up" the appearance of your macro, just as on the normal Edit screen. Neither key will affect how the macro runs.

Blank spaces within commands (i.e., between curly braces) do not have a centered dot.

Blank spaces appear with a small dot in the middle so that you can better see spaces between commands and keystrokes.

Be aware that only rudimentary editing capabilities are available in the Macro Editor. Block, Search and Replace, Undelete (F1), the Speller, and other more advanced editing capabilities are unavailable.

EDITING TEXT IN A MACRO

Inserting and deleting text in a macro is similar to inserting text at the Edit screen. However, the Macro Editor is always in Insert mode, so you cannot use Typeover. For example, Figure 15.6 shows a macro that types a name and address on the Macro Editor screen. Suppose you want to change the address from 1234 Oak Tree Lane to 6789 Oak Tree Lane.

This is a simple job: Just move the cursor to the *1* in *1234,* press Delete four times to delete *1234,* then type *6789* to insert this new text. Figure 15.7 shows the completed change.

```
Macro: Action

    File            ALTW.WPM

    Description     Transpose two words

    ┌────────────────────────────────────────────────────────┐
    │{DISPLAY OFF}{Del Word}{Word Right}{Cancel}r             │
    │                                                        │
    │                                                        │
    │                                                        │
    │                                                        │
    │                                                        │
    │                                                        │
    │                                                        │
    │                                                        │
    │                                                        │
    │                                                        │
    │                                                        │
    └────────────────────────────────────────────────────────┘

Ctrl-V to Insert next key as command;
Ctrl-PgUp for macro commands;  Press Exit when done
```

FIGURE 15.5:

A sample macro on the Macro Editor screen

```
Macro: Action

    File            ADDRESS.WPM

    Description     Type formatted company name and address

┌─────────────────────────────────────────────────────────────────┐
│ ┌───────────────────────────────────────────────────────────────┤
│ │{DISPLAY OFF}{Bold}{Font}aiMacroTech, Inc. {Right}{Right}{Enter} │
│ │1234 Oak Tree Lane{Enter}                                        │
│ │Malibu, CA  91234{Enter}                                         │
│ │                                                                 │
│ │                                                                 │
│ │                                                                 │
│ │                                                                 │
│ │                                                                 │
│ │                                                                 │
│ │                                                                 │
│ └───────────────────────────────────────────────────────────────┘
└─────────────────────────────────────────────────────────────────┘

Ctrl-PgUp for macro commands;  Press Exit when done
```

FIGURE 15.6:

A sample name-and-address macro on the Macro Editor screen

```
Macro: Action

    File            ADDRESS.WPM

    Description     Type formatted company name and address

┌─────────────────────────────────────────────────────────────────┐
│ ┌───────────────────────────────────────────────────────────────┤
│ │{DISPLAY OFF}{Bold}{Font}aiMacroTech, Inc. {Right}{Right}{Enter} │
│ │6789 Oak Tree Lane{Enter}                                        │
│ │Malibu, CA  91234{Enter}                                         │
│ │                                                                 │
│ │                                                                 │
│ │                                                                 │
│ │                                                                 │
│ │                                                                 │
│ │                                                                 │
│ │                                                                 │
│ └───────────────────────────────────────────────────────────────┘
└─────────────────────────────────────────────────────────────────┘

Ctrl-PgUp for macro commands;  Press Exit when done
```

FIGURE 15.7:

The address (text) in the sample macro has been changed.

INSERTING CURSOR-MOVEMENT KEYS IN A MACRO

As mentioned, pressing →, ←, Tab, and so forth lets you move the cursor around in the Macro Editor. But what if you want the *macro* to press → or ← or Tab while it's running? There are two ways you can insert movement keys in a macro:

◆ If you want to insert a single movement key in the macro, press **Ctrl-V**, then the key you want the macro to execute.

◆ If you want to insert several movement keys in the macro, press Macro Define (**Ctrl-F10**), type the keys you want the macro to execute, then press Ctrl-F4 again to return to normal keystroke functions.

For example, if you want your macro to "press Tab" while it's running, press Ctrl-V, then press Tab. The Macro Editor screen displays *{Tab}*, which indicates that the macro will press the Tab key at that point. If you want the macro to press → four times while it's running, you can press Ctrl-V, then → four times, or press Ctrl-F10, press → four times, then press Ctrl-F10 again. Either way, you'll see the following:

{Right}{Right}{Right}{Right}

These are the commands required to make the macro press → four times while it's running.

Note that either technique works with any editing command. For example, if you want your macro to press ↵, press Ctrl-V, then ↵. It appears as *{Enter}* on the Edit screen. This also works for Cancel (F1) and Exit (F7), among others. If you want your macro to move the cursor to the top of the document, press Ctrl-F10, press Home Home Home ↑, then press Ctrl-F10 again. This inserts the commands *{Home}{Home}{Home}{Up}* in the macro.

You can even insert a {Macro Define} command in your macro, by pressing Ctrl-V then Ctrl-F10.

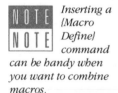

Inserting a {Macro Define} command can be handy when you want to combine macros.

EDITING MENU AND SHORTCUT KEY COMMANDS

If you want your macro to perform some action that requires selecting menu options, your macro must include the exact keystrokes to make the selections. You can use a shortcut command, such as {Format}, or actually type in the pull-down menu sequence of commands, starting with Alt-=.

For example, if you want the macro to activate the Speller when it runs, you can press Spell (Ctrl-F2) while editing the macro. WordPerfect automatically converts your Ctrl-F2 keystroke to the command *{Spell}* and displays that on the Macro Editor screen. Optionally, you can press Ctrl-V, then Alt-=, to display the command *{Menu Bar}* so that the macro displays the menu bar, then type *TE* so that the macro selects **T**ools ➤ Sp**e**ll. The Macro Editor displays *{Menu Bar}TE* if you use this approach.

While you are in the Macro Editor, the shortcut keys don't actually do anything other than insert the command. That is, pressing Ctrl-F2 doesn't activate the Speller; it just inserts the {Spell} command. Furthermore, the pulldown menus aren't available from within the Macro Editor, so you need to know the exact sequence of selections you want to make from the menu bar.

If you're not exactly sure of the keystrokes required to perform a given task, try them at the normal Edit screen and jot them down. Then go into the Macro Editor, and perform those exact keystrokes.

For example, to activate single spacing at the Edit screen, you can press Shift-F8, then L to select Line, then S to select Line Spacing. Next, type 1 to initiate single line spacing, then press ↵ and Exit (F7) to return to the Edit screen. (A quick peek at the Reveal Codes screen will show [Ln Spacing:1], indicating you've pressed all the right keys.)

If you write down the exact keystrokes you press along the way, your written text will look like this:

Shift-F8 L S 1 Enter F7

These are the exact keystrokes you want to insert using the Macro Editor. So first, bring the macro onto the Macro Editor screen as discussed earlier. Next, position the cursor where you want these keystrokes to be played back (at the beginning of the macro, in this example). Press Shift-F8, then type *L,* then *S,* then *1,* which looks like this on the Edit screen:

{Format}ls1

It looks like this if you use uppercase letters, though case is unimportant:

{Format}LS1

But you're not finished, because you still have to get the ↵ and Exit (F7) keystrokes in there. These double as editing keys in the Macro Editor, so you need to press Ctrl-V and ↵, then Ctrl-V and Exit (F7). You've added this series of commands and keystrokes to your macro:

{Format}ls1{Enter}{Exit}

Figure 15.8 shows an example where these keystrokes were added just after the {DISPLAY OFF} command in a sample macro. You can save the edited macro by pressing Exit (F7).

As an alternative to trying to get every keystroke just right, you can record a set of keystrokes in a small, temporary macro (perhaps called *CHUNK*), then read these keystrokes into a larger, existing macro, as described in "Combining Macros" later in this chapter.

EDITING MACRO PROGRAMMING COMMANDS

Always use the techniques described here to insert macro programming commands in your macro. Do not try to type them as regular text, because your macro won't work properly.

You can use the Macro Editor to insert and delete macro programming commands in any macro, as follows:

1. Bring the macro that you want to edit to the Macro Editor, as described in "Using the Macro Editor" earlier in this chapter.

2. Move the cursor to where you want to insert a macro programming command.

3. Press **Ctrl-Page Up** to display the macro commands menu, shown near the upper-right corner of Figure 15.9.

4. Use the ↑, ↓, Page Up, and Page Down keys to scroll through available commands, or use Name Search to move the highlight to the general vicinity of the command you want. (To use Name Search, type the first character of the command, then press ↵.)

```
Macro: Action

    File            ADDRESS.WPM

    Description     Type formatted company name and address

 ┌──────────────────────────────────────────────────────────────────┐
 │{DISPLAY OFF}{Format}lsl{Enter}{Exit}                               │
 │{Bold}{Font}aiMacroTech, ·Inc.{Right}{Right}{Enter}                 │
 │6789·Oak·Tree·Lane{Enter}                                           │
 │Malibu,·CA··91234{Enter}                                            │
 │─                                                                   │
 │                                                                    │
 │                                                                    │
 │                                                                    │
 │                                                                    │
 │                                                                    │
 │                                                                    │
 │                                                                    │
 │                                                                    │
 │                                                                    │
 │                                                                    │
 │                                                                    │
 └──────────────────────────────────────────────────────────────────┘

Ctrl-PgUp for macro commands;   Press Exit when done
```

FIGURE 15.8:

A name-and-address macro with commands for single line spacing just after the {DISPLAY OFF} command

If "Press Macro Define to enable editing" appears in the lower-left corner of the Macro Editor screen, you're in command-insertion mode. Press Ctrl-F10 to turn off this mode, before trying to access the macro programming commands menu.

5. When the highlight is on the command you want, press ↵ to select the command.

6. You can repeat steps 2 through 5 as many times as necessary. When finished, press Exit (**F7**) to save your edited macro.

If you want to delete a macro programming command, use the Delete or Backspace key.

SAVING OR CANCELING YOUR EDITED MACRO

When you are finished editing your macro, you can save your changes and exit the Macro Editor simply by pressing Exit (F7). You'll be returned to the Edit screen immediately, where you can run your edited macro if you want to test your changes.

If you make a mess of things while editing your macro, and you want to start over, press Cancel (F1) instead. You'll see these options:

Cancel changes? No (Yes)

Select Yes if you want to abandon all changes made during the current editing session, or select No if you change your mind and want to continue editing the macro as it is.

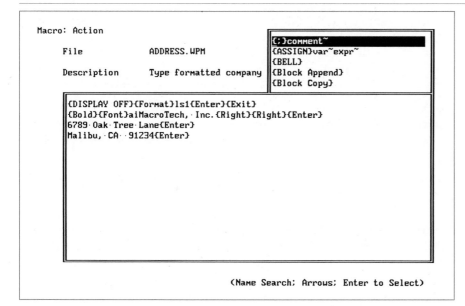

```
Macro: Action

     File          ADDRESS.WPM        {;}comment~
                                      {ASSIGN}var~expr~
                                      {BELL}
     Description   Type formatted company  {Block Append}
                                      {Block Copy}

  {DISPLAY OFF}{Format}ls1{Enter}{Exit}
  {Bold}{Font}aiMacroTech, Inc.{Right}{Right}{Enter}
  6789 Oak Tree Lane{Enter}
  Malibu, CA  91234{Enter}














                (Name Search; Arrows; Enter to Select)
```

FIGURE 15.9:

The macro programming commands menu

SOME MORE ADVANCED MACROS

Here are some additional tips and some advanced techniques that will help you create more powerful macros.

DESIGNING MACROS THAT ACTIVATE STYLES

If your macro is designed to select an option from any list that's subject to change, including List Files, Base Font, or Styles, you should always use Name Search to position the highlight while recording the macro keystrokes.

If you create a style (Chapter 14) and then decide you want to create a macro to activate the style (e.g., so you can just press Alt-H whenever you want to turn on your heading style), be sure to use the Name Search feature—instead of just highlighting the desired style with the cursor keys or mouse—to pick the style name while recording the macro keystrokes. Otherwise, if you add or delete styles in the future, the macro may select the wrong style.

If you want to create a macro that activates a style named *Heading,* follow these steps:

1. Start recording your macro normally.

2. While recording the macro keystrokes, select **T**ools ➤ **S**tyles, or press **Alt-F8** to get to the Styles menu.

3. Press **N** to activate Name Search.

4. Type the complete name of the style you want to activate, and when the highlight is on the style, press ↵.

5. Press **O** to select On.

You'll be returned to the Edit screen, where you can continue recording additional keystrokes or stop recording keystrokes by pressing Ctrl-F10.

MAKING MACROS DISPLAY PULL-DOWN MENUS

Even if you choose to have your macro display each keystroke as it is typed, the macro will not display pull-down menus, because all pull-down menu selections are automatically converted to shortcut keystrokes when you record the macro keystrokes. If your macro is designed as a training tool to show others the exact menus that must be pulled down to execute a task, you may prefer to have the macro display the menus.

If so, you must convert every shortcut keystroke in the macro to its pull-down menu equivalent; you'll need to use the Macro Editor. For example, to display the pull-down menus that lead to the menu for changing the left and right margins, you need to change

{Format}LM

(i.e., Shift-F8 L M) in your macro to

{Menu Bar}LLM

(**L**ayout ➤ **L**ine ➤ **M**argin). In the Macro Editor, you can insert the {Menu Bar} command by pressing Ctrl-V, then Alt-=.

Be sure to delete any {DELETE OFF} and {MENU OFF} commands from the macro as well, to be sure that all menus appear on the screen when the macro is running. Also, to prevent the pull-down menus from whizzing by too quickly, you may need to insert {SPEED} commands that slow down the execution of the macro.

As an example, Figure 15.10 shows a macro that was created by recording keystrokes to change the left, right, top, and bottom margins. This macro shows the familiar shortcut keystrokes. Figure 15.11 shows a macro that performs the same keystrokes, but runs much more slowly and displays pull-down menus in the process.

A careful look at the macro in Figure 15.11 reveals an interesting feature on the third line. The commands

{Menu Bar} l {Down}{Enter}

were used to select the Page: Format menu, instead of

{Menu Bar} lp

TIP ▼ *If you decide to run the macros in these examples, you might want to turn on Reveal Codes first, so you can see the codes appear as the macros insert them in your document.*

```
Macro: Action

     File            SHORTCUT.WPM

     Description     Recorded macro to change margins

┌─────────────────────────────────────────────────┐
│ {DISPLAY OFF}{Format}lm2{Enter}                   │
│ 2{Enter}                                          │
│ {Exit}{Format}pm2{Enter}                          │
│ 2{Enter}                                          │
│ {Exit}                                            │
│                                                   │
│                                                   │
│                                                   │
│                                                   │
│                                                   │
│                                                   │
│                                                   │
│                                                   │
│                                                   │
│                                                   │
└─────────────────────────────────────────────────┘

 Ctrl-PgUp for macro commands;  Press Exit when done
```

FIGURE 15.10:

An example of a recorded-keystroke macro to change margins

This also will work, but won't display the move downward to select the Page option from the Layout pull-down menu (Page is the second option on the Layout menu). If you want to clearly see each option as it's being selected by a macro, you must insert the cursor movements that will highlight the option name, then insert the {Enter} command to select that option. Simply typing the letters used to select an option from a pull-down submenu won't clearly show the selection unless the macro is the *first* option.

RUNNING MACROS AUTOMATICALLY

You can have WordPerfect run a macro automatically as soon as WordPerfect is started from DOS. Such a macro can be designed to reset some of WordPerfect's default format settings to your preferences—a handy macro if you share your computer and can't make your preferences permanent.

To run a macro as soon as you start WordPerfect, you must use the /M-*macroname* start-up switch along with the WP command you type at the DOS command prompt, where *macroname* is the name of the macro you want to run. For example, to start WordPerfect and run a macro named *MYSETUP,* you enter the following at the DOS command prompt:

NOTE NOTE

To "auto-execute" a macro or program means to run it automatically.

WP /M-MYSETUP

```
Macro: Action

    File              PDMENU.WPM

    Description       Pull-down menu macro to change margins

  {SPEED}50~
  {Menu Bar}11m2{Enter}2{Enter}{Exit}
  {Menu Bar}1{Down}{Enter}m2{Enter}2{Enter}{Exit}




Ctrl-PgUp for macro commands;   Press Exit when done
```

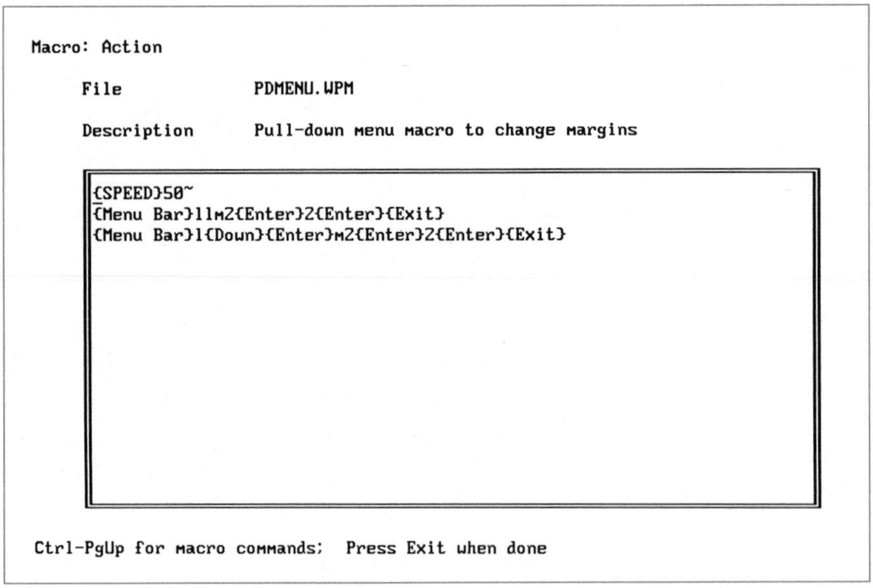

FIGURE 15.11:

A macro to change margins, displaying pull-down menus along the way

Auto-executing a Macro Every Time

 *Be careful **never** to save your AUTOEXEC.-BAT file in WordPerfect format; you must save it as DOS text. See your DOS book or manual if you need more information about this file or the SET command.*

If you want a particular macro to be executed every time WordPerfect is started from the DOS command prompt, you can change the DOS environment so that it adds the /M-*macroname* command automatically. Add the SET command to your DOS AUTOEXEC.BAT file, with the general format

SET WP = /M-*macroname*

where *macroname* is the name of the macro you want executed. For example, if you want your computer to run a macro named *ALWAYS.WPM* every time you enter the WP command at the DOS command prompt, add this command to your AUTOEXEC.BAT file:

SET WP = /m-always

In the future, when DOS receives the command *WP* from the keyboard, it will convert that command to *WP /m-always* before executing it.

Auto-executing a Macro at Boot-up Only

If you want to run WordPerfect and a macro just once when you first start your computer, you need to include the appropriate WP /M-*macroname* command in your AUTOEXEC.BAT file. This should be the last line; otherwise, the commands after the instruction will not be executed until you exit WordPerfect.

Chapter 8 shows an example of a macro used to download soft fonts to the printer once (presumably at the start of each day) during boot-up, so there's no need to wait for these fonts during future print jobs. Once the fonts are downloaded to the printer, the macro exits you from WordPerfect so that the AUTOEXEC.BAT file can resume its job.

COMBINING MACROS

Sometimes it's handy to be able to combine two or more macros into one. Doing so is a tad tricky, but not too difficult. One of the macros, which I'll refer to as the "incoming" macro, must have an Alt-*letter* name. If it does not, you can use the List Files screen to copy it to or rename it as an Alt-*letter* file name (for example, to rename it from *MYMACRO.WPM* to *ALTM.WPM*). Next, you must bring that macro into the Macro Editor. Figure 15.12 shows a sample macro, named *ALTZ.WPM*.

Once this incoming macro is on the Edit screen, here's how you can prepare it to be read into a separate macro file:

1. Move the cursor to the start of the macro, press Ctrl-V, then press Ctrl-F10. This inserts a {Macro Define} command at the start of the macro.

2. Press **Home Home ↓, Ctrl-V,** then **Ctrl-F10** again to insert a {Macro Define} command at the end of the macro, as in the example in Figure 15.13.

3. Press Exit (**F7**) to save the modified macro.

4. Bring the other macro (the one that you want to read the incoming macro into) onto the macro-editing screen.

5. Position the cursor wherever you want to insert the incoming macro, then press the incoming macro's Alt-*letter* name to execute that macro (*Alt-Z* in this example).

If you plan to continue using the previous incoming macro on its own, you must go back and remove the {Macro Define} commands you added to it.

The incoming macro, without its leading and ending {Macro Define} commands, will be inserted in the current macro. You can move the cursor throughout the macro and press ↵ wherever you want to insert a line break to make the entire macro visible (and more readable) on the narrow Macro Editor screen. Press Exit (F7) to save the new macro.

```
Macro: Action

    File            ALTZ.WPM

    Description

  ┌─────────────────────────────────────────────────────┐
  │{Format}ls2{Enter}                                    │
  │{Exit}THIS·IS·A·SIMPLE·MACRO·THAT·STARTS·WITH·A·SIMPLE·LINE·SPACING·│
  │COMMAND,·AND·ENDS·WITH·A·SIMPLE·LINE·SPACING·COMMAND.{Format}LS1│
  │{Enter}                                               │
  │{Exit}                                                │
  └─────────────────────────────────────────────────────┘

Ctrl-PgUp for macro commands:  Press Exit when done
```

FIGURE 15.12:
A sample macro named ALTZ.WPM

CONVERTING VERSION 4 MACROS FOR USE IN 5.1

WordPerfect version 4.x macros have a .MAC file-name extension. Version 5.x macros have a .WPM file-name extension.

WordPerfect 5.1 cannot run macros that were originally created for Word-Perfect version 4.x (that is, 4.0, 4.1, or 4.2). To run these macros, you'll need to convert them by using the WordPerfect 5.1 conversion program, which is called MACROCNV. This program is installed automatically on your hard disk when you install the WordPerfect Utility programs, which are usually on the same drive as WordPerfect 5.1 (C:\WP51).

To use the macro conversion program, follow these steps:

1. Go to the DOS command prompt and to the directory where the MACROCNV program is stored.

*For some online help in using the conversion program, enter the command **macrocnv /b** at the DOS command prompt.*

2. Enter the command **macrocnv *macroname*,** where *macroname* is the name of the macro you want to convert. You can use wildcards; for example, **macrocnv *** converts all the macros in the current directory from 4.x to 5.1 format.

When the conversion is complete, you'll see the message "Done"; a detailed report is printed. If the converted macro is extremely large, the conversion program automatically breaks it down into smaller macros, no larger than 4.5K (approximately 4500 characters), so that the converted macro will fit in the Macro Editor. You may also need to make additional changes and refinements with the Macro Editor to get the converted macro to run properly.

```
Macro: Action

    File            ALTZ.WPM

    Description

    ┌─────────────────────────────────────────────────────────────────┐
    │{Macro Define}{Format}ls2{Enter}                                   │
    │{Exit}THIS·IS·A·SIMPLE·MACRO·THAT·STARTS·WITH·A·SIMPLE·LINE·SPACING·│
    │COMMAND,·AND·ENDS·WITH·A·SIMPLE·LINE·SPACING·COMMAND.{Format}LS1    │
    │{Enter}                                                            │
    │{Exit}{Macro Define}_                                              │
    │                                                                   │
    │                                                                   │
    │                                                                   │
    │                                                                   │
    │                                                                   │
    │                                                                   │
    │                                                                   │
    │                                                                   │
    │                                                                   │
    └─────────────────────────────────────────────────────────────────┘

Ctrl-PgUp for macro commands;  Press Exit when done
```

FIGURE 15.13:

A {Macro Define} command added to the ALTZ.WPM macro

CONVERTING 5.0 MACROS FOR USE IN 5.1

Macros created with version 5.0 need no conversion to run with 5.1. However, because the keystrokes to perform some operations have changed with version 5.1, you may need to use the Macro Editor to modify the 5.0 macros.

This chapter has taken you from the basics of recording and playing back basic macros to some of the more advanced macro techniques. Be sure to try Lesson 8 in Part 9 if you need help getting started on creating your own macros.

In Part 5, you'll learn how to use a variety of tools that will make your office work easier, including mail merge and WordPerfect's Sort and Math features.

PART FIVE

Office Tools

! n this part you'll learn about specialized features of Word-Perfect that are particularly useful in a business setting. The Merge feature lets you merge data and text, and is particularly useful for mass-producing form letters, mailing labels, envelopes, and fill-in forms. The Sort and Select features can be used in conjunction with merges to let you better control mass mailings; they are also handy for managing just about any type of document that needs to be alphabetized or reorganized. WordPerfect's Math feature performs basic math calculations with numbers.

CHAPTER 16

Form Letters, Mailing Labels, and Other Merges

HANDS-ON
········
LESSON 9

For a hands-on lesson in using WordPerfect's Merge feature, see Lesson 9 in Part 9.

! f you ever need to send mass mailings, you're sure to appreciate WordPerfect's Merge feature. With it you can create a list of names and addresses, type up a single letter, and then have WordPerfect automatically print a personalized copy of that letter to everyone on the list, along with envelopes or mailing labels. Once you create your basic list of names and addresses, you can use it over and over again to print letters, invoices, envelopes, and mailing labels, as often as you need to without ever retyping a single name or address.

As you'll see, the Merge feature is useful for more than just mass mailings. It can be used to fill in blank forms, create invoices and packing slips, create sorted, alphabetized lists, and much more.

MERGE TERMINOLOGY

Merging always uses two files, the primary merge file and the secondary merge file. The primary file can be a form letter, a mailing label, an envelope, an invoice,

Once you put information in a secondary merge file, you can use it over and over again, without ever retyping it!

a packing slip, a fill-in form, or any other kind of document. The secondary file is a list that contains the data (variable information) to be printed on each copy of the document. Figure 16.1 shows an example of a primary merge file.

The primary file contains fixed information, which does not change from document to document. For example, in Figure 16.1, the letterhead, date, and all the text of the letter will be the same on every copy of the letter. The variable information will be inserted in the primary merge file wherever you have placed commands enclosed in curly braces, like this:

{FIELD}First Name~ {FIELD}Last Name~

The secondary merge file contains variable information, which changes from letter to letter. Figure 16.2 shows a secondary merge file that contains a list of *field names* (e.g., First Name, Last Name, Address) and actual names and addresses.

Acme Furniture
P.O. Box 1234
Los Angeles, CA 91234

August 11, 1991

{FIELD}First Name~ {FIELD}Last Name~
{FIELD}Address~
{FIELD}City~, {FIELD}State~ {FIELD}Zip~

Dear {FIELD}Salutation~:

Just a quick note to remind you that our annual clearance sale is happening next weekend at the Los Angeles Civic Center.

As usual, prices will be slashed below *our* production costs, so don't miss this important event.

Hope to see you there!

Best Regards:

Jason Klemmer
Vice President

FIGURE 16.1:
An example of a primary merge file

If your signature has been scanned and stored on-disk, you can have it printed automatically on each merged document.

When you merge the primary and secondary file, WordPerfect automatically replaces the {FIELD} commands in the primary file with data from the secondary file document, producing a third document with information from both files. Figure 16.3 shows the results of merging the primary and secondary merge files displayed in the preceding figures. Notice how WordPerfect has correctly produced a copy of the letter for each person in the secondary merge file.

Two terms that go along with secondary merge files are *field* and *record*, which originated in database management. In database management, data is organized into columns (fields) and rows (records), as the example in Figure 16.4 shows.

As you can see in the figure, a field is a column of similar information. For example, the third field in Figure 16.4 contains addresses. A record is all the information (that is, all the fields) for one item in the list. In Figure 16.4, the first record consists of all the data for Frank Fleinder.

A secondary merge file with field names and actual names and addresses

```
{FIELD NAMES}
        First Name~
        Last Name~
        Address~
        City~
        State~
        Zip~
        Salutation~~
{END RECORD}
==================================================================
Frank{END FIELD}
Fleinder{END FIELD}
123 Oak St.{END FIELD}
Glendora{END FIELD}
KS{END FIELD}
54321{END FIELD}
Frank{END FIELD}
{END RECORD}
==================================================================
Nita{END FIELD}
Bonita{END FIELD}
P.O. Box 5432{END FIELD}
Glendora{END FIELD}
KS{END FIELD}
54320{END FIELD}
Miss Bonita{END FIELD}
{END RECORD}
==================================================================
Jane{END FIELD}
Tarzana{END FIELD}
555 Apple St.{END FIELD}
Jackson{END FIELD}
KS{END FIELD}
54300{END FIELD}
Jane{END FIELD}
{END RECORD}
==================================================================
```

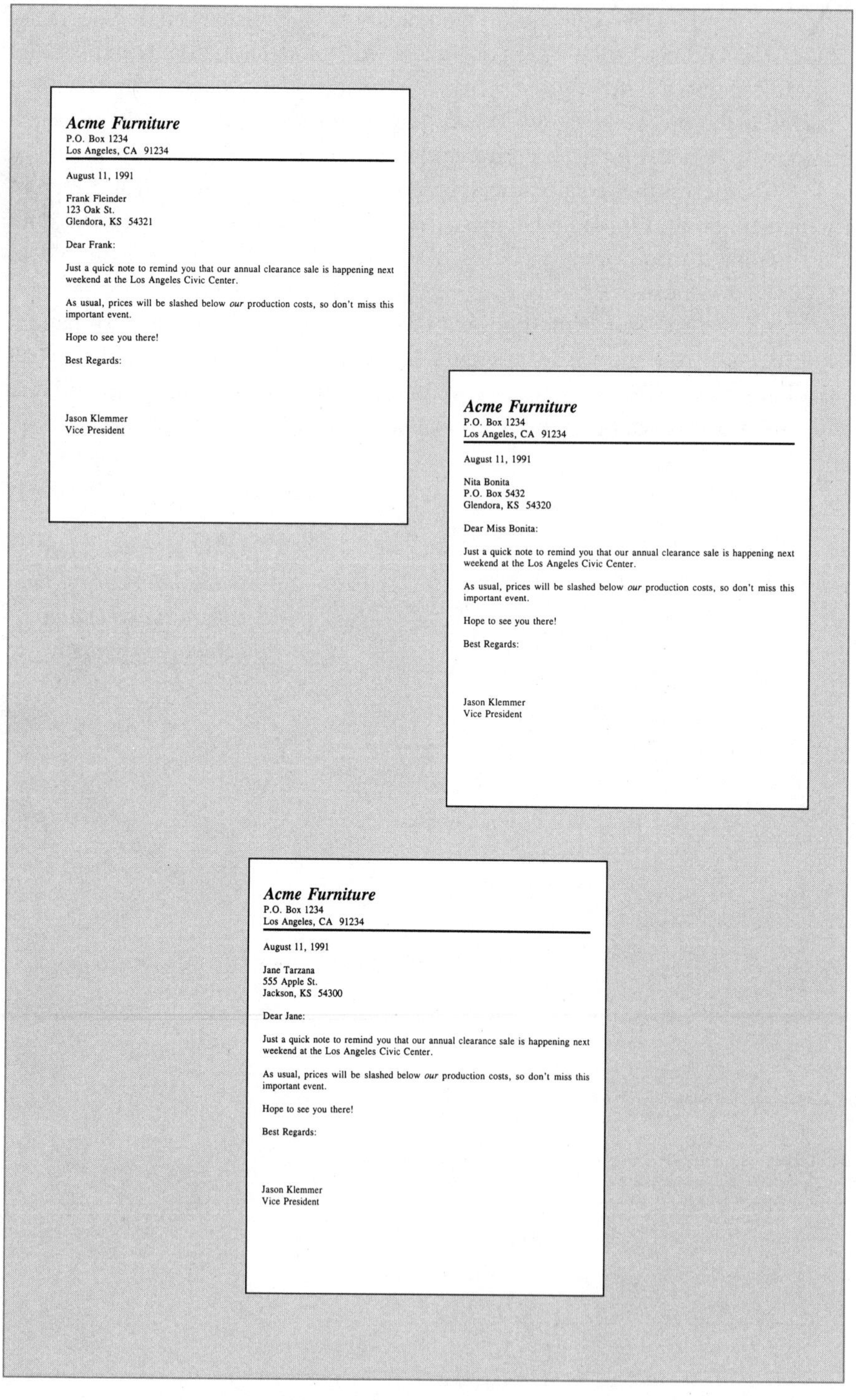

Acme Furniture
P.O. Box 1234
Los Angeles, CA 91234

August 11, 1991

Frank Fleinder
123 Oak St.
Glendora, KS 54321

Dear Frank:

Just a quick note to remind you that our annual clearance sale is happening next weekend at the Los Angeles Civic Center.

As usual, prices will be slashed below *our* production costs, so don't miss this important event.

Hope to see you there!

Best Regards:

Jason Klemmer
Vice President

Acme Furniture
P.O. Box 1234
Los Angeles, CA 91234

August 11, 1991

Nita Bonita
P.O. Box 5432
Glendora, KS 54320

Dear Miss Bonita:

Just a quick note to remind you that our annual clearance sale is happening next weekend at the Los Angeles Civic Center.

As usual, prices will be slashed below *our* production costs, so don't miss this important event.

Hope to see you there!

Best Regards:

Jason Klemmer
Vice President

Acme Furniture
P.O. Box 1234
Los Angeles, CA 91234

August 11, 1991

Jane Tarzana
555 Apple St.
Jackson, KS 54300

Dear Jane:

Just a quick note to remind you that our annual clearance sale is happening next weekend at the Los Angeles Civic Center.

As usual, prices will be slashed below *our* production costs, so don't miss this important event.

Hope to see you there!

Best Regards:

Jason Klemmer
Vice President

FIGURE 16.3:
Results of merging the files shown in figures 16.1 and 16.2

PLANNING A MERGE

Before you start creating your own merge files, you will need to decide the following:

◆ What information is fixed and therefore belongs in the primary merge file?

◆ What information varies and therefore belongs in the secondary merge file?

One way to get started is to pre-write a finished document. Then, circle the information that will vary from one document to the next, and give each circled item a unique name. For example, Figure 16.5 shows a form letter with variable information circled, and a brief name jotted down next to each item.

When creating your list of field names, first keep in mind that each field must have a unique name. For example, you cannot have two separate fields with the name *Date*. You could, however, have a field named *Date 1* and a field named *Date 2*.

Second, use brief, descriptive names no more than a word or two in length. So perhaps rather than having two fields named *Date 1* and *Date 2,* you'd want to use the names *Date Hired* and *Date Discharged,* or some other, more descriptive names. This makes it easier for you to keep track of what each field actually contains.

Also, be sure to include enough fields to cover every possible situation. For instance, if you are indeed creating a secondary merge file for mass mailings, do you need to include a job title with some names and addresses? Do you need two address lines for some? If you think you'll only need a job title or second line address in *some* cases, you still must include these in your list of field names, because every record in a secondary merge file must have exactly the same number of fields.

Also, try to break the information down into discrete, independent fields. There's no advantage to combining different types of information into a single field. So even though you typically print city, state, and zip code information

First Name	Last Name	Address	City	State	Zip	Salutation
Frank	Fleinder	123 Oak St.	Glendora	KS	54321	Frank
Nita	Bonita	P.O. Box 5432	Glendora	KS	54320	Miss Bonita
Jane	Tarzana	555 Apple St.	Jackson	KS	54300	Jane
William	Handroid	12 Main St.	Jackson	MI	54222	Willy

records

fields

FIGURE 16.4:

Fields and records in a database

in the format

Albuquerque, NM 76543

your best bet is to store this information as three separate fields in your secondary merge file, like this:

City	State	Zip
Albuquerque	NM	76543

As you'll see later, this gives you the greatest flexibility in managing the information in the future. For example, if you later decide to sort this information into zip-code order for bulk mailing, or to print letters, labels, or envelopes for people in a certain city or state only, you can easily do so, because the city, state, and zip codes are each in their own fields.

Don't worry about the comma between the city and state, or the spacing between the city, state, and zip fields. That comma is a fixed format that won't vary from letter to letter (or label to label, or envelope to envelope), and so can be handled in the primary merge file. All you want to store in the secondary

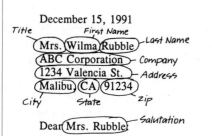

FIGURE 16.5:

A form letter with variable information circled

December 15, 1991

Title   First Name

Mrs. Wilma Rubble — Last Name

ABC Corporation — Company

1234 Valencia St. — Address

Malibu CA 91234

City   State   Zip

Dear Mrs. Rubble — Salutation

           Amount

Thank you for your donation of $500.00 to get our local Little League into action. Your donation will help us purchase outfits and equipment for the league.

Our next goal will be recruitment. We hope to call for players early in the next season, and start practicing before the big leagues start their pre-season games. If you have, or know of any children, who will be interested in playing next season, please have them send us their name and mailing address so we can keep them posted on dates and times.

Thanks again,

Willie B. Good
Director

When designing your secondary merge file, include data that may be useful in future projects. You can then use any of the fields in your primary merge files.

file is the pure, unformatted ("raw") data that varies from one document to the next, broken down into independent fields of information.

Finally, think of the long-range possibilities of your merge file. Suppose you're creating a list of names and addresses. Perhaps you'd like to send birthday cards to these people once a year. If so, include a field for their birthdates (perhaps named *Birthday*) so that you can easily isolate names and addresses with birthdates in the current month, then print some envelopes and birthday greetings for these people. When you've decided on your fields, jot them down on a piece of paper.

CREATING A SECONDARY MERGE FILE

TO CREATE A SECONDARY MERGE FILE,

1. **Select Tools ➤ Merge Codes ➤ More (or press Shift-F9 M).**

2. **Choose the {FIELD NAMES} command.**

3. **Type the name of every field in the secondary file, pressing ⏎ after each name (press ⏎ twice after typing the last field name).**

4. **Type in the data, ending each field (including empty fields) with an {END FIELD} command (by pressing F9), and ending each record with an {END RECORD} command (by selecting Tools ➤ Merge Codes ➤ End Record or pressing Shift-F9 E).**

As with earlier versions of Word-Perfect, it's not absolutely necessary to create a list of field names in a secondary merge file. But doing so makes your work easier in the long run. If you omit the field name list, each field will be numbered sequentially, starting with 1.

Once you've determined the individual fields that you'll need, you can create your secondary merge file. Follow these steps:

1. Start at a blank WordPerfect Edit screen.

2. Select **T**ools ➤ Me**r**ge Codes ➤ **M**ore to get to the merge commands, or press **Shift-F9 M**.

3. Type the letters **FN** to move the highlight to the {FIELD NAMES}name1~...nameN~~ option, as shown in Figure 16.6.

4. Press ⏎ to select that option.

5. Notice the prompt "Enter Field 1:" near the lower-left corner of the screen.

6. Type in a field name from your handwritten list of field names, and press ⏎.

7. Repeat step 6 for each field in your list of field names.

8. After you've entered all your field names, and WordPerfect asks for the next field name, just press ↵.

The merge commands menu disappears and your field names are displayed across the top of the screen, starting with a {FIELD NAMES} command. A hard page break appears beneath the list.

If your list of names is wider than the screen, some field names may be scrolled off the right edge of the screen. If so, you can move the cursor to the start of any field name (or each field name), and press ↵ to start each name on a separate line. You can also press Tab (but not the spacebar or any other key) to indent each field name if you wish. When you're finished, just make sure that

◆ The list of field names begins with a {FIELD NAMES} command (which appears as *[Mrg:FIELD NAMES]* on the Reveal Codes screen).

◆ Each field name is followed by a tilde (~).

◆ The last field name is followed by two tildes (~~).

◆ The entire list is followed by an {END RECORD} command and a hard page break (which appear as *[Mrg:END RECORD][HPg]* on the Reveal Codes screen).

The order of fields in a second- ary merge file is not important, but for your own con- venience, you should list them in whatever order seems most natural for typing them in—for ex- ample, Address, City, State, Zip is more com- mon than State, Ad- dress, Zip, City.

Merge com- mands in curly braces must be entered by using the menus; you cannot simply type a merge command, like {FIELD NAMES}, at your keyboard.

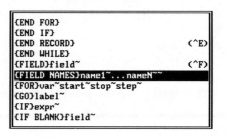

```
{END FOR}
{END IF}
{END RECORD}                        (^E)
{END WHILE}
{FIELD}field~                       (^F)
{FIELD NAMES}name1~...nameN~~
{FOR}var~start~stop~step~
{GO}label~
{IF}expr~
{IF BLANK}field~
```

(Name Search; Arrows; Enter to Select)

FIGURE 16.6:

The {FIELD NAMES} op- tion highlighted on the merge commands menu

Figure 16.7 shows an example where the field names from Figure 16.6 have been entered on the screen, following the steps described earlier. WordPerfect has automatically word-wrapped the names at the blank space in the Last Name field, but in some cases, it may simply scroll the field names off the right edge of the screen.

Figure 16.8 shows the field names from Figure 16.7 after using the ↵ and Tab keys to reformat the field name list. This format is not required, but makes it much easier to see each field name at a glance, which will come in handy later.

FILLING IN SECONDARY MERGE RECORDS

After deciding what fields your secondary merge file needs and completing the steps above for entering field names, you can start typing your secondary merge data. Remember these three important points:

◆ You must press End Field (**F9**) after typing the contents of a single field (the Edit screen displays {END FIELD} at the end of the field).

◆ You must select **T**ools ➤ Me**r**ge Codes, or press Merge Codes (**Shift-F9**), then select **E**nd Record after typing the last field to mark the end of the record.

◆ Don't forget that each record must contain the same number of fields, even if this means leaving a field empty. If there is no information for

---

```
{FIELD NAMES}Title~First Name~Last
Name~Company~Address~City~State~Zip~Salutation~Amount~~{END RECORD}
================================================================================
—




















Field: Title                              Doc 1 Pg 2 Ln 1" Pos 1"
```

FIGURE 16.7:

The field names from Figure 16.6 initially entered into a secondary merge file

a given field, press End Field (F9) to leave it blank. The field will then contain only an {END FIELD} command.

Let's take it from the top, step by step, to add records to a new (or existing) secondary merge file:

1. If the secondary merge file is not currently on your Edit screen, retrieve it.

2. Move the cursor to the bottom of the secondary merge file (press **Home Home** ↓). Note that the lower-left corner of the screen indicates which field you need to type, as shown in the example in Figure 16.9.

NOTE *You can enter several lines or paragraphs as the value for a single field. Keep in mind that pressing ⏎ just places a [HRt] code in your document; it doesn't end the field.*

3. Type in the field data (i.e., the information to be stored in that field). The field value can be a single line of text, many lines, or several paragraphs. If there is no information for this field, don't type anything, but *do* proceed to the next step.

4. Press End Field (**F9**) even if you left this field blank in the preceding step. The {END FIELD} command appears to the right of your entry (or in the otherwise blank field), the cursor moves down a line, and the name of the next field appears in the lower-left corner of the screen, as shown in Figure 16.10.

5. Repeat steps 3 and 4 for every field in the record.

```
{FIELD NAMES}
    Title~
    First Name~
    Last Name~
    Company~
    Address~
    City~
    State~
    Zip~
    Salutation~
    Amount~~
{END RECORD}
================================================================================



                      Doc 1 Pg 1 Ln 2.83" Pos 1"
```

FIGURE 16.8:

The field name list from Figure 16.7 reformatted to make it easier to view the field names

6. After you type in the last field for the record and press F9 to end that field, the cursor waits on the next line (as usual), but the lower-left corner of the screen shows a field number rather than a field name (for example, *Field: 11*). Select **T**ools ➤ Me**r**ge Codes, or press **Shift-F9**, and select **E**nd Record to indicate that you've finished typing this record.

At this point, an {END RECORD} command followed by a hard page break (double underline) appears on the screen, and the cursor moves down to the next row. Now the cursor is waiting for you to type the first field of the next record in the secondary merge file, as shown in the example in Figure 16.11.

At this point, you can repeat the basic steps above to type in as many records as you wish. Figure 16.12 shows a second record added to the sample secondary merge file presented in Figure 16.11.

Notice in Figure 16.12 that the Company field for the second record is left blank, containing only an {END FIELD} command. Why is it so important to leave the field blank when there is no information for that field? Simply because WordPerfect knows nothing about the information in each field—it can't tell a name from an address, from a zip code, from a bologna sandwich. Hence, if you type the wrong information into a field, WordPerfect won't know the difference.

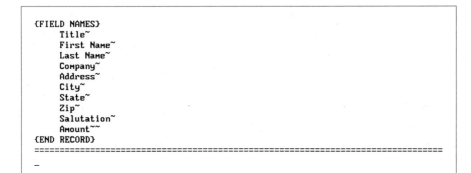

FIGURE 16.9:

WordPerfect ready to accept a Title entry

```
{FIELD NAMES}
     Title~
     First Name~
     Last Name~
     Company~
     Address~
     City~
     State~
     Zip~
     Salutation~
     Amount~~
{END RECORD}
==================================================================
 _



Field: Title                        Doc 1 Pg 2 Ln 1" Pos 1"
```

```
{FIELD NAMES}
     Title~
     First Name~
     Last Name~
     Company~
     Address~
     City~
     State~
     Zip~
     Salutation~
     Amount~~
{END RECORD}
===========================================================================
Mrs.{END FIELD}
     _




Field: First Name                        Doc 1 Pg 2 Ln 1.17" Pos 1"
```

FIGURE 16.10:

After you type "Mrs." as the first field entry, the cursor waits for the First Name for this record.

```
     First Name~
     Last Name~
     Company~
     Address~
     City~
     State~
     Zip~
     Salutation~
     Amount~~
{END RECORD}
===========================================================================
Mrs.{END FIELD}
Wilma{END FIELD}
Rubble{END FIELD}
ABC Corporation{END FIELD}
1234 Valencia St.{END FIELD}
Malibu{END FIELD}
CA{END FIELD}
91234{END FIELD}
Mrs. Rubble{END FIELD}
$500.00{END FIELD}
{END RECORD}
===========================================================================
Field: Title                             Doc 1 Pg 3 Ln 1" Pos 1"
```

FIGURE 16.11:

One complete record is entered on the screen. The cursor is waiting for the first field of the next record.

For example, if you completely omit the Company field by forgetting to place an {END FIELD} command in it, like this,

Mr.{END FIELD}
Dustin{END FIELD}
Seeburg, III{END FIELD}
P.O. Box 1221{END FIELD}
Montecito{END FIELD}
CA{END FIELD}
91121{END FIELD}
Dusty{END FIELD}
$100.00{END FIELD}
{END RECORD}

WordPerfect will accept your entry, and at first glance it will seem correct. However, when you perform the merge later, the top of the letter will come out looking something like this,

Mr. Dustin Seeburg, III
P.O. Box 1221
Montecito
CA, 91121 Dusty

Dear $100.00:

```
Wilma{END FIELD}
Rubble{END FIELD}
ABC Corporation{END FIELD}
1234 Valencia St.{END FIELD}
Malibu{END FIELD}
CA{END FIELD}
91234{END FIELD}
Mrs. Rubble{END FIELD}
$500.00{END FIELD}
{END RECORD}
================================================================
Mr.{END FIELD}
Dustin{END FIELD}
Seeburg, III{END FIELD}
{END FIELD}
P.O. Box 1221{END FIELD}
Montecito{END FIELD}
CA{END FIELD}
91121{END FIELD}
Dusty{END FIELD}
$100.00{END FIELD}
{END RECORD}
================================================================
Field: Title                          Doc 1 Pg 4 Ln 1" Pos 1"
```

FIGURE 16.12:

A second record has been added to the secondary merge file. Notice the "blank" Company field above the address.

If you for-get to leave a field blank, you can move the cursor to the beginning of the field, then press End Field (F9) to insert an {END FIELD} command. Doing so will move data below the cursor into its correct field position.

Why? Because in the secondary merge file you've placed the address where the company belongs, the city where the address belongs, the state where the city belongs, and so forth. You can see the problem quite clearly by scrolling the cursor through each field in the secondary file and noting the field name shown in the lower-left corner of the screen. For example, if you place your cursor on the field entered above as *$100.00,* you'll see the field name Salutation (not Amount) displayed in the lower-left corner of the screen.

In short, you must make sure that you correctly type each item of information in its correct place in the secondary merge file. If there is no entry for a particular field, you must press End Field (F9) to mark the end of the field, so WordPerfect knows that the field has been intentionally left blank.

SAVING YOUR SECONDARY MERGE FILE

When you're set-ting up a merge for the first time, start with a "dry run" by adding just a few records to your secon-dary merge file; then create the primary merge file and per-form a merge.

After creating your secondary merge file, you must save it as you would any other document, using **File ➤ S**ave, the Save key (F10), or **File ➤ E**xit. You may want to use a file-name extension, such as *.SCD,* that will make it easy for you to recognize this as a secondary merge file in the future. For example, you could save the sample file above as *NAD.SCD;* NAD is a commonly used abbreviation (in computer circles) for "name and address," and SCD is short for "secondary."

CREATING A PRIMARY MERGE FILE

TO CREATE A PRIMARY MERGE FILE,

> **type the fixed text as you normally would, but where you want to incorporate text from the secondary merge files, select Tools ➤ Merge Codes ➤ Field (or press Shift-F9 F) to insert a {FIELD} command, fol-lowed by the name (or number) of the field you want to insert and a tilde (~).**

A primary merge file can use any com-bination of fields, in any order, from a secondary merge file, and can use any single field more than once.

Creating a primary merge file is much like creating any other document in WordPerfect—you start with a clear Edit screen and type and edit as necessary. The only difference is that, wherever you want to merge variable text from your secondary merge file, you need to insert a command that tells Word-Perfect exactly where to place that text. Here's the complete procedure:

1. Start with a clear Edit screen (if the secondary merge file is still on the screen, save it and clear the screen).

2. Type your primary merge file as you would any other document. However, whenever you want to use text from the secondary merge file, position the cursor where you want that text to appear.

3. Select **T**ools ➤ Me**r**ge Codes, or press Merge Codes (**Shift-F9**).

4. Select **F**ield.

5. Type the name of the field that you want to place at the cursor position, and press ↵. The command {FIELD} followed by the field name and a tilde appears. (If you created the secondary file without using the {FIELD NAMES} command, your fields will be numbered sequentially, starting with 1; if so, type a field number instead of a name.)

6. Repeat steps 2–5 for whatever fields you want to place in the current primary merge file.

7. When you've finished creating the primary merge file, save it and clear the screen, as you would for any other document.

When inserting codes in your primary merge file, be sure to include any necessary blank spaces and punctuation marks, just as though you were typing the actual information. For example, if your secondary merge file contains the fields City, State, and Zip, and you place these commands in your primary merge file as

{FIELD}City~{FIELD}State~{FIELD}Zip~

they will be printed as

EncinitasCA92024

However, if you place the commands in your primary merge file as

{FIELD}City~, {FIELD}State~ {FIELD}Zip~

they will be printed as

Encinitas, CA 92024

Figure 16.13 shows a sample primary merge file for the secondary merge file presented earlier in this chapter.

When typing the field name for the primary merge file, be sure to spell it exactly as you did in the secondary merge file. If you type it incorrectly, the field will be ignored during the merge.

To make it easier to keep track of primary merge files, you may want to give them all the same file-name extension, such as .PRM.

PERFORMING THE MERGE

TO MERGE YOUR PRIMARY AND SECONDARY MERGE FILES,

1. Be sure to save each one, get to a blank Edit screen, then select Tools ➤ Merge or press Merge/Sort (Ctrl-F9), and choose Merge.

2. Enter the name of the primary and secondary merge files as prompted.

3. To print the merged documents, select File ➤ Print ➤ Full Document (or press Shift-F7 F).

After you've created and saved your primary and secondary merge files, you're ready to merge them. Follow these steps:

1. Start from a clear Edit screen.

2. Select **T**ools ➤ **M**erge or press Merge/Sort (**Ctrl-F9**), and choose **M**erge.

3. As prompted on the screen, type the name of the primary file, including the extension (for example, *FORMLET.PRM*), and press ⏎.

4. As prompted on the screen, type the name of the secondary file, including the extension (for example, *NAD.SCD*), and press ⏎.

December 15, 1991

{FIELD}Title~ {FIELD}First Name~ {FIELD}Last Name~
{FIELD}Company~
{FIELD}Address~
{FIELD}City~, {FIELD}State~ {FIELD}Zip~

Dear {FIELD}Salutation~:

Thank you for your donation of {FIELD}Amount~ to get our local Little League into action. Your donation will help us purchase outfits and equipment for the league.

Our next goal will be recruitment. We hope to call for players early in the next season, and start practicing before the big leagues start their pre-season games. If you have, or know of any children, who will be interested in playing next season, please have them send us their name and mailing address so we can keep them posted on dates and times.

Thanks again,

Doc 1 Pg 1 Ln 1" Pos 1"

FIGURE 16.13:

A sample primary merge file

5. Wait for the "* Merging *" message to disappear from the lower-left corner of the screen.

You can also view the results on-screen by selecting File ➤ Print ➤ View Document (or pressing Shift-F7 V). This is especially handy when you're experimenting with merges and want to preview the results without wasting paper.

The merge combines both documents into one new merge document on your Edit screen, with the cursor positioned at the end of the document. You can press Home Home ↑ to move to the top of the document, then scroll through the document with the usual cursor-movement keys, including Page Up, Page Down, and the gray + and − keys. To print the results, select **F**ile ➤ **P**rint ➤ **F**ull Document (or press Shift-F7 F).

After the merge, your original primary and secondary merge files are still on the disk, so you can reuse either in the future, if need be. In fact, there really is no reason to save the results of the merge on your screen, because once you've printed those documents, the job is finished.

If you happen to notice an error in the merged document, you're better off clearing the merged document from the Edit screen, correcting the primary or secondary file, saving the corrected file, then repeating the merge. This way, you can clean up the problem at its source, so it won't pop up again the next time you perform the merge.

If the error is just in the variable information on one page (a misspelled name or address, for example), you needn't reprint the entire merged file. Just make your corrections to the secondary merge file and repeat the merge as described above. Then move the cursor to the page you want to reprint and select **F**ile ➤ **P**rint ➤ **P**age (or press Shift-F7 P). See Chapter 8 for more information on printing selected pages of a document.

PRINTING ENVELOPES AND LABELS

TO MERGE TEXT TO ENVELOPES OR MAILING LABELS,

1. **Insert the appropriate paper size in the Document Initial Codes area of the primary merge file.**

2. **Arrange the {FIELD} commands in the primary merge file to print on a single envelope or label.**

3. **Save that file and merge it with the secondary merge file.**

You can create any number of primary merge files for a single secondary merge file. Hence, you can use the same secondary merge file repeatedly to print a monthly newsletter, form letters, fliers, lists, envelopes, and labels.

Your primary merge file can use any size of paper—even form letters or mailing labels. Just be sure to place the appropriate paper size for the primary merge file in the Document Initial Codes area (so it's not repeated on each merged document). If you've installed WordPerfect for use with multiple printers, be sure to choose the appropriate printer before defining a primary merge file for envelopes or labels, so you can find or create the correct paper size. Here are the basic steps:

1. At a blank Edit screen or at the top of an existing document, select **L**ayout ➤ **D**ocument ➤ Initial **C**odes or press **Shift-F8 D C**.

2. Select **L**ayout ➤ **P**age ➤ Paper **S**ize or press **Shift-F8 P S**.

3. Move the highlight to the paper size you want to print on (see Chapter 7 if you need a refresher or need to create a paper size), and choose Select to select it.

4. Press Exit (**F7**) until you return to the Edit screen.

5. Create and save your primary merge file as you normally would, as described under "Creating a Primary Merge File."

6. Perform the merge and print the resulting document, as described under "Performing the Merge."

 *Techniques for formatting individual envelopes and letters will also work for primary merge files. The View Document screen can also help you define your format.*

As an example, Figure 16.14 shows a primary merge file for printing envelopes, which is very similar to the envelope format shown in Chapter 7. Figure 16.15 shows a primary merge file for printing labels. You can see the basic formatting codes on the Reveal Codes screen. Note, however, that the [Paper Sz/Typ] code is not visible on the Reveal Codes screen simply because that code was placed in the Document Initial Codes area for each document, to prevent it from being repeated throughout the final merge document.

Refining Label Alignment

If you use a merge file to print labels, and your labels are not properly aligned, here are a few tips that may help you align them:

◆ Because labels are much more expensive than paper, you may want to use plain paper while initially trying to align your label text correctly. After printing, align the sheet of paper directly over the blank labels and hold both sheets together up to a light, so you can see how the text lines up with the label outlines.

◆ If the name and address are printed too high on each label, edit the primary merge file for printing labels, and press ↵ to move all the {FIELD} codes down one or more lines (or, if you are using tractor-fed labels, align the first label to be printed a little higher above the print head).

◆ If the name and address are printed too far to the left, edit the primary merge file, and use the Tab key (and tab stops) to move each row of {FIELD} codes a little to the right (or, if you are using tractor-fed labels, position the labels a little farther to the left before printing).

```
West L.A. Little League
123 Santa Monica Blvd.
Santa Monica, CA  92222




                                {FIELD}Title~ {FIELD}First Name~ {FIELD}Last Name~
                                {FIELD}Company~
                                {FIELD}Address~
                                {FIELD}City~, {FIELD}State~  {FIELD}Zip~
                                         Doc 1 Pg 1 Ln 0.29" Pos 0.25"
[
[T/B Mar:0.29",1"][L/R Mar:0.25",1"]West L.A. Little League[HRt]
123 Santa Monica Blvd.[HRt]
Santa Monica, CA  92222[HRt]
[HRt]
[HRt]
[HRt]
[HRt]
[L/R Mar:3.25",1"][Mrg:FIELD]Title~ [Mrg:FIELD]First Name~ [Mrg:FIELD]Last Name~
[HRt]
[Mrg:FIELD]Company~[HRt]

Press Reveal Codes to restore screen
```

FIGURE 16.14:

A sample primary merge file for printing envelopes

```
{FIELD}Title~ {FIELD}First Name~ {FIELD}Last Name~
{FIELD}Company~
{FIELD}Address~
{FIELD}City~, {FIELD}State~  {FIELD}Zip~







                                 Doc 1 Pg 1 Ln 0" Pos 0.165"
[                           ]
[Center Pg][Mrg:FIELD]Title~ [Mrg:FIELD]First Name~ [Mrg:FIELD]Last Name~[HRt]
[Mrg:FIELD]Company~[HRt]
[Mrg:FIELD]Address~[HRt]
[Mrg:FIELD]City~, [Mrg:FIELD]State~  [Mrg:FIELD]Zip~[HRt]




Press Reveal Codes to restore screen
```

FIGURE 16.15:

A sample primary merge file for printing labels

◆ If the first label prints correctly but the labels that follow are out of alignment, the label size or page size definition is incorrect. Select **L**ayout from the menu or press Format (Shift-F8), then select **P**age ➤ Paper **S**ize, and move the highlight to the paper type definition for printing labels. Then do one of the following:

WordPerfect may make adjustments to your label entries to accommodate the printer. Or, it may reject an "impossible" label size, such as when the labels could not possibly fit on the label sheet.

  ◆ If you are using tractor-fed labels, select **E**dit. Then select Paper **S**ize and **O**ther. Press ↵ to keep the defined width, and type in a larger or smaller height, depending on whether you need to increase or decrease the height of each printed label. Press ↵, then Exit (F7) until you get back to the Edit screen.

  ◆ If you are using sheet labels, select **E**dit, then La**b**els, then **Y**es. Select **D**istance Between Labels, press ↵ to leave the Column distance unchanged, and decrease or increase the Row setting to move the text on each label closer or farther apart. Press ↵, then Exit (F7) until you get back to the Edit screen.

◆ When printing labels other than for mailing (for example, when printing disk labels or ID labels), you may want to center text on each label. To center text horizontally on each label, place a [Just:Center] code at the top of the primary merge file (select **L**ayout or press Shift-F8, then choose **L**ine ➤ **J**ustification ➤ **C**enter). To center text vertically on each label, place a [Center Pg] code at the top of the primary merge file (select **L**ayout or press Shift-F8, then choose **P**age ➤ Center Page ➤ **Y**es) before merging the files.

After changing your primary merge file or label paper size, be sure to save your primary merge file, and remerge the primary and secondary files, before attempting to print the labels again.

REFINING YOUR MERGES

One problem almost invariably arises when you merge documents: Empty fields in the secondary merge file appear as blank lines or blank spaces in the primary merge file. For example, the name and address for a person who does not have a company affiliation in the secondary file will come out with a blank line above the address (where the company is normally printed), like this:

Mr. Dustin Seeburg, III

P.O. 1221
Montecito, CA 91121

There may be an extra blank space in front of people's names without an entry in the Title field (this would be caused by the blank space normally used to separate the title from the first name), like this:

Alicia Ramirez
311 Valley Parkway
Escondido, CA 92001

Fortunately, both these common problems are quite easy to solve.

ELIMINATING BLANK LINES

TO PREVENT AN EMPTY FIELD IN A SECONDARY FILE FROM PRODUCING A BLANK LINE IN THE FINISHED DOCUMENT,

insert a question mark (?) at the end of the field name (but before the tilde,~) in the primary merge file.

To prevent a blank field from becoming a blank line in your finished document, add a question mark (?) to the {FIELD} command in the primary file (not the secondary file), just before the closing tilde (~). The question mark tells WordPerfect to print nothing, rather than a blank line, if the field is empty.

For example, to prevent the blank line caused by the empty Company field, bring the primary merge file back to the Edit screen, and add a question mark to the Company field, just in front of the tilde that ends the field name, like this:

{FIELD}Company?~

Save the primary merge file, and then merge the primary and secondary files again. This time, records with blank Company fields will print properly, as below:

Mr. Dustin Seeburg
P.O. 1221
Montecito, CA 91121

 *You can type the question mark (?) right at the keyboard; you don't need to use a merge command or the menus.*

HANDLING BLANK FIELDS

If you're using several fields across a single line in a merged document, and one of those fields is empty, the blank space used to separate the fields is still printed, causing extra blank spaces in your final merged document, as shown in the Alicia Ramirez example above.

A potentially more embarrassing problem with blank fields occurs when they are required, but omitted by accident. For example, if the Salutation field is inadvertently left blank in a record, or several records, the salutation in the letter may come out looking like this:

Dear   :

WordPerfect offers two merge commands for handling blank fields, **{IF BLANK}** *field~print this* **{END IF}** and **{IF NOT BLANK}***field~print this* **{END IF}**,

where *field* is the name of the field you want to test as blank (or not blank), and *print this* is whatever you want to insert in the merged document (including any spaces and hard returns), based on whether or not the field is blank. For example, notice the command line below:

{IF NOT BLANK}Title~{FIELD}Title~ {END IF}

This sequence of commands says, "If the Title field is not blank, print the Title field, followed by a blank space." Of course, this also prevents either the title or the blank space from being printed if the title is blank.

You can add an {ELSE} command to the {IF...} statements to choose an alternative course of action should the field prove to be blank, or not blank. You must structure the commands this way:

{IF BLANK}*field~print this***{ELSE}***print this***{END IF}**

{IF NOT BLANK}*field~print this***{ELSE}***print this***{END IF}**

For example, the command below prints the word *Dear,* then decides, "If the Salutation field is blank, print the words *Valued Customer,* otherwise print the contents of the Salutation field." Then it prints the colon:

Dear **{IF BLANK}***Salutation~Valued Customer* **{ELSE}{FIELD}** Salutation~**{END IF}**:

The word *Dear* and the colon at the end are always printed, regardless of whether the Salutation field is blank or not, because both are outside the {IF} and {END IF} commands.

To use the {IF}, {END IF}, and optional {ELSE} commands in your primary merge file, follow these steps:

1. Position the cursor where you want to insert an {IF} command in your document.

2. Select **T**ools ➤ Me**r**ge Codes (or press **Shift-F9**) and select **M**ore.

3. Type the letter *I* to move to the general vicinity of the IF command you want to select, then use the arrow keys (or mouse) to highlight the specific command (either {IF BLANK}field~ or {IF NOT BLANK}field~). Press ↵ to select the highlighted command.

4. At the "Enter field:" prompt, type the name of the field that you want to test, then press ↵.

5. Type whatever you want to appear when the {IF} condition proves *true*. If you want a field inserted, press **Shift-F9**, select **F**ield, type the field name (or number), and press ↵. Remember, fields, text, spaces, and hard returns that you enter here will be included in the merged document *only* if the {IF} condition proves true.

6. If you are using the {IF} command to prevent extra blank spaces only (as in our Title example earlier in this section), skip to step 8. If, on the other hand, you want WordPerfect to print something specific when the {IF} condition proves *false* (as in our Valued Customer example), select **T**ools ➤ Me**r**ge Codes (or press **Shift-F9**), then select **M**ore. Type **E** and press ↵ to select {ELSE}.

7. Type whatever you want to appear when the {IF} condition proves *false*. As in step 5, if you want a field inserted, press **Shift-F9**, select **F**ield, type the field name (or number), and press ↵. Remember, fields, text, spaces, and hard returns that you enter here will be included in the merged document *only* if the {IF} condition proves false.

Each {IF BLANK} and {IF NOT BLANK} command must have one (and only one) {END IF} command associated with it. The {ELSE} command in between is optional.

8. Select **T**ools ➤ Me**r**ge Codes (or press **Shift-F9**), then select **M**ore. Type **E** and use the arrow keys (or mouse) to highlight the {END IF} option, then press ↵ to select it.

The {END IF} command marks the end of the "if" decision. Any fields, text, blank spaces, or hard returns to the right of the {END IF} command are part of the general primary file and will be included in the resulting merge regardless of whether the {IF} condition proves true or false.

Figure 16.16 shows a more refined version of the primary merge file commands used in previous merges. The ? next to the Company field prevents empty Company fields from being printed as blank lines, and {IF} commands control potentially blank titles and salutations.

These more complex merge commands use a pair of *nested* {IF} statements to determine the best way to print the salutation. The logic of the decision goes like this:

IF the salutation isn't blank

    Print the salutation

ELSE (the salutation is blank)

    IF the title isn't blank

        Print the title and last name

    ELSE (both salutation and title are blank)

        Print the word "Donor"

    END IF (title is not blank)

END IF (salutation is not blank)

The line scrolls past the right edge of the Edit screen, but you can see the commands on the Reveal Codes screen (where each command starts with *Mrg:* and is enclosed in square brackets rather than curly braces).

Figure 16.17 shows two sample records from a secondary merge file that might cause some problems with a basic primary merge file. The first sample record has an empty Company field and an empty Salutation field. The second example has empty Title, First Name, Last Name, and Salutation fields. (The empty fields are easy to spot because each one has just an {END FIELD} command on a line by itself, without any additional text.)

The merge commands presented in Figure 16.16, however, could handle these two records quite easily, presenting each one in the format below when the merge is complete:

Mr. Wallace Wilcox
P.O. Box 999
L.A., CA 91234

Dear Mr. Wilcox:

MegaCorp
Box 3311
L.A., CA 90023

Dear Donor:

```
{IF NOT BLANK}Title~{FIELD}Title~ {END IF}{FIELD}First Name~ {FIELD}Last Name~
{FIELD}Company?~
{FIELD}Address~
{FIELD}City~, {FIELD}State~  {FIELD}Zip~

Dear {IF NOT BLANK}Salutation~{FIELD}Salutation~{ELSE}{IF NOT BLANK}Title~{FIELD




                                                     Doc 1 Pg 1 Ln 1" Pos 1"
{                                                                             }
[Mrg:IF NOT BLANK]Title~[Mrg:FIELD]Title~ [Mrg:END IF][Mrg:FIELD]First Name~ [Mr
g:FIELD]Last Name~[HRt]
[Mrg:FIELD]Company?~[HRt]
[Mrg:FIELD]Address~[HRt]
[Mrg:FIELD]City~, [Mrg:FIELD]State~  [Mrg:FIELD]Zip~[HRt]
[HRt]
Dear [Mrg:IF NOT BLANK]Salutation~[Mrg:FIELD]Salutation~[Mrg:ELSE][Mrg:IF NOT BL
ANK]Title~[Mrg:FIELD]Title~ [Mrg:FIELD]Last Name~[Mrg:ELSE]Donor[Mrg:END IF][Mrg
:END IF]:[HRt]


Press Reveal Codes to restore screen
```

FIGURE 16.16:

A more refined primary merge file capable of handling empty fields

```
Mr.{END FIELD}
Wallace{END FIELD}
Wilcox{END FIELD}
{END FIELD}
P.O. Box 999{END FIELD}
L.A.{END FIELD}
CA{END FIELD}
91234{END FIELD}
{END FIELD}
$50.00{END FIELD}
{END RECORD}
================================================================================
{END FIELD}
{END FIELD}
{END FIELD}
MegaCorp{END FIELD}
Box 3311{END FIELD}
L.A.{END FIELD}
CA{END FIELD}
90023{END FIELD}
{END FIELD}
$1,000.00{END FIELD}
{END RECORD}
================================================================================
Field: Title                                         Doc 1 Pg 2 Ln 1" Pos 1"
```

FIGURE 16.17:

A sample secondary merge file with some empty fields and missing data

You can use many additional commands to further refine your WordPerfect merges, as will be discussed later in this chapter. Before I talk about these, however, let's return our attention to the secondary merge file.

MANAGING YOUR SECONDARY MERGE FILE

Use the Search feature (select Search from the menu bar or press F2) to search through a large secondary merge file to locate a specific record.

Chances are that you will use your secondary file many times in the future. And as situations change, you'll need to add new records, change them, and delete them. For the most part, you'll use the standard WordPerfect editing techniques to do so. But in this section, I'll discuss techniques that pertain specifically to secondary merge files.

ADDING OR CHANGING RECORDS IN A SECONDARY MERGE FILE

You need not be concerned about the alphabetical order of names in your secondary merge file because you can sort the names anytime (see Chapter 17).

To add new records to a secondary merge file, use the exact sequence of steps listed in "Filling in Secondary Merge Records" earlier in this chapter. You can also change the information in the secondary merge file by using the same editing keys and techniques you use at the regular Edit screen. Just be sure to keep an eye on the current field name, shown in the lower-left corner of the screen, to make sure you put the right information in the right field (for instance, you don't want to put a zip code in the City field).

If you simply forget to leave a field blank when typing in information, you can insert a new (blank) field in a record by moving the cursor to wherever the blank field should appear and pressing F9. Then you can scroll the cursor through the fields and check the prompt near the bottom of the screen to make sure the correct information is in each field.

If you want to delete an entire record, be sure to delete all the text and codes from the first character of the record to the [HPg] code that ends the record. Alternatively, you can use the Select feature (Chapter 17) to limit your merges to certain types of records in your secondary merge file. This feature isolates certain types of records (for example, all New York residents or all orders for a particular part number) and makes it unnecessary to delete records from your secondary merge file.

Remember to save the entire file after making any changes to your secondary merge file.

ADDING OR DELETING A FIELD

Any field in a secondary merge file can contain a hard return. So in a pinch, you can split the contents of a single field into two rows of text by pressing ⏎ after typing the first line. For example, Figure 16.18 shows a record with the job title *Vice President,* as well as the name *WaterSport, Inc.,* in the Company field of a secondary merge file.

But as mentioned earlier, if you want to manage your secondary merge file by using the sorting and selection techniques described in Chapter 17, your best bet is to break the information into several fields, and use the fields consistently in each record.

If you've already created your secondary merge file and added some records, then later decide to add a field to the overall structure, you should first add the field name to the {FIELD NAMES} section of the secondary merge file. Be sure to start the field name after a tilde (~), and add a new tilde after typing your new field name. For example, Figure 16.19 shows the field name Job Title added to the list of field names shown in Figure 16.11.

Next, save the entire secondary merge file and clear the screen, then retrieve the secondary merge file. As you scroll down through existing fields, the new field name will appear in the lower-left corner of the screen when the cursor is positioned on it. Press End Field (F9) to insert a blank field at the new position, or type an entry, then press F9.

Figure 16.20 shows a blank Job Title field properly inserted in Wilma Rubbles's record (after the new Job Title field was inserted in the list of field names and the secondary file was saved, then retrieved again).

You can use the same basic technique to delete a field from a secondary merge file: Move the cursor to the field name you want to delete (between the {FIELD NAMES} and the {END RECORD} commands), then delete the entire field

Be sure to update every record in the secondary merge file to match the new list of field names. You can then use the new field name in any primary merge files.

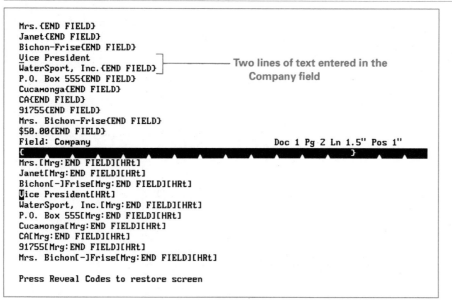

FIGURE 16.18:

A field that uses a hard return to split text into two lines within a secondary merge file

name, the tilde (~), and the [HRt] code (if there is one). Save the entire secondary merge file, clear the screen, then retrieve the secondary merge file. Again, as you scroll through existing text in the records, the lower-left corner of the screen shows which field the cursor is in. Press Ctrl-End, then Delete, to delete the field contents and the [HRt] code that follows the field entry.

MORE MERGE OPERATIONS

So far you've seen how to perform merges and have been introduced to several merge commands. For the remainder of this chapter, I'll present some additional types of merges and introduce some more merge commands. But first I'll review the basic steps required to select a merge command.

SELECTING MERGE COMMANDS

As you've seen in preceding examples, merging involves the use of merge commands. As a review and for future quick reference, here are the steps for selecting a merge command:

1. Position the cursor where you want to insert a merge command.

2. Select **T**ools ➤ Me**r**ge Codes, or press Merge Codes (**Shift-F9**).

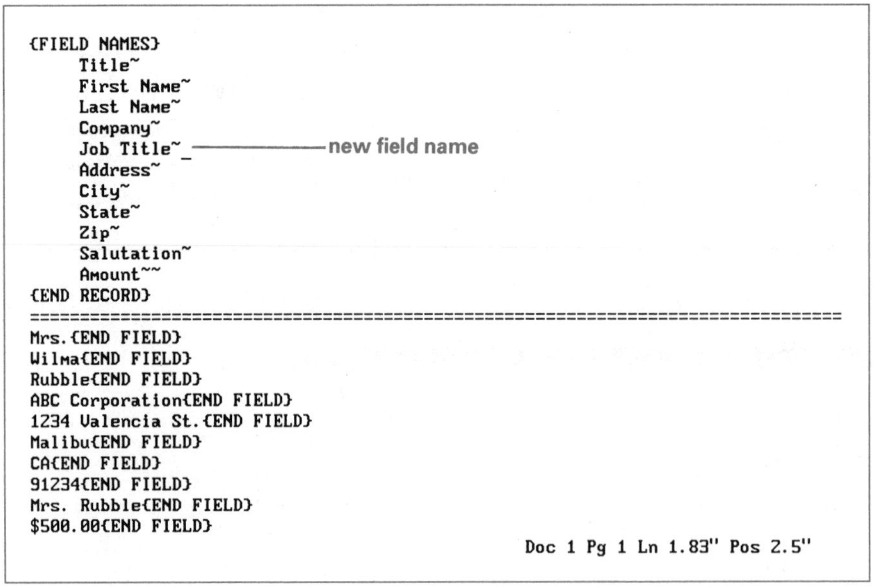

```
{FIELD NAMES}
     Title~
     First Name~
     Last Name~
     Company~
     Job Title~_————————new field name
     Address~
     City~
     State~
     Zip~
     Salutation~
     Amount~~
{END RECORD}
================================================================
Mrs.{END FIELD}
Wilma{END FIELD}
Rubble{END FIELD}
ABC Corporation{END FIELD}
1234 Valencia St.{END FIELD}
Malibu{END FIELD}
CA{END FIELD}
91234{END FIELD}
Mrs. Rubble{END FIELD}
$500.00{END FIELD}
                              Doc 1 Pg 1 Ln 1.83" Pos 2.5"
```

FIGURE 16.19:

A new Job Title field has been added to the list of field names.

3. If the merge command you want does not appear on the first menu, select **M**ore to view additional ones.

4. Move the highlight to the command you want, and press ↵ to select it. If the command requires additional information (such as {FIELD}*field~*, which requires a field name in place of the word *field*), you'll be prompted for the required information in the lower-left corner of the screen. Fill in the prompt, and press ↵. (Some commands present two or more prompts.)

5. When no (additional) information is required, the cursor returns to the document, and you can continue typing text or selecting additional merge commands.

This basic procedure can be used to select any commands used in merges, including all the examples that follow.

Word Wrap and Merge Commands When word-wrapping text on the Edit screen, WordPerfect ignores merge commands. Therefore, lines that contain merge commands often scroll off the right edge of the screen. The Reveal Codes screen, however, wraps codes at the right margin, so you can see all your text and codes.

The Reveal Codes screen also displays merge commands somewhat differently from the Edit screen. The commands are usually highlighted in square

When selecting a merge command from the More menu, you can type the first letter or letters of the command to move the highlight quickly to the command or its general vicinity.

```
{FIELD NAMES}
        Title~
        First Name~
        Last Name~
        Company~
        Job Title~
        Address~
        City~
        State~
        Zip~
        Salutation~
        Amount~~
{END RECORD}
================================================================================
Mrs.{END FIELD}
Wilma{END FIELD}
Rubble{END FIELD}
ABC Corporation{END FIELD}
{END FIELD} ──────────────────────── Every record must be updated to
1234 Valencia St.{END FIELD}           accommodate the new field
Malibu{END FIELD}
CA{END FIELD}
91234{END FIELD}
Mrs. Rubble{END FIELD}
Field: Job Title                       Doc 1 Pg 2 Ln 1.67" Pos 1"
```

FIGURE 16.20:

A blank field inserted in the first record to match the new list of field names

brackets rather than curly brackets and preceded by *Mrg:*. For example, the command {IF NOT BLANK} on the Edit screen appears as [Mrg:IF NOT BLANK] on the Reveal Codes screen.

MERGING STRAIGHT TO THE PRINTER

If your secondary merge file is very large, you may not be able to complete a merge in your computer's memory. As an alternative, you can tell WordPerfect to send the results of each merge directly to the printer instead of the Edit screen. To do so, simply bring the primary merge file to the Edit screen, move the cursor to the bottom of the merge file (press Home Home ↓), then select **T**ools ➤ Me**r**ge (or press Shift-F9) and choose **M**ore. Highlight the {PRINT} command and press ↵. This places a {PRINT} command at the bottom of the merge file, as shown in Figure 16.21.

Now you can save the primary merge file and perform the merge. Word-Perfect prints each completed document as it is merged.

CREATING LISTS FROM MERGE FILES

The sample primary merge file uses {IF} and {ENDIF} commands to omit the Last Name, Title, and First Name fields when the Last Name field is empty and to omit the company when the Company field is empty.

You can alphabetize (sort) a merged document, like the sample directory, using the Sort feature presented in the next chapter.

Normally when you perform a merge, information from each record in the secondary merge file is printed on a separate page, which is ideal for printing form letters, envelopes, and labels (the latter because WordPerfect treats each label as a page). In some cases, however, this separation into pages may not be desirable, such as when you want to print a list or directory from your secondary merge file. For instance, Figure 16.22 shows a sample directory assembled from a secondary merge file of names and addresses.

Figure 16.23 shows the primary merge file used to print the directory, in both the Edit and Reveal Codes windows. The {PAGE OFF} command at the bottom of the primary merge file prevents each name and address from being printed on a separate page. Each blank line (i.e., [HRt] code) above the {PAGE OFF} command becomes one blank line between each printed record in the merged document.

To insert a {PAGE OFF} command in a primary merge file, move the cursor to the bottom of the file (press Home Home ↓) and select **T**ools ➤ Me**r**ge ➤ **P**age Off (or press Shift-F9 P). Then save the primary merge file, and merge it with the secondary file as usual.

ADDING TEXT ON THE FLY

It's not necessary to store all the information for a merge in the secondary merge file. You can type in some or all of the fields for a merged document as the merge is taking place. This may come in handy if you need to add some variable text for a particular form letter that you'll be printing only once, and therefore don't want to bother changing the secondary merge file.

Let's suppose you have a secondary merge file of company personnel, most of whom have submitted potential passwords for the company computer. You need to send a final password to each person, but don't want to add the password to the secondary merge file. You could set up the primary

```
{FIELD}Company~
{FIELD}Address~
{FIELD}City~, {FIELD}State~  {FIELD}Zip~


Dear {FIELD}Salutation~:

Thank you for your donation of {FIELD}Amount~ to get our local Little
League into action. Your donation will help us purchase outfits and
equipment for the league.

Our next goal will be recruitment. We hope to call for players
early in the next season, and start practicing before the big
leagues start their pre-season games. If you have, or know of any
children, who will be interested in playing next season, please
have them send us their name and mailing address so we can keep
them posted on dates and times.

Thanks again,


Willie B. Good
Director
{PRINT}_
                                    Doc 1 Pg 1 Ln 5.33" Pos 1"
```

FIGURE 16.21:

A {PRINT} command at the bottom of a primary merge file

MegaCorp, Box 3311, L.A., CA 90023

Seeburg, III, Mr. Dustin, P.O. Box 1221, Montecito, CA 91121

Rubble, Mrs. Wilma, ABC Corporation, 1234 Valencia St., Malibu, CA 91234

Wilcox, Mr. Wallace, P.O. Box 999, L.A., CA 91234

FIGURE 16.22:

A sample directory printed from a secondary merge file

merge file as shown in Figure 16.24. The name, address, and so forth will come from the primary merge file, but the password will be typed in as the merge takes place, because of this command:

{INPUT}Enter user's password ~

To insert an {INPUT} command in your primary merge file, position the cursor, then select **T**ools ➤ Me**r**ge Codes (or press Shift-F9), and choose **I**nput. Type the message you want displayed during the merge, then press ↵.

Once you start merging the files, the {INPUT} command will display its prompt, as shown below for this example:

Enter user's password

At that point you can type the individual's password, then press End Field (F9) to complete the merge. You'll be prompted to enter a user password for each record in the secondary merge file.

During the merge, your first tendency might be to press ↵ after typing the password (or whatever text you're being prompted for), but you should resist this urge and press F9 instead; otherwise, you'll add an extra blank line to the merged text and WordPerfect will continue waiting until you do press F9. Of course, if you actually want to add a blank line, or even several

You might want to include the phrase "then press F9" in your message prompt (as in "Enter user's password, then press F9") as a reminder to press F9 after typing text from the keyboard.

```
{IF NOT BLANK}Last Name~{FIELD}Last Name~, {FIELD}Title~ {FIELD}First Name~,
    {END IF}{IF NOT BLANK}Company~{FIELD}Company~, {END IF}{FIELD}Address~, {FI
    {FIELD}State~  {FIELD}Zip~

{PAGE OFF}




                                              Doc 1 Pg 1 Ln 1" Pos 1"
[                                             }
[→Indent][→Mar Rel][Mrg:IF NOT BLANK]Last Name~[Mrg:FIELD]Last Name~, [Mrg:FIELD
]Title~ [Mrg:FIELD]First Name~,[SRt]
[Mrg:END IF][Mrg:IF NOT BLANK]Company~[Mrg:FIELD]Company~, [Mrg:END IF][Mrg:FIEL
D]Address~, [Mrg:FIELD]City~,[SRt]
[Mrg:FIELD]State~  [Mrg:FIELD]Zip~[HRt]
[HRt]
[Mrg:PAGE OFF]



Press Reveal Codes to restore screen
```

FIGURE 16.23:

The primary merge file uses a {PAGE OFF} command to prevent page breaks when printing the directory shown in Figure 16.22.

paragraphs, you can easily do so just by typing text as usual. You can even use bold, underline, the cursor-movement keys, and *any other* WordPerfect features (including tables and graphics) when entering your input text. Just be sure to press End Field (F9) when you're ready to proceed with the next record.

FILLING IN A BOILERPLATE FORM

The {TEXT} and {VARIABLE} commands provide another way to insert text from the keyboard in a primary merge file. These commands are particularly handy for merges that you perform only occasionally and that reuse the same information in several places. For example, Figure 16.25 shows a boilerplate will that prints the husband's name, wife's name, and wife's maiden name in several places throughout the document.

The {TEXT} and {VARIABLE} commands were entered into the primary merge file in the usual manner (by selecting Tools – Merge Codes – More or pressing Shift-F9 M, then highlighting the command). The {TEXT} commands display a message to the user (e.g., "Type husband's name"), then place whatever the user types—up to 129 characters—in a variable (e.g., Husband-Name). The {VARIABLE} commands insert the contents of a variable (e.g., HusbandName) at that place in the text. Because all the fields in this primary merge file come from {VARIABLE} commands (which get their data from {TEXT} commands), you don't even need a secondary merge file.

 Remember that boilerplate text is text that you want to repeat in several places in a document or in more than one document.

```
November 19, 1991

{FIELD}First Name~ {FIELD}Last Name~
{FIELD}Address~
{FIELD}City~, {FIELD}State~  {FIELD}Zip~

Dear {FIELD}First Name~:

Thanks for submitting potential passwords for the computer system.
Your password will be {INPUT}Enter user's password ~. Please write it
down, and store it in a safe place to prevent other users from
discovering your password.

Thanks,


Margaret Glassburg,
Computer Center
_
█
```

Doc 1 Pg 1 Ln 4" Pos 1"

FIGURE 16.24:

A primary merge file containing an {INPUT} command that asks for an entry from the keyboard during the merge

To merge text with this document, select Tools ➤ Merge, or press Merge/Sort (Ctrl-F9) and choose Merge. Then type the name of the primary merge file and press ↵. When prompted for the secondary merge file name, just press ↵ rather than typing a name. You'll be prompted to type the husband's name, wife's name, and wife's maiden name. Press ↵ after typing in each entry.

WordPerfect will then assemble your entries with the boilerplate document on the Edit screen. You can print the completed document with File ➤ Print (Shift-F7).

FILLING IN PREPRINTED FORMS

You can also use the Merge feature to fill in preprinted forms. Preprinted forms can be anything from job applications to a series of tractor-fed payroll checks—the size and shape of the form doesn't really matter, as long as your printer can handle the required paper size.

To print on preprinted forms, you first need to determine the exact location of each blank field on the form. Start with a clear Edit screen and a copy of the preprinted form in hand, and follow these steps:

1. If the preprinted form is not the standard 8.5" × 11" size, select Layout ➤ **P**age ➤ Paper **S**ize (or press **Shift-F8 P S**) to select (or first create, then select) the appropriate paper size.

```
{TEXT}HusbandName~Type husband's name (all caps), then press
Enter: ~{TEXT}WifeName~Type wife's name (all caps), then press
Enter: ~{TEXT}MaidenName~Type wife's maiden name, then press
Enter: ~            LAST WILL AND TESTAMENT
                           OF
               {VARIABLE}HusbandName~

        I, {VARIABLE}HusbandName~, a resident of Oxford County,
State of New Jersey, declare that this is my Will.
        FIRST:  I hereby revoke all wills and codicils that I
have previously made.
        SECOND:  I declare that I am married to
{VARIABLE}WifeName~, formerly known as {VARIABLE}MaidenName~, and
all references in this Will to "my wife" are to her.
        THIRD:  I hereby confirm to my wife her interest in our
community property.
        FOURTH:  I give all the residue of my estate to my
wife, {VARIABLE}WifeName~, if she survives me for sixty (60)
days.
        FIFTH:  I nominate and appoint my wife,
{VARIABLE}WifeName~, as my executor of this Will to serve without
bond.
        The term "my executor" as used in this Will shall
include any personal representative of my estate.  The executor
may administer my estate under the Independent Administration of
Estates Act.
        I subscribe my name to this Will this 31st day of July,
of 1991, at Oxford, New Jersey.
```

FIGURE 16.25:

A boilerplate will that merges text from the keyboard

2. Change the top, bottom, left, and right margins, if necessary, to match the form's margins.

3. Make sure the cursor is in the upper-left corner of the Edit screen (**Home Home ↑**) and note the Ln and Pos measurements near the lower-right corner of the screen.

4. Type a character (such as *X*).

5. Insert a copy of the preprinted form in the printer. If you are using a dot-matrix or other printer, insert the form in a manner that will be easy to repeat in the future (because you'll need to insert future blank forms in exactly the same way to align the text properly).

6. Print the current document (select **File ➤ Print ➤ P**age or press **Shift-F7 P**).

7. Using a ruler, measure from the upper-left corner of the page to where the base of the *X* actually appears on your preprinted form. (If this measurement is not the same as what the Ln and Pos indicators showed in step 3, you'll need to make some adjustments in the next step.)

8. Measure the distance, from the upper-left corner of the page, of every blank that needs to be filled in on the form, and write each measurement on the form, as shown in Figure 16.26. (See below for making any necessary adjustments.)

To prevent waste, use photocopies of the preprinted form, rather than originals, when first trying to get text aligned on the form.

If the measurement in step 7 was different from the measurement in step 3, you'll need to adjust your measurements accordingly. For example, if the Edit screen shows the cursor at Ln 1" and Pos 1" in step 3, but the *X* actually appears at .5" and .5" in step 7, the page is ½ inch higher and ½ inch to the left of what the Edit screen shows. You will need to compensate by adding ½ inch to all your measurements. What you do next depends on whether you prefer to print multiple preprinted forms from a secondary merge file or fill in and print one form at a time.

Filling in Multiple Preprinted Forms

If you want to merge data from a secondary merge file to multiple preprinted forms, you'll need to set up a secondary merge file with the appropriate fields defined. Figure 16.27 shows a sample record in a secondary merge file, with

The Advance feature is covered in more detail in Chapter 20.

field names at the top, which can be used to fill in the blanks on the form shown in Figure 16.26.

Next, create a primary merge file with the {FIELD} commands to print data at specific locations on the page. Be sure to use the proper page size and margins, as determined in the first two steps above. You can use the Advance

FIGURE 16.26:

Location of each blank on the preprinted form

Saturnine Lending Corporation

"Our rates are out of this world."

NOTICE OF RIGHT TO CANCEL

IDENTIFICATION OF LOAN TRANSACTION

Customer	Amount	Security
Ln 2.82", Pos 1.1"		Ln 2.82", Pos 5.7"
Ln 3.15", Pos 1.1"		Ln 3.15", Pos 5.7"
Ln 3.46", Pos 1.1"	Ln 3.46" Pos 3.5"	Ln 3.46", Pos 5.7"

YOUR RIGHT TO CANCEL

We have agreed to establish an open-end credit account for you, and you have agreed to give us the security interest in your home as security for the account. You have a legal right under federal law to cancel the account, without cost, within three business days after the latest of the following events:

  (1) the opening date of your account which is ___Ln 4.85", Pos 5.2"___ ; or
  (2) the date you received your Truth-in-Lending disclosures; or
  (3) the date you received this notice of your right to cancel the account.

If you cancel the account, the security interest in your home is also canceled. Within 20 days of receiving your notice, we must take the necessary steps to reflect the fact that the security interest in your home has been canceled. We must return to you any money or property you have given to us or to anyone else in connection with this account.

You may keep any money or property we have given you until we have done the things mentioned above, but you must then offer to return the money or property. If it is impractical or unfair for you to return the property, you must offer its reasonable value. You may offer to return the property at your home or at the location of the property. Money must be returned to the address below. If we do not take possession of the money or property within 20 calendar days of your offer, you may keep it without further obligation.

HOW TO CANCEL

If you decide to cancel this account, do so by notifying us in writing at ___Ln 7.55", Pos 5.2"___
___Ln 7.80", Pos 1.1"___

You may use any written statement that is signed and dated by you and states intention to cancel, or you may use this notice by dating and signing below. Keep one copy of this notice no matter how you notify us because it contains important information about your rights.

If you cancel by mail or telegram, you must send the notice no later than midnight of ___Ln 8.55", Pos 6.0"___ (or midnight of the third business day following the latest of the three events listed above).

I WISH TO CANCEL

Customer's Signature   Date

feature to ensure that the text in each field appears just where you want it, by following these steps:

1. Select **L**ayout or press Format (**Shift-F8**). Then choose **O**ther ➤ **A**dvance ➤ **L**ine, type a vertical (line) measurement for where you want an item of text to appear, then press ↵. (This corresponds to the Ln measurements you jotted down earlier.)

2. Select **A**dvance ➤ **P**osition, enter a horizontal measurement for where you want the same item of text to appear, and press ↵. (This corresponds to the Pos measurements you jotted down earlier.)

3. Press Exit (**F7**) to return to the Edit screen.

4. Select **T**ools ➤ Me**r**ge Codes ➤ **F**ield (or press **Shift-F9 F**). Then type the name (or number) of the field that you want to position at the location defined in the preceding two steps, and press ↵.

5. Repeat steps 1–4 for each field that needs to be filled in on the form.

6. When you're finished, save the entire document.

At this point, your document is a primary merge file that merges text from a secondary merge file to the exact locations required to fill in the form.

```
{FIELD NAMES}
      Customer 1~
      Customer 2~
      Customer 3~
      Amount~
      Security 1~
      Security 2~
      Security 3~
      Open Date~
      Office Name~
      Office Add~
      Close Date~~
{END RECORD}
=================================================================
Robert Fulsome{END FIELD}
Wanda Fulsome{END FIELD}
{END FIELD}
$150,000{END FIELD}
123 Oak St.{END FIELD}
Glendora, CA{END FIELD}
91740{END FIELD}
June 1, 1991{END FIELD}
Azusa Office{END FIELD}
225 Arrow Hwy., Azusa, CA   91234{END FIELD}
June 4, 1991{END FIELD}
{END RECORD}
=================================================================
```

FIGURE 16.27:

A secondary merge file that can be used to fill in a form

Figure 16.28 shows how that primary merge file might look in the Edit and Reveal Codes windows. (In Figure 16.28, you can't see the Advance code that advances text to Ln 8.55" and Pos 6" for the Close Date field in the Reveal Codes window, but it's really there.)

To actually print on the preprinted forms, first merge the primary and secondary merge files in the usual manner. Then load the blank forms in the printer, and print the entire merged document. If you made all your measurements accurately and loaded the blank forms in the printer correctly, your text should be aligned properly on the form, as shown in Figure 16.29.

Filling in a Single Preprinted Form

If you only need to fill in one blank form at a time, you may not want to bother with merge files. You can place Advance codes (as in the preceding example) to position the cursor exactly where you want text to be printed on the form. Next to each pair of Advance codes, place a comment (select **E**dit ➤ **Co**mment ➤ **C**reate or press Ctrl-F5 C C) that describes the text to be typed on the form. Press ↵ after typing each comment.

Repeat this basic procedure for each blank on the fill-in form. Figure 16.30 shows an example that advances the cursor to each blank on the sample form

Check out Chapter 3 if you want to learn more about creating document comments.

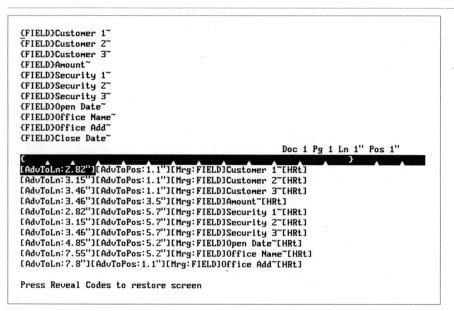

FIGURE 16.28:

A primary merge file for merging text to a preprinted form

shown earlier in Figure 16.26. Note the comments in the Edit window and the Advance codes in the Reveal Codes window.

Figure 16.31 shows text for the same fill-in form. Here, the text to be printed on the form is typed below each comment (though on your Edit screen, you'll

Saturnine Lending Corporation
"Our rates are out of this world."

NOTICE OF RIGHT TO CANCEL

IDENTIFICATION OF LOAN TRANSACTION

Customer	Amount	Security
Robert Fulsome		123 Oak St.
Wanda Fulsome		Glendora, CA
	$150,000	91740

YOUR RIGHT TO CANCEL

We have agreed to establish an open-end credit account for you, and you have agreed to give us the security interest in your home as security for the account. You have a legal right under federal law to cancel the account, without cost, within three business days after the latest of the following events:

(1) the opening date of your account which is June 1, 1991   ; or
(2) the date you received your Truth-in-Lending disclosures; or
(3) the date you received this notice of your right to cancel the account.

If you cancel the account, the security interest in your home is also canceled. Within 20 days of receiving your notice, we must take the necessary steps to reflect the fact that the security interest in your home has been canceled. We must return to you any money or property you have given to us or to anyone else in connection with this account.

You may keep any money or property we have given you until we have done the things mentioned above, but you must then offer to return the money or property. If it is impractical or unfair for you to return the property, you must offer its reasonable value. You may offer to return the property at your home or at the location of the property. Money must be returned to the address below. If we do not take possession of the money or property within 20 calendar days of your offer, you may keep it without further obligation.

HOW TO CANCEL

If you decide to cancel this account, do so by notifying us in writing at Azusa Office
225 Arrow Hwy., Azusa, CA 91234

You may use any written statement that is signed and dated by you and states intention to cancel, or you may use this notice by dating and signing below. Keep one copy of this notice no matter how you notify us because it contains important information about your rights.
If you cancel by mail or telegram, you must send the notice no later than midnight of June 4, 1991
(or midnight of the third business day following the latest of the three events listed above).

I WISH TO CANCEL

Customer's Signature   Date

FIGURE 16.29:

Data from a secondary merge file merged to a fill-in form

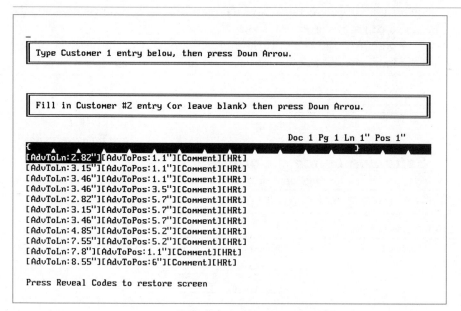

FIGURE 16.30:

*A document to fill in
a single fill-in form
without merging*

need to scroll to view all the comments in this lengthy document). Once you've typed the text to be printed on the fill-in form, you can print the entire document on your preprinted form. Since document comments never print, only the typed text will be printed on the form, producing a neatly filled-in form, just like the example shown in Figure 16.29.

OTHER ADVANCED MERGE COMMANDS

NOTE *Word-
Perfect of-
NOTE fers still
more
merge options and
techniques, described
in Chapter 26.*

If you want to merge data to documents that involve math, use the math capabilities of the Tables feature, discussed in Chapter 18. If you want to use data from other programs, such as a database management system or a spreadsheet program, for your merges, refer to Chapter 25.

In the next chapter, you'll learn how to sort lists and how to select data from lists, including secondary merge files. These techniques will add a lot of power to your merging capabilities.

```
Type Customer #1 entry below, then press Down Arrow.
```
Robert Fulsome
```
Type Customer #2 entry (or leave blank) then press Down Arrow.
```
Wanda Fulsome
```
Type Customer #3 entry (or leave blank) then press Down Arrow.
```

```
Type in the Amount below, then press Down Arrow.
```
$150,000
```
Type Security address line 1 below, then press Down Arrow.
```
123 Oak St.
```
Type Security address line 2 below, then press Down Arrow.
```
Glendora, CA
```
Type Security address line 3 below, then press Down Arrow.
```
91740
```
Enter account Opening Date below, then press Down Arrow.
```
June 1, 1991
```
Type Branch Office, then press Down Arrow.
```
Azusa Office
```
Type complete Branch address below, then press Down arrow.
```
225 Arrow Hwy., Azusa, CA 91234
```
Type Closing Date below, then press Down Arrow.
```
June 4, 1991

FIGURE 16.31:

Text to be printed on the fill-in form is typed between the document comments.

CHAPTER 17

Sorting and Selecting

I f you work with lists, tables, or secondary merge files, chances are you often need to sort (alphabetize) and select those lists. By *sort,* I mean to put the items into some kind of order, such as alphabetical order, or zip-code order for bulk mailing. By *select,* I mean to "pull out" certain items from the list. For example, when using a secondary merge file, you might need to pull out New York residents only or customers with past-due accounts to send a mailing to only those customers. This chapter describes both how to sort and select from any kind of document.

SORTING TERMINOLOGY

Like merging, sorting borrows some terms from the field of database management, which offers, among other things, comprehensive sorting and selecting capabilities.

RECORDS AND FIELDS

The terms "tab and indent codes" in this chapter refer to all codes that align text on, or between, tab stops and margins, including [Tab], [→ Indent], [Center], [Flsh Rgt], [Dec Tab], and others described in Chapter 4.

Before you can properly sort your text, you first need to envision your text as being organized into records and fields. WordPerfect sorts your text, based on fields within each record. Generally, records are separated by one or more returns ([HRt] or [SRt] codes). Fields are separated by tab and indent codes. But the exact definition of these terms depends on how the text being sorted is organized in the first place.

In a *line sort,* a record is any line of text that ends with a single hard return ([HRt]) or soft return ([SRt]). Each *field* is separated by a single tab or indent code. For example, Figure 17.1 shows some text organized into rows and columns in the Edit and Reveal Codes windows and illustrates how you define records and fields for sorting purposes.

In a *paragraph sort,* each record is separated by two or more hard-return ([HRt]) codes. Any given record in a paragraph might contain several lines of text, each line ending with a single hard return ([HRt]) or soft return ([SRt]). Furthermore, any given line within the paragraph might be separated into fields, where each field is separated by a tab or indent code. Figure 17.2 shows an example of some paragraphs separated by two hard returns and illustrates how the terms *record, line,* and *field* are defined in a paragraph sort. Only the top line of each record includes indent codes in this example ([Center] and [Flsh Rgt], visible in the Reveal Codes window), so only that line in each record is divided into fields.

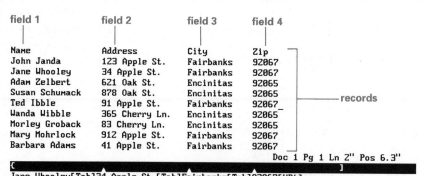

Records and fields for performing a line sort; records are separated by single hard returns.

Merge sorts are used for sorting secondary merge files (Chapter 16). Here, the terms *record* and *field* mean the same as they do in merges. Each field ends with an {END FIELD} command, and each record ends with an {END RECORD} command, as shown in Figure 17.3. The fields in this example aren't divided into lines, because no field contains a hard- or soft-return code (the hard return at the end of each field is not part of the text within the field). WordPerfect does allow you to sort secondary merge files whose fields consist of multiple lines.

In *table sorts,* a record is simply a row. A line is any single line of text that ends with a hard or soft return within the row. The term *field* is not used when sorting tables. Instead, each record (row) is separated into cells, each cell being a column of text. That is, the leftmost column is cell 1, the next column is cell 2, and so forth, as shown in Figure 17.4.

> **NOTE NOTE** *Figure 17.4 doesn't show any entries with multiple lines, but you can certainly use them in your own tables.*

WORDS

Often, you need to define exactly which word in a field (or table cell) you want to use for sorting. A *word* is any text that's preceded by a blank space, rather than a tab or indent. For example, take a look at this list of names:

> **NOTE NOTE** *As you'll see later, words can also be separated by forward slashes (/) or hard hyphens (Home -). This is handy for sorting dates.*

Martha Mellor

Andy Bowers

Bonnie Zeepers

Wanda Carneros

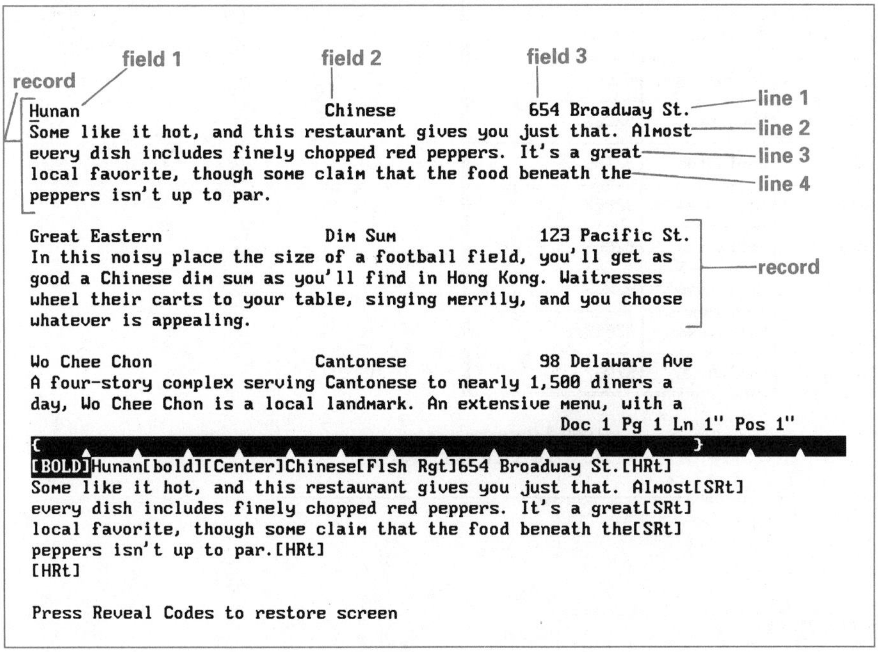

FIGURE 17.2:
Records, lines, and fields for paragraph sorts, where records are separated by two hard returns

```
{FIELD NAMES}
    First Name~
    Last Name~
    Address~
    City~
    State~
record  Zip~
    Salutation~~
{END RECORD}
================================================================
Frank{END FIELD}────────────field 1
Fleinder{END FIELD}─────────field 2
123 Oak St.{END FIELD}──────field 3
Glendora{END FIELD}─────────field 4
KS{END FIELD}───────────────field 5
54321{END FIELD}────────────field 6
Frank{END FIELD}────────────field 7
{END RECORD}
================================================================
Nita{END FIELD}
Bonita{END FIELD}
P.O. Box 5432{END FIELD}
Glendora{END FIELD}
KS{END FIELD}

                                    Doc 1 Pg 1 Ln 1" Pos 1"
```

FIGURE 17.3:

A secondary merge file, with records and fields defined for sorting purposes

Name	Address	City	Zip
John Janda	123 Apple St.	Fairbanks	92067
Jane Whooley	34 Apple St.	Fairbanks	92067
Adam Zelbert	621 Oak St.	Encinitas	92065
Susan Schumack	878 Oak St.	Encinitas	92065
Ted Ibble	91 Apple St.	Fairbanks	92067
Wanda Wibble	365 Cherry Ln.	Encinitas	92065
Morley Groback	83 Cherry Ln.	Encinitas	92065
Mary Mohrlock	912 Apple St.	Fairbanks	92067
Barbara Adams	41 Apple St.	Fairbanks	92067

cell 1   cell 2   cell 3   cell 4

Doc 1 Pg 1 Ln 4.2" Pos 1"

FIGURE 17.4:

A table, with records (rows) and cells defined for sorting tables

If you sort these names on the first word, the names are displayed in this order:

Andy Bowers

Bonnie Zeepers

Martha Mellor

Wanda Carneros

Notice how the names are sorted by each person's first name. If you want these names alphabetized by each person's last name, you sort on the second word (that is, the text after the first blank space). Sorting on the second word displays the names alphabetized by each person's last name, like this:

Andy Bowers

Wanda Carneros

Martha Mellor

Bonnie Zeepers

NOTE
NOTE
You can also "count backward" by line when doing a table or merge sort. For example, line number −1 would be the last line.

When identifying a word to sort on within a field or line, you can "count backward" from the end of the field or line. For example, word number −1 is the last word in the line or field. So, to sort the list of names above into proper last-name order, you could also identify the sort key (see the next section) as word −1 in the name field. This technique of counting backward is especially helpful if some names have middle initials and some don't (in this case, if you sort by word number 2 instead of word number −1, some names will end up sorted by middle initial, and others will be sorted by last name).

THE SORT KEY

The *sort key* is the most important element of the sorting process, because it defines how the sort should take place. For example, when sorting information in a list of names and addresses into zip-code order for bulk mailing, the sort key is the zip code. When sorting names and addresses into alphabetical order by name, the last name must be defined as the key. You identify a sort key by its exact line, field (or cell), and word position in each record. That's why it's important to understand what each of these terms means with respect to the text you want to sort. I'll provide exact steps for performing the sort and more examples of sort keys in a moment.

THE SORT TYPE

When defining a sort key, you can also define a key type, from one of these two options:

Alphanumeric Use this option to sort text, combined text and numbers (e.g., part numbers like *123-ZY-KLM*), or numbers of equal length (e.g., five-digit zip codes).

Numeric Use this option to sort numbers that vary in length, such as quantities (e.g., 1, 999, 1,000) and currency amounts (e.g., $1.00, $1,000.00, $123.43).

SORTS WITHIN SORTS

WordPerfect lets you define up to nine sort keys for a single sort operation. If you define more than one key for a sort, the additional keys act as "tiebreakers" when the previous key or keys are identical. You can use multiple keys to produce a "sort within a sort." This is useful both for sorting large amounts of text and for grouping information.

The white pages of the phone book may be the most common example of a sort within a sort, where entries are sorted by each person's last name; within each identical last name, the names are sorted by each person's first name (e.g., *Smith, Ann* comes before *Smith, Millie*, which comes before *Smith, Zeke*).

As another example, here's a small list of eight records with four fields each—Department, Last Name, First Name, and Extension—in random order:

DEPARTMENT	LAST NAME	FIRST NAME	EXTENSION
Accounting	Smith	Zeke	2312
Marketing	Leeland	Lee	5434
Accounting	Smith	Michelle	7434
Marketing	Boorish	Babs	8433
Accounting	Smith	Adrian	5423
Marketing	Argosy	Steve	8323
Accounting	Adams	Wanda	8434
Accounting	Zastrow	Ernie	8434

Here's the same list after sorting the records by field 1, the department. Notice how within each department, employee names are in random order:

DEPARTMENT	LAST NAME	FIRST NAME	EXTENSION
Accounting	Adams	Wanda	8434
Accounting	Smith	Zeke	2312
Accounting	Smith	Adrian	5423
Accounting	Zastrow	Ernie	8434
Accounting	Smith	Michelle	7434
Marketing	Leeland	Lee	5434
Marketing	Argosy	Steve	8323
Marketing	Boorish	Babs	8433

Here's the same list sorted with two sort keys: the Department field and the Last Name field. The departments are listed in alphabetical order, and within each department, employee names are sorted by last name:

NOTE NOTE *This example also shows how sorting can be used as a means of grouping. In this case, employee names are grouped according to department.*

DEPARTMENT	LAST NAME	FIRST NAME	EXTENSION
Accounting	Adams	Wanda	8434
Accounting	Smith	Adrian	5423
Accounting	Smith	Zeke	2312
Accounting	Smith	Michelle	7434
Accounting	Zastrow	Ernie	8434
Marketing	Boorish	Babs	8433
Marketing	Argosy	Steve	8323
Marketing	Leeland	Lee	5434

In yet another example, three sort keys are used to sort the rows: the Department field, Last Name field, and First Name field. This list is almost identical to the preceding list, except that the Smiths are in alphabetical order by first name, because First Name was defined as the third sort key.

DEPARTMENT	LAST NAME	FIRST NAME	EXTENSION
Accounting	Adams	Wanda	8434
Accounting	Smith	Adrian	5423
Accounting	Smith	Michelle	7434
Accounting	Smith	Zeke	2312
Accounting	Zastrow	Ernie	8434
Marketing	Argosy	Steve	8323
Marketing	Boorish	Babs	8433
Marketing	Leeland	Lee	5434

In general, the larger your list, the more likely you'll want to use more sort keys to organize it. In the example above, it's easy to see all the Smiths in the Accounting department, so it's not crucial that they be in alphabetical order by first name. But if there were dozens of Smiths in Accounting, it would be much easier to find a particular one if they were listed alphabetically by first name.

THE SORT ORDER

The *sort order* is the direction of the sort. You can choose either *ascending* order (from A to Z, or smallest number to largest), or *descending* order (from Z to A, or largest number to smallest).

PERFORMING A SORT OPERATION

The general procedure for sorting text in a document is as follows:

1. To play it safe, save a copy of your document with **File ➤ S**ave or the Save key (**F10**), so you can easily recover from a mistake.

2. If you do *not* want to sort all the text in the document, block the text that you do want to sort (select **Edit ➤ B**lock or press **Alt-F4** or **F12**). If you want to sort a table, place your cursor anywhere within the table, or block the table rows you want to sort.

 *You will not see these prompts if you blocked the text in step 2 or if your cursor is inside a table.*

3. Select **Tools ➤ S**ort or press Merge/Sort (**Ctrl-F9**), then select **S**ort.

4. If prompted with "Input File to sort: (Screen)", press ↵ to sort the document on the Edit screen, or type the name of the file that contains the text to be sorted and press ↵. Similarly, if you are prompted with "Output file for sort: (Screen)", you can just press ↵ to

place the sorted output on the Edit screen, or type the name of a file where you want to send the results and press ↵ (see "Sorting and Selecting to and from Documents On-Disk" for more information).

The sorting options appear at the bottom of the screen, as in Figure 17.5.

5. Select **T**ype, then **L**ine, **P**aragraph, or **M**erge, depending on which type of record you want to sort (this is a very important step!).

6. Select **O**rder, then either **A**scending or **D**escending.

7. Select **K**eys and define up to nine sort keys as described in the next section. Press Exit (**F7**) when you're finished defining your keys.

8. Select **P**erform Action to perform the sort.

It may take a few seconds or minutes (depending on the amount of text you want to sort) for WordPerfect to complete the job. If your sort results are not what you expected, you can abandon the current version of the document (select **F**ile ➤ E**x**it ➤ **N**o ➤ **N**o, or press F7 N N), and retrieve the previous version (select **F**ile ➤ **R**etrieve or press Shift-F10), provided you made a safety copy.

If the cursor is within a table when you start a sort operation, WordPerfect automatically defines the sort as a table sort.

See "Troubleshooting Sorts" later in this chapter if your text is sorted in an unexpected manner.

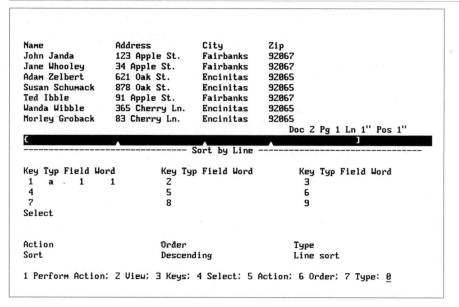

FIGURE 17.5:

The sorting options, on the bottom half of the screen

```
Name            Address         City        Zip
John Janda      123 Apple St.   Fairbanks   92067
Jane Whooley    34 Apple St.    Fairbanks   92067
Adam Zelbert    621 Oak St.     Encinitas   92065
Susan Schumack  878 Oak St.     Encinitas   92065
Ted Ibble       91 Apple St.    Fairbanks   92067
Wanda Wibble    365 Cherry Ln.  Encinitas   92065
Morley Groback  83 Cherry Ln.   Encinitas   92065
                                        Doc 2 Pg 1 Ln 1" Pos 1"
[                                                           ]
------------------------------- Sort by Line -------------------------------
Key Typ Field Word      Key Typ Field Word      Key Typ Field Word
 1   a    1    1          2                        3
 4                        5                        6
 7                        8                        9
Select

Action                  Order                   Type
Sort                    Descending              Line sort

1 Perform Action; 2 View; 3 Keys; 4 Select; 5 Action; 6 Order; 7 Type: 0
```

DEFINING SORT KEYS

After you select the Keys option from the Sort menu, you will be allowed to define up to nine sort keys. The line sort example in Figure 17.5 shows several headings for each sort key:

Key: identifies which key number you are defining.

Typ: lets you indicate whether the sort is to be alphanumeric or numeric.

Field: lets you define the field number for this key.

Word: lets you define the word number for this key.

For merge, paragraph, and table sorts, you'll also see a heading for *Line* (lets you define the line number for this key). Note that table sorts display the heading *Cell* in place of *Field* to let you define a cell (column) number for the key.

You'll see many examples of sort keys throughout this chapter, but before looking at these, let's go over the procedure for defining a sort key. Follow these steps:

1. Choose **K**eys from the Sort menu. The cursor will move to the first sort key.

2. Press → (or ↵) to move forward and ← to move backward through the table of keys, and enter the type (either *a* for alphanumeric or *n* for numeric) and the field, word, line, and cell numbers for each key (as appropriate).

3. You can change any of the existing settings by typing over them. If you make a mistake, just press **Backspace** and retype your entry. Press Ctrl-End to delete the sort keys from the cursor position to the last key.

4. When you're finished defining keys, press Exit (**F7**) to return to the Sort menu.

As a shortcut, press the ↓ or End key to move to the next undefined sort key; press ↑ to move to the first sort key.

SORTING LINES

TO SORT LINES OF TEXT,

1. Block the text you want to sort (Alt-F4 or F12).

2. Select Tools ➤ Sort ➤ Type ➤ Line (or press Ctrl-F9 S T L).

3. Define your sort Keys and Order.

4. Select Perform Action.

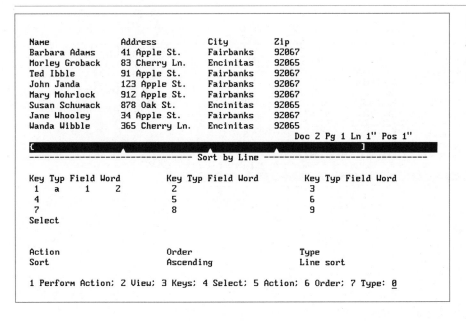

If you need to get another look at the Edit screen to scroll around, select View and use the cursor-movement keys to scroll. Press Exit (F7) when you're ready to return to the Sort menu.

Use the Line Sort option when your text is in a simple list format and each line is broken by a single hard return ([HRt] code), as in Figure 17.1. Remember to block the lines that you want to sort, and after selecting **T**ools ➤ **S**ort ➤ **T**ype ➤ **L**ine (or pressing Ctrl-F9 S T L), define your sort keys.

Figure 17.6 shows a list of records with the sort keys set up to sort the list by each person's last name. In this example, each person's last name is the second word in the first field (that is, the first field in each row is a name, the first word in each name is the person's first name, and the second word is the last name). Therefore, you want to set up the sort key as shown in the figure, and below:

KEY	TYP	FIELD	WORD
1	a	1	2

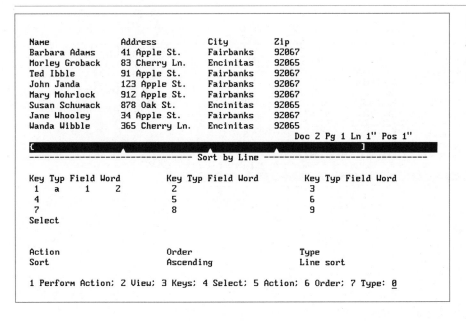

FIGURE 17.6:

Sort keys defined to sort names and addresses by last name

```
Name             Address         City        Zip
Barbara Adams    41 Apple St.    Fairbanks   92067
Morley Groback   83 Cherry Ln.   Encinitas   92065
Ted Ibble        91 Apple St.    Fairbanks   92067
John Janda       123 Apple St.   Fairbanks   92067
Mary Mohrlock    912 Apple St.   Fairbanks   92067
Susan Schumack   878 Oak St.     Encinitas   92065
Jane Whooley     34 Apple St.    Fairbanks   92067
Wanda Wibble     365 Cherry Ln.  Encinitas   92065
                                    Doc 2 Pg 1 Ln 1" Pos 1"
[                                              ]
------------------------------ Sort by Line ------------------------------

Key Typ Field Word      Key Typ Field Word      Key Typ Field Word
 1   a    1    2          2                        3
 4                        5                        6
 7                        8                        9
Select


Action                  Order                   Type
Sort                    Ascending               Line sort

1 Perform Action; 2 View; 3 Keys; 4 Select; 5 Action; 6 Order; 7 Type: 0
```

Figure 17.7 shows the same list of names and addresses with sort keys defined to sort records into zip-code order, and then by address within each zip code. Notice that the first sort key is, of course, the zip-code field (field 4). The second sort key is field 2 word 2, the street name (the second word in the Address field). The third sort key is field 2 word 1, the street number (the first "word" in the address field, sorted as a number). After selecting Perform Action, records are in zip-code order and by address within each zip-code area (as shown by the sorted results in the figure).

SORTING PARAGRAPHS

TO SORT PARAGRAPHS,

1. Block the text you want to sort.

2. Select Tools ➤ Sort ➤ Type ➤ Paragraph (or press Ctrl-F9 S T P).

3. Define sort Keys and Order.

4. Select Perform Action.

```
Name              Address         City        Zip
Morley Groback    83 Cherry Ln.   Encinitas   92065
Wanda Wibble      365 Cherry Ln.  Encinitas   92065
Adam Zelbert      621 Oak St.     Encinitas   92065
Susan Schumack    878 Oak St.     Encinitas   92065
Jane Whooley      34 Apple St.    Fairbanks   92067
Barbara Adams     41 Apple St.    Fairbanks   92067
Ted Ibble         91 Apple St.    Fairbanks   92067
John Janda        123 Apple St.   Fairbanks   92067
Mary Mohrlock     912 Apple St.   Fairbanks   92067
                                        Doc 2 Pg 1 Ln 1" Pos 1"

------------------------------ Sort by Line ------------------------------

Key Typ Field Word      Key Typ Field Word      Key Typ Field Word
 1   a    4    1          2   a    2    2          3   n    2    1
 4                         5                        6
 7                         8                        9
Select


Action                  Order                   Type
Sort                    Ascending               Line sort

1 Perform Action; 2 View; 3 Keys; 4 Select; 5 Action; 6 Order; 7 Type: 0
```

FIGURE 17.7:

Sort keys set up to sort records into street-address order within each zip code

If you want to sort a series of paragraphs, first block the paragraphs (unless you want to sort every paragraph in the document). Before defining your sort keys, remember to select **T**ype ➤ **P**aragraph from the Sort menu so that you can properly identify the sort key or keys. Notice in the lower-right corner of Figure 17.8 that the sort type is Paragraph, which lets you identify each sort key by Typ, Line, Field, and Word.

Figure 17.8 shows the paragraph sort with the zip code in each field identified as the sort key. In the figure, you can see that the only sort key is line 3, field 1, word −1. That's because the city, state, and zip code are on the third line of each record. There is only one field on that line because the city, state, and zip code are separated by blank spaces, not tabs. The zip code is the last "word" on each line, hence its position is identified as word −1.

Another example of a paragraph sort is presented in Figure 17.9, where each bibliography entry is separated by two hard returns. This is a tricky one, because the first line of each paragraph is outdented one tab stop with a combination of [→Indent] and [←Mar Rel] codes (i.e., with a hanging paragraph format, as discussed in Chapter 4). These codes are, of course, visible only on the Reveal Codes screen, which is not shown in the figure.

Take a look at the defined sort key. Line 1 is chosen because the author's name is on the first line of each record. But even though each author's name appears to be at the beginning of the line, the sort key must be defined as field 3 in this example because the [→Indent] and [←Mar Rel] codes at the start of each paragraph are treated as tab and indent codes. Therefore,

To sort by zip code, use an alphanumeric Typ for the key so that extended and foreign zip codes will be sorted properly.

The tab and indent codes define new fields.

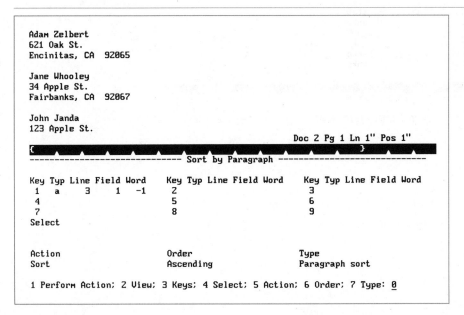

FIGURE 17.8:

A paragraph sort to list names and addresses in zip-code order

WordPerfect assumes that field 1 is to the left of the [→Indent] code, and field 2 is to the left of the [←Mar Rel] code (even though there is no text in either place), so field 3 starts at the right of the [←Mar Rel] code. Hence, each author's last name is actually in field 3, and this list will be sorted correctly only if the sort key is defined accordingly.

SORTING A SECONDARY MERGE FILE

TO SORT A SECONDARY MERGE FILE,

1. Select Tools ➤ Sort ➤ Type ➤ Merge (or press Ctrl-F9 S T M).

2. Define Sort Keys and Order.

3. Select Perform Action.

To sort a secondary merge file, just bring it to the Edit screen and remember to select **Type ➤ M**erge from the Sort menu, so you can properly define your sort keys. Remember that the [HRt] code at the end of each field is *not* included

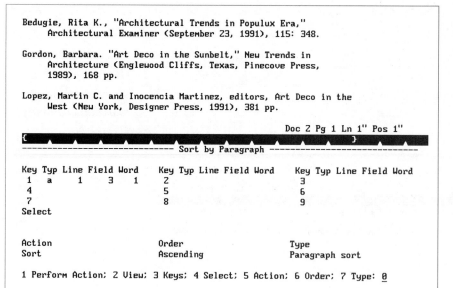

```
Bedugie, Rita K., "Architectural Trends in Populux Era,"
    Architectural Examiner (September 23, 1991), 115: 348.

Gordon, Barbara. "Art Deco in the Sunbelt," New Trends in
    Architecture (Englewood Cliffs, Texas, Pinecove Press,
    1989), 168 pp.

Lopez, Martin C. and Inocencia Martinez, editors, Art Deco in the
    West (New York, Designer Press, 1991), 381 pp.


                                      Doc 2 Pg 1 Ln 1" Pos 1"

------------------------------ Sort by Paragraph ------------------------------

Key Typ Line Field Word   Key Typ Line Field Word   Key Typ Line Field Word
 1   a   1    3    1        2                          3
 4                          5                          6
 7                          8                          9
Select


Action                    Order                     Type
Sort                      Ascending                 Paragraph sort

1 Perform Action; 2 View; 3 Keys; 4 Select; 5 Action; 6 Order; 7 Type: 0
```

FIGURE 17.9:

A bibliography with hanging paragraphs set up to be sorted by author's last name

when defining a line to sort by; you only need to specify the line number for a sort key if a particular field contains more than one line of text.

Figure 17.10 shows a secondary merge file with the sort key defined to sort the records into zip-code order (perhaps for bulk mailing). Field 6 identifies the sixth field from the top of each record (in this example, the name *Frank* is in the first field). The field is not divided into additional lines or words, so both of these options are set to 1.

If you want to sort the secondary merge file into name order, like the telephone directory (that is, by last name and by first name within identical last names), you define sort keys 1 and 2 as below:

KEY	TYP	FIELD	LINE	WORD
1	a	2	1	1

KEY	TYP	FIELD	LINE	WORD
2	a	1	1	1

This sets up each person's last name as the main sorting key and each person's first name as the tiebreaker within each identical last name.

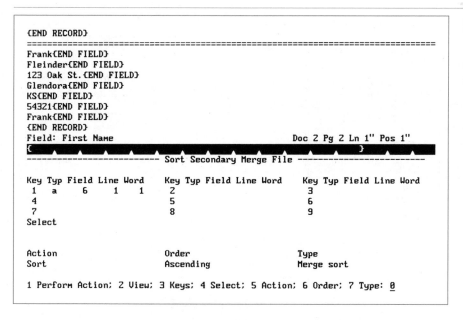

FIGURE 17.10:

A sort key set up to sort a sample secondary merge file by zip code

SORTING A TABLE

TO SORT A TABLE,

1. **Block the rows that you want to sort.**

2. **Select Tools ➤ Sort (or press Ctrl-F9 S).**

3. **Define sort Keys and Order.**

4. **Select Perform Action.**

Before sorting text in a table, be sure to do the following:

1. Leave Table Edit mode, if necessary, by pressing Exit (**F7**).

2. Move the cursor anywhere into the table.

3. Save the entire document with File ➤ **S**ave or the Save key (**F10**).

4. Block the rows you want to sort (**Alt-F4** or **F12**).

The last step is particularly important because, as with line and paragraph sorting, if you don't block any rows, all the rows in the table will be sorted. Generally, you don't want to sort column titles, table titles, totals, or other information at the bottom of the table. So be sure to block only the rows that you do want to sort, as shown in Figure 17.11, where the table title, column

```
          ┌─────────────────────────────────────────┐
          │        COMPARATIVE OPERATING EXPENSES    │
          ├──────────┬──────────┬──────────┬─────────┤
          │ Division │   1990   │   1991   │ % Change│
          ├──────────┼──────────┼──────────┼─────────┤
          │ North    │ 1,980,870│ 2,780,870│  40.0%  │
          ├──────────┼──────────┼──────────┼─────────┤
          │ South    │   987,750│   760,080│ -23.1%  │
          ├──────────┼──────────┼──────────┼─────────┤
          │ East     │   986,500│ 1,100,000│  11.5%  │
          ├──────────┼──────────┼──────────┼─────────┤
          │ West     │ 1,275,000│   987,000│ -22.6%  │
          ├──────────┼──────────┼──────────┼─────────┤
          │ Total    │ 5,230,120│ 5,627,950│   7.6%  │
          └──────────┴──────────┴──────────┴─────────┘


Block on                    Cell D6 Doc 1 Pg 1 Ln 2.54" Pos 6.08"
```

FIGURE 17.11:

The rows to be sorted in the table are blocked before starting the sort operation.

titles, and totals are excluded from the sort operation.

Also, you should avoid including rows with more, or fewer, cells than other rows in the sort. For example, if the sort included the row of joined cells at the top of the table shown in Figure 17.11, that row's position after sorting would be quite unpredictable.

After you've blocked the rows you want to sort, you can then proceed with the sort as described earlier in this chapter. You don't need to choose a sort type, because WordPerfect automatically sets the option to Table when the cursor is within a table.

Figure 17.12 shows the sort key used to sort the rows of the table in Figure 17.11 in descending order from largest to smallest percentage of change. Note that the Order is Descending, and the Type is Table sort, as shown at the bottom of the screen.

The sort key is defined as

KEY	TYP	CELL	LINE	WORD
1	n	4	1	1

because the sort key is numeric and is in the fourth column of the table.

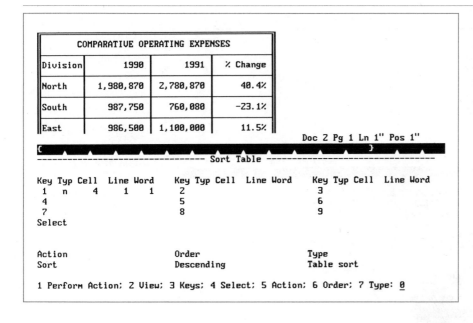

NOTE
NOTE

You may need to change the table's line styles (using the Lines option in Table Edit mode) after sorting, because lines are sorted with their rows.

FIGURE 17.12:

A sort key set up to sort a table in descending order from largest to smallest percentage of change (column 4)

TROUBLESHOOTING SORTS

If your sorted text does not come out in the order you expected, then typically one of four things is wrong:

◆ You defined the wrong text as the sort key, so the sort order appears to be random.

◆ You did not select the correct sort type (e.g., Line, Paragraph, or Merge).

◆ The fields don't correspond to one another's position in the records.

◆ You forgot to select Perform Action after correctly defining the sort keys.

The first mistake is the most common, particularly when sorting lines or paragraphs. It's important to realize that when you are sorting lines or paragraphs, *every* tab or indent defines a new field. Thus, if the first column of text is indented, then it will be in field 2, the next field will be field 3, and so forth. This situation, where the first visible column isn't actually the first field, was described earlier in the example about sorting a bibliography and is shown in Figure 17.13.

If you did not define your tab stops before typing columns, your sort may also go awry, because the fields are not positioned the same way in each

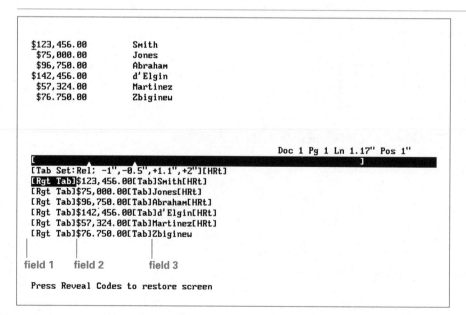

FIGURE 17.13:

Every tab or indent code counts as a field, even the first one, as in this example, where the dollar amounts are in field 2 and the names are in field 3.

record. For example, in the first of two records shown below, the address is in field 3 because it's preceded by two [Tab] codes. But in the second record, the address is in field 4 because it's preceded by three [Tab] codes (field 3 contains nothing in that record).

| John Jones[Tab] | ABC Corporation[Tab] | 123 Apple St. |
| Nancy Wilcox[Tab] | XYZ Co.[Tab][Tab] | 345 Oak St. |

Redefining tab stops is covered in Chapter 4.

To fix this problem, you must first redefine the tab stops so that only one tab code is required to separate each column of text. Then remove any extra tab codes so that text aligns properly in each column. When that's finished, you can define your sort key or keys and perform the sort.

Some text is impossible to sort simply because it is not arranged in any kind of field-and-record order. For example, you could not possibly sort the bibliography shown earlier in Figure 17.9 in Title, Publisher, or Date order, because these items are not in consistent, identifiable positions within each record.

TRICKY NAME SORTS

A common, though solvable, sort problem occurs when names are stored in a single field without a specific word to latch onto for sorting, like this:

Mr. A. H. Smith

Mr. and Mrs. George C. Lott

Windham Earl III

Winston Fitzgerald Jr.

Word-Perfect counts only normal spaces, forward slashes, and hard hyphens.

There's no hope of counting words from the front to identify each person's last name, and a −1 will incorrectly identify the *III* and the *Jr.* as the last name in two of these records. There is a solution, however.

When counting words, WordPerfect does not count hard spaces. If you always remember to use a hard space (by pressing Home spacebar) to separate the III and the Jr. from the last name in every record, you can use word −1 as the sort key in this field, and the names will be alphabetized properly.

SORTING DATES

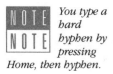

You type a hard hyphen by pressing Home, then hyphen.

If you type dates in the format **mm/dd/yy** (e.g., 12/31/91), or **mm-dd-yy** (e.g., 12-31-91) by using hard hyphens, you can sort records in date order. The slashes or hard hyphens are treated as spaces and therefore can be used to divide each date into words representing month, day, and year. When defining the sort key, define the year as the first sort key (in word -1), the month as the second key (in word 1), the day as the third key (in word 2), and the Typ of each key as numeric. Figure 17.14 shows an example where dates are in the second column of a table (cell 2), and all three fields are defined for proper sorting by date. After selecting Perform Action in this example, records will be listed in earliest to latest date order.

SELECTING TEXT

TO SELECT TEXT,

1. **Block your text and define your sort keys.**

2. **If the text you want to select is not already a sort key, define it as one.**

3. **Choose Select from the Sort menu.**

Sort keys set up to sort records in a table by date

Part No.	Date	Description	Qty	Unit Price
A-111	1/3/92	Armchair	1	$150.00
A-111	12/30/91	Armchair	1	$150.00
B-111	1/2/92	Loveseat	2	$250.00
B-111	12/30/91	Loveseat	1	$150.00

```
                                         Doc 2 Pg 1 Ln 1" Pos 1"
[                                                            }
---------------------------- Sort Table ----------------------------

Key Typ Cell  Line Word    Key Typ Cell  Line Word    Key Typ Cell  Line Word
 1   n    2    1   -1       2   n    2    1    1        3   n    2    1    2
 4                          5                           6
 7                          8                           9
Select


Action                  Order                   Type
Sort                    Ascending               Table sort

1 Perform Action; 2 View; 3 Keys; 4 Select; 5 Action; 6 Order; 7 Type: 0
```

4. Define your selection criteria.

5. Choose Perform Action.

When you're maintaining a list, such as a mailing list, you often need to isolate certain items in it. For example, you may want to send a special holiday catalog to customers who have spent above a certain amount in the last year, or tell customers living in one state about a new insurance discount available to them. WordPerfect's Select feature lets you pick out the records you need from your larger list, and optionally, sort them in the process.

To select records, follow these steps:

1. Perform steps 1-7 described in "Performing a Sort Operation" earlier in this chapter to block the text you want to sort and define the sort keys.

2. If the text you want to use to identify records for selection is not already defined as a sort key, identify that text as a sort key (it doesn't have to be the first sort key; any valid sort key will do).

3. Choose **S**elect from the menu of sort options, and define your selection criteria, as described in the sections that follow. Use the normal typing keys to enter your criteria, then press ↵ when you're ready to return to the Sort menu. If you make a mistake when typing your criteria, or you need to make some changes, you can use the normal cursor-movement and editing keys to move through the line and make corrections. To delete the selection criteria entirely, move to the beginning of the line and press **Ctrl-End**.

4. Choose **P**erform Action to sort and select records.

In short, selecting records is virtually identical to sorting them, except that you must choose the Select option from the Sort menu and define your selection criteria before selecting Perform Action.

Be sure to read the next section, "Warning! Word-Perfect Deletes When It Selects." It contains valuable advice on preventing the accidental deletion of records.

DEFINING SELECTION CRITERIA

The *selection criteria* are the conditions a record must meet to remain in the output of the select operation. A list of selection criteria has three elements:

◆ Key numbers

◆ Selection operators

◆ Search values

The key number is the number of the key as you've defined it on the Sort menu. As you know, you can define up to nine keys, numbered 1 to 9. When typed as part of a list of selection criteria, the first key is *key1,* the second is *key2,* and so on.

The selection *operator* defines the type of relationship that you are seeking. The available operators are listed below:

=	Equals
<>	Does not equal
>	Is greater than
<	Is less than
>=	Is greater than or equal to
<=	Is less than or equal to

The search value defines what you are looking for or comparing to. For example, suppose you want to limit your mailing to California residents. First, you define the state field in a secondary merge file as the second sort key (key2). Then, because you want to pull out only those records with CA in that field, the selection criterion is

key2=CA

which in English says, "Delete all records *except* those with CA in the second sort key" (which you've previously defined as the state field in your secondary merge file). The resulting merge file can then be used to print letters and labels for California residents only.

Two special operators allow you to combine search criteria:

+	OR
*	AND

When combining search criteria, you must use all three elements—key numbers, selection operators, and search values—on both sides of the * (AND) and + (OR) combination characters. For example, suppose you want to print letters and labels only for people in certain zip-code areas, such as 92000 to 92999 (which covers most of the cities in San Diego County). If you define the zip code as your first sort key (key1), your selection criteria are

key1>=92000*key1<=92999

which in English says, "Isolate records with zip codes that are greater than or equal to 92000, and are also less than or equal to 92999." Table 17.1 offers examples of other search criteria and a quick summary for future reference.

One of the most common mistakes people make when combining selection criteria is to forget to use all three elements on both sides of the * (AND) and + (OR) combination characters. For example, if you enter selection criteria like

key1>=92000*<=92999

you might think that WordPerfect would be smart enough to read this as "zip codes that are greater than or equal to 92000 and less than 92999." But neither WordPerfect nor your computer is smart enough to make this inference. Instead, your entry is interpreted as "zip codes that are greater than or equal to 92000 and who-knows-what is less than or equal to 92999."

The same holds true for the + (OR) combination operator. For example, suppose you want to send letters to people in the states of Georgia, Alabama, and Florida, and have already defined the state field as sort-key number 1 (key1). Now you need selection criteria that delete all records *except* those with GA, AL, or FL in the state field. Your selection criteria must be

key1 = GA + key1 = AL + key1 = FL

If you incorrectly enter the selection criteria as

key1 = GA + AL + FL

or

key1 = GA + = AL + = FL

WordPerfect will reject the criteria and display the "ERROR: Incorrect format" message.

It's also very important not to confuse the AND (*) and OR (+) operators, because they don't always relate directly to how you might represent criteria in English. Consider the example of mailings to residents of Georgia, Alabama,

If you enter faulty criteria, as in this example, WordPerfect will simply display the message "ERROR: Incorrect format" when you try to exit the Select option and then will place the cursor at the point where you ran into trouble.

SYMBOL	FUNCTION	EXAMPLE	MEANING
=	Equal to	key1=45	Selects all records for which key 1 is equal to 45
<>	Not equal to	key1< >45	Selects all records for which key 1 is not equal to 45
>	Greater than	key1> 45	Selects all records for which key 1 is greater than 45
<	Less than	key1< 45	Selects all records for which key 1 is less than 45
>=	Greater than or equal to	key>=45	Selects all records for which key 1 is greater than or equal to 45
<=	Less than or equal to	key<=45	Selects all records for which key 1 is less than or equal to 45
*	And	key1= 45*key2=M	Selects all records for which key 1 is equal to 45 and key 2 is equal to M
+	Or	key1= 45+key2=M	Selects all records for which key 1 is equal to 45 or key 2 is equal to M
g	Global	keyg=45	Selects all records with the value 45 in any key

TABLE 17.1:

Selection Operators

and Florida. You might think that these selection criteria will do the trick:

key1 = GA * key1 = AL * key1 = FL

In English, this says, "Delete records except those that have GA in the state field, and AL in the state field, and FL in the state field." WordPerfect, however, interprets this as meaning something like "records that have *GA AL FL* in the state field." But a single record could not possibly have all three states in its state field, so the results of the selection are no records at all!

Understanding this difference between AND and OR is crucial to creating valid selection criteria. Remember that WordPerfect performs a selection by comparing every record, individually, with the selection criteria. That is, when WordPerfect performs your selection with criteria such as

key1 = GA + key1 = AL + key1 = FL

it looks at one record at a time and asks, "Does this record have GA, *or* AL, *or* FL in the state field?" If WordPerfect can answer *Yes* to this question, it does not delete the record.

On the other hand, when WordPerfect sees selection criteria like

key1 = GA * key1 = AL * key1 = FL

*If you're not accustomed to using computers to select items from a list (or records from a merge file), your mind may be reeling with all this business of **and** and **or**. But a little practice and experience will surely help you to get things right.*

it asks, "Does this record have GA, AL, *and* FL in the state field?" WordPerfect is bound to come up with the answer No for each record it compares to these selection criteria, because it's impossible for any single record (i.e., one person's home address) to contain three different states.

When defining your selection criteria, it's important to keep in mind that you are not asking a question in English. Instead you are setting up a screen or filter through which some records will pass and some will not. That is, WordPerfect will compare each record, one at a time, with your selection criteria. If all the criteria joined by the AND operator (*) can be answered Yes for a single record, that record is retained. If any of the criteria joined by the OR (+) operator in your selection criteria can be answered Yes for a single record, that record is retained.

You and I know what the sentence "Send letters to everyone in Georgia, Alabama, *and* Florida" means. However, your computer can't understand plain English like this. You must set up your selection criteria specifically to say, "Keep only those records that have GA in the state field, *or* AL in the state field, *or* FL in the state field." And the only way to do this (assuming that the first sort key represents the state field) is with the selection criteria

key1 =GA + key1 = AL + key1 = FL

WARNING! WORDPERFECT DELETES WHEN IT SELECTS

When you make a selection, it's important to understand that WordPerfect actually deletes records that do not match the selection criteria from the list. Therefore, you should always send the results of a selection to a separate file so that you do not accidentally delete some records from your existing list (some people refer to this as the "master list").

For example, suppose you create a secondary merge file named NAMELIST.WP, with 500 names and addresses. If you then do a select operation on that file to isolate, say, Nebraska residents, WordPerfect will delete all the records except those for the Nebraska residents. If you then save the results of the selection with the original name, NAMELIST.WP, you will permanently lose every record except Nebraska residents in your NAMELIST.WP file—they cannot be recovered! You have to retype the records for residents of all the other states—not a pleasant task.

If you are going to be sorting and selecting often, I recommend that you save two copies of your list or secondary merge file, one with all the records and one that will be used to hold only the results of the most recent select operation. You might want to name this results file *SELECTED.WP.*

Always use the original secondary merge file to add and edit data. Then use the SELECTED.WP file only to store the results of selections. This will prevent confusion about which file is which by avoiding the creation of dozens of files that are simply the results of selections (which can gobble up your valuable disk space).

REFINING YOUR SELECTION CRITERIA WITH PARENTHESES

If your selection criteria start becoming rather complicated, you must be careful about how you combine AND and OR operators. For example, suppose your secondary merge file contains (among others) a field for the state where each person lives and a field for each person's credit limit. You then decide to write a form letter to all the people in Georgia and only those in Florida whose credit limits are $500 or greater, informing them that you've raised their credit limit by $1000 (perhaps because the value of their real estate has gone up).

If you want to isolate records from your secondary merge file to address only your intended customers, you must create selection criteria that combine *and* logic and *or* logic. That is, you must isolate all people who live in Georgia and only those in Florida who have credit limits of $500 or more.

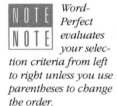
Word-Perfect evaluates your selection criteria from left to right unless you use parentheses to change the order.

If you're not careful, you may end up creating ambiguous selection criteria while trying to isolate these customers. For example, assuming that you've already defined the first sort key (key1) as the state field, and the second sort key (key2) as the credit-limit field, you might compose your selection criteria as

`key1=GA+key1=FL*key2>=$500`

But WordPerfect will interpret this as "Choose records that have GA or FL in the state field; from that list, choose records where the credit limit is greater than or equal to $500." The result includes those people in both Georgia and Florida whose credit limits are $500 or greater (but since you want to include *everyone* in Georgia, regardless of their present credit limit, this interpretation doesn't accomplish your intended goal).

To avoid potential confusion with such complicated selection criteria, you can use parentheses to refine the meaning and control how WordPerfect interprets your criteria. For example, the criteria

key1=GA+(key1=FL*key2>=$500)

say that, to avoid being deleted, a record must have GA in the state field (so all Georgians will be selected), or it must have FL in the state field and have a value that's greater than or equal to $500 in the credit-limit field. This resolves the ambiguity and ensures that *all* Georgians (with any credit limit at all) and *only* those Floridians with credit limits of $500 or more will remain after the select operation is finished.

GLOBAL SELECTIONS

You can use the *keyg* key name to search *all* the sort keys for a specific value. For example, suppose you create a secondary merge file that includes both a business address and a home address for each individual. If you want to mail to everyone who has either a home or business address in New York, define both the home and business state fields as sort keys. Then specify *keyg=NY* as the selection criterion. This will delete all records except those with NY in either the home or business state field.

SELECTING WITHOUT SORTING

You can select data from a file without sorting them. You still need to define your sort keys so that you can refer to them in your selection criteria, then specify your criteria. However, before you choose the Perform Action option, select **A**ction from the Sort menu, then choose Select **O**nly. The resulting output will contain only the selected records, but not in sorted order. This can speed things up a bit when you're performing selections from very large files.

EXAMPLES OF SELECTIONS

Figure 17.15 illustrates a sort key set up to sort a list of names and addresses in alphabetical order by last name, as shown earlier in Figure 17.6. In this example, however, only those records with *Schumack* as the last name (key1=Schumack) will be retained.

As you can see, the first sort key (key1) is defined as the second word in the first field. The selection criterion, which you can see below the Select heading in the lower portion of the screen, is

key1=Schumack

After you choose Perform Action, only records that have Schumack as the last name will remain in the document.

. . . .

Figure 17.16 shows another example, defined in Figure 17.8 to sort paragraphs in zip-code order. In this example, however, the following selection criterion has been added:

key1=92067

```
Name            Address         City        Zip
Barbara Adams   41 Apple St.    Fairbanks   92067
Morley Groback  83 Cherry Ln.   Encinitas   92065
Ted Ibble       91 Apple St.    Fairbanks   92067
John Janda      123 Apple St.   Fairbanks   92067
Mary Mohrlock   912 Apple St.   Fairbanks   92067
Susan Schumack  878 Oak St.     Encinitas   92065
Jane Whooley    34 Apple St.    Fairbanks   92067
Wanda Wibble    365 Cherry Ln.  Encinitas   92065
                                     Doc 2 Pg 1 Ln 1" Pos 1"
[                                      ]
------------------------------ Sort by Line ------------------------------

Key Typ Field Word      Key Typ Field Word      Key Typ Field Word
 1   a    1    2          2                        3
 4                        5                        6
 7                        8                        9
Select
key1=Schumack

Action                  Order                   Type
Select and sort         Ascending               Line sort

1 Perform Action; 2 View; 3 Keys; 4 Select; 5 Action; 6 Order; 7 Type: 0
```

FIGURE 17.15:
Records with Schumack as the last name will be selected after choosing Perform Action.

```
Adam Zelbert
621 Oak St.
Encinitas, CA  92065

Jane Whooley
34 Apple St.
Fairbanks, CA  92067

John Janda
123 Apple St.
                                     Doc 2 Pg 1 Ln 1" Pos 1"
[                                      ]
------------------------------ Sort by Paragraph ------------------------------

Key Typ Line Field Word    Key Typ Line Field Word    Key Typ Line Field Word
 1   a    3    1   -1        2                          3
 4                           5                          6
 7                           8                          9
Select
key1=92067

Action                  Order                   Type
Select and sort         Ascending               Paragraph sort

1 Perform Action; 2 View; 3 Keys; 4 Select; 5 Action; 6 Order; 7 Type: 0
```

FIGURE 17.16:
A sort-and-select operation that will pull out records in the 92067 zip-code area

This will select records in only the 92067 zip-code area.

Figure 17.17 shows a sample secondary merge file, with the city (field 4) defined as the first sort key and the state (field 5) defined as the second sort key. The selection criteria are defined as

key1=Layton*key2=KS

After selecting Perform Action, the secondary merge file will contain only names and addresses for residents of Layton, Kansas.

SORTING AND SELECTING TO AND FROM DOCUMENTS ON-DISK

If you don't block the text you want to sort or select, you'll see the prompt

Input file to sort: (Screen)

After you respond to that prompt, you'll see

Output file for sort: (Screen)

The input file is the file that already contains the text to be sorted or selected. The output file is generally a new file that will contain the sorted or selected text.

```
{END RECORD}
================================================================================
Nita{END FIELD}
Bonita{END FIELD}
P.O. Box 5432{END FIELD}
Glendora{END FIELD}
KS{END FIELD}
54320{END FIELD}
Miss Bonita{END FIELD}
{END RECORD}
                                        Doc 2 Pg 1 Ln 2.33" Pos 1"
{                                                          }
-------------------------- Sort Secondary Merge File --------------------------

Key Typ Field Line Word    Key Typ Field Line Word    Key Typ Field Line Word
 1   a    4    1    1       2   a    5    1    1       3
 4                          5                          6
 7                          8                          9
Select
key1=Layton * key2=KS

Action                     Order                      Type
Select                     Ascending                  Merge sort

1 Perform Action; 2 View; 3 Keys; 4 Select; 5 Action; 6 Order; 7 Type: 0
```

FIGURE 17.17:

A sort-and-select operation designed to isolate residents of Layton, KS

You can use these options to sort and select from and to any file on-disk. This is particularly handy when selecting records from secondary merge files. Keep in mind my warning about not using the same names for your input and output files; if you use NAMELIST.WP as the input file and SELECTED.WP as the output file when selecting, you don't have to worry about deleting records from your original NAMELIST.WP merge file.

In the next chapter, you'll learn another handy technique for the office: performing math calculations within a table. As you'll see, this technique can also be convenient for certain types of merges.

CHAPTER 18

Perfect Math

This chapter discusses WordPerfect's Math feature, which is handy for typing invoices, financial statements, and other documents that require some basic business computations. The easiest way to do math in WordPerfect is to use the Tables feature, introduced in Chapter 6.

If you are experienced with earlier versions of WordPerfect, you may be accustomed to working with math columns and the Math Definition screen. Be aware that you can still use these for math. However, you'll probably find that it's much easier to do math in conjunction with the Tables feature.

If you prefer to use spreadsheet programs like Lotus 1-2-3 or PlanPerfect for math, you will be glad to know that you can still use your spreadsheet program for all your math needs, and then import the spreadsheet into a WordPerfect document for printing. This topic is covered in Chapter 25.

For now, I'll review some of the basics of the WordPerfect Tables feature so that I can talk about using it for math.

TABLES AND MATH

As described in Chapter 6, every cell in a table has an *address* that identifies its position in the table. The first (leftmost) column is A, the next column is B, and so forth. The rows are numbered from top to bottom, starting with *1*.

The place where a column and row meet is called a cell, and each cell is identified by its column and row coordinates. The cell in the upper-left corner is A1 (column A, row 1), the cell to the right of that is B1, then C1, and so on. The cell beneath cell A1 is cell A2, the next cell down is cell A3, and so on.

You can always tell which cell the cursor is in by looking at the status line near the bottom of the screen. For example, Figure 18.1 shows a table with the cursor in cell C4. The figure also identifies each cell in the table.

USING MATH FORMULAS

TO ENTER A FORMULA IN A TABLE CELL,

1. **Move the cursor into the cell where you want to place the formula.**

2. **Go into Table Edit mode by selecting Layout ➤ Tables ➤ Edit or pressing Columns/Tables (Alt-F7).**

3. **Select Math ➤ Formula, type your formula, and press ⏎.**

Cell addresses in a table

Cell A1	Cell B1	Cell C1
Cell A2	Cell B2	Cell C2
Cell A3	Cell B3	Cell C3
Cell A4	Cell B4	Cell C4

Cursor is in cell C4

Cell C4 Doc 1 Pg 1 Ln 1.98" Pos 6.05"

Pressing the hyphen key or the gray– on your numeric keypad are both valid ways of expressing the leading minus sign.

Within a table, you can perform calculations by creating math formulas. The numbers can contain decimal points, commas to separate thousands, and leading dollar signs ($). For example, *1000, 1,000.00,* and *$1,000.00* are all valid ways of expressing the number one thousand. A negative number can be expressed with a leading minus sign or enclosed in parentheses. To express a negative value of one thousand, you can enter −1000, −1000.00, −1,000.00, −$1,000.00, $−1,000.00, or ($1,000.00).

You can use any combination of the following arithmetic operators in your formulas:

( )	Parentheses (used for grouping)
+	Addition
− (hyphen)	Subtraction or negative number
/	Division
*	Multiplication

You have to recalculate the entire table before WordPerfect will display the correct results of formulas, as discussed a little later in this chapter.

A formula can contain numbers, cell addresses, or both. For example, the formula *2 * 100* displays *200* in its cell. If cell A1 contains 25, cell A2 contains 10, and cell A3 contains the formula *A1 * A2,* then cell A3 displays *250* (the result of multiplying 10 times 25). If cell A1 contains *$100.00,* and cell A2 contains the formula *1.065 * A1,* then cell A2 actually displays *106.50* (a handy formula for adding a 6.5 percent sales tax to the number in another cell).

Word-Perfect calculates formulas from left to right, which is not the standard order in mathematics.

If a formula contains two or more operators, they are calculated in left-to-right order. For example, the result of the formula *1+5 * 10* is *60.* However, you can force any part of the formula to be calculated first by enclosing it in parentheses. Therefore the result of *1+(5 * 10)* is *51,* because the parentheses force the multiplication to take place first.

If you want to enter a number that involves a complex fraction into a cell and do not know the decimal equivalent of the fraction offhand, enter the number as a formula instead. For example, to enter the number $17^{15}/_{16}$ (seventeen and fifteen-sixteenths) into a cell, create a formula that calculates *17+(15/16)* in that cell. The cell will then display the correct decimal equivalent of the number.

You can *nest* up to seven pairs of parentheses in a formula. This allows you to perform quite complex calculations within a table. For example, if cell A1 contains the cost of an item, A2 the salvage value of that item, A3 the useful life in years, and A4 the current year, then the formula

A1−A2*(A3−A4+1)/(A3*(A3+1)/2)

calculates the current depreciation using the sum-of-the-years-digits method.

As I'll discuss later in this chapter, your table can also include special math functions to calculate subtotals, totals, and a grand total. These are indicated by a +, =, or * character (respectively) and are selected from menu options, not typed directly into a cell. Figure 18.2 shows a table designed for printing invoices. This figure shows math formulas (e.g., *C2*D2*) used in cells in the rightmost column.

You might not need to type each formula into a cell. If the formulas follow the same pattern, as in Figure 18.2, where each cell calculates the quantity times the unit price, you can just enter the formula in the topmost cell, and then copy the formula to the cells below. You'll learn how to copy formulas in a moment.

ENTERING FORMULAS

Once you create a table, you can enter a formula in any cell whenever you are in Table Edit mode. Follow these steps:

To determine the address of a cell that you want to use in a calculation, move the cursor to that cell and check the status line in the lower-right corner of the screen.

1. Move the cursor into the cell where you want to put the formula.

2. If you are not already in Table Edit mode, select **L**ayout ➤ **T**ables ➤ **E**dit or press Columns/Tables (**Alt-F7**).

3. Select **Math** ➤ **Formula**.

4. Type in your formula and press ↵.

Part No.	Description	Qty	Price	Total	
A-111	Spark plugs	8	$3.5	$28.00	—C2*D2
A-222	Radiator cap	1	$9.8	$9.80	—C3*D3
D-333	Fan belt	2	$12.5	$25.00	—C4*D4
B-207	Wax	2	$17.99	$35.98	—C5*D5
				$0.00	—C6*D6
				$0.00	—C7*D7
				$0.00	—C8*D8
			Subtotal:	$98.78	—+ (subtotal function)
			Sales tax:	$6.42	—0.065*E9
			Total:	$105.20	—E9+E10

=E9+E10   Cell E11 Doc 1 Pg 1 Ln 4.02" Pos 6.78"

FIGURE 18.2:

A table with formulas for an invoice

You can also see the formula in the lower-left corner of the normal Edit screen whenever you move the cursor into that cell.

Unlike a spreadsheet program, WordPerfect does not automatically recalculate the results of formulas when you change a number in a table.

The results of the calculation appear on the screen immediately, and the formula itself appears in the lower-left corner of the Table Edit screen (above the menu), preceded by an equal sign (=).

RECALCULATING FORMULAS

If you change a number in a cell that's used in a calculation, WordPerfect will not recalculate the new results of the formula automatically. To recalculate the entire table, follow these steps:

1. Move the cursor anywhere into the table.

2. If you are not already in Table Edit mode, select **L**ayout ➤ **T**ables ➤ **E**dit or press Columns/Tables (**Alt-F7**).

3. Select **M**ath ➤ **C**alculate.

All the formulas in the table will be recalculated.

CONTROLLING THE DECIMAL ACCURACY OF FORMULAS

To control the decimal accuracy of numbers in a table, you might first want to format the columns where the numbers will be stored. Follow these steps:

1. Move the cursor into any cell of the table.

2. If you are not already in Table Edit mode, select **L**ayout ➤ **T**able ➤ **E**dit or press Columns/Tables (**Alt-F7**).

3. Move the highlight to the column you want to format, or block as many columns as you want to format with the Block (**Alt-F4** or **F12**) and arrow keys.

4. Select **F**ormat ➤ Co**l**umn ➤ # **D**igits and type the number of decimal places you want displayed in each number (from 0 to 15). For example, enter *2* if you will be displaying dollar amounts. Press ↵.

If the table already contains some formulas, select **M**ath ➤ **C**alculate to recalculate their values and adjust the decimal accuracy.

CHANGING OR DELETING A FORMULA

You cannot change a formula after removing the [Table Def:] code.

If the results of a calculation are incorrect, even after you have recalculated the entire table, chances are the formula itself is incorrect. Similarly, if you add or delete table rows and columns, or you move or sort the contents of

To delete a formula, just press Delete repeatedly in step 4 until the formula is removed. You may also need to exit Table Edit mode, delete any numbers remaining in that cell, then return to Table Edit mode and recalculate the results.

cells in the table, you may need to adjust your formulas accordingly. Follow these steps:

1. Move the cursor into the cell containing the formula that you want to change.

2. If you are not already in Table Edit mode, select **L**ayout ➤ **T**ables ➤ **E**dit or press Columns/Tables (**Alt-F7**).

3. Select **M**ath ➤ **F**ormula.

4. Use the normal editing keys to make changes, or type an entirely new formula from scratch.

5. Press ↵.

6. Select **M**ath ➤ **C**alculate.

COPYING FORMULAS

If several cells perform similar calculations, you can enter the first formula and then copy it to cells in adjoining rows or columns. Like most spreadsheet programs, WordPerfect will automatically adjust the copied formulas to reflect the pattern of the original formulas. For example, if you copy a formula that adds A1 and B1 (A1+B1) to the next row down, the copied formula will automatically be adjusted to add A2 and B2 (A2+B2).

To copy a formula, follow these steps:

1. Position the cursor in the cell containing the formula you want to copy.

2. If you are not already in Table Edit mode, select **L**ayout ➤ **T**ables ➤ **E**dit or press Columns/Tables (**Alt-F7**).

3. Select **M**ath ➤ Co**p**y Formula. You'll see these options:

Copy Formula To: 1 Cell; 2 Down; 3 Right

◆ To copy the formula to a specific cell, select **C**ell, move the cursor to the cell where you want the formula copied (the destination cell), then press ↵.

◆ To copy the formula to several cells beneath the current cell, select **D**own, type the number of times to copy the formula, then press ↵.

◆ To copy the formula to several cells to the right, select **R**ight, type the number of times to copy the formula, then press ↵.

The cell addresses of the copied formulas are altered to retain the pattern of the original formula. For example, in Figure 18.2, the formula in cell E2 was

Remember to recalculate the table after copying your formulas.

entered as C2 * D2, and it correctly calculates the quantity (8) times the unit price ($3.5) for that row to come up with the total ($28.00). That formula was then copied down six rows to produce the other formulas (C3 * D3, C4 * D4, C5 * D5, and so forth), each of which correctly calculates the quantity times the price for its row.

CALCULATING SUBTOTALS, TOTALS, AND GRAND TOTALS

TO CALCULATE A SUBTOTAL, TOTAL, OR GRAND TOTAL IN A CELL,

1. Go into Table Edit mode.

2. Position the highlight on the cell in which you want to display the calculation.

3. Select Math, followed by one of the math functions: + (subtotal), = (total), or * (grand total).

You can also include in your tables special math functions to calculate subtotals, totals, and grand totals. However, you do not enter these functions directly from the keyboard. Instead, you must select them from the Table Edit menu, as outlined below:

*The total function (=) displays **0** if there are no subtotals above it, and the grand-total function (*) displays zero if there are no totals (=) above it. If you simply want to sum a column of numbers, use the subtotal (+) function.*

+   Subtotal (sums the numbers above)

=   Total (sums the subtotals above, up to the preceding total)

*   Grand total (sums the totals above)

To include a subtotal, total, or grand-total calculation in a table, follow these steps:

1. Position the cursor in the cell where you want to use the subtotal, total, or grand-total function.

2. If you are not already in Table Edit mode, select **L**ayout ➤ **T**ables ➤ **E**dit or press Columns/Tables (**Alt-F7**).

3. Select **M**ath.

    ◆ To calculate a subtotal, select + (option 4).

◆ To calculate a total (the sum of all subtotals above), select = (option 5).

◆ To calculate a grand total (the sum of all totals above), select * (option 6).

To delete a subtotal, total, or grand-total formula from a cell, select **M**ath ➤ **F**ormula from the Table Edit menu, press Delete, then press ↵. If necessary, exit Table Edit mode, delete any numbers already calculated for the cell, then return to Table Edit mode and recalculate the table.

Remember to recalculate your table after putting in (or removing) subtotal, total, and grand-total functions.

Figure 18.3 shows a sample table that uses the subtotal, total, and grand-total functions. The figure also illustrates how you can use the Math feature in a table to create common financial statements, then remove and change table lines (Chapter 6) to give the document a more traditional appearance.

Excluding Cells from Totals

The subtotal, total, and grand-total operators base their calculations on all the numbers in a column. This can cause a miscalculation if a cell contains a number that should be excluded from the calculation. For example, if the heading of a column is the year 1992, the number 1,992 will be added to the total.

```
First Quarter: Eastern Division
New Cars             $22,500,000.00
Used Cars             $7,500,000.00
Subtotal             30,000,000.00 ─────── + (subtotal function)

First Quarter: Western Division
New Cars             $18,500,000.00
Used Cars             $9,500,000.00
Subtotal             $28,000,000.00 ─────── + (subtotal function)
Qtr 1 Total          $58,000,000.00 ─────── = (total function)

Second Quarter: Eastern Division
New Cars             $21,750,000.00
Used Cars             $9,675,000.00
Subtotal             $31,425,000.00 ─────── + (subtotal function)

Second Quarter: Western Division
New Cars             $16,000,000.00
Used Cars             $8,775,000.00
Subtotal             $24,775,000.00 ─────── + (subtotal function)
Qtr 2 Total          $56,200,000.00 ─────── = (total function)

Grand Total          $114,200,000.00 ────── * (grand-total function)
```

FIGURE 18.3:

The subtotal, total, and grand-total functions

To exclude a cell from a subtotal, total, or grand-total calculation, change its type from Numeric to Text. Follow these steps:

1. If you're not already in Table Edit mode, move the cursor into the table and go into Table Edit mode (select **L**ayout ➤ **T**ables ➤ **E**dit or press **Alt-F7**).

2. Move the cursor to the cell that you want to exclude from the calculation. If you want to exclude several cells from a calculation, block those cells.

3. Select **F**ormat ➤ **C**ell ➤ **T**ype ➤ **T**ext.

4. Select **M**ath ➤ **C**alculate to recalculate the formulas.

The totals will be recalculated without the cells you've defined as Text.

INCLUDING DOLLAR SIGNS

If you want to insert a leading dollar sign ($) in a cell that shows the results of a calculation (or just a regular cell containing a number), follow these steps:

1. If you are in Table Edit mode, press Exit (**F7**) to return to the Edit screen.

2. Move the cursor to the first character of the cell that contains the formula and displays its results, or to the first character of the cell containing the number.

3. Type the dollar sign ($).

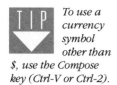
To use a currency symbol other than $, use the Compose key (Ctrl-V or Ctrl-2).

DISPLAYING NEGATIVE RESULTS IN PARENTHESES

Normally, WordPerfect displays negative results of calculations with leading minus signs. If you prefer to display negative results in parentheses, follow these steps:

1. Move the cursor into the table.

2. If you are not already in Table Edit mode, select **L**ayout ➤ **T**ables ➤ **E**dit or press Columns/Tables (**Alt-F7**).

3. Select **O**ptions ➤ **D**isplay Negative Results.

4. Type **2** to display all negative calculation results in parentheses.

5. Press ↵.

6. Press Exit (**F7**) to return to Table Edit mode.

7. If your table already contains formulas, select **M**ath ➤ **C**alculate to recalculate all the formulas and display negative results in parentheses.

Keep in mind that this option *does not* automatically put parentheses around numbers originally entered with a leading minus sign (or vice versa); it only affects the display of negative *calculation results*. So, for instance, if you want the number *−247.50* displayed with parentheses, (247.50), you must return to the Edit screen, delete the leading minus sign, and place parentheses around the number.

KEEPING NUMBERS ALIGNED

When displaying negative values in parentheses, you'll probably want to decimal-align all the numbers so that the decimal points line up. Move the cursor to the column containing the numbers you want to align, and go into Table Edit mode if you have not already done so (select **L**ayout ➤ **T**able ➤ **E**dit or press Alt-F7). If you want to align several columns, block them with the Alt-F4 or F12 key.

From the Table Edit menu, select **F**ormat ➤ **C**olumn ➤ **J**ustify ➤ **D**ecimal Align. If necessary, you can then press Ctrl-→ to widen the column to accommodate the parentheses surrounding negative numbers.

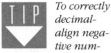

*To correctly decimal-align negative numbers displayed in parentheses, you will probably need to increase the # Digits setting of that column by selecting **F**ormat ➤ **C**olumn ➤ **#D**igits (Chapter 6).*

NEGATING A TOTAL

You can precede any formula with a minus sign (you can use the hyphen key or the minus sign on the numeric keypad) to convert its value to a negative number. This is handy in situations where you want to display income and expenses as positive values, but prefer to calculate the sum of expenses as a negative value and then use that calculation in subtotals, totals, grand totals, or other formulas.

For example, if cells B3, B4, and B5 contain expenses expressed as positive values, then the formula *−(B3+B4+B5)* in cell C6 displays their sum as a negative value. Subtotal, total, and grand-total functions in column C, and any other formulas using cell C6, also treat that cell as a negative value.

You can also negate the results of a subtotal, total, or grand-total function in the same way. Go through the usual menu selections to put the +, =, or * function in its cell in Table Edit mode. Then, leave Table Edit mode, move the cursor to the cell containing the function, and type a hyphen. When you recalculate the table, you'll see the result displayed as a negative number.

Figure 18.4 shows two examples of using negative numbers to manage income and expenses figures. In both examples, the numbers and calculation results are the same, but they're expressed somewhat differently with respect to positive and negative numbers. In the first example, the ending Inventory (7/1/90) and formulas for Total Cost of Goods Sold and Total Operating Expenses are expressed as negative numbers, with the formulas for Gross Profit on Sales and Net Profit adjusted accordingly (the figure shows the formulas used). In the second example, the ending Inventory (7/1/90) and formulas for Total Cost of Goods Sold and Total Operating Expenses are expressed as positive numbers, with the formulas for Gross Profit on Sales and Net Profit adjusted accordingly.

Sales		5,980,000.00	
Cost of Goods Sold			
Inventory (6/1/90)	1,550,000.00		
Purchases	4,550,000.00		
Inventory (7/1/90)	-3,000,000.00		
Total		-3,100,000.00	—(B4+B5+B6)
Gross Profit on Sales		2,880,000.00	C1+C7
Operating Expenses			
Salaries	1,159,200.00		
Phone	25,000.00		
Mail	57,500.00		
Utilities	47,500.00		—(B11+B12+B13+B14+B15)
Office Supplies	15,500.00		
Total Expenses		-1,304,700.00	
Net Profit		1,575,300.00	C1+C7+C16

Sales		5,980,000.00	
Cost of Goods Sold			
Inventory (6/1/90)	1,550,000.00		
Purchases	4,550,000.00		
Inventory (7/1/90)	3,000,000.00		
Total		3,100,000.00	B4+B5-B6
Gross Profit on Sales		2,880,000.00	C1-C7
Operating Expenses			
Salaries	1,159,200.00		
Phone	25,000.00		
Mail	57,500.00		
Utilities	47,500.00		B11+B12+B13+B14+B15
Office Supplies	15,500.00		
Total Expenses		1,304,700.00	
Net Profit		1,575,300.00	C1-C7-C16

FIGURE 18.4:

Two ways of representing income and expenses

LOCKING FORMULA CELLS

You can lock any cell in a table to protect it from change or erasure. This is particularly handy in tables that you want to use repeatedly for performing calculations. You can lock the cells containing formulas, fill in the numbers to be calculated, print the table, and then simply erase all the cells in the table when you want to enter a new set of numbers. Only the unlocked cells will actually be erased.

Because the formulas are locked, you won't have to worry about accidentally erasing them. Therefore, you'll be able to reuse the same table repeatedly. This technique is ideal for multiple invoices, packing slips, and similar forms.

To lock a cell or group of cells, follow these steps:

1. Move the cursor to the cell or the corner of a group of cells that you want to lock.

2. If you are not already in Table Edit mode, select **L**ayout ➤ **T**ables ➤ **E**dit or press Columns/Tables (**Alt-F7**).

3. If you want to lock several cells, use the Block key (**Alt-F4** or **F12**) to highlight the group of cells you want to lock.

4. Select **F**ormat ➤ **C**ell ➤ **L**ock ➤ **O**n.

 *On the normal Edit screen, your cursor will jump right over any locked cells.*

When a cell is locked, its address appears in brackets on the Table Edit menu's status line (e.g., [A1]). If the cell contains a formula, it will still be recalculated when you recalculate the table. Also, you can import data from spreadsheets into locked cells.

To unlock a cell or cells, repeat the steps above but select **O**ff rather than On in the last step.

PREVENTING RECALCULATION

Normally, every formula in a table is recalculated when you recalculate the table. If, for whatever reason, you do not want a particular formula to be recalculated, you can change its cell type to Text. To do so, move the cursor into the cell containing the formula that you do not want recalculated. Go to Table Edit mode (select **L**ayout ➤ **T**able ➤ **E**dit or press Alt-F7), and choose **F**ormat ➤ **C**ell ➤ **T**ype ➤ **T**ext.

Be forewarned, however, that any other cell using that changed cell's address in a formula or math function will display only ?? the next time you recalculate. That's because you cannot refer to a Text-type cell in a formula.

The ?? result occurs only if a referenced cell containing a formula is defined as Text, not if it contains a number.

If you end up with ?? in a formula, make sure that all cells referenced by that formula are of Numeric type. You can tell whether a cell is Text or Numeric by moving the cursor to the cell and checking the status line on the Edit screen or Table Edit screen. If quotation marks appear in front of the cell's address, it's a Text cell (for example, *Cell A1* indicates a Numeric cell, and *Cell "A2* indicates a text cell). To change a Text cell back to Numeric, move the highlight to the cell in Table Edit mode, then select **F**ormat ➤ **C**ell ➤ **T**ype ➤ **N**umeric.

MERGING TO TABLES

If you decimal-align columns that have {FIELD} commands in them, the commands may move partially out of the cell or be partially obscured on the Edit screen, but the merge will still be successful.

You can merge data from a secondary merge file into a table that contains {FIELD} commands. This is the same technique discussed in Chapter 16. The primary file contains {FIELD} commands that indicate which field goes where. Figure 18.5 shows an example where 18 fields have been placed in a primary merge file that resembles an invoice (the form is intentionally small to fit on one screen in this example).

You create the primary merge file in the normal way (without being in Table Edit mode), using **T**ools ➤ Me**r**ge Codes ➤ **F**ield (Shift-F9 F) to enter each {FIELD} command, as discussed in Chapter 16. Some columns may expand to accommodate the {FIELD} command. Use the View Document screen rather than the Edit screen to see the actual width of each column in your table.

```
Invoice Number: {FIELD}Invoice Number~
Invoice Date: {FIELD}Invoice Date:~

Bill To:

{FIELD}Name~
{FIELD}Address 1~
{FIELD}Address 2?~
{FIELD}City State Zip~
```

Code	Description	Hours	Rate	Total
{FIELD}Code 1~	{FIELD}Descript 1~	{FIELD}Hours 1~	{FIELD}Rate 1~	$1.00
{FIELD}Code 2~	{FIELD}Descript 2~	{FIELD}Hours 2~	{FIELD}Rate 2~	$4.00
{FIELD}Code 3~	{FIELD}Descript 3~	{FIELD}Hours 3~	{FIELD}Rate 3~	$9.00
			Total:	$14.00

```
=C2*D2 Align char = .          Cell E2 Doc 1 Pg 1 Ln 2.79" Pos 5.31"
```

FIGURE 18.5:
A primary merge file with merge fields and formulas

The rightmost column of the table in Figure 18.5 contains the formulas required to perform calculations. The cursor is in cell E2, which contains the formula C2*D2 to calculate the hours times the rate. (You can see the formula in the lower-left corner of the screen.) The cell in the bottom-right corner of the table contains the subtotal function, + (not visible on the screen), to calculate the total. Currently, all the calculated results are incorrect because the data from the secondary merge file has not been merged with this file yet.

Figure 18.6 shows a secondary merge file for this example. You can see the field names and one sample record (though, of course, this file could have enough data to print dozens of invoices).

```
{FIELD NAMES}
      Invoice Number~
      Date~
      Name~
      Address 1~
      Address 2~
      City State Zip~
      Code 1~
      Descript 1~
      Hours 1~
      Rate 1~
      Code 2~
      Descript 2~
      Hours 2~
      Rate 2~
      Code 3~
      Descript 3~
      Hours 3~
      Rate 3~~
{END RECORD}
================================================================
11101{END FIELD}
June 11, 1991{END FIELD}
Izzy Hartunian{END FIELD}
ABC Corporation{END FIELD}
P.O. Box 17007{END FIELD}
New York, NY  10010{END FIELD}
105{END FIELD}
Word Processing{END FIELD}
10{END FIELD}
$55.00{END FIELD}
107{END FIELD}
Form Letters{END FIELD}
2{END FIELD}
$90.00{END FIELD}
{END FIELD}
{END FIELD}
{END FIELD}
{END FIELD}
{END RECORD}
================================================================
```

FIGURE 18.6:

A secondary merge file with invoice data

After merging the primary and secondary files, you can scroll through the results on your Edit screen as usual. Figure 18.7 shows an example, where the first record from the sample secondary merge file has been merged with the primary merge file.

There's one catch, though. As you can see in Figure 18.7, the figures for the Total column do not reflect the actual numbers in the table. All of the tables involved in the merge need to be recalculated before printing. Needless to say, you wouldn't want to recalculate the tables one at a time, so you can create a macro to make this job easier, which starts at the top of the document, locates each table in the document, and recalculates it.

Figure 18.8 shows just such a macro. To create it, you'll need to know about macros and the Macro Editor (Chapter 15), and a little bit about the advanced macro commands (Chapter 26). Once it's created, you can use it in any document containing multiple tables (whether or not that document is the result of a merge) to recalculate all the tables.

Starting in the next chapter, you'll learn about integrating text and graphics in your WordPerfect documents, the foundation of desktop publishing.

Because you have to recalculate tables after a merge, you cannot merge straight to the printer when there's math involved.

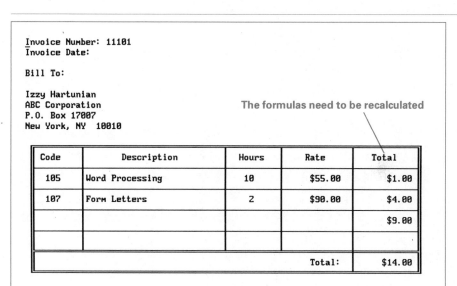

The files merged but not yet calculated

```
Invoice Number: 11101
Invoice Date:

Bill To:

Izzy Hartunian
ABC Corporation          The formulas need to be recalculated
P.O. Box 17007
New York, NY  10010
```

Code	Description	Hours	Rate	Total
105	Word Processing	10	$55.00	$1.00
107	Form Letters	2	$90.00	$4.00
				$9.00
			Total:	$14.00

```
Doc 1 Pg 1 Ln 1" Pos 1"
```

```
Macro: Action

    File              RECALC.WPM

    Description       Recalculate all tables in a document


  ┌─────────────────────────────────────────────────────────────────┐
  │{Home}{Home}{Home}{Up}            {;}Start·at·top·of·doc~          │
  │{LABEL}NextTable~                                                  │
  │{ON NOT FOUND}{GO}NoMore~~        {;}End·when·no·more·tables.~     │
  │   {Search}{Columns/Tables}td{Search}  {;}Locate·next·table~      │
  │   {Columns/Tables}mc             {;}Recalc·current·table~         │
  │   {Exit}{Right}                  {;}Exit·edit·mode,·move·cursor~  │
  │{GO}NextTable~                    {;}Repeat·steps·above~           │
  │                                                                   │
  │{LABEL}NoMore~                    {;}No·more·tables·in·doc~        │
  │{Home}{Home}{Up}                                                  │
  │                                                                   │
  │                                                                   │
  │                                                                   │
  │                                                                   │
  └─────────────────────────────────────────────────────────────────┘

Ctrl-V to Insert next key as commmand;
Ctrl-PgUp for macro commands;  Press Exit when done
```

FIGURE 18.8:

A macro to recalculate every table in a document

PART SIX

Desktop Publishing

! n this part you'll build upon the basic desktop publishing skills you've acquired in previous chapters and learn to create truly dazzling documents. You'll learn how to position and size graphic images, and to combine graphics and text. Then you'll learn to create more advanced documents that use newspaper and parallel columns. Finally, you'll learn how to create equations, which is handy if you work with mathematical or scientific literature.

CHAPTER 19

Using Graphics in Your Documents

It's an old cliché, but certainly true: A picture is worth a thousand words. Pictures are not only informative, they are also appealing to the eye, and they can be used to make any document more attractive and more readable. For example, take a look at the "plain-text" document in Figure 19.1. Then take a look at the same document in Figure 19.2 with some graphics and fonts called into play. Granted, both documents say the same thing; but which one would *you* be more inclined to read?

HANDS-ON
....
LESSON 7

For a hands-on lesson in using graphic boxes, see Lesson 7 in Part 9.

In this chapter, you'll learn about some techniques for adding graphics to your own documents. This will let you move from the realm of word processing into more advanced document generation and desktop publishing.

UNDERSTANDING GRAPHIC BOXES

Using graphics is basically a matter of positioning a *graphic box* in the text, then filling the box. WordPerfect offers five different types of graphic boxes:

Figure box, Text box, Table box, User box, and Equation box. The names have nothing to do with their usage. Each has an initial border style, shading, and caption position, and each has its own independent, automatic numbering system to help you manage and reference boxes from within your text. If you like, you can put text in a Table box, a figure in an Equation box—it makes no difference.

Figure 19.3 shows examples of empty graphic boxes with their default borders, shading, and caption positions. As you'll find out later in this chapter,

By default, Equation boxes are borderless, like User boxes, and they have no shading (see Chapter 21).

Another BRIGHT IDEA from BulbCo

A Lightbulb Guaranteed
to Last a Lifetime

Your life or the bulb's (we're betting on the bulb, by the way). That's right, with BulbCo's new Perennial Lightbulb, you and your descendants will never again need to replace another lightbulb. Sure, these babies cost almost $300 apiece, and we don't recommend juggling with them, but think of the savings!

They Pay for Themselves in
Just Ten Years (Or So)

Waitaminit! you're thinking now. These lightbulbs we're talking about here cost a fortune! Well, sure they do, <u>at first</u>. You can get a lightbulb from one of the other guys for just over one-hundredth of the cost. But just think, in six months to two years (see chart, above), you'll be browsing through the hardware store looking for another replacement. Add it up for yourself, in twenty, twenty-five, fifty years ...tops... our Perennial bulbs will have paid for themselves.

Breakage Insurance Available

So, what's in it for BulbCo, you may wonder. Well, first, we should point out that we're going to do land-office business with this product. Planned obsolescence? Pfuui! Give us a good, solid (unbeatable, that is) product and just let us sell 'em one at a time. Of course, you're going to want to protect your investment. We'll guarantee these lightbulbs for a lifetime, yours or theirs, as we've asserted, but we'll only guarantee that they'll continue operating **as long as they remain intact.** If that sounds to you like a mighty big if, you're right. You drop one of our Perennials on the linoleum and you've dropped about three hundred dollars and smashed them into shards all over your kitchen floor. Give one of our Perennials to baby to use as a rattle. Shake, shake, shake, and there goes the filament. We build 'em sturdy, but, face it, they're lightbulbs.

Easy Terms

So what are we going to do for you? Glad you asked. We'll <u>insure</u> every single one of your lightbulbs for a small premium, ranging from $.50 a year for the 30-watt model to a still-negligible $1.97 a year for our superpowerful 250-watt bulbs. See the table to the left for details.

you can easily change the border style, shading, or caption position of any box, or all the boxes of a given type (e.g., all the Figure boxes).

The automatic numbering feature is especially helpful for saving you time and trouble. For example, you could put all your document figures in Figure boxes, and let WordPerfect number them automatically (e.g., Figure 1.1,

FIGURE 19.2:

The document with some graphics and fonts added

Another *BRIGHT IDEA* from *BULBCO*

A Lightbulb Guaranteed to Last a Lifetime
Your life or the bulb's (we're betting on the bulb, by the way). That's right, with BulbCo's new Perennial Lightbulb you and your descendants will never again need to replace another lightbulb. Sure, these baby's cost almost $300 apiece, and we don't recommend juggling with them, but think of the savings!

They Pay for Themselves in Just Ten Years (Or So)
Waitaminit! you're thinking now, these lightbulbs we're talking about here cost a fortune! Well, sure they do, <u>at first</u>. You can get a lightbulb from one of the other guys for just over one-hundredth of the cost but just think, in six months to two years (see chart, above), you'll be browsing through the hardware store looking for another replacement. Add it up for yourself, in twenty, twenty-five, fifty years ...tops... our Perennial bulbs will have paid for themselves.

The Perennial outlasts even our old favorite, the Superior, and makes mincemeat of the competition. (The chart only shows ten years projected, but the Perennial will, of course, last forever.)

Breakage Insurance Available
So, what's in it for BulbCo, you may wonder. Well, first, we should point out that we're going to do land-office business with this product. Planned obsolescence? Pfuui! Give us a good, solid (unbeatable, that is) product and just let us sell 'em one at a time. Of course, however, you are going to want to protect your investment. We'll guarantee these lightbulbs for a lifetime, yours or theirs, as we've asserted, but we'll only guarantee that they'll continue operating **as long as they remain intact.** If that sounds to you like that might be a big if, you're right. You drop one of our Perennials on the linoleum and you've dropped about three hundred dollars and smashed them into shards all over your kitchen floor. Give one of our Perennials to baby to use as a rattle. Shake, shake, shake, and there goes the filament. We build 'em sturdy, but, face it, they're lightbulbs.

Insurance Rates

Model	Premium	Deductible
30 watt	$.50	$25
75 watt	$.75	$35
100 watt	$.99	$50
150 watt	$1.49	$70
250 watt	$1.97	$99

Easy Terms
So what are we going to do for you? Glad you asked. We'll <u>insure</u> every single one of your lightbulbs for a small premium, ranging from $.50 a year for the 30-watt model to a still-negligible $1.97 a year for our superpowerful 250-watt bulbs. See the table to the left for details.

A single document can have any combination of up to 999 boxes, with a maximum of 100 boxes per page (however, your computer's memory may impose additional limitations).

Figure 1.2, and so forth). In the same document, you could place all your tables in Table boxes, and let WordPerfect number them separately and automatically (e.g., Table 1.1, Table 1.2, and so forth). Whenever you insert, move, and delete tables and figures, WordPerfect will renumber them for you. What's more, WordPerfect can also automatically generate figure lists and table lists from these figures and tables, using the List option in Automatic Referencing, as described in Chapter 23.

As mentioned earlier, each box type initially has its own unique border style. For example, in Figure 19.2, the light bulb in the upper-right corner of the document is in a User box (no border). The bar graph is in a Figure box

Empty Table Box: Thick lines at top and bottom, caption above.

Empty Figure Box: Single line border on all sides, caption below.

Empty Text Box: Thick lines at top and bottom, shaded, caption below.

Empty User Box: No border lines or shading, caption below.

FIGURE 19.3:
Examples of empty Figure, Table, Text, and User boxes with their default borders, shading, and caption positions

(full, single-line border), and the table in the lower-left corner is in a Table box (thick lines at the top and bottom and no lines on the sides).

But you can change the border style for any single graphic box or all the graphic boxes of a particular type, as described in "Changing the Appearance of Boxes" later in this chapter. Using different border styles can add variety and texture to your document.

WHAT CAN GO IN A BOX

Every box you create is initially empty. But you can fill any empty box with a graphic figure, a table, text, or an equation, as described below.

GRAPHIC IMAGES

Graphic images come from files stored outside of your document, which you can read into a box. Your WordPerfect package comes with 30 WordPerfect graphics files, which you can see in Figure 19.4. Each of these files has the file-name extension .WPG (for *WordPerfect graphic*). If you have a hard disk and installed WordPerfect properly, these are stored in the same directory as your WordPerfect program by default.

If you have an earlier version of WordPerfect, or DrawPerfect, you can also use any .WPG files from those packages.

You can also create your own graphics, using spreadsheet and graphics programs, screen-capture programs, and scanners. See the section titled "Sources of Graphics" later in this chapter for additional information.

TABLES

You can display a table in your document with or without the aid of a box. Either way, you still use the Tables feature to create and edit the table. However, there are a few advantages to placing tables in boxes:

◆ If the table is in a Table box, you can wrap text around it (like the table in the lower-left corner of Figure 19.2 and the lower-right corner of Figure 19.6).

◆ If the table is in a box and is small enough to fit on one page, WordPerfect will never split the table across two pages.

◆ You can display two or more tables side by side if each table is in a box.

◆ If you caption and number each table (e.g., Table I.1, Table I.2, and so forth), WordPerfect can handle all the numbering automatically, letting

FIGURE 19.4:

WordPerfect graphic images

you add, delete, and move Table boxes without having to readjust all the numbers manually.

◆ You can automatically generate a list of tables for your completed document if all the tables are in Table boxes (see Chapter 23).

NOTE
NOTE

The box in the center of Figure 19.6 contains the text "WordPerfect has lots of tools...."

TEXT

A box can also contain text, using whatever fonts and features your printer offers for printing text. Text boxes are commonly used to display quotations or catchy phrases from the document.

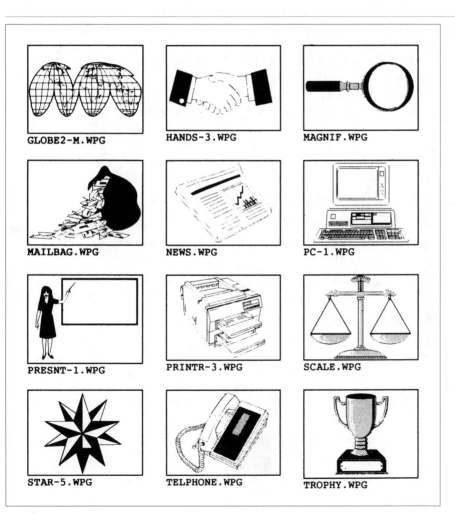

FIGURE 19.4:

WordPerfect graphic images (continued)

GLOBE2-M.WPG

HANDS-3.WPG

MAGNIF.WPG

MAILBAG.WPG

NEWS.WPG

PC-1.WPG

PRESNT-1.WPG

PRINTR-3.WPG

SCALE.WPG

STAR-5.WPG

TELPHONE.WPG

TROPHY.WPG

EQUATIONS

A box can also contain an equation that you create using the WordPerfect Equation Editor. For information on using the Equation Editor, refer to Chapter 21.

A BOX IS JUST A BOX

Remember that the only reason that WordPerfect offers different types of boxes is to simplify the automatic numbering of boxes and to let you define a unique border style for boxes within a particular category. WordPerfect categorizes boxes as Figure, Table, Text, User, and Equation simply because many documents use these types of boxes. This means that any box, regardless of its type, can contain a graphic figure, a table, text, or an equation. For example, you can use Figure boxes for business graphs, graphic images, photos, diagrams, and so forth; Table boxes for tables; Text boxes for sidebars, quotes, catchy phrases, and other text that's set off from the main body text; Equation boxes for mathematical and scientific equations; and User boxes for additional graphics that don't fit into any of the other categories.

CREATING A BOX

TO CREATE A GRAPHICS BOX,

1. Position the cursor.

2. Select Graphics from the menu or press the Graphics key (Alt-F9).

3. Select the type of box you want to create, then choose Create.

4. Use options on the box Definition menu to position, size, and fill the box.

The general steps for creating any box are summarized below:

1. Position the cursor at the character or paragraph to which you want to attach the box or, if the box will be anchored to the page, at the top of the document (discussed in more detail in "Anchoring a Box").

2. Pull down the Graphics menu, or press Graphics (**Alt-F9**).

3. Select a box type from the options offered (**F**igure, **T**able Box, Text **B**ox, **U**ser Box, or **E**quation).

4. Select **C**reate. The box Definition menu, shown in Figure 19.5, appears.

5. Select Anchor **T**ype, and then **P**aragraph, P**a**ge, or **C**haracter. Then choose the **V**ertical Position or **H**orizontal Position options to position the box vertically and horizontally on the page, as described later in this chapter.

You can use List Files (F5) to select the graphic image in step 6.

6. To add text or a table to the box, select **E**dit, create the box contents, and then press Exit (**F7**). Alternatively, to copy a graphic image (or text or a table stored in a file) into the box, select **F**ilename, and enter the directory location and full name of the file.

7. Select any other options to define **C**aption, **S**ize, or **W**rap Text Around Box (as described in the sections that follow).

8. Press Exit (**F7**) to return to the Edit screen.

Only an empty "ghost" image of the box appears on the Edit screen. But the View document screen (**F**ile ➤ **P**rint ➤ **V**iew Document or Shift-F7 V) displays the box as well as its contents.

```
Definition: Figure

    1 - Filename

    2 - Contents           Empty

    3 - Caption

    4 - Anchor Type        Paragraph

    5 - Vertical Position  0"

    6 - Horizontal Position Right

    7 - Size               3.25" wide x 3.25" (high)

    8 - Wrap Text Around Box Yes

    9 - Edit




Selection: 0
```

FIGURE 19.5:
The box Definition menu

ANCHORING A BOX

You have three options when choosing how you want to anchor a box; you must position the cursor accordingly before going through the steps to create the box:

Paragraph: A paragraph-anchored box floats with its paragraph as you add and delete surrounding text. You use such a box when the text refers to "this figure" or "the figure at the left," or when you want to make sure that "Figure X.X" stays near the first reference to Figure X.X in a paragraph. Place the cursor to the left of the paragraph before defining the box.

Page: This type of box is anchored to the page and never moves, no matter what happens to the text around it. You use it for a graphic headline or a graphic or text box centered in the middle of a page, where it spans two or more columns. Place the cursor at the top of the document before defining the box.

Character: This type of box is anchored to a specific character. You use it for small in-line graphics and graphic boxes in page headers, footers, footnotes, and endnotes. Place the cursor to the right of the character before defining the box.

Multi-column layouts are covered in the next chapter.

Figure 19.6 shows a few examples of different kinds of boxes and explains how they are anchored. The figure uses a multicolumn layout, but the basic anchoring principles work with single-column layouts as well.

VERTICALLY POSITIONING A BOX

You can just estimate the vertical position of a box when first defining it, because you can easily make adjustments later.

Whereas anchoring a box defines what the box is fixed to, *positioning* the box defines the box's position with respect to the anchor point. To vertically position a box, select the Vertical Position option from the box Definition menu. The options available to you at that point depend on how you've anchored the box.

Vertically Positioning a Paragraph-Anchored Box

*When editing the paragraph later, do not add text in front of the graphic-box code; the box must always be placed **before** the paragraph text.*

Before you create a paragraph-anchored box, position the cursor at the first character of the paragraph where you want to anchor the box. Create the box and select Paragraph as the anchor type, as described above. Then specify a vertical position for the box with respect to the paragraph by selecting the Vertical Position option. You'll see this prompt:

Offset from top of paragraph: 0"

If you leave the position at 0", the top of the box will be even with the top of the paragraph. Any measurement you enter other than zero will move the box down with respect to the top of the paragraph, as in the example shown in Figure 19.7.

FIGURE 19.6:

Examples of anchored boxes

Examples of Anchoring Boxes

CHECK BOX
We start with a small graphic image that is anchored to his paragraph (the box's hidden code is just before the first character of this paragraph.

The box is sized small, and the text of the paragraph wraps around it.

DIPLOMA
Another case for anchoring a figure to a paragraph is when you want a figure to closely follow its callout in text.

For example, Figure 1 shows a diploma. To keep that figure near, but below, it's anchored to the top of the next paragraph. Its Horizontal Position is Full (the width of the column.)

Figure 1.

Because the box is as wide as this column, no text wraps around the side of it.

TEXT BOX
The text box in the center of the page is anchored to the page. Its hidden code is at the top of the page. All text wraps around it. Page anchoring is the only way to create boxes that cross columns.

TABLE BOX
The Table box in the lower right corner of the page is

WordPerfect has lots of tools for aligning graphic boxes in columns

also anchored to the page (bottom right corner). Page anchoring was required here because we needed the table to be wider than one column.

FOOTER
The star symbol at the lower left corner of the page is actually in a footer. It's character-anchored, because that's the

only anchor type allowed in headers and footers.

IN-LINE GRAPHIC
Next we have a small graphic mouse in text. The mouse graphic is in a character anchored User Box, and is sized small enough to fit on a line of text.

Small character-anchored graphics like that can be used as icons in text, margins, or in margin notes -- or perhaps for amusing pictures in children's books.

COLUMNS & LINES
The columns in this example are newspaper columns with a distance of .4" between them. Chapter 20 discusses multi-column layouts in detail.

The lines are all graphic lines with the Graphics ▸ Line menu options (see Chapter 19).

The table below shows the Column (horizontal) and Vertical position, as the length, of each vertical line.

Line	1ˢᵗ	2ⁿᵈ	3ʳᵈ	4ᵗʰ
Column	1	2	1	2
Vertical	1.51	1.51	6.35	6.35
Length	2.83	2.83	3.45	2.08

Page 1

WordPerfect never splits a graphic box across two pages. If there isn't enough room to print the entire graphic box on the current page, WordPerfect automatically bumps the entire box to the next page.

Getting the vertical measurement just right can be tricky for two reasons:

◆ Text always wraps around the outside border space defined for the box (by means of the Outside Border Space options, described later).

◆ WordPerfect always adds 2 points of leading to the top of proportionally spaced fonts, but no leading to monospaced fonts.

Therefore, to center the box on the right in Figure 19.7 relative to the text surrounding it, the outside border space for the box was set at the top and bottom to 0". The vertical position of the box was set to 29p (29 points): 28 points to compensate for two 12-point lines of text, each with 2 points of additional leading, and one additional point based on a visual inspection after printing, which indicated that the box was a little too close to the line of text above it.

Vertically Positioning a Page-Anchored Box

Before you create a page-anchored box, move the cursor to the top of the document so that it precedes the first character of text, but follows any codes that define margins, headers, or footers. Create the box as described earlier, then choose Anchor Type and select Page. When you choose to anchor the box to the page, you'll see a prompt asking

Number of pages to skip: 0

Press ↵ to accept 0 and place the box on the current page, or enter the number of pages to skip (e.g., entering *1* will place the box on the next page, page 2).

To vertically position the box on its page, select Vertical Position and one of the options that appears:

Full Page	The box will fill the entire page.
Top	The top of the box will line up with the top margin of the page (below the page header, if any).

In this example, the figure is anchored to this paragraph, with a vertical position of 0", so the top of the box is aligned with the top of the paragraph. To reduce extra blank space at the bottom of the box, we set the Outside Border Space at the bottom of the box (via Options) to 0".

In this example, we set the vertical position of the box to 29p, which causes the box to be placed a little lower in the paragraph. We also set the Outside Border Space at the top and bottom of the box to 0" to reduce extraneous white space surrounding the box (picky picky!).

FIGURE 19.7:

Examples of vertically positioning a paragraph-anchored box

Center	The box will be centered between the top and bottom margins of the page.
Bottom	The bottom of the box will line up with the bottom margin of the page (above the page footer, if any).
Set Position	This lets you place the box at an exact distance from the top of the page (not from the top margin).

Vertically Positioning a Character-Anchored Box

If the current box is anchored to a character, and you select Vertical Position to position it, you'll be given the following options:

Top	The top of the box will be aligned with the top of the character.
Center	The box will be centered next to the character—the most commonly used option for aligning small in-line graphics.
Bottom	The bottom of the box will be aligned with the bottom (baseline) of the character.
Baseline	The baseline of the text or equation within the box will line up with the baseline of the text. This option is generally used to align in-line equations with their surrounding text.

Be aware that aligning a box with a character causes the space allotted to the line to be as tall as the box, in much the same way that placing a single large character within a line of text causes the entire line to be as tall as that one character.

To maintain an equal line height among lines of text that do and do not contain boxes, you must either adjust the height of the box so that it does not change the line height (using the Size option on the box Definition menu) or set a fixed line height for the entire paragraph that matches the line height of the box (by selecting **Layout ➤ Line ➤ Line Height** from the menus or by pressing Shift-F8 L H; see Chapter 20).

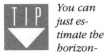

You can just estimate the horizontal position of a box when first defining it, because you can easily make adjustments later.

HORIZONTALLY POSITIONING A BOX

The Horizontal Position option on the box Definition menu lets you specify the horizontal position of the box relative to its anchor point. Again, the options available to you depend on how you've chosen to anchor the box. (The horizontal position of a character-anchored box is determined solely by the position of the character it's anchored to, so this option is not available or needed for character-anchored boxes.)

Horizontally Positioning a Paragraph-Anchored Box

If the box is anchored to a paragraph, you'll be given these options when you select Horizontal Position from the box Definition menu:

Left	The box will be aligned at the left side of the paragraph.
Right	The box will be aligned at the right side of the paragraph.
Center	The box will be in the center of the paragraph, but only text to the left of the box will wrap around it.
Full	The box will be placed above the paragraph it's anchored to and will fill the page's left and right margins.

Horizontally Positioning a Page-Anchored Box

If the box is anchored to the page, selecting Horizontal Position offers these options:

1 Margins; 2 Columns; 3 Set Position

If you select Margins, your choices are

Left	The left edge of the box will be aligned with the left margin.
Right	The right edge of the box will be aligned with the right margin.
Center	The box will be centered between the left and right margins.
Full	The box will be expanded to fill all the space between the left and right margins.

If you select Set Position, you'll see this prompt:

Offset from left of page: 0"

Type in a measurement (in inches), and press ↵. The measurement you enter is the distance from the left edge of the page, not the distance from the left margin. For example, if the left margin is 1", and you enter a measurement of 1.5", the figure will be one-half inch from the left margin.

Horizontal Positioning in a Multicolumn Layout

See Chapter 20 for more information mation on how to work with multicolumn layouts.

If your document uses a multicolumn layout (like a newsletter), you can select Columns as an option for horizontally positioning the box. You'll first see this prompt:

Enter column(s): 1

You can type in a single column number (such as *1* or *2*) or type in a range of columns (such as *1–2*, or *2–4*) if you want the box to be wider than a single column. After selecting a column or range, press ↵. You will then see the same options as with margins, but they now refer to the columns:

Left	The box will be aligned with the left edge of the column (or the left edge of the leftmost column if you specified two or more columns).
Right	The box will be aligned with the right edge of the column (or the right edge of the rightmost column if you specified two or more columns).
Center	The box will be centered in the column you specified (or centered between the columns if you specified two or more columns).
Full	The box will be as wide as the column (or as wide as several columns if you specified two or more columns).

SIZING A BOX

Measurements are initially set for inches, but you can change the unit of measure by using Setup (see Chapter 13).

The Size option on the box Definition menu lets you control the size of the box. When selected, it provides these options:

Set Width/Auto Height	Lets you enter the width (in inches). WordPerfect will calculate the height to retain the box shape.
Set Height/Auto Width	Lets you enter the height of the box (in inches). WordPerfect will calculate the width to retain the box shape.
Set Both	Lets you enter both the width and height (in inches).

Auto Both   WordPerfect calculates both the width and the height automatically. If the box contains a graphic image, the box is sized to fit the original dimensions of the image. If the box contains text or a table, the box is sized to fit snugly around its contents.

WRAPPING TEXT AROUND A BOX

Use the Advance feature (Chapter 20) to position text precisely, either on the Edit screen or within a graphic box.

The Wrap Text Around Box option on the box Definition menu controls how the text adjacent to the box is printed. If you choose **Y**es, text outside of the box wraps around the box (as in all the boxes shown in Figure 19.6). If you choose **N**o, text outside the box writes over the box.

The No option is useful for combining text with graphics, as in the examples shown in Figure 19.8. The text in this figure also explains how each example was created.

CAPTIONING A BOX

You can change the appearance and numbering style for caption numbers and adjust the caption's position relative to the box, as described later under "Changing the Appearance of All Boxes of a Given Type."

You can add a caption to any box. To add a caption to the current box (at the box Definition menu), select Caption. You'll be taken to an editing screen for typing the caption (the title "Box Caption" appears at the bottom of this screen). You can use all the general editing techniques and most menu options (including fonts, sizes, and appearances) to help you create your caption.

By default, the [Box Num] hidden code, which defines the style of caption numbers, appears at the beginning of your entry. You can see this code by turning on Reveal Codes while editing your caption.

You cannot caption boxes in page headers or footers.

Type your caption, up to a maximum of 256 characters in length, to the right of the [Box Num] code. Optionally, you can delete the [Box Num] code by using the Backspace or Delete key. If you inadvertently delete the [Box Num] code and want to reinsert it, press Graphics (Alt-F9). When you're finished typing your caption, press Exit (F7) to return to the box Definition menu.

FILLING A BOX

As you've seen, the box Definition menu is used for both positioning and sizing a box, as well as for filling the box with a graphic, a table, or text. In this section, I'll describe the options for filling a box in a little more detail. To start with, note that three options on the box Definition menu are used for filling boxes, as summarized below:

Filename | Use this option to import a copy of an external file into a box (the only way to fill a box with a graphic image).

Contents | If you select Filename to pull in the box contents, this setting is adjusted automatically. Optionally, you can select this option to specify a different content for the box, such as text or an equation.

Here the PRESNT-1.WPG graphic is in a Figure box, with Wrap Text Around Box set to No. Normally this causes this text to write over the box. But a User box the same size as the Figure box, with Wrap Text Around Box set to Yes, is printed at exactly the same position. This text is wrapping around that User box. The text on the teacher's blackboard is in the User box.

On a PostScript printer, the Shadow text appearance is opaque white. In this example, similar to the one above, the BUTTRFLY.WPG graphic is in a Figure box with Wrap Text Around Box set to No. The shadow text is in a User box, at the same position, and the same size, as the Figure box, with Wrap Text set to Yes. This text wraps around the User box.

This could be a full-page sign with the margins set to about 0.25 inch around the page. A User box, containing the BORDER-8.WPG graphic, is anchored to the page, with vertical and horizontal positions set to Full and Wrap Text Around Box set to No. The words Wet Paint are centered horizontally and vertically on the page (on the regular Edit screen).

FIGURE 19.8:

Examples of combining text with graphics

Edit   Use this option to enter text, equations, or a table into a
                        box, or to change the existing text, equations, table, or
                        graphic image in a box.

Each of these options is described in more detail in the sections that follow.

Filling a Box with a Graphic Image

The Filename option on the box Definition menu lets you specify the name
of a file stored on-disk as the contents of the box. You use this option when
importing a graphic from a disk into a box (including the .WPG graphics files
that came with your WordPerfect package).

When you select Filename, WordPerfect displays this prompt:

Enter filename:

Type in the complete name (including the three-letter extension) of the file
that you want to pull into the box, and press ↵.

If the file is not on the disk drive and in the directory where WordPerfect
expects to find graphic images, you must specify the complete location of the
file. For example, to import a Lotus 1-2-3 graph file named MYGRAPH.PIC that
is stored in the directory named *123* on hard-disk-drive C, you have to enter
the complete name *C:\123\MYGRAPH.PIC*.

You can also use the Filename option to import text, a table, or equations
stored as text. For example, if you use the Tables feature to create and save a
table in a document named TABLE1.WP, you can use the Filename option to
pull a copy of the table stored in TABLE1.WP into the box.

Note, however, that when you pull a graphic figure into a box, Word-
Perfect adjusts the size of the graphic so that the graphic fits into the box. If
you pull text or a table into a box that is not large enough to hold that text or
table, WordPerfect does not adjust the size of the box. The table may extend
beyond the right edge of the box; with excess text, only as much text as can
fit in the box is displayed. If this occurs, use the Size option described earlier
in this chapter to change the size of the box.

Once you import a file into a box, its name is listed to the right of
the Filename option, and "Graphics," "Text," or "Equation" appears to the
right of the Contents option. To some extent, you can also change the
appearance of a graphic image that has been imported into a box, using
the Edit option on the box Definition menu, as described under "Editing
a Graphic Image" later in this chapter.

When prompted for the name of a graphic image file, you can press F5 to switch to the List Files screen (see Chapter 12).

If you didn't initially choose to create an Equation box, you must set the box contents to Equation before importing an equation from an external text file.

Filling a Box with Text or a Table

*To move existing text or a table into a box, block the text or table on the Edit screen, then select **E**dit ▶ **M**ove (Cut) from the menu. Next, create or edit the graphic box as described earlier, select Edit from the box Definition menu, and press ↵ to complete the move.*

If you want to fill the current box with text or a table, select Edit from the box Definition menu. You'll be taken to an editing screen that has the title "Box:" at the bottom. Here you can type your text, or create your table as you would at the normal Edit screen. (If you're working with an Equation box, you'll be taken directly to the Equation Editor after selecting Edit, as described in Chapter 21.)

You can select fonts and use centering, right alignment, or the Advance feature (Chapter 20)—just about any normal editing option—to control the appearance of your text or table. Any selections you make will affect only the contents of the box, not the text outside the box.

Rotating Text in a Box

While editing the contents of a box that contains text or a table, you can choose to rotate the box. After selecting Edit from the box Definition menu, you'll notice the message "Graphics to rotate text" near the bottom of the screen. If you press the Graphics key (Alt-F9), you'll see the following options:

Rotate Text: 1 0°; **2** 90°; **3** 180°; **4** 270°

You can select an option to rotate the contents by 0, 90, 180, or 270 degrees, respectively. (The box will also be resized, if necessary, to hold the rotated text.) Figure 19.9 shows examples of Text boxes rotated by using each of the options.

Check your printer manual for information on how much you can rotate text.

Note, however, that the amount of rotation is limited by your printer. Many printers can print at only 0-degree rotation (normal right-side-up). Many laser printers can print at only 0-degree and 90-degree rotation. PostScript and HP LaserJet III printers can usually print at all degrees of rotation.

When you've finished filling the box with your text or table, press Exit (F7) to leave the box-editing screen and return to the box Definition menu.

The "Too Much Text" Error Message

If you add more to a Text or Table box than the page size can handle, WordPerfect will immediately display a soft page break (a line of hyphens) at the place where you've typed beyond the boundaries. If this happens, you should use the Backspace key to erase text until the page break disappears. Otherwise, when you try to leave the editing screen, you'll see the message

ERROR: Too much text

and you won't be able to get back to the box Definition menu.

After you delete enough text to get rid of the page break, then you can press Exit (F7) to return to the Definition menu. From there, select Size; then increase the size of the box, and select Edit to resume your editing. When you're finished editing, press Exit once again.

SAVING AND VIEWING YOUR COMPLETED BOX

After you've finished anchoring, positioning, sizing, and filling a box, press Exit (F7) to leave the box Definition menu and return to the Edit screen. On the Edit screen, the box will appear empty (if it's visible at all). But you can see the box as well as its contents by switching to the View Document screen.

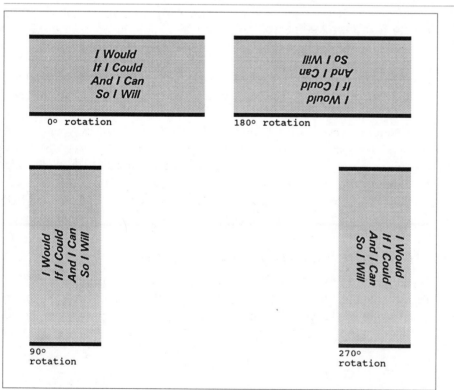

FIGURE 19.9:

Examples of rotated Text boxes

CHANGING THE APPEARANCE OF
AN INDIVIDUAL BOX

TO CHANGE AN EXISTING BOX,

1. Select Graphics from the menu or press Graphics (Alt-F9).

2. Choose the type of box you want to change.

3. Select Edit, and enter the number of the box you want to change. You'll be taken to the box Definition menu for that box, where you can make any selections to change the box.

If you want to change the general style of all boxes in a category (e.g., all the Figure boxes), you should refer to "Changing the Appearance of All Boxes of a Given Type" later in this chapter.

If you aren't sure whether you're editing the right box, you can select Edit from the box Definition menu to view the contents of the box you've selected.

If you are not happy with the size, location, or contents of a box, you can easily make a change by using the same basic options you used to create the box:

1. Select **G**raphics from the menu bar, or press Graphics (**Alt-F9**).

2. Select the type of box that you want to change.

3. Select **E**dit. (The next higher number or the number of the next box below the cursor appears as a suggestion in the prompt.)

4. Type the number of the box you want to change, then press ↵.

You're returned to the box Definition menu for that particular box. At this point, you can change any of your initial entries for the box. For example, you can select the Caption, Anchor Type, Vertical Position, Horizontal Position, Size, or Wrap Text Around Box option, then make a different selection to change your original one. When finished, press the Exit (F7) key until you return to the Edit screen; from there you can use the View Document screen to check your work. There are also a number of techniques you can use to refine your existing selections, as described in the sections that follow.

CHANGING THE TYPE OF A BOX

Let's suppose that you create a particular type of box, such as a Text box, then later decide to change it to a Table box. There is no option on the box Definition menu to do this, but it can be done very easily. Follow these steps:

1. Select **G**raphics from the menu bar, or press Graphics (**Alt-F9**). Select the type of the box that you want to change, choose **E**dit, then type the number of the box you want to change, and press ↵.

2. Note the current type of the box (next to "Definition:" in the upper-left corner of the screen).

3. Press Graphics (**Alt-F9**).

4. Select the new type for the current box from the menu at the bottom of the screen. Your choices are **F**igure, **T**able Box, Text **B**ox, **U**ser Box, and **E**quation.

The only immediate change you'll see is that the box type near the top of the screen has changed. However, when you return to the Edit or View Document screen, you'll see that the caption numbers (if any) have changed as well, to reflect the proper sequence of numbers for the various types of boxes in the document. If you look at the figure on the View Document screen, you'll also see that the borders have changed to match those of the box type you've switched to. For instance, if you convert from a Figure box to a Text box, your borders will change from a single line all the way around to a thick line above and below the box.

CHANGING THE CONTENTS OF A BOX

Suppose you place a graphic image in a box and then decide to use a different graphic image instead. It's easy to replace the contents of any box that contains a file with the contents of a new file by following these steps:

1. Use the usual techniques to edit the existing box and gain access to the Definition menu.

2. Select Filename.

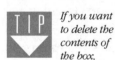

If you want to delete the contents of the box, without deleting the box itself, select Filename, press Ctrl-End, press ↵, then press Y to confirm the deletion.

3. Type in the complete name of the new file that you want to display in the box and press ↵ (or press **F5** to select a file from the List Files screen).

4. When the screen displays

Replace contents with *filename*? No (Yes)

press **Y** if you are sure you want to display *filename* (the new file) in the box. You'll see the change the next time you preview the document or print it.

DETERMINING THE TYPE OF CONTENTS A BOX WILL CONTAIN

If you are not yet ready to fill a box, but you know what type of information the box will contain, you can use the Contents option on the Definition menu. This sets the box to the default size for the type of information that will eventually be in the box, which can help you correctly place boxes that are still empty.

When you select Contents, you'll see these options:

1 Graphic; **2 G**raphic on **D**isk; **3 T**ext; **4 E**quation

In addition to defining the contents as graphic, text, or equation, you can use this option to tell WordPerfect not to make an imported graphic file part of the document, but to read the file from disk whenever it's needed for viewing or printing. Because documents containing imported graphics can be very large, setting this option to read the file from disk can be useful for conserving your hard-disk space.

To reduce the size of the file, you can choose Graphic on Disk rather than Graphic. WordPerfect will not permanently copy the graphic into the document; it will use the graphic only as needed. The only disadvantage of this option is that if you copy the document to another computer that does not have the referenced graphic on its own disk, you will not be able to view or print the graphic image.

 When placing a graphic image in a style, the Graphic on Disk option is your only choice.

EDITING A GRAPHIC IMAGE

TO CHANGE THE SCALE, ANGLE, POSITION, LOCATION, OR SIZE OF A GRAPHIC IMAGE WITHIN A BOX,

1. **Select Graphics from the menu bar, or press Graphics (Alt-F9).**

2. **Choose the box type, then Edit, and enter the box number.**

3. **Select Edit from the box Definition menu.**

Selecting Edit from the box Definition menu also lets you change the contents of a box that contains text or a table, using the normal Edit screen techniques.

If the box you are editing contains a graphic, you have many options for changing the appearance of the graphic. First, you need to follow the general steps listed earlier for changing an existing box by means of the menus. Then choose Edit from the box Definition menu.

The keys and commands that you can use to manipulate the image appear on two lines at the bottom of the screen (see Figure 19.10). The keys on the top line let you adjust the graphic interactively, and the options on the bottom line let you make changes by exact measurements, as discussed in the sections that follow. Feel free to experiment—you can always return the image to its original form simply by pressing the Goto key (Ctrl-Home).

If you need more control over graphic images than Word-Perfect provides, you should consider using a graphics package, such as DrawPerfect.

The frame surrounding the graphic image on the screen (if any) is actually the frame of the box being used to display the graphic within your document. The graphic-editing options control the appearance of the graphic image *within* the box, but do not change the size and shape of the box itself.

Moving the Graphic within Its Box

To move the graphic within its box, press the ↑, ↓, →, and ← keys. The graphic will move in the direction of the arrow key you press. For example, Figure 19.10 shows the BULB.WPG graphic, which was originally centered in its box, after pressing ← a few times.

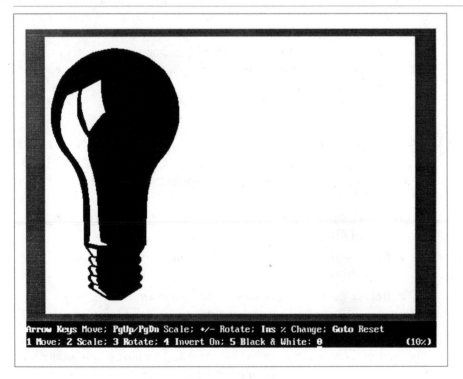

The light-bulb graphic

```
Arrow Keys Move; PgUp/PgDn Scale; +/- Rotate; Ins % Change; Goto Reset
1 Move; 2 Scale; 3 Rotate; 4 Invert On; 5 Black & White: 0          (10%)
```

If you move a portion of the image outside of the box, that portion will not be printed. Note that moving part of the image outside the box creates an equal amount of white space within the box on the other end, which you may not want.

You can also move the graphic within its box by selecting Move at the bottom of the screen. You'll be prompted to enter the distances to move horizontally and vertically in inches (unless you've changed the Units of Measure setting in Setup). Positive numbers move the graphic right or up; negative numbers move it left or down.

SCALING THE GRAPHIC WITHIN ITS BOX

To *scale* the graphic within its box (that is, to make it larger or smaller), press the Page Up or Page Down key. The image will grow each time you press Page Up and shrink each time you press Page Down. For example, Figure 19.11 shows the bulb graphic after pressing Page Up several times to increase its size.

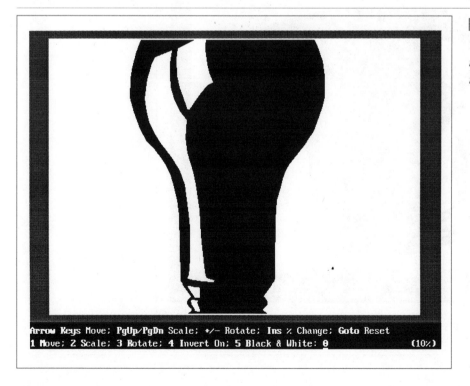

FIGURE 19.11:

The graphic scaled to a larger size with the Page Up key

Scaling an image larger is an excellent way to take unnecessary background out of an image and highlight the parts you really want the reader to notice. (It's often very helpful with figures imported from scanners.)

You can also scale a graphic within its box by selecting the Scale option from the menu at the bottom of the screen. When you select this option, you are prompted to enter the percentage by which to scale the image larger or smaller, where *100* equals 100 percent (the original scaling factor), *50* equals 50 percent (half) size, *200* equals 200 percent (twice the original size), and so forth.

You can scale both the x-axis (the graphic's width) and the y-axis (its height). For example, Figure 19.12 shows the bulb graphic with 250 as the x-scale and 100 as the y-scale.

Remember, if your scaling gets out of hand and you want to go back to the original scaling factor, you can simply press the Goto key (Ctrl-Home).

> **TIP**
> *You can use the Scale ⟩ option to scale a graphic border, like BORDER8-.WPG, to page size after setting the vertical and horizontal positions to Full.*

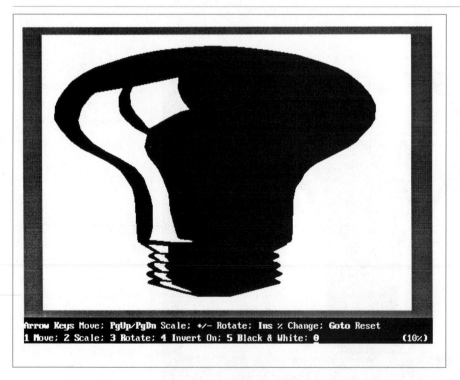

FIGURE 19.12:

The graphic scaled at 250 percent of its width and at its original height

ROTATING THE GRAPHIC WITHIN ITS BOX

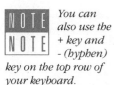

You can also use the + key and - (hyphen) key on the top row of your keyboard.

The gray + key rotates the graphic clockwise, and the gray - key rotates it counterclockwise. Figure 19.13 shows the bulb after pressing the gray + key several times to rotate the graphic a full 180 degrees.

You can also rotate a graphic by selecting the Rotate option from the menu at the bottom of the screen. You'll be prompted to enter the number of degrees (1–360) you want to rotate the image. Type in the number of degrees (for example, 180 to flip it upside down), then press *f*.

You'll then be asked whether you want a mirror image of the graphic as well. If you select No, the image remains unchanged. If you select Yes, the image is reversed as though you were viewing it in a mirror. Figure 19.14 shows examples of the WordPerfect BICYCLE.WPG and BKGRND-1.WPG graphics (on the left) and their mirror images (on the right).

Note that if you only want to produce a mirror image of the graphic, you still must first select the Rotate option from the bottom of the screen. When asked for the degrees of rotation, just press ↵ to accept the suggested value, 0. Then select Yes to convert the graphic to its mirror image.

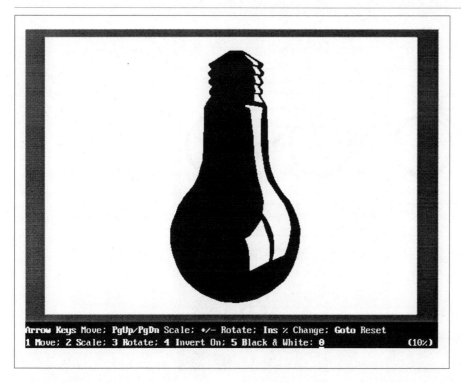

FIGURE 19.13:

The graphic rotated 180 degrees with the gray + key

CONTROLLING THE DEGREE OF CHANGE

The Insert key adjusts the percentage of change shown in parentheses in the lower-right corner of the Graphics Edit screen. This percentage indicates the degree to which the ↑, ↓, →, ←, Page Up, Page Down, gray +, and gray – keys will affect the image.

Each press of the Insert key switches the percentage among 25, 10, 5, and 1. Choose a smaller percentage if you want the keys to make more precise changes. Choose a larger percentage if you want to work with broad increments. This feature is very helpful when you are trying to fine-tune a graphic to fit just right in its box.

SELECTING A COLOR STYLE FOR THE GRAPHIC

You can change the display of a color graphic to black and white on a color screen by selecting the Black & White option at the bottom of the screen. You'll be prompted to confirm your change by selecting Yes or No. Be aware that switching a graphic to black and white—regardless of whether or not your printer can print in color—may affect the printout, because colors print as shades of gray on noncolor printers.

FIGURE 19.14:

Examples of normal and mirror-image graphics

INVERTING AN IMAGE

To invert (or reverse) the black and white in a graphic, select the Invert On option at the bottom of the screen. This converts black to white and white to black (like the negative of a black-and-white photograph). Note that colors and shades of gray may be unaffected by inverting the graphic. Figure 19.15 shows a graphic image printed in color, black and white, and black and white with Invert turned on.

SAVING A MODIFIED GRAPHIC IMAGE

When you've finished changing a graphic image, press Exit (F7). You'll be returned to the box Definition menu, where you can make additional changes or press Exit (F7) to return to the Edit screen. Any changes to your graphic will appear on the next printout and on the View Document screen.

CHANGING THE APPEARANCE
OF ALL BOXES OF A GIVEN TYPE

TO CHANGE THE BORDER, CAPTION, OR NUMBER-ING STYLE, OR THE SPACING OF ALL BOXES OF A GIVEN TYPE,

1. **Position the cursor before the code for the first box that you want to change.**

2. **Select Graphics from the menu bar or press Graphics (Alt-F9).**

3. **Choose the type of box you want to change, then choose Options.**

color   black and white   black and white and inverted

FIGURE 19.15:

A graphic image in "color," black and white, and black and white with Invert turned on

Up to this point, I've focused on ways to refine the appearance of an individual box in a document. But WordPerfect also lets you change the appearance of *all* boxes of a given type in one fell swoop. For example, you can change the appearance of all Figure boxes or of all Table boxes.

Such selections do not affect the contents of any individual box. Rather, they alter the general appearance of that box style, such as the border style, the numbering style, the caption style, the spacing between boxes and text, and other features associated with a particular type (or style) of box.

If you are satisfied with the general appearance of all the types of boxes in a document, there's no need for you to change any of the default values. But as you gain experience, you may want an extra level of refinement. Follow these steps:

NOTE   *You can change the appearance of Figure, Text, Table, User, and Equation boxes at any time, before or after creating the boxes.*

1. Position the cursor before the code for the first box of the type whose style you want to set. If you haven't created any boxes yet, put the cursor at the top of the document or somewhere before the spot where you expect to place the first box.

2. Pull down the Graphics menu or press Graphics (**Alt-F9**).

3. Select the type of box you'll be working with: Figure, Table, Text, User, or Equation.

4. Select **O**ptions. The Options menu for the selected box type appears, as in Figure 19.16.

```
Options: Figure

    1 - Border Style
            Left                          Single
            Right                         Single
            Top                           Single
            Bottom                        Single
    2 - Outside Border Space
            Left                          0.167"
            Right                         0.167"
            Top                           0.167"
            Bottom                        0.167"
    3 - Inside Border Space
            Left                          0"
            Right                         0"
            Top                           0"
            Bottom                        0"
    4 - First Level Numbering Method      Numbers
    5 - Second Level Numbering Method     Off
    6 - Caption Number Style              [BOLD]Figure 1[bold]
    7 - Position of Caption               Below box, Outside borders
    8 - Minimum Offset from Paragraph     0"
    9 - Gray Shading (% of black)         0%

Selection: 0
```

FIGURE 19.16:

The Options menu for Figure boxes

5. Set the options as discussed in the sections that follow.

6. Press Exit (**F7**) to return to the Edit screen.

Whenever you access an Options menu, WordPerfect puts a hidden code—[Fig Opt], [Tbl Opt], [Txt Opt], [Usr Opt], or [Equ Opt], depending on the box type—in your document at the cursor position. The settings represented by that code affect all boxes of the given type that follow the code's position in the document.

The following sections describe the various items on the Options menus.

SETTING BORDER STYLE

The border style is the type of line used to frame the box. When you select Border Style from the Options menu, the following menu line appears at the bottom of your screen:

1 None; **2 S**ingle; **3 D**ouble; **4 D**ashed; **5 D**otted; **6 T**hick; **7 E**xtra Thick

Figure 19.17 shows examples of each style of line.

Choose one of these styles or a combination of styles for your border. As you can see on the Options menu, you can select different styles for each of the four sides of the box. The first option, None, lets you hide the border on some or all sides of the box.

You can also draw a border around text by placing that text in a single-cell table (Chapter 6). An easy way to create a coupon like the one in Figure 19.17 is to use a single-cell table (Chapter 6) with the **L**ines ➤ **O**utside options on the Table Edit menu set to Dashed for the outermost border. The text, lines, and check boxes (Zapf Dingbat graphics in this example) are placed right in the cell. The sunburst graphic surrounding "Free Offer!" is in a borderless User box, also within the cell, with Wrap Text Around Box set to No.

SETTING OUTSIDE BORDER SPACE

The Outside Border Space option sets the amount of space between each border and the text outside your box, as Figure 19.18 shows. The default width is usually acceptable, but can easily be changed for special requirements. Ensuring a certain amount of white space around your graphic box is important to the layout of a document and makes the document easier to read.

Because WordPerfect generally reserves space under the box for the caption, you may find the white space under boxes without captions to be too wide. Setting the outside border space at the bottom of the figure to 0" helps close up that extra white space.

SETTING INSIDE BORDER SPACE

The Inside Border Space options prevents the text or graphic within the box from being printed right against the border, as shown in Figure 19.18. Select the exact amount of space that should remain blank inside each border, or accept the default—either 0.167 inches (12 points) or 0 inches, depending on the box type.

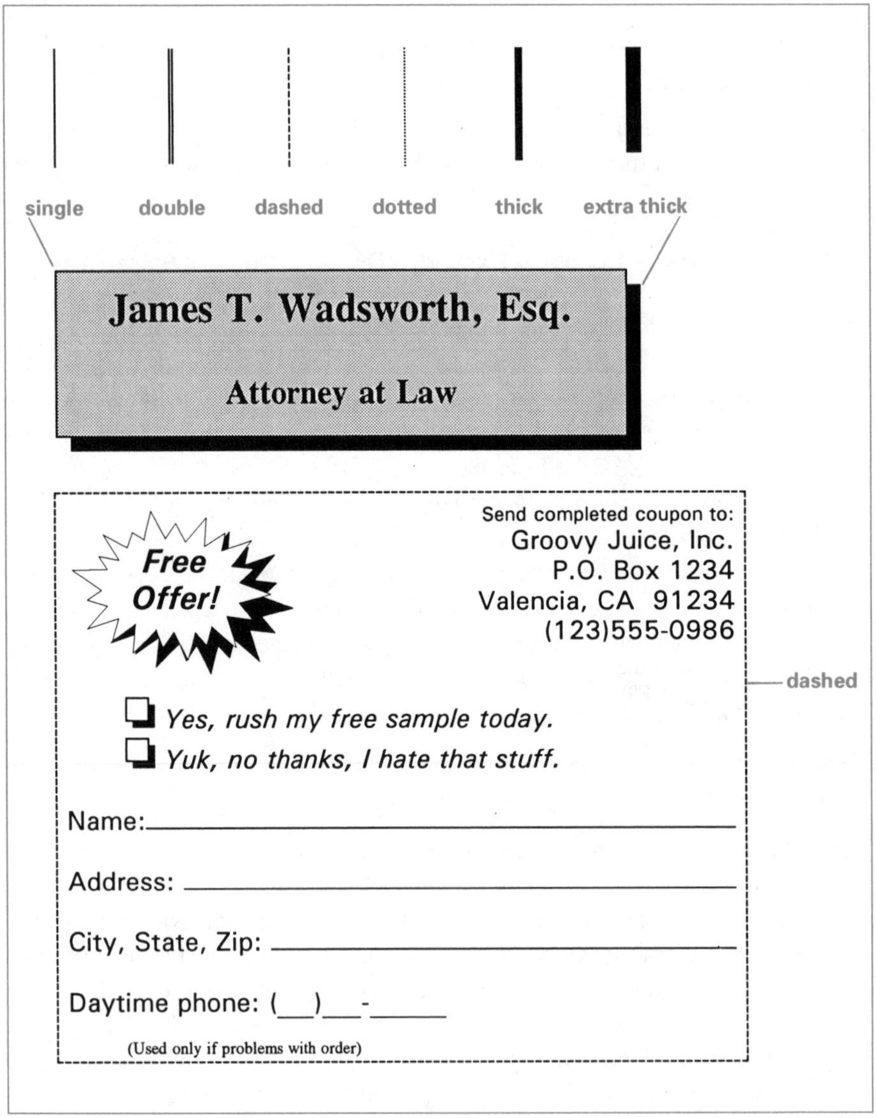

FIGURE 19.17:

The available border styles

NUMBERING THE BOXES

The First Level Numbering Method option controls the numbering of the boxes. *Level* is an organizational term that refers to the numbering of graphics by subsection. For example, in this book a two-level system of figure numbering is used. *Figure 19.1* is the first figure in the nineteenth chapter; *19* is the first level and *1* is the second level.

The following line appears at the bottom of the Options menu when you choose First Level Numbering Method:

1 Off; **2 N**umbers; **3 L**etters; **4 R**oman Numerals

The option you choose here will be the first level used to number all captions for the particular box type.

The Second Level Numbering Method option is used to create multilevel numbering for graphic boxes. For example, if you specify Roman Numerals for the first level and choose Letters for the second level, the boxes you create will be numbered *I-a, I-b, I-c,* and so on. However, the second level will not appear in the captions unless you refer to it in the Caption Number Style setting (discussed next).

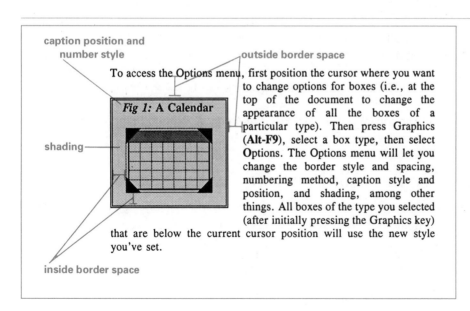

caption position and
number style

outside border space

shading

inside border space

To access the Options menu, first position the cursor where you want to change options for boxes (i.e., at the top of the document to change the appearance of all the boxes of a particular type). Then press Graphics (**Alt-F9**), select a box type, then select Options. The Options menu will let you change the border style and spacing, numbering method, caption style and position, and shading, among other things. All boxes of the type you selected (after initially pressing the Graphics key) that are below the current cursor position will use the new style you've set.

Fig 1: A Calendar

FIGURE 19.18:

Other graphics features you can control

CHOOSING A CAPTION NUMBER STYLE

 This option controls the format and position of the caption number and caption. To add a caption to an individual box, use the Caption option on the box Definition menu.

The Caption Number Style option lets you tell WordPerfect how to print the caption number and related text, such as the word *Figure,* in boxes that have captions. Your caption number style can include text, formatting codes, and numbering levels (these are inserted in the [Box Num] code, which automatically appears in captions when you select the Caption option on the box Definition menu). Formatting features (such as bold and italic) are switched on using the same keys that you use on the Edit screen. For example, to boldface the word *Figure* for Caption Number Style, you press Bold (F6), type the word *Figure,* then press Bold again. Press ↵ after defining your caption number style.

 Use the numbers 1 and 2 when defining Caption Number Style, even if you chose letters or Roman numerals for the numbering methods.

Caption Number Style is important to the printed numbering of boxes. The default style for each box type, while varying from box type to box type, always includes the number *1,* representing the first numbering level. If you want to print the second numbering level, you must include the number *2* in the Caption Number Style entry. For example, the entry

[BOLD][ITALC]Figure 1**[italc][bold]**

 See "Selecting a Font for Captions" later in this chapter for information on selecting a font for all captions.

will print captions using only the first-level number (or letter), even if you switched on a second level with the Second Level Numbering Method option. Your captions will print like this: ***Figure 1*** , ***Figure 2*** , ***Figure 3*** , and so on.

The following entry for Caption Number Style will produce two-level caption numbers like the ones used in this book:

[BOLD][ITALC]Figure 1.2**[italc][bold]**

Your captions will print like this: ***Figure 19.1*** , ***Figure 19.2*** , ***Figure 19.3*** , and so on.

POSITIONING THE CAPTION

 With Equation boxes, you can place the caption above or below the borders, or to the left or right of the box (inside the box borders).

The Position of Caption option places the caption in one of four places around and in the box. The choices are

◆ Below Box, Outside of Border

◆ Below Box, Inside of Border

◆ Above Box, Outside of Border

◆ Above Box, Inside of Border

SETTING MINIMUM OFFSET FROM PARAGRAPH

The Minimum Offset from Paragraph option limits how much a paragraph-anchored box can move up in a paragraph before being bumped to the next page. Normally, WordPerfect honors the Vertical Position setting on the box Definition menu. But when a graphic box would otherwise be split by a page break, WordPerfect tries to keep the box on the same page by moving it up in the paragraph until the box fits on the page or its top border is flush with the first line of the paragraph (a minimum offset of 0 inches). If the box still won't fit on the page, it is bumped to the next page. If you prefer not to have the graphic box moved up as far as the first line of the paragraph, you can set a minimum amount for the box offset.

For example, let's suppose you anchor a rather large box to a paragraph near the bottom of a page. If the vertical position of the box is set to 1 inch (below the top of the paragraph), and the Minimum Offset from Paragraph setting is 0.5 inches, WordPerfect will move up the box only 0.5 inches into the paragraph (instead of as much as 1 inch) before bumping the box to the next page.

SHADING THE BOX BACKGROUND

The Gray Shading option controls the background on which the box contents will be printed. WordPerfect lets you print with gray backgrounds of various intensities; the higher the percentage you choose, the darker the background. Only Text boxes are shaded by default, but you can set gray shading for any type of box by using the Gray Shading box options. Figure 19.19 shows examples of a box with different levels of shading.

A WARNING ABOUT BOX OPTION CODES

As mentioned before, whenever you make selections from the Options menu, WordPerfect inserts a hidden [Opt] code at the cursor position, which affects all boxes of that type from the code position forward—or until the next [Opt] code of the same box type, if any. Therefore, if an old [Opt] code follows a newer one, the old code takes precedence over the new one. To avoid confusion and prevent code clutter, make a habit of deleting any old [Opt] codes at the cursor position.

One shortcut might be worth mentioning at this point. Let's suppose you have set some Figure box options and are satisfied with most, but not all, of the settings. You can move your cursor just to the right of the existing [Fig Opt] code (most easily done after turning on the Reveal Codes screen), then select the Figure box options as usual. Since your cursor is to the right of an older [Fig Opt] code, WordPerfect will remember all the existing settings, and you can just change the few settings that need fine-tuning. After making your changes, delete the old code to prevent clutter.

SAVING YOUR CHANGES

When you're finished defining your box style, press Exit (F7) to return to the Edit screen. You will not be able to see the new box style on the Edit screen, but you can use View Document to see it.

RENUMBERING BOXES

TO RENUMBER ALL THE BOXES IN A DOCUMENT,

1. **Move the cursor above the box where you want to start the new numbering.**

2. **Select Graphics from the menu bar or press Graphics (Alt-F9).**

0% Shading

20% Shading

40% Shading

FIGURE 19.19:
A box with different levels of shading

3. Choose the box type, then New Number.

4. Type the new box number and press ↵.

This is the figure-numbering style used in this book.

Let's say your document is divided into several chapters and you're numbering the figures within each chapter using a two-level system. Perhaps the first number is the chapter number, and the second number is the number of the figure within that chapter. WordPerfect cannot recognize the start of a new chapter and update the numbering automatically; you must tell it where to update the numbering. Follow these steps to adjust your box numbers:

1. Position the cursor before the first box to be renumbered, but *after* the preceding box. WordPerfect renumbers the boxes from the cursor position forward.

2. Pull down the Graphics menu or press Graphics (**Alt-F9**).

3. Select the type of box you want to renumber: Figure, Table, Text, User, or Equation.

4. Select **N**ew Number. WordPerfect prompts you for the number of the next box of the selected type.

5. Type the number and press ↵. WordPerfect inserts a hidden code at the cursor position, indicating the new number you just selected.

If the Edit screen doesn't immediately reflect the new box numbers, press Home Home ↓, then press Ctrl-Home twice.

This will automatically renumber the boxes on the Edit screen and will adjust all caption numbers for the type of box you selected. For example, to restart figure numbering at the beginning of Chapter 2, just enter *2* in step 5. WordPerfect knows to restart the second numbering level, if one is set, and to renumber correctly all remaining boxes or all boxes up to the next New Number code.

SELECTING A PRINT QUALITY FOR GRAPHICS

If your printer does not have enough memory to print text and graphics, you can print just the text, then reload the same pages and print just the graphics (see Chapter 8).

If your printer can print graphics, it may also be able to print them with various levels of quality. You can even prevent graphics from being printed. Basically, the higher quality printing you use, the longer it takes to print the graphics. So you might want to omit graphics or use Draft quality to print the initial rough drafts of your document. When you are ready for the final draft, you can switch to Medium or High quality.

Here are the general steps for selecting the graphics quality for your printout:

1. At the Edit screen, select **F**ile ➤ **P**rint, or press Print (**Shift-F7**).

2. Select **G**raphics Quality.

3. Select one of the options shown:

1 Do **N**ot Print; **2 D**raft; **3 M**edium; **4 H**igh

You can then use the Full Document or Page option to print the document as usual.

MOVING AND DELETING GRAPHIC BOXES

Like most WordPerfect features, boxes are controlled by hidden codes in your document. When you attach a box to a paragraph, the code is placed before the first character in the paragraph. The code starts with the type of box—Fig Box, Text Box, Tbl Box, Usr Box, or Equ Box—followed by a colon, the box number, and a semicolon.

If the contents of the box came from a file, the file name follows the first semicolon. If the box has a caption, the [Box Num] code (which displays the box number next to the caption) and the caption follow. For example, the code below is for Figure-box number 1, which contains the BALLOONS.WPG graphic image with a caption.

[Fig Box:1;BALLOONS.WPG;[Box Num]: This is a Figure box]

Because WordPerfect uses hidden codes to manage figures, you can use the Reveal Codes screen to help you move, delete, and edit figures in a document. If you discover that you've created an extra box, or you want to move a box from one place to another, you can simply delete or move the hidden code for the box.

To delete a box from a document, move the cursor to the hidden code for the box and press Delete. Similarly, if you anchor a box to a paragraph or character, then decide to move it to some other character, you must move the hidden code. One of the easiest ways to move a box is to delete the box's hidden code from its current position, move the cursor to where you want the new box to appear, then press Cancel (F1) and choose Restore.

You can copy a box quickly by deleting it (press Del), restoring it (press F1), then moving the cursor to a new position, and restoring it again (press F1).

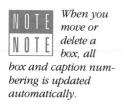

When you move or delete a box, all box and caption numbering is updated automatically.

To move a page-anchored graphic box, select Graphics (or press Alt-F9), choose a box type, then choose Edit to redefine the number of pages to skip and the vertical and horizontal position of the box.

LINKING A REFERENCE TO ITS BOX

Automatic numbering of boxes is a great convenience. If you currently have figures 1.1 to 1.20 in a document, and then add a new figure above Figure 1.2, WordPerfect automatically renumbers all the figures below the new one; the captions show the new, correct figure numbers. But any text references to those figures (for example, a phrase that says "see Figure 1.6") will not be updated to match the new figure numbers, unless you use automatic cross-referencing, as discussed in Chapter 23.

PLACING BOXES IN TABLES

You can place a box in any single table cell. To do so, move the cursor into the cell where you want the graphic box to appear. If you are currently in Table Edit mode, press Exit (F7) to return to the normal Edit screen. Then just go through the normal steps of creating a box. Here are some general tips to make the procedure easier and to help ensure that the table cell is nicely filled with the graphic image:

◆ Set the outside border space for User boxes to 0 for all four borders, so each box best fills the cell. To do so, move the cursor to just before the [Table Def] code that defines the table (use Reveal Codes to see the [Table Def] code), then select Graphics ➤ User Box ➤ Options (or press Alt-F9 U O) to get to the Outside Border Space options.

◆ Define every box that you place within a cell as a User box, so the frame surrounding each table cell becomes the frame surrounding each graphic box.

◆ While defining a box in a table cell, anchor it to a paragraph. Also, set the horizontal position to Full to best fill the box.

NOTE NOTE *A table was also used to produce Figure 19.4 earlier in this chapter, which explains why the boxes are so neatly aligned on the page.*

Of course, these guidelines are just general. You may want to experiment with boxes in table cells to create your own unique effects. Figure 19.20 shows an example of a storyboard, where these guidelines were used to place graphic boxes in table cells. Each graphic figure is in a borderless User box within a table cell, and the text beneath each graphic is in the cell immediately below. The lines in the table were then removed or modified to give the desired appearance.

SELECTING A FONT FOR CAPTIONS

You can choose a font for all the captions of a given box type (e.g., all Figure boxes, or all Table boxes) by preceding the options code for the box type with a font selection for the captions and following the code with a font for the normal text. For example, the codes below define the font for Figure box captions as Courier 8 cpi and the font for normal text as Courier 10 cpi:

[Font:Courier 10cpi][Fig Opt][Font:Courier 12cpi]

Chapter 5 covers how to select fonts.

Select Font ➤ Base Font (or press Ctrl-F8 F) to select the fonts. Then select **G**raphics from the menu bar or press Graphics (Alt-F9), choose a box type, then select **O**ptions to create the [Opt] code. Finally, move the cursor past the [Opt] code, and select the font you want to use for the normal text of the document. (See "A Warning about Box Option Codes," earlier in this chapter, for information on cleaning up old box-option codes.)

Bob is born

Bob becomes Bob boy

Bob graduates from college

Bob enters the business world, and starts his own company

Bob goes public

Stock market goes berserk

Bob makes a bundle

Bob's a happy dude

FIGURE 19.20:

A storyboard created by placing graphic images in User boxes within a table

STORING GRAPHIC FILES IN A UNIQUE DIRECTORY

See Chapter 13 for more information about the Setup options for customizing WordPerfect.

To prevent file clutter in your WordPerfect directory, you may want to create a separate directory just for storing WordPerfect graphic images. To do so, create a directory of your choosing, such as C:\WP51\GRAPHICS, using DOS or List Files, then change the location of files to that directory by selecting **F**ile ➤ **S**etup ➤ **L**ocation of Files ➤ **G**raphic Files or by pressing Shift-F1 L G. Finally, move any existing .WPG files to that directory, again using List Files.

SOURCES OF GRAPHICS

Any printed graphic can be digitized with a scanner and stored on-disk as a file. You can then read a copy of the scanned image into any graphic box, using the Filename option on the box Definition menu, to put a copy of that image in a WordPerfect document. (If the format of the scanned image is not compatible with WordPerfect, however, you must convert it by using the GRAPHCNV program described later). Figure 19.21 shows a few examples of scanned images that were imported into WordPerfect using techniques described in the sections that follow.

Another source of graphics is screen captures, where you "capture" the image displayed on your screen in a graphics file. These graphics are useful

FIGURE 19.21:

Examples of graphic images

Clip art

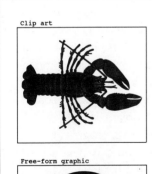

Scanned images

Business graphic

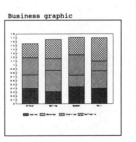

Free-form graphic

Photo/video frame

Special character

when you're writing about a computer program and want to show the reader something that appears on the screen. Figure 19.22 shows examples of captured screens, which are also discussed below.

CLIP ART AND SCANNED IMAGES

*Don't assume **all** clip art is free of copyright—you cannot use copyrighted art without permission.*

Clip-art images are small pieces of art often used to jazz up newsletters and other documents. Thousands of ready-to-use clip art images are available, as a trip to your local computer store will confirm. Most clip art is free of copyright restrictions, so you can just purchase it for a onetime fee, then use it freely in your work without paying a royalty to the artist.

You can make your own clip art by scanning a printed image of the art (as long as you have permission). If you don't have a scanner, typically you can have a commercial-printing house or desktop-publishing bureau scan the image for you. You can even scan your signature, company logo, photographs—whatever—then place them in graphic boxes in your WordPerfect documents or primary merge files.

Scanned images are generally stored as TIFF (Tagged Image File Format) files (with the .TIF extension). You can use the GRAPHCNV program (see "Importing Graphic Images" later in this chapter) to convert these to .WPG files.

BUSINESS AND FREE-FORM GRAPHICS

Most spreadsheet programs let you display data in bar graphs, pie charts, and other business graphic formats. Most graphics programs let you create free-form graphics, as well as business graphs. Specialized graphics programs are also available for scientific, engineering, and other types of graphics.

Virtually any image created by any program can be read into a WordPerfect graphic box by using the Filename option on the box Definition menu. You just need to specify the directory location and complete file name of the graphic you are importing (e.g., C:\123\MYGRAPH.PIC to import a Lotus 1-2-3 business graph that's stored in the 123 directory of drive C).

In some cases, you may prefer to use the GRAB program (described below) to capture a graph that's on the screen. Or, you may need to convert the graphic image to a .WPG file (see "Importing Graphic Images").

Refer to your Windows 3 manual for details on capturing Windows screens.

CAPTURED WINDOWS SCREENS

If you're using WordPerfect 5.1 in the Windows 3 environment, the following information might be of interest. Although you can't use the WordPerfect 5.1

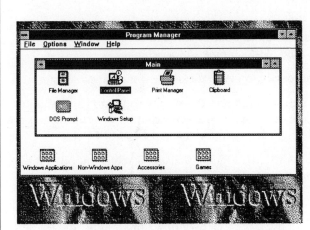

captured
Windows screen

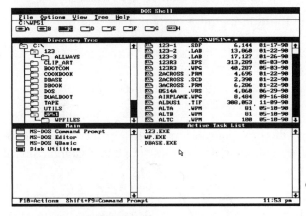

captured
graphics screen

captured text screen

FIGURE 19.22:

*Examples of captured
screens*

GRAB program to capture Windows 3 screens, you can get them in other ways. Follow these steps:

1. Run Windows in the usual manner (if you don't have a color printer, you might want to use the Control Panel in the Main window to switch Colors to the Monochrome Color Scheme).

2. Do whatever is necessary to get to the screen you want to capture.

3. To capture the entire screen, press **Print Screen**, or, to capture only the active window, press **Alt-Print Screen**. A copy of the screen is placed in the default Clipboard file, named DEFAULT.CLP.

4. Work your way back to the Program Manager screen, and open the Accessories window.

5. Select the Paintbrush icon.

6. Maximize the size of the Paintbrush window, and remove the borders (select **V**iew ➤ **T**ools and Linesize, then **V**iew ➤ **P**alette).

7. Select **P**aste from the **E**dit menu. A copy of the captured screen appears.

8. Select **F**ile ➤ **S**ave As ➤ **O**ptions ➤ **P**CX.

9. Enter a path and file name (e.g., C:\WP51\GRAPHICS\ WINDOW1.PCX), and select OK.

Now you can return to the box Definition menu in WordPerfect and import the WINDOW1.PCX file into a graphic box (see "Importing Graphic Images" below for additional information).

CAPTURED GRAPHICS SCREENS

GRAB works only with graphics programs and Word-Perfect graphics screens (like the View Document, Graphics Edit, and Equation Editor screens), not with text screens (like the WordPerfect Edit screen) or Windows 3 screens.

WordPerfect comes with a program named *GRAB* that lets you take a snapshot of any graphic image that's currently on the screen. The snapshot is stored in a .WPG file, ready for use with WordPerfect. To run GRAB, follow these steps:

1. Exit any programs that you are currently running to get to the DOS command prompt (don't "suspend" a program to get to the prompt; completely exit the program to remove it from memory).

2. Go to the WordPerfect directory, and run GRAB. Typically, you enter these commands at the DOS command prompt:

```
cd \wp51 ↵
grab ↵
```

For help with the GRAB program, enter **grab /b** *rather than just* **grab** *at the DOS command prompt.*

A copy of the GRAB program will stay in memory for the remainder of your session (until you turn off the computer). To capture an image, follow these steps:

1. Do whatever is required to get to the screen you want to capture (your computer will behave normally, even though GRAB is loaded).

2. Hold down the Alt and Shift keys, and press **F9** (**Alt-Shift-F9**). If the current screen is "capturable," you'll hear two brief tones and see a blinking frame on your screen.

3. Use the arrow keys to move the frame, or hold down Shift and press the arrow keys to size the frame, until the area you want to capture is within the frame. If the arrow keys won't let you zero in close enough, press **Insert** to reduce the effect of the arrow keys, then try again. Press Insert again if you want to return the arrow keys to their old effects.

4. Press ⏎. You'll hear two tones indicating that the capture is complete.

The file you just created will be in the current directory, with the file name GRAB.WPG (or GRABx.WPG, where x is a number, to make the file name unique). You can now place this grabbed image in any graphic box by specifying its name with the Filename option on WordPerfect's box Definition menu.

CAPTURED TEXT SCREENS

Ironically, the simple text screen is one of the hardest to capture in Word-Perfect. Your best bet is to use a third-party screen capture and graphics conversion program, such as HiJaak from Inset Systems or HotShot Graphics from SymSoft.

PHOTOS AND VIDEOTAPE IMAGES

See "Importing Graphic Images" for more information on importing TIFF and other graphic file types.

To include photographs in your documents, first have the photo scanned to produce a TIFF file, which you can then import into a graphic box. You can also capture still images from TV, video games, or videotapes if you have a video digitizer card and appropriate software. See your computer dealer for more information.

If you want to retouch a photo or video image to improve its appearance before printing it, you need a gray-scale-image editing program, such as Gray F/X from Xerox, available at any computer store.

SPECIAL CHARACTERS

For added spice, you can use any of more than one thousand special characters that WordPerfect offers as graphics, particularly if your printer can print these characters in large sizes. For example, the right-pointing finger in Figure 19.21 is special character 5,21 enlarged to 100 points within a User box.

If you have a PostScript printer, or the Zapf Dingbats font on some other printer, you also can use the special characters shown in Figure 19.23. Just

> **NOTE** *Character codes are described in Chapter 5.*

12,33	12,72	12,111	12,184	12,223
12,34	12,73	12,112	12,185	12,224
12,35	12,74	12,113	12,186	12,225
12,36	12,75	12,114	12,187	12,226
12,37	12,76	12,115	12,188	12,227
12,38	12,77	12,116	12,189	12,228
12,39	12,78	12,117	12,190	12,229
12,40	12,79	12,118	12,191	12,230
12,41	12,80	12,119	12,192	12,231
12,42	12,81	12,120	12,193	12,232
12,43	12,82	12,121	12,194	12,233
12,44	12,83	12,122	12,195	12,234
12,45	12,84	12,123	12,196	12,235
12,46	12,85	12,124	12,197	12,236
12,47	12,86	12,125	12,198	12,237
12,48	12,87	12,126	12,199	12,238
12,49	12,88	12,161	12,200	12,239
12,50	12,89	12,162	12,201	12,240
12,51	12,90	12,163	12,202	12,241
12,52	12,91	12,164	12,203	12,242
12,53	12,92	12,165	12,204	12,243
12,54	12,93	12,166	12,205	12,244
12,55	12,94	12,167	12,206	12,245
12,56	12,95	12,168	12,207	12,246
12,57	12,96	12,169	12,208	12,247
12,58	12,97	12,170	12,209	12,248
12,59	12,98	12,171	12,210	12,249
12,60	12,99	12,172	12,211	12,250
12,61	12,100	12,173	12,212	12,251
12,62	12,101	12,174	12,213	12,252
12,63	12,102	12,175	12,214	12,253
12,64	12,103	12,176	12,215	12,254
12,65	12,104	12,177	12,216	
12,66	12,105	12,178	12,217	
12,67	12,106	12,179	12,218	
12,68	12,107	12,180	12,219	
12,69	12,108	12,181	12,220	
12,70	12,109	12,182	12,221	
12,71	12,110	12,183	12,222	

FIGURE 19.23:

The Zapf Dingbats special characters

select Fonts ➤ Base Font (or press Ctrl-F8 F), then select the Dingbats font and a point size. When you're ready to insert the character, press Ctrl-V and the code shown in the chart.

IMPORTING GRAPHIC IMAGES

Many different formats are used to store graphic images in files on a disk. Although WordPerfect directly supports only the WordPerfect Graphics (.WPG) format, you can typically import files from any of these popular graphic formats:

◆ Computer Graphics Metafiles (.CGM)

◆ Dr. Halo (.CUT)

◆ Encapsulated PostScript (.EPS), for output only

◆ GEM (.IMG)

◆ Hewlett-Packard plotter files

◆ Lotus (.PIC)

◆ Macintosh Paint

◆ PC Paint and PC Paint Plus

◆ PC Paintbrush and Publisher's Paintbrush (.PCX)

◆ Tagged Image Format File (.TIF)

◆ WordPerfect and DrawPerfect Graphics (.WPG)

In most cases, just entering the proper directory location and full name of the graphic file you want to import is sufficient. For example, if you select Filename from the box Definition menu, and enter **D:\windows\myart.pcx** as the name of the file to import, WordPerfect will know that the file is in PCX format and convert it to WPG format as the import takes place.

Some conversions are a little more difficult; if WordPerfect reports that it cannot convert a file, you might try using the GRAPHCNV program that comes with WordPerfect to convert the file.

To use GRAPHCNV, exit WordPerfect and get to the DOS command prompt. Then go to your WordPerfect directory and enter **graphcnv**, followed by the directory location and name of the file to convert, and the location and name of the converted file.

For example, if you are at the DOS command prompt, and you want to convert all the .PCX files in your D:\windows directory to .WPG files stored

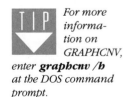

*For more information on GRAPHCNV, enter **graphcnv /b** at the DOS command prompt.*

in your C:\wp51\graphics directory, you enter these commands at the DOS prompt:

```
cd \wp51 ↵
graphcnv d:\windows\*.pcx c:\wp51\graphics\*.wpg ↵
```

Now you should be able to import the converted .WPG files into your graphic boxes by using the Filename option on the box Definition menu in WordPerfect.

Once you've mastered these techniques of adding graphics to your documents, you can move further into the realm of desktop publishing by learning more about columns and page layout, discussed in the next chapter.

CHAPTER 20

Working with Columns and Creating Layouts

 lthough graphics can enhance any document, a truly polished, publication-quality finished product requires some additional touches. Using multiple columns is one way to make a document more inviting and even easier to read (which is one reason that newspapers use them).

Beyond using columns, there are other elements of your document's layout that you can make changes to, such as the amount of space between lines, spacing between letters, and exact positioning of text. This chapter covers these more advanced desktop publishing features, which you can use to gain accurate control over the appearance of your text.

HANDS-ON
....
LESSON 7

For a hands-on lesson in creating a newsletter, see Lesson 7.

CREATING NEWSPAPER-STYLE COLUMNS

TO CREATE NEWSPAPER-STYLE COLUMNS,

1. Move the cursor to where the columns should start.

2. Select Layout ➤ Columns ➤ Define (or press Alt-F7 C D).

3. Choose Type ➤ Newspaper ➤ Number of Columns.

4. Enter the number of columns to place across each page.

> **5. Optionally, select Distance Between Columns and Margins.**
>
> **6. Press Exit (F7), then choose On to activate the columns.**

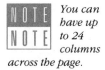 *You can have up to 24 columns across the page.*

Newspaper columns (also called snaking columns) organize your text like the text in a newspaper: Text runs down the leftmost column to the bottom of the page, wraps to the top of the next column, continues to the bottom of the page, and then wraps either to the next column or, if there are only two columns, to the leftmost column on the next page. Figure 20.1 shows an example of a newsletter, where the text snakes through three columns.

WordPerfect automatically takes care of all the business of wrapping, even as you add, change, and delete text. You can activate your columns before or after you type your text.

DEFINING NEWSPAPER COLUMNS

The first step in using newspaper-style columns is to define how you want the columns to look: How many columns do you want across the page? How much space do you want between the columns (often called *gutter space*)? Follow these steps:

1. Position the cursor above (or at) the place where you want to start arranging text into columns, either before or after you've typed the text.

2. Select **L**ayout ➤ **C**olumns ➤ **D**efine (or press **Alt-F7 C D**). The Text Column Definition menu appears, as shown in Figure 20.2.

3. If Newspaper is not already shown for Type, select **T**ype then **N**ewspaper.

4. Select **N**umber of Columns, and enter the number of columns you want   across each page. For example, if you want three columns, type **3** and press ↵.

5. By default, WordPerfect allows ½" of empty space between each column. If you want more or less space, select **D**istance Between Columns, and enter a measurement (e.g., *.25* or *¼* for ¼ inch, or *24p* for 24 points).

6. By default, WordPerfect makes each column the same width. These widths are listed under the Margins option on the menu. If you want

FIGURE 20.1:

A newsletter with text in three newspaper-style columns

The Vacationer

Vol. 1 No. 1 · Travel fun for everyone · January 1991

Newsletter debut
by Joan Smith

We're pleased to bring this first issue of our newsletter, *The Vacationer*, to our many loyal customers. The newsletter was inspired by your ideas and questions. You've asked us about where to find the best travel fares, where to go for the person who has been everywhere, what to eat and how to eat it when visiting faraway countries. We've responded by creating this newsletter.

Here we'll bring you the latest news about great deals on vacations in exotic corners of our planet, fun places for inexpensive weekend getaways, and out-of-the-way spots you might never have thought to ask us about. We'll include handy vacation planning tips and introduce you to exciting foods, puzzling customs, and important laws you'll encounter during sojourns to foreign lands. So relax, enjoy, and travel with us as we bring you a new issue every season. ✿

Celebrate with us
by Jill Evans

In honor of our newsletter's maiden voyage, we'd like to invite you to an Open House at 7:00pm on January 11, 1991, at our offices. Please dress casually or come in your most fashionable travel togs. ✿

Tropical travel
by Elizabeth Olson

Travel to tropical islands is on the increase. Just look at the graph showing our

Inside...

to set manually the width of each margin, select **M**argins, then enter the left and right margin positions of each column.

Column margin measurements are from the left edge of the page. Therefore, if the margins for the first column are 1" and 2.5", that column starts at the 1" left margin and is 1.5" wide. If the margins for the second column are 2.75" and 5.75", that leaves 0.25" between the first and second column, and the second column is 3" wide.

7. Press Exit (**F7**) when you're finished. The following menu appears:

   Columns: 1 On; 2 Off; 3 Define

8. If you want to activate (turn on) the columns at the cursor position right now, select **O**n. Otherwise, press ↵ to return to the Edit screen without activating the columns, or select Define to change your column definition.

The steps above insert a [Col Def:] code in your document at the cursor position, which might look something like this on the Reveal Codes screen (depending on your selections):

[Col Def:Newspaper;2;1",4";4.5",7.5"]

Once this code is in place, you can activate or deactivate columns anyplace below (or to the right of) the code (see the next section).

```
Text Column Definition

     1 - Type                          Newspaper

     2 - Number of Columns             2

     3 - Distance Between Columns

     4 - Margins

     Column    Left      Right     Column    Left      Right
      1:        1"        4"         13:
      2:        4.5"      7.5"       14:
      3:                             15:
      4:                             16:
      5:                             17:
      6:                             18:
      7:                             19:
      8:                             20:
      9:                             21:
     10:                             22:
     11:                             23:
     12:                             24:

   Selection: 0
```

FIGURE 20.2:

The Text Column Definition menu

ACTIVATING NEWSPAPER COLUMNS

If you selected On in step 8 in "Defining Newspaper Columns," your columns are already activated.

Once the columns are defined, you can turn them on at any time by following these steps:

1. Move the cursor to where you want to activate (or deactivate) columns (the cursor must be to the right of or below the [Col Def] code).

2. Select **L**ayout ➤ **C**olumns ➤ **O**n (or press **Alt-F7 C O**).

Narrow margins often make text look too loose, particularly when text is fully justified. You can use WordPerfect's hyphenation feature (Chapter 11) to tighten the text.

A [Col On] code is inserted in your document at the cursor position. Any text to the right of and below is formatted into columns, on both the Edit and View Document screens. A look at the Reveal Codes screen will show a [Col On] code where you activated the columns. You'll also notice that the Col indicator on the Edit-screen status line shows the column number where the cursor is currently resting.

TYPING AND EDITING IN NEWSPAPER COLUMNS

Typing and editing within columns can be a little tricky, and for this reason, many experienced WordPerfect users simply type and edit all their text before putting it in columns. But it helps to know that WordPerfect treats each column as though it were a page.

For example, when you are typing along and reach the end of a column, the cursor automatically wraps to the top of the next column (just as typing off the end of a page automatically takes you to the top of the next page). If you insert a hard page break (Ctrl-↵) in a column, the cursor is automatically positioned at the top of the next column. This is useful when you want to force text, such as an article title, to start at the top of a new column. You can prevent text from splitting across two columns with the Conditional End of Page feature (Chapter 7).

Editing text in columns can be confusing because of the way the cursor behaves. When the cursor is at the end of a line and you press →, the cursor moves down to the next line in the column (not across to the next column). If you're in the last line of the column and press ↓, the cursor moves to the first line of the same column on the next page. But if you press → enough times to go beyond the end of the last line of the column, you'll wind up at the top of the next column on the page (or in the leftmost column on the next page if you were in the rightmost column of the previous one).

As you can imagine, trying to place the cursor on a specific error that's a few lines and columns away can be pretty confusing. Here are some tips to help you control the cursor when editing text in a multicolumn layout:

◆ If you have a mouse, move the mouse pointer to the mistake, and click the left button to place the cursor there.

◆ If you want to move across to the next column, press Goto (Ctrl-Home), then the ← or → key, depending on whether you want to move left or right. To move the cursor to the rightmost column on the page, press Ctrl-Home Home →; to move to the leftmost column, press Ctrl-Home Home ←.

◆ When adding new text at the end of the last column, make sure the cursor is above and to the left of the [Col Off] code (if any) so that the new text is also in the column format.

◆ If you need to do a lot of editing and want to get rid of the columns, just delete the [Col On] code at the top of the text. Then do all your editing, go back to the top of the text (just to the right of the [Col Def] code), and reactivate the columns. Optionally, just turn off side-by-side column display, as discussed below.

On en-
hanced
keyboards,
you can
press Alt-← or Alt-→
to move from column
to column.

As an alternative to deactivating columns to help with editing, you can just turn off the side-by-side display of the columns. This still lets you edit within the columns and see where one column ends and another begins, but without the confusion of having multiple columns across the Edit screen. Follow these steps:

1. With the cursor anywhere in any document, select **F**ile ➤ Setup ➤ **D**isplay (or press **Shift-F1 D**).

2. Select **E**dit-Screen Options ➤ **S**ide-by-side Columns Display.

3. Select **N**o.

4. Press Exit (**F7**) to return to the Edit screen.

In this format, each column is on a separate page on the Edit screen, and you can use the arrow, PgUp, and PgDn keys to scroll from one column to another, as though each were a separate page. (Of course, on the View Document screen and printed copy, the columns will still be side by side.) The side-by-side display will remain turned off until you repeat the steps above and select **Y**es in step 3.

DEACTIVATING NEWSPAPER COLUMNS

If you use a graphic box, you don't have to deactivate columns before inserting text or graphics that span two or more columns, as described later in this chapter.

If, for whatever reason, you want to deactivate the columns so that text below the cursor spans the page normally again, follow these simple steps:

1. Position the cursor where you want to deactivate the columns.

2. Select **L**ayout ➤ Columns ➤ O**ff** (or press **Alt-F7 C F**).

WordPerfect inserts a [Col Off] code at the cursor position, and text below the cursor ignores the previous column definitions. You can reactivate columns at any point below in the document or define a different set of columns if you wish.

CREATING PARALLEL COLUMNS

> ### TO CREATE PARALLEL COLUMNS,
>
> **follow the same steps as for creating newspaper-style columns, except select Type of Parallel or Parallel with Block Protect (instead of Newspaper).**

When using the Tables feature, processing is slowed down dramatically as the table gets larger. You can use parallel columns instead to create large, multi-column tables.

Parallel columns are like newspaper columns except that text does not "snake" from one column to the next. When text reaches the end of a column, it simply moves to the top of the same column on the next page.

WordPerfect offers two types of parallel columns:

Parallel Columns: Text in one column stays aligned with text in the next column, but text in any given column can be broken across two or more pages. Useful for scripts and text with margin notes.

Parallel Columns with Block Protect: Same as above, but text in any given column does not break across pages, as with tables. Hence, if the page can't hold all the text in a column, all columns are bumped to the next page. Useful for trip itineraries and schedules.

Figure 20.18, near the end of this chapter, shows an example of parallel columns (without Block Protect), where the main text of the document is in the right column, and a margin note and graphic are in the left margin. As text in the right margin is added and deleted, the margin note to the left will stay with the paragraph to its right.

Parallel columns with Block Protect are often used to type large (multiple-page) tables. In general, using the Tables feature is easier, but it can slow down processing dramatically when the table spans several pages. So if you need to type a lengthy document formatted like a table, and you want to make sure text across each column stays aligned, you probably want to use the Parallel Columns with Block Protect feature to format your text.

DEFINING AND ACTIVATING PARALLEL COLUMNS

Unlike newspaper columns, parallel columns are not very simple or convenient if they're activated after you've typed your text. So to simplify matters, it's a good idea to define and activate your parallel columns before typing the text that goes into the columns. The basic procedure for defining and activating parallel columns is practically identical to that for defining and activating newspaper columns:

1. Move the cursor to where you want to begin the parallel columns.

2. Select **Layout ➤ Columns ➤ Define** (or press **Alt-F7 C D**). The Text Column Definition menu appears.

3. Select **Type**, then either **Parallel** or Parallel with **Block** Protect.

4. Specify the number of columns, the distance between columns, and, optionally, the column margins, using the same techniques described in "Defining Newspaper Columns" earlier in this chapter.

5. Press Exit (**F7**) to exit the Text Column Definition menu.

6. If you want to activate the parallel columns now, select **On**. Otherwise, press ⏎ to return to the Edit screen without activating the columns, or select Define if you want to change your column definition.

Just as with newspaper columns, if you do not activate the columns immediately after defining them, you can activate them later by moving the cursor to the top of the text (to the right of or below the [Col Def] code) and selecting **Layout ➤ Columns ➤ On** (or pressing Alt-F7 C O).

TYPING AND EDITING IN PARALLEL COLUMNS

As with newspaper columns, WordPerfect treats each parallel column as a page. Therefore, to type in parallel columns, type the text in the current column, then press Ctrl-⏎ to move to the next column. Each time you press Ctrl-⏎, the cursor moves to the next column (or back to the previous column if there is no column to the right).

Pressing Ctrl-⏎ in parallel columns usually inserts a hard page break ([HPg]) code at the cursor position and moves the cursor to the next column. However, if there is no column to the right of the current column when you press Ctrl-⏎, WordPerfect inserts [Col Off] and [Col On] codes, which move the cursor back to the first (leftmost) column.

*Block
protection
is intro-
duced in
Chapter 7.*

If you defined Parallel Columns with Block Protect, the text in the first column begins with a [Block Pro:On] code, and the text in the last column ends with a [Block Pro:Off] code. These codes prevent the text across the columns from being split across two pages.

If you need to leave a column blank, either permanently or temporarily (because you don't yet know what to enter), you should still press Ctrl-↵ to move the cursor to the "blank" column, then move on to the next entry by pressing Ctrl-↵ again.

When editing, you move the cursor just as you do with newspaper columns:

◆ To move across columns, press Goto (Ctrl-Home) then ← or → (or Alt-← or Alt-→ if you have an enhanced keyboard), depending on which direction you want to move.

◆ To move to the leftmost column, press Ctrl-Home Home ←.

◆ To move to the last column, press Ctrl-Home Home →.

If you discover that a section of text is in the wrong column while typing or editing, you can easily correct the problem by managing the codes (with Reveal Codes turned on), as summarized below:

◆ To move text one column to the left, delete the [HPg] code at the top of the text.

◆ To move text one column to the right, move the cursor to where you want to divide the text and press Ctrl-↵.

◆ To move text back from the first (leftmost) column to the last (rightmost) column, first delete the [Col On] code that appears just before the text you want to move. Then press ← until you have highlighted the [Col Off] code that appears at the end of the last column. Delete that code and remove any extra [HRt] codes that you do not want. (If you defined Parallel Columns with Block Protect, you can also delete the [Block Pro:On] and [Block Pro:Off] codes.) This is handy if you accidentally press Ctrl-↵ in the last column and then type text in the first column that really belonged with the text in the last column.

DEACTIVATING PARALLEL COLUMNS

You deactivate parallel columns the same way you deactivate newspaper columns: Position the cursor where you want the columns to end, and select **L**ayout ➤ **C**olumns ➤ **O**ff (or press Alt-F7 C F). From the cursor position down, you can resume typing with the normal margins or define a new set of columns. This lets you combine regular text with text that's formatted into parallel columns.

For example, Figure 20.3 shows text in two parallel columns after a [Col Def] code and [Col On] code. The final [Col Off] code after the word *almonds* deactivates the columns, and text typed beneath that code is in paragraph format.

THE EFFECT OF COLUMNS ON MARGINS

Once you've defined and activated newspaper or parallel columns, the position of the cursor in relation to the [Col On] and [Col Off] codes that mark the beginning and end of columns affects formatting options in a variety of ways, which can be summarized like this:

◆ When the cursor is not between a [Col On] and a [Col Off] code, the terms *page* and *margin* have their usual meanings.

◆ When the cursor is between a [Col On] and a [Col Off] code, the left and right margins *always* mean the left and right margins of the current column (not the left and right margins of the page), and each column is essentially a "page."

Consider two examples of the latter point. When you are typing within a column and press Center (Shift-F6) or Flush Right (Alt-F6) to center or right-justify text, the text is centered or right-justified within the column, *not* the page margins. And if you add a ¼-inch tab stop just beneath a [Col On] code by using **L**ayout ➤ **L**ine ➤ **T**ab Set (Shift-F8 L T), that tab stop is available at the left side of each column, not just at the left of each page.

```
    —        3/4 cup butter              1/3 cup brandy

             2-1/2 cups                  2-1/2 cups blanched
             confectioner's sugar        almonds

Cream the butter and add the sugar, gradually alternating it with

brandy until both are used. Beat until blended and smooth. Toast

the almonds in a 350° oven for 20 minutes or until lightly browned,

A:\RECIPES.WP                              Doc 1 Pg 1 Ln 1" POS 1"
[                                                        ]
[Col Def:Parallel;2;2",4";5",7"][Col On]3/4 cup butter[HPg]
1/3 cup brandy[Col Off]
[Col On][HRt]
2[-]1/2 cups[SRt]
confectioner's sugar[HPg]
[HRt]
2[-]1/2 cups blanched[SRt]
almonds [Col Off]
[HRt]
[Ln Spacing:2]Cream the butter and add the sugar, gradually alternating it with[
SRt]
Press Reveal Codes to restore screen
```

FIGURE 20.3:

Combining parallel columns and regular text

USING COLUMNS
WITH GRAPHIC BOXES AND LINES

Without a doubt, the snazziest desktop-published documents often use a combination of columns, graphic boxes, and lines. For a WordPerfect user, these documents can also be the most intimidating, since it's hard to imagine how to create such things. But, if you remember the two basic points described in the preceding section, even combining graphics, lines, and columns can be fairly simple.

If you want a graphic box to flow with text in a column, anchor the box to a paragraph or character in the column. When defining the horizontal position of the box, selecting Full will make the box as wide as the column (not the page margins), Right will place the box against the right edge of the column (not the right edge of the page), and Left will place the box against the left edge of the column.

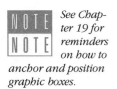

See Chapter 19 for reminders on how to anchor and position graphic boxes.

If you want the text in the columns to flow around the graphic box, or if you want the graphic box to be wider than a single column, you must anchor the box to the page. Ideally, you'll first want to position the cursor at the top of the document (above [Col Def], [Col On], and all text). Then you can define the horizontal position in relation to the page margins or a column or range of columns.

Graphic lines follow the same basic rules as graphic boxes and formatting features in columns. For example, if you define a horizontal graphic line while the cursor is within a column and set the line's horizontal position as Full, the line will be as wide as the column.

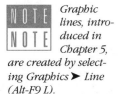

Graphic lines, introduced in Chapter 5, are created by selecting Graphics ➤ Line (Alt-F9 L).

When defining the horizontal position of a vertical graphic line, you're given the option to place it between columns. If you do so, WordPerfect automatically centers the line to the right of the column you choose, so it's quite easy to embellish your document with lines between columns—a common technique used in newsletters and magazines.

USING WORDPERFECT'S TYPESETTING FEATURES

Whether or not your desktop-published document uses columns, WordPerfect offers quite a few features that give you more precise control over your page layout and the positioning and appearance of text. These "typesetting" features (as they are sometimes called) are discussed in the following sections.

CONTROLLING THE EXACT POSITION OF TEXT

TO POSITION TEXT PRECISELY ON THE PAGE,

1. Move the cursor to the text you want to position or to the place where you're about to type.

2. Select Layout ➤ Other ➤ Advance (or press Shift-F8 O A).

3. Choose a direction to move the text, then type the amount (distance) to move it.

WordPerfect's Advance feature lets you position text exactly on the page, relative to the cursor position on the screen. This can be helpful when you need to print at an exact position on a preprinted form (Chapter 16) or when you need to combine text and graphics. To use the Advance feature, follow these steps:

I discuss the Advance feature in terms of inches, but you can use any unit of measure allowed by WordPerfect (see Chapter 13).

1. Move the cursor to the start of the text that you want repositioned on the page (or where you are about to type the text).

2. Select **L**ayout ➤ **O**ther ➤ **A**dvance (or press **Shift-F8 O A**).

3. Select the direction in which you want to move the text, as summarized below:

Up	Moves the text up without changing its horizontal position
Down	Moves the text down without changing its horizontal position
Line	Moves the text to a specific line (vertical position) on the page, measured in inches from the top edge of the page
Left	Moves the text to the left on the same line
Right	Moves the text to the right on the same line
Position	Moves the text to an exact horizontal position, measured from the left edge of the page

You can enter your measurement in any unit recognized by WordPerfect, regardless of your Units of Measure selection.

4. Enter the distance you want to move the text, in inches (e.g., *2.5* for 2½ inches) or in points followed by a *p* (e.g., *2p* for 2 points).

5. You can repeat the three steps above as needed, for example, to move text both up and to the right, or to an exact vertical and horizontal position on the page.

6. Press Exit (**F7**) to return to your document.

The steps above place a hidden [Adv] code in the document, which affects only the printed document and the View Document screen. For example, if you advance the print 2.5 inches to the right, WordPerfect places the hidden code [AdvRgt:2.5"] in the document. The text remains in its original position on the Edit screen. However, when the cursor is to the right of the advanced text, the Ln and Pos indicators in the lower-right corner of the screen indicate the actual cursor position in relation to the printed page.

It's important to keep in mind that Advance codes are additive. That is, if you advance 2 inches to the right, then change your mind and advance 2.5 inches to the right, the net result is a 4.5-inch advance to the right if you don't delete the original [Adv] code.

Resuming Normal Printing

If you want to advance only a portion of text, you'll need to use Advance a second time to determine where the text that follows will be printed. If you moved the cursor up, down, left, or right slightly, you can get back on track by moving the cursor in the opposite direction by the same amount. For example, if you use Advance to move text up by 0.02 inches, then type the text to be moved up, you must use Advance to move text down by 0.02 inches to resume printing at the baseline.

You may want to resume printing exactly where you left off before you advanced a certain chunk of text. The easiest way to do this is to position the cursor one character to the left of the [Adv] codes. Then, check the Ln and Pos indicators to determine the cursor position (jot these down). Next, move the cursor to the start of the text that should print at the original cursor position (past the text that's already been advanced). Finally, use the Line and Position options on the Advance menu to position the text according to the Ln and Pos measurements.

CONTROLLING LETTER, WORD, AND LINE SPACING

If your printer does not support a feature that the printer functions offer, it ignores any settings you change.

Some printers allow precise control over the placement and spacing of text, and WordPerfect offers several *printer functions* to support that control. To use the printer functions, follow these steps:

1. Move the cursor to where you want the feature to start in your document.

2. Select **L**ayout ➤ **O**ther ➤ **P**rinter Functions (or press **Shift-F8 O P**). The Printer Functions menu appears, shown in Figure 20.4.

3. Select an option and enter your settings.

4. When you're finished making your changes, press Exit (**F7**) to return to the Edit screen.

Each of the options available on the Printer Functions menu is described in the sections that follow.

Using Kerning

If you require even more control than WordPerfect's built-in kerning offers, you can kern letters manually by using the Advance feature to position each letter precisely.

Your WordPerfect package includes a file named KERN.TST that lets you print a kerning table for your printer and base font.

Kerning is a technique used to reduce the amount of white space between certain combinations of letters by "tucking" smaller letters under larger ones. For example, look carefully at the word *Tools* on the first two lines of Figure 20.5. The top example is not kerned, and the bottom example is kerned so that the letter *o* is slightly tucked under the letter *T*. Similarly, the first sentence beginning with the word *Wonderful* is somewhat tighter because of kerning.

To activate kerning, follow the general steps for using the printer functions, and set Kerning to Yes. Kerning does not affect the appearance of text on the Edit screen, but it is visible on the View Document screen and the printed document.

If you want to turn off kerning at some other place in your document, position the cursor, repeat the same steps, but select No. WordPerfect inserts a hidden [Kern:On] code where you activate kerning and a [Kern:Off] code where you deactivate it.

```
Format: Printer Functions

   1 - Kerning                              No

   2 - Printer Command

   3 - Word Spacing                         Optimal
       Letter Spacing                       Optimal

   4 - Word Spacing Justification Limits
       Compressed to (0% - 100%)            60%
       Expanded to (100% - unlimited)       400%

   5 - Baseline Placement for Typesetters   No
       (First baseline at top margin)

   6 - Leading Adjustment
       Primary   - [SRt]                    0''
       Secondary - [HRt]                    0''




   Selection: 0
```

FIGURE 20.4:

The Printer Functions menu

Setting Word and Letter Spacing

The Word Spacing and Letter Spacing options on the Printer Functions menu let you control the spacing between words and letters on some printers. After selecting Word Spacing (option 3), you'll be prompted first to enter word spacing, then letter spacing. You can choose from the options summarized below:

Normal	Uses the spacing the printer manufacturer considers best
Optimal	Uses the spacing that WordPerfect Corporation considers best (this is the default and may be the same as Normal)

_____**Kerning**

Tools
Tools

Wonderful Available Radar, VA: Unkerned
Wonderful Available Radar, VA: Kerned

_____**Word and Letter Spacing**

Optimal Word and Letter Spacing
2 0 0 %   o f   O p t i m a l
75% of Optimal

_____**Word Spacing Justification Limits**

This line demonstrates the word spacing justification limits (normal)

This line demonstrates the word spacing justification limits (100%)

E   V   E   N   L   Y

_____**Baseline**

The baseline is the invisible line that text is printed on. Line height is the distance between two baselines, and includes any leading between the top of tall letters and the next baseline above.

FIGURE 20.5:

Examples of Word-Perfect printer functions

Percent of Optimal	Lets you modify the Optimal setting by increasing or decreasing the spacing between letters and words as a percentage (for example, entering *110* increases spacing by 10 percent, entering *90* decreases spacing by 10 percent)
Set Pitch	Lets you enter your own pitch (characters per inch) for spacing

Figure 20.5 shows examples of word and letter spacing at optimal, 200 percent of optimal (i.e., the spacing is double its normal amount), and 75 percent of optimal (the spacing is three-fourths its normal amount). If you choose Set Pitch, you can enter word or letter spacing as a characters-per-inch measurement. Your entry is automatically converted to a percentage of optimal. For example, if the optimal setting is 10 characters per inch, and you set the pitch to 12 characters per inch, your selection is converted to 84 percent of optimal ($^{10}/_{12}$ is about 0.84 inches).

Setting Word-Spacing Justification Limits

You can also adjust the compression and expansion used for printing fully justified paragraphs by selecting option 4. Normally, WordPerfect allows for 60 percent compression and 400 percent expansion of spacing between letters and words when printing fully justified text. A percentage is a percentage of an existing space. In lines that require expansion to be fully justified, WordPerfect first expands the spacing between words. When the limit for spacing between words is reached, WordPerfect then starts adjusting the spacing between characters.

The first paragraph starting with "This line demonstrates" in Figure 20.5 shows an example of the default spacing justification. The paragraph beneath it shows an example of 100 percent compression and expansion. Because WordPerfect can only expand the space between words to 100 percent (rather than 400 percent), it must also expand the space between letters; thus, the space between words is reduced, and the space between letters is increased.

When you select option 4, you can enter a maximum compression limit in the range 0 to 100 (percent) and an expansion limit in the range 100 percent to unlimited (0). WordPerfect inserts a hidden [Just Lim:] code at the current cursor position.

If you want to space a few characters evenly across a line, like the word *EVENLY* in Figure 20.5, it's not necessary to change the word/letter spacing or word justification. Instead, try this trick:

1. Make sure the justification is set to Full (select **Layout ➤ Line ➤ Jus**tification **➤ Full**, or press **Shift-F8 L J F**) and Reveal Codes is on.

2. Type the word or words that you want to spread across the line.

3. Press the spacebar once to insert a blank space.

4. Repeatedly insert hard spaces (by pressing **Home spacebar**—they appear as [ ] on the Reveal Codes screen) until WordPerfect inserts a soft return [SRt] after the word or words you typed.

When you switch to the View Document screen, you'll see that the text is spaced evenly across the line.

Placing Baselines

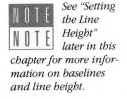

A spec is a precise description of the font, size, spacing, and placement of various text elements on a page.

The *baseline* is the invisible line that each letter rests on (see the bottom of Figure 20.5 for an illustration). If you need to control the exact position of each baseline on a page to match some publishing specs, you should first lock in the position of the first baseline on the page. Otherwise, if you increase the size of text printed at the first baseline, WordPerfect will move that baseline (and all the baselines beneath it) to avoid pushing up the text into the top margin.

When you change the Baseline Placement for Typesetters option (5) on the Printer Functions menu to Yes, WordPerfect will print the first line of text inside the top margin, so the first baseline on the page does not move if you change the size of the print on that line. Consequently, all baselines below the first line also remain fixed. This option is especially useful for publications with facing pages or multiple columns, where you want text to line up evenly across the pages or columns.

To use this feature, follow these steps:

See "Setting the Line Height" later in this chapter for more information on baselines and line height.

1. Set the top margin with **Layout ➤ Page ➤ Margin** (**Shift-F8 P M**).

2. Change the Baseline Placement for Typesetters option to Yes on the Printer Functions menu.

3. Set a fixed line height by selecting **➤ Line ➤ Line Height ➤ Fixed** (**Shift-F8 L H**).

Once you've completed these steps, the baselines on the page will be spaced at exactly the intervals you specified for fixed line height, regardless of the fonts used on any line.

Adjusting Leading

The term leading comes from earlier typesetting days, where line spacing was determined by strips of lead.

Leading (pronounced "ledding") is a typesetting term that refers to the vertical spacing of lines (the distance between two baselines). The Leading Adjustment option (6) on the Printer Functions menu lets you change both the *primary* and *secondary* leading. Primary leading is used to control the vertical spacing of lines within paragraphs; that is, lines that are separated by soft returns ([SRt] codes). Secondary leading is used to control the vertical spacing of lines between paragraphs; that is, lines that are separated by hard returns ([HRt] codes), which are entered whenever you press ↵. Figure 20.6 shows examples of leading used to control the spacing between lines within paragraphs and between paragraph titles and the paragraphs themselves.

When you change the leading, WordPerfect inserts a hidden [Leading Adj:] code at the cursor position. All text below the hidden code up to the next [Leading Adj:] code (if any) uses the leading measurements defined in the code. The text on the Edit screen will not look any different, but you can see the change on the View Document screen and the printed document.

The Leading option is great for expanding or contracting text to fill out a page. If the text is running a little short (that is, it doesn't quite reach the bottom of the page), you can increase the leading to increase the spacing between lines and better fill the space. If the text is running a little long (a couple of lines extend to the next page), you can decrease the leading a little to move some text back from the next page.

NOTE NOTE *You can enter a leading adjustment in inches or fractions (e.g., 1/72) or in points (e.g., 1p for 1 point). You can also use negative numbers to reduce leading (e.g., −1p to remove a point of leading).*

Leading Adjustment

WordPerfect adds two points of leading to proportionally spaced fonts, no leading to monospaced fonts. Here is the default leading with a proportionally spaced font.

Primary Leading

In this example we've added 4 points (4p) of primary leading, so the lines in this paragraph are spaced wider.

Secondary Leading

In this example we've added 8 points (8p) of secondary leading, so the gap between this paragraph's title and this text is widened.

Using Alien Printer Commands

In the unlikely event that your printer offers some feature that WordPerfect can't access, you can use the Printer Command option on the Printer Functions menu to send a code directly to the printer and activate that feature.

When defining the code to send to the printer, you must express in angle brackets (<>) command codes that are less than 32 or greater than 126. For example, if your printer requires the code Escape-E to activate a feature, that code must be expressed as *<027>E* (the ASCII code for the Escape character is number 27). You can create a file of the codes to send to the printer by using BASIC or an ASCII text editor.

To insert a printer command code in a document, move the cursor to the place in your document where you want the special code to be sent to the printer, then go to the Printer Functions menu and select Printer Command. If you want to type the printer code directly, select Command, type the printer code, and press ↵. If you've already stored the printer code in a file, select Filename and enter the name of the file.

If you view the document on the Reveal Codes screen, you'll see that WordPerfect has inserted a [Ptr Cmnd:] code at the current cursor position. If you change your mind about sending this code to your printer, you can delete it.

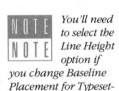

To determine the code required to activate a feature on your printer, refer to the documentation for that printer.

SETTING THE LINE HEIGHT

Normally, WordPerfect automatically determines the height of a line by the height of the largest character on that line. You, in turn, can add or delete a little space between lines by changing the leading. You can also change the line height directly by turning off the automatic line height feature and entering a fixed line height. This gives you greater control over the spacing of lines and can be handy when you want to print on preprinted forms that also use fixed line heights, or when you need to control line spacing for publication specs.

You'll need to select the Line Height option if you change Baseline Placement for Typesetters to Yes.

To change the line height method to Fixed, follow these steps:

You cannot change the line height on printers that can only print six lines to the inch.

1. Move the cursor to where you want the new line height to take effect (above or to the left of the lines).

2. Select **Layout** ➤ **Line** ➤ Line **H**eight (or press **Shift-F8 L H**).

3. Select **F**ixed.

4. Enter a height in inches or in points followed by a lowercase *p*.

5. Press ↵.

6. Press Exit (**F7**) to return to your document.

WordPerfect inserts a hidden [Ln Height:] code in the document at the cursor position, which affects all text to the end of the document or to the next [Ln Height:] code. (You can delete this code on the Reveal Codes screen if you change your mind about the line height you've selected.)

If you want to resume automatic line height later in the document, position the cursor and repeat the steps above, but select Auto rather than Fixed in the third step.

If you need very precise line-height measurements, remember that line height is the measurement from one baseline to the next and is not based solely on the height of the tallest letter in that font. The line height also includes any leading that's built into the font.

WordPerfect does not add any leading to monospaced fonts; any extra leading is generally built in by the manufacturer of the font. Thus, if you are using a 10-point monospaced font from a manufacturer that has not added any leading, the line height for that font is 10 points.

For proportionally spaced fonts, WordPerfect adds two points of leading, in addition to any leading that the manufacturer adds. Thus, if you are using a 10-point proportionally spaced font from a manufacturer that has not added any leading, WordPerfect still adds two points of leading to the font, making the actual line height 12 points.

SOME DESKTOP PUBLISHING EXAMPLES

WordPerfect offers many advanced features to precisely control the appearance of your text and graphics, but it's not always easy to envision productive and creative ways of using these features without some examples to follow. In the sections that follow, I'll present some examples and a graphic presentation of the exact keystrokes used to create each example.

You may want to try duplicating the examples by following the keystroke figure for each document at your computer. As you do so, keep an eye on the screen, and check the View Document screen every once in a while to monitor your progress and get an understanding of how each series of commands progresses toward the finished document.

 *Many of the features presented here are printer-specific, so when you print the finished example, it may not look exactly like the one you see in the figure.*

When following the keystroke figures, keep in mind that some elements of the examples may not be available to you; these are presented in square brackets, as in [Times Roman 14pt]. In such cases, you may need to substitute a font or graphic image that is available to you if you want to continue following along.

TEXT WRAPPED AROUND A GRAPHIC

Figure 20.7 shows an example of text combined with a graphic with the aid of the Advance feature. Figure 20.8 shows the exact keystrokes used to create the example. This example uses two graphic boxes to accomplish the goal: The graphic image is in a box that has Wrap Text set to No, and the large text is in a User box that's printed right over the graphic (its Wrap Text option is set to Yes to make text in the outside paragraph wrap around the second, borderless box).

```
In this example, the computer is
in a Figure box that has Wrap
Text Around Box set to No. The
text (Hi!) is in a User box.
Both boxes are the same size and
in the same position.

The User box prints over the
Figure box because the Figure
box's Wrap Text Around Box
option is Set to No. But the
Wrap Text Around Box option is
set to Yes for the User box, so
text wraps around the User box.

Make sure that the hidden code
for the box that wraps text comes after the code for the box that
doesn't wrap the text.
```

FIGURE 20.7:

Text combined with a graphic, with outside text wrapping around

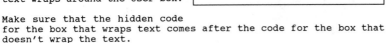

FIGURE 20.8:

The keystrokes used to create the example shown in Figure 20.7

[Alt]-[=] Graphics ▸ Figure ▸ Create ▸ Filename ▸PC-1.WPG[↵] ▸ Wrap Text Around Box ▸ No[F7]
[Alt]-[=] Graphics ▸ User Box ▸ Create ▸ Edit
[Alt]-[=] Font ▸ Base Font ▸ [Helvetica Bold 36pt] ▸ Select
[Alt]-[=] Layout ▸ Other ▸ Advance ▸ Line ▸0.45[↵] ▸ Advance ▸ Position
▸1.23[↵][F7]Hi![F7] ▸ Size ▸ Set Both ▸3.25[↵]2.35[↵][F7]

```
In this example, the computer
is in a Figure box that has
Wrap Text Around Box set to
No. The text (Hi!) is in a
User box. Both boxes are the
same size and in the same
position.[↵]
[↵]
The User box prints over the
Figure box because the Figure
box's Wrap Text Around Box
option is Set to No. But the
Wrap Text Around Box option is
set to Yes for the User box,
so text wraps around the User
box.[↵]
[↵]
Make sure that the hidden code for the box that wraps text comes
after the code for the box that doesn't wrap the text.
```

DROP CAPS

Figure 20.9 shows an example of a *drop cap,* where the first letter of a paragraph is large and dropped down. (Figure 20.10 shows the exact keystrokes used.) To create this, you put the large letter in a graphic User box at the start of the paragraph. But because WordPerfect allows room for a caption in graphic boxes, you may have trouble getting the spacing around the box just right.

To deal with the extra-space problem in this example, Wrap Text was set to No around the User box where the letter *S* is stored. Then a smaller User box was created in the same position as the first one, and Wrap Text was set to Yes so that the outside text wraps tighter around the drop cap.

Sometimes work itself can be a form of work avoidance. Recently, while writing a chapter that absolutely had to be done by 3:00, I suddenly had the urge to vacuum my closet. While waving the vacuum nozzle around without paying attention, I (or rather, the vacuum cleaner) sucked some ties off my tie rack. They came out of the hose looking like little silk prunes. So now there was another job to do--iron some ties.

FIGURE 20.9:

An example of drop-cap text

```
Alt-= Graphics ▸ User Box ▸ Create ▸ Horizontal Position ▸ Left ▸ Edit
Alt-= Font ▸ Base Font ▸ [Times Bold 72pt] ▸ Select
S F7 ▸ Wrap Text Around Box ▸ No ▸ Size ▸ Set Both ▸ .55↵ .8↵ F7
Alt-= Graphics ▸ User Box ▸ Create ▸ Horizontal Position ▸ Left ▸ Size ▸ Set Both
▸ .5↵ .65↵ F7
Alt-= Font ▸ Base Font ▸ [Times 14pt] ▸ Select
ometimes work itself can be a form of work avoidance. Recently,
while writing a chapter that absolutely had to be done by 3:00, I
suddenly had the urge to vacuum my closet. While waving the vacuum
nozzle around without paying attention, I (or rather, the vacuum
cleaner) sucked some ties off my tie rack. They came out of the
hose looking like little silk prunes. So now there was another job
to do--iron some ties.
```

FIGURE 20.10:

The keystrokes used to create the drop cap shown in Figure 20.9

WHITE TEXT ON A BLACK BACKGROUND

If your printer can print white or shades of gray, you can print white text on a black background. Just create a graphic box with the gray shading set at 100 percent of black, and within that box, set the print color to white and type your text. Figure 20.11 shows an example, with the exact keystrokes used to create the example listed below it.

NEWSLETTER

Styles are covered in detail in Chapter 14.

Newsletters are one of the most common applications of WordPerfect's desktop publishing features and generally use some combination of fonts, columns, graphic images, and graphic lines. Figure 20.1 at the start of this chapter shows one example. Figure 20.12 shows the keystrokes used to create the basic layout for that newsletter.

When creating documents of this complexity on your own, you'll probably want to use styles for the main elements, such as article titles, bylines, and body text.

TWO-FOLD MAILER

Figure 20.13 shows an empty two-fold mailer format, and Figure 20.14 shows the exact keystrokes used to create it. Figure 20.15 completes the sequence by showing an example of the basic layout put to use. Essentially, this is a three-column newspaper-style format, so once the basic layout is complete, you just press ⌐ a few times, then type the text for the brochure ("Do you know the true value…"), changing the fonts as desired. When you're ready to format the text and graphics on the opposite flap of the brochure, you press Ctrl-Enter twice to move to the last column.

Reversed -- White on Black

(Alt)-(=) **Graphics** ▸ **Text Box** ▸ **Options** ▸ **Border Style**▸ **None** ▸ **None** ▸ **None** ▸ **None** ▸ **Gray Shading** ▸ 100⌐⌐
(Alt)-(=) **Graphics** ▸ **Text Box** ▸ **Create** ▸ **Size** ▸ **Width** 6.5⌐ ▸ **Edit**
(Alt)-(=) **Font** ▸ **Base Font** [Helvetica Bold Italic 32pt] ▸ **Select**
(Alt)-(=) **Font** ▸ **Print Color** ▸ **White** ⌐Reversed -- White on Black(F7)(F7)

FIGURE 20.11:

White text on a black background, and the keystrokes used to create the example

FLIER

The sample flier in Figure 20.16 was printed on a PostScript printer and uses graphic images from the DrawPerfect package. Obviously, not everyone has this much printer power or the need to create documents quite so complex. But in case you're interested in giving it a whirl, Figure 20.17 shows the exact keystrokes used to create this example.

MARGIN NOTES

Figure 20.18 shows a small passage of text with a margin note in the left margin, which illustrates a practical application of the Parallel Columns feature. Using this complicated format for a long document can grow tiresome, so I created a style and macro to simplify things. Figure 20.19 shows the exact keystrokes used to type the example *after* creating the style and macro discussed in a moment.

 *Styles and macros are covered in detail in Part 4.*

After creating the style and macro, it is easy to type a margin note with the light-bulb icon next to it: You need only press Alt-N, then type the text of the note. The macro handles all the tedious tasks of creating the note: It switches to the left column, creates the bulb graphic, waits for you to type the text of the note, then switches back to the right column.

Alt-= Graphics ▸ Text Box ▸ Create ▸ Anchor Type ▸ Page ▸0⏎ ▸ Horizontal Position ▸ Margins ▸ Full ▸ Edit
Alt-= Font ▸ Base Font [Main Headline font (62pt)] F7 ▸ Size ▸ Set Both ▸6.5⏎2.24⏎F7

Alt-= Graphics ▸ Text Box ▸ Create ▸ Anchor Type ▸ Page ▸0⏎ ▸ Vertical Position ▸ Bottom ▸ Horizontal Position ▸ Margin ▸ Right ▸ Edit
Alt-= Font ▸ Base Font ▸ [Font and Inside...] F7 ▸ Size ▸ Set Both ▸ 4.12⏎2.12⏎F7

Alt-= Font ▸ Base Font ▸ [Helvetical 14pt] ▸ Select
Vol.Shift-F6   Centered Alt-F6   Date
Alt-= Graphics ▸ Line ▸ Create Horizontal ⏎⏎⏎

Alt-= Layout ▸ Columns ▸ Define ▸ Type ▸ Newspaper ▸ Number of Columns ▸ 3⏎ ▸ Distance Between Columns ▸.35⏎⏎⏎ ▸ On
F7F7

FIGURE 20.12:

The keystrokes used to create the basic layout of the newsletter shown in Figure 20.1

You'll need some sample text to work with to create the macro, so if you'd like to try this yourself, set up two parallel columns and activate them, press Ctrl-↵ to move the cursor into the right column, and type three or more paragraphs of text, ending each paragraph with two hard returns. You can use the text in the right column of Figure 20.19 as an example (but don't worry about typing the margin note just yet). Then, you can create the style for formatting margin notes, described next.

FIGURE 20.13:

A basic two-fold mailer layout

Your Return
Address Goes
Here

Creating the Style

To keep this style for use in other documents, you must select Layout ➤ Styles ➤ Save (or press Alt-F8 S).

Follow these steps to create the style for the margin note, which you can name *Tip:*

1. Start at the WordPerfect Edit screen, and select **L**ayout ➤ **S**tyles ➤ **C**reate ➤ **N**ame (or press **Alt-F8 C N**).

2. Type the style name (e.g., *Tip*) and press ↵.

3. Select **T**ype ➤ **O**pen.

4. Optionally, select **D**escription and type a description, such as *Tip margin note,* then press ↵.

5. Select **C**odes to start adding formatting codes.

[Alt]-[=] Layout ▸ Page ▸ Paper Size [Standard – Wide] Select ▸ Margins ▸0.3[↵]0.3[↵][↵] ▸ Line ▸ Margins ▸0.3[↵]0.3[↵][F7]

[Alt]-[=] Layout ▸ Columns ▸ Define ▸ Type ▸ Newspaper ▸ Number of Columns ▸ 3[↵][↵] ▸ On

[Alt]-[=] Graphics ▸ Line ▸ Create Horizontal ▸ Vertical Position ▸ Set Position ▸ 0.3[↵] Width of Line ▸0.13[↵] [F7]

[Alt]-[=] Graphics ▸ Line ▸ Create Horizontal ▸ Vertical Position ▸ Set Position ▸ 8.07[↵] Width of Line ▸0.13[↵][F7]

[Alt]-[=] Graphics ▸ Line ▸ Create Horizontal ▸ Horizontal Position ▸ Set Position ▸7.5[↵] ▸ Vertical Position ▸ Set Position ▸0.3[↵] ▸ Length of Line ▸ 3.13[↵] Width of Line ▸ 0.13[↵] [F7]

[Alt]-[=] Graphics ▸ Line ▸ Create Horizontal ▸ Horizontal Position ▸ Set Position ▸ 7.5[↵] ▸ Vertical Position ▸ Set Position ▸8.07[↵] ▸Length of Line ▸3.13[↵] ▸ Width of Line ▸0.13[↵] [F7]

[Alt]-[=] Graphics ▸ User Box ▸ Create ▸ Anchor Type ▸ Page ▸0[↵] Horizontal Position ▸ Columns ▸2[↵] ▸ Left ▸ Wrap Text Around Box ▸ No ▸ Edit

[Alt]-[=] Font ▸ Base Font ▸ [Courier 12cpi] ▸ Select [↵] [↵]

[Alt]-[=] Layout ▸ Tables ▸ Create ▸1[↵] ▸1[↵] ▸ Lines ▸ Outside ▸ Dotted ▸ Options ▸ Position ▸ Right [F7] [Size using [Ctrl]-[←] and [Ctrl]-[→] until [Tbl Def::] code in Reveal Codes screen indicates column width of about 0.8] [F7] [↵] [↵] [↵] [F7] Size ▸ Set Both ▸ 1.05[↵] ▸1.1[↵] [F7]

[Alt]-[=] Graphics ▸ Figure ▸ Options ▸ Inside Border Space ▸.3[↵] ▸.3[↵] ▸.3[↵] ▸.3[↵] [↵]

[Alt]-[=] Graphics ▸ Figure ▸ Create ▸ Type ▸ Page ▸0[↵] ▸ Vertical Position ▸ Full Page ▸ Horizontal Position ▸ Columns ▸2[↵] ▸ Full ▸ Edit

[Alt]-[=] Font ▸ Base Font ▸ [font for return address] ▸ Select [type return address] [Alt]-[F9] ▸ 2 90° [F7][F7]

FIGURE 20.14:

The keystrokes used to create the layout in Figure 20.13

6. From the pull-down menus, select **G**raphics ➤ User Box ➤ **O**ptions (or press **Alt-F9 U O**).

7. Select **O**utside Border Space and set the options to Left = 0, Right = 0.08, Top = 0, Bottom = 0. Then press Exit (**F7**) to return to the code-editing screen.

8. Select **G**raphics ➤ User Box ➤ **C**reate (or press **Alt-F9 U C**).

9. Now you can create your graphic icon. You can use any WordPerfect-compatible figure or large special character. For the example, I selected **F**ilename and entered *BULB.WPG* as the name.

10. Select **H**orizontal Position ➤ **L**eft.

11. Select **S**ize ➤ Set **B**oth, and size the graphic-icon box. (I used 0.36" wide and 0.45" high.)

12. If you're using a graphic figure (i.e., a .WPG file), select **E**dit and, if necessary, rescale the figure to fit the box better. You can use the PgUp, PgDn, and arrow keys to size and position the figure (press Ins to

FIGURE 20.15:

An example of the two-fold mailer layout put to use

Do you know the true value of your home?

Few people realize the value of their home in today's market. If you'd like to find out the current market value of your home, just call Apgar Realty for a free appraisal. One of our qualified professionals will gladly stop by to appraise your property. And it won't cost you a penny.

Of course, should you decide to sell your home now, and cash in on some of that wonderful equity, we can help you do that as well.

Just think of what you could do with all that cash. You could buy fancy cars, jewelry, yachts, or just take an ocean cruise around the world. Or if you're more frugal than that, you could buy another house exactly like the one you're in now (don't forget, yours isn't the *only* house on the block that's gone up in value).

For more information on what Apgar Realty can do for you today, just look inside this wonderful brochure. Trust us, you'll be glad you did.

Apgar Realty
P.O. Box 1234
Cuesta Verde, CA 92067

Apgar Realty

Sold

Serving Cuesta Verde Since 1991

change the effect of these keys as necessary). Press Exit (**F7**) when you're satisfied with the size and position of the figure within its frame.

13. Press Exit (**F7**) to return to the code-editing screen.

14. Select Font ➤ Base Font (or press **Ctrl-F8 F**), and select the font for your margin notes (I used Times 10-point).

15. If you want your margin notes left-justified (like the example), select Layout ➤ Line ➤ Justification ➤ Left (or press **Shift-F8 L J L**), then press Exit (**F7**) to return to the code-editing screen.

16. If you want to reduce the white space between the lines, as in the example, select Layout ➤ Other ➤ Printer Functions ➤ Leading Adjustment (or press **Shift-F8 O P L**). (I took out one point of primary leading by entering *–1p* for that measurement, and I left the secondary leading at zero.) Press Exit (**F7**) to return to the code-editing screen.

17. If you want to align the text near the middle of the icon, as in the example (rather than at the top of the icon), press ↵.

18. Press Exit (**F7**) to return to the Styles: Edit menu.

19. Select **T**ype ➤ **P**aired.

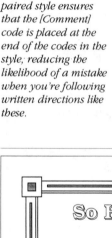

Starting the style as an open style and changing it to a paired style ensures that the [Comment] code is placed at the end of the codes in the style, reducing the likelihood of a mistake when you're following written directions like these.

FIGURE 20.16:

A sample flier, printed with a PostScript printer

20. Select **Enter** ➤ **Off**. This will turn off the style automatically when you press ↵ after typing the margin note.

21. Press Exit (**F7**) twice to return to the Edit screen.

Now you're ready to create the macro that activates the style and also takes care of placing the note in the left column.

```
Alt-= Layout ▸ Page ▸ Paper Size [Standard Wide] Select F7
Alt-= Layout ▸ Page ▸ Margins ▸0.3 ↵ 0.3 ↵ Center Page ▸ Yes ↵
▸ Line ▸ Margins ▸0.3 ↵ 0.3 ↵ ▸ Justification ▸ Center F7

Alt-= Graphics ▸ User Box ▸ Create ▸ File Name ▸ [Border Graphic] ↵
▸ Anchor Type ▸ Page ▸0 ↵ ▸ Vertical Position ▸ Full Page ▸ Horizontal Position ▸ Margins ▸
Full ▸ Wrap Text Around Box ▸ No F7

Alt-= Graphics ▸ User Box ▸ Create ▸ File Name ▸ [Dog Graphic] ↵
▸ Anchor Type ▸ Page ▸0 ↵ ▸ Vertical Position ▸ Set Position ▸2.45 ↵ ▸ Horizontal
Position ▸ Set Position ▸1 ↵ ▸ Size ▸ Width ▸3 ↵
▸ Wrap Text Around Box ▸ No F7

Alt-= Graphics ▸ User Box ▸ Create ▸ File Name ▸ [Dog Graphic] ↵
▸ Anchor Type ▸ Page ▸0 ↵ ▸ Vertical Position ▸ Set Position ▸2.45 ↵ ▸ Horizontal Position
▸ Set Position ▸7 ↵ ▸ Size ▸ Width ▸3 ↵
▸ Wrap Text Around Box ▸ No ▸ Edit ▸ Rotate ▸0 ↵ ▸ Yes F7 F7

Alt-= Font ▸ Base Font ▸ [ITC Bookman Demi] ▸ Select ▸36 ↵
Alt-= Font ▸ Appearance ▸ Outline Alt-= Font ▸ Appearance ▸ Shadow
So How's About a Donation? → → ↵
↵
Alt-= Font ▸ Print Color ▸ Other ▸90 ↵ 90 ↵ 90 ↵ ↵
Alt-= Font ▸ Base Font ▸ [ITC Zapf Dingbats] ▸ Select ▸36 ↵ Ctrl-V 12,113 ↵
Alt-= Font ▸ Base Font ▸ [Palatino Italic] ▸ Select ▸36 ↵ $10.00 ↵
Alt-= Font ▸ Print Color ▸ Other ▸70 ↵ 70 ↵ 70 ↵ ↵
Alt-= Font ▸ Base Font ▸ [ITC Zapf Dingbats] ▸ Select ▸36 ↵ Ctrl-V 12,113 ↵
Alt-= Font ▸ Base Font ▸ [Palatino Italic] ▸ Select ▸36 ↵ $49.99 ↵
Alt-= Font ▸ Print Color ▸ Other ▸ Gray ↵
Alt-= Font ▸ Base Font ▸ [ITC Zapf Dingbats] ▸ Select ▸36 ↵ Ctrl-V 12,113 ↵
Alt-= Font ▸ Base Font ▸ [Palatino Italic] ▸ Select ▸36 ↵ $74.99 ↵
Alt-= Font ▸ Print Color ▸ Other ▸Black ↵
Alt-= Font ▸ Base Font ▸ [ITC Zapf Dingbats] ▸ Select ▸36 ↵ Ctrl-V 12,113 ↵
  Alt-= ▸ Base Font ▸ [Palatino Italic] ▸ Select ▸36 ↵ $99.99 ↵
↵
Alt-= Font ▸ Base Font ▸ [ITC Bookman Light] ▸ Select ▸18 ↵
for the Alt-= Font ▸ Base Font ▸ [ITC Zapf Dingbats] ▸ Select ▸30 ↵
Alt-= Layout ▸ Other ▸ Advance ▸ Down ▸0.05 ↵ F7
Alt-= Font ▸ Appearance ▸ Outline Ctrl-V 12,100 ↵
Alt-= Font ▸ Base Font ▸ [ITC Bookman Demi] ▸ Select ▸30 ↵
Alt-= Layout ▸ Other ▸ Advance ▸ Up ▸.02 ↵ F7
Alt-= Font ▸ Appearance ▸ Shadow Save the Snowflake →
Alt-= Layout ▸ Other ▸ Advance ▸ Down ▸.02 ↵ F7
Alt-= Font ▸ Base Font ▸ [ITC Zapf Dingbats] ▸ Select ▸30 ↵ Ctrl-V 12,100 ↵
Alt-= Font ▸ Base Font ▸ [ITC Bookman Light] ▸ Select ▸18 ↵
Alt-= Layout ▸ Other ▸ Advance ▸ Up ▸0.05 ↵ F7 society ↵
↵
Alt-= Font ▸ Base Font ▸ [Palatino] ▸ Select ▸22 ↵
P.O. Box 1234 ↵
Corn Flake, CA  91234
```

FIGURE 20.17:

The keystrokes used to create the flier in Figure 20.16

Creating the Macro

As mentioned, you should already have typed at least three paragraphs, each separated by two hard returns, in the right column of the parallel columns, so you can actually record some keystrokes in the steps below:

1. Position the cursor at the start of the second paragraph, then press **Ctrl-F10** and enter the macro name (Alt-N was used in the example).

This small passage illustrates a practical application of parallel columns; notes in the left margin. It also demonstrates a way to combine two of WordPerfect's more advanced features to simplify your work, Styles and Macros.

This is a margin note, created with a macro, but formatted with a style.

In this example, parallel columns were defined and activated at the top of the document. Then a style was created, named Tip, to format the margin notes and put in the graphic. Then a macro was created, named Alt-N, so that a margin note could be typed at any time simply by pressing Alt-N, typing the note, and pressing enter.

This combination of features makes it easy to type even a seemingly complex document like this one. Furthermore, you can create styles for other kinds of margin notes, such as Notes and Warnings, as well as icons.

FIGURE 20.18:

Sample text from a document with a margin note and icon

Alt-= Layout ▸ Line ▸ Justification ▸ Left F7
Alt-= Layout ▸ Columns ▸ Define ▸ Type ▸ Parallel ▸ Margins
▸1⏎2.5⏎2.75⏎7.5⏎⏎ ▸ On
Alt-= Font ▸ Base Font ▸ [Times 12pt] ▸ Select
Ctrl-⏎

This small passage illustrates a practical application of parallel columns; notes in the left margin. It also demonstrates a way to combine two of WordPerfect's more advanced features to simplify your work, Styles and Macros.
⏎
⏎
This is a margin note, created with a macro, but formatted with a style.⏎

Alt-N In this example, parallel columns were defined and activated at the top of the document. Then a style was created, named Tip, to format the margin notes and put in the graphic. Then a macro was created, named Alt-N, so that a margin note could be typed at any time simply by pressing Alt-N, typing the note, and pressing enter.
⏎
⏎
This combination of features makes it easy to type even a seemingly complex document like this one. Furthermore, you create styles for other kinds of margin notes, such as Notes and Warnings, as well as icons.

FIGURE 20.19:

The keystrokes used to create Figure 20.18 after creating the style and Alt-N macro

2. If you see a message indicating that the macro already exists, you'll have to decide whether to replace the existing macro or to press Cancel (**F1**) and start over, using a different name.

3. When prompted for a description, you can type a brief description, such as *Enter a margin note,* and press ↵. You should see "Macro Def" blinking, indicating that WordPerfect is recording your keystrokes.

4. Press **Backspace** twice. (This step assumes you've separated paragraphs with two hard returns, by pressing ↵ twice at the end of each paragraph, as in the example, and helps align the note with the text. You may need to experiment later if you're using a different format.)

5. Press **Ctrl-↵** to insert a hard page break (this will move the cursor to the left column).

6. Select **L**ayout ➤ **S**tyles (or press **Alt-F8**) to get to the Styles menu.

7. Press **N** to select Name Search, then type the name of the style you want to turn on (*Tip* in the example), and press ↵.

8. Press **O** to select On and leave the menu.

9. Press **Ctrl-PgUp,** and select **P**ause so that the macro will pause later to let you type in the margin-note text. Press ↵ to complete the Pause selection.

10. Press → to move the cursor past the [Style Off] code for the margin note.

11. Press **Ctrl-↵** to move the cursor back to the right column.

12. Press **Ctrl-F10** to stop recording macro keystrokes.

When you're creating a macro that chooses a style, don't just highlight the style name and press ↵ to select it: Use Name Search instead. That way, the macro will always select the correct style even if you add or delete styles in your style library.

While creating the macro, you placed an empty note in the margin. Ignore that note when checking your macro.

To use the macro properly, the cursor must be positioned either at the start of an existing paragraph or where you're about to type a new paragraph in the right column. During this trial run, you can move the cursor to the start of the third paragraph of text or anywhere below that paragraph. Then press Alt-N, type the text of your margin note, and press ↵. To observe your success, check the View Document screen or print the page.

The advantage of the combined macro and style is that you can easily type a margin note with a graphic by pressing Alt-N, typing the note, and pressing ↵. If you later decide to change the font or other appearance of all the Tip margin notes, you need only change the appearance of the Tip style. You can also make styles for other kinds of margin notes (e.g., Note, Warning, Icon, etc.), make a separate macro to type each kind, and create an otherwise complex document with minimal effort.

With the help of Chapter 19 and this chapter, you've mastered some new techniques for working with text, lines, graphics, and multiple columns—key ingredients for producing publication-quality documents. In the next chapter, I'll look at a somewhat specialized task in desktop publishing: creating equations. If your work involves mathematical, scientific, or engineering publications, you're sure to appreciate WordPerfect's Equation Editor.

CHAPTER 21

Adding Equations to Your Documents

For mathematicians, scientists, and the people who type their documents, WordPerfect offers the Equations feature. This feature lets you type complex mathematical equations into a document and print them using all the special symbols and typesetting standards. Note, however, that the Equations feature does not *solve* the equations for you; it just lets you *edit* them. Figure 21.1 shows a sample equation typed with WordPerfect.

NOTE NOTE

Like the View Document screen, the Equation Editor requires that you have a graphics monitor.

WordPerfect follows standard rules of typesetting when printing equations:

◆ The equation is centered horizontally and vertically on its own line.

◆ Variables are printed in italics.

◆ Numbers and mathematical functions are printed in a roman (non-italicized) font.

As you'll learn later, you can change any of these defaults.

CREATING EQUATIONS

TO CREATE AN EQUATION,

Move the cursor to where you want to place the equation, select Graphics ➤ Equation ➤ Create (Alt-F9 E C), and select Edit.

You can place equations in any of the five types of graphic boxes discussed in Chapter 19, although it's often simplest to stick with using Equation boxes for this purpose. WordPerfect offers a special *Equation Editor* for creating, editing, and previewing your equations. To add an equation to a document and access the Equation Editor, follow these steps:

1. If you've already typed some or all of the text in the document, move the cursor to the line where you want to place the equation.

2. Select **G**raphics ➤ **E**quation ➤ **C**reate, or press **Alt-F9 E C**.

3. Select **E**dit.

Figure 21.2 shows a sample Equation Editor screen, after an equation has been typed. It's divided into three major sections, as shown in the figure: the Display window in the upper portion shows the equation graphically (much as it will be printed); the Edit window in the bottom portion is used to type in and edit the equation; and the equation palette on the right contains commands, symbols, and functions you can insert in the equation instead of, or in addition to, typing them from the keyboard.

The equation below demonstrates some of the capabilities of WordPerfect's equation editor. You can find a similar equation in the WordPerfect PRINTER.TST file to see how it looks in the equation editor.

$$\int_0^\infty x^{n-1} e^{-x} dx = \int_0^1 \left(\log \frac{1}{x} \right) dx = \frac{1}{n} \prod_{m=1}^\infty \frac{\left(1 + \frac{1}{m} \right)}{1 + \frac{n}{m}} = \Gamma(n) , \quad n > 0$$

Equations follow typesetting standards; they are centered on their own lines, and variable names are printed in italics. However, you can change those standards, and put an equation anywhere you wish, even right in your text.

FIGURE 21.1:

An example of an equation typed with WordPerfect

Typing Equations

Typing and editing an equation in the Edit window is much like typing and editing any other text in WordPerfect, although there are some differences. For the most part, you can type symbols and special operators either from the keyboard or from the various equation palettes, as described a little later.

While the cursor is in the Equation Edit window, you can use the usual editing techniques to modify the equation. For example, you can use the ← and → keys to position the cursor, the Backspace and Delete keys to delete characters, and the Insert key to switch between Insert and Typeover modes. You can also use your mouse to position the cursor.

When you're ready to see a graphical representation of the equation you've typed so far, you can press Screen (Ctrl-F3), then look at the top Display window.

> **NOTE** *You can also press the Graphics (F9) key or click on Screen Redisplay at the bottom of the Editor screen to refresh the Display window.*

The Role of Curly Braces

When you're entering equations in WordPerfect, you should type them as they might be spoken aloud and use curly braces ({ }) to group items together. For example, the formula shown in Figure 21.2 could be expressed verbally as "the

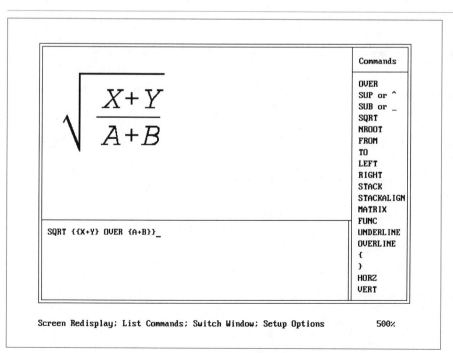

The Equation Editor screen

square root of X + Y over A + B." This equation is expressed in the Equation Editor as

SQRT {{X+Y} OVER {A+B}}

Because everything to the right of the SQRT command must be under the radical, this entire portion of the equation is enclosed in curly braces. And, because the entire X + Y portion should be placed over the entire A + B portion, each of these is also contained in its own curly braces. Figure 21.3 shows more examples illustrating the important role played by the curly braces.

It's important that the curly braces in an equation make sense. For example, if you have more open curly braces than closing curly braces, or vice versa, the Equation Editor will not be able to make sense of the grouping. Hence, when you press Screen (Ctrl-F3) to view such a formula, you'll see the message "ERROR: Incorrect format" displayed briefly at the bottom of the screen, and the Display window will be left blank.

The same error message might be displayed if your equation uses equation commands improperly, even though the curly braces are correct.

Entering Blanks and New Lines

Blanks entered with the spacebar are used to separate equation commands, but these blank spaces are *not* part of the final equation. If you want to include a blank space in an equation, type a tilde (~) where you want the blank space to appear.

SQRT X+Y OVER A+B	$\sqrt{X}+\dfrac{Y}{A}+B$
SQRT {X+Y} OVER A+B	$\dfrac{\sqrt{X+Y}}{A}+B$
SQRT X+Y OVER {A+B}	$\sqrt{X}+\dfrac{Y}{A+B}$
SQRT X+{Y OVER A}+B	$\sqrt{X}+\dfrac{Y}{A}+B$
SQRT {X+Y OVER A+B}	$\sqrt{X+\dfrac{Y}{A}+B}$
SQRT {{X+Y} OVER {A+B}}	$\sqrt{\dfrac{X+Y}{A+B}}$

FIGURE 21.3:

Examples of the usage of curly braces in equations

Four thin spaces are equal to one normal space.

You can also insert a thin space (a quarter space) using the backward accent character (`). (It's on the same key as the tilde on most keyboards.) Use one accent to add a quarter space, two accents to add a half space, and so forth. The tilde and accent appear only in the Edit window, never in the printed document.

Pressing ↵ while editing an equation moves the cursor to the next line, as on the normal Edit screen. However, this does not insert a line break in the actual equation (it just gives you more room to type the equation and makes the Edit window easier to read). To stack items in an equation, use the STACK, STACKALIGN, MATRIX, #, or similar commands described later.

Typing Numbers, Variables, and Operators

When typing a real number containing a decimal point or negative sign, you must surround the number in curly braces, like this: {−1.47}.

You will need to type numbers and variables (such as $X, Y, A,$ and B) directly from the keyboard. And because the following operators and symbols aren't on the equation palette, you'll also need to type them from the keyboard:

$$+ \; - \; * \; / \; = \; < \; > \; ! \; ? \; . \; | \; @ \; " \; , \; ;$$

In addition, you can type commands like SQRT and OVER directly from the keyboard, in either upper- or lowercase letters, provided that you know the exact command to use. Similarly, you can type special symbols with the Compose key (Ctrl-2). However, when first learning to use the Equation Editor, you'll probably prefer to select most commands and symbols from the equation palettes.

USING THE EQUATION PALETTES

You can select commands or special symbols from the equation palette anytime you are in the Equation Editor by following these steps:

1. With the cursor in the Equation Edit window, move the cursor to where you want to place an item from a palette.

2. Press List (**F5**) to move to the palette area, or click with the left mouse button on List Commands at the bottom of the screen.

3. Press **Page Up** or **Page Down**, or click on PgUp or PgDn in the lower-right corner of the screen, to scroll through the various palettes until you find the one you want.

4. Move the cursor to the item you want.

5. Press ↵ (or **Ctrl-↵**, as described later) to select the item.

6. To view the equation, press Screen (**Ctrl-F3**) or Graphics (**F9**), or click on Screen Redisplay at the bottom of the screen.

Figure 21.4 shows examples of a number of equations created with the Equation Editor. Keywords in the examples that don't come directly from the Commands palette (described in the next section) were selected from other palettes. For example, ALPHA, OMEGA, and THETA were selected from the Greek palette; SUM and INT were selected from the Large palette; INF and THEREFORE were selected from the Symbols palette. (As you scroll through these palettes, you'll see the palette name above the palette.)

Numbers, letters, and operators such as m + n = 0 were typed in directly from the keyboard. The techniques used were the same as those described earlier for Figure 21.2.

The ways in which you can combine equation commands and symbols are nearly endless. When you are first learning, it may take some trial-and-error practice to get everything just right. You should build your formula gradually, pressing Screen (Ctrl-F3) often to see how things are progressing. That way, you can correct mistakes and refine your equation as you type it.

The sections that follow describe the various palettes. As you read these sections, be sure to refer back to Figure 21.4 for examples of how to type these commands and what they look like when printed or when displayed in the Display window.

The Commands Palette

NOTE

Remember that any command or character from the Commands palette, such as { }, can be typed in the Equation Edit window directly or selected from the equation palette; it's entirely a matter of personal preference.

The Commands palette offers commands that are used to organize and position values in an equation and to draw some special characters, such as the radical (SQRT) sign. As you scroll through the palette, the lower-left corner of the screen displays the purpose of the command and shows an example of its usage.

As you saw in figures 21.2 and 21.3 earlier, how you group items with curly braces has a major effect on the results. See Table 21.1 for complete descriptions of the equation commands. The italicized word *variable* refers to either a single character or a group of characters enclosed in curly braces. (See Figure 21.4 for printed examples of these commands.)

The Other Palettes

The various other palettes in the Equation Editor offer a visual means of selecting special symbols. There are eight palettes in all (counting the Commands palette). After pressing List (F5) to move from the Equation Edit window into

ALIGNC 10 OVER 100000	$\dfrac{10}{100000}$
ALIGNL 10 OVER 100000	$\dfrac{10}{100000}$
ALIGNR 10 OVER 100000	$\dfrac{10}{100000}$
BINOM ALPHA OMEGA	$\left(\begin{matrix}A\\\Omega\end{matrix}\right)$
BINOMSM ALPHA OMEGA	$\left(\begin{smallmatrix}A\\\Omega\end{smallmatrix}\right)$
BOLD THETA	$\boldsymbol{\theta}$
SUM FROM {x=0} TO INF	$\displaystyle\sum_{x=0}^{\infty}$
FUNC {no˜italics}	no italics
ITAL cosine	*cosine*
123 HORZ 100 45	123 45
LEFT ({1^x} OVER m RIGHT)	$\left(\dfrac{1^x}{m}\right)$
MATRIX {MATFORM {ALIGNL & ALIGNR} 1&2 # 10&20 # 100&200}	1 2 10 20 100 200
LEFT DLINE MATRIX {a & b & c # x & y & z} RIGHT DLINE	$\left\|\begin{matrix}a & b & c\\x & y & z\end{matrix}\right\|$
NROOT 3 {-{x OVER y}}	$\sqrt[3]{-\dfrac{x}{y}}$
tan ``THETA`=`{sin``THETA} OVER {cos``THETA}	$\tan\theta=\dfrac{\sin\theta}{\cos\theta}$

FIGURE 21.4:

Examples of equation commands and symbols

OVERLINE {n != 0}	$\overline{n \ne 0}$
1 OVER {x OVERSM {y+1}}	$\dfrac{1}{\frac{x}{y-1}}$
STACK {m+n=0 # m PHANTOM {+n}=2}	$\begin{array}{l} m+n=0 \\ m=2 \end{array}$
LEFT. {X^1} OVER {Y_2} RIGHT LINE	$\left. \dfrac{X^1}{Y_2} \right|$
SQRT {a^2 + b^2}''=c	$\sqrt{a^2+b^2}=c$
STACK {x+y # a+b # m+n}	$\begin{array}{l} x+y \\ a+b \\ m+n \end{array}$
STACK {ALIGNR x+y # a+b+c # ALIGNL m+n}	$\begin{array}{c} y+z \\ a+b+c \\ m+n \end{array}$
STACKALIGN {a&<=b-c # x-y&>=z}	$\begin{array}{l} a \le b-c \\ x-y \ge z \end{array}$
x SUB 1 (or x_1)	x_1
x SUP 1 (or x^1)	x^1
x SUB y SUP 1 (or x_y^1)	x_y^1
INT SUB 0 SUP INF	$\displaystyle\int_0^\infty$
UNDERLINE THEREFORE	$\underline{\therefore}$
A VERT 100 B VERT 100 C	$\begin{array}{c} C \\ B \\ A \end{array}$
THEREFORE ~\THEREFORE	$\therefore \ \textit{THEREFORE}$

FIGURE 21.4:

Examples of equation commands and symbols (continued)

COMMAND	DESCRIPTION
ALIGNC	Center-aligns a *variable* over a line or in a matrix
ALIGNL	Left-aligns a *variable* over a line or in a matrix
ALIGNR	Right-aligns a *variable* over a line or in a matrix
BINOM	Creates a binomial construction from two *variables* that follow
BINOMSM	Creates a binomial construction from two *variables* that follow, but in the next smaller font (printer- and font- dependent)
BOLD	Boldfaces the *variable,* symbol, or function that follows
FROM	Provides beginning and ending limits for a symbol, and must be used in conjunction with the TO command
FUNC	Treats a *variable* name as a mathematical function so that it will not be printed in italics
HORZ	Specifies a distance to move horizontally, in increments that are a percentage of the current font size (for example, *HORZ 100* moves the cursor 12 points to the right if you're using a 12-point font; *HORZ −100* moves the cursor 12 points to the left for a 12-point font)
ITAL	Italicizes a *variable,* symbol, or function
LEFT	Defines a delimiter that will expand to the size of the sub-group it encloses; if LEFT is used in an equation, RIGHT must also be used, but you don't have to use identical (or matched) left and right delimiter symbols
MATFORM	Used with MATRIX to align *variables,* where ALIGNC, ALIGNL, and ALIGNR specify the alignment, *&* separates columns, and *#* separates rows
MATRIX	Creates a matrix of *variables,* where *&* separates columns and *#* separates rows (think of *&* as meaning "and" and *#* as meaning "over," e.g., *x & y # a & b* means "x and y over a and b")
NROOT	Creates the *n*th root sign over a *variable,* such as *NROOT 3 {x+y}* (the cube root of x + y).
OVER	Creates a fraction by placing one *variable* over a second *variable*
OVERLINE	Places a line over a *variable*
OVERSM	Same as OVER, but reduces the entire construction to the next smaller available font (printer- and font-dependent)

TABLE 21.1:

Equation Commands

COMMAND	DESCRIPTION
PHANTOM	Occupies the same space as the *variable* that follows, but displays only blank space; useful for lining up stacked equations
RIGHT	Used in conjunction with LEFT to display the right delimiter (*see* LEFT)
SQRT	Places a square-root radical over *variable*
STACK	Stacks equations; # is used to start a new line for *variables* that appear on separate rows
STACKALIGN	Stacks *variables* on specified characters; & precedes the character used for alignment in each row and # separates the rows
SUB *or* _	Changes into a subscript the *variable* to its right
SUP *or* ^	Changes into a superscript the *variable* to its right
TO	Used in conjunction with FROM to set starting and ending limits for a symbol
UNDERLINE	Places a bar under the *variable*
VERT	Like HORZ, but moves the cursor vertically in increments that are a percentage of the current point size
{ *and* }	Delineates a group
~	Inserts a full space
`	Inserts a quarter space
&	Used with the MATRIX and MATFORM commands to delineate columns; used with STACKALIGN to indicate the alignment character
#	Used with MATRIX, STACK, and STACKALIGN to delineate rows
.	Used with LEFT and RIGHT to display an invisible delimiter
\	Prints a command literally; for example, *THETA* alone displays the Greek letter theta (Θ), but \ *THETA* displays the word *THETA*

TABLE 21.1:

Equation Commands (continued)

the palette area, you can scroll through the various palettes by pressing Page Up and Page Down.

You can select a symbol from one of these palettes by moving the highlight to the symbol you want and then pressing either ↵ or Ctrl-↵. Pressing ↵ copies the *keyword* for the symbol into the Equation Edit window. For example, pressing ↵ when the Greek letter Θ is highlighted copies the word *theta*. Pressing Ctrl-↵ copies the *actual symbol* for theta to the Equation Edit window.

If you have a mouse, you can select a command or symbol from a palette by first clicking with the left button on the List Commands option at the bottom of the screen. Press Page Down or click on the PgDn option at the bottom of the screen to scroll through the palettes, then double-click with the left button on the symbol you want to use. This method is the same as selecting a command or symbol by pressing ↵.

Note that regardless of whether you use ↵ or Ctrl-↵ to select a symbol, the Display window and printed copy of your document always display the actual symbol. The only exception is if you type a backslash (\), select a symbol such as *theta,* then press ↵. In this case, your equation will contain *theta,* which will be spelled out rather than displayed as the Greek letter.

The other palettes are summarized below, and you can see exactly which symbols are available on each by scrolling through them with the Page Up and Page Down keys:

Large	Offers many symbols that can be sized as either small or large, and delimiters that can be sized with the LEFT and RIGHT commands
Arrows	Contains arrows, circles, triangles, and squares
Sets	Contains set symbols (though union and intersection are on the Large palette)
Greek	Contains uppercase and lowercase Greek letters
Symbols	Contains a set of miscellaneous symbols used in math and logic
Functions	Contains functions such as *cos* and *sin,* which the Equation Editor recognizes as mathematical functions and does not print in italics
Other	Provides diacritical marks and ellipses that are attached to the variable that precedes them

USING THE DISPLAY WINDOW

Keep in mind that nothing you do in the Display window affects the printed equation; this window is provided solely for checking your work as you build your equation.

The Display window in the Equation Editor lets you preview how the equation will look when printed. The Display window is updated when you press Screen (Ctrl-F3) or Graphics (F9), and when you move the cursor into it. You can move the cursor into the Display window at any time by pressing Switch (Shift-F3) or clicking on Switch Window at the bottom of the screen.

Once you are in the Display window, you can move about the equation with the arrow keys, change the magnification by pressing Page Up and Page Down (or by clicking on PgUp and PgDn), and restore the formula to its original position and magnification by pressing Goto (Ctrl-Home) or clicking on Goto Reset at the bottom of the screen. When you've finished checking your formula in the Display window, press Switch (Shift-F3) again to move the cursor back to the Equation Edit window, where you can make additional changes if you wish.

HIDDEN CODES FOR EQUATIONS

The automatic numbering of Equation boxes is the same as the automatic numbering of other boxes, as explained in Chapter 19.

Every equation in a document is stored in a box identified as a hidden code that begins with *Equ Box.* Each Equation box is numbered, so the first Equation box in a document is identified as *Equ Box:1,* the second is identified by *Equ Box:2,* and so forth.

If you add a new equation above others that are already in the document, WordPerfect automatically assigns that box its correct number in the sequence and automatically renumbers all boxes beneath the new Equation box accordingly.

CHANGING AN EQUATION

To change an equation, you first need to know its box number. You can see the number of an Equation box if you move the cursor to the equation's approximate position in the document, or you can turn on the Reveal Codes screen to view its hidden code, which also contains the box number. Then follow these steps to make your changes:

1. Select **G**raphics ➤ Equation ➤ Edit (or press **Alt-F9 E E**).

2. Type the number of the Equation box you want to change and then press ↵.

At this point, you can select options from the box's Definition menu to change the size or placement of the box where the equation is stored, or you can select Edit to return to the Equation Editor and work directly on the equation. When you've finished making your changes, just press Exit (F7) as many times as necessary to return to the Edit screen.

DELETING OR MOVING AN EQUATION

If you want to delete an equation from a document, you must delete the hidden code that displays the equation. You move the cursor to the approximate location of the equation in the document, turn on Reveal Codes, highlight the code of the equation you want to delete, then press Delete.

If you want to move an equation in a document, perhaps so that it is printed below a certain paragraph rather than above it, follow the steps for deleting the equation, then move the cursor to where you want the equation to appear (perhaps below the current paragraph), press Cancel (F1), and select Restore to restore the hidden code at the new cursor location. Then you can turn off the Reveal Codes screen if you wish.

CONTROLLING THE SIZE OF PRINTED EQUATIONS

The size and style of characters used for printing an equation are controlled by two factors: what the current font is and whether or not equations are printed graphically. Most important is the current (or base) font. By default, WordPerfect will print all equations using whatever font is in effect for the rest of the document.

If you want a particular equation to be printed in a different font (including a smaller or larger point size), you must change the base font just before the hidden [Equ Box:] code for that equation. Then, change the base font back to the font used for printing text after the code. You may want to use the Reveal Codes screen to ensure that you're placing the [Font:] codes correctly.

 When selecting a typeface for equations, it's best to use Helvetica, Times Roman, or Courier, because these are the three that WordPerfect can best emulate ("draw") graphically.

As an example, suppose you want a particular equation to be printed in 18-point size and text to be printed in 10-point size. The sequence of hidden codes on the Reveal Codes screen might be as follows:

[Font:Helvetica 18pt][Equ Box:1;;][Font:Times Roman 10pt]

If you want to print all the equations in a document in the same special font (one that's different from the font used for the rest of the document), you don't need to change the font for each [Equ Box:] code. Instead, you can insert an equation options code at the top of the document. Follow these steps:

1. Move the cursor to the top of the document (to the left of the first [Equ Box:] code).

2. Select **G**raphics ➤ **E**quation ➤ **O**ptions, or press **Alt-F9 E O**. This will bring you to a menu for controlling the appearance of the Equation boxes.

3. Change any of the options if you wish. Press Exit (**F7**) to return to the document.

This procedure inserts a hidden [Equ Opt] code in the document at the current cursor position.

Now you can move to the left of the [Equ Opt] code and set the base font for printing equations, then you can move to the right of the code and set the base font for printing text, as below:

[Font:Helvetica 18pt][Equ Opt][Font:Times Roman 10pt]

Unless you make another font change elsewhere, all equations will be printed in the 18-point size, and all text will be printed in the 10-point size.

CONTROLLING
GRAPHICS PRINTING AND ALIGNMENT

By default, WordPerfect prints all equations graphically, "drawing" each character rather than selecting it from the current font. This may make your equations look a little different from the rest of text (which in most cases is probably acceptable). It also centers your equation both vertically and horizontally in an "invisible" box.

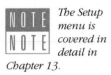

The Setup menu is covered in detail in Chapter 13.

You can change either or both of these defaults through the Setup menu. You can also change them for a single equation or for all equations (globally). Follow these steps:

1. If you want to change the options for a single equation only, select **G**raphics ➤ **E**quation ➤ **E**dit (or press **Alt-F9 E E**), enter the box number, and choose **E**dit. If you want to change the defaults for all equations, start from the normal Edit screen.

2. If you are starting from the Equation Editor, just press Setup (**Shift-F1**). You will see the Equation: Options menu. If you're starting from the Edit screen, select **F**ile ➤ Se**t**up ➤ Initial Settings ➤ **E**quations, or press **Shift-F1 I E**. The Setup:Equation Options menu, shown in Figure 21.5, will appear.

To print equations using characters from the current font, change the **P**rint as Graphics option to No. WordPerfect will then print characters graphically only if they cannot be found in the current font. To print the entire equation graphically, leave the setting at Yes.

The **G**raphical Font Size option lets you determine the size of graphically printed equation characters. Leave this setting at Default if you want to use the size determined by the current font. However, if the Print as Graphics option is set to Yes, you can choose Graphical Font Size, then select **S**et Point Size and enter a point size to print the entire equation at the selected size. (Set Point Size has no effect if the Print as Graphics option is set to No.)

Normally, equations are centered both vertically and horizontally in their boxes. The **H**orizontal Alignment and **V**ertical Alignment options let you change that alignment if you wish. For Horizontal Alignment, you can choose Left (align at the left edge of the box), Center (center horizontally within the box), or Right (align at the right edge of the box). For Vertical Alignment, you can choose Top

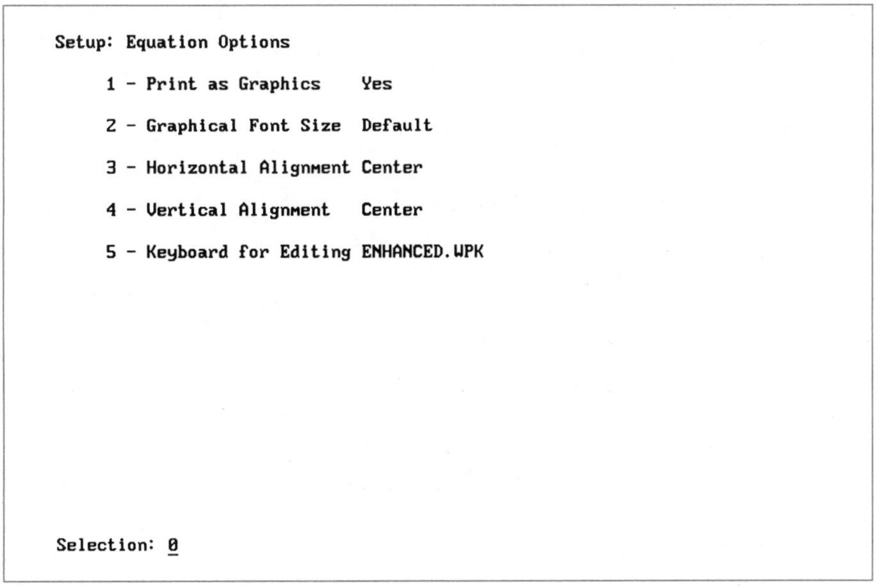

You can control the quality of graphically printed equation characters by setting the Graphics Quality option on the Print menu (see Chapter 8).

```
Setup: Equation Options

     1 - Print as Graphics     Yes

     2 - Graphical Font Size  Default

     3 - Horizontal Alignment Center

     4 - Vertical Alignment   Center

     5 - Keyboard for Editing ENHANCED.WPK













     Selection: 0
```

FIGURE 21.5:

The Equations Options menu

(align at the top edge of the box), Center (center vertically within the box), or Bottom (align at the bottom edge of the box).

If you start from the Edit screen (to set defaults for all equations), you will also see an option for selecting a keyboard. WordPerfect comes with a keyboard named *EQUATION* that lets you enter equations and special symbols without using the palettes. See Chapter 27 for additional information about alternative keyboards.

After making your selections from the menu, you can press Exit (F7) to return to the Edit screen or the Equation Editor (whichever you started from).

USING THE SAME EQUATION IN MULTIPLE DOCUMENTS

Saving an equation does not save the entire document. If you want to keep the equation and the current document, save the document normally when you exit WordPerfect.

If you want to use the same equation in multiple documents, you can save a text version of the equation in its own file. You must first be in the Equation Editor with the equation you want to save displayed on that screen. Then press Save (F10), type in a file name for the equation, and press ↵.

In the future, you can retrieve a copy of that equation onto any blank (or partially filled) Equation Edit screen. To do so, leave the cursor in the Edit window and press Retrieve (Shift-F10). Type in the same path, file name, and extension that you specified when saving the equation, and press ↵. A copy of the equation will be brought into the Equation Editor. You can also retrieve this saved equation by selecting the Filename option on the box Definition menu and typing in the file name.

POSITIONING EQUATIONS

Chapter 19 provides detailed information about working with boxes. Using the techniques described there, you can present equations in a variety of formats, some of which are shown in Figure 21.6.

Keep in mind that an equation can be placed in any type of box. For example, if you want to present an equation as a figure (like the top example in Figure 21.6), go through the steps required to create a Figure box (not an Equation box). When you get to the box Definition menu, select Contents, then select Equation. In the future, whenever you select Edit from that same menu, you'll be taken to the Equation Editor.

This chapter concludes our discussion of desktop publishing techniques. Part 7 of this book introduces you to some of the features that will make your work with large documents a lot easier, including automatic outlining and numbering, the subject of the next chapter.

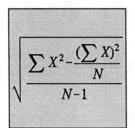

You can put equations into any type of box and adjust the appearance of the box using techniques described in Chapter 19. This equation is in a shaded Figure box. To put an equation into a box, define the box's Contents as Equation on the box definition menu. Then, when you select Edit, you'll be taken to the Equation editor to create or change your equation.

The base font determines the size of the characters in the equation. We changed the base font to 18 point to the left of the hidden code that displays the equation above. Then we changed the base font back to Courier 10 pitch before typing these paragraphs.

An equation can be placed in a line, like $\cos\theta = \sqrt{1-\sin^2\theta}$, by anchoring its box to a character. In this example, the equation is in a User box that's anchored to the comma following the equation, and has a vertical position of Baseline. You may also need to increase the line height so that all lines are equally spaced.

In the example below, the equation is in a centered, auto-sized User box. The box itself is in a table cell.

PROD FROM {x=1} TO INF	$\prod\limits_{x-1}^{\infty}$

PART SEVEN

Managing the Big Jobs

This part covers WordPerfect's powerful automatic referencing features, which help you to automatically create outlines, tables of contents, indexes, tables of authorities, figure lists, table lists, and cross-references. You'll also learn about the Master Document feature, which expands your automatic reference skills by letting you use those same features across multiple documents. These features are particularly useful if you develop larger documents, like books, dissertations, and corporate reports.

CHAPTER 22

Automatic Numbering and Outlining

Automatic numbering is a powerful and versatile tool that you can use for any type of numbering, including items in numbered lists and section numbers. The advantage of using automatic, as opposed to manual, numbering of items is that if you add, change, or delete a numbered item, all the other numbered items are updated instantly and automatically to reflect your change. For many people, this one feature alone is worth the price of the WordPerfect product, and as you'll see, is also quite easy to use.

AUTOMATIC PARAGRAPH NUMBERING

If you need to number items in a list or sections in a document, you can use the *paragraph-numbering* feature. You can use a simple, single-level numbering scheme, like a numbered list (1, 2, 3, 4, 5, and so on), or a hierarchical scheme with up to eight levels (for example, 1, 1.1, 1.1.1, 1.1.1.1, and so on).

Because there are so many ways to number items in documents, Word-Perfect offers many different numbering schemes, as well as the ability to create your own scheme. The basic procedure is simple:

1. Move the cursor to where you want to begin using automatic numbering.

2. Define your numbering scheme.

3. Use your defined numbering scheme.

If you number items or sections in your document, then change your mind about your numbering scheme, you can easily switch to a different scheme without retyping. And you can use as many different numbering schemes as you wish throughout a document.

DEFINING YOUR NUMBERING SCHEME

TO DEFINE A NUMBERING SCHEME FOR AUTOMATIC NUMBERING,

1. Select Tools ➤ Define (or press Shift-F5 D).

2. Choose Paragraph, Outline, Legal, Bullets, or User-defined (to create your own scheme).

3. When you're finished, press Exit (F7) twice.

A numbering scheme is simply a way of numbering items. Figure 22.1 shows two examples: a simple list, with one level of indentation, and a more complex numbering scheme, with three levels of indentation, used in a contract.

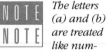 *The letters (a) and (b) are treated like numbers in the numbering scheme.*

If your numbering scheme requires several levels, like the second example shown in Figure 22.1, the automatic number that appears in your document is determined by how far the cursor is indented when you insert the automatic number. For example, in Figure 22.1, the numbers *1* and *2* are not indented; the numbers *2.1, 2.2,* and *2.3* are each indented one tab stop; *(a)* and *(b)* are each indented two tab stops.

As a convenience, WordPerfect offers four predefined numbering schemes, named Paragraph, Outline, Legal, and Bullets, any one of which might suit you well. However, if none of these schemes meets your needs, you can easily create your own, "user-defined," numbering scheme. (Keep in mind that you can define a numbering scheme for a document you've already typed.)

To choose your numbering scheme, follow these steps:

1. Move the cursor to where you want to start using automatic numbering.

2. Select **T**ools ➤ **D**efine (or press **Shift-F5 D**). The Paragraph Number Definition menu, shown in Figure 22.2, appears.

3. Choose one of the predefined schemes (**P**aragraph, **O**utline, **L**egal, **B**ullets), or create your own scheme (as described below).

4. Press Exit (**F7**) twice to return to the Edit screen.

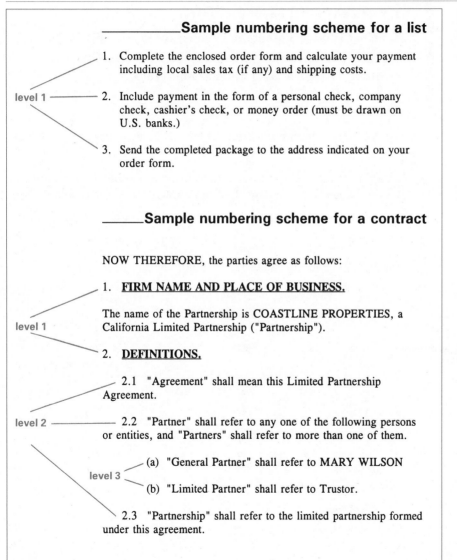

FIGURE 22.1:

Two examples of numbering schemes

_____Sample numbering scheme for a list

1. Complete the enclosed order form and calculate your payment including local sales tax (if any) and shipping costs.

level 1

2. Include payment in the form of a personal check, company check, cashier's check, or money order (must be drawn on U.S. banks.)

3. Send the completed package to the address indicated on your order form.

_____Sample numbering scheme for a contract

NOW THEREFORE, the parties agree as follows:

1. <u>**FIRM NAME AND PLACE OF BUSINESS.**</u>

The name of the Partnership is COASTLINE PROPERTIES, a California Limited Partnership ("Partnership").

level 1

2. <u>**DEFINITIONS.**</u>

2.1 "Agreement" shall mean this Limited Partnership Agreement.

level 2

2.2 "Partner" shall refer to any one of the following persons or entities, and "Partners" shall refer to more than one of them.

(a) "General Partner" shall refer to MARY WILSON

level 3

(b) "Limited Partner" shall refer to Trustor.

2.3 "Partnership" shall refer to the limited partnership formed under this agreement.

WordPerfect inserts a [Par Num Def] code at the cursor position, and any automatic numbers that you insert below that point will adhere to the numbering scheme you've chosen.

INSERTING AUTOMATIC NUMBERS

TO INSERT AN AUTOMATIC NUMBER,

1. Press an indent key if necessary.

2. Select Tools ➤ Paragraph Number (or press Shift-F5 P).

3. Press ↵ to have the numbering level based on the indent, or type a level number and press ↵.

Once you've defined your numbering scheme, it's easy to insert the automatic numbers:

1. Position the cursor where you want to insert a number. If you want to indent, press Tab, →Indent (F4), or →Indent← (Shift-F4) as necessary.

2. Select **T**ools ➤ **P**aragraph Number (or press **Shift F5 P**). This prompt appears:

Paragraph Level (Press Enter for Automatic):

Basic indentation and alignment with tab stops and the Tab, →Indent (F4), and →Indent← (Shift-F4) keys are introduced in Chapter 4.

```
Paragraph Number Definition

     1 - Starting Paragraph Number             1
         (in legal style)
                                           Levels
                           1    2    3    4    5    6    7    8
     2 - Paragraph         1.   a.   i.   (1)  (a)  (i)  1)   a)
     3 - Outline           I.   A.   1.   a.   (1)  (a)  i)   a)
     4 - Legal (1.1.1)     1    .1   .1   .1   .1   .1   .1   .1
     5 - Bullets           •    o    -    ■    *    +    •    x
     6 - User-defined

     Current Definition    I.   A.   1.   a.   (1)  (a)  i)   a)
     Attach Previous Level      No   No   No   No   No   No   No

     7 - Enter Inserts Paragraph Number        Yes

     8 - Automatically Adjust to Current Level  Yes

     9 - Outline Style Name


Selection: 0
```

FIGURE 22.2:

The Paragraph Number Definition menu

3. If you want WordPerfect to automatically determine the level based on how far the cursor is currently indented, press ↵. If you want to choose the level yourself, type the level and press ↵. (For example, if you are using the Legal style and enter *2* as the level, the number will be in the format "X.X" regardless of how far the cursor is indented, because "X.X" is the format of level-2 numbers in the Legal style.)

The Edit screen shows the automatic number; the Reveal Codes screen shows the hidden codes for numbers.

WordPerfect inserts a [Par Num] code at the cursor position, which appears as the appropriate number on the Edit screen. You can then press the spacebar, or Tab, →Indent, or →Indent←, and type your text next to the number.

If you're using automatic numbering, you can easily change the level number and indentation of your paragraph after you've typed it. Just turn on the Reveal Codes screen, move your cursor to highlight the [Par Num:Auto] code, then press Tab to insert a tab code and indent a level, or press Backspace to delete a tab code and outdent a level. Each time you press Tab, you'll indent and move down one level; each time you delete a tab, you'll outdent and move up one level.

If you've chosen a fixed-level number (i.e., typed a level number in step 3 above), inserting and deleting tabs will change the indent level, but will have no effect on the paragraph number.

If the wrong automatic number appears on your screen, keep in mind that the number is determined by three factors: 1) the currently defined numbering scheme, 2) how far the cursor is indented with tab or indent codes, and 3) whether you let WordPerfect determine the level or enter the level yourself. If necessary, you can delete the [Par Num] code on the Reveal Codes screen to delete the number, then change your numbering scheme or tab ruler and try again.

Note also that if you insert or delete an automatic number, or change the paragraph-numbering scheme, WordPerfect does not adjust automatic numbers below the cursor until you move the cursor past those numbers.

To save time and keystrokes, you can create a macro (Chapter 15) that inserts an automatic number and any tab, →Indent, →Indent←, or margin-release codes associated with it.

CREATING YOUR OWN NUMBERING SCHEME

TO DEFINE YOUR OWN NUMBERING SCHEME,

1. **Select Tools ➤ Define (or press Shift-F5 D).**

2. **Select User-defined and define the format of each automatic number at each indent level. Press Exit (F7) when finished.**

3. **Select other Paragraph Number Definition options as desired, then press Exit (F7).**

If none of WordPerfect's predefined numbering schemes fits the bill for you, you can create your own by following these steps:

1. Position the cursor where you want to start your numbering scheme. (Remove any previous [Par Num Def] codes on the Reveal Codes screen so they don't cancel your new definition.)

2. Select **Tools ➤ Define** (or press **Shift-F5 D**) to get to the Paragraph Number Definition menu.

3. Select **U**ser-defined and describe the format of each automatic number at each level of indentation, using the menu that appears near the lower-left corner of your screen as a guide.

4. Select any other options (described in the following section) to define your numbering scheme.

5. Press Exit (**F7**) to return to the Edit screen. WordPerfect inserts a [Par Num Def] code at the current cursor position, and any [Par Num] codes beneath the cursor position adhere to the defined numbering scheme.

Remember that any existing automatic paragraph numbers will not be updated to reflect the new numbering scheme until after you move the cursor past them.

After you've selected User-defined as your numbering scheme, symbols that you can use to define the format of each number at each level appear near the lower-left corner of the screen, as in Figure 22.3. Remember that these symbols are just examples, not the actual letters or numbers that appear in your document, except in the case of other characters (bullets or punctuation marks) not listed as symbols.

The symbols are the following:

1	Digits (1, 2, 3, 4, etc.)
A	Uppercase letters (A, B, C, D)
a	Lowercase letters (a, b, c, d)
I	Uppercase Roman numerals (I, II, III, IV, V)
i	Lowercase Roman numerals (i, ii, iii, iv, v)
X	Uppercase Roman/Digits if Attached (I, II, III if attached to previous level; 1, 2, 3 if not attached to previous level)
x	Lowercase Roman/Digits if Attached (i, ii, iii if attached to previous level; 1, 2, 3 if not attached to previous level)
Other Character	Any character other than 1, A, a, I, i, X, or x is printed literally (not interpreted as a symbol)

The numbers, letters, and symbols you type for each level will appear on the Current Definition line on the screen. Press Tab (or ↵) to move right across levels and Margin Release (Shift-Tab) to move left across levels. (If you continue pressing Tab or ↵, your cursor will move past the last-level number format and into the Attach Previous Level line.) Press Exit (F7) when finished.

Attaching to the Previous Level

If one of the default numbering formats is already close to what you want, you can first select that format, then choose User-defined and customize it as needed.

When defining the format for each numbering level, you can press ↓ to move to the Attach Previous Level line, shown in Figure 22.3. This lets you determine whether or not to attach the current level number to the previous one. For example, if you define the level-1 number format as *1* and the level-2 format as *.1*, and set the Attach Previous Level option for the level-2 number to Yes, the automatic numbers appear in this format:

9
   9.1
   9.2
   9.3

```
Paragraph Number Definition

    1 - Starting Paragraph Number              1
        (in legal style)
                                        Levels
                            1     2     3     4     5     6     7     8
    2 - Paragraph           1.    a.    i.    (1)   (a)   (i)   1)    a)
    3 - Outline             I.    A.    1.    a.    (1)   (a)   i)    a)
    4 - Legal (1.1.1)       1     .1    .1    .1    .1    .1    .1    .1
    5 - Bullets             •     o     -     ■     ✕     +     •     ✕
    6 - User-defined

    Current Definition     _I.    A.    1.    a.    (1)   (a)   i)    a)
    Attach Previous Level         No    No    No    No    No    No    No

    7 - Enter Inserts Paragraph Number         Yes

    8 - Automatically Adjust to Current Level  Yes

    9 - Outline Style Name

1 - Digits, A - Uppercase Letters, a - Lowercase Letters
I - Uppercase Roman, i - Lowercase Roman
X - Uppercase Roman/Digits if Attached, x - Lowercase Roman/Digits if Attached
Other character - Bullet or Punctuation
```

FIGURE 22.3:

The number formats available for User-defined numbering schemes appear in the lower-left corner of the screen.

If, however, the Attach Previous Level for the level-2 number is set to No, the automatic numbers appear in this format:

9
.1
.2
.3

Using Characters in the Numbering Format

If you want to use a character as part of a number (or all by itself, for that matter), simply type the character. For example, you can include a period or parenthesis with each number, as in the predefined Paragraph and Outline numbering schemes on the Paragraph Number Definition menu. If you want to use special characters, as in the predefined Bullets scheme, press Compose (Ctrl-2), then type the code of the special character you want to use (see Chapter 5). For instance, you can press Ctrl-2 and type two asterisks to produce a bullet.

Other Numbering Options

In the sections that follow, I'll describe the other options available to you on the Paragraph Number Definition menu.

Starting Paragraph Number This option lets you determine the starting number of the first automatic number below the cursor. Normally this number is *1*, but you may need to change it. For example, if the current document is actually Part 3 of a large document (or a master document, covered in Chapter 24), you might want to number the sections as 3.1, 3.1.1, 3.2, and so forth. Your starting number in that particular document is *3*, not *1*.

You can change the starting number scheme at the start of the document or anywhere within the document.

When entering the starting number, be sure to use a number. For example, even if your level-1 "numbers" are A), B), C), and so forth, and you want to start numbering at C), enter *3* as your starting number. WordPerfect will automatically convert that to C) when you use the numbering scheme.

Enter Inserts Paragraph Number This option determines whether pressing ↵ automatically inserts the next automatic number when you are using your numbering scheme in Outline mode, as described under "Automatic Outlining" later in this chapter. If this option is set to No, you must select **Tools ➤ P**aragraph Number (or press Shift-F5 P) to enter automatic numbers, even when you are in Outline mode. If you leave this option set to Yes, automatic numbers are automatically inserted when you press ↵ if Outline mode is on. (As you'll learn later, you can still omit the numbers with Outline mode turned on by pressing Ctrl-V then ↵.)

Automatically Adjust to Current Level This option determines whether pressing ↵ causes the next line to be at the same level as the current line. When this option is set to Yes (the default), pressing ↵ in Outline mode creates a new sister topic—a topic at the same level as the one just completed—and you must press Margin Release (Shift-Tab) to remove a level of indentation, or Tab to add one. When this option is set to No, WordPerfect automatically brings the cursor back to the leftmost level of the outline whenever you press ↵.

Outline Style Name This option lets you choose a previously defined outline style for your numbering scheme (discussed later in this chapter).

AUTOMATIC OUTLINING

TO TURN ON AUTOMATIC OUTLINING,

select Tools ➤ Outline ➤ On (or press Shift-F5 O O).

As we all learned in school, an outline is a great way to get started with any large document. But as we also know, developing an outline is usually a trial-and-error effort. You start with a basic list, add topics and subtopics, then often add, delete, change, and move ideas and topics.

Developing and refining an outline manually is often a messy job, involving lots of erasing, cutting, pasting, and rewriting, simply because the outline changes as you refine your thoughts. But WordPerfect's Outline feature lets you easily change and even reorganize your outline to match your latest whim and, as you may have guessed, automatically renumbers every item as you make changes.

USING AUTOMATIC OUTLINING

In a nutshell, WordPerfect's Outline mode is just a minor variation of automatic paragraph numbering. When you are not in Outline mode, you must position the cursor and select **T**ools ➤ **P**aragraph Number (or press Shift-F5 P) to insert a new automatic number. But in Outline mode, just pressing ↵ automatically inserts the next automatic number for you, which can save a lot of keystrokes. Outline mode also lets you move, copy, or delete entire chunks of outline text without losing the numbering sequence.

To use automatic outlining, follow these steps:

1. Move the cursor to where you want to start typing your outline.

2. Select **Tools** ➤ Outline ➤ **On** (or press **Shift-F5 O O**). The word "Outline" appears in the lower-left corner of your screen as a reminder that Outline mode is turned on, and WordPerfect inserts an [Outline On] code at the cursor position.

3. Press ↵ to insert automatically the first outline number.

4. Press the spacebar, Tab, or other indent key, then type the text of this outline item.

5. Press ↵ to move to the next item; WordPerfect inserts the next number at the current outline level. You can press ↵ more than once if you want to add blank lines between items and move the outline number down. If you want to insert a new line of text without adding another outline number, press Ctrl-V before pressing ↵.

6. If you want to *promote* (indent a level), press Tab once for each level; if you want to *demote* (outdent a level), press Margin Release (Shift-Tab) once for each level.

7. Repeat steps 4–6 as many times as you wish.

8. When you are ready to start working with normal, unnumbered paragraph text, deactivate Outline mode by selecting **Tools** ➤ **Outline** ➤ **Off** (or pressing **Shift-F5 O F**). (If there's a leftover outline number above the cursor, press ↑, then press Delete as many times as needed to remove it.)

When you turn off Outline, WordPerfect inserts an [Outline Off] code at the cursor position. Anytime the cursor is between the [Outline On] and [Outline Off] codes, automatic outlining is available. Hence, there is no need to reactivate the Outline feature should you decide to add to your outline later; just move the cursor anywhere within the existing outline.

MODIFYING YOUR OUTLINE

The outline scheme is WordPerfect's default numbering scheme.

Because an outline is just a specialized mode of paragraph numbering, modifying it is as easy as modifying any automatic number. For example, to change the numbering scheme of your outline, move the cursor to the top of the outline (*before* the [Outline On] code), select **Tools** ➤ **Define** (or press Shift-F5 D), and define your numbering scheme as explained earlier in this chapter. (Remember that any existing numbers remain unchanged until you move the cursor past them.)

To indent or outdent an item, turn on Reveal Codes and insert or delete [Tab] codes until the item is at the level you want. To insert an item, move the cursor to the end of the item above your insertion point and press ↵, then press Tab or Margin Release (Shift-Tab) to change the level of indentation (if necessary).

You can use all the usual deletion techniques, including blocking, to delete any text, as well as [Par Num:Auto] codes that display the item number. However, if you want to delete entire line items or groups of line items, you'll find the Delete Family option, described next, much easier and more convenient.

MOVING, COPYING, AND DELETING OUTLINE FAMILIES

An outline consists of groups of related topics. Each topic is placed on a line by itself. Ideas related to the main topic are placed one level below the topic as subtopics, or *daughters,* of the main topic. Topics at the same organizational level are called *sisters.* A topic and all its subtopics make up a *family,* as illustrated in Figure 22.4.

WordPerfect provides a few special options for manipulating entire families of topics in an outline: Move Family, Copy Family, and Delete Family. To use one of these options, follow these steps:

1. Position the cursor on the number of the topmost topic of the family you want to move, copy, or delete.

2. Select **T**ools ➤ **O**utline (or press **Shift-F5 O**).

3. Choose **M**ove Family, **C**opy Family, or **D**elete Family. The entire family is highlighted. You can now choose to do one of the following:

   ◆ If you chose Move Family or Copy Family, use the arrow keys to position the highlighted family within the outline. As you move through the outline, the highlighted family will also move and its numbering levels will be adjusted accordingly. Press ↵ to complete the move or copy operation.

   ◆ If you chose Delete Family, select either **Y**es to delete the highlighted family or **N**o if you change your mind.

   ◆ Press Cancel (**F1**) to leave the highlighted family unchanged.

USING OUTLINE STYLES

TO CREATE AN OUTLINE STYLE,

1. Select Tools ➤ Define ➤ Outline Style Name (or press Shift-F5 D N).

2. Select Create ➤ Name, then enter a name for your outline style. Optionally, enter a description.

3. For each numbering level, define the type (Paired or Open), the formatting and paragraph-numbering codes, and the role for the ↵ key. When finished, press Exit (F7) until you return to the Edit screen.

OUTLINE

I. Prologue
    A. Introduction of Child Secret-Keeping
       1. Overview of Topic Area
       2. Purpose of the Study
    B. Hypotheses

II. Assessment of Secret-Keeping
    A. Literature Review
       1. Research Findings
       2. Family Background Factors
    B. Family Systems Theory
    C. Theory of Conditions
    D. Theory About Secrecy

III. Patterns of Secrecy
    A. Method
       1. Description of Subjects
       2. Protection of Subjects
    B. Design Considerations

IV. Description of Research
    A. Secret-Keeping Behavior
    B. Description of Procedure
    C. Examples of Secret-Keeping
    D. Design and Data Analysis

V. Results
    A. Tests of the Hypotheses
    B. Summary of Results

VI. BIBLIOGRAPHY

VII. APPENDICES

sister topics, both daughters to topic A. above

family

FIGURE 22.4:

A sample outline

A user-defined numbering scheme lets you define the general numbering scheme (e.g., digits, Roman numerals, letters, etc.); an outline style lets you define the actual appearance of numbers and text at each level.

Chapter 14 discusses WordPerfect styles, which are a great tool for using design elements easily and consistently throughout a document. The general techniques for creating and using paired and open styles are discussed in detail there.

Outline styles, discussed in this chapter, are unique in that you can assign different codes and other attributes to each numbering level, all within a single style. This lets you create numbering schemes that are more refined than those created at the Paragraph Number Definition menu, primarily because you can include formatting codes.

CREATING OUTLINE STYLES

You can create an outline style from either the general Styles menu or the special Outline Styles menu. In fact, the only difference between the two menus is that the Styles menu displays all the styles in the current style library; the Outline Styles menu displays only outline styles (i.e., no paired or open styles). To avoid unnecessary confusion, I'll stick with the Outline Styles menu in this section.

To create an outline style, follow these steps:

1. Select **T**ools ➤ **D**efine ➤ Outline Style **N**ame (or press **Shift-F5 D N**) to get to the Outline Styles menu (Figure 22.5).

2. Select **C**reate to get to the Outline Styles: Edit menu (Figure 22.6).

3. Select **N**ame, and enter a name for your outline style (up to 17 characters; it can include blank spaces).

4. Optionally, select **D**escription and enter a brief description of the style, up to 54 characters.

5. Use the ↑ and ↓ keys to move the highlight to the numbering level whose style you want to define. For example, to define the style of the first-level number, the highlight should be on level 1 (see Figure 22.6).

6. Select **T**ype, then either **P**aired or **O**pen. (In most cases, you'll want to select Paired so that the style codes for the current level do not affect other levels).

7. Select **C**odes. This takes you to the screen for entering formatting codes. You can use the pull-down menus or shortcut keys to select formatting codes defining the appearance of text at this outline level

(see the next section, "Codes for Outline Levels"). Press Exit (**F7**) after defining your codes.

The Enter option is available only for paired outline styles.

8. Select **E**nter and choose the role played by the ↵ key after you type the text for the level. Your choices are

Hrt	Inserts a hard return normally, without turning off the style; you must press → then ↵ to insert another paragraph number (in Outline mode).
Off	Turns off the style; you must press ↵ again to insert another paragraph number (in Outline mode).
Off/**On**	Turns the style off and then on so that you can insert the next numbered item. If you want to insert a blank line between items, include one or more hard returns below the [Comment] code.

9. Repeat steps 5–8 for each level where you want to define a style.

10. Press Exit (**F7**) to work your way back to the Edit screen.

CODES FOR OUTLINE LEVELS

When defining the style of the number and text at a given outline level, you'll see the same screen used for defining regular styles, except that the [Par Num] code

```
Outline Styles

   Name              Description

   -- NONE --        Use paragraph numbers only
   Document          Document Style
   Right Par         Right-Aligned Paragraph Numbers
   Technical         Technical Document Style















 1 Select; 2 Create; 3 Edit; 4 Delete; 5 Save; 6 Retrieve; 7 Update: 1
```

FIGURE 22.5:

The Outline Styles menu

is inserted automatically to display the paragraph number. For example, you'll see [Par Num:1] when defining level 1, [Par Num:2] when defining level 2, and so on. If you want to use an automatic paragraph number instead of a manual paragraph number, you must delete the existing [Par Num] code, then insert a [Par Num:Auto] code by selecting **T**ools ➤ **P**aragraph Number, then Automatic (by pressing ↵).

In Figure 22.1, at the start of this chapter, the style for level-1 topics in the second example is Bold and Underlined.

You can also use any formatting codes that you'd use with other kinds of styles, including fonts, print attributes (bold, underline, and so forth), print sizes, tab and indent codes, and graphics. Place your formatting codes either before or after the [Par Num] code to determine whether the paragraph number itself or just the text that follows the number will be formatted. If you are using a paired style to define the current outline level, codes above the [Comment] code are turned on when the style is activated, and codes below the [Comment] code are turned off when the style is deactivated.

Figure 22.7 shows an example of a style definition for a single paragraph level. Here's the role played by each code:

[DEC TAB]   Decimal-aligns the automatic paragraph number at the next tab stop (entered by selecting **L**ayout ➤ **A**lign ➤ **T**ab Align or pressing Ctrl-F6)

```
Outline Styles: Edit

  Name:

  Description:


  Level  Type        Enter

    1    Open
    2    Open
    3    Open
    4    Open
    5    Open
    6    Open
    7    Open
    8    Open





 1 Name; 2 Description; 3 Type; 4 Enter; 5 Codes: 0
```

FIGURE 22.6:

The Outline Styles: Edit menu

[Par Num:Auto]	Displays the automatic number (entered by selecting **T**ools ➤ **P**aragraph Number, and pressing ↵ for automatic level numbering)
[→Indent]	Indents the cursor to the next tab stop (entered by pressing F4)
[BOLD][UND]	Boldfaces and underlines the text to the right of the automatic number at this level (entered by pressing F6 and F8)
[Comment]	Separates the [Style On] codes from the [Style Off] codes and appears automatically when defining a paired style
[HRt][HRt]	Inserts two hard returns after the text typed next to the automatic number when you later put this style to use (entered by pressing ↵ twice after pressing ↓ to move the cursor past the [Comment] code)

NOTE *Because the [BOLD] and [UND] codes follow the [Par Num] code, only the text, not the number, will be bold and underlined. The closing [bold] and [und] codes are not necessary because this is a paired style.*

ACTIVATING OUTLINE STYLES

TO ACTIVATE AN OUTLINE STYLE,

1. **Select Tools ➤ Define ➤ Outline Style Name (or press Shift-F5 D N).**

2. **Highlight the outline style you want to activate, press ↵ or choose Select, then press Exit (F7).**

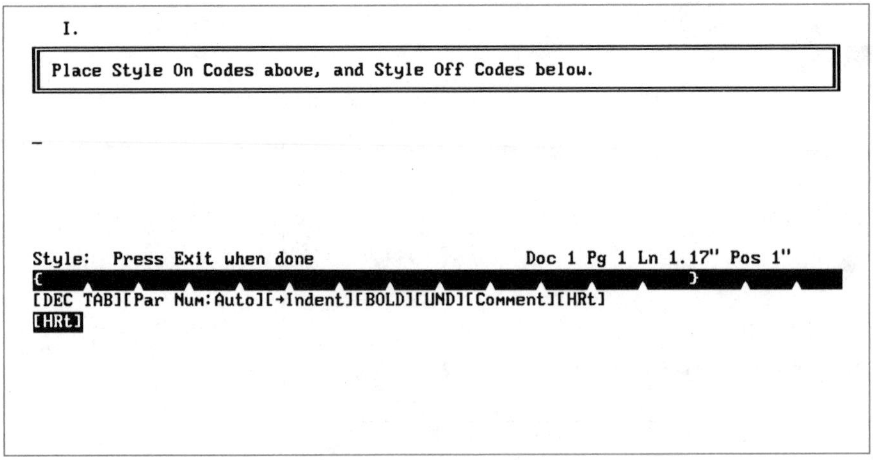

```
   I.

┌──────────────────────────────────────────────────────────────┐
│ Place Style On Codes above, and Style Off Codes below.         │
└──────────────────────────────────────────────────────────────┘


   ─



Style:   Press Exit when done              Doc 1 Pg 1 Ln 1.17" Pos 1"
{                                                   }
[DEC TAB][Par Num:Auto][→Indent][BOLD][UND][Comment][HRt]
[HRt]
```

FIGURE 22.7:

Sample style codes for a single outline level

> **3. Choose Outline ➤ On if you want to turn on the Outline mode, or press ↵ to leave the Outline mode turned off.**

Outline styles are displayed on both the Styles menu and the Outline Styles menu. However, you can only activate outline styles from the Outline Styles menu. Follow these steps:

1. At the Edit screen, move the cursor to where you want to use the outline style.

2. Select **T**ools ➤ **D**efine ➤ Outline Style **N**ame (or press **Shift-F5 D N**), which brings you to the menu of existing outline styles.

3. Move the highlight to the name of the outline style you want to activate, then press ↵ or choose Se**l**ect.

4. You are returned to the Paragraph Number Definition menu, and the name of the outline style you just selected is listed next to the Outline Style Name option. Press Exit (F7).

5. From the bottom menu that appears, you can choose **O**utline then **O**n if you want to turn on the Outline mode, or press ↵ to leave the Outline mode turned off.

As a shortcut, you can activate an outline style as soon as you're finished creating it by highlighting its name on the Outline Styles menu and choosing Select.

The outline style determines the format of numbers and text at each level in an outline. The current numbering scheme still determines what kind of numbering is used at each level (Digit, Roman, Letter, Bullet, etc.).

Outline styles are stored in the same libraries as other paired and open styles. See Chapter 14 for reminders on how to manage style libraries.

At this point, WordPerfect inserts a [Par Num Def:] code in your document at the cursor position, with the name of the outline style after the colon. This code acts like the [Par Num Def] code for any of the predefined numbering schemes described earlier (Paragraph, Legal, Bullets, etc). That is, if you turn on the Outline mode, you can press ↵ to start inserting numbers automatically. If you do not turn on the Outline mode, you can still activate the styles by inserting paragraph numbers with the **T**ools ➤ **P**aragraph Number options (Shift-F5 P).

MANIPULATING OUTLINE STYLES

Outline styles are saved with the document and can be stored in libraries, just like other styles. You can manipulate your outline styles from the Outline Styles menu the same way you manipulate ordinary styles from the Styles menu; the same options (Create, Edit, Delete, Save, Retrieve, and Update) are available. (On the Outline Styles menu, however, Update updates only outline styles, not all the styles in the current library. Also, the Outline Styles menu uses the Select option in place of the On and Off options on the Styles menu.)

SAMPLE OUTLINE STYLES

The sample style library, LIBRARY.STY, that comes with your WordPerfect package includes the three sample outline styles described below:

Document: Each level sets the style of a section heading in a document and includes codes for automatically generating a table of contents. For example, level 1 is large type and might be a main heading, level 2 is underlined, level 3 is boldface, and so forth.

Right Par: This style right-aligns automatic numbers at the current tab stop; this is useful for typing general numbered lists.

Technical: Like Document, this includes table-of-contents codes, but has different spacing and formatting styles at each level.

You might want to explore these styles on your own to learn more about outline styles. Start with an empty Edit screen and retrieve the LIBRARY.STY style library (select **T**ools ➤ **D**efine or press Shift-F5 D; then choose Outline Style **N**ame ➤ **R**etrieve ➤ LIBRARY.STY). If you see the message "Style(s) already exist. Replace? **N**o (**Y**es)", choose Yes. Then highlight a style name and press ↵ to select it. Press Exit (F7), then select **O**utline ➤ **O**n if you want to activate Outline mode.

Experiment with the Tab, Margin Release (Shift-Tab), and ↵ keys, and (if you did not activate the Outline mode) try inserting some paragraph numbers. Check the View Document screen to see how the outline style affects your text.

To learn more about the style, you can select **T**ools ➤ **D**efine ➤ Outline Style **N**ame ➤ **E**dit (Shift-F5 D N E). You'll see the name and description of the style, as well as the type (paired or open) and the role of the Enter key for each level in the style. To view the codes for a particular level in the style, highlight the level you are curious about and select Codes.

NUMBERING LINES

TO TURN ON AUTOMATIC LINE NUMBERING,

select Layout ➤ Line ➤ Line Numbering ➤ Yes (or press Shift-F8 L N Y), choose the line number options you want, then press Exit (F7).

NOTE NOTE *The verti-
cal line
separating
the line
numbers from the text
in Figure 22.8 is a
graphic line, dis-
cussed a little later in
this section.*

WordPerfect can number each line in your document or just certain sections, formats that are commonly used in the legal profession. The numbers are generally printed in the left margin of the document, as in the example shown in Figure 22.8. As you'll see, however, you can print the numbers anywhere on the page.

Line numbering is a completely separate feature from automatic and outline numbering. You cannot devise your own numbering schemes or use multiple levels. In fact, line numbering is activated as a formatting option from the Layout menu rather than from the Tools menu.

```
 1 │ STEVEN C. SMITH
 2 │ 53505 Orange Avenue
 3 │ Los Angeles, CA  90025
 4 │
 5 │ Telephone:  (123) 435-1200
 6 │
 7 │
 8 │ STEVEN C. SMITH, Complainant
 9 │
10 │
11 │
12 │
13 │               UNITED STATES OF AMERICA
14 │
15 │                     BEFORE THE
16 │
17 │        COMMODITY FUTURES TRADING COMMISSION
18 │
19 │
20 │
21 │ In the Matter of the Reparations  )   CFTC DOCKET NO.  90-S205
22 │ Proceeding Between:                )
23 │                                    )   COMPLAINANT'S APPEAL
24 │ STEVEN C. SMITH                    )   INFORMAL DOCUMENT
25 │                                    )
26 │      Complainant,                  )
27 │                                    )
28 │ and                                )
29 │                                    )
30 │ LEVER BROTHERS, INC.               )
31 │ and JOHN JONES                     )
32 │                                    )
33 │      Respondents.                  )
34 │ ─────────────────────────────────
35 │
36 │
37 │               INTRODUCTION
38 │   My Work Priority Policy - A prerequisite to other outside
39 │ involvement activities.  My work requires that I have no outside
40 │ interruption of any kind, except in an emergency.
41 │   As an introduction to any discussion of my undertaking with
42 │ others, including financial investments that could disturb me at my
43 │ work, except for emergencies, that the above policy be carefully
                          -1-
```

FIGURE 22.8:

A sample document with line numbers

ADDING LINE NUMBERS

To add line numbers to a document automatically, follow these steps:

1. Position the cursor where you want the line numbering to start.

2. Select **L**ayout ➤ **L**ine ➤ Line **N**umbering ➤ **Y**es (or press **Shift-F8 L N Y**). The Line Numbering menu appears (Figure 22.9).

3. Select the options you want, if any, as explained in the following sections.

4. Press Exit (**F7**) to return to your document.

WordPerfect inserts a hidden [Ln Num:On] code at the cursor position, marking the spot in the document where line numbering will start. The following sections explain the options available on the Line Numbering menu.

Count Blank Lines This option determines whether blank lines created by multiple hard returns will be counted in the numbering. Turn this option off if you only want to number lines that contain text. Note that lines left blank by your line-spacing setting are never numbered.

Number Every n Lines, Where n Is This option sets the increment for the *printed* line number. When set to 1, every line number is printed. When set to 2, only every other line number is printed. This option does not affect how the line numbers are calculated, only how often WordPerfect actually prints the numbers.

Position of Number from Left Edge This option sets the position of the line number from the left edge of the page, inside the margin. Be careful not to set the line numbers between the page margins. For example, if you have a 1-inch left margin, your entry should be some number that's less than *1*. Otherwise, the line numbers will be printed on top of your text.

Starting Number This option lets you set a new starting number for the lines. Normally, line numbering starts at *1* whenever you activate it. You might need this option if you stop line numbering in the middle of a document and then want to pick it up again later, using numbers relative to the previous numbering rather than starting over again from *1*.

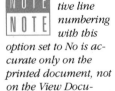

Restart Numbering on Each Page This option determines whether line numbering will start anew on each page. When Yes (the default) is selected, each page will be numbered with the value specified by the Starting Number option (usually *1*). Otherwise, the value used will be carried over from the previous page.

Chapter 5 explains how to change fonts, and Chapter 7 discusses headers and footers. Endnotes and footnotes are introduced in Chapter 23.

The line numbers are printed using the base font in effect at (or before) the position of the [Ln Num:On] code. To change the font of the line numbers, turn on Reveal Codes and place your font selection code just to the left of the [Ln Num:On] code. Then move the cursor to the right of the [Ln Num:On] code, and choose the font you want to use in the rest of the document. Footnotes and endnotes are included in line numbering, but page headers and footers are not. To ensure that new codes and text do not affect line numbering, you may want to place the line-numbering code in the Document Initial Codes area.

TURNING OFF LINE NUMBERING

To turn off line numbering, follow these steps:

1. Position the cursor where you want the numbering to stop.

2. Select **Layout** ➤ **Line** ➤ **Line Numbering** ➤ **No** (or press **Shift-F8 L N N**).

```
Format: Line Numbering

     1 - Count Blank Lines              Yes

     2 - Number Every n Lines, where n is   1

     3 - Position of Number from Left Edge  0.6"

     4 - Starting Number               1

     5 - Restart Numbering on Each Page   Yes











Selection: 0
```

FIGURE 22.9:

The Line Numbering menu

ADDING A SEPARATOR LINE

NOTE
NOTE
You can print graphic lines only if you have a printer that can print graphics.

If you want to add a line that separates the line numbers from the text, as in Figure 22.8, and you want that line to appear on every page, place a vertical graphic line in a header that's printed on every page. Follow these steps:

1. Move the cursor to the top of the document.

2. Select **L**ayout ➤ **P**age (or press **Shift-F8 P**). Then choose **H**eaders ➤ Header **A** *or* Header **B** ➤ Every **P**age.

3. Select **G**raphics ➤ **L**ine ➤ Create **V**ertical (or press **Alt-F9 L V**).

4. Define the line from the options shown on the screen (Figure 22.8 uses these default options: left margin, full page, 0.013", and 100 percent shading).

5. Press Exit (**F7**) three times to return to the Edit screen.

You'll need to switch to the View Document screen or print a page to verify your new header.

In the next chapter, I'll look at automatic referencing, a tool that helps you create tables of contents, indexes, figure lists, table lists, footnotes, and endnotes, and also lets you update them automatically as you make changes to your document.

CHAPTER 23

Automatic Referencing

Many documents require referencing with footnotes and endnotes, tables of contents, indexes, figure and table lists, cross-referencing, and more. As you'll see in this chapter, WordPerfect can simplify the creation and management of all these items and, in true WordPerfect style, can automatically update them as you add, change, and delete text in your document.

ADDING FOOTNOTES AND ENDNOTES

Many scholarly, scientific, and technical documents use footnotes and endnotes to reference additional reading material or to provide parenthetical or related information that is not essential to the flow of the text. Footnotes are typed at the bottom of the page, and endnotes are generally typed at the end of the document.

Figure 23.1 shows an example of a page printed with two footnotes at the bottom. These footnotes refer to the superscripted numbers 1 and 2 in the text. Figure 23.2 shows an example of endnotes used as a bibliography at the end of a document.

If you've ever had to use a standard typewriter to type a document with footnotes, you know what an unpleasant task this can be. As you might expect, this process is much easier with WordPerfect, because you just type the note right at its reference point in the document, and WordPerfect automatically places it at the bottom of the page or at the end of the document. You can easily add and delete notes without having to worry about renumbering them, since WordPerfect handles this automatically. If you add, change, or delete text later, WordPerfect will properly reposition the note, if necessary, the next time you print the document.

Only two of Archimedes' works on mechanics have been handed down to us. These are titled *On the Equilibrium of Planes or Centers of Gravity of Plane Figures* and *On Floating Bodies*. Both were published in 1543 by Nicolo Tartaglia, and Italian mathematician. In the *Equilibrium*, Archimedes dealt with the lever which, along with the wedge, roller, pulley, and inclined plane, belonged to the simple machines of his time. Archimedes used the concept of the center of gravity, or barycenter, throughout his discussion of the lever, but never explicitly defined this notion.[1]

Great progress in the theory of equilibria followed Archimedes' time. In 1717 Johann Bernoulli proposed the principle of virtual work[2] as the fundamental law of statics. The law states that

> in equilibrium, no work is needed to achieve an infinitesimal displacement of a given mechanical system.

The rule captures both stable and unstable configurations. That is, imagine a steel ball that is free to roll on a landscape with depressions and elevations. If the ball is at the top of a hill, it lies in unstable equilibrium. In the center of a

---

[1] There have been many speculations about why Archimedes never defined the center of gravity. Most scholars believe that the concept had already been defined elsewhere, either by Archimedes or earlier scientists, in a work that has since been lost.

[2] This principle was stated in a letter by Bernoulli to the French physicist Pierre Varignon (1654-1722), written January 26, 1717. It was first published in Varignon's *Nouvelle Mécanique*, vol 2, p. 174, in 1725.

FIGURE 23.1:
An example of Word-Perfect footnotes

TYPING FOOTNOTES AND ENDNOTES

TO TYPE A FOOTNOTE OR AN ENDNOTE,

1. Position the cursor.

2. Select Layout ➤ Footnote *or* Endnote ➤ Create (or press Ctrl-F7 F or E, C).

3. Press the spacebar, Tab, or the indent key (F4), then type the text of your note.

4. Press Exit (F7) when finished.

Other than their positions when printed, footnotes and endnotes are virtually the same in WordPerfect, so I'll just refer to both as "notes" and indicate differences where appropriate.

WordPerfect numbers footnotes automatically; you need not type a number.

All notes consist of two elements: a superscripted number that appears in the text to alert the reader to the note and the note itself. Typing either kind of note is a simple procedure:

1. Move the cursor to where you want the superscripted note number to appear in the text (usually at the end of a sentence, after the period).

2. Select **L**ayout (or press **Ctrl-F7**), then select either **F**ootnote or **E**ndnote, depending on where you want the note positioned.

3. Select **C**reate.

FIGURE 23.2:

An example of Word-Perfect endnotes

NOTES

1. Cf. Bernard Williams, "Tertullian's Paradox" in Antony Flew and Alasdair MacIntyre, eds., *New Essays in Philosophical Theology* (London: Macmillan, 1963), esp. pp 203-205.

2. From a contradiction *anything* follows, see Copi, *Symbolic Logic* (New York: Macmillan, 1954), or any other introductory text in logic.

3. For more remarks on this topic see Ronald Hepburn, *Christianity and Paradox* (London: Watts, 1966), Chs. 9 and 10; and Paul Tillich, *Systematic Theology* (London: Nisbet, 1955) Vol. 1 pp. 231-243.

4. These are ways set forth in the *Summa Theologica*, I q.2, a.3. (Cf. Text Number 3 in the Texts Without Comment at the end of the volume.) We propose to restate the same arguments, however, divesting them of all examples borrowed from ancient physics and formulating them in a language appropriate to modern times.

5. In *De Aeternitate Mundi* (written in 1270-71) St. Thomas made room in advance for the speculations of modern mathematics on infinite multitude.

4. You will see the note number at the top, and the message "Footnote" or "Endnote" at the bottom of an otherwise empty Edit screen.

5. Depending on how you want to space or indent the text following the note number, you can press the spacebar, Tab, or the indent key (F4), then type the text of your note. You can use all the usual editing and formatting features of WordPerfect, including fonts, print attributes, graphics, special characters, Reveal Codes, the Speller, and the Thesaurus, just as you would at the normal Edit screen.

6. When you've typed the entire footnote, press Exit (**F7**) to return to your document.

You'll be returned to the Edit screen. WordPerfect inserts a [Footnote] or [Endnote] code at the cursor position. This code actually contains the text of the note, and some of the text is visible when you move the cursor to the hidden code on the Reveal Codes screen. When you print the document or preview it on the View Document screen, WordPerfect will then put the note in the appropriate place.

If you press ⏎ after typing a footnote, WordPerfect will print an extra blank line beneath your note. If you press ⏎ accidentally, just press Backspace to delete the hard return.

The text of an endnote or footnote is never visible on the Edit screen.

EDITING NOTES

TO EDIT AN EXISTING FOOTNOTE OR ENDNOTE,

1. Move the cursor to the start of the page containing the faulty note.

2. Select Layout ➤ Footnote *or* Endnote ➤ Edit (or press Ctrl-F7 F or E, E).

3. Type the number of the note you want to edit and press ⏎.

4. Edit your note, then press Exit (F7) when finished.

You can use the Search feature (F2, then Ctrl-F7) to look for notes in a large document. See Chapter 9 for more information.

If you make an error in the text of a note, you can easily go back and fix it. Follow these steps:

1. If you have chosen to start note numbering with *1* on each page, move the cursor to the start of the page containing the faulty note. Alternatively, if you're using consecutive note numbering, the cursor can be anywhere in the document.

2. Select **L**ayout (or press **Ctrl-F7**), then select either **F**ootnote or **E**ndnote, depending on which kind of note you need to change.

3. Select **E**dit.

4. Type the number of the note you want to edit and press ↵.

5. Use the normal WordPerfect editing techniques to edit your note.

6. Press Exit (**F7**) when finished.

A single note can contain up to 65,000 bytes, which is basically the same as 65,000 characters.

MOVING AND DELETING NOTES

You can move the superscripted number that refers to a note from one place in your document to another simply by moving the [Footnote] or [Endnote] code for that note. Briefly, the technique is the following: Activate the Reveal Codes screen, place the cursor on the note number you want to move, press Delete, move the cursor to the new position for the note number, press Cancel (F1), then choose **R**estore. WordPerfect will automatically renumber all the notes (as necessary) as you scroll through the document and will print them in their proper places the next time you print the document.

If you inadvertently type regular text inside of your footnote or endnote (or vice versa), you can use the Move feature to move that text. For example, if you need to move some text out of your footnote into your document, go to the Edit screen for that footnote, block the text that needs to be moved, then select **E**dit ➤ **M**ove (Cut) or press Ctrl-Del. Next, press Exit (F7) to leave the note-editing screen, position the cursor wherever you want to move the text, and press ↵ to complete the move.

To delete a footnote or endnote, use the Reveal Codes screen to locate its [Footnote] or [Endnote] code, and delete the code as you would any other. WordPerfect will renumber all the other notes accordingly as you scroll through the document.

RENUMBERING NOTES

As an alternative to remarking the note starting numbers in multiple files, you can use the Master Document feature (Chapter 24) to number notes consecutively in multiple documents.

Normally, the first note in a document is numbered *1,* and any others are numbered consecutively. You can change the starting number at any place in your document. This might be handy if, say, your document is divided into several files, and you need the numbering in one file to pick up where the numbering in another file left off. To set a new note starting number, follow these steps:

1. Move the cursor to wherever you want to restart the numbering sequence (before the code for the first note that you want to renumber).

2. Select **L**ayout (or press **Ctrl-F7**), then select either **F**ootnote or **E**ndnote, depending on which kind of note you want to resequence.

3. Select **N**ew Number.

4. Type the new starting number and press ↵.

WordPerfect inserts a hidden [New Ftn Num:n] or [New End Num:n] code, where n indicates the new starting number, at the cursor position. All notes below that hidden code will be renumbered starting at the new number when you scroll through the document.

CHANGING THE APPEARANCE OF FOOTNOTES

By default, footnotes are printed in the format shown in Figure 23.1 near the start of this chapter. However, you can change the appearance of footnotes in several ways, by means of the Options selection on the Footnote menu. Here's the general procedure:

If you previously changed the footnote options, delete the old [Ftn Opt] code to prevent conflicting codes.

1. Move the cursor to where you want to define the new footnote appearance (e.g., to the top of the document if you want to define the appearance of all the footnotes in the document).

2. Select **Layout ➤** Footnote **➤ O**ptions (or press **Ctrl-F7 F O**). You'll see the menu shown in Figure 23.3.

3. Select the options for the appearances you want, as described in the following sections.

4. Press Exit (**F7**) to return to the Edit screen.

```
Footnote Options

    1 - Spacing Within Footnotes          1
            Between Footnotes             0.167"

    2 - Amount of Note to Keep Together   0.5"

    3 - Style for Number in Text          [SUPRSCPT][Note Num][suprscpt]

    4 - Style for Number in Note                    [SUPRSCPT][Note Num][suprscpt

    5 - Footnote Numbering Method         Numbers

    6 - Start Footnote Numbers each Page  No

    7 - Line Separating Text and Footnotes 2-inch Line

    8 - Print Continued Message           No

    9 - Footnotes at Bottom of Page       Yes




Selection: 0
```

FIGURE 23.3:

The Footnote Options menu

WordPerfect inserts a [Ftn Opt] code at the cursor position, and all footnotes below this code will adhere to the selections you made in step 3. You can check the notes on the View Document screen or by printing the document.

Changing the Spacing of Footnotes

By default, WordPerfect prints one blank line between each footnote at the bottom of the page and single-spaces the text within the footnote. The first option on the Footnote Options menu lets you change both kinds of spacing.

After selecting **S**pacing Within Footnotes (option 1), you can enter a spacing for lines within the note (e.g., *1* for single spacing, *1.5* for one-and-a-half spacing, and *2* for double spacing), then press ↵. Next, you can enter a measurement for spacing between footnotes, either in inches (such as *0.167,* the default) or in points, followed by a *p* (for example, *12p,* which is automatically converted to 0.167 inches because Units of Measure is set to inches).

NOTE NOTE
As mentioned previously, if you press ↵ after typing a footnote, that hard return is printed beneath the footnote as a blank line and will be added to the measurement you enter for option 1.

Keeping Footnotes Together

Footnotes are usually brief, but some situations call for longer footnotes. By default, WordPerfect will print about $1/2$ inch of a lengthy footnote at the bottom of each page, and then "spill" the rest of the note in 0.5-inch increments onto the pages that follow.

To change this, select **A**mount of Note to Keep Together (option 2) from the Footnote Options menu, type a new measurement, and press ↵. For example, if you want each page to display up to 1 inch of text from a lengthy footnote, type *1.*

Changing the Appearance of Footnote Numbers

By default, the numbers that identify footnotes in text are superscripted. Within the note, the number is superscripted and also indented. However, you can change the appearance of these numbers with Style for Number in **T**ext (option 3) and Style for Number in **N**ote (option 4) on the Footnote Options menu.

After selecting either option, you'll see the current format, as in the example below:

[SUPRSCPT][Note Num][suprscpt]

where [SUPRSCPT] and [suprscpt] are the starting and ending codes for the superscript appearance, and [Note Num] is the code that calculates and prints the note number.

If you accidentally delete the [Note Num] code while changing the appearance of the note number, simply press Ctrl-F7 to reinsert the code.

You can delete any existing blank spaces or codes with the Delete key and can insert codes with the shortcut keys (e.g., press Ctrl-F8 to choose a text size, appearance, or font). You can also add text, such as a period, parenthesis, words, or special characters, by using Compose (Ctrl-V). If you want extra spacing before or after your note number, press the spacebar as needed, not Tab or the indent (F4) key. Keep in mind that the position of the note number with respect to the text or any formatting codes will be the same as the position of the [Note Num] code. After defining the appearance of the number, press ↵ (*not* F7).

Changing the Footnote-Marking Style

As you know, WordPerfect normally uses numbers to mark notes. But you can use letters (like *A, B,* and *C*) or special characters (like *, †, and ‡) to mark footnotes instead. To change the appearance of the numbering marker in both the text and the notes, select Footnote Numbering **M**ethod (option 5) from the Footnote Options menu. You'll see the following choices:

1 Numbers; 2 Letters; 3 Characters

Here are your options:

Numbers	Each note is numbered, starting with *1.*
Letters	Each note is lettered, starting with *A.*
Characters	Each note is marked by the character or characters you specify.

The dagger (†) and double dagger (‡) are the special characters 4,39 and 4,40. To enter a special character, press Ctrl-2 (not Ctrl-V), type the code, then press ↵. Special characters may appear as small squares on the screen. See Chapter 5 for more information.

The third option, Characters, merits some explanation. You can choose a single character, such as the asterisk (*), to mark notes. In this case, the first note will be marked with one asterisk, the second note with two asterisks, the third with three asterisks, and so on. When the character has been repeated 15 times to identify a note, WordPerfect starts over with one character.

Alternatively, you can specify up to five characters, each separated by a single blank space. For example, if you specify the three characters

* † ‡

the first note will be marked with an asterisk, the second with a dagger, and the third with a double dagger (note the blank space between each one). A fourth note will be marked with two asterisks, a fifth by two daggers, and so forth, up to 15 repetitions.

Renumbering Footnotes on Each Page

When using special characters instead of numbers to mark footnotes in a document with lots of them, it's best to restart the numbers on each page to prevent having lengthy groups of characters (this way, your characters will "recycle" on each page, starting again with one instance of the first special character).

Normally, WordPerfect numbers footnotes consecutively throughout the document. As an alternative, you can have WordPerfect assign the number *1* (or the first special character in your list) to the first footnote on each page. To have WordPerfect restart numbering on each page, select Start Footnote Numbers each **P**age (option 6) from the Footnote Options menu, and change its setting to Yes.

Separating Footnotes from Text

As you saw in Figure 23.1 early in this chapter, WordPerfect automatically uses a 2-inch horizontal line to separate text from footnotes. To change this format, choose **L**ine Separating Text and Footnotes (option 7) from the Footnote Options menu, then one of these options:

1 No Line; **2** 2-inch Line; **3** Margin to Margin

If you select No Line, WordPerfect does not draw a line separating the text from the footnotes. If you select Margin to Margin, WordPerfect draws a horizontal line from the left margin to the right margin.

Printing "Continued..." on Lengthy Footnotes

If you have a lengthy footnote that spreads across two or more pages, you can have WordPerfect automatically print the message *(Continued...)* below the part of the footnote that is continued to the next page and above the part that is continued from the previous page. To do so, select Print **C**ontinued Message (option 8) from the Footnote Options menu, and change its setting to Yes. Only lengthy footnotes that cross pages will be affected by this change.

Positioning Footnotes

You can place footnotes immediately following the text on a page that is not completely filled, rather than at the bottom of the page. This method is sometimes used in books to keep the footnotes close to the text on the last page of a chapter, which may be only partly filled with text. If you need to use this feature in your own work, select Footnotes at **B**ottom of Page (option 9) from the Footnote Options menu, then select No.

CHANGING THE APPEARANCE OF ENDNOTES

If your document uses endnotes instead of, or in addition to, footnotes, you can refine your endnotes by using many of the techniques described above in the section "Changing the Appearance of Footnotes." Even though you use a different menu, the techniques are generally the same. However, whereas WordPerfect uses [Ftn Opt] as the hidden code to mark the starting position for footnote appearance changes, it uses the code [End Opt] for endnote appearance changes.

To change the appearance of all the endnotes in your document, first move the cursor to the top of the document. Then follow these steps:

1. Select **Layout ➤ Endnote ➤ O**ptions (or press **Ctrl-F7 E O**). The Endnote Options menu, shown in Figure 23.4, appears.

2. Select the options for the appearance and numbering you want to use for the endnotes.

3. Press Exit (**F7**) to return to the Edit screen.

WordPerfect inserts an [End Opt] code at the cursor position, and all endnotes beneath that code adhere to the format and numbering selections you made in step 2. The options on the Endnote Options menu are basically the same as the corresponding ones on the Footnote Options menu (see the preceding section).

```
Endnote Options

     1 - Spacing Within Endnotes           1
              Between Endnotes             0.167"

     2 - Amount of Endnote to Keep Together  0.5"

     3 - Style for Numbers in Text         [SUPRSCPT][Note Num][suprscpt]

     4 - Style for Numbers in Note         [Note Num].

     5 - Endnote Numbering Method          Numbers
```

FIGURE 23.4:

The Endnote Options menu

```
Selection: 0
```

DETERMINING WHERE ENDNOTES WILL APPEAR

WordPerfect endnotes are automatically numbered and placed at the end of a document. But if you have combined several sections or chapters in a single file, you may want to place endnotes closer to their source; for example, at the end of each section or chapter. To change the location of the endnotes, follow these steps:

1. Move the cursor to where you want the endnotes to appear. (To ensure that endnotes start on a new page, you can press Ctrl-↵ to insert a hard page break.)

2. Select **L**ayout ➤ **E**ndnote ➤ **P**lacement (or press **Ctrl-F7 E P**).

3. When prompted with "Restart endnote numbering?", select **Y**es if you want to renumber any remaining endnotes, starting with *1*. Otherwise, select **N**o to continue numbering any remaining endnotes consecutively from where the preceding note left off.

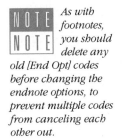

As with footnotes, you should delete any old [End Opt] codes before changing the endnote options, to prevent multiple codes from canceling each other out.

A box containing this message appears on your Edit screen:

Endnote Placement
It is not known how much space endnotes will occupy here.
Generate to determine.

WordPerfect is telling you that until it actually has to print the endnotes, it will not know how much space is needed to print them. You can complete the following steps to have WordPerfect insert the endnotes in your document now:

1. Select **M**ark ➤ **G**enerate ➤ **G**enerate Tables, Indexes, Cross-References, etc. (or press **Alt-F5 G G**).

2. You will see a message indicating that any existing tables, lists, and indexes will be replaced.

3. Select **Y**es.

To title all your endnote pages, you can place a page header at the end of your document with the appropriate title. Or, if you have changed the endnote placement, put the page header between the [HPg] code that ends the body text and the [Endnote Placement] code.

At this point you can press Ctrl-Home twice to move the cursor back to the page where you placed the endnotes. You'll see a box containing the message

Endnote Placement

indicating where the endnotes will be printed. You will also see that WordPerfect places a hard page break (a line of equal signs) below the boxed message. Any text you type above that page break will be printed on the same page as the endnotes. Any text you type below that page break will be printed on a new page, after the last endnote. If you switch to the View Document screen with the cursor on the endnotes page, you'll see the actual endnotes.

CHOOSING A FONT FOR NOTES

See Chapter 5 for more information on fonts.

By default, footnotes and endnotes are printed in the same font as the rest of the text, or using whatever base font is in effect at the location of the [Ftn Opt] or [End Opt] code. This means that you can set a font for all notes by moving the cursor to the left of a [Ftn Opt] or an [End Opt] code and selecting a base font for the notes, then moving the cursor to the right of the options code and selecting a base font for the regular body text. For example, in the following code sequence, all the footnotes will be printed in Times Roman Italic 10-point; regular body text will be printed in Times Roman 12-point:

[Font:Times Roman Italic 10pt][Ftn Opt][Font:Times Roman 12pt]

Of course, any font selection within the text of a note will override the base font selection specified here.

If you want to insert a [Ftn Opt] or an [End Opt] code at the cursor position without changing the default settings, just choose **Layout ➤ Footnote ➤ Options** (Ctrl-F7 F O) or **Layout ➤ Endnote ➤ Options** (Ctrl-F7 E O) and press Exit (F7) without making selections from the Options menu.

USING AUTOMATIC REFERENCE LISTS

TO MARK AND GENERATE LISTS AND CROSS-REFERENCES,

1. **Block the items to be referenced, then choose an option from the Mark menu (select Mark or press Alt-F5).**

2. **Move the cursor to where you want the generated list to appear, and select an option from the Mark ➤ Define menu (Alt-F5 D) to define the list.**

3. **Choose Mark ➤ Generate ➤ Generate Tables, Indexes, Cross-References, etc. ➤ Yes (Alt-F5 G G Y) to generate the lists or cross-references.**

The Master Document feature (Chapter 24) lets you generate reference lists from multiple documents stored in separate files.

A *reference list* is a list of items in a document and the page numbers on which they appear. With WordPerfect you can *mark* items to be placed in a reference list and define the location and format of the list. Then, before printing the document, you can instruct WordPerfect to *generate* the final list, complete with the proper page-number references. You can regenerate your reference list at any time to reflect changes in page numbers resulting from changes made to your document. WordPerfect documents can have four types of reference lists:

◆ Table of contents

◆ Index

◆ General list (useful for lists of figures and tables)

◆ Table of authorities (a legal-style bibliography)

The general steps for creating each kind of list are basically the same:

◆ Mark all the items in the document that belong in the list, using options on the Mark pull-down menu, shown in Figure 23.5, or options shown after you press the Alt-F5 shortcut key.

◆ Define the list (i.e., specify its format and its position in the document).

◆ Adjust the page numbers if necessary.

◆ Generate the list.

You can do any of these steps at any time, so you can create your lists as you write your document or after your document is complete. And of course, you can

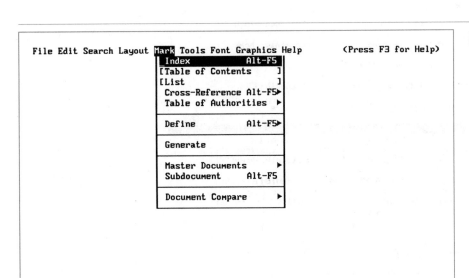

FIGURE 23.5:

The Mark pull-down menu, used for automatic referencing

make any additions, deletions, and changes to your document, and have WordPerfect automatically update all the lists to reflect your changes. I'll discuss the specific steps for marking items and defining each type of list in the sections that follow.

Marking Table-of-Contents Entries

If you want to mark titles, headings, or any other text for inclusion in a table of contents (ToC), follow these steps:

1. Block the text that you want to include in the ToC with your mouse or the Block (Alt-F4 or F12) and arrow keys, as in the example shown in Figure 23.6.

2. Select **M**ark ➤ Table of **C**ontents (or press **Alt-F5 C**). You'll see the prompt

   ToC Level:

3. Enter the level of indentation (1–5) for the entry, where *1* is the leftmost level.

4. Press ↵.

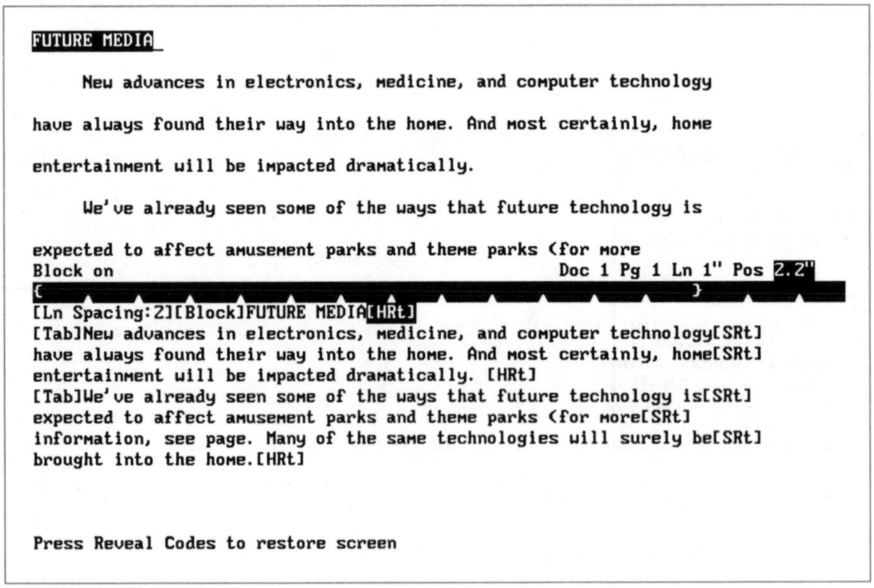

```
FUTURE MEDIA

     New advances in electronics, medicine, and computer technology

have always found their way into the home. And most certainly, home

entertainment will be impacted dramatically.

     We've already seen some of the ways that future technology is

expected to affect amusement parks and theme parks (for more
Block on                                    Doc 1 Pg 1 Ln 1" Pos 2.2"
[
[Ln Spacing:2][Block]FUTURE MEDIA[HRt]
[Tab]New advances in electronics, medicine, and computer technology[SRt]
have always found their way into the home. And most certainly, home[SRt]
entertainment will be impacted dramatically. [HRt]
[Tab]We've already seen some of the ways that future technology is[SRt]
expected to affect amusement parks and theme parks (for more[SRt]
information, see page. Many of the same technologies will surely be[SRt]
brought into the home.[HRt]


Press Reveal Codes to restore screen
```

FIGURE 23.6:

A sample heading blocked for inclusion in a table of contents

WordPerfect surrounds the blocked text with [Mark:ToC] and [End Mark:ToC] codes, visible on the Reveal Codes screen.

DEFINING A TABLE OF CONTENTS

After marking all (or some) ToC entries, you can define the position and format of the ToC by following these steps:

1. Move the cursor to the start of your document with **Home Home** ↑ (or wherever you want to place the table of contents).

2. Create a page break (**Ctrl-↵**) to put the ToC on its own page.

3. To ensure proper page numbering, move the cursor to the top of the first numbered page (i.e., page number 1 after the title page, ToC, figure lists, and any other front matter). Then select **Layout ➤ Page ➤ Page Numbering ➤ New** Page Number (or press **Shift-F8 P N N**) and assign page number 1 to that page. Press Exit (**F7**) to return to the Edit screen.

4. Move the cursor back to the page where you want to print the ToC (on or above the [HPg] code you inserted in step 2).

5. Select **Mark ➤ Define ➤** Table of **C**ontents (or press **Alt-F5 D C**). You'll see the Table of Contents Definition menu, shown in Figure 23.7.

6. Choose whatever options you need to specify the format of each level within your ToC (described in "Formatting the Table of Contents").

7. Press Exit (**F7**) to return to the Edit screen.

*You can also use Layout ➤ Page ➤ PageNumbering ➤ New Page Number (or press Shift-F8 P N N) to number the front-matter pages with Roman numerals (e.g., **i, ii**), as described in Chapter 7.*

WordPerfect inserts a hidden [Def Mark:ToC] code at the cursor position. When you generate the lists, WordPerfect inserts the table of contents below that.

Position the cursor on or above the code before typing a title or creating a page heading.

FORMATTING THE TABLE OF CONTENTS

The options on the Definition menu let you specify the format of your table of contents, as summarized below:

Number of Levels: Lets you choose how many levels are displayed in your table of contents, in the range 1 to 5.

Display Last Level in Wrapped Format: If this is set to Yes, WordPerfect word-wraps the last level in the ToC if it's longer than one line (you cannot choose a flush-right style for this level).

Page Numbering: Lets you choose a format for printing page numbers at each level in the ToC.

The formats for Page Numbering are

None	No page numbers
Pg # Follows	Page number follows the entry, separated by a space
(Pg #) Follows	Page number, enclosed in parentheses, follows the entry, separated by a space
Flush Rt	Page numbers flush with right margin next to the entry
Flush Rt with **L**eader	Flush-right page numbers preceded with dot leaders (as in Figure 23.8)

MARKING TABLE-OF-CONTENTS ENTRIES WITH STYLES

You can use the Styles feature to format section or chapter titles and headings by including codes for the table of contents right in the styles. For example,

```
Table of Contents Definition

    1 - Number of Levels        1

    2 - Display Last Level in   No
          Wrapped Format

    3 - Page Numbering - Level 1  Flush right with leader
                          Level 2
                          Level 3
                          Level 4
                          Level 5




Selection: 0
```

FIGURE 23.7:

The Table of Contents Definition menu

you can mark all the chapter titles as ToC level-1 entries, all the main headings as ToC level-2 entries, all the subheadings as ToC level-3 entries, and so forth.

See Chapter 14 if you need more information on creating or using styles.

To do this, first define the style for whichever design element you want to format (e.g., the chapter title or main headings). Then, edit the codes for that style and move the highlight to the [Comment] code. Then press Block (Alt-F4 or F12) and →. The entire comment will appear highlighted in the upper portion of the screen, and "Block on" will blink in the lower-left corner.

Next, select **M**ark ➤ Table of **C**ontents (or press Alt-F5 C), and enter the level for this style (e.g., *1* for chapter titles and *2* for main headings). Press ⏎. You'll see the [Mark:Toc] code to the left of the [Comment] code and the [End Mark:Toc] code to the right. Save the style as you normally would.

While (or after) creating your document, use the styles to format the chapter titles, headings, and so forth. Then define the ToC, as described in the preceding sections, and generate the list, as described later.

MARKING INDEX ENTRIES

To generate an index from a document stored in two or more separate files, use the Master Document feature (Chapter 24).

You can also mark entries for inclusion in an index. WordPerfect indexes offer two levels of entries: the index heading and the subheading, as shown in Figure 23.9. You can define your index entry at either or both of these levels.

Here's how to identify an index entry:

1. Move the cursor to the word you want to include in the index, or, if you want to include a phrase (two or more words) as a single entry, block those words with your mouse or the Block (Alt-F4 or F12) and arrow keys.

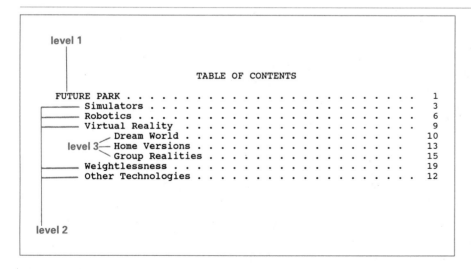

FIGURE 23.8:

A sample generated table of contents

You can select a particular word or phrase in the text (step 1), but use an entirely different heading (step 3) or subheading (step 4) for its printed index entry. For instance, you can select an occurrence of the word "gander" and print its index entry with the heading "goose" and the subheading "male."

You can press Cancel (F1) to erase the suggested subheading, leaving the subheading blank for this entry.

2. Select **Mark** ➤ **Index** (or press **Alt-F5 I**).

3. The prompt

Index Heading:

followed by the selected word or phrase appears. If you want the entry to be a heading, press ↵. If you want the entry to be a subheading, or if you want to use a different heading for this entry, type the index heading you want and press ↵.

4. The prompt

Subheading:

appears. If you typed a heading in step 3, the selected word or phrase appears as the suggested subheading; otherwise, the subheading is blank. Press ↵ to use the displayed entry (if any) as a subheading, or type a different subheading and press ↵.

USING AN INDEX CONCORDANCE FILE

As an alternative to marking items individually in a document for inclusion in an index, you can simply make a file consisting of a list of all the words you want included. This word list is called a *concordance file*. When creating a concordance file, you must end each entry with a hard-return [HRt] code (by typing the entry, then pressing ↵). Figure 23.10 shows a sample concordance file on the Edit screen.

```
                         INDEX

        Amusement  1, 2
            engineers  1
        Questor  1, 6
        Robotics  1, 9, 12─────────────────── index heading
            entertainment  15─┐
            industrial  10    ├───────── subheading
            home  11,14──────┘
        Simulators  1, 15
        Star Tours  1, 25
        Theme parks  1, 12
        Toontown  1, 16
        Universal  1
        Virtual reality  1, 10, 24
```

FIGURE 23.9:

A sample index illustrating a heading and subheadings

WordPerfect will be able to generate the index more quickly if the concordance file entries are in alphabetical order. You can use the Sort feature (Chapter 17) to alphabetize the entries.

By default, each entry in the concordance file is a main heading. To convert an entry to a subheading, mark it as a subheading in the concordance file by following the steps in "Marking Index Entries." If you want the entry to be matched as both a heading and subheading, mark the entry twice: once as a heading and once as a subheading. After creating your concordance file, save it as you would any other WordPerfect document.

DEFINING THE INDEX

Before you generate the index, you must mark its location, define its format, and, if you plan to use a concordance file, specify the concordance file name. Follow these steps:

1. Move the cursor to where you want the index to appear in your document. (Press Home Home ↓ to move to the end of the document.)

2. If you want to start the index on a new page, press **Ctrl-↵** to insert a hard page break.

3. Select **Mark ➤ Define ➤ Index** (or press **Alt-F5 D I**).

4. If you have created a concordance file, type its complete file name at the "Concordance Filename" prompt that appears. If you did not create a concordance file, press ↵.

```
amusement
audio
computers
energy
engineers
entertainment
HDTV
home
industrial
lasers
masers
medicine
questor
research
robotics
simulators
star tours
theme parks
toontown
travel
universal
video
virtual reality_

                         Doc 1 Pg 1 Ln 4.67" Pos 2.5"
```

FIGURE 23.10:

A sample concordance file

5. The Index Definition menu appears (see Figure 23.11). Select a format for the page numbers. The choices on this menu are the same as those you saw when defining the table of contents, as described earlier.

WordPerfect inserts a [Def Mark:Index] code at the cursor position, marking the spot where the index will appear when you generate the lists (described in "Generating the Lists" later in this chapter). The index is alphabetized automatically.

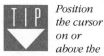

Position the cursor on or above the code before typing a title or creating a page heading.

MARKING GENERAL-LIST ENTRIES

To generate general lists from a document stored in two or more separate files, use the Master Document file (Chapter 24).

General lists are lists of items that don't necessarily fit into the index or table-of-contents format. For example, you might want to mark words or phrases in text for inclusion in a glossary or bibliography. You can have up to five such general lists (lists 1–5).

WordPerfect can also automatically create lists of numbers and captions from graphic boxes. Figure 23.12 shows a sample list of figures.

```
Index Definition

    1 - No Page Numbers

    2 - Page Numbers Follow Entries

    3 - (Page Numbers) Follow Entries

    4 - Flush Right Page Numbers

    5 - Flush Right Page Numbers with Leaders












Selection: 5
```

FIGURE 23.11:

The Index Definition menu

You need not mark graphic boxes to generate a list for them. Instead, WordPerfect has predefined lists 6 through 10 as follows:

LIST NUMBER	CONTENTS
6	Numbers and captions from all Figure boxes
7	Numbers and captions from all Table boxes
8	Numbers and captions from all Text boxes
9	Numbers and captions from all User boxes
10	Numbers and captions from all Equation boxes

> **NOTE NOTE** *Only numbered and captioned boxes are included in lists 6–10. Also, only tables in graphic Table boxes are included in list 7.*

To mark an item for inclusion in one of the general lists (1–5), follow these steps:

1. Use your mouse or the Block (Alt-F4 or F12) and arrow keys to block the word or phrase you want to put in a general list.

2. Select **Mark** ➤ **List** (or press **Alt-F5 L**).

> **NOTE NOTE** *You can include other items in lists 6–10 if you wish, but those entries will be mixed in with the graphic-box entries (if any).*

3. When prompted, type a list number (1–5) and press ↵. (If you're creating multiple general lists, it's up to you to remember which list is which; e.g., list 1 is the glossary, list 2 is the bibliography, and so forth.)

WordPerfect surrounds the word or phrase with [Mark:List,*x*] and [End Mark:List,*x*] codes, where *x* indicates the number of the list that will contain the word or phrase after you define and generate that list.

DEFINING A GENERAL LIST

After defining the items for your list, or if you're simply generating a list of graphic-box numbers and captions using the predefined lists, you must define the list's location and format by following these steps:

1. Move the cursor to where you want to create the list in your document.

```
                    LIST OF FIGURES
Figure 1. Projected and Actual Cash Flow, 1991  . . . . . . . .  1
Figure 2. Projected Cash Flow, 1992 . . . . . . . . . . . . .  3
Figure 3. Quarterly Sales for 1991  . . . . . . . . . . . . .  6
```

FIGURE 23.12:
A sample list of figures

2. If you want the list to appear on its own page, insert a hard page break by pressing **Ctrl-↵**.

3. If you are placing the list before numbered page 1 (e.g., in the document's front matter), move to the first numbered page and select **Layout ➤ Page ➤ Page Numbering ➤ New** Page Number (**Shift-F8 P N N**) to ensure that page 1 is numbered properly, as explained earlier in "Defining a Table of Contents."

4. Select **Mark ➤ Define ➤ List** (or press **Alt-F5 D L**).

5. Type the number of the list you're defining (1–10) and press ↵. The List Definition menu appears (Figure 23.13).

6. From the menu, choose a format for the page numbers in the generated list (see the table-of-contents sections if you need more information about each option).

7. Optionally, press **Ctrl-↵** to have a new page start after the list.

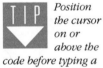 *Position the cursor on or above the code before typing a title or creating a page heading.*

You'll be returned to the Edit screen. WordPerfect inserts a [Def Mark:List,*x.y*] code at the cursor position, where *x* is the list number and *y* is the number of the option you've selected from the List Definition menu. When you generate the lists, as described later in this chapter, the list will be placed just below this code.

```
List 1  Definition

    1 - No Page Numbers

    2 - Page Numbers Follow Entries

    3 - (Page Numbers) Follow Entries

    4 - Flush Right Page Numbers

    5 - Flush Right Page Numbers with Leaders




Selection: 5
```

FIGURE 23.13:

The List Definition menu

Marking Table-of-Authorities Entries

A table of authorities (ToA) is a list of citations in a legal document (see Figure 23.14). It is typically divided into several sections, such as *Cases, Statutes,* and *Regulations,* with each section having a different format.

The document itself (typically a brief) generally contains two types of citations: a long form, which is usually the first reference in the document, and a short form, which is an abbreviated way of indicating subsequent references to the same authority. When using WordPerfect to generate a ToA, you initially mark all instances of the long form. Then you assign a short form to that authority, and from that point onward in the document you can mark all references to the same authority by using the short form.

NOTE
NOTE

As with all forms of automatic referencing, if your document is lengthy and divided into several files, you can use the Master Document feature (Chapter 24) to generate a table of authorities for all the files.

Marking the Long Form

To create the initial long-form ToA entry, follow these steps:

1. Use your mouse or the Block (Alt-F4 or F12) and arrow keys to block the long form of the citation, as in the example shown in Figure 23.15.

2. Select **M**ark ➤ Table of **A**uthorities ➤ Mark **F**ull (or press **Alt-F5 A**).

```
                    TABLE OF AUTHORITIES

Cases                                                    Page

Association of General Contractors v.
City and County of San Francisco
813 F.2d 922 (1987) . . . . . . . . . . . . . . . . 1, 9

City of Richmond v. Croson, 109 S.Ct. 706 (1989) . . . . . 1, 13

Fullilove v. Klutznick, 448 U.S. 448, 100 S.Ct 2758,
65 L.Ed. 2d 902 (1980) . . . . . . . . . . . . . . . 2, 13

Gregory Construction Co. v. Blanchard
691 F.Supp. 17 (W.D. Mich. 1988) . . . . . . . . . 12, 14, 15

Jackson v. Conway, D.C. Montana 1979, 472 F.Supp. 896 . . . 8, 11

London v. Coopers & Lybrand
C.A. Cal 1981, 644 F.2d 811 (1981) . . . . . . . . . . . 12


Statutes

California Public Contract Code, Section 10115 . . . . . . . 12
```

FIGURE 23.14:

A sample table of authorities

3. Enter a section number (1–16), based on your own organization of the table. For example, you might use section 1 for cases, section 2 for statutes, and so forth. As with general lists, it's up to you to keep track of which section is which.

4. You are taken to a special editing screen where you can change the ToA entry. Changes here are reflected in the table, but not in the document. Press Exit (**F7**) to proceed.

5. When prompted, enter the short-form name. Press ↵ to accept the suggested entry, or type a short form of your choosing, then press ↵.

NOTE NOTE
Each short-form entry must be unique, since each identifies a separate authority.

Marking the Short Forms

After you mark the long form of the citation, mark all the subsequent occurrences of the short form. You can use the Search feature to help:

NOTE NOTE
The Search feature is optional; you can mark any short-form entry simply by blocking it and selecting **M**ark ➤ *Table of* **A**uthorities ➤ *Mark* **S**hort *(or by pressing Alt-F5 A).*

1. Move the cursor to the top of the document (**Home Home ↑**).

2. Select **S**earch ➤ **E**xtended ➤ **F**orward (or press **Home F2**).

3. Type the short form (or part of the short form).

4. Press Search (**F2**).

5. If the cursor lands to the right of a valid short form, as in Figure 23.16, select **M**ark Text ➤ Table of **A**uthorities ➤ Mark **S**hort (or press **Alt-F5 A**). (If this isn't a valid short form, return to step 2 and repeat the search.)

Construing plaintiff's claims liberally, especially in light of United States Supreme Court decision in `City of Richmond v. Croson, 109 S.Ct. 706 (1989)`, plaintiff has established the patent invalidity of the "quotas", since such quotas have been found to violate Sections 1981, 1983 and 2000(d). See, for example, Association of General Contractors v. City and County of San Francisco, Ninth Circuit Court of Appeals, 813 F.2d 922 (1987).

VI

PLAINTIFF'S CAUSE OF ACTION FOR DECLARATORY RELIEF IS IDENTICAL TO THE CASE PRESENTED IN GREGORY CONSTRUCTION V. BLANCHARD, 691 F. SUPP. 17 (See Exhibit "A").

Block on   Doc 1 Pg 1 Ln 1.5" Pos `3.8"`

FIGURE 23.15:
A sample long-form ToA entry blocked on the Edit screen

6. Press ↵ to accept the suggested short-form name, or enter the correct short-form name and then press ↵.

7. Repeat steps 2–6 for each remaining short form in the document.

After completing these steps, you've defined the long and short form of a single authority in a single section. You must repeat the general procedure for each authority in the document.

DEFINING THE TABLE OF AUTHORITIES

You define a table of authorities one section at a time. Follow these steps:

1. Position the cursor where you want the table of authorities listed (usually at or near the beginning of the document).

2. To insert a hard page break, press Ctrl-↵.

3. To ensure proper page numbers, move the cursor to page 1 (beyond the ToA and any other front matter), and select **Layout** ➤ **P**age ➤ Page **N**umbering ➤ **N**ew Page Number (or press **Shift-F8 P N N**) to mark that page as page 1.

4. Move the cursor wherever you want the next section heading for the ToA to appear, and type the heading (e.g., *Cases, Statutes,* or *Regulations*). Typically this will be on or above the hard page break you entered in step 2.

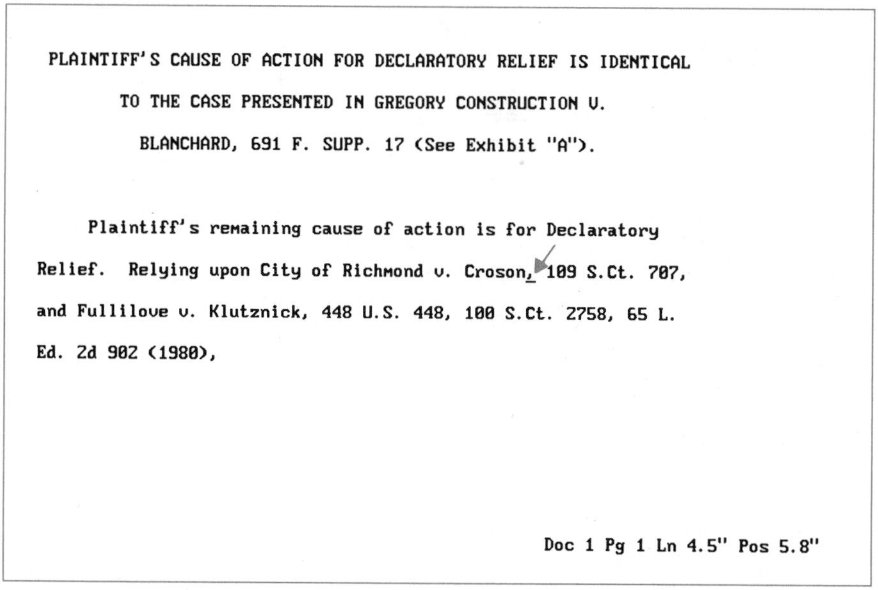

NOTE
NOTE
If you fail to indicate a new page number beyond the ToA page, WordPerfect will warn you later when you generate the lists. You can simply press any key to continue generating the lists, then make any changes or corrections later.

PLAINTIFF'S CAUSE OF ACTION FOR DECLARATORY RELIEF IS IDENTICAL

TO THE CASE PRESENTED IN GREGORY CONSTRUCTION V.

BLANCHARD, 691 F. SUPP. 17 (See Exhibit "A").

Plaintiff's remaining cause of action is for Declaratory

Relief. Relying upon City of Richmond v. Croson, 109 S.Ct. 707,

and Fullilove v. Klutznick, 448 U.S. 448, 100 S.Ct. 2758, 65 L.

Ed. 2d 902 (1980),

Doc 1 Pg 1 Ln 4.5" Pos 5.8"

FIGURE 23.16:
The cursor is just to the right of a short form of the authority blocked in Figure 23.15.

5. Select **M**ark ➤ **D**efine ➤ Table of **A**uthorities (or press **Alt-F5 D A**).

6. Type the number of the section (1–16) that you want to define, and press ↵. The Definition for Table of Authorities menu appears, shown in Figure 23.17.

7. Select formatting options for the current section to suit your needs:

Dot Leaders	If Yes, dot leaders precede page numbers, which are flush with the right margin. If No, dot leaders won't appear.
Underlining Allowed	If Yes, any underlining from the original document entries is retained. If No, any underlining is removed.
Blank Line Between Authorities	If Yes, authorities are double-spaced. If No, authorities are single-spaced.

8. Press Exit (**F7**) to return to the Edit screen.

Repeat steps 4–8 for each section in the ToA. WordPerfect inserts a [Def Mark:ToA,*x*] mark at the cursor position, where *x* is the number of the current section. When you generate the lists, as described later in this chapter, the citations for each section will be listed beneath each section's [Def Mark:ToA] code.

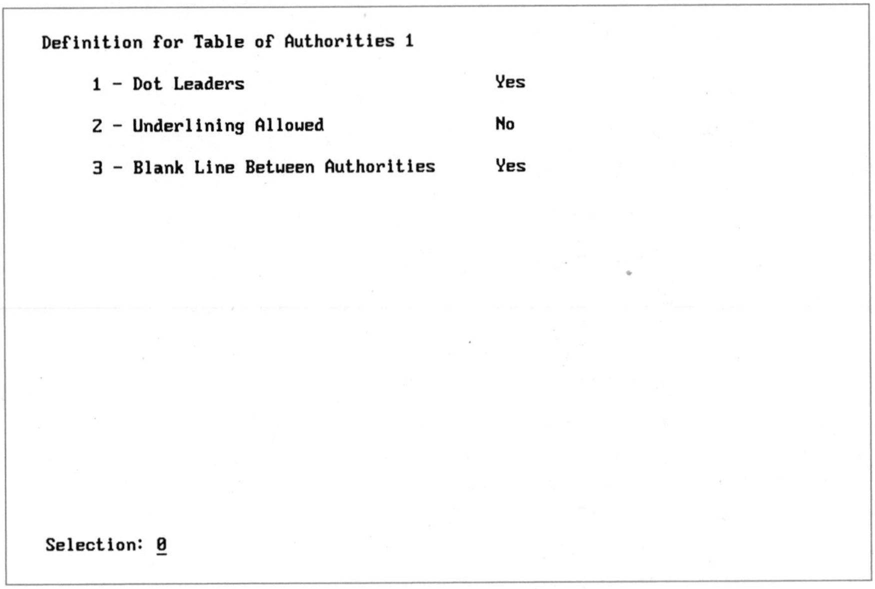

> **NOTE**
> *You can change the default setting for tables of authorities by selecting **F**ile ➤ Set up ➤ **I**nitial Settings ➤ Table of **A**uthorities (Shift-F1 I A).*

```
Definition for Table of Authorities 1

    1 - Dot Leaders                     Yes

    2 - Underlining Allowed             No

    3 - Blank Line Between Authorities  Yes
```

```
Selection: 0
```

FIGURE 23.17:

The Definition for Table of Authorities menu

AUTOMATIC CROSS-REFERENCING

Suppose that somewhere in your document you refer to a table a few pages back. At the current cursor position, you want to type a cross-reference, such as "see the table on page 14." But perhaps you don't know the page number, or (more likely) you don't know what the page number will be after a few more hours (or days) of writing and editing.

To keep the terms "target" and "reference" straight, just remember that a reference always points to its target.

WordPerfect offers a cross-reference feature that will keep track of such cross-references automatically. The item referred to (the table on page 14 in the example) is known as a *target*. The place where you mention the target is known as a *reference*.

Your cross-references need not be to page numbers. As you'll see, you can also refer to an automatic paragraph number, a footnote or an endnote number, or a graphic-box number.

MARKING A REFERENCE

To mark a reference in your document, follow these steps:

1. Move the cursor to the place in your document where you want to reference the page number, note number, or graphic-box number.

When generating references to graphic boxes, WordPerfect automatically inserts text from the caption number style defined for the referenced box type. For example, WordPerfect will automatically insert the word "Figure" before the referenced number of a Figure box (assuming the default caption number style for Figure boxes).

2. Type any introductory text as you normally would (e.g., *see page* or *as shown in*). Be sure to press the spacebar if you want a space between the last word and the number.

3. Select **M**ark ➤ Cross-**R**eference ➤ **R**eference (or press **Alt-F5 R R**). The Tie Reference menu appears (Figure 23.18).

4. Choose the type of target you're referencing from the menu.

5. If you chose Graphics Box Number, select the type of box you are referencing from the options shown below:

1 Figure; **2 T**able Box; **3 T**ext Box; **4 U**ser Box; **5 E**quation

6. Type a name for the target—it can be up to 31 characters long and can contain spaces. Press ↵ when finished.

7. If necessary, finish typing the introductory text for the reference (for example, type a space, then], for a reference that should look like *[see page 10]* after it's generated).

When entering a target name, use something that's clear and easy to remember. For example, don't use *Fig 3* as a target name, because, if you later insert a figure in front of that one, it won't be *Fig 3* any more. Instead, use a descriptive name like *Quarterly Sales Fig*.

After you enter the target name, you're returned to the Edit screen. WordPerfect inserts the [Ref(*target*)] code at the cursor position, where *target* is the name you entered in step 6 above. Depending on the type of reference, the code appears as a question mark on the Edit screen for now.

MARKING A TARGET

To identify a referenced target in your document, follow these steps:

1. Move the cursor to the right of the target. (Activate the Reveal Codes screen to make sure that the cursor is properly positioned just past the target.)

2. Select **Mark** ➤ Cross-**R**eference ➤ **T**arget (or press **Alt-F5 R T**).

3. Enter the name of the target, making sure to use the exact spelling you used when defining the reference (e.g., *Quarterly Sales Fig*), and press ↵.

WordPerfect inserts a [Target(*target*)] code at the cursor position, where *target* is the target name you entered in step 3.

After you've marked your references and targets, you can replace all the question marks by generating the cross-references, using the same steps you use to generate lists (see "Generating the Lists" later in this chapter).

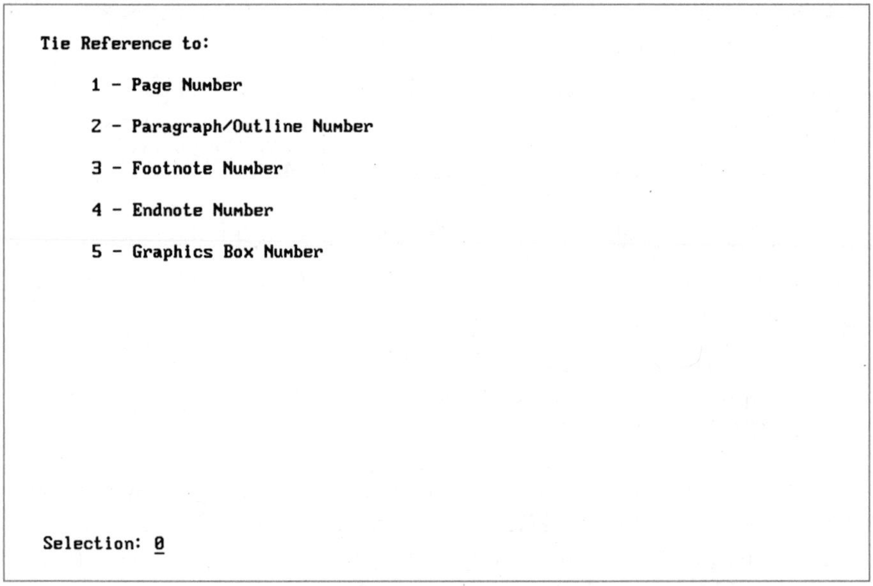

```
Tie Reference to:

     1 - Page Number

     2 - Paragraph/Outline Number

     3 - Footnote Number

     4 - Endnote Number

     5 - Graphics Box Number












Selection: 0
```

FIGURE 23.18:

The Tie Reference menu

MARKING A REFERENCE AND A TARGET AT THE SAME TIME

As an alternative to marking references and targets independently, Word-Perfect lets you mark them both at the same time. Follow these steps:

1. Position the cursor where you want the referenced page, note, or graphic-box number to appear and type the introductory text.

2. Select **Mark** ➤ Cross-**R**eference ➤ **B**oth (or press **Alt-F5 R B**).

3. From the Tie Reference menu, select the type of target, as discussed earlier.

4. When prompted, move the cursor to the target point in the document with the cursor-movement keys.

5. Press ↵.

6. If prompted, enter the name of the target.

7. If necessary, finish typing the introductory text for the reference.

PAGE X OF Y PAGE NUMBERS

By cross-referencing the last page of a document, you can set up "page x of y" page numbering for your page headers or footers, where x is the current page, and y is the last page. Follow these steps:

1. Move the cursor to the last page of the document (**Home Home** ↓).

2. Select **Mark** ➤ Cross-**R**eference ➤ **T**arget (or press **Alt-F5 R T**). Give the target an obvious name, such as *LAST PAGE*.

3. Move the cursor back to the top of the document (**Home Home** ↑).

4. Create a page header or footer by selecting **L**ayout ➤ **P**age ➤ **H**eader *or* **F**ooter (**Shift-F8 P, H** *or* **F**).

5. Within the header or footer, position the cursor where you want the page number to appear.

6. Type **Page** and press the spacebar, then press **Ctrl-B** to insert the current page number code, ^B.

7. Press the spacebar, type **of**, and press the spacebar again.

8. Select **M**ark ➤ **C**ross-**R**eference ➤ **R**eference ➤ **P**age Number (**Alt-F5 R R P**).

9. Type (or accept) the target name *LAST PAGE* and press ↵.

10. Press Exit (**F7**) twice to return to the Edit screen.

Before printing the document, remember to generate the lists (described in the next section). Also, when adding new text to the end of the document, be sure to place that new text above the [Target(LAST PAGE)] code that identifies the number of the last page.

GENERATING THE LISTS

After marking your reference list items or cross-references, you can generate all lists and referenced items in the document by following these simple steps:

1. Select **M**ark ➤ **G**enerate (or press **Alt-F5 G**). The menu shown in Figure 23.19 appears.

2. Select **G**enerate Tables, Indexes, Cross-References, etc.

3. WordPerfect prompts you to confirm the generation:

   Existing tables, lists, and indexes will be replaced. Continue? Yes (No)

4. Select **Y**es to proceed.

If your index is not acceptable, delete it before changing the definition and regenerating the index.

WordPerfect generates the lists and cross-references, giving you a progress report as it works. Then you'll be returned to the Edit screen. You can scroll through the document on the Edit screen to verify your work (though any generated references in headers, footers, notes, and so forth will only be visible on the View Document screen or printed document).

All reference lists in the document are generated whenever you go through these steps. Previously generated reference lists are replaced with a new list reflecting any changes in the content or pagination of the document.

Note that WordPerfect does not automatically update the lists when you add, delete, or change text in the future. If you make any changes to the document, you should repeat the steps above to regenerate all the lists before printing the document, to make sure all reference material is up-to-date.

Whenever you print a document that contains reference lists and has been edited since it was last generated, WordPerfect will remind you that the lists or indexes in the document may need to be generated for the lists to be current.

You can cancel the print job and regenerate the lists or indexes before printing the document, or you can tell WordPerfect to print the document anyway.

EDITING A GENERATED REFERENCE LIST

When you generate reference lists, each list begins at the location of the [Def Mark:] code that was inserted in the document when you defined the list. At the end of each generated list a new code appears: [End Def]. This code is important, because it marks the end of the material that will be replaced if the document is regenerated.

You can edit the contents of a generated reference list, refining it the same way you edit any WordPerfect text. However, your changes will be discarded if you regenerate the list in the future, because everything between a [Def Mark:] and [End Def] code is replaced with a newly generated list whenever you regenerate the document.

If you must edit text in a reference list, you're better off doing so at the source: within the main body of the text. That way, when you regenerate the list, the correction will be included in both the document proper and the generated list.

In the next chapter, I'll conclude this part with coverage of the Master Document feature, which lets you treat separate files as one file for purposes of referencing and consistency of style.

```
Mark Text: Generate

    1 - Remove Redline Markings and Strikeout Text from Document

    2 - Compare Screen and Disk Documents and Add Redline and Strikeout

    3 - Expand Master Document

    4 - Condense Master Document

    5 - Generate Tables, Indexes, Cross-References, etc.
```

```
Selection: 0
```

FIGURE 23.19:

The Mark Text: Generate menu

CHAPTER 24

Using Master Document to Work with Large Files

If you write large documents, such as books with several chapters or reports with multiple large sections, you'll undoubtedly find it easiest to store each chapter or section in a separate file. This helps prevent any individual document from becoming so large that it is unwieldy to work with on the Edit screen.

If you store chapters or large sections as separate files, you can use the Master Document feature to *link* these files into one large, master document. This lets you consistently apply or change a style, search and replace, and make formatting changes throughout all the separate files as though they were one large file. You can also generate automatic references, like a table of contents, an index, figure and table lists, tables of authorities, and cross-references for all the combined files at once.

When you link several files into a master document, WordPerfect also sequentially numbers all the pages, footnotes and endnotes, automatic (paragraph) numbers, and graphic boxes in the overall master document. This gives you all the advantages of automatic numbering, which you may have grown accustomed to in a single document, across many documents stored as separate files.

WHAT IS A MASTER DOCUMENT?

A master document is like any other WordPerfect document that you create on the Edit screen, and it can contain text and hidden codes just like any other document. The only difference is that the master document contains links to other documents, which are referred to as *subdocuments*. Each subdocument, in turn, is also just a regular WordPerfect document that you've previously created and saved in the usual manner.

Equivalent shortcut keys are Alt-F5 S for the Subdocument feature, Alt-F5 G E for Master Documents Expand, and Alt-F5 G O for Master Documents Condense.

The Master Document options are on the Mark pull-down menu and its Master Document submenu, as shown in Figure 24.1. These features share a menu with the automatic-referencing features, because they are so often used to link separate files for referencing, as I'll discuss shortly.

BEFORE YOU USE MASTER DOCUMENT

Before you use the Master Document feature for numbering pages, notes, or boxes, or for generating references, you need to be aware of the following:

◆ If you'll be using any front matter before page number 1, you should include a [Pg Num:1] code at the appropriate place to start numbering at page 1 (select **L**ayout ➤ **P**age ➤ Page **N**umbering ➤ **N**ew Page Number, or press Shift-F8 P N N). None of the subsequent documents

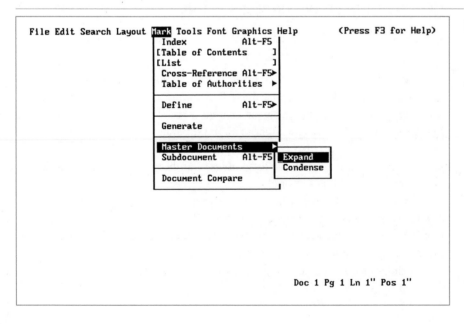

should contain [Pg Num:] codes, unless you want to interrupt the consecutive numbering sequence. You might, for example, put a [Pg Num:1] code at the beginning of each of your subdocument files to restart numbering at page 1 for each chapter of a book.

◆ If you want each chapter or section to start on an odd-numbered page, each chapter or section should include a [Force:Odd] code at the top (select **L**ayout ➤ **P**age ➤ **Fo**rce Odd/Even ➤ **O**dd, or press Shift-F8 P O O).

◆ Sequential numbering of footnotes, endnotes, graphic boxes, and automatic paragraph numbers throughout the files will not be accurate if subdocuments contain codes that activate a numbering change for any of these items.

◆ If you will be generating tables of contents, lists, or any other automatic reference lists, you may want to store the necessary [Def Mark] definition codes in a separate file, perhaps named *FRONTMAT.WP*. Remember to use hard page breaks to separate various lists within the document.

◆ If you'll be generating back matter, such as an index, you may want to store the necessary [Def Mark:Index] definition code in a separate document, perhaps named *BACKMAT.WP*.

As an alternative to the last two options, you can store the generated lists within the master document itself by placing the [Def Mark] codes above (for front matter) and below (for back matter) the subdocuments, then generating the lists.

NOTE NOTE	*You can use Roman numerals to number*

front-matter pages. Any material on these pages can also be marked for inclusion in reference lists.

CREATING A MASTER DOCUMENT

TO CREATE A MASTER DOCUMENT,

start with a blank Edit screen and select Mark ➤ Subdocument (or press Alt-F5 S) to define links to other documents.

To create a master document, follow these steps:

1. Start from a blank WordPerfect Edit screen.

2. Select **Mark ➤ S**ubdocument (or press **Alt-F5 S**). The following prompt appears in the lower-left corner of your screen:

Subdoc Filename:

WordPerfect is asking you for the file name of the first subdocument that will be linked to your master document.

The sub-document doesn't have to exist at the time you create your master document.

3. Type the name of the file you want inserted in the document and press ↵. If the file is not in the current directory, be sure to include the complete path to that file. A link to the document appears in a comment box.

4. If you want to ensure that the next document starts on a new page, insert a hard page break (press **Ctrl-↵**).

5. Repeat steps 3 and 4 for each document you want to include in the master document, making sure to link the files in proper order (e.g., FRONTMAT.WP, CHAP1.WP, CHAP2.WP, and so forth).

When you're finished, you'll see comments for each subdocument on the screen. If you inserted hard page breaks, you'll also see the double underlines used to signify those breaks on the Edit screen, as in Figure 24.2.

```
┌─────────────────────────────────────────────────────────┐
│  Subdoc: FRONTMAT.WP                                     │
└─────────────────────────────────────────────────────────┘
 _
=============================================================

┌─────────────────────────────────────────────────────────┐
│  Subdoc: CHAP1.WP                                        │
└─────────────────────────────────────────────────────────┘

=============================================================

┌─────────────────────────────────────────────────────────┐
│  Subdoc: CHAP2.WP                                        │
└─────────────────────────────────────────────────────────┘

=============================================================

┌─────────────────────────────────────────────────────────┐
│  Subdoc: CHAP3.WP                                        │
└─────────────────────────────────────────────────────────┘

=============================================================
                         Doc 1 Pg 1 Ln 1" Pos 1"
```

FIGURE 24.2:

An example of several subdocuments on the Edit screen

GENERATING REFERENCES FROM A MASTER DOCUMENT

If the page or other automatic numbers are inaccurate in your generated lists, check to see whether one or more subdocuments contain codes that incorrectly restart numbering; also, you may not have inserted hard page breaks everywhere that text needs to start on a new page.

If you've already positioned and defined reference lists that you want to generate from your subdocuments, you can just choose **Mark ➤ Generate ➤ G**enerate Tables, Indexes, Cross-References, etc. (Alt-F5 G G) to generate them now.

Optionally, you can position the cursor where you want these lists to appear within the master document, insert hard page breaks where appropriate, and define the lists right in the master document. Then generate the references as you normally would. In this case, the generated lists will be part of the master document, rather than one of the subdocuments. You can print the lists and save them as described later in this chapter.

EXPANDING THE MASTER DOCUMENT

TO EXPAND THE MASTER DOCUMENT,

select Mark ➤ Master Documents ➤ Expand (or press Alt-F5 G E).

When you generate references from a master document, WordPerfect automatically expands and condenses each document "behind the scenes" as necessary.

You can edit and save subdocuments individually, just like any other WordPerfect files. But often, you'll want to work with all your subdocuments at once—to make global changes, for example. If you want to work with subdocuments as a whole within the master document, you must *expand* the master document. This retrieves the documents to the Edit screen for normal editing. Although it's not necessary to expand the master document to generate reference lists, it *is* necessary to do so for most other types of operations. Follow these steps:

1. With the master document on the Edit screen, select **Mark ➤ Master Documents ➤ Expand** (or press **Alt-F5 G E**).

2. WordPerfect retrieves all the subdocuments in your master document (which could take some time) and places them on the normal Edit screen. (If WordPerfect cannot find a subdocument, it displays the message "Subdoc not found" and gives you a chance to type a different file name, or press ↵ to skip to the next subdocument.)

Never move or delete the [Subdoc Start] and [Subdoc End] codes that surround a subdocument in an expanded master document.

Your retrieved subdocuments on the Edit screen are essentially one large file, and you can edit this file like any other. Each subdocument is placed between a [Subdoc Start] code and [Subdoc End] code.

EDITING A MASTER DOCUMENT

You can make any editing changes to any document within the master document, but keep four points in mind:

◆ Any codes outside of [Subdoc Start] and [Subdoc End] codes are part of the master document and will be saved as part of the master document only.

◆ Any codes inside [Subdoc Start] and [Subdoc End] codes are part of that subdocument and will be saved only as part of that subdocument when you condense the master document (see "Condensing a Master Document" later in this chapter).

◆ As with single documents, later codes take precedence over earlier ones. For example, if you set the left and right margins to 2 inches each at the top of the master document, all the subdocuments will have 2-inch margins, unless one of the documents contains codes to set the margins differently. Margin codes in that subdocument will then override the codes in the master document, from where they first appear to the end of the master document (or until overridden by subsequent margin codes).

◆ Any changes that you make within a subdocument are saved *only* if you condense and save the master document (discussed later).

NOTE NOTE *Codes in subdocuments don't have any effect until the master document is expanded. If the codes conflict, you won't be able to tell while the master document is condensed.*

Once the document is expanded, you can edit normally. You can also use Search to locate text or Search and Replace to make global corrections.

CHANGING A STYLE THROUGHOUT SUBDOCUMENTS

If you have used styles to format the text of individual files, and you are not sure that each document is using the most recent set of styles, you can use the Master Document feature to bring all the styles up to date. Normally, when you expand the master document, all styles in the subdocuments (and any styles that are defined within the master document) are combined on the Style menu. If any two styles have the same name, WordPerfect uses the style in the document nearest the top of the master document.

If you know which document has the most recent "correct" set of styles, you can use that document to create an up-to-date style library for the first document in the master document, before expanding the master document.

For example, let's suppose that a document named *CHAP20.WP* has the most recent, complete set of styles for the overall project. Follow these steps:

1. Start with a clear Edit screen (no master document or subdocuments).

2. Retrieve CHAP20.WP, and select **L**ayout ➤ **S**tyles ➤ **S**ave (**Alt-F8 S**) to save its style library. (For purposes of illustration, let's say you name this style library *LATEST.STY*.)

3. Clear the Edit screen, and then retrieve whichever document is listed at the top of your master document, perhaps FRONTMAT.WP or CHAPT1.WP.

4. Select **L**ayout ➤ **S**tyles ➤ **R**etrieve (**Alt-F8 R**) to read in the style library you just created (LATEST.STY). If asked about replacing existing styles, select Yes.

5. Save that document and clear the Edit screen.

Now you can create (or retrieve) your master document, then expand it. Because the topmost subdocument now has the most recent set of styles, all documents beneath it will share these styles. When you condense the master document again, each document will inherit this style library.

PRINTING A MASTER DOCUMENT

If you print a condensed master document that contains hard page breaks, WordPerfect prints a blank page for each page break.

To print the entire master document, you first need to expand it. Then select **F**ile ➤ **P**rint ➤ **F**ull Document (Shift-F7 F) as usual. Optionally, to print only sections of the expanded document, you can either block the sections you want to print and press Print (F7) or use **F**ile ➤ **P**rint ➤ **M**ultiple Pages (Shift-F7 M) to print specified pages from the expanded document.

CONDENSING A MASTER DOCUMENT

TO CONDENSE A MASTER DOCUMENT AND SAVE ALL YOUR CHANGES,

select **Mark ➤ Master Documents ➤ Condense** (or press **Alt-F5 G O**). Then choose **Yes ➤ Replace all Remaining**.

Once you're finished working with an expanded master document, you should *condense* it before saving it again. This procedure takes the subdocuments out of the master document, but retains the links to the subdocuments.

Follow these steps:

1. Select **Mark** ➤ **M**aster Documents ➤ **C**ondense (or press **Alt-F5 G O**). You'll see the prompt

> Save Subdocs? Yes (**No**)

2. If you select No, WordPerfect will condense the master document right away, and any changes you have made to the subdocuments between their [Subdoc Start] and [Subdoc End] codes will be lost. If you select Yes (the default), WordPerfect will ask whether you want to save the first subdocument:

> Replace *filename*? **1 Yes; 2 No; 3 Replace All Remaining**

3. If you select Yes, WordPerfect will save the subdocument indicated by filename and will proceed to the next subdocument. If you select No, WordPerfect will allow you to save the subdocument under another name. (The new name will appear in the master document in place of the old one.) If you select Replace All Remaining, WordPerfect will go ahead and save all the subdocuments without prompting you on each one.

If you do not choose to condense a master document, but choose to save it under its own name, a prompt will remind you:

> Document is expanded, condense it? Yes (**No**)

There is no need to save an expanded master document (it just wastes disk space and is best generated fresh each time you want to use it), so you should select Yes. You'll then be given the same basic options described in the preceding steps.

Incidentally, you need only create a master document once, provided that you remember to save it (as with any other document). When you retrieve an existing master document, you retrieve all the links to its subdocuments, and you can then expand and condense at will.

> **TIP** *You can save some time by not saving the subdocuments if you have not made any changes to them.*

USING A MACRO TO LOAD SUBDOCUMENTS

> **NOTE NOTE** *You can't use wild-cards to retrieve sub-documents. For example, CHAP*.WP will not retrieve CHAP1.WP, CHAP2.WP, and so forth.*

Even though you need only create the master document for a given project once, it can still be tedious to enter each subdocument name, particularly if many files are involved. Figure 24.3 shows a sample macro that quickly sets up a master document for files named CHAP1.WP, CHAP2.WP, CHAP3.WP, up to CHAP25.WP, and places a hard page break between each. Note that these files don't have to exist ahead of time for the macro to work.

You can change the *CHAP*, the *.WP*, and the range of values in the {FOR} loop to identify a different set of file names for your own master document. For example, changing the second and third lines of the macro to

{FOR}Counter~1~40~1~
   {Mark Text}sMANUAL**{VARIABLE}**Counter.DOC

creates a master document for files named MANUAL1.DOC, MANUAL2.DOC, up to MANUAL40.DOC.

This chapter completes Part 7, in which you've learned many valuable techniques to help you manage larger projects. The next part takes you into more specialized, and in some ways more advanced, territories, such as interfacing with other programs and using advanced macro and merge commands.

```
Macro: Action

    File            MASTER.WPM

    Description     Load CHAP1.WP → CHAP25.WP into MD

    ┌────────────────────────────────────────────────────┐
    │{;}*********************************** MASTER.WPM~    │
    │{FOR}Counter~1~25~1~                                 │
    │    {Mark Text}sCHAP{VARIABLE}Counter~.WP            │
    │    {Enter}{HPg}                                     │
    │{END FOR}                                            │
    │_                                                    │
    │                                                     │
    │                                                     │
    │                                                     │
    │                                                     │
    │                                                     │
    └────────────────────────────────────────────────────┘

Ctrl-V to Insert next key as command;
Ctrl-PgUp for macro commands;  Press Exit when done
```

FIGURE 24.3:

A sample macro to load files named CHAP1.WP through CHAP25.WP into a master document

PART EIGHT

Techniques for Power Users

This part of the book delves into the more advanced options that WordPerfect offers for power users. You'll learn about interfacing with other programs, including spreadsheets, database managers, and other word processing programs. Then you'll learn about some of WordPerfect's more widely used advanced macro and merge commands. Finally, you'll learn about customizing your keyboard layout—a particularly handy skill for authors and editorial teams who work on diverse projects to produce a wide variety of documents.

CHAPTER 25

Interfacing
with Other Programs

our WordPerfect package includes several tools that let you share documents and data with other programs. This chapter gives you the basic information you need to know to convert files to and from other formats, but it's your responsibility to know what formats you'll need and also to keep track of the locations and names of files that you are importing or exporting. If necessary, refer to the documentation for the software whose data you are trying to import or export for further information.

CONVERTING FILES
TO AND FROM OTHER WORD PROCESSOR FORMATS

TO IMPORT A DOCUMENT FROM OR EXPORT A DOCUMENT TO ANOTHER WORD PROCESSOR,

run the CONVERT program from the DOS command prompt.

The CONVERT program supplied with your WordPerfect package lets you convert WordPerfect documents to other popular word-processing formats, and vice versa. Though referred to as "conversion," this process actually works on a copy of the original file, leaving you with both a converted file and the intact original.

If your computer has a hard disk, the CONVERT.EXE program is stored in your WordPerfect 5.1 directory (usually C:\WP51) during normal installation. If you installed WordPerfect on floppy disks only, the program is on the disk you labeled *Utilities*. To use the CONVERT program, follow these steps:

1. At the DOS command prompt, switch to the WordPerfect 5.1 directory (typically by entering **C:** then **CD\WP51** at the prompt).

2. Type **CONVERT** and press ↵. You'll see the prompt

   ### Name of Input File?

3. Type the name of the file you are converting, including the full path name, and press ↵ (e.g., A:\CHAP1.DOC).

4. You'll see the prompt

   ### Name of Output File:

   Type the name and optionally the path (if it's not the same as the current directory) for the file you are converting to (e.g., C:\MYDOCS\CHAP1.WP), and press ↵. The CONVERT menu appears, as shown in Figure 25.1.

5. If you're converting the file from WordPerfect to another format, select option 1, then an option from the export format options (Figure 25.2). If you're converting the file from another format to WordPerfect, select the format of the file from options 2 through C.

When the conversion is complete, you're returned to the DOS command prompt, and the converted file is stored on the drive, in the directory, and with the file name you specified in step 4.

*You can use the DOS wildcard characters ? and * when specifying input and output file names to convert multiple files.*

To cancel the conversion without making a selection, press Cancel (F1).

A WordPerfect macro can send the CONVERT command to the DOS command line and execute a batch file. See "Exiting Temporarily to DOS" later in this chapter.

USING DOS BATCH FILES TO CONVERT FILES

As an alternative to going through the CONVERT program menus, you can perform a conversion from the DOS command prompt. This is particularly useful when you want to automate the conversion process for less experienced users, because you can perform the conversion commands from within a batch file and start WordPerfect with an auto-executing macro that brings the converted data right to the Edit screen or uses it in a merge.

The basic syntax for using CONVERT at the command prompt without menus is

CONVERT *inputfilename outputfilename inputfiletype outputfiletype fielddelimeter recorddelimiter deletecharacters*

where *inputfilename* and *outputfilename* are the paths and names of the input and output files; *inputfiletype* is the type of the file being converted, using the number or letter option on the CONVERT menu; and *outputfiletype* is the format you want for the converted file, using the number on the second CONVERT menu. You only need to specify an output file type if the input file type is WordPerfect (1).

For example, the command

CONVERT A:\CHAP*.DOC C:\WP51\CHAP*.WP 5

imports WordStar 3.3 documents named *CHAP1.DOC, CHAP2.DOC,* and so forth from the floppy disk in drive A and converts them to WordPerfect 5.1 files named *CHAP1.WP, CHAP2.WP,* and so forth on C:\WP51. The *5* at the end is the option number for the WordStar 3.3 input file type listed on the CONVERT menu. (For information on the three optional delimiters you can add to the command, see "Importing Data for Secondary Merge Files" later in this chapter.)

NOTE *Be sure to separate each parameter in a CONVERT command with a blank space.*

FIGURE 25.1:
The CONVERT menu

```
0 EXIT
1 WordPerfect to another format
2 Revisable-Form-Text (IBM DCA Format) to WordPerfect
3 Final-Form-Text (IBM DCA Format) to WordPerfect
4 Navy DIF Standard to WordPerfect
5 WordStar 3.3 to WordPerfect
6 MultiMate Advantage II to WordPerfect
7 Seven-Bit Transfer Format to WordPerfect
8 WordPerfect 4.2 to WordPerfect 5.1
9 Mail Merge to WordPerfect Secondary Merge
A Spreadsheet DIF to WordPerfect Secondary Merge
B Word 4.0 to WordPerfect
C DisplayWrite to WordPerfect

Enter number of Conversion desired _
```

CHOOSING AN INTERMEDIATE DATA FORMAT

Practically every program can export to ASCII text files, which WordPerfect can import by means of **F**ile ► *Text* **I** *n (Ctrl-F5 T).*

If you cannot use CONVERT to convert a particular file directly to or from WordPerfect format, try to find an intermediate data format common to both programs. For example, suppose you want to import text from a hypothetical program named *WonderWords* into WordPerfect format, but you see no option for WonderWords on the CONVERT program menu. Then you check the documentation for WonderWords and discover that it can export text to Navy DIF Standard format. If that's the case, your problem is solved, because you can use WonderWords to export text to Navy DIF format, then use the Word-Perfect CONVERT program to convert the Navy DIF file to WordPerfect format.

IMPORTING DATA FOR SECONDARY MERGE FILES

Check the documentation of the program whose data you are exporting for information about exporting to delimited text files.

Many programming languages and database management systems and some spreadsheets let you export data to ASCII *delimited* text files, where each field is separated by a comma, and each record is terminated by a CR/LF (carriage return/line feed). Character strings (textual data) may be enclosed in quotation marks. Dates are typically stored in YYYYMMDD format (e.g., *19911115* for 11/15/91), as in Figure 25.3.

```
0 EXIT
1 Revisable-Form-Text (IBM DCA Format)
2 Final-Form-Text (IBM DCA Format)
3 Navy DIF Standard
4 WordStar 3.3
5 MultiMate Advantage II
6 Seven-Bit Transfer Format
7 ASCII Text File
8 WordPerfect Secondary Merge to Spreadsheet DIF

Enter number of output file format desired _
```

FIGURE 25.2:

The options for converting a WordPerfect document to another format

Chapter 16 covers secondary merges and field names.

When you use data from text files as a secondary merge file, the fields have no names. Therefore, you must refer to each field by number in your primary merge file. The first (leftmost) field is {FIELD}1~, the second field is {FIELD}2~, and so forth.

USING CONVERT TO IMPORT TEXT FILES

You can use option 9, Mail Merge to WordPerfect Secondary Merge, on the CONVERT menu to convert an ASCII delimited text file to a secondary merge file. For example, suppose you have a dBASE application that exports data from a .DBF file to a text file named *TOWP.TXT*, using the dBASE command COPY TO TOWP.TXT DELIMITED. The TOWP.TXT file will then have the basic structure shown in Figure 25.3.

After dBASE creates the file, you can run CONVERT from the DOS command prompt, specifying C:\DBASE\TOWP.TXT as the input file and perhaps C:\WP51\FROMDB.SCD as the output file. Then you can select option 9 from the CONVERT menu. You'll see the following prompt:

Enter **Field delimiter** characters or decimal ASCII values enclosed in { }

If you type a comma as the field delimiter, then press ↵, you see this prompt:

Enter **Record delimiter** characters or decimal ASCII values enclosed in { }

The record delimiter is typically a carriage return (ASCII 13, typed as *{13}*) , line feed (typed as *{10}*) , or both. If you type *{13}{10}* and press ↵, you see this prompt:

Enter characters to be **stripped** from the file or press Enter if none

---

```
1001,"Smith","John",19911115,Y
1002,"Adams","Annie",19910101,F
1003,"Watson","Wilbur",19911115,T
1004,"Mahoney","Mary",19911201,T
1005,"Newell","John",19911215,T
1006,"Beach","Sandy",19911215,T
1007,"Kenney","Ralph",19911230,F
1008,"Schumack","Susita",19911230,T
1009,"Smith","Anita",19910101,T
```

FIGURE 25.3:

A sample ASCII delimited text file

If you want to strip the quotation marks from the string fields, type a double quote (") and press ↵. When the conversion is complete, you can run WordPerfect and use **File ➤ Retrieve** (Shift-F10) to retrieve the secondary merge file—for example, to add field names at the top.

As an alternative to going through the CONVERT program menus, you can specify the delimiters and characters to be stripped at the DOS command prompt. For example, entering the command

CONVERT C:\DBASE\TOWP.TXT C:\WP51\FROMDB.SCD 9 , {13}{10} {34}

at the DOS prompt imports the TOWP.TXT file from the C:\DBASE directory to a WordPerfect 5.1 secondary merge file named *FROMDB.SCD* on C:\WP51. The *9* is the input file type on the CONVERT menu (Mail Merge to WordPerfect Secondary Merge), the comma is the field delimiter, *{13}{10}* is the record delimiter (carriage return plus line feed), and *{34}* is the double quote (") to be deleted during the conversion.

IMPORTING DELIMITED TEXT FILES WITHOUT USING CONVERT

If your ASCII text file does not require you to strip any characters, WordPerfect can use it as a secondary merge file without your having to convert it. For example, Figure 25.4 shows a sample text file that does not enclose strings in quotation marks, and hence can be used directly as a secondary merge file.

Follow these steps:

1. At the WordPerfect Edit screen, select **Tools ➤ Merge** (or press **Ctrl-F9 M**).

```
1001,Smith,John,19911115,Y
1002,Adams,Annie,19910101,F
1003,Watson,Wilbur,19911115,T
1004,Mahoney,Mary,19911201,T
1005,Newell,John,19911215,T
1006,Beach,Sandy,19911215,T
1007,Kenney,Ralph,19911230,F
1008,Schumack,Susita,19911230,T
1009,Smith,Anita,19910101,T
```

FIGURE 25.4:

An ASCII text file that can be used as a secondary merge file without conversion

Because the secondary merge file contains no field names, the primary merge file must refer to fields as {FIELD}1~, {FIELD}2~, and so forth.

You can change the default delimiters used for importing secondary merge data from text files by selecting File ➤ Setup ➤ Initial Settings ➤ Merge (Shift-F1 I M).

2. Type the name of the primary merge file and press ↵.

3. When prompted for the name of the secondary merge file, press Text In/Out (**Ctrl-F5**). The prompt asks for the name of the DOS delimited text file.

4. Type the drive and directory location (if necessary) and name of the text file, and press ↵.

5. Select **F**ield Delimiters and enter the characters used to mark the start and end of each field, pressing ↓ (not ↵) after typing the characters. Then select **R**ecord Delimiters, and enter the characters used to start and end each record, again pressing ↓ after typing the characters. Then press Exit (**F7**) to start the merge.

Figure 25.5 shows how to define the field and record delimiters to import the text file shown in Figure 25.4. To enter the [CR] character, press Ctrl-M. To enter the [LF] character, press ↵. Field and record start delimiters are optional, but you must use end delimiters.

CONVERTING IMPORTED DATES

When using text files as secondary merge files, the dates may be in the YYYYMMDD format. To convert this format to a more usable one, use the {MID} command in your primary merge file to isolate specific parts of the date. The {MID} command extracts a portion of a string from a larger string (called the *expression*), given a starting position (*offset*) and a length (*count*).

The first character in the string is counted as number *0,* the second character as number *1,* and so forth. In a date in YYYYMMDD format, the month starts at character 4 and is two characters long. The day starts at character 6 and is two characters long. The year starts at character 0 and is four characters long. Therefore, assuming that the date is in {FIELD}4~ of the secondary merge file, the series of {MID} commands next to *Date:* in the primary merge file shown in Figure 25.6 will display that date in MM/DD/YY format.

When creating your primary merge file, you must use **T**ools ➤ Me**r**ge Codes ➤ **M**ore (Shift-F9 M) to choose the {MID} command and **T**ools ➤ Me**r**ge Codes ➤ **F**ield (Shift-F9 F) to choose the {FIELD} command; you cannot simply type these commands at the keyboard. To show you how this works (because it's a bit tricky), here are the steps for inserting the first {MID} command shown in Figure 25.6:

Primary and secondary merge files are covered in detail in Chapter 16.

1. Position the cursor after *Date:* and press **Tab**.

2. Select **T**ools ➤ Me**r**ge Codes ➤ **M**ore (or press **Shift-F9 M**).

3. Type **M**, highlight the {MID} command in the command list, then press ↵.

4. Type **X** (or any other letter), and press ↵ at the "Enter Expression:" prompt.

5. Type **4** and press ↵ at the "Enter Offset:" prompt.

6. Type **2** and press ↵ at the "Enter Count:" prompt.

7. Move the cursor to the letter *X* and press **Delete**, being careful not to delete the tilde (~) after the *X*.

8. Select **T**ools ➤ Me**r**ge Codes ➤ Field (or press **Shift-F9 F**), type **4**, and press ↵ at the "Enter Field:" prompt.

Now press the End key and type a slash (/), which separates the month from the day. To enter the {MID} commands for the day and the year, just repeat steps 2 through 8, adjusting the offset in step 5 and the count in step 6 accordingly, type another slash at the end of the line, and repeat steps 2 through 8 once more (again adjusting the numbers in steps 5 and 6).

```
Merge: DOS Text File

     1 - Field delimiters  - Begin
                             End        ,

     2 - Record delimiters - Begin
                             End        [CR][LF]

Selection: 0
```

Field and record delimiters for merging the data from the file shown in Figure 25.4

INTERFACING WITH SPREADSHEETS

TO IMPORT OR LINK TO A SPREADSHEET,

1. **Select File ➤ Text In ➤ Spreadsheet (or press Ctrl-F5 S).**

2. **Select either Import or Create Link.**

3. **Choose options from the menu presented.**

WordPerfect can import or link to PlanPerfect spreadsheets (versions 3.0 and 5.0), Lotus 1-2-3 (releases 1.0 through 3.0), Microsoft Excel (versions 2.*x*), Quattro, and Quattro Pro. The differences between importing and linking are summarized below:

◆ If you *link* to the spreadsheet, changes made in your spreadsheet program to the spreadsheet file will be reflected in the WordPerfect document after you save the spreadsheet.

◆ If you *import* the spreadsheet, any subsequent changes to the spreadsheet are not reflected in the copy stored in your WordPerfect document unless you reimport the spreadsheet.

```
No.       {FIELD}1~
Name:     {FIELD}2~, {FIELD}3~
Date:     {MID}{FIELD}4~~4~2~/{MID}{FIELD}4~~6~2~/{MID}{FIELD}4~~0~4~
Active:   {FIELD}5~




                                        Doc 1 Pg 1 Ln 1.17" Pos 2.3"
{                                                              }
No.[Tab][Tab][Mrg:FIELD]1~[HRt]
Name:[Tab][Mrg:FIELD]2~, [Mrg:FIELD]3~[HRt]
Date:[Tab][Mrg:MID][Mrg:FIELD]4~~4~2~/[Mrg:MID][Mrg:FIELD]4~~6~2~/[Mrg:MID][Mrg:
FIELD]4~~0~4~  [HRt]
Active:[Tab][Mrg:FIELD]5~



Press Reveal Codes to restore screen
```

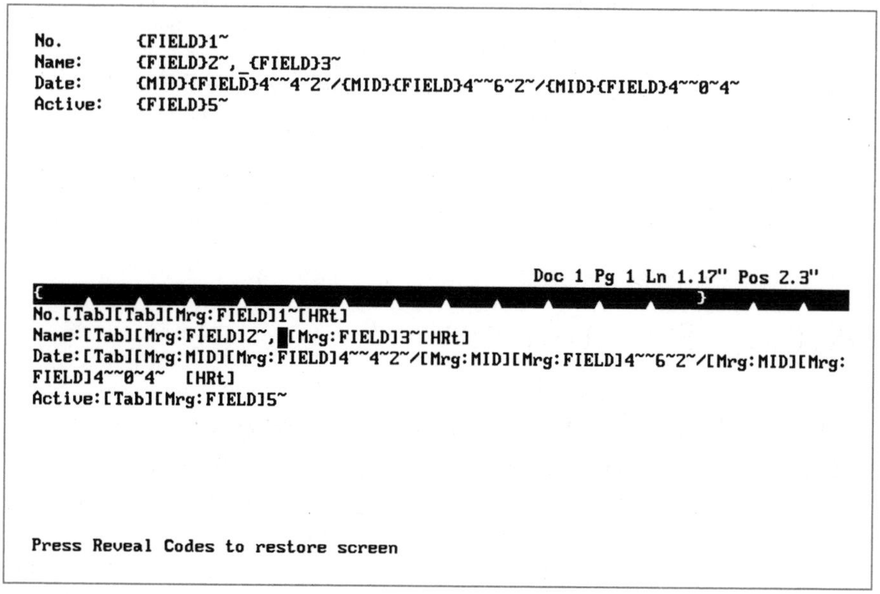

FIGURE 25.6:

{MID} commands used in a primary merge file to convert YYYYMMDD dates to MM/DD/YY format

Regardless of whether you import or link, it's important to understand that only the results of formulas are imported, not the formulas themselves. You can edit the spreadsheet in WordPerfect as you would any other document (this has no effect on the underlying spreadsheet file). However, if you change some numbers in the spreadsheet and try to recalculate the math, nothing will happen, because there are no formulas in the imported spreadsheet.

To import or link a spreadsheet file, follow these steps:

1. Move the cursor to where you want the spreadsheet to appear in the document.

2. Select File ➤ Text In ➤ **S**preadsheet (or press **Ctrl-F5 S**).

3. Select **I**mport (to import a copy of the spreadsheet without a link) or **C**reate Link (to link to the spreadsheet).

4. Select **F**ilename and enter the complete path, file name, and extension for the file you are importing (for example, C:\123\LOAN.WK1 to import a 1-2-3 worksheet named *LOAN.WK1* from the \123 directory of drive C). Optionally, you can press List (F5), use List Files to locate the file, and then select Retrieve to retrieve it.

5. Optionally, select **R**ange and specify a range to import (described in more detail below).

6. Select **T**ype, then either Ta**b**le (to import the spreadsheet into a WordPerfect table) or T**e**xt (to import the spreadsheet data as text in tabular columns).

7. Select **P**erform Import (if you're importing the spreadsheet) or **P**erform Link (if you're linking).

WordPerfect imports the spreadsheet and displays it on the Edit screen. The sections that follow describe the options available to you on the spreadsheet menu.

IMPORTING A SPREADSHEET AS A TABLE OR AS TEXT

If you import the spreadsheet into a table, WordPerfect will create the table automatically, and each cell in the spreadsheet will be copied to a cell in the table. If you import the cell as text, columns in the imported spreadsheet will be separated by [Tab] codes, and rows will be separated by [HRt] codes.

If the imported spreadsheet is too wide to fit between the current page margins, you'll see a brief warning near the bottom of the screen, and the table will be wider than the screen. Text beyond the right edge of the page will not be printed. You can use Ctrl-← in Table Edit mode to narrow columns as necessary.

You can also change the font, margins, and paper size (or any combination thereof) to better format spreadsheet text that's too wide for the page.

If you import a spreadsheet as text, and it's too wide to fit on the page, some columns will wrap to the next line.

IMPORTING A RANGE

You can import a range from a spreadsheet, provided that you know the range coordinates you want or have already named the range in the spreadsheet program. To import a specific range, select the Range option. The full size of the spreadsheet will be displayed next to the prompt, and you will be able to edit with the WordPerfect editing keys or by typing entirely new range coordinates.

If you are importing to a table, the maximum number of columns you can import is 32. If you are importing as text, the maximum is 20.

Optionally, you can press List (F5) before pressing any other key to see a list of range names in the file you are importing. Then you can highlight the name of the range you want to import and press ↵. Even if you define a range, you must still select Perform Import or Perform Link after defining the range.

MANAGING LINKED SPREADSHEETS

If you link rather than import a spreadsheet, you'll notice that your imported spreadsheet is surrounded by two link messages indicating where the link begins and ends (these messages are never printed). You can remove these messages from the screen and also control when the link is updated. Follow these steps:

1. Position the cursor anywhere within the imported spreadsheet (between the [Link] and [Link End] codes on the Reveal Codes screen).

2. Select **File ➤ Text In ➤ S**preadsheet **➤ Link** Options (or press **Ctrl-F5 S L**).

3. Your options are

Update on **R**etrieve	If Yes, ensures that each time you retrieve the document, it automatically updates the copy of the spreadsheet. (The update is based on the most recently *saved* version of the spreadsheet.)
Show Link Codes	If No, the Link and Link End boxes on the Edit screen are not displayed.
Update All Links	Updates all the linked spreadsheets in the document immediately, using the most recently *saved* versions of the spreadsheets.

EDITING THE LINK

If you link a spreadsheet to a document, then need to change one of your previous settings, move the cursor between the [Link] and [Link End] codes and select **F**ile ➤ Text **In** ➤ **Sp**readsheet ➤ **E**dit Link (or press **Ctrl-F5 S E**). You'll be taken to a menu that lets you change the settings for the current link.

IMPORTING SPREADSHEETS TO GRAPHIC BOXES

You can import a spreadsheet into a graphic box so that you can anchor it to a page and wrap text around it. To do so, create the box as you normally would. Select Edit at the box's Definition menu to get to the screen for editing the graphic-box contents. From there, you can use the **F**ile ➤ Text **In** ➤ **Sp**readsheet options to link or import the spreadsheet.

EXITING TEMPORARILY TO DOS

If you need to use DOS for a few commands but do not want to save your document and exit WordPerfect, you can temporarily exit to DOS by selecting File ➤ Go to DOS or by pressing Go to DOS (**Ctrl-F1**). You'll be given these two options:

*Exiting to DOS temporarily is not the same as exiting to DOS by selecting **F**ile ➤ **E**xit or pressing F7. Always return to WordPerfect and exit properly before turning off your computer.*

Go to DOS	Takes you to the DOS command prompt, where you can enter one or more DOS commands. When you've finished entering DOS commands, type **EXIT** and press ↵ to return to your document.
DOS **C**ommand	Allows you to type one DOS command only (press ↵ after typing the command). After the command finishes, you'll see a message indicating that you can press any key to return to WordPerfect.

A macro can send a single command to DOS with this option.

Be forewarned that loading a memory-resident program after temporarily exiting to DOS can prevent you from getting back into WordPerfect and hence can cause you to lose the document currently on your screen. Just to play it safe, you might want to do a quick save with **F**ile ➤ **S**ave or the Save (F10) key before going to DOS.

IMPORTING DOS OUTPUT

If you want to use the output from a DOS command in your WordPerfect document, use the > redirection symbol at the end of the DOS command to send its output to a file. For example, the following command sends the output from the DIR command to a file named *FILELIST.TXT*:

```
DIR *.WP >C:\WP51\FILELIST.TXT
```

You can then use the **File ➤** Text **In** (Ctrl-F5 T) commands to read the file (C:\WP51\FILELIST.TXT in this example) into your WordPerfect document.

EDITING DOS (ASCII) TEXT FILES

TO EDIT DOS TEXT FILES WITH WORDPERFECT,

use the File ➤ Text In options (Ctrl-F5 T R or Ctrl-F5 T E) to retrieve the file and the File ➤ Text Out options (Ctrl-F5 T S) to save the file.

Many programs store their *source code* files as DOS text files (also called ASCII text files). This includes DOS batch (.BAT) files, dBASE command (.PRG) files, Paradox script (.SC) files, and others. You can edit such files with WordPerfect (with some degree of risk). To do so, start with a clear Edit screen, select **File ➤** Text **In ➤** DOS Text CR/LF to **H**Rt (or press Ctrl-F5 T R), type the complete path and file name, including the extension (for example, C:\AUTOEXEC.BAT), and press ↵.

After making your changes, save the file by selecting **File ➤** Text **Out ➤** DOS **Text** (or by pressing Ctrl-F5 T S), and entering the complete path and name of the file. Then clear the Edit screen *without* saving the file by selecting **File ➤** Exit **➤** No **➤** No (F7 N N).

There are risks, however:

◆ If you inadvertently save the text file as a WordPerfect document by using Save (F10), Exit (F7), or the equivalent pull-down menu options, WordPerfect will add hidden codes to the file, rendering it unusable as an ASCII file. If that happens, you'll need to retrieve the file as a WordPerfect document (Shift-F10), then resave it as a DOS text file.

◆   WordPerfect will word-wrap lines that extend past the right margin, but most programs (including DOS) cannot execute a wrapped line. To prevent word wrap, you'll need to use a wide paper size and narrow margins whenever you edit text files.

IMPORTING DOS TEXT FILES

The **File** ➤ Text **In** options (Ctrl-F5 T) can also be used to simply import a text file into a document. This is handy because many programs let you "print" (or save) reports to disk in ASCII (DOS) text format. Most often, these files are saved with the extension .PRN (or perhaps .TXT). You can retrieve such a file directly into WordPerfect.

For example, suppose you use the Paradox database management system and want your WordPerfect document to include a report that Paradox generates. First, run Paradox and use its Report, Output, and File commands to "print" a report to disk. When prompted, you could name this file something like C:\WP51\PDOX2WP.PRN so that it is stored in the \WP51 directory.

After you exit Paradox and run WordPerfect, you can retrieve the Word-Perfect document in which you want to display the Paradox report, with the Retrieve or List Files commands. Then position the cursor where you want the Paradox report to appear, and select **File** ➤ Text **In** (or press Ctrl-F5 T).

CR/LF stands for carriage return/line feed, the ASCII equivalent of a Word-Perfect [HRt] code.

At this point, there are two ways to retrieve the file. If you want it to retain its original width (even if it's wider than the margins), select DOS Text (CR/LF to **H**Rt) if you're using the pull-down menus, or **R**etrieve (CR/LF to [HRt]) if you're using the a shortcut keys. If you want it to be wrapped to fit within the margins, select DOS Text (CR/LF to **S**Rt) or **R**etrieve (CR/LF to [SRt] in HZone). Be sure to include the file name and extension when prompted (PDOX2WP.PRN in this example).

The Text Out pull-down menu also offers a generic format for saving files. This option lets you save a WordPerfect file for use with any word processor not included in the CONVERT program's menus. You'll also find options here to save the file to WordPerfect 5.0 or 4.2 format, useful for sending your 5.1 documents to friends with an older version of the program.

In the next chapter, I'll delve into advanced uses of macro and merge commands, introduced earlier in chapters 15 and 16.

CHAPTER 26

Advanced Macro
and Merge Commands

ordPerfect offers a substantial *macro programming language,* which gives you refined control over how macros and merges behave. It's called a language because it offers many features of more traditional programming languages, such as BASIC, C, and dBASE. The WordPerfect language is unique, however, because it is specifically designed to work with WordPerfect macros and primary merge files.

. . . .
LESSON 10

For a hands-on lesson in using advanced macro programs, see Lesson 10 in Part 9.

It's important to understand that you don't need to learn how to use the macro language to run WordPerfect; it will be of interest mostly to programmers. You can create many useful macros without programming simply by recording keystrokes, as described in Chapter 15. And you can create very sophisticated merges with just the basic merge commands presented in Chapter 16. You may, however, want to delve into the more advanced macro and merge commands if

◆ You want to automate the assembly of complex documents based on data in secondary merge files.

◆ You want to develop macros that repeat some sequence of steps many times over (like the example in Chapter 24, which set up a master document to assemble many subdocuments).

◆ You want to build custom *applications* that simplify and automate complex tasks for less experienced computer users.

◆ You want to develop utilities that enhance the capabilities of Word-Perfect, adding features that WordPerfect does not have.

Complete macro wizardry is not a skill you learn overnight. Like all programming languages, thorough mastery of WordPerfect's macro command language requires a solid background in basic programming concepts (such as variables, looping, branching, and event handling), familiarity with all the commands and syntax of the language, and knowledge of how to use WordPerfect features and shortcut keystrokes.

Unfortunately, there is not enough space to cover programming concepts and the entire macro language within this book. However, appendices I through L in the documentation that came with your WordPerfect package document all the commands and introduce some basic programming concepts. You can also find in-depth treatments of these topics in any WordPerfect book that's dedicated to the subject of macros, such as *WordPerfect 5.1 Macro Handbook,* by Kay Nelson, SYBEX, 1990.

In this chapter, I'll present some practical merges and macros that demonstrate the macro command language and concepts in action. You may find these examples quite useful, because you can use them to accomplish "real-life" tasks, and because they illustrate applications of these advanced commands. In addition to studying these examples, you might also want to take a look at several macros that came with your WordPerfect package, including those in the MACROS soft keyboard (see Chapter 27) and the macros listed below:

*To look at macros in the MACROS keyboard definition, select **F**ile ➤ **S**et up ➤ **K**eyboard Layout (Shift-F1 K), highlight MACROS and choose **E**dit, then highlight the macro you want to look at and choose **A**ction.*

*You can execute these macros by selecting **T**ools ➤ **M**acro ➤ **Ex**-ecute (or by pressing Alt-F10), then typing the macro name and pressing ↵.*

Labels	Sets up handy label formats for sheet labels
Calc	An online calculator
Codes	Converts codes to text and lets you print the resulting document
Endfoot	Converts endnotes to footnotes
Footend	Converts footnotes to endnotes
Inline	Sets up the proper codes for creating an equation in a line of text

Before looking at any examples, however, you'll first need to know some basic rules (or *syntax*) of the WordPerfect macro language.

MACROS VS. MERGES

In some ways, macros and merges are similar. They both use a similar programming language, can often be used to accomplish similar tasks, and are well suited to repetitive jobs. You can start a merge from a macro and vice versa.

There are many differences, however, with some of the most important ones listed below:

◆ Generally speaking, a macro is executed as if you were typing keystrokes at your computer; the macro programming commands determine which keystrokes are executed in which order. A merge deals with text rather than keystrokes, combining text from several sources into a single document; merge programming commands determine which text is merged in which order.

◆ Although you can record macro keystrokes from the normal Edit screen, you insert all macro programming commands by using the Macro Editor (Home Ctrl-F10). No equivalent editor is available for merges: You enter all merge commands from the normal Edit screen by selecting pull-down menu options (Tools ➤ Merge Codes) or pressing equivalent shortcut keys (Shift-F9).

The macro commands menu shows the full syntax of each command, including parameters, arguments, and tildes. To use the command access box from the Macro Editor, press Ctrl-Page Up, then highlight the command you want and press ↵.

◆ When you insert a macro programming command using the Macro Editor's command access box, only the command itself is inserted. You must then type in the tildes (~) and other information required by the command. On the other hand, when you select a merge command, WordPerfect will prompt for all the information the command needs and will insert the tildes for you.

◆ Macros are stored in special files with a .WPM extension. Merge commands are stored in normal WordPerfect primary merge files, which can have any extension.

◆ Pressing Tab or ↵ in the Macro Editor formats the macro for easier reading but does not insert any codes in the macro. In a merge document, however, these keystrokes have the usual effect of inserting codes in the document. As described later, you can use a {COMMENT} command to insert tabs and blank lines in merge documents, without inserting codes.

◆ Macros can contain both programming commands and keystroke commands (e.g., {Home} {Left} {Right} {Search}). Merge files can contain only merge programming commands, not keystroke commands.

BUILDING MACRO AND MERGE COMMANDS

Macro and merge commands, like all programming language commands, must be entered in a specific format, or *syntax,* or they won't work properly. Many such commands use parameters or arguments, which require a tilde (~) to separate them and end the command.

As an example, the command {ASSIGN} stores a value (i.e., a number or text) in a *variable.* Its syntax is

{ASSIGN}*variable~value~*

where *variable* is the name of the variable, and *value* is the value to store in the variable. (A variable is like a "placeholder" that stores information in memory. The text or number stays in memory until you exit WordPerfect.) The command below stores the number *10* in a variable named *HowMany:*

{ASSIGN}HowMany~10~

In the following example, the {FOR} command, which executes a series of commands a certain number of times, uses the general syntax

{FOR}var~start~stop~step~

where *var* is a variable, *start* is the starting value for *var, stop* is the ending value, and *step* is the increment.

Another frequently used command is {VARIABLE}, which accesses the contents of a variable. Its general form is

{VARIABLE}var~

Now, if you want to use the variable named HowMany for the *stop* value in the {FOR} command, you have to enter the command like this

{FOR}LoopCount~1~**{VARIABLE}**HowMany~~1~

Notice the two tildes after HowMany. The first tilde ends the {VARIABLE} command; the second marks the end of the "stop" portion of the {FOR} command. If one of the tildes is missing, the macro or merge will not work properly. Be sure to check these tildes first if your macro or merge doesn't seem to be working correctly.

TYPES OF COMMANDS

As mentioned earlier, a thorough explanation of all WordPerfect's macro commands would require a hefty book of its own. However, you can get a good idea of the capabilities of the macro language just by studying the various categories of commands that are available to you:

CATEGORY	USAGE
User Interface	Communicate with the user by displaying a prompt, allowing input from the keyboard, or both
Flow Control	Change the flow of a macro or merge execution
Macro, Merge, or Subroutine Termination	End a macro, merge, or subroutine
External Condition Handling	Determine how to respond to a condition that occurs outside a macro (e.g., the user presses the Cancel key) or create a condition
Macro Execution	Start a macro
Variables	Assign a value to a variable, determine the state of a variable, or execute (write out) a variable
System Variables	Determine the value of system variables
Execution Control	Affect speed or visibility of execution on the user's screen
Programming Aids	Provide tools that can help you debug your macros when they aren't working properly
Keystroke Commands	Select these from the macro commands menu if you don't have an enhanced BIOS keyboard

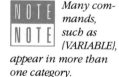

The term "user" simply refers to the person using the macro at the moment.

Many commands, such as {VARIABLE}, appear in more than one category.

Table 26.1 lists commands in each of these categories and indicates whether they are merge or macro commands, or both. It also indicates which commands appear in the examples in this chapter (discussed in more detail later).

COMMAND	MACRO	MERGE	EXAMPLES
USER INTERFACE			
{BELL}	X	X	X
{CHAR}	X	X	X
{INPUT}	X	X	
{KEYBOARD}		X	
{LOOK}	X	X	
{ORIGINAL KEY}	X		
{PAUSE}	X		X
{PAUSE KEY}	X		
{PROMPT}	X	X	X
{STATUS PROMPT}	X	X	
{TEXT}	X	X	
FLOW CONTROL			
{BREAK}	X	X	
{CALL}	X	X	X
{CASE}	X	X	X
{CASE CALL}	X	X	
{CHAIN}	X		
{CHAIN MACRO}	X		
{CHAIN PRIMARY}	X		
{CHAIN SECONDARY}	X		
{ELSE}	X	X	X
{END FOR}	X	X	X
{END IF}	X	X	X
{END WHILE}	X	X	X
{FOR}	X	X	X
{FOR EACH}	X		

TABLE 26.1:

Categories of Macro and Merge Commands

COMMAND	MACRO	MERGE	EXAMPLES
FLOW CONTROL			
{GO}	X	X	X
{IF}	X	X	X
{IF BLANK}	X		
{IF EXISTS}	X	X	
{IF NOT BLANK}		X	
{LABEL}	X	X	X
{NEST}	X		
{NEST MACRO}		X	
{NEST PRIMARY}		X	
{NEST SECONDARY}		X	
{NEXT}	X	X	X
{ON CANCEL}	X	X	
{ON ERROR}	X	X	
{ON NOT FOUND}	X		X
{OTHERWISE}	X	X	
{PROCESS}		X	
{QUIT}	X	X	X
{RESTART}	X		
{RETURN}	X	X	X
{RETURN CANCEL}	X	X	
{RETURN ERROR}	X	X	
{RETURN NOT FOUND}	X		
{SHELL MACRO}	X		
{STOP}		X	
{SUBST PRIMARY}		X	
{SUBST SECONDARY}		X	
{WHILE}	X	X	X

TABLE 26.1:

Categories of Macro and Merge Commands (continued)

COMMAND	MACRO	MERGE	EXAMPLES
MACRO, MERGE, OR SUBROUTINE TERMINATION			
{BREAK}	X	X	
{QUIT}	X	X	X
{RESTART}	X		
{RETURN}	X	X	X
{RETURN CANCEL}	X	X	
{RETURN ERROR}	X	X	
{RETURN NOT FOUND}	X		
{STOP}		X	
EXTERNAL CONDITION HANDLING			
{CANCEL OFF}	X	X	
{CANCEL ON}	X	X	
{ON CANCEL}	X	X	
{ON ERROR}	X	X	
{ON NOT FOUND}	X		X
{RETURN CANCEL}	X	X	
{RETURN ERROR}	X	X	
{RETURN NOT FOUND}	X		
MACRO EXECUTION			
{ALT *letter*}	X		
{CHAIN}	X		
{CHAIN MACRO}		X	
{KEY MACRO *n*}	X		
{NEST}	X		
{NEST MACRO}		X	

TABLE 26.1:
Categories of Macro and Merge Commands (continued)

COMMAND	MACRO	MERGE	EXAMPLES
MACRO EXECUTION			
{SHELL MACRO}	X		
{VAR n}	X		
{VARIABLE}	X	X	X
VARIABLES			
{ASSIGN}	X	X	X
{CHAR}	X	X	X
{IF EXISTS}	X	X	
{LEN}	X	X	
{LOCAL}		X	
{LOOK}	X	X	
{MID}	X	X	
{NEXT}	X	X	
{SYSTEM}	X	X	X
{TEXT}	X	X	
{VAR n}	X		
{VARIABLE}	X	X	X
SYSTEM VARIABLES			
{DATE}		X	
{ORIGINAL KEY}	X		
{STATE}	X		X
{SYSTEM}	X	X	X
EXECUTION CONTROL			
{DISPLAY OFF}	X		X
{DISPLAY ON}	X		
{MENU OFF}	X		

TABLE 26.1:

Categories of Macro and Merge Commands (continued)

COMMAND	MACRO	MERGE	EXAMPLES
EXECUTION CONTROL			
{MENU ON}	X		
{REWRITE}		X	
{SPEED}	X		
{WAIT}	X	X	
PROGRAMMING AIDS			
{;} (Comment)	X		X
{BELL}	X	X	X
{COMMENT}		X	X
{DISPLAY OFF}	X		X
{DISPLAY ON}	X		
{SPEED}	X		
{STEP OFF}	X	X	
{STEP ON}	X	X	
KEYSTROKE COMMANDS			
{Block Append}	X		
{Block Copy}	X		
{Block Move}	X		
{Item Down}	X		
{Item Left}	X		
{Item Right}	X		
{Item Up}	X		
{Para Down}	X		
{Para Up}	X		

TABLE 26.1:

Categories of Macro and Merge Commands (continued)

ASSEMBLING DOCUMENTS
WITH ADVANCED MERGE COMMANDS

In Chapter 16 you learned to use numerous merge commands to create primary and secondary files for merging, and to merge text from the keyboard into an existing document. As you may recall, selecting **T**ools ➤ Me**r**ge Codes ➤ **M**ore (or pressing Shift-F9 M) takes you to a menu for accessing advanced merge commands, such as {IF BLANK}...{ENDIF}, which you can insert in your primary merge files.

You can also use the {IF} command with any of the operators shown below to make decisions within a primary merge, based on information in the secondary merge file:

OPERATOR	FUNCTION
=	Equal to
!=	Not equal to
>	Greater than
<	Less than
&	And
¦	Or
!	Not

By combining the {IF} command with the {DOCUMENT} command (which reads an entire document from disk into the primary merge file), you can decide which document to include as a merge is progressing. Such techniques are especially useful when you want to insert variable paragraphs in contracts, dunning notices, and other documents that must be customized for a particular situation.

Figure 26.1 shows a sample primary merge file that uses {IF} statements to build a letter based on information in a secondary merge file. Depending on the value in a field named *Days_Late* in the secondary merge file, the primary merge file reads in a document named *OVER30.WP, OVER60.WP,* or *OVER90.WP.*

Take a look at the first {IF}...{ENDIF} clause in the document, as shown below:

NOTE NOTE
NOTE

Like all primary merge files, the example in Figure 26.1 was created at the normal Edit screen, using Tools ➤ Merge Codes to insert merge commands.

{IF}{FIELD}Days_Late~>29~&**{FIELD}**Days_Late~<60~**{COMMENT}**
    ~**{DOCUMENT}**OVER30.WP~**{COMMENT}**
~**{END IF}{COMMENT}**

The first line says, "If the Days_Late field contains a number that's greater than 29 *and* a value that's less than 60." Now if the Days_Late field satisfies the test, the {DOCUMENT}OVER30.WP~ command reads the OVER30.WP document into this primary merge file. The closing {END IF} command marks the close of the {IF} command. The other two {IF}…{END IF} statements test for Days_Late between 59 and 89 (inserting OVER60.WP) and Days_Late greater than 89 (inserting OVER90.WP). The resulting merge file will contain one letter for each person in the mailing list, where the content of each letter depends on how late the person is in paying.

Using Comments to Control Spaces and Blank Lines

NOTE *As with all merge commands, you must select {COMMENT} from the merge commands menu; you cannot simply type the word {COMMENT} on the screen.*

A comment (or programmer comment) is a block of text in a macro or primary merge file that WordPerfect ignores. You use them to write reminder notes to yourself (or other people) explaining the purpose of a particular set of commands and also to make your program easier to read and understand. Every comment in a primary merge file starts with a {COMMENT} command and ends with one tilde (~). In between the {COMMENT} and tilde, you can type text and enter tabs and hard returns.

```
{FIELD}First~ {FIELD}Last~
{FIELD}Address~
{FIELD}City~, {FIELD}State~  {FIELD}Zip~

{FIELD}Salutation~:

{IF}{FIELD}Days_Late~>29&{FIELD}Days_Late~<60~{COMMENT}
    ~{DOCUMENT}OVER30.WP~{COMMENT}
~{END IF}{COMMENT}

~{IF}{FIELD}Days_Late~>59&{FIELD}Days_Late~<90~{COMMENT}
    ~{DOCUMENT}OVER60.WP~{COMMENT}
~{END IF}{COMMENT}

~{IF}{FIELD}Days_Late~>89~{COMMENT}
    ~{DOCUMENT}OVER90.WP~{COMMENT}
~{END IF}

Sincerely:


Wilma Dunning
Accounts Receivable
                                    Doc 1 Pg 1 Ln 1" Pos 1"
```

FIGURE 26.1:
A primary merge file that assembles a document based on information in the secondary merge file

As mentioned earlier, the tabs or hard returns you enter in a merge file will appear as extra spaces or hard returns in the merged file, unless you hide them in some way. This hiding is accomplished with a {COMMENT} command. In a primary merge file, comments are especially useful for structuring your {IF} and {END IF} commands in blocks (a common practice in most programming languages), without inserting hard returns or extra spaces into the primary merge file.

If you look back at Figure 26.1, you'll notice that some {COMMENT} commands are used with each {IF} command. The {COMMENT} at the end of the first {IF}{FIELD}... line allows a hard return and tab to be inserted, which indents the command on the next line without showing the hard return and tab in the resulting merge. The tilde before the {DOCUMENT}OVER30.WP line ends the first comment. Likewise, {COMMENT} commands are used after the lines containing the {DOCUMENT} and {END IF} commands, again simply to allow hard returns to be inserted in the primary merge file without printing blank lines on the final merged document. Ultimately, WordPerfect just interprets all these comments as if the three sets of {IF}...{END IF} commands had been strung together without any intervening tabs or hard returns.

A MACRO TO LOCATE A SPECIFIC FONT

Figure 26.2 shows a macro that can locate a specific font within your document, as opposed to a generic [Font] code. For instance, you can use it to place the cursor on the next Helvetica or Courier font code. This handy macro demonstrates several basic principles that will be useful when you start developing advanced macros on your own.

Like all advanced macros, the examples in figures 26.2 through 26.4 were created with the Macro Editor, not at the Edit screen.

You'll notice that the figure has line numbers and a vertical line to the left of the macro text and commands. These are shown only to make this macro (and the two that follow) easier to understand as you learn about their inner workings. If you try to create these macros on your own, please do not type the line numbers or vertical lines: Line numbers and vertical lines are *never* included in macros.

SUMMARY OF THE MACRO

One way to learn macro programming is to read a few completed macros, thoroughly understand their logic and commands, type them into the Macro

Editor, run them, and then try to write some macros on your own. To help you through this process, I'll discuss a few sample macros step by step, first describing them in plain English, then discussing details of the commands used.

```
1   {;}************************* FF.WPM (Find font)
2       Macro to locate a specific font in a document~
3
4   {;}Note state of Reveal Codes screen, then turn it off.~
5   {ASSIGN}RevealCodes~WasOff~
6   {IF}{STATE}&512~
7       {ASSIGN}RevealCodes~WasOn~
8       {Reveal Codes}                      {;}Turn off Reveal Codes~
9   {END IF}
10
11  {;}Note current position in a document~
12  {ASSIGN}PageNo~{SYSTEM}Page~~
13  {ASSIGN}LinePos~{SYSTEM}Line~~
14  {ASSIGN}RowPos~{SYSTEM}Pos~~
15
16  {;}Ask user for font search for, and store selection in LookFor~
17  {Font}4
18  {PROMPT}Highlight font to look for, and press Enter to select it.~
19  {PAUSE}
20  {ASSIGN}LookFor~{SYSTEM}Entry~~
21  {Exit}
22
23  {;}Turn off screen activity and do the job.~
24  {DISPLAY OFF}
25  {ON NOT FOUND}{GO}NotFound~~     {;}If font not found, tell user~
26
27  {LABEL}NextFont~
28      {Search}{Font}4{Search}
29      {Font}4
30      {;}Is this the font we're looking for?~
31      {IF}"{SYSTEM}Entry~"="{VARIABLE}LookFor~"~
32          {Cancel}{GO}Found~    {;}If yes, go to Found~
33      {ELSE}
34          {Cancel}                {;}Otherwise, leave Fonts menu and proceed.~
35      {END IF}
36  {GO}NextFont~
37
38  {;}NotFound --- Requested font not found below cursor~
39  {LABEL}NotFound~
40      {;}Inform the user~
41      {CHAR}Dummy~Font not found, press any key to continue~
42
43      {;}Return to original cursor position in document~
44      {Home}{Home}{Up}
45      {Goto}{VARIABLE}PageNo~~{Enter}
46      {WHILE}{SYSTEM}Line~<{VARIABLE}LinePos~~
47          {Down}
48      {END WHILE}
49      {WHILE}{SYSTEM}Pos~<{VARIABLE}RowPos~~
50          {Right}
51      {END WHILE}
52
53      {;}Turn on Reveal Codes if it was on at the start~
54      {IF}"{VARIABLE}RevealCodes~"="WasOn"~
55          {Reveal Codes}
56      {END IF}
57  {QUIT}                  {;}End the macro~
58
59  {;}Found -- Requested font was found: Show it on Reveal Codes~
60  {LABEL}Found~
61      {Reveal Codes}          {;}Turn on Reveal Codes~
62  {QUIT}                  {;}End the macro~
```

FIGURE 26.2:

A macro to locate a specific font in a document. The line numbers and vertical line are shown for discussion purposes only and are not part of the macro.

Here is an explanation of what's happening in the macro shown in Figure 26.2. The numbers in parentheses correspond to the line numbers in the figure:

Lines 1–2, 4, 11, etc.: These are comments to be read; WordPerfect ignores them.

Lines 5–9: The macro starts by assuming Reveal Codes is off (line 5). If Reveal Codes is on (line 6), the macro stores the phrase *WasOn* in the variable named *RevealCodes* for future reference (line 7), then turns off the Reveal Codes screen (line 8).

Lines 11–14: Macro stores the current page number (line 12), line number (line 13), and position within the line (line 14) in the document so that it can restore the cursor to that position if it cannot find the requested font. (This way the macro will work like WordPerfect's Search command, which returns the cursor to its original position if a search is unsuccessful.)

Lines 16–21: Displays the font list (line 17), asks the user to highlight the font he or she is looking for (line 18), waits for the user to highlight it and press ↵ (line 19), saves the user's selection in a variable named *LookFor* (line 20), and leaves the font list (line 21).

Line 24: Turns off the screen display to reduce screen activity.

Line 25: If the Search fails, will pass control to the routine named *NotFound* in line 39.

Line 27: The routine named *NextFont* repeats the steps in lines 28–36 until there are no more fonts or until you find the font you want:

Lines 28–29: Searches for the next generic [Font] code in the document (line 28), then goes to the font list (line 29). At this point, the highlighted entry in the font list will match the currently set font in the document.

Lines 31–36: Line 31 asks, "Is the currently highlighted font on the menu the same as the font stored in the variable named *LookFor*?" If yes, leave the font menu and go to the routine named *Found* in line 60 (line 32). If no (line 33), cancel the Font menu and try again (lines 34–36).

Line 39: The routine named *NotFound* is executed if no fonts match the one the macro is looking for (lines 41–57).

Line 41: Displays a message informing the user and waits for a single keypress. The keypress is stored in a variable named *Dummy* (so named because it is not necessary to know what

*A **routine** is a group of commands designed to do a specific job.*

key the user pressed, but the {CHAR} command requires that the keypress be stored in a variable).

Lines 44–51: Returns the cursor to its original position by moving to the top of the document (line 44), going to the previously saved page number (line 45), moving down until the previously saved line number is reached (lines 46–48), then moving across the line until the previously saved position within the line is reached (lines 49-51).

Lines 54–56: Turns Reveal Codes back on if it was on at the start.

Line 57: Ends the macro.

Lines 60–62: The Found routine is executed if the macro finds the requested font. Turns on Reveal Codes so that the user can see the font code (line 61), then ends the macro (line 62).

USING THE SAMPLE MACRO COMMANDS

Now that I've discussed the logic of how the macro operates, here's an explanation of the macro commands used (in order of appearance). Again, I've included line numbers so that you can refer back to Figure 26.2 to see where these commands are used in the example.

{;}comment~ Comments are notes to the macro programmer (or other programmers) about the purpose of various lines and routines. Everything between the {;} command and the tilde (~) is ignored by WordPerfect as it executes the macro. A comment can appear on a line by itself (lines 1, 2, 4, etc.) or at the end of a line (Lines 8, 25, 32, etc.) if you use the Tab key to move the cursor beyond the end of the command on that line.

{ASSIGN}var~expr~ Assigns the value of the expression (*expr*) to a variable (*var*). For example, the {ASSIGN} command on line 5 assigns the value *WasOff* to the variable named *RevealCodes*.

{IF}expr~ Executes a set of commands if the expression (*expr*) is true (lines 6–9, 31–35, 54–56). For example, lines 6–9 assign the value *WasOn* to the RevealCodes variable (line 7) and turn Reveal Codes off (line 8) if the {STATE} command (described next) indicates that Reveal Codes was on. All {IF} command sequences must end with an {END IF} command, as in line 9. If you want to execute certain commands only when the {IF} expression is false, use the {ELSE} command, as in line 33.

{STATE} Returns a number representing the current state of WordPerfect (line 6). You can find out what state WordPerfect is in by forming an AND expression (using &) and combining this with an {IF} command. The {STATE} command lets you test for several different states, including 512 (Reveal Codes active) and 2048 (cursor is in a list).

{SYSTEM}sysvar~ Returns the value of the given system variable (*sysvar*). For examples of the {SYSTEM} command, see lines 12–14, 20, 31, 46, and 49. WordPerfect has many system variables, including Page (returns the current page number), Line (returns the current line number), Pos (returns the current horizontal position within a line), Entry (returns a copy of the entry being highlighted in a list of fonts, styles, etc.), and List (returns the number of items in a list).

{PROMPT}message~ Displays a message on the status line at the bottom of the screen (line 18) and is useful for sending a message to the user. Be sure to follow this with a {PAUSE} command to give the user time to read your message.

{PAUSE} Pauses the macro until the user presses ↵ (line 19).

{DISPLAY OFF} Turns off the display so that the user can't see the macro executing (line 24). Use {DISPLAY ON} if you want to turn the display back on.

{ON NOT FOUND}action~ Performs the specified action if a Search command fails to find what it's looking for. On line 25, the action is a {GO} command, which sends the macro to the NotFound label. Two tildes are required in this example: one to end the {ON NOT FOUND} command and one to end the {GO} command.

{GO}label~ WordPerfect's "Go To" command, this transfers execution to the specified label (lines 25 and 36). Normally a macro executes from top to bottom, unless you use a command like {GO} (or others listed under "Flow Control" in Table 26.1).

{LABEL}label~ Marks a particular line in the macro (lines 27, 39, and 60), which is typically the first line in a routine that's designed to perform some specific job. Several commands, including {GO}, can cause the macro to skip directly to the position marked by the label. For example, the {GO}NextFont~ command in line 36 causes the macro to loop back to the {LABEL}NextFont~ command in line 27. Labels can be any length and can include spaces. Upper- and lowercase are treated the same (e.g., NEXTFONT and NextFont are equivalent).

{VARIABLE}var~ Accesses the contents of a variable (lines 31, 45, 46, 49, 54). For example, the following command from line 31 tests to see whether the value of the highlighted font is equal to the value in the variable named *LookFor:*

{IF}"{SYSTEM}Entry~"="{VARIABLE}LookFor~"~

{CHAR}var~message~ Displays a message and waits for the user to type a single keystroke, which is then stored in the variable (*var*). This command is useful for simulating WordPerfect menus. In line 41, the user's response is stored in the variable named *Dummy*. Later in this chapter, you'll see a more elaborate use of the {CHAR} command to create a menu at the bottom of the screen.

{WHILE}expr~ Executes the commands between {WHILE} and {END WHILE} statements as long as the expression (*expr*) is true (lines 46–48 and 49–51). For example, the commands in lines 46–48 move the cursor down as long as the current line number returned by {SYSTEM}Line~ is less than the line number stored in the LinePos variable in line 13.

{QUIT} Stops the macro or merge dead in its tracks (lines 57 and 62).

Using Keystroke Commands in a Macro

As mentioned earlier, a macro is just a series of recorded keystrokes and macro commands. You can record the keystrokes right at the Edit screen, as described in Chapter 15, or in the Macro Editor. When composing macro programs like the ones in this chapter, you use the Macro Editor to enter the keystroke commands and any text you want.

Like macro programming commands, shortcut keystrokes and cursor-movement keys appear in your macro as boldface text enclosed in curly braces; however, unlike programming commands (which are uppercase only), these will be in lowercase letters, except for an initial capital letter. Examples include {Font}, {Home}, {Down}, {Exit}, {Cancel}, and so on.

To record a shortcut keystroke, press the shortcut key (e.g., F1 for {Cancel}, F7 for {Exit}, Ctrl-F8 for {Font}, or Alt-F8 for {Styles}). If the shortcut key normally leads to a menu or requires you to make other selections, simply type

NOTE *When comparing strings of text in an {IF} command, place quotes (") around the values being compared. When comparing numbers, quotes aren't necessary.*

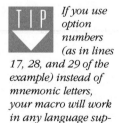
TIP *If you use option numbers (as in lines 17, 28, and 29 of the example) instead of mnemonic letters, your macro will work in any language supported by WordPerfect.*

the mnemonic letter or number of your selection, or enter any required text, exactly as you would if you were working at the normal Edit screen.

Remember that the keys you press in the Macro Editor are stored as command codes in your macro file: They do not activate WordPerfect features until you execute the macro. For instance, when you press the {Font} key (Ctrl-F8) in the Macro Editor, you won't actually see the font menu, only the {Font} code. Therefore, before composing your macro, you should either write down the exact keypresses required or record them in a short macro that you combine with the main macro.

As mentioned in Chapter 15, cursor-movement keypresses, Exit (F7), Cancel (F1), and Macro Define (Ctrl-F10) cannot be inserted in your macro just by pressing the keys themselves. Instead, you must press Ctrl-V, then the key you want (e.g., press Ctrl-V then ↵ to insert the {Enter} keypress). Looking back at Figure 26.2, you can see that entered shortcut keypresses, text, and cursor movements were entered in lines 17, 21, 28–29, 32, 34, 44–45, 47, 50, 55, and 61. In some cases, these were combined with macro programming commands on the same lines.

A MACRO TO LOCATE A SPECIFIC PAIRED STYLE

This macro finds only paired styles, not open styles.

The macro to locate a specific paired style, shown in Figure 26.3, is virtually identical to the previous macro to locate a specific font, except that it lets the user search for a specific style within the document. You'll find the main differences in lines 17, 28, and 29, which access the styles list using the {Style} shortcut key rather than the font list using the {Font} key.

A MACRO TO CHANGE FONTS

The macro to change fonts throughout a document, shown in Figure 26.4, builds on the basic principles presented in the macro to find a specific font, letting the user search for and replace a particular font. Be aware, however, that if the currently selected printer has scalable fonts, this macro actually replaces a *typeface,* not a font per se. That is, you can replace all the Courier codes (regardless of size) with a new typeface, but you cannot replace Courier 10-point with Courier 12-point. The reason is that the {SYSTEM}Entry command (line 83) can only grab exactly what's highlighted on a menu, which does not include the point size if the currently selected printer has scalable fonts.

FIGURE 26.3:

*A macro to locate a
specific style in a
document*

```
 1  {;}************************ FS.WPM (Find a paired style)
 2      Macro to locate a specific paired style in a document~
 3
 4  {;}Note state of Reveal Codes screen, then turn it off.~
 5  {ASSIGN}RevealCodes~WasOff~
 6  {IF}{STATE}&512~
 7      {ASSIGN}RevealCodes~WasOn~
 8      {Reveal Codes}                    {;}Turn off Reveal Codes~
 9  {END IF}
10
11  {;}Note current position in a document~
12  {ASSIGN}PageNo~{SYSTEM}Page~~
13  {ASSIGN}LinePos~{SYSTEM}Line~~
14  {ASSIGN}RowPos~{SYSTEM}Pos~~
15
16  {;}Ask user for style to search for, and store selection in LookFor~
17  {Style}
18  {PROMPT}Highlight style to look for, and press Enter to select it.~
19  {PAUSE}
20  {ASSIGN}LookFor~{SYSTEM}Entry~~
21  {Exit}
22
23  {;}Turn off screen activity and do the job.~
24  {DISPLAY OFF}
25  {ON NOT FOUND}{GO}NotFound~~     {;}If font not found, tell user~
26
27  {LABEL}NextStyle~
28      {Search}{Style}1{Search}
29      {Style}
30      {;}Is this the style we're looking for?~
31      {IF}"{SYSTEM}Entry~"="{VARIABLE}LookFor~"~
32          {Cancel}{GO}Found~    {;}If yes, go to Found~
33      {ELSE}
34          {Cancel}                {;}Otherwise, leave styles menu and proceed.~
35      {END IF}
36  {GO}NextStyle~
37
38  {;}NotFound --- Requested style not found below cursor~
39  {LABEL}NotFound~
40      {;}Inform the user~
41      {CHAR}Dummy~Style not found, press any key to continue~
42
43      {;}Return to original cursor position in document~
44      {Home}{Home}{Up}
45      {Goto}{VARIABLE}PageNo~~{Enter}
46      {WHILE}{SYSTEM}Line~<{VARIABLE}LinePos~~
47          {Down}
48      {END WHILE}
49      {WHILE}{SYSTEM}Pos~<{VARIABLE}RowPos~~
50          {Right}
51      {END WHILE}
52
53      {;}Turn on Reveal Codes if it was off at the start~
54      {IF}"{VARIABLE}RevealCodes~"="WasOn"~
55          {Reveal Codes}
56      {END IF}
57  {QUIT}                    {;}End the macro~
58
59  {;}Found -- Requested style was found: Show it on Reveal Codes~
60  {LABEL}Found~
61      {Reveal Codes}          {;}else turn on Reveal Codes~
62  {QUIT}                {;}End the macro~
```

FIGURE 26.4:

*A macro to change a
font throughout a
document*

```
1   {;}******************************** ChFont.wpm (Change Font)
2        Macro to change a font in document and/or styles~
3
4   {;}Determine, and remember, initial state of Reveal Codes screen.~
5   {ASSIGN}RevealCodes~WasOff~
6   {IF}{STATE}&512~
7        {ASSIGN}RevealCodes~WasOn~
8   {END IF}
9
10  {;}Ask user for font to be replaced, and store as OldFont~
11  {Font}4
12  {PROMPT}Highlight font to be replaced, and press Enter to select it.~
13  {PAUSE}
14  {ASSIGN}OldFont~{SYSTEM}Entry~~
15
16  {;}Ask user for new font, and store as NewFont.~
17  {PROMPT}Highlight new (replacement) font, and press Enter~
18  {PAUSE}
19  {ASSIGN}NewFont~{SYSTEM}Entry~~
20  {Exit}
21
22  {;}Display main menu~
23  {LABEL}MainMenu~
24  {CHAR}Choice~{^Q}Change where?;
25       {^]}1{^\} {^]}D{^\}ocument;
26       {^]}2{^\} {^]}S{^\}tyles;
27       {^]}3{^\} {^]}B{^\}oth Styles and Document;
28       {^]}4{^\} {^]}C{^\}ancel~
29
30       {;}Perform request, or redisplay menu if invalid entry~
31       {CASE}{VARIABLE}Choice~~
32            1~Document~D~Document~d~Document~
33            2~Styles~S~Styles~s~Styles~
34            3~Both~B~Both~b~Both~
35            4~Cancel~C~Cancel~c~Cancel~
36            {ELSE}~BadChoice~
37       ~
38  {;}Document -- Change font in the document~
39       {LABEL}Document~
40       {;}Need consistent Reveal Codes state~.
41       {IF}"{VARIABLE}RevealCodes~"="WasOff"~{Reveal Codes}{END IF}
42       {DISPLAY OFF}
43       {ASSIGN}StartPoint~1~
44       {CHAR}StartPoint~
45            {^]}1{^\} {^]}E{^\}ntire document;
46            {^]}2{^\} {^]}B{^\}elow cursor only~
47
48       {CASE}{VARIABLE}StartPoint~~
49            2~StartHere~B~StartHere~b~StartHere~~
50            {Home}{Home}{Home}{Up}
51       {LABEL}StartHere~
52       {CALL}NextChange~
53       {RETURN}
54
55  {;}Styles -- Change font in Styles~
56       {LABEL}Styles~
57       {DISPLAY OFF}
58       {Style}
59       {ASSIGN}HowMany~{SYSTEM}List~~
60       {Home}{Home}{Home}{Up}
61       {FOR}LoopCount~1~{VARIABLE}Howmany~~1~
62            EC        {;}edit codes~
63            {CALL}NextChange~
64            {Exit}{Exit}{Down}
65       {END FOR}
66  {Exit}{RETURN}         {;}Leave the styles menu~
67
68  {;}Both -- Change fonts in both the Document and Styles.~
69       {LABEL}Both~
70       {CALL}Document~
71       {CALL}Styles~
72
73  {;}Cancel -- Macro is finished, or user canceled.~
74       {LABEL}Cancel~
75       {QUIT}
76
```

SUMMARY OF THE MACRO

As you can see, this macro is much more complex than the two previous ones, but it uses many of the concepts you've seen before. Here's what's happening:

Lines 5–8: Saves the state of Reveal Codes.

Lines 10–14: Displays the list of available fonts (line 11). Asks the user to highlight the old font to replace (lines 12–13) and stores that selection as OldFont (line 14).

Lines 17–20: Asks the user to highlight the new (substitute) font (lines 17–18) and stores that selection as NewFont (line 19). Exits the font list (line 20).

Lines 23–28: The MainMenu displays the main menu on the status line at the bottom of the screen and waits for the user to type a single character:

◆ **1** or **D** to change the font in the document only

◆ **2** or **S** to change the font in the styles only

◆ **3** or **B** to change the font in both the styles and the document

◆ **4** or **C** to cancel the selection

Lines 31–37: Uses a {CASE} command (described below) to branch to one of the following routines, depending on the user's response:

◆ If the user types *1, D,* or *d,* branches to Document routine in line 39.

◆ If the user types *2, S,* or *s,* branches to Styles routine in line 56.

```
77  {;}NextChange -- Change the next font.~
78      {LABEL}NextChange~
79      {ON NOT FOUND}{RETURN}~
80      {Search}{Font}4{Search}
81      {Font}4
82
83      {IF}"{SYSTEM}Entry~"="{VARIABLE}OldFont~"~
84      n{VARIABLE}NewFont~{Enter}{Enter}
85
86      {;}If asking for point size, press Enter again~
87      {IF}{STATE}&2048~{Enter}{END IF}
88
89      {;}Delete the old font (to the left of the current one)~
90      {Left}{Left}
91      {Del}{Right}
92      {ELSE}          {;}If not what we're looking for, leave fonts menu~
93          {Cancel}
94      {END IF}
95  {GO}NextChange~      {;}Check next [Font] code.~
96
97  {;}BadChoice -- Give user another chance at the menu selection.~
98      {LABEL}BadChoice~
99      {BELL}
100     {GO}MainMenu~
101
102 {;}End of ChFont.wpm macro.~
```

FIGURE 26.4:

A macro to change a font throughout a document (continued)

◆ If the user types *3, B,* or *b,* branches to Both routine in line 69.

◆ If the user types *4, C,* or *c,* branches to Cancel routine in line 74.

◆ If the user types anything else, branches to BadChoice routine in line 98.

Line 39: The Document routine changes the font in the document only (lines 40–53).

Lines 41–42: Turns off Reveal Codes if it was previously on, then turns off the screen display.

Line 43: Stores the value *1* in a variable named *StartPoint,* for future use.

Lines 44–46: Displays a menu asking the user how much of the document to change and waits for a response. The user can change the entire document by typing either *1* or *E,* or change only the portion below the cursor by typing *2* or *B.*

Lines 48–51: If the user wants to change only the portion below the cursor, skips to the label StartHere without executing {Home}{Home}{Home}{Up} commands, thereby beginning the search at current cursor position. If the user wants to change the font in the entire document, these commands are not skipped over, so they do move the cursor to the top of the document before execution gets to the label StartHere.

Line 52: Calls the subroutine NextChange, which actually performs the font switch (see lines 78–95).

Line 53: Returns control to calling routine if executed as a subroutine by a {CALL} command (i.e., from the routine named *Both*).

Line 56: The Styles routine changes the font in styles only (lines 57–66).

Line 57: Turns off the screen display.

Line 58: Turns on the style list.

Line 59: Counts the number of styles in the list and saves this number in HowMany.

Line 60: Moves the highlight to the top of the style list.

Lines 61–65: For each item in the list, edits the style codes (line 62), calls the NextChange subroutine to change the font from the old font to the new font (line 63), returns to the styles list, and moves down to the next style (line 64).

If Reveal Codes is off, WordPerfect asks for permission before deleting a hidden code, but not if Reveal Codes is on. Therefore, any macro that deletes codes must turn Reveal Codes on or off, so you can include or exclude keystrokes to respond to the prompt.

*A **sub-routine** is a routine that, after doing its job, passes control back to the first command line beneath the command line that called it.*

Line 66: When finished changing the styles, exits the style list and returns to wherever this routine was called from (routine named *Both*), or if the user is changing a font in styles only, ends the macro.

Lines 69–71: The Both routine changes the fonts in both the document and the styles by calling these as subroutines.

Lines 74–75: The Cancel label ends the macro.

Line 78: The NextChange subroutine does the work of changing from the old font to the new font (lines 79–95).

Line 79: Prepares to return to the calling routine if and when a search fails (i.e., there are no more [Font] codes below the cursor.)

Lines 80–81: Finds the next [Font] code, then opens the font list. The highlighted entry in the font list will match the currently set font in the document.

Line 83–95: Asks, "Does the currently highlighted font match the one we stored as OldFont?" If it does, perform a Name Search (line 84) to move the highlight to the font that matches the one stored in New-Font and select that font. If it's a scalable font, press ↵ again to respond to the point-size prompt (line 87). Then delete the old font (lines 90–91) and loop back to NextChange (line 95). If the current font did not match the font being changed, just leave the font list (line 93). Either way, check the next generic [Font] code by repeating the NextChange routine (line 95).

Lines 98–100: The BadChoice label tells the user that he or she didn't choose the correct option from the main menu, beeps at the user, and returns to the MainMenu.

In macros, it's best to select fonts, styles, and other items that are chosen from a list by using the **N***ame Search feature. You can activate Name Search within a macro by having it type* **n** *or* **=** *when the font list is displayed (*= *is the international version.)*

DISPLAYING A CUSTOM MENU

The macro in Figure 26.4 includes commands for displaying a WordPerfect-style menu on the status line at the bottom of the screen (see lines 24–28 and 44–46). The {CHAR} command allows you to print a message and store a one-character user response to that message. You can enhance the appearance of your message by typing special Ctrl-*letter* combinations along with the message text. Some commonly used combinations are

Ctrl-]	Turns on bold; displayed as {^]} on the Macro Editor screen
Ctrl-\	Turns off bold; displayed as {^\} on the Macro Editor screen
Ctrl-Q	Turns off all display attributes; displayed as {^Q} on the Macro Editor screen

Therefore, you would use the keystrokes shown in Figure 26.4 (lines 24–28) to display the following menu at the bottom of the screen:

Change where?; **1 D**ocument; **2 S**tyles; **3 B**oth Styles and Document; **4** Cancel

SOME NEW COMMANDS

I've covered most of the commands used in Figure 26.4, but a few are new:

{CASE}expr ̃ case1 ̃ label1 ̃ ...caseN ̃ labelN ̃ Branches to one of several locations, depending on the value of the expression (*expr*). The value of the expression is compared with each case. When a match is found, execution branches to the label associated with that case. You can use an {OTHERWISE} or {ELSE} command to handle situations where the expression doesn't match any of the cases listed. Figure 26.4 shows {CASE} commands in lines 31–37 and 48–49. In lines 31 and 32, for example, the expression being tested is the value in the Choice variable. If it's *1, D,* or *d,* the case statement branches to the Document label.

{CALL}label ̃ Transfers execution to the *label* subroutine. When the subroutine is completed, the macro returns to the command following the call.

{RETURN} Marks the end of a subroutine and causes execution to resume with the command following a {CALL} or {CASE CALL} statement. If there isn't a {CALL} or {CASE CALL} to return to, the macro ends (see lines 53, 66, and 79).

{FOR}var ̃ start ̃ stop ̃ step ̃ Executes a series of commands between {FOR} and {END FOR} a certain number of times. The {FOR} command initializes the variable (*var*) to the start value. Each time through the loop, {FOR} increments the variable by the step. The loop stops after the variable is greater than or equal to the stop value. The start, stop, and step can be expressions, variables, or other commands. See lines 61–65 for an example using {FOR}.

{BELL} Causes the computer to beep (line 99).

Having studied the macros in this chapter, you may be ready to build a few on your own. Again, keep in mind that macro programming is not something that you have to learn; recorded-keystroke macros like those discussed in Chapter 15 work just fine for most people. In the next chapter, you'll learn ways to attach macros (recorded or otherwise) to specific keys, and how to build personalized or project-specific collections or macros.

CHAPTER 27

Customizing the Keyboard Layout

very key on your keyboard performs some action when pressed. When you press a letter or number key, that letter or number appears on the screen. When you press a cursor-movement key or function key, Word-Perfect moves the cursor or inserts a hidden code. WordPerfect lets you change the action assigned to nearly every key on your keyboard. You may find this feature handy if

◆ You want to change some WordPerfect keystrokes to act like other programs you're familiar with.

◆ You want to be able to type special characters without using the Compose (Ctrl-V) key and remembering special codes.

◆ You share your computer with other users, and you want to create your own set of Alt-*letter* key macros.

◆ You'd like to create unique sets of Alt-*letter* key macros for individual projects.

◆ You want more than the 26 combination keystroke macros available with Alt-*letter* names.

To change the roles played by various keys on your keyboard, you need to create a *soft keyboard,* define the roles played by the various keys on that keyboard, and then activate the keyboard. You can create any number of soft keyboards, each of which has a unique set of custom keys assigned to it. You can activate or deactivate a soft keyboard at any time.

When you create a soft keyboard, you can change the role of virtually any key or key combination, except for the few "hard-wired" keys: ↵, Print Screen, Scroll Lock, Pause/Break, Caps Lock, and Num Lock. You can also assign actions to unused key combinations, such as Ctrl and any letter.

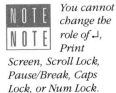
You cannot change the role of ↵, Print Screen, Scroll Lock, Pause/Break, Caps Lock, or Num Lock.

SAMPLE SOFT KEYBOARDS

Your WordPerfect package comes with a set of six sample soft keyboards that you may want to explore on your own. Their names are

Altrnat	Redefines F1 as the Help key, F3 as the Escape key, and Escape as the Cancel key, to match the conventions of many popular programs
Enhanced	Adds definitions for Ctrl, Shift, and Alt with F11 and F12, and the cursor-movement keys for use with an enhanced keyboard
Equation	Has special mathematical characters as Alt-*letter* and Ctrl-*letter* combinations
Fastkeys	Adds definitions for Ctrl-*letter* combinations, such as Ctrl-B for boldface
Macros	Offers popular macros as Alt-*letter* and Ctrl-*letter* combinations
Shortcut	Provides quick routes through common menu sequences (most of the Size and Appearance options are assigned to Ctrl-key and Alt-key combinations)

The sections that follow describe how to activate and use a soft keyboard, then describe how to create your own.

ACTIVATING A SOFT KEYBOARD

▌ **TO ACTIVATE A SOFT KEYBOARD,**

select File ➤ Setup ➤ Keyboard Layout (or press Shift-F1 K), move the highlight to the keyboard you want to activate, and choose Select.

To activate an existing soft keyboard, follow these steps:

1. Select **F**ile ➤ Se**t**up ➤ **K**eyboard Layout (or press **Shift-F1 K**). A list of available soft keyboards appears, as in Figure 27.1.

2. Highlight the name of the layout you want to use, and choose **S**elect.

3. Press Exit (**F7**) to return to the Edit screen.

The key definitions of the soft keyboard you selected go immediately into effect.

EXPLORING THE NEW KEYBOARD

To determine which key does what on a soft keyboard, you can go through the basic steps required to edit the keyboard, or you can look at the keyboard

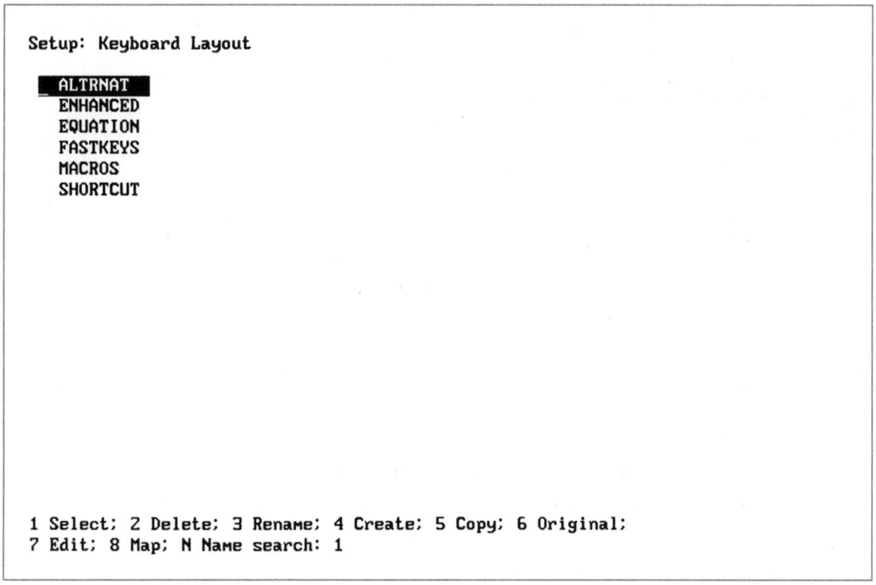

```
Setup: Keyboard Layout

  ALTRNAT
  ENHANCED
  EQUATION
  FASTKEYS
  MACROS
  SHORTCUT
```

```
1 Select; 2 Delete; 3 Rename; 4 Create; 5 Copy; 6 Original;
7 Edit; 8 Map; N Name search: 1
```

FIGURE 27.1:

The Keyboard Layout screen, with the six prepackaged soft keyboards

map (described later in this chapter). Start from the Edit screen, and follow these steps:

1. Select **F**ile ➤ **S**etup ➤ **K**eyboard Layout (**Shift-F1 K**).

2. Move the highlight to the keyboard you want to edit, and select **E**dit.

NOTE NOTE

The list of keys may be longer than what appears on the screen. You can use the movement keys to scroll through the complete list.

A brief description of each custom key's action appears (an example is shown for the SHORTCUT keyboard in Figure 27.2). In the example, you can see that pressing Alt-W will change the appearance of the text to Shadow. In other words, while the SHORTCUT keyboard is in effect, there are two ways you can change the text appearance to Shadow: with the standard method (i.e., using the Font menu or Ctrl-F8 key) and with the shortcut method (i.e., simply by pressing Alt-W).

You might want to explore the various soft keyboards that come with WordPerfect to see if one is particularly well suited to your needs. When you've finished viewing the descriptions of the actions assigned to the keys, press Exit (F7) twice to return to the Edit screen.

To try a key at the Edit screen, just press it (for example, press Alt-W to try the Shadow key on the SHORTCUT keyboard). You can also look behind the scenes to see what takes place by turning on the Reveal Codes screen.

```
Keyboard: Edit

  Name: SHORTCUT

  Key            Action          Description

  Alt-W          {KEY MACRO 26}  Shadow
  Alt-E          {KEY MACRO 15}  Edit a Code
  Alt-R          {KEY MACRO 8}   Redline
  Alt-T          {KEY MACRO 27}  Strikeout
  Alt-I          {KEY MACRO 1}   Italics
  Alt-O          {KEY MACRO 25}  Outline
  Alt-P          {KEY MACRO 21}  Superscript
  Alt-A          {KEY MACRO 32}  Add an Attribute
  Alt-S          {KEY MACRO 6}   Small
  Alt-D          {KEY MACRO 2}   Double Underline
  Alt-F          {KEY MACRO 7}   Fine
  Alt-G          {KEY MACRO 30}  Go Printer
  Alt-L          {KEY MACRO 5}   Large
  Alt-X          {KEY MACRO 3}   Extra Large
  Alt-V          {KEY MACRO 4}   Very Large
  Alt-B          {KEY MACRO 20}  Subscript
  Ctrl-B         {KEY MACRO 23}  Base Font

 1 Action; 2 Dscrptn; 3 Original; 4 Create; 5 Move; Macro: 6 Save; 7 Retrieve: 1
```

FIGURE 27.2:

The custom keys on the SHORTCUT keyboard

RETURNING TO THE ORIGINAL KEYBOARD LAYOUT

Pressing Ctrl-6 restores the keyboard for the current editing session only (until you exit WordPerfect), whereas the Original option restores the keyboard permanently (or until you select a new one).

To deactivate a soft keyboard and return to the normal WordPerfect keyboard, select **F**ile ➤ Se**t**up ➤ **K**eyboard Layout ➤ **O**riginal (or press Shift-F1 K O). Then press Exit (F7) to return to the Edit screen. As a shortcut, you can just press Ctrl-6. Nothing will appear to happen, but WordPerfect immediately deactivates the soft keyboard and restores all the keys to their normal functions. Your normal Alt-key macros (if any) will also be available.

SOFT KEY/MACRO PRECEDENCE

*If you need to activate an Alt-letter macro while a soft key has precedence, press Alt-F10 and enter the file name of the macro (e.g., **altj** to execute your Alt-J macro).*

If you have an Alt-letter macro on-disk, and the current soft keyboard also has an action assigned to that Alt-letter combination, the soft key takes precedence over the macro. That is, an Alt-letter macro is temporarily deactivated when you use a soft keyboard that has another definition for the same Alt-letter combination.

Of course, the advantage of soft-key precedence is that you can create different soft keyboards for different projects. For example, you might have an Alt-H macro on one soft keyboard that formats headings according to one project's specifications and an Alt-H keystroke on another soft keyboard that formats headings according to another project's specs. So, regardless of how many different projects you have going, you can always use Alt-H to format headings.

CREATING YOUR OWN SOFT KEYBOARD

TO CREATE A SOFT KEYBOARD,

select File ➤ Setup ➤ Keyboard Layout ➤ Create (or press Shift-F1 K C), and enter a file name for the keyboard.

Each soft keyboard is stored as a file with the extension .WPK in the directory specified in Location of Files.

You can easily create your own soft keyboard by following these steps:

1. From the Edit screen, select File ➤ Setup ➤ Keyboard Layout ➤ Create (or press **Shift-F1 K C**). You'll see the following prompt:

   Keyboard Filename:

2. Type a file name (up to eight characters, with no extension) for the soft keyboard and press ↵. The name appears on the list of available soft keyboards and is highlighted for selection.

The new soft-keyboard name appears on the list, along with any existing soft keyboards. You can then assign new actions to existing keystrokes or to new keystrokes, as described in "Assigning Actions to Soft Keys" later in this chapter. You can activate the new soft keyboard at any time.

DELETING, RENAMING, AND COPYING KEYBOARDS

Use a copy of an existing keyboard as your starting point to create a new soft keyboard that has some keys in common with it.

Soft keyboards are stored as files and therefore can be copied, renamed, or deleted, by choosing the Cop**y**, **R**ename, or **D**elete option on the Keyboard Layout menu. There's also a **N**ame Search option on the menu that lets you type the name of the soft keyboard that you want to highlight.

If you want a macro to select a soft keyboard, be sure the macro uses the Name Search feature to choose the keyboard. That way, if the list of available keyboards changes (because you've added or deleted keyboards), the macro will still be able to locate the correct keyboard, by name instead of by position in the list.

ASSIGNING ACTIONS TO SOFT KEYS

TO ASSIGN AN ACTION TO A KEY IN THE CURRENT SOFT KEYBOARD,

1. **Select File ➤ Setup ➤ Keyboard Layout (or press Shift-F1 K).**

2. **Highlight the name of the soft keyboard in which you want to assign the key.**

3. **Choose Edit ➤ Create and define the key, description, and action as prompted.**

To assign a new action to a key or combination keystroke in a soft keyboard, follow these steps:

1. If you are starting at the Edit screen, select **File ➤ Setup ➤ K**eyboard Layout (or press **Shift-F1 K**) to get to the Keyboard Layout menu.

2. Move the highlight to the soft keyboard in which you want to add or change a key definition, then select **E**dit.

3. The Edit screen for that keyboard appears, listing the currently defined keys (if any).

While the Keyboard: Edit screen is displayed, you can define a key as follows:

1. Select **C**reate. You'll see the prompt

   ## Key:

2. Press the key you want to redefine. For example, to assign an action to the Ctrl-P combination, press Ctrl-P. You see the prompt

   ## Description:

3. You can type in a brief description (up to 39 characters), or just leave this entry blank if you prefer, then press ↵. The Key: Action screen appears, shown in Figure 27.3. Except for its title, this screen is the same as the Macro Editor screen (discussed in chapters 15 and 26).

4. Press **Delete** to erase the original definition of the key, which, unless some other definition has already been assigned, is just the key's name in macro format (e.g., *{^P}* for Ctrl-P in Figure 27.3).

5. Press the keys that produce the action you're assigning to the key, exactly as you do when defining keystrokes for a macro in the Macro Editor. You can use any combination of the following options:

   ◆ If you want the key to type text, type that text.

   ◆ If you want the key to type a special character, press Ctrl-2, the special character's code (e.g. *4, 0*), then ↵.

> **NOTE** *If you want to assign an existing macro to a key definition, see "Converting a Key Definition to a Macro" later in this chapter.*

```
Key: Action

    Key          Ctrl-P

    Description  The key description appears here

  ┌─────────────────────────────────────────────────┐
  │ {^P}                                            │
  │                                                 │
  │                                                 │
  │                                                 │
  │                                                 │
  │                                                 │
  │                                                 │
  │                                                 │
  │                                                 │
  │                                                 │
  └─────────────────────────────────────────────────┘

Ctrl-V to Insert next key as command;
Ctrl-PgUp for macro commands;  Press Exit when done
```

FIGURE 27.3:

The Key: Action screen for a sample key redefinition

◆ If you want the key to activate a feature, press the shortcut key for that feature (e.g., F4 for →Indent or Ctrl-F8 for Font).

◆ If you want the key to activate a cursor-movement key, or ⏎, Tab, Insert, Delete, Home, Exit (F7), Cancel (F1), Help (F3), Ctrl-V, or Delete to EOL (Ctrl-End), press Ctrl-V then the key.

◆ If you want to insert macro programming commands, press Ctrl-PgUp and select your command from the menu.

6. Press Exit (**F7**) to return to the Keyboard: Edit screen. Your newly redefined key is listed on the menu, along with the description you entered.

The lower-case-letter macro commands, such as {Para Up} and {Para Down}, represent keystrokes usually available only on enhanced BIOS keyboards; but you can assign these actions to a key on any keyboard when defining a soft keyboard or a macro.

You may be curious about the Action heading on the Keyboard: Edit screen. Entries in this column tell you whether a key has been redefined from its original action. If you redefine a key, the Action entry for that key will be {KEY MACRO *nn*}, where *nn* is a sequential macro number. If you didn't actually change the key's original definition (i.e., you skipped steps 4 and 5 above), the Action entry will be just the key name (e.g., F, {Home}, or {^P}) .

Figure 27.4 shows a sample key definition for Alt-I that italicizes the word at the cursor position. The commands for cursor-movement and editing actions, such as {Right}, {Del to EOL}, and {Word Right}, were entered by pressing Ctrl-V then the desired key (→, Ctrl-End, and Ctrl-→, respectively). The commands {Search Left}, {Search}, and {Font} were entered with shortcut keystrokes (Shift-F2, F2, and Ctrl-F8, respectively). The text, including the blank space to the right of the {Del to EOL} command and the letters *ai* (which choose **A**ttributes ➤ **I**talics from the Font menu), were typed directly from the keyboard.

You can record the keystrokes that you want to assign to a soft key at the Edit screen, as you would any other macro, then copy that macro to the soft key.

Figure 27.5 shows a more advanced example, which uses macro programming commands. The Ctrl-Q key has been defined to display this bottom menu:

S Left; **D** Right; **Y** Delete EOL

If the user of this keyboard presses Ctrl-Q then S, the cursor moves to the beginning of the line. If the user presses D, the cursor moves to the end of the line. If the user presses Y, the text from the cursor position to the end of the line is deleted. This makes the Ctrl-Q key combination act the way it does in WordStar and in the many text editors that follow WordStar conventions.

You can continue selecting Create to redefine additional keys. When you've finished defining keys, press Exit (F7) to return to the Keyboard Layout screen.

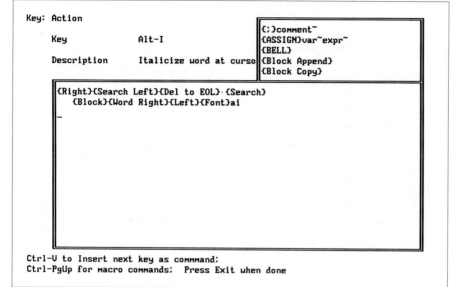

```
Key: Action

       Key              Alt-I                {;}comment~
                                             {ASSIGN}var~expr~
       Description      Italicize word at curso {BELL}
                                             {Block Append}
                                             {Block Copy}
   ┌─────────────────────────────────────────────────────────────┐
   │{Right}{Search Left}{Del to EOL} {Search}                     │
   │   {Block}{Word Right}{Left}{Font}ai                          │
   │_                                                             │
   │                                                             │
   │                                                             │
   │                                                             │
   │                                                             │
   │                                                             │
   │                                                             │
   │                                                             │
   └─────────────────────────────────────────────────────────────┘
Ctrl-V to Insert next key as commmand;
Ctrl-PgUp for macro commands;  Press Exit when done
```

FIGURE 27.4:

A sample soft-key definition that italicizes the word at the cursor

```
Key: Action

       Key              Ctrl-Q

       Description      Ctrl-Q macro

   ┌─────────────────────────────────────────────────────────────┐
   │{;}Define an action for Ctrl-Q and next key pressed~          │
   │                                                             │
   │{CHAR}NextKey~{^Q}S{^U} Left; {^Q}D{^U} Right; {^Q}Y{^U} Delete EOL~│
   │{CASE}{VARIABLE}NextKey~~                                     │
   │   s~Left~S~Left~                                             │
   │   d~Right~D~Right~                                           │
   │   y~DelRest~Y~DelRest~                                       │
   │~                                                            │
   │{LABEL}Left~                                                 │
   │   {Home}{Home}{Left}{QUIT}                                   │
   │{LABEL}Right~                                                │
   │   {Home}{Home}{Right}{QUIT}                                  │
   │{LABEL}DelRest~                                              │
   │   {Del to EOL}                                              │
   └─────────────────────────────────────────────────────────────┘
Ctrl-V to Insert next key as commmand;
Ctrl-PgUp for macro commands;  Press Exit when done
```

FIGURE 27.5:

A soft keyboard that makes Ctrl-Q act as it does in text editors that follow WordStar conventions

EDITING A SOFT KEYBOARD

The menu at the bottom of the Keyboard: Edit screen lets you manage the soft-key definitions within the current keyboard as follows:

Remember to move the highlight to the key you want to edit before choosing an option from the bottom menu of the Keyboard: Edit screen.

Action	Lets you change the action assigned to the currently highlighted key
Dscrptn	Lets you change the description assigned to the currently highlighted key
Original	Deletes the currently highlighted soft key, returning the key to its original action
Create	Lets you define a soft key, as described in the previous section
Move; Macro	Lets you move the action assigned to the currently highlighted key to a new key (for example, if you assign an action to Ctrl-X and decide you want Alt-X to execute that action instead, select Move, then press Alt-X)

The **S**ave and **R**etrieve options let you retrieve a macro from disk to a soft key and vice versa, as described in the next two sections.

CONVERTING A KEY DEFINITION TO A MACRO

To copy a key definition from one soft keyboard to another, save its definition as a macro, then retrieve that macro into a key definition in the other keyboard.

Conveniently, WordPerfect lets you create a macro from any key you define in a soft keyboard. This places a copy of the definition on-disk so that it becomes a regular macro. This makes the key definition universally accessible, like any other macro, rather than tying it to a soft keyboard.

To convert (copy) a key definition to a macro, follow these steps:

The MACROS soft keyboard has some particularly good keys for conversion to macros, including a macro to replace paired Size and Attribute codes (Alt-R).

1. Starting at the Edit screen, select **F**ile ➤ Se**t**up ➤ **K**eyboard Layout (or press **Shift-F1 K**).

2. Highlight the keyboard containing the key definition you want to save as a macro, and select **E**dit.

3. Highlight the key whose action you want to convert to a macro.

4. Select **S**ave.

5. Press an Alt-*letter* combination, or type a name (up to eight characters) for the macro and press ⏎.

6. Press Exit (**F7**) twice to return to the Edit screen.

The macro you name in step 5 will be available just like any other macro (regardless of which soft keyboard is active). You can use the Alt-*letter* name to execute the macro, or, if you saved the macro with a longer name, you can press Alt-F10 to execute it. You can also explore or change the macro with the Macro Editor.

COPYING A MACRO TO A KEY DEFINITION

If you want to assign one of your favorite macros to a key definition, follow these steps:

1. Starting at the Edit screen, select **F**ile ➤ Setup ➤ **K**eyboard Layout (or press **Shift-F1 K**).

2. Move the highlight to the keyboard where you want the macro copied, and select **E**dit.

3. Select **R**etrieve.

4. At the "Key:" prompt, press the key or key combination you are assigning the macro to (e.g., Ctrl-M if you want to execute the macro by pressing Ctrl-M when this soft keyboard is active). If this key has already been defined, you'll be asked whether you want to replace it. Select **Y**es to replace the definition for the key, or select **N**o to return to the Keyboard: Edit screen.

5. At the "Macro:" prompt, press the Alt-*letter* combination, or type the name (up to eight characters) for the existing macro that will be assigned to this key, then press ↵.

6. Press Exit (**F7**) to return to the Keyboard Layout menu.

7. If you want to use the keyboard layout now, choose **S**elect.

8. Press Exit (**F7**) to return to the Edit screen.

Your macro still exists on-disk, but a copy is also in the soft keyboard.

USING THE KEYBOARD MAP

Besides the Keyboard: Edit screen, WordPerfect offers you a second way to manage the key assignments in a soft keyboard: the *keyboard map*. The keyboard map gives you the "big picture" of the current soft keyboard, showing a brief description of all the Alt and Ctrl characters, punctuation marks, numbers, and uppercase and lowercase letters on the keyboard. The keyboard map also offers several options for assigning and changing key definitions.

To view the map for a soft keyboard, follow these steps:

1. Select **File ➤** Setup **➤ K**eyboard Layout (or press **Shift-F1 K**).

2. Highlight the name of the soft keyboard you want to work with.

3. Select **M**ap to display the keyboard map. As an example, Figure 27.6 shows the keyboard map for the SHORTCUT keyboard.

Five Key/Action tables make up the bulk of the map. *Key* refers to the character on the keyboard, and *Action* refers to what the key does in that particular soft keyboard. Keys that have not been changed are marked with a *C* (because they still perform their original *command,* if any). Keys that have been modified are marked with an *M* (because they are now *macros*). Keys that type a single character are marked by that character.

The description of what a particular key does is near the bottom of the screen. For example, in Figure 27.6, the cursor is currently under Alt-A, near the top of the screen. Near the bottom of the screen, you can see that this macro key can be used to add an attribute. You can use the arrow keys to move to other keys to see their descriptions.

```
Keyboard: Map

 Name: SHORTCUT

 Alt   Key      ABCDEFGHIJKLMNOPQRSTUUWXYZ1234567890-=\`[];',./
       Action   MMCMMMMCMCCMCCMMCMMMCMMMCCCCCCCCCCCCCCC

 Ctrl  Key      ABCDEFGHIJKLMNOPQRSTUUWXYZ[\]_            C = Command
       Action   CMMMMMMMMMCMMCMMMCMMCCCCCCCCCC           M = Keyboard Macro

       Key      !"#$%&'()*+,-./0123456789:;<=>?@
       Action   !"#$%&'()*+,-./0123456789:;<=>?@

       Key      ABCDEFGHIJKLMNOPQRSTUUWXYZ[\]^_`
       Action   ABCDEFGHIJKLMNOPQRSTUUWXYZ[\]^_`

       Key      abcdefghijklmnopqrstuvwxyz{|}~
       Action   abcdefghijklmnopqrstuvwxyz{|}~


 Key           Action          Description
 Alt-A         {KEY MACRO 32}  Add an Attribute


 1 Key; 2 Macro; 3 Description; 4 Original; 5 Compose; N Key Name Search: 1
```

The keyboard map for the SHORTCUT keyboard

The keyboard map doesn't have the function keys (F1 to F12), but you can still change the actions assigned to them with the Keyboard: Edit screen's Create option.

The Map screen lets you perform many of the same operations as the Keyboard: Edit screen. Here is a summary of the options available to you:

Key — Lets you assign the action assigned to another key on the keyboard to the currently highlighted key (for example, pressing F4 while Ctrl-I is highlighted assigns the action →Indent to the Ctrl-I key combination)

Macro — Takes you to the Macro Edit screen, where you can define or change the action assigned to the currently highlighted key

Description — Lets you change the description of the currently highlighted key

Original — Returns the action assigned to the currently highlighted key to its original role, deleting the current soft-key definition

Compose — Lets you assign a special character to the currently highlighted key; after choosing Compose, type the character's code (e.g., *4, 0* for a bullet), and press ↵

Key **N**ame Search — Lets you highlight a key or combination keystroke

When you've finished working with the keyboard map, you can press Exit (F7) to save any changes, or press Cancel (F1) and select **Y**es to cancel any changes. You return to the Keyboard Layout menu.

PART NINE

Hands-On Lessons

This part of the book presents ten hands-on lessons designed to teach you how to use many of WordPerfect's features right at your keyboard. Each lesson takes you step by step through the keystrokes required to produce a sample document or reach a particular goal. Though doing these lessons is optional, they help illustrate features explained in the chapters so that you can see the features in action while using them. (Look at the bottom of each lesson page for a handy cross-reference to the appropriate chapter in the book.) If you're a beginning or an intermediate WordPerfect user, these lessons will help you get up to speed fast.

Typing and Printing a Letter

In this exercise you'll type, print, and save your first document, a business letter, and then exit WordPerfect.

BEFORE YOU BEGIN

Before you begin this lesson, start WordPerfect and get to the blank Edit screen. You should also be familiar with the location of the Backspace, ↵, and other special keys and, if you have a mouse, how to move the mouse pointer. If you need any help with these topics, refer to Chapter 1.

TYPING THE LETTER

Figure L1.1 shows a rough draft of a sample business letter. The sections that follow provide step-by-step instructions for creating, printing, and saving this document.

TYPING THE NAME, ADDRESS, AND SALUTATION

You should be at the top of the blank WordPerfect Edit screen to start this lesson. To type the short lines at the top of the letter, just type each line and press ↵ to end each one. If you make a mistake at any time while typing in WordPerfect, you can press the Backspace key to back up and make corrections.

Here are the exact steps:

1. Type **Mrs. Adrian Smith** and press ↵.

2. Type **123 Oak Ave.** and press ↵.

3. Type **San Diego, CA   92123** and press ↵.

4. Press ↵ again to add a blank line.

5. Type **Dear Mrs. Smith:** and press ↵.

6. Press ↵ again to add another blank line.

Your screen should look like Figure L1.2. In the next section, when you type paragraphs, you'll only press ↵ at the end of each paragraph.

TYPING THE PARAGRAPHS AND CLOSING

1. Type the following paragraph as though it were one long line of text. Don't indent, and don't try to break the lines to match those shown below or those in the figure.

Thank you for your letter regarding our Hawaiian outer-island tour packages. Currently, we offer two travel packages with no overnight stays on Oahu.

2. Press ↵.

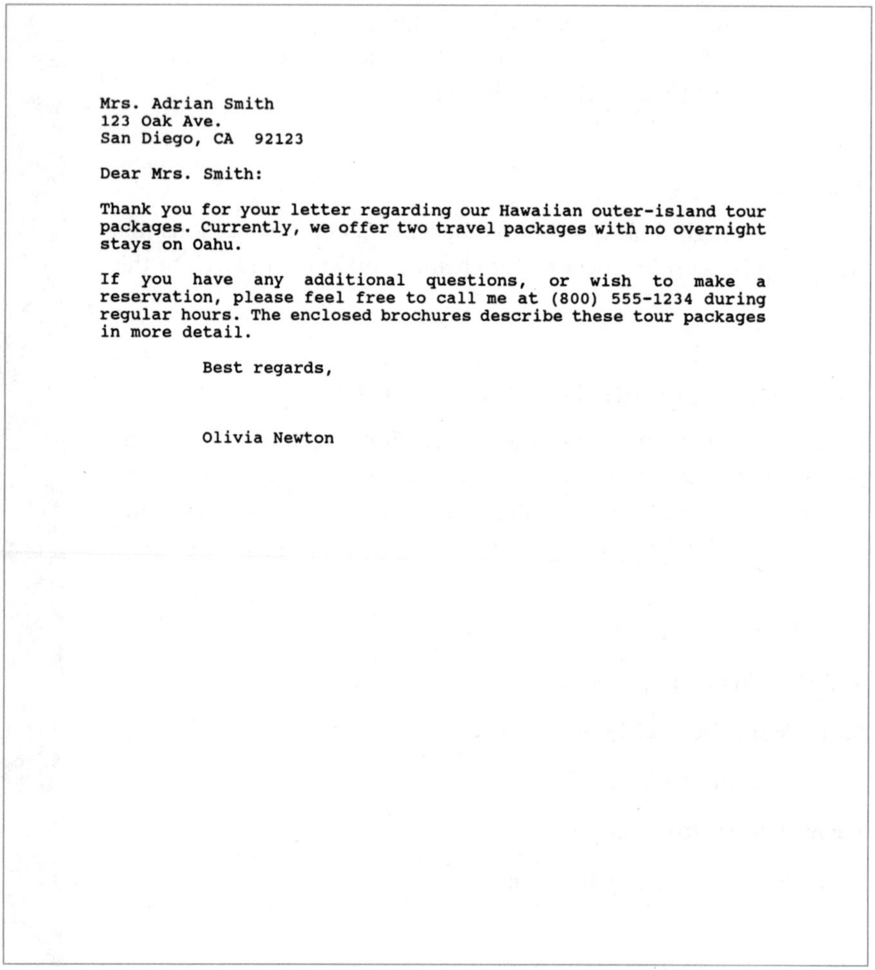

Mrs. Adrian Smith
123 Oak Ave.
San Diego, CA 92123

Dear Mrs. Smith:

Thank you for your letter regarding our Hawaiian outer-island tour packages. Currently, we offer two travel packages with no overnight stays on Oahu.

If you have any additional questions, or wish to make a reservation, please feel free to call me at (800) 555-1234 during regular hours. The enclosed brochures describe these tour packages in more detail.

　　Best regards,

　　Olivia Newton

FIGURE L1.1:

A sample business letter

Now follow these steps to add a blank line and type the second paragraph:

1. Press ⏎ again to add a blank line.

2. Type the following paragraph, again as though it were one long line of text, without indenting or pressing ⏎:

   If you have any additional questions, or wish to make a reservation, please feel free to call me at (800) 555-1234 during regular hours. The enclosed brochures describe these tour packages in more detail.

3. Press ⏎.

Now you are ready to add the closing and signature lines. Just to get a little practice indenting with the Tab key, which works much as it does on a typewriter, follow these steps:

1. Press ⏎ to add a blank line.

2. Press the **Tab** key twice.

3. Type **Best regards,** and press ⏎.

4. Press ⏎ three times to add three blank lines.

5. Press the **Tab** key twice.

6. Type **Olivia Newton** and press ⏎.

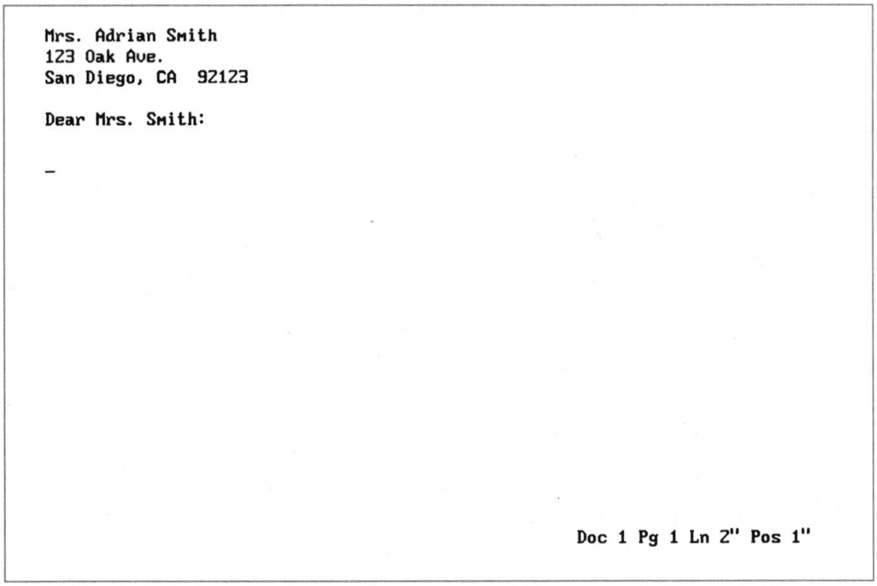

```
Mrs. Adrian Smith
123 Oak Ave.
San Diego, CA  92123

Dear Mrs. Smith:


_




                                   Doc 1 Pg 1 Ln 2" Pos 1"
```

FIGURE L1.2:

The sample business letter is started.

Refer to Chapter 1

Your letter is complete now, and your screen should look something like Figure L1.3. Don't worry if you made mistakes; you'll learn how to correct them in Chapter 2. For now, let's print a copy of the letter.

PRINTING YOUR DOCUMENT

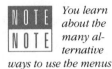

You learn about the many alternative ways to use the menus in Chapter 3.

Make sure that your printer is turned on, is online, and has paper in it. Follow these steps to print your letter now:

1. Press **Alt-=** (hold down the Alt key, press the = key, then release both keys) or click your right mouse button to display the menu bar at the top of the screen.

2. Press **F** to pull down the File menu.

3. Press **P** to select Print.

4. Press **F** to select Full Document.

You should see a printed copy of your document in just a few seconds. If your printer does not print, check Chapter 8 for additional information on using your printer.

```
Mrs. Adrian Smith
123 Oak Ave.
San Diego, CA  92123

Dear Mrs. Smith:

Thank you for your letter regarding our Hawaiian outer-island
tour packages. Currently, we offer two travel packages with no
overnight stays on Oahu.

If you have any additional questions, or wish to make a
reservation, please feel free to call me at (800) 555-1234 during
regular hours. The enclosed brochures describe these tour
packages in more detail.

        Best regards,


        Olivia Newton
_



                        Doc 1 Pg 1 Ln 4.33" Pos 1"
```

FIGURE L1.3:

The completed letter on the Edit screen

Refer to Chapter 1

SAVING YOUR DOCUMENT AND EXITING WORDPERFECT

You'll use this same letter in Lesson 2 to practice editing. So let's save the letter now, then exit WordPerfect.

1. Press **Alt-=** or click your right mouse button to get to the menu bar.

2. Press **F** to select File.

3. Press **X** to select Exit. You'll see the message

   Save document? Yes (No)

4. Press **Y** (or ↵) to select **Yes**. The screen shows

   Document to be saved:

5. Type the file name **SMITH.WP**.

6. Press ↵. If WordPerfect asks whether it should replace the existing SMITH.WP file, press **Y** to answer Yes. (This only happens if you or somebody else has already taken this lesson and saved the SMITH.WP file. If you think there is another document named *SMITH.WP* on-disk already, perhaps you should give this file a different name.)

If you use an operating system other than DOS, or you use a DOS shell, exiting WordPerfect takes you back to that operating system or shell.

7. When WordPerfect asks

   Exit WP? No (Yes)

   press **Y** to select Yes and exit WordPerfect.

This will take you back to DOS; your work is saved, and you are back to where you started from (before running WordPerfect). You can now go to Lesson 2 or return to Chapter 1 for more information.

Refer to Chapter 1

Editing a Document

Figure L2.1 shows the sample letter you created in Lesson 1, marked with some changes. In this lesson, you'll use some of the techniques described in Chapter 2 to make these changes.

RETRIEVING THE LETTER

Chances are you've exited WordPerfect since Lesson 1 or at least have cleared your Edit screen. Either way, the sample letter is probably not on your Edit screen, so you need to retrieve it. Follow these steps:

1. If WordPerfect is not up and running on your computer, you need to get it running (as described in Chapter 1) to get to the blank Word-Perfect Edit screen.

2. At the Edit screen, press **Alt-=** or click the right mouse button to view the menu bar.

3. Press **F** or click on File with the left mouse button to pull down the File menu.

4. Press **R** or click on Retrieve to select Retrieve.

5. In response to the prompt "Document to be retrieved:" near the bottom of the screen, type **SMITH.WP** and press ↵.

The letter appears on your screen, ready for editing, looking just as it did at the end of Lesson 1.

INSERTING THE DATE

In Lesson 1, you didn't insert the date at the top of the letter, so you can do that now (as well as inserting a couple of blank lines). Follow these steps:

1. The cursor should already be at the top of the document, but if you've moved it, press **Home Home** ↑, or move the mouse

Refer to Chapter 2

pointer to the upper-left corner of the screen and click the left button. This moves the cursor to the *M* in *Mrs.*

2. Press ↵ three times to insert three blank lines.

3. Move the cursor back to the top line, by clicking in the upper-left corner of the Edit screen with your mouse or by pressing **Home Home** ↑ (or just ↑ three times).

4. Type the date (*August 1, 1992* is used in the example).As a shortcut to typing today's date, select Date **T**ext on the **T**ools menu.

The Num Lock key must be off for the arrow, Delete, and other special keys on the numeric keypad to work properly.

The date should now be at the top of the document, with a couple of blank lines beneath, as in Figure L2.2. If you'd like to experiment with adding and deleting blank lines, just move the cursor to any blank line, press Delete to delete it, or press ↵ to insert a new one.

DELETING A WORD

Now you'll delete the word *additional,* as marked in Figure L2.1. Follow these steps:

1. If you have a mouse, move the pointer to the word *additional* and click the left button, or just press the ↓, →, ↑, and ← keys as needed until the cursor is at the word *additional.*

2. Press **Ctrl-Backspace** (hold down the Ctrl key and press the Back-space key) once, or press Delete or Backspace as many times as necessary to delete the entire word.

August 1, 1992

Mrs. Adrian Smith
123 Oak Ave.
San Diego, CA 92123

Dear Mrs. Smith:

Thank you for your letter regarding our Hawaiian outer-island tour packages. Currently, we offer two travel packages with no overnight stays on Oahu.

If you have any ~~additional~~ questions, or wish to make a reservation, please feel free to call me at (800) 555-1234 during regular hours. The enclosed brochures describe these tour packages in more detail.

                Best regards,

                Olivia Newton

FIGURE L2.1:

The sample letter with suggested changes

Refer to Chapter 2

3. Press ↓ once to move the cursor down a line and to reformat the paragraph.

INSERTING A WORD

Now insert the word *business* by following these steps:

1. Move the cursor to the letter *h* in the word *hours* near the end of the first sentence in the second paragraph. You can click on the letter *h* with your mouse or use the arrow keys.

2. Make sure you are in Insert mode so that your new text is inserted at the cursor position. If you see the word "Typeover" in the lower-left corner of the screen, press the Insert key to switch to Insert mode.

3. Type the word **business**.

4. Press the spacebar to insert a blank space.

5. Press ↑ to reformat the paragraph.

As you may have noticed in the preceding exercises, the text on the screen may look "out of whack" right after you insert or delete text. But as soon as you move the cursor up or down a line, WordPerfect reformats the entire paragraph for you.

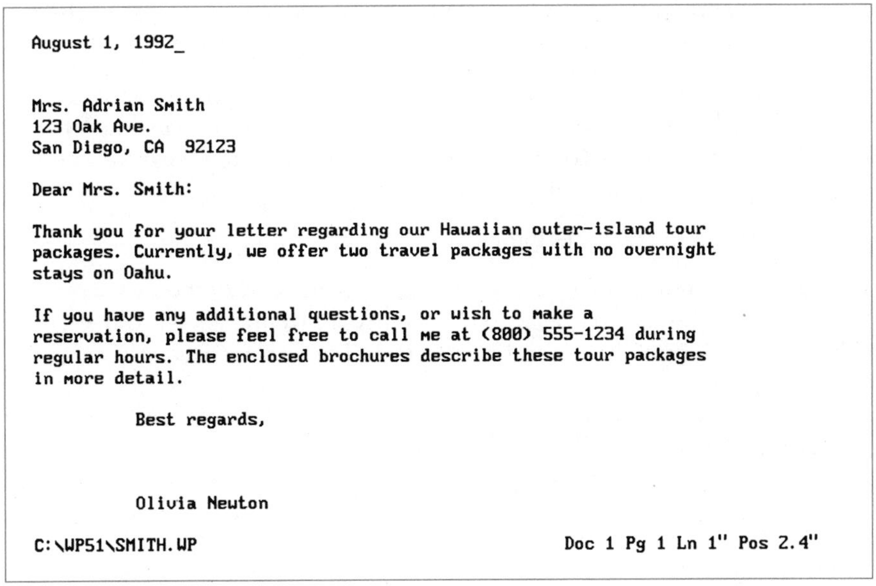

```
August 1, 1992_

Mrs. Adrian Smith
123 Oak Ave.
San Diego, CA  92123

Dear Mrs. Smith:

Thank you for your letter regarding our Hawaiian outer-island tour
packages. Currently, we offer two travel packages with no overnight
stays on Oahu.

If you have any additional questions, or wish to make a
reservation, please feel free to call me at (800) 555-1234 during
regular hours. The enclosed brochures describe these tour packages
in more detail.

        Best regards,


        Olivia Newton

C:\WP51\SMITH.WP                         Doc 1 Pg 1 Ln 1" Pos 2.4"
```

FIGURE L2.2:

The letter, with the date inserted at the top

MOVING TEXT

Next you'll move the sentence at the end of the second paragraph to the start of that paragraph. This requires a basic cut-and-paste operation:

1. Move the cursor to the letter *T* at the start of the last sentence in the second paragraph. You can either click on the *T* with your mouse or use the ↑, ↓, →, and ← keys.

2. Block (highlight) that sentence by using one of the following techniques:

   ◆ If you have a mouse, place the pointer on the *T,* hold down the left button, and move the mouse downward slightly until the sentence is highlighted.

   ◆ If you prefer to use the menus, press **Alt-=** to access the menu bar, press **E** to select Edit, press **B** to select Block, then type a period (.) to highlight the entire sentence.

   ◆ If you prefer to use shortcut keystrokes, press **F12** or **Alt-F4**, then type a period (.) to highlight the entire sentence.

If you block the wrong text, just press Cancel (F1) or Block (F12) to remove the flashing "Block on" indicator, then try again.

Regardless of which method you use, your screen should look like Figure L2.3 when you've blocked the correct text.

3. While "Block on" is blinking in the lower-left corner of the screen, press **Alt-=** (or click your right mouse button) to display the menu bar.

4. Press **E** to select Edit, then press **M** to select Move (Cut). The blocked text disappears, and the message in the lower-left corner of the screen instructs you to move the cursor and press ↵.

5. Move the cursor to the *I* in *If* at the start of the second paragraph, either by clicking on the *I* with your mouse or by pressing ↑ twice, Home, and ← (or whatever combination of arrow keys you need to press to position the cursor properly).

If pressing the spacebar in step 7 erases the letter I, you're not in Insert mode; press Insert, then type **I**.

6. Press ↵ to complete the move.

7. To insert a space between the period at the end of the first sentence and the start of the second sentence, move the cursor to the letter *I* at the start of the second sentence, and press the spacebar.

Figure L2.4 shows how your edited letter should look. Now you can print a copy.

```
August 1, 1992


Mrs. Adrian Smith
123 Oak Ave.
San Diego, CA  92123

Dear Mrs. Smith:

Thank you for your letter regarding our Hawaiian outer-island tour
packages. Currently, we offer two travel packages with no overnight
stays on Oahu.

If you have any questions, or wish to make a reservation, please
feel free to call me at (800) 555-1234 during regular business
hours. The enclosed brochures describe these tour packages in more
detail.

        Best regards,



        Olivia Newton

Block on                              Doc 1 Pg 1 Ln 3.67" Pos 1.7"
```

FIGURE L2.3:

The sentence to be moved is blocked (highlighted) on the screen.

PRINTING YOUR EDITED LETTER

The steps for printing the edited letter are exactly the same as for printing the letter the first time:

1. Press **Alt-=** or click the right mouse button to access the menu bar.

```
August 1, 1992


Mrs. Adrian Smith
123 Oak Ave.
San Diego, CA  92123

Dear Mrs. Smith:

Thank you for your letter regarding our Hawaiian outer-island tour
packages. Currently, we offer two travel packages with no overnight
stays on Oahu.

The enclosed brochures describe these tour packages in more detail.
If you have any questions, or wish to make a reservation, please
feel free to call me at (800) 555-1234 during regular business
hours.

        Best regards,



        Olivia Newton

C:\WP51\SMITH.WP                      Doc 1 Pg 1 Ln 3.33" Pos 1"
```

FIGURE L2.4:

The edited letter on the Edit screen

Refer to Chapter 2

2. Press **F** or click on File to pull down the File menu.

3. Press **P** or click on Print to select Print.

4. Press **F** or click on Full Document to select Full Document.

In a few seconds, your letter will be printed.

SAVING YOUR CHANGES

The changes you've made in this lesson are visible on the screen and in the printed document, but have not been saved permanently to disk (they're only in the computer's RAM). To save this copy of the letter, you must save the document again. You can use the same basic steps you used in Lesson 1 to replace the old copy of the document with this new, edited copy. Follow these steps:

1. Press **Alt-=** or click the right mouse button to access the menu bar.

2. Press **F** or click on File to pull down the File menu.

3. Press **X** or click on Exit to select Exit.

4. When you see "Save document? **Y**es (**N**o)", select Yes by clicking on that option or by pressing **Y**.

5. Press ↵ to accept the suggested file name, *SMITH.WP*.

6. When asked about replacing the old copy of SMITH.WP, select **Y**es, by clicking on that option or pressing **Y**.

7. When asked about exiting, you decide what to do. If you want to call it quits for now, select Yes. If you want to keep using WordPerfect, click on No, press ↵, or press **N**.

If you select No in step 7, the letter is cleared from the Edit screen, but you're still in WordPerfect, where you can start a new document or retrieve an existing one. If you select Yes, you return to DOS, where you can run another program or turn off your computer.

This concludes Lesson 2. Don't forget to read Chapter 2 for more information on editing documents and Chapter 3 for tips on using the menus. If you've had many difficulties with these first two lessons, you may want to read chapters 1–3 to get some more background, then try these lessons again.

Refer to Chapter 2

A Guided Tour of WordPerfect

Now that you've had a chance to do some basic typing and editing with WordPerfect, in this lesson you'll learn more about the Word-Perfect interface in general. This will give you the flexibility required to use advanced features and solve formatting problems on your own and to get information when you need it.

HANDS-ON

LESSON

3

BEFORE YOU BEGIN

You'll need some sample text to work with in this lesson, so go ahead and retrieve the SMITH.WP document that you worked with in the first two lessons. Remember, you need to get to the WordPerfect Edit screen first, then select the Retrieve option from the File pull-down menu. Then type **SMITH.WP** and press ↵ to retrieve that document.

USING THE MENUS

Using the pull-down menus is the easiest way to access most of WordPerfect's many features, particularly for beginners; you've already had some experience with the menus in the preceding lessons. In this lesson you'll explore the three main techniques for using the menus so that you can decide which method is most comfortable for you.

Throughout this book and these lessons, I present a series of menu selections as options separated by the symbol ➤. And, where appropriate, I point out optional shortcut keys like this:

Select **L**ayout ➤ **A**lign ➤ **C**enter (or press Shift-F6).

Let's try three different ways of following this instruction.

Refer to Chapter 3

USING THE MOUSE

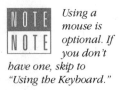

Using a mouse is optional. If you don't have one, skip to "Using the Keyboard."

To select these menu options with your mouse, follow these steps (if necessary, first move the cursor to the top of the document by pressing Home Home ↑):

1. Click the right mouse button to display the menu bar.

2. Move the mouse pointer to the Layout option, and click the left mouse button.

3. Move the mouse pointer to the Align option, and click the left mouse button.

4. Move the mouse pointer to the Center option, and click the left mouse button.

The date is now centered on the page. Let's do this again, this time using the keyboard. First, uncenter the date by pressing ←, then Delete.

USING THE KEYBOARD

If you don't have a mouse or prefer not to use it, you can use the keyboard to select menu options. You can do so either by typing the boldface letters after the menu bar is displayed (e.g., type *LAC* or *lac;* uppercase/lowercase doesn't matter) to select **L**ayout ➤ **A**lign ➤ **C**enter or by positioning the highlight on each option and pressing ↵. Follow these steps:

1. Press **Alt-=** to display the menu bar.

2. To pull down the Layout menu, press → three times to highlight **L**ayout and press ↵, or just press the letter **L**.

3. To select **A**lign, press ↓ ten times and press ↵, or just press the letter **A**.

4. To select **C**enter, press ↓ three times and press ↵, or just press the letter **C**.

The date is centered. Now try the shortcut-key method. First, uncenter the date by pressing ←, then Delete.

USING THE SHORTCUT KEYS

The shortcut key for choosing the Center option is Shift-F6, which is a *combination keystroke.* Anytime you see a combination keystroke—that is, two keys joined with a hyphen—that means "hold down the first key, press the

Refer to Chapter 3

second key, then release both keys." To center the date, follow this single step:

◆ Press **Shift-F6** (hold down the Shift key, press the F6 key, then release both keys).

You need not know all the shortcut keys off the top of your head to use Word-Perfect. Instead, you can learn them as you go along, memorizing only those that you use often. A shortcut key, when available, is shown next to the option right on the menu. For example, you know that Shift-F6 is the shortcut to choosing **L**ayout ➤ **A**lign ➤ **C**enter because, after choosing **L**ayout ➤ **A**lign, *Shft-F6* appears just to the right of the Center option on the menu, as Figure L3.1 shows.

CANCELING MENU CHOICES

Occasionally, you may accidentally select some menu options and end up at an unfamiliar menu, or you may just change your mind and want to back up. Follow these steps:

1. Select **L**ayout ➤ **A**lign.

2. To change your mind and back out of these selections, try any of the following:

◆ Press Cancel (**F1**), **Alt-=**, or **Escape** as many times as necessary.

◆ Click the right mouse button.

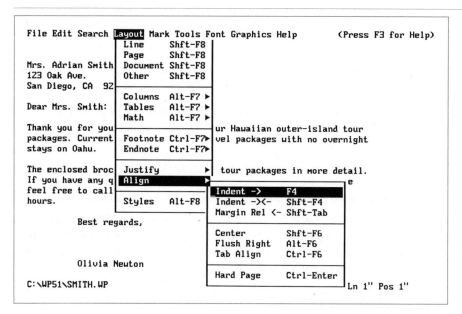

FIGURE L3.1:

The shortcut keystroke Shft-F6 is shown next to the Center option.

Refer to Chapter 3

Remember, there's no need to feel stuck with a menu or selection, because there are lots of ways to back out and return to more familiar territory.

As discussed in Chapter 3, some menus are full-screen menus, and others are bottom menus that appear only at the bottom of the screen. But the techniques for choosing options and backing out are generally the same for each type of menu. Getting the hang of using the menus is just a matter of experience, and with time it will become second nature.

USING THE REVEAL CODES SCREEN

I've just discussed how to back out of menus *while* you're making selections, but what if you make a series of selections, get all the way back to the Edit screen, and then change your mind? For example, in your SMITH.WP document, the date is already centered at the top because you've already completed the action required to do the centering, and the menus are off the screen. So how do you back up from here?

The answer is you don't. Once you've completed your action, WordPerfect inserts a *hidden code* in your document that reflects whatever choices you've made. So to undo that action, you must remove the hidden code. And as you may have guessed, it's much easier to delete a hidden code if you can see it. The Reveal Codes screen lets you see all the hidden codes in your document.

To activate the Reveal Codes screen, follow this single step:

◆ Select **Edit** ➤ **Reveal Codes**, or press **Alt-F3**.

If your keyboard has 12 function keys, F1–F12, you can also press F11 to turn Reveal Codes on and off.

Your screen is now divided in half. The top half shows part of your document as it appears normally. The bottom half shows about the same amount of text, but with the hidden codes displayed, as shown in Figure L3.2.

Notice that there is a [Center] code to the left of the date near the top of the Reveal Codes screen. This is the code that WordPerfect inserted when you centered the date. If you want to uncenter the date, just delete that code:

1. Position the cursor on the letter *A* in the word *August*. Notice that the *A* is highlighted in the Reveal Codes portion of the screen.

2. Press ←, and notice that the cursor is now in the upper-left corner of the Edit screen, and the [Center] code is highlighted on the Reveal Codes screen.

3. Press **Delete** to delete the [Center] code.

Now that you've deleted the [Center] code, the date is no longer centered. Earlier, you uncentered the date simply by pressing ← then Delete, with the Reveal Codes screen turned off. It may have seemed odd at the time that just pressing Delete once could have deleted all the space that pushed the date out to the center of the screen.

Refer to Chapter 3

But with the Reveal Codes screen turned on, it's much easier to see why that single press of the Delete key uncentered the date: You deleted the code. Whether you do this kind of editing with the Reveal Codes screen turned on or off is entirely up to you. But with experience, you'll probably find it much easier to do your editing with Reveal Codes turned on.

The Reveal Codes screen for your letter also shows other codes; these include [HRt] (hard-return) codes, which were inserted anytime you pressed ↵, and some [Tab] codes, which were inserted when you pressed Tab near the bottom of the document. (Press Home Home ↓ to move the cursor to the bottom of the document to see the [Tab] codes.)

If you want to see your full screen again, without all these codes, just turn off the Reveal codes screen, using the same steps you used to turn it on:

◆ Select **E**dit ➤ **R**eveal Codes, or press **Alt-F3** or **F11**.

Be sure to read the section on the Reveal Codes screen in Chapter 3, where you'll learn about deleting and moving hidden codes. You'll also learn about some other useful features, including the built-in Help system and the View Document screen, which gives you a preview of your printed document.

If you want to try some more hands-on exercises first, go to Lesson 4, with the current document on your screen. If you want to call it quits for now, you can clear the Edit screen by selecting **F**ile ➤ **Ex**it ➤ **N**o (the changes you've made to the document aren't worth saving), then selecting either **N**o to stay in WordPerfect or **Y**es to exit WordPerfect and return to DOS.

```
                      August 1, 1992


Mrs. Adrian Smith
123 Oak Ave.
San Diego, CA  92123

Dear Mrs. Smith:

Thank you for your letter regarding our Hawaiian outer-island tour
packages. Currently, we offer two travel packages with no overnight
C:\WP51\SMITH.WP                              Doc 1 Pg 1 Ln 1" Pos 3.55"
[                                                             ]
[Center]August 1, 1992[HRt]
[HRt]
[HRt]
Mrs. Adrian Smith[HRt]
123 Oak Ave.[HRt]
San Diego, CA  92123[HRt]
[HRt]
Dear Mrs. Smith:[HRt]
[HRt]
Thank you for your letter regarding our Hawaiian outer[-]island tour[SRt]

Press Reveal Codes to restore screen
```

FIGURE L3.2:

The activated Reveal Codes screen

Refer to Chapter 3

Using Indents, Special Characters, and Fonts

In this lesson you'll get some hands-on experience using some of the basic techniques described in chapters 4 and 5, including indenting, changing the tab stops, and using fonts.

BEFORE YOU BEGIN

Figure L4.1 shows the sample letter you created and edited in lessons 1 and 2, with some additions and changes that you'll make in this lesson. If you've cleared the Edit screen or exited WordPerfect, be sure to get WordPerfect up and running again. Then select **File ➤ R**etrieve and type **SMITH.WP** to retrieve the letter.

SWITCHING TO LEFT JUSTIFICATION

When you printed the SMITH.WP document, you may have noticed that it had a smooth right margin, because WordPerfect prints text fully justified by default. Switch to a ragged right margin now, by switching to left justification:

1. Make sure the cursor is at the top of the document by pressing **Home Home** ↑ or by moving the cursor to the upper-left corner of the document and clicking the left mouse button.

2. Select **Layout ➤ J**ustify **➤ L**eft from the menus. (You cannot see any changes on the Edit screen.)

3. To view this change, select **File ➤ P**rint **➤ V**iew Document (or press **Shift-F7**), then press **1** to choose 100%. If you have a graphics monitor, you should now see a preview of your printed document with a ragged right margin in the paragraphs, as in Figure L4.2.

4. To return to the Edit screen, press Exit (**F7**).

Refer to Chapters 4 and 5

The sample letter after making changes presented in this lesson

August 1, 1992

— Left-justify the text

Change the font to Times (Dutch)

Mrs. Adrian Smith
123 Oak Ave.
San Diego, CA 92123

Add bulleted paragraphs

Dear Mrs. Smith:

Thank you for your letter regarding our Hawaiian outer-island tour packages. Currently, we offer two travel packages with no overnight stays on Oahu.

● Paradise Vacations' *Outer Islands Getaway*; offering three days each on Maui, Kauai, and Hawaii

● Heavenly Cruises' *Pristine Island Fun Pack*; offering three days each on Maui, Molokai, and Kauai, travelling by boat between islands

The enclosed brochures describe these tour packages in more detail. If you have any questions, or wish to make a reservation, please feel free to call me at (800) 555-1234 during regular business hours.

Best Regards,

Delete tabs in closing

Olivia Newton

FIGURE L4.2:

The sample letter on the View Document screen, with a ragged right margin

Refer to Chapters 4 and 5

If you want to see what happened behind the scenes, turn on the Reveal Codes screen (select **E**dit ➤ **R**eveal Codes, or press Alt-F3 or F11). You'll see a [Just:Left] code to the left of the date. (If you changed your mind and wanted to go back to full justification, you could just move the highlight to that code and press Delete to delete it.)

ADDING A BULLETED ITEM

Now add the first bulleted item to the letter. This time, leave the Reveal Codes screen on, so you can see what's going on behind the scenes as you type.

1. Move the cursor to the blank line that separates the first paragraph from the second one (so that the cursor is above the letter *T* in the word *The*).

2. Press ↵ to insert another blank line.

3. Press the **Tab** key to indent.

4. You'll use special character 4,0 for a bullet. Select **F**ont ➤ **C**haracters from the menus, or press Compose (**Ctrl-V**).

5. Type **4,0** and press ↵. The bullet appears on the screen.

6. To indent, press →Indent← (**Shift-F4**) or choose **L**ayout ➤ **A**lign ➤ **I**nden t → ←.

7. Start the text by typing **Paradise Vacations'**, and then press the spacebar to insert a blank space.

8. Activate the Italics print attribute by selecting **F**ont ➤ **A**ppearance ➤ **I**talics from the pull-down menus (or by pressing **Ctrl-F8 A I**). Notice that [ITALC] and [italc] codes appear on the Reveal Codes screen at the cursor position.

9. Type **Outer Islands Getaway** and notice how, on the Reveal Codes screen, the text stays between the [ITALC] and [italc] codes.

10. Press → to move the cursor past the closing [italc] code to resume typing regular text.

11. Type **;** (semicolon), press the spacebar, then type

    offering three days each on Maui, Kauai, and Hawaii

12. Press ↵ twice.

13. Press **Tab** to indent before typing the next bulleted item.

NOTE **NOTE** *After you press Shift-F4, your text will be indented until you press ↵.*

Refer to Chapters 4 and 5

14. Type another bullet, again by pressing **Ctrl-V** (or selecting Font ➤ Characters), typing **4,0**, then pressing ↵.

15. Press →Indent← (**Shift-F4**) or select **L**ayout ➤ **A**lign ➤ **In**dent =><= to indent.

16. Type

Heavenly Cruises' Pristine Island Fun Pack; offering three days each on Maui, Molokai, and Kauai, travelling by boat between islands

Press ↵ to end that paragraph.

You may want to turn off the Reveal Codes screen (by pressing Alt-F3 or F11) to get a better look at your document.

CHOOSING A PRINT ATTRIBUTE AFTER TYPING

In step 16 above, you didn't italicize the name of the travel package. But that's no problem, since you can just block it and select the print attribute now. Follow these steps:

1. Using your mouse or arrow keys, move the cursor to the letter *P* in the word *Pristine.*

2. Select **E**dit ➤ **B**lock or press **Alt-F4** (or **F12**) to turn on blocking.

3. Highlight the words *Pristine Island Fun Pack* by pressing → as many times as necessary or simply by pressing the letter **K**.

4. Activate italics by selecting **F**ont ➤ **A**ppearance ➤ **I**talics (or pressing **Ctrl-F8 A I**).

Depending on your monitor, the italicized text may be colored or shaded differently from the regular text. To verify your change, you can turn on Reveal Codes (Alt-F3 or F11) to view the [ITALC] and [italc] codes surrounding the text you blocked in step 3.

CHANGING THE TAB STOPS

Currently your document is using WordPerfect's default ½-inch tab stops, and your bulleted items are indented accordingly. To change that amount of indentation, you need to change the tab stops. Follow these steps:

1. Move the cursor above the first bulleted item (anywhere above the first bullet).

2. Select **L**ayout ➤ **L**ine ➤ **T**ab Set (or press **Shift-F8 L T**). You'll see the tab ruler at the bottom of the screen, as in Figure L4.3.

Refer to Chapters 4 and 5

3. Press → seven times to move the cursor a little to the right of the second tab stop (L).

4. Press **L** to insert a left-aligned tab stop. On the Edit screen, the text to the right of each bullet moves in to the new tab stop, tightening the gap between each bullet and its text.

5. Press Exit (**F7**) twice to save your change and return to the Edit screen.

Now your document should look more like the example in Figure L4.1. If you turn on the Reveal Codes screen, you'll see that WordPerfect has inserted a [Tab Set] code, showing the position of every tab stop, at the cursor position.

> NOTE NOTE
>
> *If you want to change the tab stops again, you first have to delete this existing [Tab Set] code, as discussed in Chapter 5.*

UNINDENTING THE CLOSING

In Lesson 1 you indented the closing of the letter (*Best regards* and *Olivia Newton*). Suppose you change your mind and decide to align the closing at the left margin. No problem—just delete the [Tab] codes that are pushing it out to the second tab stop:

1. If Reveal Codes is currently off, turn it on by selecting **Edit ➤ R**eveal Codes or by pressing **Alt-F3** or **F11**.

2. Press **Home Home** ↓ to move the cursor to the bottom of the document.

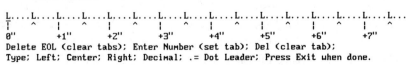

```
    •    Paradise Vacations' Outer Islands Getaway;
         offering three days each on Maui, Kauai, and
         Hawaii

    •    Heavenly Cruises' Pristine Island Fun Pack;
         offering three days each on Maui, Molokai,
         and Kauai, travelling by boat between islands

The enclosed brochures describe these tour packages in more
detail. If you have any questions, or wish to make a reservation,
please feel free to call me at (800) 555-1234 during regular
business hours.

    Best Regards,


    Olivia Newton

L....L....L....L....L....L....L....L....L....L....L....L....L....L...
T    ^    T    ^    T    ^    T    ^    T    ^    T    ^    T    ^
0"        +1"       +2"       +3"       +4"       +5"       +6"       +7"
Delete EOL (clear tabs); Enter Number (set tab); Del (clear tab);
Type; Left; Center; Right; Decimal; .= Dot Leader; Press Exit when done.
```

FIGURE L4.3:

The tab ruler is at the bottom of the Edit screen.

Refer to Chapters 4 and 5

3. Press the ↑ key (or whatever key is required) to move the highlight to the first [Tab] code to the left of *Olivia Newton,* near the bottom of the document.

4. Press **Delete** twice to delete the [Tab] codes.

5. Repeat steps 3 and 4 to delete the two [Tab] codes to the left of *Best regards.*

Notice that you did nothing to the tab ruler here. The tab ruler is just for setting tab stops (like on a typewriter). Hidden codes for indenting, such as [Tab], actually align the text at the tab stop.

CHANGING THE BASE FONT

Now let's take a look at the fonts your printer has to offer and try one out in the letter. Follow these steps:

1. Press **Home Home** ↑ to move the cursor to the top of the document (because you want to change the font for all the text in the letter).

2. Select **Font ➤ Base Font** from the pull-down menus (or press **Ctrl-F8 F**).

3. If your printer has more than one font available, you'll see a list of fonts. You can move the highlight to any font of your choosing (if your fonts show sizes, you may want to start with a fairly normal-size font, about 10 or 12 points or characters per inch). A Times (or Dutch) font was used in the example.

4. Press **S** to select the currently highlighted font.

5. If your printer has scalable fonts, you'll be asked for a size. Type a size (*10* or *12* is "normal" print size), and press ↵.

You won't see any change on your Edit screen. However, on the Reveal Codes screen, you can see that WordPerfect inserted a [Font] code, which has the name and size of the font you chose.

PRINTING AND SAVING YOUR CHANGES

Now you can print and save your edited document, using the same steps you followed in previous lessons. To print, select **File ➤ Print ➤ F**ull Document (or press Shift-F7 F). To save your document and clear the screen, select **File ➤ Exit** (or press F7). Choose **Yes**, press ↵ to reuse the existing file name, choose **Yes** to replace the old copy of the file, then choose either **Yes** or **No,**

Refer to Chapters 4 and 5

depending on whether or not you want to exit WordPerfect now.

With Lesson 4 complete, you might want to go back and read chapters 4 and 5, or you might prefer to plunge into the next lesson, where you'll learn how to create tables.

Refer to Chapters 4 and 5

Creating a Table

In this lesson you'll create the table shown in Figure L5.1, using techniques presented in Chapter 6. You'll use this table again in Lesson 7, where you create a sample newsletter.

BEFORE YOU BEGIN

If you've exited WordPerfect, be sure to get WordPerfect up and running again, as described in Chapter 1. If you're already in WordPerfect, and there's a document on your Edit screen at the moment, you can save that document and clear the Edit screen by selecting **F**ile ➤ E**x**it. If you want to save that document, choose **Y**es, type a file name, and press ↵. Otherwise, just choose **N**o. When you see the prompt asking whether you want to exit WordPerfect, choose **N**o.

COLUMNS, ROWS, AND CELLS

Tables provide a convenient way to work with information in rows and columns, without having to enter tabs or tab settings. Creating a table involves defining the number of columns and rows for the table, typing in the text for the table, and refining the format of table text and numbers.

A table consists of vertical *columns* and horizontal *rows,* which intersect to form *cells.* Columns are labeled alphabetically from left to right, and rows are labeled numerically from top to bottom. Each cell has a unique *address,* which is its row and column position in the table. For instance, A1 is the first cell in a table (column A, row 1); B1 is the cell just to the right of A1; and A2 is the cell just below A1. The address of the cell that the cursor is in appears on the status line near the lower-right corner of the screen.

DEFINING THE TABLE

Follow these steps to define the number of columns and rows for the table shown in Figure L5.1:

Refer to Chapter 6

	INSURANCE RATES	
Model	Premium	Deductible
30 watt	$.50	$25.00
75 watt	$.75	$35.00
100 watt	$1.49	$70.00
250 watt	$1.97	$100.00

1. Press **Alt-=** or click the right mouse button to access the menu bar.

2. Select **Layout** ➤ **T**ables ➤ **C**reate (or press **Alt-F7 C**).

3. Type **3** and press ↵ at the prompt for number of columns.

4. Type **6** and press ↵ at the prompt for number of rows.

After you define the number of columns and rows, WordPerfect displays the empty table and the Table Edit menu, as shown in Figure L5.2. You'll use the Table Edit menu later when you change the appearance of the table. For now, exit Table Edit mode and return to the normal Edit screen by pressing Exit (F7).

```
Table Edit:   Press Exit when done        Cell A1 Doc 1 Pg 1 Ln 1.14" Pos 1.12"

Ctrl-Arrows Column Widths; Ins Insert; Del Delete; Move Move/Copy;
1 Size; 2 Format; 3 Lines; 4 Header; 5 Math; 6 Options; 7 Join; 8 Split: 0
```

ENTERING THE TABLE TEXT

You use the normal Edit screen to add text and numbers to the table. You use the Table Edit mode to change the structure of the table, add lines and other formatting, and do math.

Now that you've defined the structure of the table and exited Table Edit mode, you're ready to type in text. Here are the steps for entering the first column in the table. Notice how the status line in the lower-right corner of the screen shows the current cell address as you move from cell to cell:

1. Make sure the cursor is in the first cell of the table (cell A1). If it isn't, use the arrow keys to move to cell A1, or click in cell A1 with your mouse.

2. Type **INSURANCE RATES** and press ↓.

3. Type **Model** and press ↓.

4. Type **30 watt** and press ↓.

5. Type **75 watt** and press ↓.

6. Type **100 watt** and press ↓.

7. Type **250 watt**.

Chapter 6 lists the many ways to move around in the table, both on the Edit screen and in Table Edit mode.

Now you're ready to move to the top of the next column and add some more text.

1. Press **Ctrl-Home** then **Home** ↑ to move to the top of the column.

2. Press **Tab** to move one cell to the right (to cell B1).

3. Press ↓ to move to cell B2.

4. Type **Premium** and press ↓.

5. Type **$.50** and press ↓.

6. Type **$.75** and press ↓.

7. Type **$1.49** and press ↓.

8. Type **$1.97**.

Column B is now complete, and you're ready to enter column C:

1. Press ↑ four times to move to cell B2, then press **Tab** to move to cell C2.

2. Type **Deductible** and press ↓.

3. Type **$25.00** and press ↓.

4. Type **$35.00** and press ↓.

5. Type **$70.00** and press ↓.

Refer to Chapter 6

6. Type **$100.00**. The table on your screen should now look like Figure L5.3.

CHANGING THE APPEARANCE OF THE TABLE

If you compare the table you have now with the one shown in Figure L5.1 at the beginning of this lesson, you'll see that the basic structure and all the text are the same, but there are some important differences. In the next few exercises, you'll use Table Edit mode to change the format of your table so that it matches the finished product shown earlier.

To get into Table Edit mode (also called the Table Editor), follow these steps:

1. Make sure your cursor is in any cell in the table.

2. Select **L**ayout ➤ **T**ables ➤ **E**dit (or press **Alt-F7**).

You'll see the Table Edit menu near the bottom of the screen.

NOTE
NOTE

Your cursor is in a table when the status line at the bottom of the screen shows the current cell address, as in Figure L5.3.

JOINING CELLS

Your first task is to combine the three cells at the top of the table into a single cell. Follow these steps:

1. Press **Home Home** ↑ to move to the top of the table (cell A1).

INSURANCE RATES		
Model	Premium	Deductible
30 watt	$.50	$25.00
75 watt	$.75	$35.00
100 watt	$1.49	$70.00
250 watt	$1.97	$100.00_

Cell C6 Doc 1 Pg 1 Ln 2.54" Pos 6.13"

FIGURE L5.3:

The table after adding text on the Edit screen

Refer to Chapter 6

2. Press Block (**Alt-F4** or **F12**) to begin blocking the cells you want to join. The "Block on" message will blink at the bottom of the screen.

3. Press → twice to highlight all three cells in the first row.

4. Choose **J**oin from the Table Edit menu.

5. Choose **Y**es when prompted with "Join cells? **N**o (**Y**es)".

The three cells in the first row are now combined into a single cell, A1.

You can also use your mouse to highlight cells when "Block on" is blinking in Table Edit mode: Just move the mouse pointer to the cell that you want to extend the highlight to, and click the left mouse button.

CENTERING TEXT IN A CELL

Next, center the title "INSURANCE RATES." Follow these steps:

1. Make sure your cursor is still in cell A1. If it isn't, use the arrow keys to move to A1, or click in cell A1 with your mouse.

2. Choose **F**ormat ➤ **C**ell ➤ **J**ustify ➤ **C**enter from the Table Edit menu.

BOLDFACING TEXT IN A CELL

You can also boldface text and make other size and appearance changes from the normal Edit screen.

Now you're ready to boldface the INSURANCE RATES text. Follow these steps:

1. Make sure your cursor is still in cell A1.

2. Choose **F**ormat ➤ **C**ell ➤ **A**ttributes ➤ **A**ppearance ➤ **B**old from the Table Edit menu.

CHANGING THE LINE STYLES

Next, you'll add double lines at the tops of the cells in row 2 and change the double lines around the outside of the table to single lines. As you will see, WordPerfect offers many line styles, as well as shading, to help you create professional-looking tables. Follow these steps:

1. Using the arrow keys or your mouse, move the highlight to cell A2, which contains the word *Model*. (The status line shows cell A2 when you're in that cell.)

2. Press Block (**Alt-F4** or **F12**), then press **End** to highlight all the cells across the current row.

3. Select **L**ines from the Table Edit menu. Notice that near the bottom of the screen is a description of all the lines in that cell, starting with *Top=Single*. You will change the top line of every cell in that row to double lines.

4. Select **T**op ➤ **D**ouble.

Refer to Chapter 6

5. Next change the outside lines to single. Press ↑ to move the highlight to cell A1.

6. Press Block (**Alt-F4** or **F12**) to begin blocking.

7. Press **Home Home** ↓ to block the entire table.

8. Choose Lines ➤ Outside ➤ **S**ingle from the Table Edit menu.

If the single line at the left edge of your screen display disappears, just press ← twice to redisplay it. Now your screen should look like Figure L5.4.

JUSTIFYING COLUMNS AND CELLS

Now it's time to align the text and numbers in the columns. Your goal is to center the column headings in cells A2, B2, and C2, and to right-align numbers and text in the columns below the headings. Follow these steps:

1. Move the cursor to any cell in column A by using the arrow keys or by clicking your mouse (A2 is a convenient cell to use).

2. Press Block (**Alt-F4** or **F12**) then **End** to highlight all the cells across the row.

3. Choose Format ➤ Column ➤ Justify ➤ **R**ight from the Table Edit menu.

```
                  ┌─────────────────────────────────────────────────┐
                  │                 INSURANCE RATES                 │
                  ├────────────────┬──────────────┬─────────────────┤
                  │ Model          │ Premium      │ Deductible      │
                  ├────────────────┼──────────────┼─────────────────┤
                  │ 30 watt        │ $.50         │ $25.00          │
                  ├────────────────┼──────────────┼─────────────────┤
                  │ 75 watt        │ $.75         │ $35.00          │
                  ├────────────────┼──────────────┼─────────────────┤
                  │ 100 watt       │ $1.49        │ $70.00          │
                  ├────────────────┼──────────────┼─────────────────┤
                  │ 250 watt       │ $1.97        │ $100.00         │
                  └────────────────┴──────────────┴─────────────────┘


Table Edit:  Press Exit when done        Cell A6 Doc 1 Pg 1 Ln 2.54" Pos 1.1"
═══════════════════════════════════════════════════════════════════════════════
Ctrl-Arrows Column Widths; Ins Insert; Del Delete; Move Move/Copy;
1 Size; 2 Format; 3 Lines; 4 Header; 5 Math; 6 Options; 7 Join; 8 Split: 0
```

FIGURE L5.4:

The table after changing line styles

Refer to Chapter 6

You'll notice that right-justifying these columns has no effect on the IN-SURANCE RATES text in cell A1. That's because earlier you formatted cell A1 with the **F**ormat ➤ **C**ell options, and formatting for a cell has precedence over formatting for a column. Therefore, the centered formatting for cell A1 remains, even though the columns below are right-justified.

Next, center the column headings in cells A2, B2, and C2 by following these steps:

1. Move the cursor to cell A2, which contains the word *Model,* using the arrow keys or your mouse.

2. Press Block (**Alt-F4** or **F12**).

3. Press **End** to extend the highlight across all three columns.

4. Choose **F**ormat ➤ **C**ell ➤ **J**ustify ➤ **C**enter from the Table Edit menu.

Figure L5.5 shows how the table should now look on your screen.

ADDING SHADING TO THE TABLE

You can emphasize the low cost of the insurance premium in the table by shading cells B2 through B6. Follow these steps:

1. Move the cursor to cell B2, which contains the word *Premium*.

2. Press Block (**Alt-F4** or **F12**) to begin blocking.

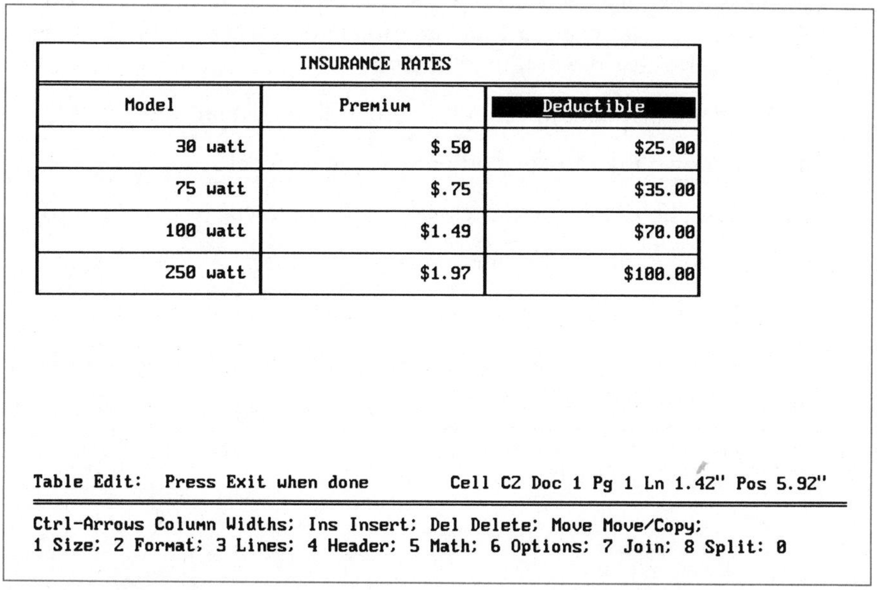

FIGURE L5.5:

The table after changing the justification of text and numbers in the cells

INSURANCE RATES		
Model	Premium	Deductible
30 watt	$.50	$25.00
75 watt	$.75	$35.00
100 watt	$1.49	$70.00
250 watt	$1.97	$100.00

```
Table Edit:  Press Exit when done        Cell C2 Doc 1 Pg 1 Ln 1.42" Pos 5.92"

Ctrl-Arrows Column Widths; Ins Insert; Del Delete; Move Move/Copy;
1 Size; 2 Format; 3 Lines; 4 Header; 5 Math; 6 Options; 7 Join; 8 Split: 0
```

Refer to Chapter 6

3. Press **Home** ↓ to block the entire column.

4. Choose **Lines ➤ Shade ➤ On** from the Table Edit menu to shade the highlighted cells.

At this point, you won't be able to see the shading on your screen. But if you have a graphics monitor, you can see the shading on the View Document screen. Follow these steps:

1. Press Exit (**F7**) to leave Table Edit mode.

2. Select **File ➤ Print ➤ View Document ➤ 1** 100% (or press **Shift-F7 V 1**). The shading in column B will probably look more like dots than actual shading, but will be more like shading when you print the table.

3. Press Exit (**F7**) after viewing the table to return to the Edit screen.

4. Press **Home Home** ↑ to move the cursor to the top of the Edit screen.

ADJUSTING COLUMN WIDTHS

Now the only remaining task is to narrow the columns so that the table will look better. To adjust column widths, you move the cursor to the column you want to adjust, then in Table Edit mode, repeatedly press Ctrl-← to narrow the column or Ctrl-→ to widen it. To do this for the three columns in your table, follow these steps:

1. Press ↓ to move the cursor into the table.

2. Press **Alt-F7**, or choose **Layout ➤ Tables ➤ Edit** from the pull-down menus, to go back to Table Edit mode (so that the Table Edit menu appears near the bottom of the screen).

3. Move the highlight to cell A2 (or any cell in column A except A1).

4. Hold down the Ctrl key and press ← nine times.

5. Release the Ctrl key and press → to move the cursor to column B.

6. Hold down the Ctrl key and press ← ten times.

7. Release the Ctrl key and press → to move the cursor to column C.

8. Hold down the Ctrl key and press ← eight times. Your screen should now look like Figure L5.6.

If the text in a cell wraps to the next line, press Ctrl-→ to widen the column.

PREVIEWING AND PRINTING THE TABLE

You preview and print a table the same way you do any other WordPerfect document. Just follow these steps:

1. Press Exit (**F7**) to leave Table Edit mode.

2. Select **File ➤ Print** (or press **Shift-F7**).

3. If you want to preview your printed table, select **View Document**. After viewing the table, press Cancel (**F1**) to return to the Print menu.

4. Select **F**ull Document to print your table, which should now look like the one shown in Figure L5.1 at the beginning of this lesson.

SAVING YOUR WORK

You'll use this table in Lesson 7 to create a sample newsletter, so you'll want to save it now. Follow these steps:

1. Select **File ➤ Exit** (or press **F7**).

2. When asked about saving the document, choose **Y**es by pressing **Y** or clicking on the Yes option with your mouse.

3. Type **LESSON5.WP** and press ↵.

4. If you're asked whether you want to replace an existing copy of LESSON5.WP, press **Y** to choose Yes.

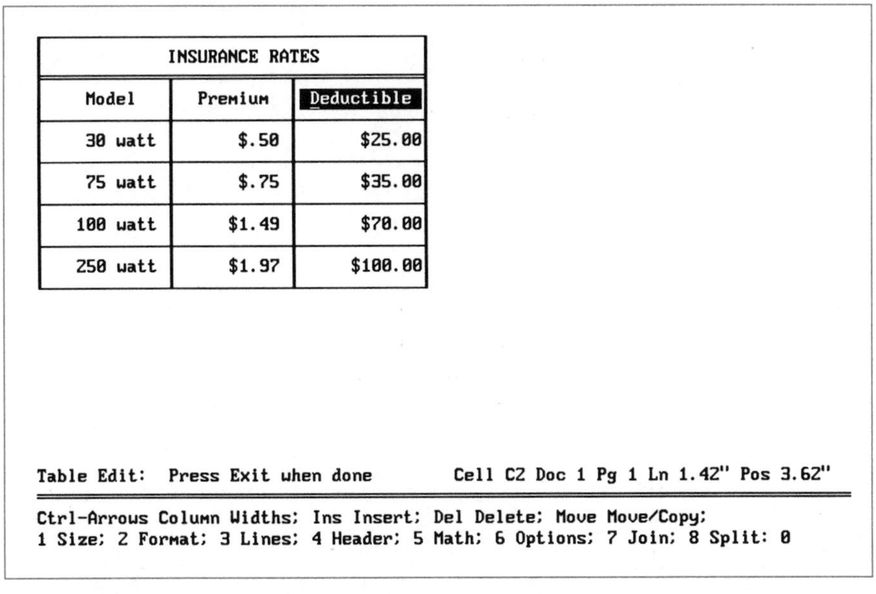

FIGURE L5.6:

The table after narrowing the columns

```
              INSURANCE RATES

     Model     Premium    Deductible

    30 watt     $.50       $25.00

    75 watt     $.75       $35.00

    100 watt    $1.49      $70.00

    250 watt    $1.97      $100.00


 Table Edit:  Press Exit when done      Cell C2 Doc 1 Pg 1 Ln 1.42" Pos 3.62"

 Ctrl-Arrows Column Widths; Ins Insert; Del Delete; Move Move/Copy;
 1 Size; 2 Format; 3 Lines; 4 Header; 5 Math; 6 Options; 7 Join; 8 Split; 0
```

Refer to Chapter 6

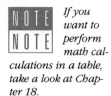

If you want to perform math calculations in a table, take a look at Chapter 18.

5. When you see the prompt "Exit WP? No (Yes)", you can either select No, if you want to continue using WordPerfect, or select Yes, if you want to leave WordPerfect now.

Now that you've had a chance to create a table, you can go back and read Chapter 6 to learn more about tables. Or if you prefer to forge ahead with the hands-on lessons, continue with Lesson 6, which shows you how to create the styles you'll be using for the newsletter in Lesson 7.

Refer to Chapter 6

Creating Some Sample Styles

In this lesson, you'll create and apply the three sample styles shown in Figure L6.1 for headlines, author bylines, and body text, and use them to help create the sample newsletter in the next lesson.

BEFORE YOU BEGIN

If you've exited WordPerfect, be sure to get WordPerfect up and running again, as described in Chapter 1, with a clear screen.

DELETING EXISTING STYLES

WordPerfect comes with some sample styles in a style library named LIBRARY.STY; these are the default styles that are normally loaded when you first start WordPerfect. You won't be using any of these styles in this document, however, so you can just delete them. Follow these steps to get started:

1. Press **Alt-=** or click your right mouse button to view the menu bar.

2. Select **L**ayout ➤ **S**tyles (or press **Alt-F8**). You'll see some existing styles, most likely the ones that come with your WordPerfect package, as shown in Figure L6.2.

3. Select **D**elete ➤ **I**ncluding Codes.

4. Repeat step 3 six more times (or once for every style in your default library) until none of the existing styles remains.

Now you can start creating a new set of styles.

A Perennial Favorite — headline style

by Jo Brightman — byline style

Your life or your bulb's? That's what we asked ourselves when we designed the new Perennial Lightbulb. We know how important your life is, so we designed a bulb that never dies. Buy the Perennial and you'll never have to replace another lightbulb. A surefire winner at only $300 apiece, only from BulbCo -- the brightest idea in lights. ☼

body-text style

FIGURE L6.1:

The sample styles presented in this lesson

CREATING THE HEADLINE STYLE

Now you're going to create a paired headline style that sets the font for article headlines. Follow these steps:

1. Select **C**reate from the menu at the bottom of the Styles screen.
2. Choose **N**ame.
3. Type **Headline** and press ↵.
4. Choose **D**escription.
5. Type **Style for headlines** and press ↵.
6. Choose **C**odes. You're taken to the screen for entering formatting codes for a style.

```
Styles

  Name          Type      Description

  Bibliogrphy   Paired    Bibliography
  Doc Init      Paired    Initialize Document Style
  Document      Outline   Document Style
  Pleading      Open      Header for numbered pleading paper
  Right Par     Outline   Right-Aligned Paragraph Numbers
  Tech Init     Open      Initialize Technical Style
  Technical     Outline   Technical Document Style

1 On; 2 Off; 3 Create; 4 Edit; 5 Delete; 6 Save; 7 Retrieve; 8 Update: 1
```

FIGURE L6.2:

The sample styles that come with WordPerfect

Refer to Chapter 14

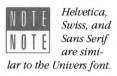

Helvetica, Swiss, and Sans Serif are similar to the Univers font.

7. Select Font ➤ Base Font (or press **Ctrl-F8 F**).

8. Use ↑ or ↓ to highlight the font you want—I used Univers Bold (Scalable) 18pt, but you must highlight a font from the options shown on your own screen.

9. Choose **S**elect or press ↵ to select the highlighted font.

10. If prompted, type a point size and press ↵ (I used 18-point).

11. Press → to move past the [Comment] code.

12. Press ↵ to add the hard return [HRt] to be inserted when you turn the style off.

You can see the [Font:] code for your selection in the lower portion of the screen, as shown in Figure L6.3, although your font may be different. The [HRt] code is to the right of the [Comment] code and will ensure that any text after the headline starts on a new line.

Now you can save the style:

1. Press Exit (**F7**) to return to the Styles: Edit screen.

2. Choose **E**nter.

3. Choose **O**ff.

4. Press Exit (**F7**) to return to the Styles menu.

Choosing **E**nter ➤ **O**ff will cause the style to be turned off automatically when you press ↵ when using the style later. Before you try out the style, however, create the next one.

```
┌─────────────────────────────────────────────────────────┐
│ Place Style On Codes above, and Style Off Codes below.   │
└─────────────────────────────────────────────────────────┘

 ─



Style:   Press Exit when done              Doc 1 Pg 1 Ln 1.28" Pos 1"
[                                                      }
[Font:Univers Bold (Scalable) 18pt][Comment][HRt]
█
```

FIGURE L6.3:

The completed headline style on the style-codes editing screen

Refer to Chapter 14

CREATING THE BYLINE STYLE

Now create the author byline style, which is almost identical to the headline style created above, except that it uses a different font. Follow these steps:

1. Select **C**reate from the menu at the bottom of the screen.

2. Choose **N**ame.

3. Type **Byline** and press ↵.

4. Choose **D**escription.

5. Type **Style for author bylines** and press ↵.

6. Choose **C**odes.

7. Select F**o**nt ➤ Base Font (or press **Ctrl-F8 F**).

8. Use ↑ and ↓ to highlight Univers Italic 12pt or some similar font from the list of available fonts.

9. Choose **S**elect or press ↵.

10. If prompted for a size, type **12** and press ↵.

11. Press → to move past the [Comment] code.

12. Press ↵ to insert the hard-return [HRt] code.

13. Press Exit (**F7**) to return to the Styles: Edit menu.

14. Choose **E**nter ➤ O**ff**.

15. Press Exit (**F7**) to return to the Styles menu.

Now you have two styles in your current document, named *Byline* and *Heading*. Let's forge ahead and create the third style now.

CREATING THE BODY-TEXT STYLE

Now you'll create the style for defining the body text within each article, including the small special character that ends each article. Follow these steps to get started:

1. Choose **C**reate.

2. Choose **N**ame.

3. Type **Body text** and press ↵.

4. Choose **D**escription.

5. Type **Style for body text** and press ↵.

Refer to Chapter 14

6. Choose **C**odes.

7. Select Font ➤ Base Font (or press **Ctrl-F8 F**).

8. Use the ↑ or ↓ keys to highlight the font you want. CG Times (Scalable) 12pt was used in this example.

Dutch Roman and Times Roman are similar to the CG Times font.

9. Choose **S**elect or press ↵.

10. If prompted for a point size, type **12** and press ↵.

Now you've defined the codes to use when the style is turned on. The next step is to define the [Style Off] codes, which include a right-aligned special character and a hard return. Follow these steps:

Special characters are covered in Chapter 5.

1. Press → to move past the [Comment] code.

2. Select **L**ayout ➤ **A**lign ➤ **F**lush Right (or press **Alt-F6**).

3. Press **Ctrl-V**.

4. Type **5,6** and press ↵ to insert the Compass special character.

5. Press ↵ to insert a hard-return [HRt] code.

Your completed style should now resemble Figure L6.4, although your font selection may be different. Press Exit (F7) twice to return to the Styles menu, where you can see that you now have three styles.

TRYING OUT THE HEADLINE STYLE

If you're ready to try out the headline style now, follow these steps:

1. Press Exit (**F7**) to return to the Edit screen.

2. If the Reveal Codes screen isn't on already, activate the menu bar and select **E**dit ➤ **R**eveal Codes (or press **Alt-F3** or **F11**) to turn it on. This way you'll be able to see what's happening behind the scenes.

3. Select **L**ayout ➤ **S**tyles or press Style (**Alt-F8**).

4. Use the ↓ key to highlight Headline.

5. Choose **O**n or press ↵.

6. Type **A Perennial Favorite** and press ↵.

Refer to Chapter 14

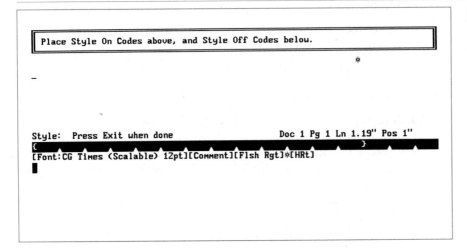

```
┌─────────────────────────────────────────────────────────────┐
│ Place Style On Codes above, and Style Off Codes below.       │
└─────────────────────────────────────────────────────────────┘
                                                        *

 _




Style:   Press Exit when done              Doc 1 Pg 1 Ln 1.19" Pos 1"
{                                                      }
[Font:CG Times (Scalable) 12pt][Comment][Flsh Rgt]*[HRt]
█
```

Your screen should now look like Figure L6.5. Notice the [Style On:Headline] and [Style Off:Headline] codes with the text between them, and see how pressing ↵ in step 6 automatically turned the headline style off, moving the cursor to the next line.

Your style doesn't look like much right now because fonts don't show up on the Edit screen. But you can preview the printed document by using

```
A Perennial Favorite
 _




                                          Doc 1 Pg 1 Ln 1.28" Pos 1"
{                                                      }
[Style On:Headline]A Perennial Favorite[Style Off:Headline]█




Press Reveal Codes to restore screen
```

the View Document screen:

1. Select **File** ➤ **Print** ➤ **View** Document (or press **Shift-F7 V**) to preview your headline.

2. Press Exit (**F7**) to return to the Edit screen.

TRYING OUT THE BYLINE STYLE ON EXISTING TEXT

Applying a style to existing text is a lot like applying boldface or other formatting: You block the text, then apply the style.

Now try the body-text style—this time, just for practice, you'll apply the style to *existing* text. Follow these steps:

1. Type

   by Jo Brightman

2. Press **Home** ← to move to the beginning of the line.

3. Select **Edit** ➤ **Block** (or press **Alt-F4** or **F12**) to begin blocking the line.

4. Press **End** to block to the end of the line.

5. Select **Layout** ➤ **Styles** or press Style (**Alt-F8**).

6. Use ↓ to highlight Byline.

7. Choose **On** or press ↵.

Notice how applying this style to existing text inserted the appropriate [Style On] and [Style Off] codes. You can again preview this on the View Document screen.

TRYING OUT THE NEW BODY-TEXT STYLE

Test the body-text style now by following these steps:

1. Press **Home Home** ↓ to make sure you're at the bottom of the document.

2. Press ↵ to insert an extra blank line.

3. Select **Layout** ➤ **Styles**, or press Style (**Alt-F8**).

4. If necessary, use the ↑ or ↓ keys to highlight *Body text*.

5. Choose **On** or press ↵ to turn on the style.

6. Type the following text without pressing ↵:

   Your life or the bulb's? That's what we asked ourselves when we designed the new Perennial Lightbulb. We know how important your life is, so we designed a bulb that never dies. Buy the Perennial and you'll never have to replace another lightbulb. A surefire winner at only $300 apiece, only from BulbCo—the brightest idea in lights.

Refer to Chapter 14

7. Press → to move past the [Style Off] code and turn off the style. Your screen should now look like Figure L6.6 (don't worry if part of your screen is cut off at the right; this will happen if you are using a narrow font).

Again, you can use the View Document screen to check your progress. Figure L6.7 shows the results with the document at 100 percent (normal) size. Press Exit (F7) to return to the Edit screen after viewing the document.

COMPLETING THE TEXT

Remember, don't press ↵ while typing the articles; let WordPerfect word-wrap the text for you automatically.

Figure L6.8 shows two more articles added to the sample document. Go ahead and type them now, using your styles to format the headings, bylines, and body text. Remember, you use a style before typing text by activating the style, typing your text, then pressing → to end the style. Or, if you prefer, you can type the text, then block it and activate the style. Also, press ↵ an extra time before typing each headline and after typing each byline, to insert the blank lines shown in the figure.

PRINTING AND SAVING YOUR WORK

If you wish, you can print a copy of your document now, and then save it.

```
A Perennial Favorite
by Jo Brightman

Your life or your bulb's? That's what we asked ourselves when we designed the ne
Lightbulb. We know how important your life is, so we designed a bulb that never
Perennial and you'll never have to replace another lightbulb. A surefire winner
apiece, only from BulbCo -- the brightest idea in lights                    *
_



                                        Doc 1 Pg 1 Ln 2.42" Pos 1"
[                                                                        ]
Lightbulb. We know how important your life is, so we designed a bulb that never
dies. Buy the[SRt]
Perennial and you'll never have to replace another lightbulb. A surefire winner
at only $300[SRt]
apiece, only from BulbCo [-][-] the brightest idea in lights[Style Off:Body text
]




Press Reveal Codes to restore screen
```

FIGURE L6.6:

The Edit and Reveal Codes screens after applying the body-text style to some text

Refer to Chapter 14

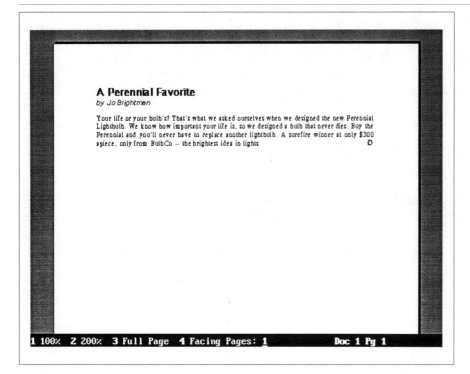

A Perennial Favorite
by Jo Brightman

Your life or your bulb's? That's what we asked ourselves when we designed the new Perennial Lightbulb. We know how important your life is, so we designed a bulb that never dies. Buy the Perennial and you'll never have to replace another lightbulb. A surefire winner at only $300 apiece, only from BulbCo -- the brightest idea in lights.   ☼

Insure it with ease
by G Ubetter

Now that we've got your attention, we'd like to tell you that Perennial Lightbulbs are guaranteed for a lifetime -- yours or theirs. As long as the bulbs remain intact. You drop one of our Perennials on the linoleum and your three hundred dollars aren't worth a filament. That's why we're offering insurance. Yep! We'll insure every one of these babies for a small premium, as shown in the accompanying table.   ☼

Festival of Lights
by Les Pardee

Don't miss our Festival of Lights, for a firsthand look at all of our great products, including the new Perennial. There will be free refreshments at our offices, and the first 20 guests will get two years of Perennial insurance -- absolutely free! See you July 15.   ☼

FIGURE L6.8:

Use the styles you created in this lesson to add two more articles and complete the document.

Refer to Chapter 14

Follow the same steps presented in previous lessons:

1. If you want to print the document now, choose **File ➤ Print ➤ Full Document** (or press **Shift-F7 F**).

2. To save the document, select **File ➤ Exit ➤ Yes** (or press **F7 Y**).

3. Type **LESSON6.WP** as the name of the file, then press ↵.

4. If you want to leave WordPerfect now, select Yes. If you want to go straight to Lesson 7 and continue developing the newsletter, press Cancel (**F1**) to leave the current document on the screen.

Now that you've created a few styles, you can go back and read Chapter 14 to learn more, or you can continue with the hands-on lessons. In the next lesson, you'll create a newsletter using the table from Lesson 5 and the text and styles you created in this lesson. You'll also learn about graphics, lines, and columns.

Refer to Chapter 14

Creating a Newsletter

In this lesson, you'll use the table created in Lesson 5, the articles and styles created in Lesson 6, and the graphics and multicolumn layout techniques presented in chapters 19 and 20 to create the one-page newsletter shown in Figure L7.1.

Newsletters are one of the most popular desktop publishing applications for WordPerfect, because they bring together three of the program's most dazzling features: styles, graphics, and multicolumn layouts. Once you've mastered the techniques shown here, you'll be able to adapt them to your own publications, including newsletters, fliers, memos, invitations, and any other documents requiring extra sparkle and pizazz.

BEFORE YOU BEGIN

If you haven't completed Lesson 5 on Tables and Lesson 6 on Styles, you should do so before starting this lesson. If you've exited WordPerfect, be sure to get WordPerfect up and running again. Then retrieve the document you created in Lesson 6, LESSON6.WP. You should see the three short articles you created in Lesson 6.

CREATING THE NAMEPLATE

We'll take it from the top by creating the nameplate, which consists of the shaded-text graphic with the name of the newsletter, the drop-shadowed light bulb, and the issue information followed by a horizontal line.

Text boxes are auto-matically shaded, with thick horizontal lines drawn above and below the box. For more informa-tion, see Chapter 19.

CREATING THE TEXT BOX

Here are the steps for creating the shaded Text box:

1. Press **Home Home Home** ↑, then ↵, then ← again to put a blank line above the existing text and move the cursor back to that line. This will give you some room in which to work.

FIGURE L7.1:

The sample newsletter you'll create in this lesson

BulbCo
BLURBS

 Volume 1, Number 1   June 1992

A Perennial Favorite
by Jo Brightman

Your life or your bulb's? That's what we asked ourselves when we designed the new Perennial Lightbulb. We know how important your life is, so we designed a bulb that never dies. Buy the Perennial and you'll never have to replace another lightbulb. A surefire winner at only $300 apiece, only from BulbCo -- the brightest idea in lights. ♀

Insure it with ease
by G Ubetter

Now that we've got your attention, we'd like to tell you that Perennial

Lightbulbs are guaranteed for a lifetime -- yours or theirs. As long as the bulbs remain intact. You drop one of our Perennials on the linoleum and your three hundred dollars aren't worth a filament. That's why we're offering insurance. Yep! We'll insure every one of these babies for a small premium, as shown in the accompanying table. ♀

Festival of Lights
by Les Pardee

Don't miss our Festival of Lights, for a firsthand look at all of our great products, including the new Perennial. There will be free refreshments at our offices, and the first 20 guests will get two years of Perennial insurance -- absolutely free! See you July 15. ♀

INSURANCE RATES		
Model	Premium	Deductible
30 watt	$.50	$25.00
75 watt	$.75	$35.00
100 watt	$1.49	$70.00
250 watt	$1.97	$100.00

Refer to Chapters 19 and 20

2. Select **G**raphics ➤ Text **B**ox ➤ **C**reate (or press **Alt-F9 B C**). You'll see the Text box Definition screen.

3. Choose Anchor **T**ype.

4. WordPerfect will prompt with

Anchor Type: **1** Paragraph; **2** Page; **3** Character

5. Choose **P**age to anchor the graphic to the page.

6. Type **0** and press ↵ (or just press ↵) when prompted with "Number of pages to skip:". This places the graphic on the current page.

7. Choose **H**orizontal Position.

8. Choose **M**argins to set the position with respect to the margins.

9. Choose **F**ull to have the box fill the space between the left and right margins.

10. Choose **S**ize.

11. Choose Set **H**eight/Auto Width to set a height for the graphic box and let WordPerfect calculate the width automatically.

12. Type **2.25** (for inches) and press ↵.

Now you're ready to type in the newsletter name. Follow these steps:

1. Choose **E**dit to start defining the contents of the empty box you just created.

2. Press ↵ to insert a blank line.

3. Select **F**ont ➤ Base **F**ont from the pull-down menus (or press **Ctrl-F8 F**).

4. Use the ↑ or ↓ key to highlight the font you want. (I used the CG Times Bold Italic (Scalable) 48-point font.)

5. Choose **S**elect or press ↵.

6. If you're using a scalable font, type the point size (*48* to match this example) and press ↵.

7. Select **L**ayout ➤ **A**lign ➤ **F**lush Right (or press **Alt-F6**) to align the text flush-right.

8. Type **BulbCo** and press ↵.

The next line of the nameplate should be much larger, so again you'll select a font and type the text:

1. Select **F**ont ➤ Base **F**ont (or press **Ctrl-F8 F**).

Page-anchored graphics are placed at a particular spot on a page. Paragraph-anchored graphics float with the paragraph to which they're anchored. Character-anchored graphics float with the character to which they're anchored.

The Dutch font is similar to Times.

Refer to Chapters 19 and 20

2. Use the ↑ or ↓ key to highlight the font you want. (Again I used CG Times Bold Italic (Scalable) —this time at 64 points.)

3. Choose **S**elect or press ↵.

4. If you're using a scalable font, type the point size (*64* to match our example) and press ↵.

5. Select **L**ayout ➤ **A**lign ➤ **F**lush Right (or press **Alt-F6**) to align the text flush-right.

6. Type **B L U R B S** and press ↵. Don't forget to include a blank space in between each letter, by pressing the spacebar, and to type the word in capital letters.

7. Press Exit (**F7**) twice to return to the Edit screen.

The Edit screen doesn't reveal the contents of graphic boxes, so you'll need to check your work on the View Document screen. Follow these steps:

1. Select **F**ile ➤ **P**rint ➤ **V**iew Document (or press **Shift-F7 V**), then type **3** to look at your handiwork so far, as shown in Figure L7.2.

2. Press Exit (**F7**) to return to the Edit screen.

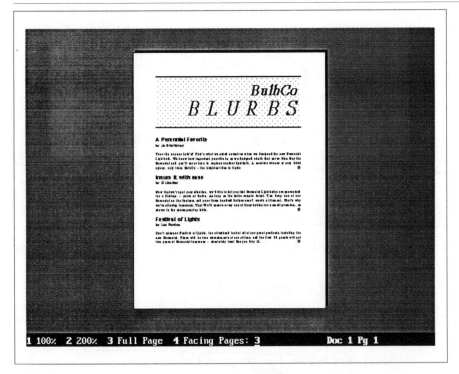

FIGURE L7.2:

The View Document screen after setting up the Text box

Refer to Chapters 19 and 20

DEFINING THE FIGURE BORDERS

TIP *To create a drop shadow, just use a thick or extra-thick line at the left and bottom edges or at the right and top edges of the graphic border.*

Next you'll create the light-bulb graphic in a Figure box. An ordinary Figure box has a border style with single lines at the left, right, top, and bottom. But adding a drop shadow will put a little more sizzle into your light bulb. To do this, you'll define some Figure options. Follow these steps:

1. Select **G**raphics ➤ **F**igure ➤ **O**ptions (or press **Alt-F9 F O**). This displays the screen shown in Figure L7.3.

2. Choose **B**order Style to define the border style for any subsequent Figure boxes.

3. WordPerfect will present these options for the border lines:

   1 None; **2 S**ingle; **3 D**ouble; **4 D**ashed; **5 D**otted; **6 T**hick; **7 E**xtra Thick

4. Choose **T**hick for the left border.

5. Press ↵ to leave the right border as a single line.

6. Press ↵ to leave the top border as a single line.

7. Choose **T**hick for the bottom border.

8. Press Exit (**F7**) to return to the Edit screen.

Any Figure boxes that you create to the right of the current cursor position will use the border style you've just defined. Let's go ahead and create a Figure box now.

```
Options: Figure

     1 - Border Style
             Left                 Single
             Right                Single
             Top                  Single
             Bottom               Single
     2 - Outside Border Space
             Left                 0.167"
             Right                0.167"
             Top                  0.167"
             Bottom               0.167"
     3 - Inside Border Space
             Left                 0"
             Right                0"
             Top                  0"
             Bottom               0"
     4 - First Level Numbering Method    Numbers
     5 - Second Level Numbering Method    Off
     6 - Caption Number Style            [BOLD]Figure 1[bold]
     7 - Position of Caption             Below box, Outside borders
     8 - Minimum Offset from Paragraph   0"
     9 - Gray Shading (% of black)       0%

Selection: 0
```

FIGURE L7.3:

The Figure Options screen

Refer to Chapters 19 and 20

CREATING THE FIGURE BOX

Now you're ready to define the light-bulb Figure box. Follow these steps:

1. On the Reveal codes screen, make sure the highlight is still on the [HRt] code following the [FigOpt] code.

2. Select **G**raphics ➤ **F**igure ➤ **C**reate (or press **Alt-F9 F C**) to create a Figure box.

3. Choose **F**ilename to select a graphic from the disk.

4. Type **BULB.WPG** and press ↵ (this assumes you installed WordPerfect graphics files).

5. Choose **H**orizontal Position ➤ **L**eft to place the graphic at the left margin.

6. Choose **S**ize ➤ Set **W**idth/Auto Height to define the width of the graphic.

7. Type **.75** and press ↵ to set the width to 0.75 inches (the height will be set automatically to 0.563 inches).

8. If you want to view the graphic, select **E**dit. Then press Exit (**F7**) to return to the menu.

9. Press Exit (**F7**) to return to the Edit screen.

10. Select **F**ile ➤ **P**rint ➤ **V**iew Document (or press **Shift-F7 V**) to view your progress so far. Your screen will resemble Figure L7.4.

11. Press Exit (**F7**) when you're ready to return to the Edit screen.

The View Document screen displays a true-to-life view of your document, but the Edit screen looks a lot like gobbledygook. All you'll typically see on the Edit screen is an outline of where the graphics will appear, and if Reveal Codes is on, the bottom of the screen will show the graphics codes.

ADDING NAMEPLATE TEXT

You've just about completed the nameplate—all that's left to do is to include the information about the newsletter issue and to draw the horizontal dividing line below it. Follow these steps:

Helvetica and Swiss fonts are similar to Univers.

1. Select **F**ont ➤ **B**ase Font (or press **Ctrl-F8 F**).

2. Use the ↑ or ↓ key to highlight the font you want. (I used the Univers (Scalable) 12-point font.)

3. Choose **S**elect or press ↵.

Refer to Chapters 19 and 20

4. If prompted for a size, type the point size (*12* to match this example) and press ↵.

5. Press ↵ to add a blank line above the text.

6. Type

   Volume 1, Number 1

7. Select **L**ayout ➤ **A**lign ➤ **F**lush Right (or press **Alt-F6**).

8. Type **June 1992** and press ↵.

ADDING THE HORIZONTAL LINE

The next task is to define the horizontal line:

1. Select **G**raphics ➤ **L**ine ➤ **C**reate **H**orizontal (or press **Alt-F9 L H**). For this line, you can just use the default settings.

2. Press Exit (**F7**) to return to the Edit screen.

3. Press ↵ twice to allow some space beneath the horizontal line.

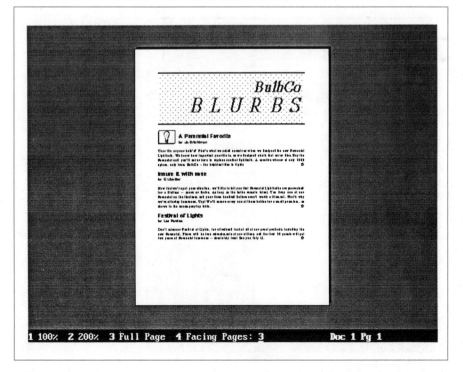

FIGURE L7.4:

The View Document screen, with the sized graphic

Refer to Chapters 19 and 20

The nameplate is now complete. To view it on your own screen, you'll again have to switch to the View Document screen. It should look like Figure L7.5. Press Exit (F7) when you're finished viewing the newsletter.

DEFINING THE NEWSPAPER-STYLE COLUMNS

NOTE
NOTE

With news-paper-style columns, text flows continuously up and down through the columns of the page, like a newspaper or magazine.

The newsletter consists of three newspaper-style columns, with vertical lines, a table, and, of course, the text of the stories. To create multiple columns, you first must define the columns, then activate them. Follow these steps:

1. Press → then ← to move the highlight to the [Style On] code for the first article.

2. Select **L**ayout ➤ **C**olumns ➤ **D**efine (or press **Alt-F7 C D**).

3. Choose **N**umber of Columns.

4. Type **3** and press ↵.

Notice on your screen that WordPerfect has predefined the left and right margins for each column, with an initial distance between columns of $1/2$ inch.

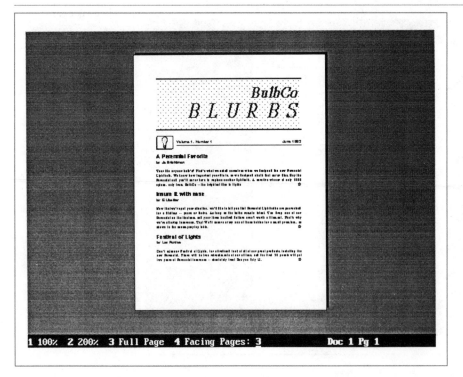

FIGURE L7.5:

The completed nameplate

Refer to Chapters 19 and 20

For example, column 1 ends at 2.83" and column 2 begins at 3.33", $1/2$ inch to the right.

5. Press ↵ to return to the prompt:

> **Columns: 1 On; 2 Off; 3 Define**

6. Choose **On** to activate the columns.

The columns may not look very good on your Edit screen, but will look fine on the View Document screen. The highlight should still be on the [Style **On**] code for the first headline. Jot down the measurement next to Ln near the bottom of the Edit screen.

ADDING THE VERTICAL LINES

Defining vertical lines is similar to defining horizontal lines. Follow these steps:

1. Select **G**raphics ➤ **L**ine ➤ Create **V**ertical (or press **Alt-F9 L V**).

2. Choose **H**orizontal Position ➤ **B**etween Columns.

3. When prompted with "Place line to right of column", type **1** and press ↵.

4. Choose **V**ertical Position ➤ **S**et Position.

5. Type **4.29** (or whatever number you jotted down earlier), and press ↵. This will set the top of the vertical line even with the first line of text in the first column. Note that the Length of Line setting was calculated for you automatically.

6. Press Exit (**F7**) to return to the Edit screen.

The line does not appear on the Edit screen, but you'll see it in a moment. First, use the same basic steps you just used to create the second vertical line, but with a different horizontal position:

1. Select **G**raphics ➤ **L**ine ➤ Create **V**ertical (or press **Alt-F9 L V**).

2. Choose **H**orizontal Position ➤ **B**etween Columns.

3. Type **2** and press ↵ to place the line to the right of column 2.

4. Choose **V**ertical Position ➤ **S**et Position.

Refer to Chapters 19 and 20

5. Type **4.29** (or whatever number you jotted down earlier) and press ↵ to set the vertical line even with the first line of text in the second column.

6. Press Exit (**F7**) to return to the Edit screen.

Now you can switch to the View Document screen to check your progress. Press Exit (F7) to return to the Edit screen.

DEFINING THE TABLE BOX

The last graphic you need to create is the Table box, which appears at the bottom of the page between columns 2 and 3. By default, WordPerfect places a thick horizontal line above and below a Table box. Follow these steps:

1. Select **G**raphics ➤ **T**able Box ➤ **C**reate (or press **Alt-F9 T C**).

2. Choose **F**ilename.

3. Type **LESSON5.WP** and press ↵ to select the table you created in Lesson 5.

4. Choose Anchor **T**ype ➤ **P**age.

5. Type **0** and press ↵ to place the graphic on this page.

6. Choose **V**ertical Position ➤ **B**ottom to place the graphic at the bottom of the page.

7. Choose **H**orizontal Position ➤ **C**olumns to choose the columns where the graphic should appear.

8. You'll see the prompt

   Enter column(s):

9. Type **2-3** and press ↵ to place the graphic across columns 2 and 3.

10. You'll see the prompt

    Horizontal Position: 1 Left; 2 Right; 3 Center; 4 Full

11. Choose **F**ull to have the graphic fill the space between the left and right margins of columns 2 and 3.

12. To verify that the table has been added to the box, choose **E**dit to view the box's contents. You should see the table you created in Lesson 5.

13. Press Exit (**F7**) twice to return to the Edit screen.

The Columns option is only available when you've defined multiple columns.

Refer to Chapters 19 and 20

Once again you'll want to check your progress on the View Document screen. Your screen should look like Figure L7.6. Press Exit (F7) when you're ready to return to the Edit screen.

EDITING THE GRAPHIC LINE

Whoops! Do you see a problem? Is the vertical line between column 2 and column 3 too long? At this point, you could print the page and measure how long the line should be. (For the example, I determined that the line should be about 3.25 inches long.) Here's how to edit that line:

1. Select **G**raphics ➤ **L**ine ➤ Edit V**e**rtical (or press **Alt-F9 L E**).

2. Choose **L**ength of Line.

3. Type **3.25** (or whatever measurement seems right for you), and press ↵.

4. Press Exit (**F7**) to return to the Edit screen.

5. Select **F**ile ➤ **P**rint ➤ **V**iew Document (**Shift-F7 V**) to take a look at the revised line, then press Exit (**F7**) to return to the Edit screen.

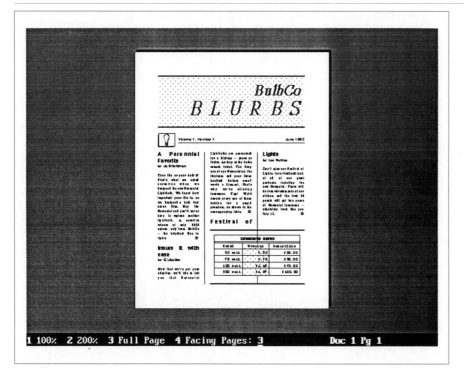

FIGURE L7.6:

The View Document screen after defining the Table box

Refer to Chapters 19 and 20

CHANGING THE JUSTIFICATION

In narrow columns, particularly when using a large font size, left justification generally looks better than full justification. Let's change the justification now:

1. Press →, then select **Layout ➤ Line ➤ Justification ➤ Left** (or press **Shift-F8 L J**).

2. Press Exit (**F7**) to return to the Edit screen.

Feel free to check out the document on the View Document screen, or just go on to the next section.

CHANGING THE BODY-TEXT STYLE

Suppose now that you decide you want to end each article with a small graphic light bulb rather than the compass character you defined earlier. This will be easy because you created a style to format all the articles, so you just need to change the style. Here's how:

1. Select **Layout ➤ S**tyles (or press **Alt-F8**).

2. Use the arrow keys to move the highlight to the body-text style.

3. Select **E**dit from the menu at the bottom of the screen.

4. Select **C**odes, which brings you to the screen for defining and changing codes.

5. Move the cursor to the compass character.

6. Press **Delete** to delete that character.

7. Select **G**raphics ➤ User Box ➤ **C**reate (or press **Alt-F9 U C**) to create a user-defined graphic box (which, by default, has no borders).

8. Choose **F**ilename, type **BULB.WPG**, and press ↵.

9. Choose Anchor **T**ype ➤ **C**haracter, because you want this graphic to "stick to" its neighboring character.

10. Select **S**ize ➤ Set **H**eight/Auto Width.

11. Type **.125** and press ↵ to make the graphic very small.

12. Press Exit (**F7**) to return to the codes editing screen. The graphic appears as only a small box on this screen and as a [Usr Box:1; BULB.WPG] code on the bottom half of the screen.

13. Press Exit (**F7**) three times to return to the Edit screen.

Refer to Chapters 19 and 20

MOVING TEXT TO A NEW COLUMN

Your printed document may not look exactly like Figure L7.1, because your printer may not have the same fonts. You may find that the words *Festival of* are at the end of column 2, rather than at the top of column 3. You can force text to a new column by moving the cursor to the start of the text that you want to bump over to the next column and pressing Ctrl-↵ to insert a hard page break ([HPg]).

If you need to bump the article heading over to column 3, follow these steps:

1. Press Search (**F2**), type **Fest**, then press Search again. This moves the cursor to the article heading.

2. Press ← five times to move the cursor to the [Style On] code for the headline.

3. Press **Ctrl-↵**. This inserts a hard page break, which forces text to the next column.

4. To view the document, select **F**ile ➤ **P**rint ➤ **V**iew Document (or press **Shift-F7 V**). It should look something like Figure L7.7.

5. Press Exit (**F7**) to return to the Edit screen.

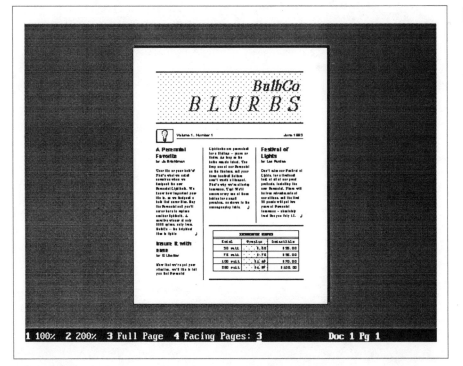

FIGURE L7.7:

The completed newsletter on the View Document screen

Refer to Chapters 19 and 20

PRINTING AND SAVING THE DOCUMENT

Now you're ready to print and save your document. Follow these steps:

1. Select File ➤ **P**rint (or press **Shift-F7**).

2. For the highest-quality graphic output, choose **G**raphics Quality ➤ **H**igh.

3. Select **F**ull Document. Be patient—it takes a while for most printers to print high-quality graphics.

4. When the printing is finished, choose File ➤ E**x**it (or press **F7**).

5. When asked about saving the document, select **Y**es, type **LESSON7.WP**, and press ↵.

6. If you want to call it a day and leave WordPerfect, choose **Y**es. If you want to work with your newsletter some more, press Cancel (**F1**). If you want to stay in WordPerfect but with a clear Edit screen, choose **N**o.

Standard fonts on a Hewlett-Packard LaserJet III printer were used for all these lessons.

Congratulations! You've just created a sophisticated WordPerfect document with columns, lines, and graphics. To learn more about the features used here, see chapters 19 and 20. Or, if you prefer, dive into the next hands-on lesson to learn how to create macros.

Refer to Chapters 19 and 20

Creating Some Handy Macros

Macros are terrific time-savers because they let you capture many keystrokes—much as tape and video recorders capture sound and images—then play them back with push-button ease. In this lesson, you'll create several very handy macros that you can use right away to make working with WordPerfect faster and easier.

BEFORE YOU BEGIN

If you've exited WordPerfect, be sure to get WordPerfect up and running again, with a clear screen.

SIG: A MACRO TO CLOSE CORRESPONDENCE

Suppose you usually end all correspondence this way:

Fred Stevens
Vice President, Marketing
MegaMamaToid Corp.

Follow these steps to store these keystrokes in a macro named *SIG*:

1. Press ↵ a couple of times to move to the beginning of a new line.

2. Select **T**ools ➤ **M**acro ➤ **D**efine from the pull-down menus, or press Macro Define (**Ctrl-F10**).

3. You'll see the prompt

    Define macro:

4. Type **SIG** and press ↵ to give your macro a name.

Refer to Chapter 15

5. If you see the prompt

   SIG.WPM Already Exists: **1 R**eplace; **2 E**dit; **3 D**escription

   someone has probably done this lesson before. It's probably safe to do
   the following:

   ◆ Press **R** to choose **R**eplace.

   ◆ Press **Y** when prompted with "Replace C:\WP51\SIG.WPM? **N**o
   (**Y**es)".

   You'll see the prompt

   Description:

6. Type **My signature** and press ↵ to describe your macro. Notice the
   flashing "Macro Def" message at the bottom of the screen, which
   indicates that keystrokes are now being recorded.

7. Type your signature, using whatever text you wish. For this example,
   you can type

   Fred Stevens
   Vice President, Marketing
   MegaMamaToid Corp.

   Remember to press ↵ at the end of each line. Your screen should now
   look something like Figure L8.1.

TIP *If you want to cancel a macro definition when "Macro Def" is flashing, just select Tools ➤ Macro ➤ Define or press Macro Define (Ctrl-F10) again.*

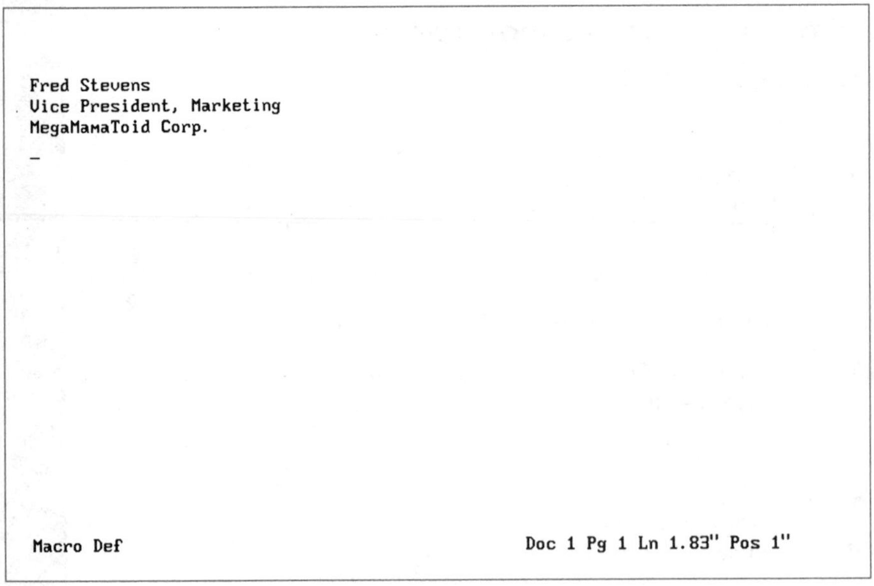

```
Fred Stevens
Vice President, Marketing
MegaMamaToid Corp.
_




Macro Def                        Doc 1 Pg 1 Ln 1.83" Pos 1"
```

FIGURE L8.1:

The screen, just before ending the macro definition

Refer to Chapter 15

8. Select **T**ools ➤ **M**acro ➤ **D**efine or press Macro Define (**Ctrl-F10**) to finish the macro. The flashing "Macro Def" message disappears, and your macro is recorded.

Now when you're at the end of a document, where you would normally type your signature, you can use the SIG macro. To try it now, follow these steps:

1. Select **F**ile ➤ E**x**it ➤ **N**o ➤ **N**o (or press **F7 N N**) to clear your screen now without saving the current document.

2. Type the letter closing:

Sincerely yours,

3. Press ↵ three times to insert some blank lines.

4. Select **T**ools ➤ **M**acro ➤ E**x**ecute or press Macro (**Alt-F10**).

5. Type **SIG** and press ↵ at the "Macro:" prompt.

Your signature will be typed automatically at the cursor position.

ALT-S: A QUICK-SAVE MACRO

By now you should be in the habit of saving your work frequently by using **F**ile ➤ **S**ave or the Save (F10) key. The following macro makes this easier by "quick-saving" a document to disk. It assumes that the document on the screen has already been saved at least once. Therefore, you need to start from a previously saved document before recording this macro. Or you can just save the text that's on your screen now and use it as the starting point. Follow these steps:

1. Select **F**ile ➤ **S**ave, or press Save (**F10**).

2. Type a file name, such as **SIG.WP**, and press ↵.

3. If you're asked whether you want to replace the file, press **Y** (assuming you don't mind replacing SIG.WP; otherwise, press **N** and return to step 2, where you can enter a different file name).

Because you'll be using the quick-save macro frequently, you'll assign an Alt-*letter* name to it so that you can play it back later without using the **T**ools ➤ **M**acro ➤ E**x**ecute pull-down menu options or the Macro (Alt-F10) key. You'll name this macro Alt-S, because the letter *S* helps to remind you that this macro is used to save a document. Follow these steps to define the macro:

1. Select **T**ools ➤ **M**acro ➤ **D**efine, or press Macro Define (**Ctrl-F10**).

Refer to Chapter 15

2. When you see the "Define macro:" prompt, press **Alt-S**. This creates the macro ALTS.WPM.

3. Choose **R**eplace if you see the prompt

   ALTS.WPM Already Exists: 1 Replace; 2 Edit; 3 Description

   Then press **Y** to verify the replacement.

4. Type **Quick Save** and press ↵ when prompted for the description. "Macro Def" now flashes at the bottom of the screen.

5. Select **File ➤ S**ave or press Save (**F10**). WordPerfect prompts

   Document to be saved:

   followed by the name of the file.

6. Press ↵ to accept the name. WordPerfect now asks whether you want to replace the file.

7. Press **Y** for Yes, indicating that you want to update the old version with the new one. The file is saved to disk, and the "Macro Def" message resumes flashing.

Use this macro just before printing, doing a Search and Replace operation, or spell-checking.

8. Select **T**ools ➤ **M**acro ➤ **D**efine or press Macro Define (**Ctrl-F10**) to stop recording the macro, since the macro is now complete.

Using the quick-save macro is very easy. Anytime you're working in the Edit screen of a document that's already been saved once, just press Alt-S. This activates the macro and quickly saves your document to disk.

TIPS ON OTHER EASY-TO-CREATE MACROS

You can use these same basic steps to simplify access to other frequently used features, such as creating an Alt-V macro to switch to the View Document screen (File ➤ Print ➤ View Document), or an Alt-F macro to take you to the list of available fonts easily (Font ➤ Base Font).

Another handy use of macros is for typing special characters. If you regularly use a special character (such as a bullet) in your work, why not record the keystrokes required to type the bullet in a macro, perhaps named Alt-B? Then in the future, you need only press Alt-B to type the bullet, rather than going through the entire "compose" sequence with the Ctrl-V keys.

ALT-T: A MACRO TO TRANSPOSE CHARACTERS

One of the most common typing mistakes is swapping two letters or numbers, such as typing *hte* instead of *the*. It's annoying to have to switch the two misplaced characters using the ordinary editing keys. But you can create a macro that does this job for you.

You can call this one Alt-T, to remind you that the macro transposes letters. Follow these steps:

1. Press ↵ to start on a new line.

2. Type the misspelled word **hte** and press ↵.

3. Move the cursor beneath the letter *h*.

4. Select **T**ools ➤ **M**acro ➤ **D**efine, or press Macro Define (**Ctrl-F10**).

5. Name the macro by pressing **Alt-T.**

6. If WordPerfect indicates that this macro already exists, choose **R**eplace, then press **Y** to verify the replacement, or press Cancel (**F1**), repeat steps 1–4, and choose a new name in step 5.

7. For the macro description, type **Transpose two letters** and press ↵.

8. Press the **Delete** key.

9. Press → once to move the cursor one character to the right.

10. Press Cancel (**F1**) to undelete the character.

11. Choose **R**estore. The two characters have been transposed.

12. Select **T**ools ➤ **M**acro ➤ **D**efine or press Macro Define (**Ctrl-F10**) to stop recording keystrokes.

To see just how handy this macro can be, intentionally mistype another word, then use the new Alt-T macro to transpose the letters. Follow these steps:

1. Press **Home** → to move to the end of the word *the.*

2. Press the spacebar to insert a blank space.

3. Type the misspelled word **smiple**.

4. Position the cursor beneath the letter *m*.

5. Press **Alt-T** to switch the *m* and the *i,* transforming *smiple* into *simple*.

Now anytime you need to transpose two characters, you can just move the cursor to the first letter to be transposed, then press Alt-T.

ALT-W: A MACRO TO TRANSPOSE WORDS

Another common mistake is transposing two words, such as typing *important really* instead of *really important*. You can create a macro named Alt-W that

Refer to Chapter 15

reverses their order. Follow these steps:

1. Press **End** to move to the end of the current line.

2. Press the spacebar to insert a blank space.

3. Type the words

   cat black yelped

4. Move the cursor to the *c* in *cat*.

5. Select **T**ools ➤ **M**acro ➤ **D**efine, or press Macro Define (**Ctrl-F10**).

6. Name the macro by pressing **Alt-W**.

7. If WordPerfect indicates that this macro already exists, choose **R**eplace, then press **Y** to verify the replacement.

8. For the macro description, type **Transpose two words** and press ↵.

9. Press **Ctrl-Backspace** to delete the word *cat*.

10. Press **Ctrl-→** to move to the start of the word *yelped*.

11. Press Cancel (**F1**).

12. Press **R** to select Restore.

13. Select **T**ools ➤ **M**acro ➤ **D**efine or press Macro Define (**Ctrl-F10**) to stop recording keystrokes.

You can try the macro now by positioning the cursor on the first character of any word that has another word to the right of it, then pressing Alt-W to reverse the order of the words.

STARTMEM: A MACRO THAT PAUSES FOR INPUT FROM THE KEYBOARD

In many cases, you might want a macro to perform a few keystrokes, then wait for you to type something, then perform a few more keystrokes. One example is if you type a memo where you want the macro to type automatically the lines shown below, pausing after each line to let you fill in the missing information:

DATE:
TO:
FROM:
SUBJECT:

Refer to Chapter 15

To create such a macro in WordPerfect, you need to insert a *pause* in your macro. Follow these steps to create STARTMEM, so-named because it is useful for starting a memo:

1. Clear the Edit screen.

2. Select **T**ools ➤ **M**acro ➤ **D**efine, or press Macro Define (**Ctrl-F10**).

3. Type **STARTMEM** and press ↵ to name the macro.

4. If WordPerfect indicates that this macro already exists, choose **R**eplace, then press **Y** to verify the replacement.

5. For a macro description, type **Start a memo, with pauses** and press ↵.

6. Type **DATE:** and press **Tab** once.

7. Press the Macro Commands key (**Ctrl-Page Up**). You'll see the following menu line:

   1 Pause; 2 Display; 3 Assign; 4 Comment

8. Choose **P**ause to have the macro pause.

9. Press ↵ to signal the end of the Pause command.

10. Press ↵ twice to insert a blank line.

If you are at a menu choice, you see only the first two options: Pause and Display.

The remaining steps pretty much repeat steps 6–10:

11. Type **TO:** and press **Tab** twice (to place the recipient's name below the date, assuming that your default tab stops are set every half inch).

12. Press the Macro Commands key (**Ctrl-Page Up**).

13. Choose **P**ause.

14. Press ↵ to signal the end of the Pause command.

15. Press ↵ twice to insert a blank line.

16. Type **FROM:** and press **Tab** once.

17. Press the Macro Commands key (**Ctrl-Page Up**).

18. Choose **P**ause.

19. Press ↵ to signal the end of the Pause command.

20. Press ↵ twice to insert a blank line.

21. Type **SUBJECT:** and press **Tab** once.

22. Press the Macro Commands key (**Ctrl-Page Up**).

23. Choose **P**ause.

Refer to Chapter 15

24. Press ↵ to signal the end of the Pause command.

25. Now press ↵ three more times, to add two blank lines after the subject line.

26. Select **T**ools ➤ **Ma**cro ➤ **D**efine or press Macro Define (**Ctrl-F10**) to stop recording keystrokes.

You use a macro that has a pause in it the same way you use any other macro. When the macro reaches the point where you entered the pause, it will stop and wait for you to take action. Type in your entry, and then press ↵ to play back the rest of the keystrokes.

To try your new macro, follow these steps:

1. Clear the Edit screen.

2. Select **T**ools ➤ **Ma**cro ➤ **Ex**ecute, or press Macro (**Alt-F10**).

3. Type **STARTMEM** and press ↵. The macro will enter *DATE:* and a tab, then wait for you to type something, as shown in Figure L8.2.

4. Type today's date and press ↵. The macro will enter *TO:* and two tabs, and wait again.

5. Type the recipient's name and press ↵. The macro will enter *FROM:* and a tab, then wait again.

```
DATE:    _
```
```
                          Doc 1 Pg 1 Ln 1" Pos 2"
```

FIGURE L8.2:

The macro types the initial keystrokes, then pauses.

Refer to Chapter 15

6. Type your name and press ↵. The macro will enter *SUBJECT:* and a tab, then wait again.

7. Type a subject for your memo and press ↵. With the heading information complete, you can now start typing the body of your memo.

Now that you've created several macros on your own, you can explore macros in more detail by reading Chapter 15 if you haven't already. Then you might want to tackle the "power macros" in Chapter 26 and Lesson 10.

Refer to Chapter 15

Creating Form Letters and Mailing Labels

In this lesson you'll create some sample form letters and mailing labels by merging primary and secondary merge files. This lesson illustrates some of the information presented in Chapter 16.

BEFORE YOU BEGIN

Before you begin this lesson, you need to start WordPerfect and get to the blank Edit screen. You should have completed at least the first few lessons so that you know the basics of creating, editing, saving, and printing a document.

CREATING A SECONDARY MERGE FILE

Let's suppose that you want to write a form letter to everyone in your Rolodex, and each card in the Rolodex has a name and address on it, in this form:

Marie Abzug
ABC Corporation
123 Ocean Way
Los Angeles, CA 91234
(213)555-0134

To write a form letter to each person, you first need to create a secondary merge file with the information from each card broken into *fields* and *records*. Each record represents a single Rolodex card; each field represents some unit of information that's repeated on most, or all, of the cards. For this lesson, you'll divide the information on each card (i.e., in each record) into the nine fields shown in Figure L9.1.

Refer to Chapter 16

DEFINING THE FIELD NAMES

You don't have to define field names, but it makes the merge procedure easier in the long run.

The first step in creating your secondary merge file will be to define the field names you'll be using. You need to start at a blank WordPerfect Edit screen, then follow these steps:

1. Select **Tools** ➤ **Merge Codes** ➤ **More** (or press **Shift-F9 M**).

2. Type **FN** to move the highlight, then press ↵ to select the {FIELD NAMES} command. The prompt "Enter Field 1:" appears at the bottom of the screen.

3. Type **LastName** for field 1 and press ↵.

4. Type **FirstName** for field 2 and press ↵.

5. Type **Company** for field 3 and press ↵.

6. Type **Address** for field 4 and press ↵.

7. Type **City** for field 5 and press ↵.

8. Type **State** for field 6 and press ↵.

9. Type **ZipCode** for field 7 and press ↵.

10. Type **Phone** for field 8 and press ↵.

11. Type **Salutation** for field 9 and press ↵.

12. Instead of entering field 10, just press ↵ to stop entering names.

After you type the last field name, you'll see the list of names followed by a double dashed line, as shown in Figure L9.2.

```
FIELD NAME          EXAMPLE

LastName            Abzug
FirstName           Marie
Company             ABC Corporation
Address             123 Ocean Way
City                Los Angeles
State               CA
ZipCode             91234
Phone               (213)555-0134
Salutation          Ms. Abzug
```

FIGURE L9.1:

The nine fields for the secondary merge file

Refer to Chapter 16

REFINING THE FIELD-NAME LIST

If you'd like to make the field names easier to read, you can move the cursor to the start of each name, then press ↵ and Tab to place each on a separate line and indent it. The text will appear to wrap incorrectly at first, because there are no blank spaces for WordPerfect to use for wrapping. But don't worry about that. You can also move the cursor to the second tilde (~) after the Salutation~ field name and press ↵. That way, the field names stand out clearly and you can read them at a glance (as shown at the top of Figure L9.3 later on).

You can also make any corrections, such as correcting a misspelled field name, with the usual editing keys. When you're finished, just make sure that all the field names and tildes are in place, like at the top of Figure L9.3 (above the double dashed line).

NOTE *If you had not defined field names earlier in this lesson, a field number rather than a field name would appear at the bottom of the screen, making it harder to keep track of which field Word-Perfect is expecting data for at the moment.*

ADDING THE NAMES

Now you're ready to add the first person's record (i.e., Rolodex card) to the secondary merge file. Make sure the cursor is below the double dashed line (press Home Home ↓), then follow the steps below. As you type, notice that the lower-left corner of the screen displays which field WordPerfect is expecting next.

1. Type **Abzug** for LastName and press End Field (F9).

```
{FIELD NAMES}LastName~FirstName~Company~Address~City~State~ZipCode~Phone~Salut
ation~~{END RECORD}
===============================================================================
_
```

```
Field: LastName                          Doc 1 Pg 2 Ln 1" Pos 1"
```

FIGURE L9.2:

The screen after defining field names for the secondary merge file

Refer to Chapter 16

2. Type **Marie** for FirstName and press End Field (F9).

3. Type **ABC Corporation** for Company and press End Field (F9).

4. Type **123 Ocean Way** for Address and press End Field (F9).

5. Type **Los Angeles** for City and press End Field (F9).

6. Type **CA** for State and press End Field (F9).

7. Type **91234** for ZipCode and press End Field (F9).

8. Type **(213)555-0134** for Phone and press End Field (F9).

9. Type **Ms. Abzug** for Salutation and press End Field (F9).

10. Select **T**ools ➤ Me**r**ge Codes (or press **Shift-F9**), and select **E**nd Record to mark the end of the first record.

Figure L9.3 shows how this record should look on your screen, below the field names. The double dashed line beneath the record is a hard page break, which WordPerfect automatically places at the end of each record.

The cursor is now positioned for typing the second record; in the lower-left corner of your screen, you can see that WordPerfect is expecting an entry for the LastName field. You'll add this record next:

Izzy Hartunian
XYZ Corporation

```
{FIELD NAMES}
     LastName~
     FirstName~
     Company~
     Address~
     City~
     State~
     ZipCode~
     Phone~
     Salutation~
~{END RECORD}
============================================================================
Abzug{END FIELD}
Marie{END FIELD}
ABC Corporation{END FIELD}
123 Ocean Way{END FIELD}
Los Angeles{END FIELD}
CA{END FIELD}
91234{END FIELD}
(213)555-0134{END FIELD}
Ms. Abzug{END FIELD}
{END RECORD}
============================================================================

Field: LastName                            Doc 1 Pg 3 Ln 1" Pos 1"
```

FIGURE L9.3:

The first record in a secondary merge file

Refer to Chapter 16

2345 Salamander Rd.
San Diego, CA 92067
(619)555-9320

Follow these steps:

1. Type **Hartunian** for LastName and press End Field (F9).

2. Type **Izzy** for FirstName and press End Field (F9).

3. Type **XYZ Corporation** for Company and press End Field (F9).

4. Type **2345 Salamander Rd.** for Address and press End Field (F9).

5. Type **San Diego** for City and press End Field (F9).

6. Type **CA** for State and press End Field (F9).

7. Type **92067** for ZipCode and press End Field (F9).

8. Type **(619)555-9320** for Phone and press End Field (F9).

9. Type **Mr. Hartunian** for Salutation and press End Field (F9).

10. Select **T**ools ➤ M**e**rge Codes (or press **Shift-F9**), and select **E**nd Record to mark the end of the first record.

Figure L9.4 shows how your screen should look now, with the second record added to the secondary merge file.

```
===================================================================
Abzug{END FIELD}
Marie{END FIELD}
ABC Corporation{END FIELD}
123 Ocean Way{END FIELD}
Los Angeles{END FIELD}
CA{END FIELD}
91234{END FIELD}
(213)555-0134{END FIELD}
Ms. Abzug{END FIELD}
{END RECORD}
===================================================================
Hartunian{END FIELD}
Izzy{END FIELD}
XYZ Corporation{END FIELD}
2345 Salamander Rd.{END FIELD}
San Diego{END FIELD}
CA{END FIELD}
92067{END FIELD}
(619)555-9320{END FIELD}
Mr. Hartunian{END FIELD}
{END RECORD}
===================================================================
Field: LastName                    Doc 1 Pg 4 Ln 1" Pos 1"
```

FIGURE L9.4:

The second record added to the secondary merge file

Refer to Chapter 16

The third record, shown below, presents a bit of a switch, because this person has no company affiliation:

Wilbur Watson
123 Apple St.
Encinitas, CA 92024
(619)555-1234

Because you've defined your field names, however, with a company name in each record, you must include the Company field in every record of the secondary merge file. To do so, press End Field (F9) when you get to the Company field, to indicate that the field is empty. Follow these steps:

Glance at the bottom of the screen to see what field information is expected, so you don't accidentally type information in the wrong field.

1. Type **Watson** for LastName and press End Field (F9).

2. Type **Wilbur** for FirstName and press End Field (F9).

3. Press End Field (F9) to leave the Company field empty.

4. Type **123 Apple St.** for Address and press End Field (F9).

5. Type **Encinitas** for City and press End Field (F9).

6. Type **CA** for State and press End Field (F9).

7. Type **92024** for ZipCode and press End Field (F9).

8. Type **(619)555-1234** for Phone and press End Field (F9).

9. Type **Mr. Watson** for Salutation and press End Field (F9).

The sample secondary merge file contains only three records and nine fields, but yours can contain any number of records and fields.

10. Select **T**ools ➤ Me**r**ge Codes (or press **Shift-F9**), and select **E**nd Record.

SAVING THE SECONDARY MERGE FILE

Your secondary merge file should now look like Figure L9.5 (the field names and first record have scrolled off the top of the screen). You don't need to do anything else with this file right now, so you can save the completed secondary merge file and clear the screen:

1. Select **F**ile ➤ E**x**it, or press Exit (**F7**).

2. Select **Y**es.

Using .SCD as the filename extension will remind you that this file contains a secondary merge file.

3. Type the file name **NAMELIST.SCD** (though you can use any valid file name), and press ↵.

4. If asked for permission to replace a previous NAMELIST.SCD file, press **Y** (this may happen if you or someone else has already taken this lesson).

Refer to Chapter 16

5. When asked about exiting WordPerfect, press **N** for No.

Now you've created a secondary merge file, which you can use over and over again in the future to print form letters, mailing labels, envelopes, and so forth. You need never retype any of that information. But to use the information, you must create a primary merge file, described in the next part of this lesson.

CREATING A PRIMARY MERGE FILE

Creating a primary merge file is much like creating any other document in WordPerfect. However, you need to tell WordPerfect where to place information that will come from the secondary merge file, and you need to include the usual blank spaces and punctuation between each piece of information. In this section, you'll create a form letter.

Follow these steps from the blank Edit screen:

1. Enter the current date at the top of the letter by selecting **T**ools ➤ Date **C**ode (or pressing **Shift-F5 C**).

2. Press ↵ twice.

3. To place the first name at the cursor position, first select **T**ools ➤ M**er**ge Codes or press (**Shift-F9**).

4. Select **F**ield.

> [NOTE NOTE] *For more information on dates and times in WordPerfect, see Chapter 3.*

```
=====================================================================
Hartunian{END FIELD}
Izzy{END FIELD}
XYZ Corporation{END FIELD}
2345 Salamander Rd.{END FIELD}
San Diego{END FIELD}
CA{END FIELD}
92067{END FIELD}
(619)555-9320{END FIELD}
Mr. Hartunian{END FIELD}
{END RECORD}
=====================================================================
Watson{END FIELD}
Wilbur{END FIELD}
{END FIELD}
123 Apple St.{END FIELD}
Encinitas{END FIELD}
CA{END FIELD}
92024{END FIELD}
(619)555-1234{END FIELD}
Mr. Watson{END FIELD}
{END RECORD}
=====================================================================

Field: LastName                    Doc 1 Pg 5 Ln 1" Pos 1"
```

FIGURE L9.5:

The complete secondary merge file

5. Type **FirstName** and press ↵.

6. Press the spacebar to add a blank space.

7. Press **Shift-F9** and select **F**ield.

8. Type **LastName** and press ↵.

9. Press ↵ to move to the next line.

10. Press **Shift-F9** and select **F**ield.

11. Type **Company?** and press ↵.

 The question mark after the field name prevents an extra blank line from appearing in your merged output when the corresponding field is empty in the secondary file.

12. Press ↵ to move to the next line.

13. Press **Shift-F9** and select **F**ield.

14. Type **Address** and press ↵.

15. Press ↵ to move to the next line.

16. Press **Shift-F9** and select **F**ield.

17. Type **City** and press ↵.

18. Type a comma and press the spacebar so that there will be a comma and a blank space after the city in your printed letter.

19. Press **Shift-F9** and select **F**ield.

20. Type **State** and press ↵.

21. Press the spacebar twice to add a couple of blank spaces.

22. Press **Shift-F9** and select **F**ield.

23. Type **ZipCode** and press ↵.

24. Press ↵ twice to move down a couple of lines.

25. Type **Dear** and then press the spacebar to add a blank space.

26. Press **Shift-F9** and select **F**ield.

27. Type **Salutation** and press ↵.

28. Type **:** (a colon) to end the salutation.

29. Press ↵ twice to add a couple of blank lines.

 You don't have to include every field from the secondary merge file in the primary file. For example, the phone number was omitted in this primary file. But that field might come in handy in another document, such as a phone list or directory, so it was worth including in the secondary file.

Your screen should look like Figure L9.6 (though the date at the top of your screen will probably be different). As you can see, it looks kind of like a "skeleton" for the start of a letter (which is exactly what it is).

Refer to Chapter 16

Use the .PRM file extension to remind yourself that this file contains a primary merge file.

As a convenience, just so you don't have to repeat all these steps in the future when creating new form letters, save your work right now:

1. Select **File ➤ Save**, or press Save (**F10**).

2. Type the file name **STARTLET.PRM** and press ↵.

3. If asked for permission to replace a previous STARTLET.PRM file, press **Y**.

Now it's time to create a complete form letter. Follow these steps:

1. Type this paragraph and letter closing:

Just a brief reminder that the next annual meeting of cave dwellers is just a few weeks away. Please call if you can volunteer any time to this momentous occasion.

Sincerely,

Wanda K. Doorknob

2. Press ↵ after typing the last line.

```
July 16, 1992

{FIELD}FirstName~ {FIELD}LastName~
{FIELD}Company?~
{FIELD}Address~
{FIELD}City~, {FIELD}State~  {FIELD}ZipCode~

Dear {FIELD}Salutation~:


—




                                  Doc 1 Pg 1 Ln 2.5" Pos 1"
```

Refer to Chapter 16

SAVING THE PRIMARY MERGE FILE

Your letter should now look like Figure L9.7. Save it as LETTER1.PRM:

1. Select **F**ile ➤ E**x**it, or press Exit (**F7**).

2. Select **Y**es to save the document.

3. Type **LETTER1.PRM** and press ↵.

4. If asked for permission to replace a previous LETTER1.PRM file, press **Y**.

5. When asked about exiting, press **N**.

MERGING THE PRIMARY AND SECONDARY FILES

Now you have a secondary merge file named NAMELIST.SCD and a primary merge file named LETTER1.PRM that can merge information from that file into a form letter. Follow these steps to merge the two files:

1. Select **T**ools ➤ **M**erge (or press **Ctrl-F9 M**).

2. In response to the prompt at the bottom of the screen, type **LETTER1.PRM** as the name of the primary file and press ↵.

3. In response to the next prompt, type **NAMELIST.SCD** as the name of the secondary file and press ↵.

```
July 16, 1992

{FIELD}FirstName~ {FIELD}LastName~
{FIELD}Company?~
{FIELD}Address~
{FIELD}City~, {FIELD}State~  {FIELD}ZipCode~

Dear {FIELD}Salutation~:

Just a brief reminder that the next annual meeting of cave dwellers
is just a few weeks away. Please call if you can volunteer any time
to this momentous occasion.

Sincerely,


Wanda K. Doorknob
_



                              Doc 1 Pg 1 Ln 3.83" Pos 1"
```

The completed primary file, a form letter

Refer to Chapter 16

4. When the merge is complete, a letter appears on your screen. You can press Page Up and Page Down to scroll through the completed, merged letters. Notice that each letter is addressed to one person from your secondary merge file. Each will be printed on a separate page, as indicated by the hard page break line between letters.

5. To print the letters, select **File ➤ Print ➤ Full** Document (or press **Shift-F7 F**).

6. There is no need to save this sample merged file after printing the letters, so select **File ➤ Exit** or press Exit (**F7**).

7. Press **N** twice to answer No to the prompts that follow to clear the screen and stay in WordPerfect.

Figure L9.8 shows one of the completed form letters. As you can see, Word-Perfect has filled in the skeleton at the top part of the original LETTER1.PRM primary merge file ({FIELD}FirstName~, {FIELD}LastName~, and so forth) with the contents of the corresponding fields from the NAMELIST.SCD file.

PRINTING MAILING LABELS

Now you'll create and print mailing labels, which requires adding a paper size for printing on labels rather than on standard 8.5 × 11" paper. First, you have to find out whether there's already a label size available for you to use. Follow these steps:

1. Start at a clear Edit screen.

```
July 16, 1992

Marie Abzug
ABC Corporation
123 Ocean Way
Los Angeles, CA   91234

Dear Ms. Abzug:

Just a brief reminder that the next annual meeting of cave dwellers
is just a few weeks away. Please call if you can volunteer any time
to this momentous occasion.

Sincerely,


Wanda K. Doorknob
```

FIGURE L9.8:

A printed form letter

Refer to Chapter 16

2. If you've installed multiple printers, select the printer you want to use for printing labels: Select **F**ile ➤ **P**rint ➤ **S**elect Printer (or press **Shift-F7 S**), highlight the printer, press ↵, and press Exit (**F7**).

3. Select **L**ayout ➤ **P**age ➤ Paper **S**ize (or press **Shift-F8 P S**).

You'll see a screen similar to the one shown in Figure L9.9, except that the options available on your screen will depend on the formats that have already been set up for your printer.

What you do next depends on what's currently available for your printer:

◆ If you see a label paper type that's suitable for your needs, press Exit (F7) twice and skip to "Creating a Primary Merge File for Labels."

◆ If you do not see a paper type that's suitable for your needs, press Exit (F7) twice and read "Creating a Label Paper Size."

CREATING A LABEL PAPER SIZE

To create a paper size for printing labels, you can use the LABELS.WPM macro that came with your WordPerfect package. Follow these steps:

1. Select **T**ools ➤ **M**acro ➤ **E**xecute, or press Macro (**Alt-F10**).

2. Type **LABELS** and press ↵.

The rightmost column on your screen, titled "Labels," contains a measurement for the paper type if the paper size can be used to print labels.

If you see the message "ERROR: File not found" when trying to run the Labels macro, or you have questions about the options it presents, refer to Chapter 7 for more information.

```
Format: Paper Size/Type

                                                 Font  Double
Paper type and Orientation   Paper Size  Prompt Loc  Type  Sided  Labels

2 1/2" round labels          8.5" x 11"   No   Contin Port  No    3 x 4
3.5" disk labels -Avery 5196 8.5" x 11"   Yes  Manual Port  No    3 x 3
5.25" disk labels-Avery 5197 8.5" x 11"   Yes  Manual Port  No    2 x 6
Address labels - Avery 5162  8.5" x 11"   Yes  Manual Port  No    2 x 6
Envelope                     8.5" x 11"   No   Contin Port  No    2 x 6
Envelope - Wide              9.5" x 4"    No   Manual Land  No
File folder labels - Av 5266 8.5" x 11"   Yes  Manual Port  No    2 x 15
Hello Labels                 8.5" x 11"   No   Contin Port  No    2 x 3
Legal                        8.5" x 14"   No   Contin Port  No
Legal - Wide                 14" x 8.5"   No   Contin Land  No
Pre-printed labels           4" x 4"      Yes  Manual Port  No    1 x 1
Price tags - Avery 5267      8.5" x 11"   Yes  Manual Port  No    4 x 20
Standard                     8.5" x 11"   No   Contin Port  No
Standard - Wide              11" x 8.5"   No   Contin Land  No
Transparencies - Avery 5182  8.5" x 11"   Yes  Manual Port  No    1 x 1
[ALL OTHERS]                 Width ≤ 8.5" Yes  Manual       No


1 Select; 2 Add (Create); 3 Copy; 4 Delete; 5 Edit; N Name Search: 1
```

FIGURE L9.9:

A sample Paper Size/Type list, including several sizes of labels

Refer to Chapter 16

3. Use the ↑ and ↓ keys to move the cursor through the options on the screen. (If you are using a 5/31/91 or later release of WordPerfect, you can press Shift-F3 to switch between laser and tractor-fed labels.)

4. When the label size you want is highlighted, press ↵.

5. If prompted, select **C**ontinuous for this example.

6. If you see the "Prompt to Load" prompt, press **N** for this example.

7. If you see a prompt asking about inserting the label definition in Document Initial Codes, select **N**o for this example. Otherwise, press **E**xit (**F7**) to return to the Edit screen.

Now you have a label paper size to experiment with, which you'll use in a moment to print some sample labels.

CREATING A PRIMARY MERGE FILE FOR LABELS

The name and address format on a mailing label or envelope is identical to that of the heading on a letter. So, rather than going through all the steps to insert the merge codes into a new primary merge file, you'll just modify the format you already created earlier in this lesson as a starting point. Follow these steps:

1. Select **F**ile ➤ **R**etrieve, or press Retrieve (**Shift-F10**).

2. Type **STARTLET.PRM** and press ↵.

3. Press **Delete** three times to delete the date and the two blank lines beneath.

4. Press ↓ four times to move the cursor to the blank line above *Dear*.

5. Press **End** to move the cursor to the end of the line.

6. Press **Ctrl-Page Down** to delete all text below the cursor position.

7. Press **Y** when asked for permission. Your new format should look like Figure L9.10, which is a good layout for printing mailing labels.

Placing the label format in Document Initial Codes ensures that your labels will be properly formatted after you merge the primary and secondary files.

This approach is a shortcut to individually placing each field on the Edit screen as you did when creating the primary merge file for the form letter. The same basic arrangement of fields will work fine for labels.

CHOOSING A LABEL SIZE

Now you need to tell WordPerfect to print each name and address on a separate label, rather than on a separate page, by choosing a label paper size.

Refer to Chapter 16

Follow these steps:

1. Select **L**ayout from the menu bar, or press Layout (**Shift-F8**).

2. Choose **D**ocument ➤ Initial **C**odes. You'll see a screen that looks like the Reveal Codes screen.

3. Select **L**ayout ➤ **P**age ➤ Paper **S**ize (or press **Shift-F8 P S**).

4. Use the ↑ and ↓ keys to move the highlight to the label format you want.

5. Choose **S**elect.

6. Press Exit (**F7**) three times to return to the Edit screen.

7. Press Exit (**F7**) again to start saving the document.

8. Select **Y**es to save the document.

9. Type **LABELS.PRM** and then press ↵ (though you can use any file name you want).

10. If asked for permission to replace a previous LABELS.PRM file, press **Y**.

11. When asked for permission to exit WordPerfect, press **N** to select No.

If you have a laser printer, you must use labels that are specifically designed for laser printers, available at most stationery stores.

Now you've completed the primary merge file for printing labels and have saved it with the file name LABELS.PRM. Before you can print labels, you need to merge that file with the NAMELIST.SCD secondary merge file that you

---

```
{FIELD}FirstName~ {FIELD}LastName~
{FIELD}Company?~
{FIELD}Address~
{FIELD}City~, {FIELD}State~  {FIELD}ZipCode~_




                              Doc 1 Pg 1 Ln 0.5" Pos 2.47"
```

FIGURE L9.10:

A primary merge file for mailing labels

Refer to Chapter 16

created earlier in this lesson, so there will be a properly formatted label for each record in that file.

MERGING AND PRINTING THE LABELS

Follow these steps now to merge the LABELS.PRM primary merge file with the NAMELIST.SCD secondary merge file that you created earlier in this lesson:

1. Select **T**ools ➤ **M**erge (or press **Ctrl-F9 M**).

2. Type **LABELS.PRM** for the name of the primary file and press ↵.

3. Type **NAMELIST.SCD** for the name of the secondary file and then press ↵.

4. Your screen should look like Figure L9.11. Don't worry that the labels don't appear in their final format on the Edit screen. They will print properly.

5. To print or view the labels, select **F**ile ➤ **P**rint (or press **Shift-F7**).

6. If you want to print the labels now, select **F**ull Document. If you just want to see how they will look when printed, select **V**iew Document, then press Exit (**F7**) to return to the Edit screen.

7. There is no need to save the merged file, so select **F**ile ➤ E**x**it or press Exit (**F7**).

> **TIP** *If you want to create more form letters from the sample secondary merge file, you can save some time by retrieving STARTLET.PRM and using that as your starting point for the next form letter.*

```
Marie Abzug
ABC Corporation
123 Ocean Way
Los Angeles, CA  91234
============================================================================
Izzy Hartunian
XYZ Corporation
2345 Salamander Rd.
San Diego, CA  92067
============================================================================
Wilbur Watson
123 Apple St.
Encinitas, CA  92024_




                              Doc 1 Pg 3 Ln 0.333" Pos 2.17"
```

FIGURE L9.11:

The Edit screen just after merging the primary and secondary files

Refer to Chapter 16

8. Press **N** twice to answer No to the prompts that follow.

Now that you've created a secondary merge file and have merged it with a couple of sample primary merge files, read Chapter 16 to learn more about merging if you haven't done so already.

Refer to Chapter 16

Creating a Power Macro

This lesson will give you some hands-on experience in using the Macro Editor to create a complex macro that capitalizes the first letter of a word and lowercases the rest.

BEFORE YOU BEGIN

If you've exited WordPerfect, be sure to get WordPerfect up and running again to get to the Edit screen. You should already be familiar with creating, naming, and running recorded-keystroke macros, as described in Chapter 15 and Lesson 8.

HOW THE SAMPLE MACRO WORKS

Before creating this macro, you should understand something about what it does. Figure L10.1 shows the finished macro. I've added line numbers to make it easier to explain this macro; actual macros *never* contain line numbers. (For a line-by-line explanation of the macro, see "Summary of the Macro" at the end of the chapter.)

In a nutshell, the macro moves to the beginning of the word, then starts checking each character. If it finds a hidden code or an opening punctuation mark, it skips over that character and moves on to the next one. As soon as it finds a "normal" character, it capitalizes the character, moves to the next character, then lowercases the rest of the characters.

This macro, which is named Alt-U, is handy for converting upper- or lowercase passages to initial caps. For example, if you have a heading like

EXPLORING THE SOUTH SEA ISLANDS

or

exploring the south sea islands

and want to convert it to initial caps, just move the cursor to the first character of the first word, and press Alt-U five times (once for each word) to convert that line to

Exploring The South Sea Islands

CREATING THE MACRO

Chapter 12 describes techniques for renaming and copying files.

You'll name this macro Alt-U. If you already have a macro by that name on your computer, you'll either have to use a different name for the macro you create in this lesson or rename the existing macro. Then, proceed with these steps:

1. Press **Home Home** ↑, press **Home,** then press **Ctrl-F10**.

2. Press **Alt-U** at the "Define macro:" prompt.

3. Type **Convert to initial caps** and press ↵ at the "Description:" prompt.Your screen should now look like Figure L10.2.

To select a macro programming command, type the first characters in the command name, or use the cursor-movement keys to highlight the command, and press ↵.

Now you're ready to begin entering macro commands. If you make a mistake when typing any text, just use the normal cursor-movement and editing keys to make corrections. If you accidentally choose an incorrect macro programming command, move the cursor to that command and press Delete, then select the correct command. Follow these steps to create line 1 of the macro:

1. Press **Delete** to remove the {DISPLAY OFF} command.

```
 1  {IF}!{STATE}&4~              {;}Change only at editing screen~
 2      {RETURN}
 3  {END IF}
 4  {Word Right}{Word Left}      {;}Move to beginning of word~
 5  {LABEL}SkipIt~
 6      {ASSIGN}Char~{SYSTEM}18~~  {;}Char = Character cursor is on now~
 7      {Right}                    {;}Move right 1 character~
 8      {IF}{LEN}Char~=1~          {;}Length is 1 if regular character~
 9          {CASE}{VARIABLE}Char~~ {;}Ignore leading punctuation~
10              "~SkipIt~
11              '~SkipIt~
12              `~SkipIt~
13              (~SkipIt~
14              [~SkipIt~
15              {~SkipIt~
16              <~SkipIt~
17              ~
18      {ELSE}
19          {GO}SkipIt~            {;}Length > 1 if code; skip codes~
20      {END IF}
21  {Block}{Left}{Left}           {;}Found good character; block it~
22  {Switch}1                     {;}Switch to uppercase~
23  {Right}{Block}{Word Right}    {;}Block rest of word~
24  {Switch}2                     {;}Switch to lowercase~
```

FIGURE L10.1:

A power macro to convert words to initial caps

Refer to Chapter 26

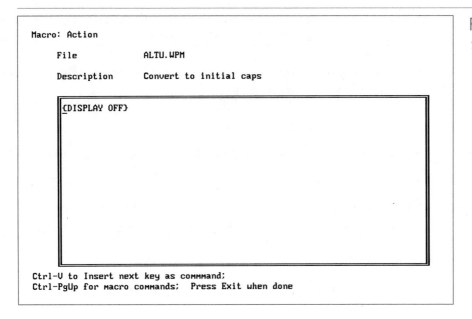

```
Macro: Action

    File           ALTU.WPM

    Description    Convert to initial caps

    ┌─────────────────────────────────────┐
    │ {DISPLAY OFF}                        │
    │                                      │
    │                                      │
    │                                      │
    │                                      │
    │                                      │
    │                                      │
    │                                      │
    │                                   ·  │
    │                                      │
    └─────────────────────────────────────┘

Ctrl-V to Insert next key as command;
Ctrl-PgUp for macro commands;  Press Exit when done
```

2. Press **Ctrl-Page Up** to display the macro programming commands.

3. Press **I**; note how the cursor immediately highlights the {IF} command.

4. Press ↵ to select the {IF} command and insert it on the macro editing screen, as shown in Figure L10.3.

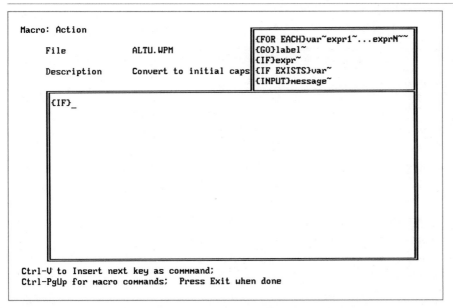

FIGURE L10.3:

The macro editing screen after selecting the {IF} command

```
Macro: Action
                                    ┌──────────────────────────────────┐
    File           ALTU.WPM         │ {FOR EACH}var~expr1~...exprN~~   │
                                    │ {GO}label~                       │
    Description    Convert to initial caps {IF}expr~                   │
                                    │ {IF EXISTS}var~                  │
    ┌───────────────────────────────│ {INPUT}message~                 │
    │ {IF}_                          └──────────────────────────────────┘
    │                                      │
    │                                      │
    │                                      │
    │                                      │
    │                                      │
    │                                      │
    │                                      │
    │                                      │
    └─────────────────────────────────────┘

Ctrl-V to Insert next key as command;
Ctrl-PgUp for macro commands;  Press Exit when done
```

Refer to Chapter 26

Notice how the command you just selected remains highlighted on the macro programming commands list. This serves to remind you of the correct format for the command. For example, the command {IF}expr~ is currently highlighted, indicating that you must supply an expression (*expr*) and a tilde (~) before the {IF} command is complete.

Now go ahead and finish up the line:

1. Type an exclamation point (**!**).

2. Press **Ctrl-Page Up**, then type **ST** to highlight the {STATE} command.

3. Press ↵.

4. Type **&4~** to finish up the {STATE} command. Don't forget to type the tilde (~), which is used throughout the macro programming language to separate parts of multipart commands and to end commands.

5. Press **Tab** six times to add some space after the commands on this line.

6. Press **Ctrl-Page Up**, then type a semicolon (**;**) to highlight the {;} comment command.

7. Press ↵ to select the comment.

8. Type **Change only at editing screen~** and press ↵. Your first line is now complete, as shown in Figure L10.4.

NOTE	*Using the Tab, spacebar, and ↵ keys to format your macro on the editing screen has no effect on the macro itself, but makes the macro easier to read and understand.*

```
Macro: Action

      File          ALTU.WPM           {;}comment~
                                        {ASSIGN}var~expr~
      Description   Convert to initial caps{BELL}
                                        {Block Append}
                                        {Block Copy}

  {IF}!{STATE}&4~              {;}Change·only·at·editing·screen~
  _













  Ctrl-V to Insert next key as command;
  Ctrl-PgUp for macro commands;  Press Exit when done
```

FIGURE L10.4:

The macro editing screen after completing the first line of the macro

Refer to Chapter 26

In the resulting command, the ! symbol is the macro programming language operator for "not," and **&** is a *mask* that is like "equal." The command {IF}!{STATE}&4 means, "If the current state is not 4...," where state 4 is "normal editing screen." (Other states include 128, Block is active; 512, Reveal Codes is active; and 1024, Yes/No Question is active.)

Now you're ready to type in the second line. Follow these steps:

1. Press **Tab**.

2. Press **Ctrl-Page Up**.

3. Type **RET** and ↵ to select the {RETURN} command.

4. Press ↵ to move to the next line.

Now that you've got the hang of it, I'll condense the steps a bit. Follow these steps to enter the next few lines:

1. Press **Ctrl-Page Up**, press **E**, and select the {END IF} command.

2. Press ↵ to move to the next line.

When you're working in the Macro Editor, you can use the cursor-movement keys to move around on the screen. But if you want the macro itself to execute a cursor movement, you must press Ctrl-V before pressing the cursor-movement key. Follow these steps to enter line 4:

1. Press **Ctrl-V** then **Ctrl-→**. This inserts a {Word Right} command in the macro.

2. Press **Ctrl-V** then **Ctrl-←**. This inserts a {Word Left} command.

3. Press **Tab** four times.

4. Press **Ctrl-Page Up**, type a semicolon (**;**), and press ↵ to select the {;} comment command.

5. Type **Move to beginning of word~** and press ↵.

The steps for entering the rest of the macro use the same techniques you've already learned. It's just a matter of careful typing. Follow these steps:

1. Press **Ctrl-Page Up**, press **L**, and press ↵ to select {LABEL}.

2. Type **SkipIt~** and press ↵.

3. Press **Tab**, press **Ctrl-Page Up**, then press **A** and ↵ to select {ASSIGN}.

4. Type **Char~**

5. Press **Ctrl-Page Up**, type **SY**, and press ↵ to select {SYSTEM}.

Refer to Chapter 26

6. Type **18~~**

7. Press **Tab** twice, press **Ctrl-Page Up**, type **;** (semicolon), and press ↵ to select {;}.

8. Type **Char=Character cursor is on now~** and press ↵.

9. Press **Tab**, **Ctrl-V**, then → to insert a {Right} command.

10. Press **Tab** eight times, then press **Ctrl-Page Up**, type **;** (semicolon), and press ↵.

11. Type **Move right 1 character~** and press ↵.

12. Press **Tab**, **Ctrl-Page Up**, **I**, and ↵ to select {IF}.

13. Press **Ctrl-Page Up**, type **LE**, and press ↵ to select {LEN}.

14. Type **Char~=1~**

15. Press **Tab** five times, then press **Ctrl-Page Up**, type **;** (semicolon), and press ↵ to select {;}.

16. Type **Length is 1 if regular character~** and press ↵.

17. Press **Tab** twice, then press **Ctrl-Page Up**, type **CAS**, and press ↵ to select {CASE}.

18. Press **Ctrl-Page Up**, **V**, and ↵ to select {VARIABLE}.

19. Type **Char~~**

20. Press **Tab** twice, then **Ctrl-Page Up**, **;** (semicolon), and ↵ to select {;}.

21. Type **Ignore leading punctuation~** and press ↵.

Follow these steps to enter lines 10–14:

1. Press **Tab** three times, then type **"~SkipIt~** and press ↵.

2. Press **Tab** three times, then type **'~SkipIt~** and press ↵.

3. Press **Tab** three times, then type **'~SkipIt~** and press ↵.

4. Press **Tab** three times, then type **(~SkipIt~** and press ↵.

5. Press **Tab** three times, then type **[~SkipIt~**

At this point, your macro editing screen should be full, as in Figure L10.5. When you press ↵ to move to the next line, the screen will scroll.

To continue typing the macro, follow these steps:

1. Press ↵ to move to the next line.

2. Press **Tab** three times, then type **{~SkipIt~** and press ↵.

Refer to Chapter 26

3. Press **Tab** three times, then type **<~SkipIt~** and press ↵.

4. Press **Tab** three times, then type **~** and press ↵ to finish up the lines of the {CASE} statement.

5. Press **Tab**, press **Ctrl-Page Up**, type **E**, and press ↵ to select {ELSE}.

6. Press ↵ to move to the next line.

7. Press **Tab** twice, press **Ctrl-Page Up**, type **G**, and press ↵ to select {GO}.

8. Type **SkipIt~**

9. Press **Tab** six times, press **Ctrl-Page Up**, type **;** (semicolon), and press ↵ to select {;}.

10. Type **Length>1 if code; skip codes~** and press ↵.

11. Press **Tab**, press **Ctrl-Page Up**, type **E**, press ↓ twice, and press ↵ to select {ENDIF}.

12. Press ↵ to move to the next line.

13. Press Block (**Alt-F4** or **F12**) to insert a {Block} command.

14. Press **Ctrl-V** then ← to insert a {Left} command.

15. Press **Ctrl-V** then ←.

16. Press **Tab** five times.

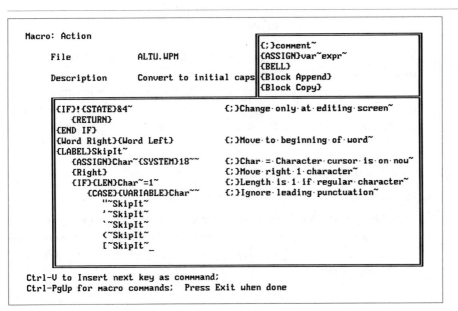

FIGURE L10.5:

The first 14 lines of the macro on the macro editing screen

```
Macro: Action

    File            ALTU.WPM        {;}comment~
                                    {ASSIGN}var~expr~
    Description     Convert to initial caps {BELL}
                                    {Block Append}
                                    {Block Copy}

    {IF}!{STATE}&4~                 {;}Change·only·at·editing·screen~
        {RETURN}
    {END IF}
    {Word Right}{Word Left}         {;}Move·to·beginning·of·word~
    {LABEL}SkipIt~
        {ASSIGN}Char~{SYSTEM}18~~   {;}Char·=·Character·cursor·is·on·now~
        {Right}                     {;}Move·right·1·character~
        {IF}{LEN}Char~=1~           {;}Length·is·1·if·regular·character~
            {CASE}{VARIABLE}Char~~  {;}Ignore·leading·punctuation~
                "~SkipIt~
                '~SkipIt~
                `~SkipIt~
                <~SkipIt~
                [~SkipIt~_

Ctrl-V to Insert next key as command;
Ctrl-PgUp for macro commands;  Press Exit when done
```

Refer to Chapter 26

17. Press **Ctrl-Page Up**, then type **;** (semicolon), and press ↵ to insert a {;} command.

18. Type **Found good character; block it~** and press ↵ to move to the next line.

19. Press Switch (**Shift-F3**) to insert a {Switch} command.

20. Type **1**.

21. Press **Tab** eight times.

22. Press **Ctrl-Page Up** and press ↵ to insert a comment command.

23. Type **Switch to uppercase~** and press ↵ to move to the next line.

24. Press **Ctrl-V** then → to insert a {Right} command.

25. Press Block (**Alt-F4** or **F12**) to insert {Block}.

26. Press **Ctrl-V** then **Ctrl-→** to insert {Word Right}.

27. Press **Tab** three times.

28. Press **Ctrl-Page Up** and press ↵ to insert a comment command.

29. Type **Block rest of word~** and press ↵ to move to the next line.

30. Press Switch (**Shift-F3**) to insert {Switch}.

31. Type **2**, then press **Tab** eight times.

32. Press **Ctrl-Page Up**, then type **;** (semicolon) and press ↵ to insert a comment.

33. Type **Switch to lowercase~**

Your screen should now look like Figure L10.6. Before saving the macro, you might want to double-check your completed macro against Figure L10.1. Be sure you have typed everything correctly. If you see a mistake, just use the cursor-movement and editing keys to make your corrections. To save the completed macro and return to the Edit screen, press Exit (F7).

When inserting function-key commands like Switch (Shift-F3), you must press the function key, then type the menu option letters or numbers exactly as if you were using the shortcut keys. Pull-down menu commands are not accessible in the Macro Editor.

The {;} followed by text in line 1 and many of the other lines is a comment. Comments are ignored when the macro executes.

SUMMARY OF THE MACRO

Let's take a look at how the macro does its job:

Lines 1–2: Line 1 translates to "if we're not at the normal Edit screen..." do whatever commands appear between the {IF} and {END IF} commands. In this case, just return to the Edit screen without doing anything (line 2).

Refer to Chapter 26

Line 4: Moves the cursor one word to the right, then one word to the left. This little dance guarantees that the cursor will be at the beginning of the word you want to capitalize, just in case it wasn't there already.

Line 5: This is a label named *SkipIt*. The macro jumps back to SkipIt whenever it needs to skip over a character in the word.

Appendix K in your Word-Perfect manual includes a complete list of all the macro commands and options.

Line 6: The {ASSIGN} command assigns a value to a variable. Here, the {SYSTEM} 18 command returns whatever character the cursor is on; if the character is a hidden code, {SYSTEM} returns a five-digit number instead. The value is stored in the variable named *char*.

Line 7: Moves the cursor to the right one character, which puts it into position to block the character to the left, or checks the next character if need be.

Line 8: If the length of the *Char* character is *1* (which is the length of a "normal" character), executes the commands in lines 9–16. If the length of the character is not *1* (which indicates a hidden code rather than a character), goes back to SkipIt and checks the next character (see line 19).

Lines 9–17: This is a CASE statement, which tests the value in the variable named *Char*. If *Char* is any of the opening punctuation characters,

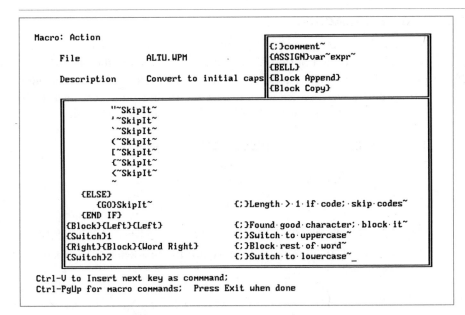

Refer to Chapter 26

" ' ` ([{ <

the macro passes control to the SkipIt label to check the next character. You can easily add tests for other punctuation marks by following the pattern used in lines 10–16.

Lines 18–20: This is the second part of the {IF} command, which started in line 8. Line 19 passes control back to SkipIt if the length of *Char* was not *1* (i.e., *Char* is a hidden code).

Line 21: Execution ends up here if the length of *Char* is *1* (a normal character) and the character isn't a punctuation mark. The macro activates blocking, then moves the cursor to the left of the character you want to capitalize.

Line 22: The macro presses Switch (Shift-F3), which, when text is blocked, presents the options to convert to upper- or lowercase. Here the macro selects option 1 to switch the blocked character to uppercase.

Line 23: These keystrokes move one character to the right, then block the rest of the word.

Line 24: Finally, the macro converts the rest of the word to lowercase by pressing Switch (Shift-F3) while Block is on and selecting option 2 (Lowercase). Since there are no commands below this command, the macro stops.

TESTING THE MACRO

With any luck, you typed your macro correctly and the macro will work perfectly the first time. If it doesn't, you can always fix it in the Macro Editor, as described later in this lesson. Type any line of text with a combination of upper- and lowercase letters, and just for testing purposes, include some punctuation and perhaps boldface. Here's an example you might try:

THE "TITANIC" WAS A **GARGANTUAN** ocean liner

Now, test the macro by completing these steps:

1. Press **Home** ← to move to the beginning of the line.

2. Press **Alt-U** to capitalize the first word.

3. Press **Alt-U** six more times to capitalize the first letter of each remaining word.

Refer to Chapter 26

EDITING THE MACRO

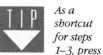

As a shortcut for steps 1–3, press Home and Ctrl-F10, then type the macro name and description.

If you discover a mistake in your macro or need to change it in some way, just follow these steps:

1. Select **T**ools ➤ **M**acro ➤ **D**efine (or press **Ctrl-F10**).

2. Press **Alt-U** at the "Define macro:" prompt. You'll see the prompt

   ALTU.WPM Already Exists: 1 Replace; 2 Edit; 3 Description

3. Choose **E**dit.

Be careful not to select Replace in step 3, or all your hard work will be thrown away and you'll be presented with an empty macro editing screen. Now make any necessary corrections to your macro, using the normal cursor-movement and editing keys. Press Exit (F7) when you're ready to replace the macro, or press Cancel (F1) then Y if you want to cancel the changes. After returning to the Edit screen, be sure to test your macro again.

Now that you've had a chance to use the Macro Editor, you can delve further into advanced macro techniques by reading Chapter 26 and explore the many ready-made macros available to you in Chapter 27.

Refer to Chapter 26

APPENDIX

Installing WordPerfect on Your Computer

 **B**efore you can use WordPerfect, it must be *installed* on your computer. You need only install WordPerfect once, not each time you plan to use it. So if you or somebody else has already installed WordPerfect on your computer, you can go straight to Chapter 1 and start using the program.

INSTALLING WORDPERFECT FOR THE FIRST TIME

If you are installing WordPerfect 5.1 for the first time, it's easiest to follow the basic installation procedure:

1. Start your computer in the usual manner and get to the DOS command prompt (typically A> or C>).

2. Insert the WordPerfect 5.1 disk labeled "Install/Learn/Utilities 1" in drive A.

3. Type **A:** and press ↵.

4. Type **INSTALL** and press ↵.

5. You'll see an initial screen asking whether you want to continue. Press ↵ to do so.

6. You'll see another screen asking whether you have a color monitor. Select either **Y**es or **N**o in response (by pressing **Y** or **N**).

7. You'll see a prompt asking whether you are installing WordPerfect on a hard disk. If you are installing on floppy disks, press **N**, label ten formatted disks as instructed on the screen, and then press **Y** to proceed. If you're installing WordPerfect on a hard disk, just press **Y**.

8. You will see the main menu for installation, as shown in Figure A.1. Select Basic by pressing **1** or **B**.

NOTE
NOTE

The lessons in this book assume that you have installed the entire WordPerfect program.

The screen will provide instructions for performing the complete installation and will inform you when to swap disks. Whenever you swap disks in drive A, press ↵ to proceed with the installation. When the entire installation procedure is completed, you'll be informed by messages on the screen.

DOING A PARTIAL INSTALLATION

If you change or add equipment, such as a graphics monitor or printer, or if you want to update your current version of WordPerfect to a more recent interim release provided by WordPerfect Corporation, you can do a partial installation.

To perform a partial installation, you need to start from the DOS prompt of your WordPerfect directory if you have a hard disk; if you're working from floppy disks, place the Install/Utilities disk in drive A, type **A:**, and press ↵.

```
Installation

     1 - Basic       Perform a standard installation to C:\WP51.

     2 - Custom      Perform a customized installation.  (User selected
                     directories.)

     3 - Network     Perform a customized installation onto a network.
                     (To be performed by the network supervisor.)

     4 - Printer     Install a new or updated Printer (.ALL) File.

     5 - Update      Install WordPerfect 5.1 Interim Release program file(s).
                     (Used for updating existing WordPerfect 5.1 software.)

     6 - Copy Disks  Install every file from an installation diskette to a
                     specified location.  (Useful for installing all the
                     Printer (.ALL) Files.)

     7 - Minimal     Install only the files for a standard configuration.

     8 - Exit        Leave Installation Program.

Selection: 1
```

FIGURE A.1:

The main menu for installing WordPerfect

Type **INSTALL** and press ↵ again. Press **Y** when asked whether you want to continue. You will see the main installation menu, with these options:

Custom	Lets you install WordPerfect files on the drive and in the directories of your choosing
Network	Used by the network supervisor to install WordPerfect for use on a network
Printer	Lets you install the driver for a new printer or several printers; you'll need to have handy the Printers 1 disk from your WordPerfect package after selecting this option (you'll then see instructions for installing the printer driver)
Update	Let's you install Interim Release files provided by the WordPerfect Corporation Software Subscription Service
Copy Disks	Decompresses and copies all the compressed files from installation disks to another disk (or other disks)

After you select an option, you'll see instructions for completing the installation, like the instructions presented during the basic installation.

TECHNICAL OPTIONS AND TROUBLESHOOTING

This section provides some technical information that will be of interest mainly to technical support personnel responsible for installing and setting up Word-Perfect, and to advanced users who are familiar with memory usage and DOS. It may also help solve some problems in getting WordPerfect to load properly.

MEMORY USAGE

NOTE
NOTE

Check Appendix N in your Word-Perfect reference manual to fine-tune your memory usage.

WordPerfect uses about 400K of conventional memory and uses all remaining memory for editing space. If LIM 3.2 or 4.0 expanded memory is available, overflow text is placed in expanded memory. (WordPerfect does not use extended memory.) Text that does not fit into conventional (and expanded) memory spills into overflow files named *WP}WP{.TV1* (for text above the cursor) and *WP}WP{.BV1* (for text below the cursor). If two documents are being edited, the overflow files for the second document have the same name, but with *2* as the last character.

On floppy-based systems, the overflow files are stored on drive A (or on the drive from which you start WordPerfect). You can redirect the overflow files to another drive (or virtual drive) using the /D option at start-up (described in the next section). This means that drive A can be freed up for other purposes while you are using WordPerfect.

If you have at least 550K of available expanded memory, you can also use it to store the WP.FIL overlay file, thereby increasing the general speed of the program. See the /R start-up option in the next section.

START-UP OPTIONS

Normally, to start WordPerfect, you just enter **WP** and press ↵ at the command prompt. This section presents some optional start-up switches that you can use to the right of the WP command to start WordPerfect with certain features enabled or disabled. All these switches are optional and can be used to solve problems if WordPerfect refuses to start or locks up the keyboard.

/CP=*code page number*	Tells WordPerfect which DOS code page your hardware is using.
/D-*drive\ directory*	Redirects overflow files to a drive other than the default drive where the WP.EXE file is located.
/F2	Starts WordPerfect with an extended screen display (more than 25 rows and 80 columns). Use this option when the /SS switch cannot solve the problem.
filename	Automatically retrieves the specified file at start-up.
/M-*macroname*	Automatically loads and executes the specified macro at start-up.
/MONO	Runs WordPerfect in monochrome. If you are using a monochrome monitor, you can add the command SET WP=/MONO to your AUTOEXEC.BAT file to force WordPerfect to always start in monochrome.
/NB	Disables the Original Backup option. This is useful when you do not have enough file space to save two copies of the same file.
/NC	Disables the Cursor Speed option, which may conflict with hardware or a TSR (terminate-and-stay-resident program). Try this option if WordPerfect refuses to run or locks the keyboard.
/NE	Disables the use of expanded memory.

/NF	Used with some IBM compatibles and windowing systems (other than TopView) to resolve problems where the screen occasionally goes blank or text is displayed over a window.
/NK	Disables the enhanced keyboard functions that are not recognized by some compatibles, and can be used to resolve the problem of WordPerfect locking up the keyboard.
/NO	Disables the Keyboard Reset key (Ctrl-6).
/PS=*path*	Instructs WordPerfect to use the Setup options stored in the .SET file in the specified path. This is generally used on a network to have WordPerfect use Setup options from a network drive rather than the local drive where WP.EXE is located.
/R	Moves about 300K of overlays, error messages, and menus into expanded memory, if available.
/SS=*rows, columns*	Used with optional monitors, such as the Genius display, to set the screen size at start-up. The settings for *rows* and *columns* must reflect the actual size of the screen. For a 50-line display with EGA or VGA, use the Setup key (Shift-F1 D T) within WordPerfect.
/X	Restores all Setup options to their original values. User-selected Setup values are restored when you exit.

Start-up options can be combined. For example, WP/R/D-F: loads overlays into expanded memory and redirects overflow files to drive F. (On a floppy-based system, this combination of switches lets you remove the WordPerfect 2 disk from drive A while using the program.)

To run the start-up options automatically, you can modify the AUTO-EXEC.BAT file to place the start-up command in the DOS environment. For example, if you want to be able to simply type *WP* to start WordPerfect, but you want to use the /R and /D start-up options, put the command

SET WP=WP/R/D-F:

in the AUTOEXEC.BAT file.

APPENDIX B

Hidden Codes

Every time you perform an action in WordPerfect, such as setting line spacing or entering a hard return, the program inserts a hidden code in your document. These codes are hidden to prevent the Edit screen from becoming cluttered (to see them, press Alt-F3 or F11). The following table lists all the codes and their meanings.

CODE	MEANING
[ ]	Hard space
[/]	No hyphenation
[–]	Hyphen character
[Adv]	Advance
[BLine]	Baseline placement
[Block Pro]	Block protection
[BOLD]	Bold
[Box Num]	Caption in graphic box
[Cell]	Table cell
[Center]	Center
[Center Page]	Center page vertically

CODE	MEANING
[Cndl EOP]	Conditional end of page
[Cntr Tab]	Centered tab
[Col Def]	Column definition
[Col Off]	End of text columns
[Col On]	Beginning of text columns
[Color]	Print color
[Comment]	Document comment
[Date]	Date/Time function
[DBL UND]	Double underline
[Dec Tab]	Decimal-aligned tab
[Decml/Algn Char]	Decimal character/thousands separator
[Def Mark:Index]	Index definition
[Def Mark:List]	List definition
[Def Mark:ToA]	Table-of-authorities definition
[Def Mark:ToC]	Table-of-contents definition
[Dorm HRt]	Dormant hard return
[DSrt]	Deletable soft return
[End.Opt]	Endnote options
[Endnote]	Endnote
[Endnote Placement]	Endnote placement
[Equ Box]	Equation box
[Equ Opt]	Equation box options
[EXT LARGE]	Extra-large print
[Fig Box]	Figure box
[Fig Opt]	Figure box options
[FINE]	Fine print
[Flsh Rgt]	Flush right

CODE	MEANING
[Font]	Base font
[Footer]	Footer
[Footnote]	Footnote
[Force]	Force odd/even page
[Ftn Opt]	Footnote options
[Full Form]	Table of authorities, full form
[Header]	Header
[HLine]	Horizontal line
[HPg]	Hard page break
[HRt]	Hard return
[HRt-SPg]	Hard return/soft page break
[Hyph Off]	Hyphenation off
[Hyph On]	Hyphenation on
[HZone]	Hyphenation zone
[→Indent]	Indent
[→Indent←]	Left/right indent
[Index]	Index entry
[Insert Pg Num]	Insert page number
[ISrt]	Invisible soft return
[ITALC]	Italics
[Just]	Justification
[Just Lim]	Word-spacing justification limits
[Kern]	Kerning
[Lang]	Language
[LARGE]	Large print
[Leading Adj]	Leading adjustment
[Link]	Spreadsheet link

CODE	**MEANING**
[Ln Height]	Line height
[Ln Num]	Line numbering
[Ln Spacing]	Line spacing
[←Mar Rel]	Left margin release
[Mark:List]	List entry
[Mark:ToA]	Table-of-authorities entry
[Mark:ToC]	Table-of-contents entry
[Math Def]	Definition of math columns
[Math Off]	End of math
[Math On]	Beginning of math
[New End Num]	New endnote number
[New Equ Num]	New Equation box number
[New Fig Num]	New Figure box number
[New Ftn Num]	New footnote number
[New Tbl Num]	New table number
[New Txt Num]	New Text box number
[New Usr Num]	New User box number
[Outline Off]	Outline off
[Outline On]	Outline on
[OUTLN]	Outline text appearance
[Ovrstk]	Overstrike
[Paper Sz/Typ]	Paper size and type
[Par Num]	Paragraph number
[Par Num Def]	Paragraph numbering definition
[Pg Num]	New page number
[Pg Num Style]	Page number style
[Pg Numbering]	Page number position

CODE	MEANING
[Ptr Cmnd]	Printer command
[REDLN]	Redline
[RGT TAB]	Right-aligned tab
[SHADW]	Shadow
[SM CAP]	Small caps
[SMALL]	Small print
[SPg]	Soft page break
[SRt]	Soft return
[STKOUT]	Strikeout
[Style Off]	Style off
[Style On]	Style on
[Subdoc]	Subdocument (master documents)
[Subdoc End]	End of subdocument
[Subdoc Start]	Beginning of subdocument
[SUBSCPT]	Subscript
[Suppress]	Suppress page format
[SUPRSCPT]	Superscript
[Tab]	Tab
[TAB]	Hard tab
[Tab Set]	Tab set
[T/B Mar]	Top and bottom margins
[Target]	Target (cross-reference)
[Tbl Box]	Table box
[Tbl Def]	Table definition
[Tbl Opt]	Table box options
[Text Box]	Text box
[Txt Opt]	Text box options

CODE	MEANING
[UND]	Underlining
[Undrln]	Underline spaces/tabs
[Usr Box]	User-defined box
[Usr Opt]	User-defined box options
[VLine]	Vertical line
[VRY LARGE]	Very large print
[W/O Off]	Widow/orphan off
[W/O On]	Widow/orphan on
[Wrd/Ltr Spacing]	Word and letter spacing

Symbols

◆ Page numbers in **bold type** are the primary source of information on a topic.

◆ Page numbers in italics refer to material in the hands-on lessons in Part 9.

◆ Page numbers followed by a *t* refer to tables.

◆ Page numbers followed by an *f* refer to figures.

Alan Simpson's Mastering WordPerfect 5.1 Companion Disk

If you want to use the sample documents, styles, and macros presented in this book without keying them in yourself, you can send for a companion disk containing all the files (excluding the files that already came with your Word-Perfect package.) You can use each file as it is, or as a starting point in creating your own document, style, or macro.

To purchase the disk, complete the order form below and return it with a check, international money order, or purchase order for $20.00 U.S. currency (plus sales tax if you are a California resident) to the address shown on the coupon. Or, use your VISA or MasterCard.

If you prefer, you can return the coupon without making a purchase to receive free, periodic newsletters and updates about Alan Simpson's latest books.

. . . .

Alan Simpson Computing
P.O. Box 945
Cardiff-by-the-Sea, CA 92007
Phone: (619) 943-7715
Fax: (619) 943-7750

☐ Please send the companion disks for *Mastering WordPerfect 5.1*

☐ No disk, thanks, but please send free newsletters from Alan Simpson Computing

_____
NAME

_____
COMPANY   PURCHASE ORDER NUMBER (IF APPLICABLE)

_____
ADDRESS

_____
CITY, STATE, ZIP

_____
COUNTRY   PHONE NUMBER (REQUIRED FOR CHARGED ORDERS)

Check one:

☐ Payment enclosed
  ($20.00, plus sales tax for California residents),
  made payable to *Alan Simpson Computing*

☐ Bill my VISA/MC Card Number_____
  Exp. Date _____

☐ No charge (newsletters only)

Check one disk size:

☐ 5¼" disk, 1.2Mb

☐ 5¼" disk, 360K

☐ 3½" disk, 1.4Mb

☐ 3½" disk, 720K

. . . .

SYBEX is not affiliated with Alan Simpson Computing and assumes no responsibility for any defect in the disk or files.

SYBEX ®

FREE BROCHURE!

Complete this form today, and we'll send you a full-color brochure of Sybex bestsellers.

Please supply the name of the Sybex book purchased.

_____

How would you rate it?

_____ Excellent   _____ Very Good   _____ Average   _____ Poor

Why did you select this particular book?

_____ Recommended to me by a friend

_____ Recommended to me by store personnel

_____ Saw an advertisement in _____

_____ Author's reputation

_____ Saw in Sybex catalog

_____ Required textbook

_____ Sybex reputation

_____ Read book review in _____

_____ In-store display

_____ Other _____

Where did you buy it?

_____ Bookstore

_____ Computer Store or Software Store

_____ Catalog (name: _____)

_____ Direct from Sybex

_____ Other: _____

Did you buy this book with your personal funds?

_____ Yes   _____ No

About how many computer books do you buy each year?

_____ 1-3   _____ 3-5   _____ 5-7   _____ 7-9   _____ 10+

About how many Sybex books do you own?

_____ 1-3   _____ 3-5   _____ 5-7   _____ 7-9   _____ 10+

Please indicate your level of experience with the software covered in this book:

_____ Beginner   _____ Intermediate   _____ Advanced

Which types of software packages do you use regularly?

_____ Accounting	_____ Databases	_____ Networks
_____ Amiga	_____ Desktop Publishing	_____ Operating Systems
_____ Apple/Mac	_____ File Utilities	_____ Spreadsheets
_____ CAD	_____ Money Management	_____ Word Processing
_____ Communications	_____ Languages	_____ Other _____

(please specify)

Which of the following best describes your job title?

____ Administrative/Secretarial   ____ President/CEO

____ Director   ____ Manager/Supervisor

____ Engineer/Technician   ____ Other _____
                                      (please specify)

Comments on the weaknesses/strengths of this book: _____

_____

_____

_____

_____

Name _____

Street _____

City/State/Zip _____

Phone _____

PLEASE FOLD, SEAL, AND MAIL TO SYBEX

SYBEX, INC.
Department M
2021 CHALLENGER DR.
ALAMEDA, CALIFORNIA USA
94501

SYBEX ®

SEAL

WORDPERFECT 5.1 FEATURE SUMMARY (continued)

FEATURE	MENU SELECTIONS	KEYSTROKES	PAGE
List (Mark Block For)	Mark ➤ List	Alt-F5 L	742
List Files	File ➤ List Files	F5	383
Location of Files	File ➤ Setup ➤ Location of Files	Shift-F1 L	428
Macro (Define)	Tools ➤ Macro ➤ Define	Ctrl-F10	468
Macro (Execute)	Tools ➤ Macro ➤ Execute	Alt-F10	471
Margin Release	Layout ➤ Align ➤ Margin Rel <-	Shift-Tab	99
Margins (Left/Right)	Layout ➤ Line M	Shift-F8 L M	91
Margins (Top/Bottom)	Layout ➤ Page M	Shift-F8 P M	93
Master Document (Condense)	Mark ➤ Master Documents ➤ Condense	Alt-F5 G O	761
Master Document (Expand)	Mark ➤ Master Documents ➤ Expand	Alt-F5 G E	759
Merge Codes	Tools ➤ Merge Codes	Shift-F9	507
Merge Documents	Tools ➤ Merge	Ctrl-F9 M	516
Move Block	Edit ➤ Move (Cut)	Ctrl-F4 B M	37
Move Sentence/ Paragraph/Page	Edit ➤ Select	Ctrl-F4	40
Outline (Define)	Tools ➤ Define	Shift-F5 D	709
Outline On/Off	Tools ➤ Outline	Shift-F5 O	707
Page Numbering	Layout ➤ Page N	Shift-F8 P N	224
Paper Size	Layout ➤ Page S	Shift-F8 P S	243
Paragraph Number	Tools ➤ Paragraph Number	Shift-F5 P	702
Password	File ➤ Password	Ctrl-F5 P	375
Print Document on Disk	File ➤ Print D	Shift-F7 D	275
Print Full Document	File ➤ Print F	Shift-F7 F	270
Print Multiple Copies	File ➤ Print U	Shift-F7 U	280
Print Multiple Pages	File ➤ Print M	Shift-F7 M	276
Print Number of Copies	File ➤ Print N	Shift-F7 N	279
Print Page	File ➤ Print P	Shift-F7 P	274
Protect Block from Page Break	Edit ➤ Protect Block	Shift-F8	237
Replace Text	Search ➤ Replace	Alt-F2	324